Women and Law

WOMEN AND LAW IN INDIA

An Omnibus comprising

Law and Gender Inequality
The Politics of Women's Rights in India
FLAVIA AGNES

Enslaved Daughters
Colonialism, Law and Women's Rights
SUDHIR CHANDRA

Hindu Women and Marriage Law
From Sacrament to Contract
MONMAYEE BASU

with an introduction by Flavia Agnes

Oxford University Press is a department of the University of Oxford. It furthers the University's objective of excellence in research, scholarship, and education by publishing worldwide. Oxford is a registered trademark of Oxford University Press in the UK and in certain other countries

Published in India by
Oxford University Press
22 Workspace, 2nd Floor, 1/22 Asaf Ali Road, New Delhi 110002, India

First Edition published in 2004
Oxford India Paperbacks 2016

ISBN-13: 978-0-19-946721-1
ISBN-10: 0-19-946721-8

Printed in India by Repro Books Limited, Thane.

Contents

LAW AND GENDER INEQUALITY
The Politics of Women's Rights in India

ENSLAVED DAUGHTERS
Colonialism, Law and Women's Rights

HINDU WOMEN AND MARRIAGE LAW
From Sacrament to Contract

INTRODUCTION

Flavia Agnes

The three books in this omnibus address a period spanning over two centuries when Indian women's rights were negotiated, rewritten, and coded. Though the centrality of the themes, their narrative style, and the concerns raised by the three books are varied, the common thread that binds them together is their engagement with the judicial discourse over women's rights within marriage in colonial and post-colonial India.

In *Enslaved Daughters*, Sudhir Chandra captures a social drama which unfolded around 'a unique event in colonial India' when a twenty-two-year-old woman, Rukhmabai, defied tradition and the colonial legal dictates by refusing to be bound to a marriage contracted when she was barely eleven. Questioning what was assumed to be natural, she offered a subversive model of assertion by women of their desire, as individuals, in a terrain dominated by family, community, and imperial notions of justice and governance.

In *Hindu Women and Marriage Law*, Monmoyee Basu traces the social and legislative history of the period ranging between two terminal points: the Hindu Widow Remarriage Act of 1856 and the Hindu Succession Act of 1956. Within these set parameters she examines social realities and the impact of legislative reforms upon a particular section of women, namely the Hindu women of Bengal.

My concerns in *Law and Gender Inequality* are situated within a broader canvas and the attempt has been to trace the origin and development of the contentious religion-based 'personal laws' within the socio-political dynamics of the period when they were evolved. Addressing the current debate around the uniform civil code (UCC), I have also argued that gender is not a neutral terrain, detached from contemporary political trends. Within a complex social, political, and economic structure, the demand of gender equality cannot be confined within a linear mould of granting uniform rights to women of all communities. An all-encompassing UCC cannot be viewed as a magic wand which will eliminate the woes and sufferings of Indian women in general, and minority women in particular.

Several contesting premises are played out in these narratives—creation of legitimizing ideologies of colonial rule, workings of patriarchies within civil societies, claims of women's identity as subjects/citizens, notions of justice as administered by an alien and adversarial legal system, contractual obligations of the state, and the supremacy of nationalist models of reform, to name just a few. Weaving some of these strands together in this introductory essay, my attempt has been to explore the complex relationship between notions of patriarchy, sexuality, and property, and the manner in which they are normalized and essentialized through state interventions. In order for this exploration to remain focused, I have narrowed down its scope to four specific segments: restitution of conjugal rights, remarriage of widows, state policies regulating property and inheritance, and notions of morality and maintenance in contemporary matrimonial litigations.

By way of methodology, apart from the secondary sources, I have relied upon cases reported in law journals as a primary source of sociological data. A legal provision has to be judged not by its legalistic wordings but its application to real-life situations. The dry words of a statute come to life only when they are contested in courtrooms and are interpreted through judicial pronouncements. Hidden in law journals is an invaluable source of empirical data on social norms and judicial attitudes.[1] An encounter with judicial records is pertinent not only to the understanding of the workings of a complex legal system but also, in a rather singular way to charting the dark and relatively unexplored area of conjugal sexuality. In an essay titled, 'Sex, Sacrament and Contract in Hindu Marriage', Patricia Uberoi comments that matrimonial cases provide

[1]Derett, J.D.M., 'Society and Family Law in India: The Problem of Hindu Marriage', in Giri Raj Gupta (ed.) *Family and Social Change in Modern India*, New Delhi: Vikas, 1976, p. 52.

an interesting illustration of the way judicial decisions amplify both the bare statutory provisions of Hindu law of marriage and the conventional legal metalanguage of sacrament versus contract as the basis of conjugal relations.[2] I have used case law in this essay to exemplify the vagaries of judicial verdicts. While in most cases the cited judgments are conservative and carry an inherent gender bias, there have also been instances of creative judicial interpretations where courts have gone beyond the statute to expand the scope of women's rights. The recent Supreme Court judgment[3] under the controversial Muslim Women (Protection of Rights on Divorce) Act (henceforth, the Muslim Women's Act or MWA) is a case in point. The dynamism between statutes, litigants, and court verdicts is what makes legal research and practice an exciting arena of intervention. This is particularly relevant to feminist legal scholarship in India.

Conjugality, Property, and the State—The Rukhmabai Case

Unfolding the events around the *Rukhmabai* case, Sudhir Chandra mentions that the social drama featured a fierce and fascinating debate about reshaping modern Indian society in which individuals, ideas, and institutions were interlocked in complex relationships of compromise and antagonism. Exposing the contradictions and hypocrisies inherent in the public debate around the high-profile case, he comments:

> Impinging disturbingly upon the nebulous world comprising women, marriage and family, Rukhmabai's case stirred up passions that ranged from the cultural to the psychic. This was a nebulous world in that it constituted the 'private' world over which many among the subject people seemed desperate to retain a reassuring sense of autonomy. But this was also a 'public' world over which the semiotic war was fought. Ironically, those most vocal in opposing the extension of colonial authority into their socio-religious affairs were the keenest, in this 'war', to utilize the colonial legal system and its alien practices.

He argues that it was not simply a 'civil war' involving different groups within the Indian society but within the colonial ambience, a war between the rulers and the ruled in which, exceptions apart,

[2]Uberoi, Patricia, 'When a marriage is not a marriage? Sex, Sacrament and Contract in Hindu Marriage', in Patricia Uberoi (ed.) *Social Reform, Sexuality and the State*, New Delhi: Sage, 1996, p. 343.

[3]*Daniel Latifi v Union of India* 2001 CriLJ 4660.

the two sought to distinguish their respective institutions, ideals, and values with regard to women, marriage, and family in order to claim superiority over the other. The issue of law and justice which figured prominently in the ensuing controversy, deepened the civilizational encounter between the ruled and the rulers.

Sudhir Chandra raises some disturbing questions. Who was responsible for the young woman's tragic predicament—those who professed that they would brook no interference with their venerable laws and usages, or the intrusive colonial masters with their alien socio-legal notions and practices who insisted on mediating in the familial affairs of the ruled? In what ways did the guiding ethico-legal assumptions of the two vary with regard to women as persons and within marriage, family, and society? The unfolding of these larger questions revealed conflicting normative and empirical claims with regard to the society and culture of the rulers and the ruled. As passions were aroused and partisan positions taken, this critical moment exposed the ideas, illusions, and contradictions of various segments of the subject and the power elites.

The battle lines in this war of words were not sharply drawn. Rather, it brought together—in a shifting pattern of confrontation and alliance—what may be distinguished as three discourses, each marked by its own internal variations and contradictions: the orthodox/reactionary, the imperialist, and the reformist. The imperialist discourse almost always sounded the most aggressively humanitarian and claimed, particularly on the women's issue, to have set afoot an irreversible process of emancipation among the colonized. But it betrayed androcentric assumptions that took women's inferiority for granted and underlined the ideological as well as institutional sexism of Victorian England. Ostensibly, however, both the orthodox and the imperialist discourses made a show of reverence and concern for women, and employed stratagems to avoid being pinned down to the actualization of that reverence and concern.

The motif of the defiance of Rukhmabai is relevant not only for its times but even for the contemporary international feminist discourse which centres largely upon violence against women. The Third World victim subject has come to represent the more victimized, that is, the real or authentic victim subject. Feminist politics in the international human rights arena, as well as in parts of the Third World, have promoted this image of the authentic victim subject while advocating for women's human rights. Ratna Kapur, a feminist legal scholar, comments that the focus on the victim subject reinforces gender and cultural essentialism in the international women's human rights arena. These have been further displaced onto a 'Third World–First World' divide, and this displacement resurrects the 'native subject' and justifies imperialist interventions.[4] She argues in favour of transcending the victim subject and disrupting the cultural and gender essentialism that have come to characterize feminist legal politics. The political and emancipatory value of focusing on the peripheral subject and identifying her locations of resistance when addressing women's human rights, then, becomes crucial for achieving this end and Rukhmabai's case is an important contribution towards achieving this goal. The motif of her defiance of both the verdict of the alien English judges and the patriarchal dictates crouched in national pride, in defence of her right over her personhood, at a time when English women were waging a battle for their right to own separate property as wives, would indeed serve to shift the rigid and fixed binaries of First World feminists/Third World victim subject which Ratna Kapur mentions in her essay.

Interspersing of Sexuality and Property—the Widow Remarriage Act

The Widow Remarriage Act of 1856 was enacted amidst two sets of contesting claims: the revivalists proclaiming that the bill, if enacted, would affect a vital part of the Hindu shastras and widows marrying under it would be regarded as social outcastes; and the reformers, at the other end, led by Ishwar Chandra Vidyasagar, claiming that the custom prohibiting widow remarriage was a modern innovation unknown in Vedic times.[5] This conflict between 'authentic' tradition and culture had been raised earlier during the debate around abolition of sati[6] and

[4]Kapur, Ratna, 'The Tragedy of Victimization Rhetoric: Resurrecting the "Native" Subject in International/Post Colonial Feminist Legal Politics', in *Harvard Human Rights Journal*, Spring 2002.

[5]Basu, Monmoyee, *Hindu Women and Marriage Law*, New Delhi: Oxford University Press, 2001, p. 69.

[6]Addressing the nineteenth-century debate around sati, Lata Mani has argued that the discourse was more on authentic culture and tradition, and Brahmanic

was reflected in the debate over the Widow Remarriage Act.[7]

These contentions are overlaid by another reality—that of caste hierarchies which Basu mentions: 'The prohibition of widow-remarriage was seen as a badge of respectability. Castes which did not allow it ranked higher in social estimation. This was carried to the extent that castes were sometimes divided into two sections, one following and the other forbidding the practice.'[8]

Basu notes further, '… a vast majority of widows never availed of the provisions of the Act and Hindu society was too conservative to accept it … by and by, the social reformers came to realize that, without the strength of education, the problems of the Hindu widows could never be solved.'[9] Later, she also raises a very pertinent question which is central to the theme of this essay—that of the economic aspects of the Act.

> Another aspect to be considered is the economic import of the Widow-Remarriage Act of 1856. Did it improve the status of the Hindu widow economically? Did it in any way give her a greater right to property? It can, however, be said that the Widow-Remarriage Act of 1856, in particular, had two serious limitations. …. Section 2 of the Act of 1856 dealt with the effect of remarriage on the right of inheritance and maintenance which a widow possessed in the property of her former husband or his lineal successors at the time of remarriage. This section deprived the widow of any right or interest which she had at the time of her remarriage in the property of her husband. … Thus the Act of 1856 did not provide the Hindu widow with an absolute right to her husband's property and she could be deprived of it as soon as she remarried.[10]

To sum up, the selected quotes from Basu reveal that there were competing claims regarding the scriptural prohibition to widow

---

scriptures were increasingly seen to be the locus of this authenticity so that, for example, the legislative prohibition of sati became a question of scriptural interpretation. Sati, widow remarriage or zenanas (seclusion of women), were not merely about women, but also instances in which the moral challenge of colonial rule was confronted and negotiated. Tradition was thus not the ground on which the status of woman was being contested. Rather the reverse was true: women in fact became the site on which tradition was debated and reformulated. What was at stake was not women but tradition. *See* Mani, Lata, 'Contentious Traditions: The Debate on Sati in Colonial India', in Sangari, Kumkum and Suresh Vaid (eds), *Recasting Women*, New Delhi: Kali for Women, 1989, p. 89.

[7]For a detailed discussion on the controversy over widow remarriage, see Kumar, Radha, *The History of Doing*, New Delhi: Kali for Women, 1993.

[8]*See* n. 4 supra, p. 72.

[9]Ibid p. 75.

[10]Ibid p. 78.

remarriage. Widows from certain lower castes had a customary right of remarriage, but a vast majority of widows (this must be read as upper-caste widows) did not avail of the legal provisions of this Act, and the Act did not improve the economic rights of a Hindu widow. On the contrary, upon remarriage, it deprived her of her right to retain her husband's property.

Taking this premise further, I wish to examine through cases reported in law journals of this period, how the Act unfolded itself upon women from the lower castes. From the brief sketch, it is evident that any woman marrying under this Act lost her right to her husband's property. Even if one can concede that it would be logical to apply these constraints to women who acquired a right of remarriage due to this statute, it is difficult to reconcile with the perverse logic through which even women who had a pre-existing right of remarriage under the custom of the caste were deprived of their property.

The statute needs to be contextualized within the legal status of English women who obtained the right to divorce, and subsequent remarriage, only in 1857 (under very stringent grounds of adultery coupled with another matrimonial offence of cruelty or desertion). The battle for the absolute and unhindered right of married women to hold property which began in 1870 went on for another half a century. The disabilities suffered by married women in respect of separate ownership of property were finally laid to rest in 1935.[11]

Despite this, the rationale for denying Hindu widows their right of retaining their property was based on judicial interpretations of Hindu law! As per the British jurists, a woman could hold property only due to the legal fiction under Hindu law that upon marriage she becomes a part of her husband's body. According to this view, a woman's personhood gets sublimated into that of her husband's. A widow could be granted a right to inherit her husband's property only on the presumption that she is the surviving part of her husband's being. Upon remarriage, a widow ceased to be a part of her former husband's body and hence she lost her right to hold his property. The prohibition against remarriage had no scriptural foundation. In any case, women from the lower castes were out of

[11]With the enactment of the *Law Reform (Married Women and Tortfeasors) Act* of 1935 the distinction between the rights of married and single women was finally abolished.

the purview of scriptural doctrines and had a customary right of remarriage. These interpretations of the principles of Hindu law governed judicial notions from 1860, when the new courts were set up, until the enactment of the Hindu Succession Act in 1956 which discarded this principle.

Regional and caste-based diversity in the property rights of women did not seem to have any bearing upon the rigid notion and the courts continued to apply these principles even to women of lower castes who were not governed by these principles. For instance, in Maraveer caste, widows could remarry even prior to the 1856 enactment. But in 1877, while deciding the case of a woman from this community, the Madras High Court held:

> The principle upon which a widow inherits is that she is the surviving half of her husband. So it cannot apply where she remarries. The law cannot permit the widow who has remarried to retain the inheritance. As per the principles embodied in Steele's Hindu Law and Custom, the custom in the shudras is that a widow on remarriage gives up all properties of her former husband's relations except what has been given her by her own parents.[12]

The court relied upon a quote which is attributed to Brihaspati: *Of him whose wife is not dead half his body survives. How should anyone else take the property while half his body lives*. This metaphor became a legal maxim in all subsequent judgments. The Madras High Court in 1884 applied this rule in the case of a woman from the Lingait Gounda community which followed the custom of remarriage prior to the Act.[13]

In the Deccan region, widow remarriages which were termed *pat* or *natra* marriages were performed among several castes. But following the trend of Madras High Court, in 1898 a judge of the Bombay High Court, Justice Ranade, held:

> So far as this Presidency is concerned it is obvious from the information collected in Steele's Law and Custom of Indian Castes in Deccan among whom *pat* marriages were allowed or forbidden. But when a widow performs *pat* her husband's relatives succeeded to her husband's estate. There is not a single caste mentioned in which any custom to the contrary prevails.[14]

The recording of customs within the Bombay Presidency which was hastily and haphazardly done by Steele during the early phase of

[12]*Murugayi v Viramakali* ILR (1877) 1 Mad 226.
[13]*Kaduthi v Madu* ILR 1884 7 Mad 321.
[14]*Vithu v Govind* ILR (1898) 22 Bom 321 FB.

the Presidency, and was published in 1827, seemed to have provided the basis for denying women from the lower castes their customary right to property in litigation several decades later.

A dissenting and more rational view was expressed by the Allahabad High Court in the year 1933. Since the Act was a beneficial legislation, the court ruled that it cannot be interpreted as to impose further disabilities upon women who were not burdened with such disabilities prior to the enactment. The court held:

> A custom of remarriage does not necessarily carry with it, a further custom of forfeiture upon marriage. Anybody who claims there has been forfeiture by reason of remarriage, must prove affirmatively that such forfeiture is an incident of the custom under which the remarriage took place.[15]

But ironically this decision was not followed by high courts of Bombay, Madras, Calcutta, or Hyderabad even in the post-independence period. These courts continued to apply the principle of forfeiture to an increasing section of lower-caste women. Since the right was so well established among many lower castes, despite a century of negative interpretations, the claims of widows continued to be litigated even in the post-independence period. Many women lost out but not without a struggle. Cases were initiated in lower courts and were followed to the high courts and from then on to the Privy Council (and hence were reported in law journals). Individual women lost out to the combined strength of local patriarchies and a gender bias inherent in the imperial legal system. Some decisions of the post-independence period are mentioned below.

In 1952, the Calcutta High Court applied the rule of forfeiture to a woman from the Bairagi community who remarried under the custom of the caste.[16] In 1954 the Bombay High Court reversed the decision of the subordinate courts and applied the rule to a woman from Kolhapur district. This was a princely state till independence and hence the Widow Remarriage Act had not been applied here and, upon remarriage, widows could retain the property of their former husbands. Ruling against the premise that as per the custom of the caste, the rule of forfeiture upon remarriage did not apply, the court declared:

[15]*Bhola Umar v Kausilla* ILR (1933) 35 All 24.

[16]*Lalit Mohan v Shyamapada Das* AIR 1952 Cal 771.

> The foundation that widow is the surviving half of her husband does not disappear merely because certain communities recognise a custom of remarriage of widows. It would indeed be a startling proposition to say that even though she takes the property of her deceased husband by inheritance as his surviving half, she is entitled to take away that property with her to her new husband on remarriage when she can no more be regarded as the surviving half of her first husband.[17]

Hyderabad was another princely state which came under the new dominion. In 1952, a full bench of the Hyderabad High Court, by a majority view, overruled several of its earlier decisions which granted women the right of retention of property, despite a strong dissenting note from a section of the judiciary which vociferously argued that Manu did not lay down rules for the shudras and was concerned only with the three higher castes and hence his views cannot govern shudra women.[18]

The significant factor here is that these decisions of the post-independence period with the constitutional mandate of equality were not even following established rules of the community. They were setting new precedents for these communities through which women's right to property was being eroded, at a point in history when the debate about the reform in Hindu law and women's rights of inheritance was raging in the country. Through an active collusion between patriarchal premises of the state and the manipulation of male relatives, women of the lower community were disempowered of their rights over property. It is indeed ironic that just two years after the Bombay High Court unsettled the established rights of women in Kolhapur district, the Hindu Succession Act came to be enacted after a prolonged and acrimonious debate. One of the salient features of the Act was the abolition of the concept of 'limited estate', besides awarding widows an absolute right over property inherited upon the death of their husbands.

During the period 1860–1930, the rights of widows in general were adversely affected through the judicial interpretation of the concept of *stridhana*. A new legal principle was gradually introduced through court decisions that whether the property is inherited by a woman through her male relatives (father, son, husband) or through her female relatives (mother, mother's mother, daughter), it is not her *stridhana* and that it would devolve on the heirs of her deceased

[17] *Rama Appa v Sakhu Dattu* AIR 1954 Bom 315.

[18] *Basappa v Parvatamma* AIR 1952 Hyd FB.

husband. The widow lost the right to will or gift away her *stridhana* and it acquired the character of a limited estate. Upon the widow's death, the property reverted back to the husband's male relatives. The introduction of this concept of 'reversioners' which is basically a legal principle under the English law, bestowed upon the male relatives the right to challenge all property dealings by Hindu widows.[19]

The establishment of a legal system based on procedures and rules of the English courts and a clear hierarchy of courts was meant to make the arbitration fora certain and definite. The legal structure was seen by the administrators as an important forte of its civilizing mission. The British interpretations of the ancient texts became binding and made the law certain, rigid, and uniform. This clear marker of modernity was welcomed by the newly evolving English-educated middle class of Bengal and provided the British a moral justification for ruling India as harbingers of enlightenment.[20] Through their interventions the Hindu society could rid itself of its 'barbarism' and enter an era of 'civilization'. An image of the cruel and superstitious natives who needed Christian salvation was deliberately constructed by the Evangelists.

An interesting strategy used by women during litigation, it appears, was to claim a shudra status and thereby application of customary law. Conversely, male relatives had to defend their right by claiming a higher Hindu status. If courts bestowed a Hindu status upon the communities, women's right would be curtailed. Most of these were borderline cases where the pendulum would swing from one end to the other. But when the issue was finally decided by the Privy Council or the respective high court as the case may be, the religious status of the community (and thereby the fate of its widows) would be sealed for all future litigations. Since the standard of proof required to prove the existence of a custom was very high, a wide range of customs which diverged from the Anglo-Hindu law were eliminated.

Lucy Carroll cites a case which was initiated by members of a tribal family claiming that on remarriage one of their widows had forfeited her right to the property that she had owned. The case

[19]For a detailed discussion on *stridhana*, see Agnes, Flavia, *Law and Gender Inequality*, New Delhi: Oxford University Press, 1999, pp. 46–52.

[20]See Note 7.

was won on a minimal show of evidence that certain Hindu practices had been adopted by some branches of the tribe (the Rajbansis). The court held this sufficient evidence to bring the entire tribe under the scope of the Act. She states that the Act provided mercenary reasons for non-Hindus to Hinduize their customs.[21] Contrary to popular belief, many of the customs that were crushed were those in favour of women.

Derrett comments that in this manner, the Anglo-Hindu law with its *dharmashastra* background spread more widely than it had ever been before. The only customs which were saved from the crushing effects of the British courts were the customs of the agricultural classes in the Punjab and matrilineal practices of the Malabar region.[22]

Land Settlements and Subversion of Women's Property Rights

British intervention carved out a space for men's individual property rights from a system based on community or joint ownership. Changes in property ownership through 'permanent settlements' developed a landowning class and conversely this served to undermine the claims of women. While this is true for the entire British India, in this section the specific focus is the Punjab region and the matrilineal practices of Kerala. The customs of these people and regions, which Derrett mentions, need to be re-examined in the light of more recent feminist scholarship. To understand the imperial policies and subversion of women's property rights in the Punjab, I find the works of Prem Chowdhry[23] and the more recent publication of Veena Talwar Oldenburg[24] particularly useful. For an analysis of land reform policies of the Malabar region, I

[21]Carroll, Lucy, 'Law, Custom and Statutory Social Reform—The Hindu Widows Remarriage Act 1856', in J. Krishnamurty (ed.), *Women in Colonial India*, Delhi: Oxford University Press, 1989.

[22]Derrett, J.D.M., *Hindu Law Past and Present*, Calcutta: Mukherjee & Co., 1957, p. 78.

[23]*See* 'Customs in a Peasant Economy: Women in Colonial Haryana', in Sangari, Kumkum and Sudesh Vaid (eds), *Recasting Women*, New Delhi: Kali for Women, 1989 p. 302–36. Also, *The Veiled Women: Shifting Gender Equations in Rural Haryana 1880–1990*, New Delhi: Oxford Univesity Press, 1994.

[24]Oldenburg, Veena Talwar, *Dowry Murder—The Imperial Origins of a Cultural Crime*, New Delhi: Oxford University Press, 2002.

shall rely upon the writings of K. Saradamoni[25] who has extensively researched this issue.

Chowdhry contends that a mere practice of widow remarriage or bride price cannot be construed as a marker of a higher status for women within the communities practising these customs. For instance, rural Haryana, one of the most backward and underdeveloped regions of the Punjab under the British, exhibited a peculiar contradiction in relation to its women. On the one hand, the region reflected accepted indices of a high status for women, i.e. bride price, widow remarriage, polyandry, and relatively greater economic participation of women in agricultural activities. At the same time, indices of women's backwardness—very low female sex ratio[26], a total neglect of and prejudice against female education, and the complete absence of women from any positions of power and decision making—were also witnessed.[27]

The importance of a wife in the agrarian economy made marriage an acknowledged economic necessity among the Jats and other agriculturist castes in the region, including Brahmins. The custom of bride price and widow remarriage have to be contextualized within this need.[28] The term for widow remarriage was *karewa*, a custom which sanctioned the remarriage of a widow with the deceased husband's younger or elder brother or an agnate cousin.

Chowdhry argues that the *karewa* form of marriage served to control a woman's sexuality in order to control her property. Even the limited right of an unmarried widow to retain her husband's property was seen as a menace and the *karewa* form of marriage served to dispossess her of her rights.[29] The widow could alienate the property for her own maintenance, for her daughter's wedding,

[25]Saradamoni, K., 'Progressive Land Legislations and Subordination of Women', in Lotika Sarkar and B. Sivaramayya (eds), *Women and Law: Contemporary Problems*, Delhi: Vikas Publishing House, 1994, pp. 155–67.

[26]The sex ratio for Haryana continues to be far below the national statistics, which in itself is adverse. As per the 1991 census, Haryana recorded a mere 865 females per 1000 males as against the national statistics of 927 females. As per the 2001 census, the national statistics improved slightly to 933 while Haryana recorded a further decline at 861 females per 1000 males.

[27]Chowdhry, Prem, 'Customs in a Peasant Economy: Women in Colonial Haryana', in Kumkum Sangari and Sudesh Vaid (eds), *Recasting Women*, New Delhi: Kali for Women, 1989, pp. 302–36.

[28]Ibid p. 312.

[29]Ibid p. 315.

or for payment of revenue—reasons termed as 'strict necessity'. That the women were able to manipulate these provisions to a certain extent to their advantage can be gauged from the constant appeals made to the deputy commissioner protesting against widows who had alienated their property 'without consent'. This self-assertion by widows in taking control of the economic resources after their husbands' death must have assumed such a proportion that for a variety of reasons government action against it became essential.

She further cites that J.M. Douie, compiler of *The Punjab Land Administration Manual*, advised the revenue officials that the widow's attempt to partition the land should be disallowed. The widow's right to control land had been legalized under the Land Revenue Act because after the husband's death she was held responsible for the payment of government revenue dues. However, since such advice could not have held much weight legally, the only solution to the fast-growing claims to partition was, according to official instruction, to be sought in a firm anchoring of the widow in remarriage. This, in the Manual instruction, 'could be the only satisfactory arrangement against which she had no appeal'.

Such advice was an inevitable outcome of the colonial policy followed in the Punjab because of its economic, political, and military importance. The imperial government had, right from the beginning, adopted the preservation of the village community as a settled policy for Punjab. The general argument of British officials was that the mass of the agricultural population of this province did not follow either the Hindu or the Muslim law. Therefore, a general code of tribal custom was prepared by settlement officers who at each settlement had compiled the *rivaj-i-am* (record of customs and rights) in consultation with the village headman of each principal landowning tribe in the district; these being, acknowledgedly, men from the most influential families in the village. Consequently, the customs of the landowning class in regard to civil matters like succession, alienation, marriage, tenure of land, adoption, and the like came to be settled primarily by the Punjab customary law which then became the first rule of decision.

The customary law of the land, backed by the full force of the colonial administrators, safeguarded the landed property from a woman's possession. Interestingly, not allowing women to inherit property was a view that struck a sympathetic, even enthusiastic, chord among many British officials. The British perception of these customs, which they also made legally binding, is significant. A curious parallel observation about the situation of women prevailing 'back home' as compared to that in the Punjab discloses the ambivalent attitude of British officials towards women:

> The proportion of females to males in England and Wales rises continuously from childhood to old age, indicative of the excessive care lavished on women in England qua women, and not merely qua child bearer. Social reformers may well stand aghast at the neglect of and the contempt for female life shown by all religious groups in the Punjab, but no less extensive, and, possibly fraught with serious consequences to the future of the race, is the excessive pampering of females in England ...

For *karewa* they held:

> ... most officers conversant with this tract of country had entertained in the existence sub rose of a system of polyandry. This institution is probably the first stage in development of a savage people after they have emerged from a mere animal condition of promiscuity. It is the concomitant of female infanticide .... The family is the first organization when all wealth including the wife are owned in common.

In Punjab, the fundamental political interest of the British transcended their less well-defined concern for social progress. This low level of civilization as signified by *karewa* had to be retained because the British concern lay in strengthening the hold of the existing peasant society over land; its break-up was inevitable if the widow was allowed to have her way.

The apprehension regarding the danger of social disequilibrium to Haryana was sharper because this region, with its insecure agricultural conditions, had provided the best recruiting ground for the British Indian Army. The *karewa* custom contributed significantly to the unceasing heavy recruitment, despite the insecurity of life and the equally heavy rate of mortality. Simultaneously, the agricultural interests of the recruits' families could not be allowed to be jeopardized by the ever-growing number of widow's claims. This could prove to be very costly to the imperial government and not only unsettle its military recruitment but also the social equilibrium upon which its rule in the state was founded. Moreover, even economically, such a demand, if conceded, would have only added to the fragmentation and subdivision of holdings, and consequently, to the fast-growing smaller uneconomic holdings in this region, as elsewhere in the Punjab, which were posing a direct threat to the agricultural prosperity of the province and hence to the collection of revenue.

Chowdhry concludes that widow remarriage—a seemingly progressive feature—continued to be applauded by the British administration. The practice, however, as it was encouraged to exist merely reinforced the social ethos that safeguarded the land in the family, clan, and community. The British administrators' own attitudes regarding female inheritance were closely identified with the primary concern of the colonial government, which did not want to disturb the patriarchal equilibrium within the rural society of Punjab[30]

This causal connection between imperial policies and subordination of women's rights is explored further by Veena Talwar Oldenburg, in her recent book, *Dowry Murder—The Imperial Origins of a Cultural Crime*.[31] Oldenburg argues that land reform policies and the creation of a masculine culture deprived women of their rights and made them vulnerable to family violence. She traces the collusion of the imperial state and the Punjabi men who reconfigured patriarchal values and manly ideals in the nineteenth-century Punjab. The two became meshed in an unsurprising alliance against the customary right of women. Pressing for a need to look beyond the statute book to comprehend a central paradox of colonial policy in India that persists in post-colonial India, she contends:

> Although the legislative record is indeed impressive and includes the outlawing of several customs that underscored the bias against women, there was in the colonial period a profound loss of women's economic power and social worth. This was a direct consequence of the radical creation of property rights in land.[32]

Oldenburg argues that modern capitalist ideas in their attenuated form seeped unevenly through the mesh of colonial needs and priorities and infiltrated the Punjabi society via two major colonial initiatives: the *ryotwari* system and the codification of 'customary' law.[33] Land was declared a marketable commodity capable of private and determinate ownership so that a fixed and settled land revenue in cash could be recovered on every plot of land in two annual instalments on two fixed dates. Annual assessments that had been customary in preceding native regimes were abruptly discontinued because they were found to be cumbersome, expensive, and

[30]Ibid p. 320.

[31]*See* n. 24 supra.

[32]Ibid p. 2.

[33]Ibid p. 100.

provided an opportunity for corruption. The British—in striving to put the administration on a rational, efficient, and economic footing—ordained that their revenue settlements for various districts stay in effect for two or three decades without regard to the situation that prevailed in any given year, be it drought, famine, or plenty. This was the policy in a nutshell, and rationalized in the British view, the jumble of competing shares, the varied annual collections, the bargaining matches and corruption that had plagued the revenue collection of the Sindh regime.

The second initiative is the codification of 'custom' as adjudicable law in the Punjab countryside.[34] These two processes worked in tandem and illuminated how the equation in gender and power came to be skewed further. By tracking the enormous change that took place when the world of peasants of the Punjab became decidedly more masculine and as land—hitherto a community-held resource—became private property, we can recapture the moment women's voices and customs were erased as men's rights and voices were recorded with singular clarity. The shared control formerly accorded to all those who worked the land came to be replaced by the arbitrary privileging of tillers as owners of the soil. Women—as those who sowed, weeded, hoed, harvested, threshed, and milled grain and vegetables, looked after dairy cattle, collected fuels, processed produce, and prepared it as food—who had been implicit coparceners in pre-colonial landholding arrangements found themselves tenuous legal dependents of men, with their access to economic resources subordinated increasingly to the control and will of the husbands.

Oldenburg comments with a note of sarcasm:

> The British had not granted their own women rights to property, so it was highly unlikely that they would shed their prejudice while introducing this 'progressive' notion of private property to the Punjab. (And progress meant assimilation to modern European norms.) They granted these rights exclusively to men so that they could collect their taxes from male proprietors who could be taken to court or sent to jail if they defaulted. Clearly women, already hindered by the custom of seclusion and veiling, could not conveniently interact with the legal machinery of the new rulers so their husband and male kin quietly subsumed their rights. A robust patriarchal mentality was reinforced in this collusion.[35]

[34]Ibid p. 101.
[35]Ibid.

According to her, that these initiatives were deployed simultaneously made them doubly powerful. At the same time, land titles were formalized and revenue settlements made for each district, and revenue officials (earlier called settlement officers) went further by collecting, organizing, and constituting oral, informal *rivaj* (literally, 'custom') from male heads of each 'tribe' or 'caste'. The officers themselves redefined these categories and reworked the information into a formal set of laws adjudicable in the new court system. The Punjab acquired a fully codified set of customary law which was laid out in a manual. By 1880 the revised recession of these laws was completed. They were to operate in lieu of the Muslim and Hindu personal laws.[36]

The registration of ownership of land was the first phase, the foundation stone of the making of the agrarian economy masculine, Oldenburg comments. The next step taken in each district of the Punjab was the attempt to translate social and customary practices into legal codes. The new regime insisted on consulting only the male heads of a village, caste, or household in order to inscribe the *rivaj-i-am* (the customs of everyday life situated in a place or region, particularizing them in the attributes of a caste or tribe). New meanings invaded the husks of many familiar words. The complex and plastic universe of oral, implicit, flexible, and informally transmitted customary practices, interpreted as much by women as by men, which ordered everyday life and relationships was systematically elicited from only males and reduced for administrative effect into a written, fixed, judicable, actionable, and enforceable corpus of laws. The timing of the project was, perhaps, as critical as the project itself. That customary laws were to be collected and written down for the first time when the record of who owned the land had just been noted, with the power and the danger of individual ownership unleashed, informed much of what the respondents, all male landowners, would call custom. Women's share in the produce of the land became meaningless but traces of what their rights might have been are discernible in these codes—they provide a faint approximation of the rights women had in a society where land was a common resource with varying levels of entitlements. According to her, the process emptied the

[36]Ibid p. 102.

female category of older, subtler meanings—of shares of birthright, and of other safeguards of the indigenous patriarchal tradition.[37]

Linking land ownership to male preference, she continues:

> Sons were the key to survival and prosperity in the relentlessly agrarian Punjab under the British. Acquiring land during auctions or sales, finding a job in the lower rungs of the imperial bureaucracy or the army, or finding a niche as a retainer in the expanding market were the new plums to fight over. The newly enhanced worth of sons with such prospects can be reflected in the confidence of some families in demanding a consideration for a marriage alliance ...

At a diagonally opposite end, Saradamoni's research[38] on the changing agrarian relations in Kerala which ranged from the colonial to the post-colonial period, addresses the manner in which tenancy statutes during colonial and post-independence periods affected women's customary rights within a system of matrilineal inheritance. 'Unfortunately there is no serious study on the relation between land and women or the status of women in the matrilineal communities,' she comments remorsefully.[39]

Matrilineal practices were prevalent among a very large section of cultivating communities including Nayars, Nambudiris, and Malabar Muslims (Moppilas). The tenurial arrangements, marriage practices, and the joint family inheritance laws served to keep the land holdings intact. The woman had a right by birth in the joint family property named as *tarawad*. A woman alone was considered progeny and the birth of a girl on whom depended the continuity of the *tarawad* was a joyous occasion. Women under *marumakkathayam* did not depend on husbands for maintenance. They entered into *sambandham* (alliance) with men of their castes or of castes above theirs. Children born to them belonged to their caste and to their *tarawad*, where they had the right of maintenance. A woman continued to live in her natal house after marriage which was termed *sambandham*. These were effected with mutual consent but was terminable at the will of either party. A woman who used the freedom to end the alliance was not looked down upon.

[37]Ibid pp. 133–4.

[38]Saradamoni, K., 'Progressive Land Legislations and Subordination of Women', in Lotika Sarkar and B. Sivaramayya (ed.), *Women and Law: Contemporary Problems*, Delhi: Vikas Publishing House, 1994, pp. 155–67.

[39]Ibid p. 157.

This system was tampered with during the British rule which led to an unrest among the tenants. According to custom, the produce of the land was equally divided among the *janmi*, the principal controller of land, the *kanakkaran*, the principal tenants who were non-cultivators, and the *verumpattakkaran*, the sub-tenants, each taking a one-third share. The British interpreted the rights and interests connected with land with their experience as well as their needs in view. They looked upon *janmi* as 'owner' of the soil, and the *kanakkaran* as the owner's lessee and as such liable to be turned out of the lands 'when the time they leased them for expires'. Earlier to this period, eviction of tenants and raising of rents were unknown. But these became common once the *janmis* became 'owners'. These set in motion agrarian unrest and struggles which, in stages, continued up to the post-independence period.

How did the tenants' struggle against the excesses of landlords get linked to the ending of *marumakkathaym*? Answering this query, Saradamoni notes that in the course of their demand for a better deal from *janmis*, they also demanded the division of joint property on the basis that individual holdings are necessary motivations for individual economic gain. Right of land alienation and abolition of the *tarawad* joint property system became a corollary and was viewed as a progressive move. The new administrative set-up introduced by the British—revenue offices, courts, schools, post offices—created new jobs which invariably went to men. These jobs necessitated setting up of separate households away from the *tarawad* which were more in the nature of a nuclear family with the man as the head of the household with a dependent wife.

Within this 'modern' set-up the *tarawads* were looked down upon and along with changes in tenancy rules, there was a demand to abolish the *tarawad* system of property ownership. During the initial phase, the voices of women, mostly Muslim and a small number of Nayar women, was recorded. But surprisingly, these voices were absent by the 1930s and 1940s. One reason the ordinary *marumakkathayam* women did not react to the above legislations and debates could be that the proposed reforms were clothed in 'modernity' and were received as 'progressive'. Saradamoni quotes from a Madras newspaper (29 January 1932): 'It is the primary duty not only of the wise but also of the government to do away with all foolish practices and customs by means of a law. It is urgent that these Bills should be passed into law immediately in view of the welfare and morals of society.'[40] The classification of the local customs and practices as outmoded or obsolete was an achievement for the alien rulers. It is one reason why the 'masculine legal culture', which they unleashed in the country went unquestioned. By their interpretation of the land laws of the region, they were able to create a section of the landed interests who were conscious of their class position and a male superiority.

One example of the new male consciousness is contained in the following text submitted before the Malabar Marriage Commission:

> That a man who begets children should be under a legal obligation to maintain them could be hardly disputed as a maxim of justice and sound policy. ... As the father, more than anyone else, is responsible for this multiplication, it can hardly be doubted that the responsibility for making a provision for the children ought to rest primarily on him. This is a dictate of natural law and the rank, position or caste of the father ought to make no difference in the case.[41]

While these ideas spread fast, evidence does not show that all men could discharge this new responsibility. Many of them did not have the wherewithal to provide for their wives and children. There was growing pressure to make women sell their share of *tarawad* property. But with each rapid division and alienation of property the individual share of many ordinary women was next to nothing. Large-scale pauperization of women was a common feature of this period. The *tarawad* which sheltered them withered away.

The later Acts, The Malabar Tenancy (Amendment) Acts of 1951 and 1954 and the Agrarian Relations Bill 1959 were meant to bring a fair deal to lower rungs of cultivating tenants and some relief to agricultural labourers. But by now, landlords and tenants came to be viewed as antagonistic categories and all progressive sympathies were with tenants. Saradamoni writes:

> Examining the comprehensive land reform legislations Kerala had passed in 1960–70s from the point of view of women, one is compelled to think that they gave further legal sanction to the protected and secondary role to which marumakkathayam women were being relegated since the British rule and the ideology that accompanied it. There was no attempt to examine how the proposed legislations would affect women. This happened even after the government's attention was drawn to the possible hardship that most women who were small landholders and who did not have any other income would face if their interests were not safeguarded. The Bill was given wide publicity

[40]Ibid p. 162.
[41]Ibid p. 163.

> to elicit public opinion and many women responded and pointed out that they had no source of income other than the lands entrusted to the tenants for cultivation. They asked for concessions to those who wished to have lands taken back from tenants for self-cultivation.

One of the questions raised during the public debate was from a person speaking on behalf of a Nayar couple both of whom had inherited *tarawad* property. The woman wanted to know the guidelines for the retention or surrender of lands if their total holding exceeded the ceiling limit. She pleaded that the wife be allowed to retain her property as often the husbands would have an independent, regular, non-agricultural income. She even mentioned the possibility of strained relations between the couple, when the wife would be deprived of any economic means if she were to surrender her lands. However, the issues raised by these women did not come up for discussion.

Saradamoni concludes:

> The arguments raised here may be criticised as trying to portray a past which met with its natural end. The answer to this could be that these legislations did not go their logical conclusion and could not bring about fairer distribution of land among the cultivators. A plea for a fresh look at *marumakkathayam* and the process of change is not to glorify it but it serves as a very good example from recent Indian history to understand the changing status of women. The plea is not for retention of private property in certain hands. The aim is to see whether questions of fairness and equality between men and women, not to leave out class, ever became the matter of debate in the process of passing 'progressive' legislations. Were all relevant questions considered? Above all, the discussion draws out attention to the role of ideas and inculcation of 'false consciousness' which is highly relevant even today especially in the context of women and change. They have a very important role in the institutionalization of relations of power, privilege and status, between classes, regions and countries. The disadvantaged sections including women sometimes show an 'objectively unfounded faith in the process of law. It is necessary for the socially committed scientists and practioners of law and activists to understand and explore what concepts like equality, freedom, justice and progress mean in any specific context, to the most disadvantaged ...[42]

There is growing evidence to suggest that the imposition of a Brahminical code served to undermine the localized, custom-based notions of women's position. The norms of the refurbished Brahminism created by colonial officials invariably implied stricter regulation of women's sexuality. At another level, the land

[42]Ibid pp. 164–5.

regulation policies of the British vested greater economic power in the hands of individual men which could now be used to control and regulate women's sexuality. The post-independence discourse on women's rights necessarily has to be viewed within this altered social reality.

Identity, Property, and State—the Hindu Succession Act

The Rukhmabai case situated within the Bombay Presidency, the consequences of the judicial verdicts regarding property rights of widows under the Widow Remarriage Act as well as *stridhana* property as reflected in litigation in the high courts of Calcutta, Bombay, and Madras Presidencies, the process of codification of customs and renegotiating land tenures in the Punjab and the Malabar region, read together provide indicators of the various processes through which patriarchal interests were strengthened through colonial initiatives. The vesting of economic rights in the hands of individual men served as a lever for control of women's sexuality in a manner that could not have been done in the precolonial period.

The conflicts and contests between the orthodox/reactionary, the imperialist, and the reformist helped to carve out a new woman for the new nation. Tradition became the site for the elaboration of state power and the power of the national state. As Partha Chatterjee[43] points out, the distinctiveness of the national culture and tradition was built around the conceptualization of a new form of femininity. This process inaugurated a new patriarchy to which the new woman was subjected. It explicitly distinguished itself from the patriarchy of indigenous tradition. The new woman, the 'bhadramahila', respectable woman, was contrasted with the characteristic of the 'common' woman who was coarse, vulgar, loud, and quarrelsome, sexually promiscuous, and subjected to brutal physical oppression by males. Since the reform of women's lives came to symbolize national sovereignty and the project of reform addressed the lives of Hindu middle-class women, this demographic section came effectively to constitute the 'nation'.

[43]*See* Chatterjee, Partha, 'The Nationalist Resolution of the Women's Question', in Kumkum Sangari and Sudesh Vaid (eds), *Recasting Women*, New Delhi: Kali for Women, 1989, pp. 233–53.

Chatterjee also shows that the nationalist resolution of the women's question, built on a system of dichotomies of the inner/outer, spiritual/material, feminine/masculine, gave birth to a national state and a notion of rights and citizenship which was exclusive in that it applied to the new middle class. The project of reform, which located the state in the nationalist resolution of the women's question, excluded those sections of the middle class which felt themselves culturally left out of the specific process of formation of the 'nation'. Indian Muslims, for example, were left out of this hegemonic cultural construct of the nation. The hegemonic 'national culture' that was built through the above process also excluded vast masses of people who could never be culturally integrated with this concept. It is within this newly evolved framework of nation, state, and identity that the discourse of patriarchy and sexuality has to be located in the post-independence period.[44]

Maitreyee Mukhopadhyay[45] argues that the debate to give women property rights in the new code was a debate about establishing a hegemonic Hindu identity and tradition. This tradition was articulated in these debates via the assertion of the jointness of the family, the corporate nature of its interest and the essentialized gender relations which characterized this unity of the family. These essentialized gender relations that characterized Hindu family and tradition also served to hierarchize an upper-caste, upper-class, propertied, patrilineal, north Indian male tradition. 'Hindu' thus became a tradition hegemonized by upper-caste, property-owning males. This tradition was not dismantled in the debates in the post-independence period, but was inscribed in the text of the new enactments. The power of this discourse about tradition lies precisely in that it operates to fix entitlements when women appeal to the state to support their rights to marital and ancestral property.

Hindu law reform in its final phase was argued on the basis that it was necessary to achieve what the new nation state stood for, namely social progress. The references to the Constitution, the eclectic use of references to the sastras and the ancient tradition, are all part of the same narrative of legitimation. The proponents tried to dissociate the new law from religion, and the state was actually

[44]Ibid p. 251.

[45]*See* Mukhopadhyay, Maitreyee, *Legally Dispossessed—Gender, Identity and the Process of Law*, Calcutta: Stree, 1998.

able to carry through legislations and the Hindu Code Bill (HCB) acquired a very special meaning in the life of the nation. It became representative of state capacities to restructure social relations. It has also come to be regarded as a secular law, secular as in 'modern' and, therefore, progressive and also separated from religion.

She contends that both of these have had implications for women. The implications are that the state became the main interlocutor in women's demands for change. This meant that the woman's fate was tied to the state's projects of progress and modernization, reducing thereby the autonomy of the woman's question. The pervasive notion that the HCB is a secular code has been strengthened in its otherness to Muslim personal law. In the present milieu in which the antagonism between political identities, Hindu and Muslim, has gained ground, the HCB has been defined as the secular code which the minorities should emulate. The implication for Hindu women is clear. The asymmetry between men's and women's rights in the family, inscribed in the law, has been obscured as a result. Examining the events around the Shah Bano judgment, she comments:

> The question of women's citizenship was taken over into a field largely defined by the antagonism between Hindu and Muslim. What began as an argument for women's right was dissipated in a vortex of patriarchal and communal formulations of the issue. The conflicts of identities that have emerged create a minefield of problems for feminist politics.[46]

Before addressing the more recent events around the Shah Bano judgment, it is relevant to examine the provisions of the succession rights of Hindu women under the new enactment. A salient feature of the much trumpeted Hindu Succession Act of 1956 was the widow's absolute right of ownership which served to erase the harm caused to widows through the Widow Remarriage Act. The second salient feature was the equal rights conferred on the daughters in the self-acquired property of the father. But the equal inheritance proclaimed by the Act was only notional. The landholdings and the agricultural property remained outside the purview of the 'egalitarian and reformed' Act. Further, even this limited property could be willed away or 'thrown into the joint stock' to convert into a coparcenary, out of the reach of the female heirs!

But even worse, these narrow provisions for women's inheritance

[46]Ibid p. 4.

are seldom utilized. Most Hindu women are not given shares of natal family property, or appear to refuse their own inheritances. The passing of the Hindu Succession Act has remained a non- event in the lives of most Hindu women. Exploring a basic question—why have laws of equal inheritance not worked for Indian women in over four decades after independence—Srimati Basu contends:

> Answers to this question cover a range of political, cultural, and economic issues, indicating how property transmission reproduces hegemonic space. The role of law needs to be considered from diverse angles: the functions of the cultural imagery [sic] created through state legislation, the cultural mechanisms that inhibit legal reform, and the ambivalence of turning to the law for women's empowerment.[47]

She further contends that one of the central tropes that codes Indian women's disentitlement to property on the grounds of customs and ancient loyalties is the spectre of the uncaring and greedy sister who claims family property. She is an overreaching woman grabbing at undeserved resources, so intent on pursuing the privileges enshrined in the letter of the law that she ignores emotional ties and destroys family harmony. This trope is not only reiterated in various forms by women explaining their voluntary forfeiture of family harmony, but also appears in other contexts such as in legal judgments or in marital negotiations.[48]

Conjugality, Morality, and Maintenance

The image of the property-grabbing woman is in sharp contrast to the new feminine woman constructed through the nationalistic discourse, the *bhadramahila* that Chatterjee refers to. This construction is shunned by women themselves at the cost of refuting their rights to property. But one place this 'common' woman—the *coarse, vulgar, loud and quarrelsome, sexually promiscuous*—becomes visible in legal discourse over property is through her claim to maintenance. Contrary to the respectable woman who does not stake her claim to property, this woman, usually of the lower class, is clearly visible under a section titled 'Maintenance' and invariably her claim to property (read economic rights) is entangled with sexual morality.

[47]Basu, Srimati, *She Comes to Take Her Rights: Indian Women, Property, and Propriety*, New Delhi: Kali for Women, 2001, p. 4.

[48]Ibid p. 5.

Husbands, with the aid of their lawyers, routinely rely upon the image of a sexually promiscuous and property-grabbing manipulator, to defeat women's claims to a paltry maintenance award. These claims are not situated under the 'codified' marriage laws but under an unpretentious and dismal provision of the Criminal Procedure Code (CrPC). The maintenance dole awarded under it has no claims of any property settlement but is meant for mere survival.[49] For these women, the maintenance applications would be their only claim to 'property' or economic rights. This otherwise innocuous section, came alive through the Shah Bano controversy in 1985 and is retained in public memory due to the furore it caused at the time, resulting in the enactment of the controversial Muslim Women's Act.[50] But rather strangely, the notions of sexual morality which this section is riddled with has not received due attention in contemporary feminist legal discourse.

The mischief is caused by Clauses 4 and 5 of S.125 CrPC which stipulate:

(4) *No woman shall be entitled to receive an allowance if she is living in adultery ...*

(5) *On proof that any wife in whose favour an order has been made under this section is living in adultery ... the magistrate shall cancel the order*

This stipulation provides the armour for husbands to entangle women in vicious and dilatory litigation over a pittance of maintenance. A careful scrutiny of reported cases in any law journal would reveal the extent to which women's chastity and morality comes into play to subvert these claims. To give an example, a journal widely used by lawyers practising matrimonial law, *Divorce and Matrimonial Cases* (DMC), in its volume for the year 2001 reports around forty-five cases under the title 'Maintenance'. In nineteen of these, the head notes reflect that chastity and morality were the core issues under litigation. The layered and multiple contexts through which sexual morality surfaces, as per the norms of patriarchy, serve only one end—to challenge the legitimacy of women's claims. It is a clear case of 'heads I win and tails you lose'. It is irrelevant whether the woman has been adulterous or the man

[49]In 2001, the ceiling of Rs 500 has been removed which has made the section more relevant to women as the maintenance awards can now be decided according to the economic status of the husband.

[50]*See* n. 19 in Chapter 7.

bigamous. As far as the woman is concerned, the purpose for which sexual morality is foregrounded is the same, to deny her maintenance. To illustrate this point, the cases are categorized as per the particular issue of sexual morality which was raised during litigation. Needless to mention that this is only a sampling of the cases around sexual morality, which are listed in DMC for the year 2001.

Allegations of Adultery

Nishi Kanta Halder v State[51]: The wife who was tortured for dowry and was compelled to leave her matrimonial home, filed for maintenance. The husband alleged that the wife is in an adulterous relationship with another man. Since he could not produce any evidence regarding the adultery, the contention was rejected and the woman was awarded Rs 400 as maintenance. The husband filed an appeal against this order in the high court.

Mahesh Chandra v Addl. Civil Judge[52]: A woman who was hearing—impaired was tortured and driven out of her home. When she filed for maintenance, in order to create evidence of immoral character, the husband made his friends file false and frivolous cases for restitution of conjugal right against the wife and later used these as proof of her immorality. Rejecting these contentions the family court granted her Rs 500 as maintenance. Against this order, the husband filed an appeal.

Jiban Krishna Das v Renu Das[53]: After the wife was subjected to dowry harassment and torture and was driven out of the matrimonial home, she filed for maintenance. The husband alleged adultery and contended that he has seen her in a 'compromising position' with another man. Rejecting this contention, the court awarded Rs 900 as maintenance. Against this order, the husband filed an appeal.

Disputing Paternity

Syed Mohd. Ghouse v Noorunnnisa Begum[54]: The husband ill-treated the wife, harassed her for dowry and then deserted her along with the child. When she filed for maintenance the husband pleaded that

[51] I (2001) DMC 119 (Cal).
[52] I (2001) DMC 229 (All).
[53] II (2001) DMC 383 (Cal).
[54] II (2001) DMC 454 (A.P.).

the wife and child are strangers. In view of this the court ordered DNA testing to ascertain the paternity of the child. The husband filed proceedings in the high court against this ruling.

Sunita More v Vivekanand More[55]: When the wife who was deserted filed for maintenance, the husband denied the marriage, cohabitation, and paternity of the child. He also alleged that she had become pregnant through illicit relationship with another person. He further alleged that since he comes from a reputed family, this was a strategy for extortion used by the woman. The woman contended that they were childhood friends and upon a promise of marriage she had conceived and subsequently they had got married. Relying upon her contention, the lower court granted her maintenance and against this order the husband filed an appeal.

Allegations of a Subsisting Previous Marriage of Wife

Pushpabai v Pratap Singh[56]: When Pushpabai, who had been deserted, filed for maintenance, the husband denied the marriage and alleged that Pushpabai had an earlier marriage subsisting and hence there was no legal marriage between them. Pushpabai pleaded that she had been married in childhood and had obtained a customary divorce as per caste customs. She was awarded Rs 500 as maintenance. Against this order, the husband went on appeal.

Ramesh Chandra v Rameshwari[57]: The wife was a divorcee at the time of the marriage and the husband was a widower. After a while, the wife left home due to cruelty and filed for maintenance. The husband denied marriage and paternity. He then alleged that she was working for him as a caretaker and that she had an earlier marriage subsisting and on this basis filed for annulment of marriage. The lower court granted her maintenance. Aganst this verdict, the husband filed an appeal.

Husband's Subsisting First Marriage and Allegations of Concubinage

Mallika v P. Kulandai[58]: Mallika got married to a man who claimed to be a widower. There was a daughter born out of this marriage. When the second wife left him on grounds of dowry harassment

[55]II (2001) DMC 693 (Bom).
[56]I (2001) DMC 110 (MP).
[57]II (2001) DMC 230 (Bom).
[58]I (2001) DMC 354 (Mad).

and claimed for maintenance, the husband challenged the validity of marriage on the ground that he had an earlier marriage subsisting and that his first wife was insane.

Malti v State of U.P.[59]: Malti, a maidservant, started cohabiting with the man in whose house she was employed. Since he was a married man, she was beaten by the first wife and was driven out. So Malti filed for maintenance. Her claim for maintenance was rejected. So she filed an appeal.

Husband's Subsequent Marriage

Sukhi Ram v Raj Dullari[60]: Due to the second marriage of the husband, the wife left the matrimonial home and filed for maintenance. The husband insisted that he would maintain her only on the condition she agrees to return to him and cohabit with him and his second wife. But the court took the view that the husband cannot insist on the wife cohabiting with him along with the second wife and granted maintenance to the wife. In appeal, the high court upheld this contention.

Sulochana Devi v State of Bihar[61]: Sulochana Devi had left her matrimonial home due to her husband's cruelty. Her contention was that the husband had remarried and driven her out of the house. The husband denied the second marriage. Since the same could not be proved, Sulochana was denied maintenance. In appeal, the court held that since the wife is a legally married first wife, even if the husband is married subsequently, this fact does not disentitle her to maintenance.

As can be observed, the issues of sexuality, morality, and polygamy, whichever way they emerge, can always be turned against the woman's claims of maintenance. For instance, it really does not matter whether the woman's previous marriage or the husband's subsequent bigamy is in dispute. So long as sexuality is pitted against property claims (read maintenance) the intention is the same.

Scanning through the judgments one can see a positive role played by the judges. Gradually, there is a change in judicial interpretations of sexuality, morality, and adultery when it is used to contest women's claims of maintenance. Despite this, the prevalence of S.125 (4) and (5) provides the scope for husbands to entangle

[59]I (2001) DMC 204 (All).
[60]II (2001) DMC 407 (J&K).
[61]II (2001) DMC 107 (Pat).

wives in prolonged litigation. The judicial proclamations are briefly summarized here.

Adultery

In the case of *Jiban* the Calcutta High Court held that a solitary act of adultery is not sufficient to prove charges of adultery against the wife. While upholding the maintenance award of Rs 700 awarded by the lower court, the high court held: 'It is well settled that the words "living in adultery" used in 125 (4) of CrPC contemplates a continuous course of conduct of adultery on the part of the wife. A single Act of unchastity or a few lapses from virtue will not disentitle the wife from claiming maintenance.'

In *Nishi*'s case, the court ruled that just the mere presence of the adulterer in the same place as the wife along with other relatives is not proof of adultery. In *Mahesh*'s case, the court held that the husband had caused incalculable harm to the wife by terming her as a woman of loose morals and awarded Rs 20,000 as exemplary costs. In another case, the Allahabad High Court[62] held: .... *The husband has levelled charges of adultery against his wife without proving the same in the court. Such habit is generally rampant. Reckless charges of corrupt life against the wife are levelled without any hesitation by the husbands. Such a conduct on the part of the husbands is incomprehensible and this practice is to be deprecated.*

Paternity

Regarding parenting in *Syed Mohd* case, the court held that though the court cannot compel a person to give a sample of blood, the court can draw inferences as a necessary corollary in sequel thereof. Since the marriage in this case was not in dispute, the court relied upon S.112 of the Indian Evidence Act to presume paternity and award maintenance to the child.

Proof of Marriage

In *Mallika*'s case, the court ruled that though the marriage could not be strictly proved there is sufficient evidence to establish that the parties lived together for a considerable period of time and continuously, long enough for a child to be born. Since the husband had misrepresented that his first wife was dead, the court granted maintenance to the second wife and her child born of that union.

[62] *Kamal Kishore v State of UP* I (2001) DMC 313 (All).

(But the amount awarded was a meagre Rs 250 for the wife and Rs 50 for the child.)

Although the majority of the judgments are in favour of women, a stray negative judgment needs to be cited in detail to highlight the humiliation a woman goes through during these litigations. In *Malti*'s case the Allahabad High Court held:

> *If the man and woman choose to live together and indulge into sex no such marriage status can be conferred automatically by their so living upon such a woman. She is not entitled to the legal status of a wife in the eyes of law and society. Law and society treat such women either as concubine or a mistress of the person with whom she is living. The two may agree to live together to satisfy their animal needs. But such a union is never called a marriage. A woman leading such a life cannot be bestowed with the sacrosanct honour of wife.*

No marital obligations accrue to such a woman against her husband. Such a wife must be termed adulterous. It really didn't seem to matter to the judge that it was the husband who had committed adultery/ bigamy. But using the language of sexual morality, the husband was absolved of the financial liability towards the woman.

To overcome the uncertainty which surfaces in matrimonial / maintenance litigation, some progressive/feminist lobbies have campaigned for compulsory registration of marriages. But such a shortsighted stance would only serve to impose an even stricter code of sexual morality upon women and would lead to invalidating all unregistered marriages and render the plight of women at the margins even more pitiable than at present. This would indeed be regressive and deprive them of the presumption of marriage due to prolonged cohabitation, and the presumption of legitimacy of children which is presently available under the Indian Evidence Act.[63]

But more positive recommendations of validating collateral and informal relationships and awarding them the right of maintenance/ residence have emerged from very unlikely quarters.

One is the recommendations by the Malimath Committee, a highly official body, constituted for suggesting reforms of criminal justice system. The recommendations of the committee are highly controversial and have met with severe criticism[64] from human rights groups for trampling upon the rights of the accused.

[63]Sections 50 and 112 of the Indian Evidence Act.

[64]See the latest publication of the Amnesty International, India, September 2003.

Nonetheless, it has come up with a suggestion: *Definition of the word 'wife' in Section 125 of the Code be amended to include a woman who was living with the man like his wife for a reasonably long period.*[65] (To quote from the report is not in the least to endorse it as the recommendations are violative of both human rights and women's rights in all other context.)

More striking is the provision in the proposed civil law on domestic violence. This bill initially drafted by activist groups and women's rights lawyers takes the issue even beyond and seeks to grant rights of residence to cohabitants and women in informal relationships. In view of the demand made by women's groups, the Parliamentary Standing Committee on Human Resource Development in its 124th Report on the Protection from Domestic Violence Bill, 2002, has made the following recommendation: *The Committee is aware of the fact that in our society there are numerous cases where a man and a woman, though not legally married, live together as husband and wife and their relationship has got social sanction too. ... The Committee, therefore, suggests that (the Bill) should be suitably amended to include those women also who have been living in relationship akin to marriages and in marriages considered invalid by law.*[66]

Conclusion

While these need to be welcomed as positive measures, the question that remains is how do we then view the claim of monogamy upon which hinges the demand of the women's movements for a uniform civil code which is then reflected in liberal claims of modernity and secular marriages. Rather surprisingly, this concern has not been foregrounded in the debates while endorsing the claims of cohabitants and second wives. The premise of a uniform civil code which mandates monogamous marriages still persists.

While these have been the collateral legal concerns, in more political discourse on uniform civil code, the only issue that gets constantly foregrounded not only in the mainstream media but also in progressive discourse is the rights of divorced Muslim women and the image of a polygamous Muslim male. What is revealing in the cases discussed for the year 2001, as reported in DMC, is that,

[65]See Point 16 (115) of the recommendations.

[66]Point 4.3 of the Parliamentary Standing Committee Recommendations.

of the nineteen cases which dealt with sexual morality, barring one solitary instance, all other cases concerned Hindu marriages.

This question brings us back to the concerns of nation, nationhood and identity, and hegemomic claims of dominant ideologies. Within the communally vitiated atmosphere, the advances made by divorced Muslim women under the provisions of the controversial *Muslim Women's Act of 1986* (which was enacted following the Shah Bano judgment and which has been labelled by women's rights and progressive lobbies as the most anti-women piece of legislation in independent India) have been rendered invisible and glossed over by the media, both mainstream and alternative.

Law is not merely an enactment but its essence lies in the manner in which it is unfolded in law courts. Right from 1988, the courts have engineered women's rights through innovative interpretation of the new statute, ushering in a new set of rights within the established principles of Muslim law. Several high courts and the lower judiciary gave a clear verdict in favour of a 'fair and reasonable provision' for life for the divorced Muslim woman in addition to the presumed maintenance for three months of *Iddat* period. What is significant is that the lump sum provision for the future does not function through a rider of sexual purity or post-divorce chastity. Can a legal provision that better secures women's rights be disregarded on the mere notion of 'uniformity' or an absurd logic of national integration as reflected in some recent judicial proclamations and popular discourse?

During the Shah Bano controversy, the denial of rights of a meagre maintenance dole was lamented by all and sundry, notwithstanding the fact that the maintenance awarded to the wife of an advocate with a flourishing practice was just Rs 25 in the first instance and Rs 179 in appeal.[67] So long as the debate could be used as a stick to beat the community, these *minor* details did not seem to matter. What did matter is the fact that a communal campaign could be mounted upon a patriarchal paradigm and thereby legitimized. The irony lay in the fact that the groundwork for mounting this campaign was laid by the women's movement, with genuine gender concerns, but firmly located within the cultural ethos of the mainstream. Within this framework, a similar appeasement of Hindus, by strengthening coparcenaries by various legislative measures, could be deliberately ignored.

[67]For a detailed discussion of this issue see Chapter 7 of *Law and Gender Inequality*.

The communal fervour could be sustained only by denying that the Act provided for an alternative remedy, far superior to the one that had been denied to Muslim women under S.125 CrPC; by negating the fact that since 1988, the Act was being positively interpreted by various high courts in the country by awarding substantial amounts as 'settlements'; by glossing over an important development in the realm of family law, that of determination of economic entitlements upon divorce, rather than the prevailing right of recurring maintenance.[68] In a series of cases, the various high courts upheld the Muslim women's rights for a 'fair and reasonable' lump sum in lieu of the paltry monthly maintenance.

But rather ironically, even while homes of poor Muslim women were looted, gutted, and razed to the ground in various communal riots which broke out in the country in the post Shah Bano phase, while teenage sons of Muslim women were killed at point-blank ranges in police firings, while Muslim women were raped under floodlights in riots following the pulling down of the Babari Masjid, the mainstream continued to lament over *Muslim appeasement* and denial of maintenance to '*poor Muslim women—the Shah Banos*'.

One could overlook even this. Perhaps there was a justification. Denial of maintenance by husbands was perhaps as loathsome as rape of women in communal riots. In the ultimate analysis, it was the Muslim woman who suffered. So far so good. But how can one logically explain the recurring motif of 'Muslim appeasement' even after the Supreme Court decision in *Daniel Latifi*[69] case, when the controversy was finally laid to rest by upholding the constitutional validity of the Act and simultaneously securing the rights of Muslim women? Unfortunately, this historic judgment proclaimed by a Constitution Bench of the Supreme Court which upheld the right of a divorced Muslim woman for a fair and reasonable settlement received hardly any publicity. Since there was no controversy through which an anti-Muslim propaganda could be mounted, it did not make a 'good story' for the media and got buried unceremoniously.

And the rhetoric was allowed to continue. And is used yet again, in defence of the Gujarat carnage. '*They had it coming ... they have been "appeased" beyond tolerance. Why should they demand a separate law in a secular country? Why should they be allowed to marry four times?*

[68]*See* Agnes, Flavia, (2001) *Judgement Call*, Mumbai: Majlis (NGO Publication), 2001.

[69]II (2001) DMC 714 (SC).

Why are Hindus alone bound by an obligation of maintenance?' What is startling is that the grievances are mouthed not only by Hindu extremists but also by centrists and liberals, the urban, cosmopolitan, middle class. Within the cultural ethos of the mainstream, an injustice to a Muslim wife gets magically transformed into a Hindu injury which could be invoked to justify communal carnage. Without this tacit approval by the middle class, the recent Gujarat carnage could never have spread so wide and so deep.

The rhetoric conveniently overlooks the fact that abandonment and destitution of wives is as rampant among Hindus; that the matrimonial faults of adultery and bigamy are evenly distributed across communities and that Hindus, Christians, and Parsees, with equal zeal, guard the patriarchal prerogatives within their respective personal laws. Further, that around 80 per cent of all women burnt in their matrimonial homes are urban middle-class Hindus!

The symbolism becomes even more stark when one is confronted with the gruesome sexual violations of women during the recent carnage in Gujarat in 2002. While exploring possible legal portals to place these blood-curdling barbarities, one hits a dead end at each turn. As one hears the narratives of young women running helter-skelter, slipping, failing, and becoming preys to the marauding mobs, their violated and mutilated bodies being thrown into open fires, the question keeps haunting: where and how does one pin down the culpability?

When violence of this scale supersedes the confines of criminal jurisprudence which is bound by conventions of proof and evidence, medical examinations and forensic reports, when criminal prosecution itself is a closed-end process in the hands of the state machinery, what legal measures can be invoked to bring justice to the dead and the surviving? It is then that the covenants of equality and equal protection mock you in the face. At the other end, there is a danger that as these violations do not form part of 'official records' they can be conveniently negated as baseless allegations or normalized as routine occurrences. There has not been so stark an instance of collusion between identity, state, and patriarachy through which the sexuality of women from marginalized communities could be violated in such a gruesome manner.

Viewed within this background, when Muslim women are increasingly getting pushed to acknowledge a community identity against a gender identity, the struggles of individual divorced

Muslim women who defied their culture and tradition and norms of patriarchy have to be acknowledged as acts of assertion. Divorced Muslim women had to fight every inch of the way for their rights, right from the trial courts in small district towns up to the Supreme Court. And they withstood the ordeal with courage and determination.

For instance, for Jaitunbi, the struggle started in the small magistrate's court in Satara way back in 1986 and in the first round she was awarded a paltry sum of Rs 60 as maintenance. Later when her husband divorced her, the courts upheld her right to a fair and reasonable settlement for life. For Amina from a small town in Kerala, the struggle was to retain the Rs 30,000 awarded to her as fair and reasonable settlement for life. For Shehnazbi from Maharashtra the struggle was to actualize the amount awarded. For Ameena Begum of Tamil Nadu the struggle was to retain the meagre amount awarded to her by way of maintenance during the postdivorce period.

All these women's claims were at stake before the Supreme Court as their husbands had filed appeals against the high court orders. In the final battle in the Supreme Court, both sides—the women's rights and progressive lobbies who had challenged the constitutionality of the Act as well as the Muslim religious leadership and the respective husbands, who had pressed for their claim that the Muslim woman's entitlement was limited to three months of *Iddat* period—lost out. Who emerged victorious was the divorced Muslim woman, the *Jaitunbis*, the *Ameena Begums* and the *Shehnazbis*, the new *Shah Banos*, who had waged a relentless battle to defend their meagre economic rights.

The political and emancipatory value of focusing on the peripheral subject and identifying her locations of resistance when addressing women's human rights, which I have mentioned in the context of Rukhmabai's case, is as relevant when we address the struggles of individual Muslim women in litigations under the Muslim Women's Act. Just as the Rukhmabai case would serve to shift the rigid and fixed binaries of First World feminists/Third World victim-subject, the struggles of Muslim women would serve to shift the binaries of mainstream feminists/Muslim victims in the contemporary Indian feminist legal discourse.

Law and Gender Inequality

LAW AND GENDER INEQUALITY

❖

The Politics of Women's Rights in India

Flavia Agnes

Dedicated to fifty years of nation building

Acknowledgements

The research that served as the foundation for this book was conducted as my M Phil dissertation with the National Law School, Bangalore. I am grateful to my guides, Professors N.S. Gopalakrishnan and M.P.P. Pillai for their useful suggestions and warm encouragement through the period of this research and to Professor Madhava Menon, Director, National Law School for not only motivating me to take on this work but also for helping me to structure it. To the faculty members and students of the National Law School I would like to express my gratitude for their participation in the various seminars, that I had presented during the course of this research and also for ensuring a lively debate which helped to formulate the study. Without NSG's gentle but constant goading I would never have found the time to complete this work.

Professors Upendra Baxi and B. Sivaramayya made comments on the first draft that have been extremely encouraging. I have tried to incorporate some of their valuable suggestions while working on the final draft.

The research could neither have been embarked upon nor completed in its present state, without the involvement of Madhusree Dutta, my friend and colleague at Majlis. Although not possessing a legal background, nevertheless her political clarity has helped me immensely in sorting out my doubts and confusion. I extend my special thanks to her.

I also extend my warm gratitude to my colleagues Saumya Uma and Veena Gowda for their help in locating source material, helping with the references and for reading through the various drafts and offering some very useful suggestions. Their contribution has enriched this work. I also extend a special thanks to them for taking on a greater burden of litigation work at the Majlis legal centre, while I was engaged in research work. I also thank each one at Majlis for the support and encouragement they extended to me while completing this work.

My thanks to Daisy Rodrigues for her help in entering the data, correcting the various drafts and all other minute editorial help which was required for completing this work in its present form. I must mention the help offered by Savita Krishnan in laboriously cross-checking all the references.

I also thank my daughters, Odile and Audrey for their gentle, unobtrusive emotional support through this venture.

Flavia Agnes
March, 1998

Contents

Abbreviations

ACJ	—	Appellate Case Journal
AIDWA	—	All India Democratic Women's Association
AIMPLB	—	All India Muslim Personal Law Board
AIR	—	All India Reporter
All	—	Allahabad
Anr	—	Another
AP	—	Andhra Pradesh
Art.s.	—	Article/s
BHCR	—	Bombay High Court Reports
BJP	—	Bharatiya Janata Party
BLR	—	Bengal Law Reporter
Bom.LR	—	Bombay Law Reporer
Bom	—	Bombay
Cal	—	Calcutta
Cr.PC	—	Code of Criminal Procedure
Cri.LJ	—	Criminal Law Journal
Cri.MC	—	Criminal Maintenance Cases
CAD	—	Constituent Assembly Debates
Del	—	Delhi
DMC	—	Divorce and Matrimonial Cases
FB	—	Full Bench
Guj	—	Gujarat
HC	—	High Court
HP	—	Himachal Pradesh
IA	—	Indian Appeals
IDA	—	Indian Divorce Act
ILR	—	Indian Law Reports
IPC	—	Indian Penal Code
J	—	Judge
JJ	—	Judges
JT	—	Judgment Today
Kar	—	Karnataka
KLT	—	Kerala Law Times

LAD	—	Legislative Assembly Debates
LC	—	Law Commission
LSD	—	Lok Sabha Debates
MIA	—	Moore's Indian Appeals
Mad	—	Madras
Madh Bh	—	Madhya Bharat
MLJ	—	Madras Law Journal
MP	—	Madhya Pradesh
Nag	—	Nagpur
Ori	—	Orissa
Ors	—	Others
P	—	Page
PP	—	Pages
Pat	—	Patna
PC	—	Privy Council
PD	—	Parliamentary Debates
P&H	—	Punjab and Haryana
PLJ	—	Pakistan Law Journal
PLD	—	Pakistan Law Digest
POC	—	Perry's Oriental Cases
Punj	—	Punjab
Rpt	—	Reprint
Raj	—	Rajasthan
RSD	—	Rajya Sabha Debates
R/w	—	Read with
S/s	—	Section/s
SB	—	Special Bench
SC	—	Supreme Court
SCC	—	Suprme Court Cases
SCR	—	Supreme Court Reporter
SCW	—	Supreme Court Weekly
SDA	—	Sudder Diwani Adawlut
TLLS	—	Tagore Law Lecture Series
Tra—Co	—	Travancore and Cochin
UCC	—	Uniform Civil Code
v	—	Versus
WEF	—	With Effect From
WR	—	Weekly Reporter
WP	—	Writ Petition
WRAG	—	Women's Research Action Group

Table of Cases

1

INTRODUCTION—*A Need for Rescrutiny*

1.1 The Dilemma

The issue of women's rights and family law reform has been increasingly entangled within the polemics of identity politics and minority rights. At one level, there is a tendency among social activists to project the demand for an all-encompassing Uniform Civil Code (UCC) as a magic wand which will eliminate the woes and sufferings of Indian women in general and of minority women in particular. At another level, within a communally vitiated political climate, the demand carries an agenda of 'national integration' and 'communal harmony'. The demand is also laden with a moral undertone of abolishing polygamy and other 'barbaric' customs of the minorities and extending to them the egalitarian code of the 'enlightened majority'.

The sharp polarization between the pro-UCC lobby (with women's rights' groups sharing an uneasy alliance with the Hindu fundamentalists) and the anti-UCC lobby symbolized by Muslim fundamentalists, leaves very little space for voicing misgivings about the feasibility of an all-encompassing code, within a culturally diverse pluralistic society.

The secular lobbies demanding the protection of women's rights, place gender as a neutral terrain which is disjunct from the contemporary political events. In this context, it would be relevant to take note of the historical fact that although the plank of social reform has been 'women's welfare' the political manoeuverings at each stage of reform have resulted in bartering away crucial economic rights of women. In the current political context, the binaries within which the demand is located, postulates similar dangers.

It is true that the hardships and sufferings experienced by women of all communities, minority as well as majority, cannot be swept under the carpet nor glossed over with the rhetoric of freedom of religion. But within a complex social, political and economic structure, the demand of gender equality cannot be confined within a linear mould of granting uniform rights to women of all communities. In order to be relevant to women's lives, there is an urgent need to contextualize the proposed reforms within a comprehensive framework, inclusive of political and economic diversities.

The Bar Council Review on Uniform Civil Code articulates this premise as follows:

> The production of a new, progressive code, overnight, sought to be enforced from above, may be seen as a quick solution. Let us however remember, that there are well meaning, genuinely secular-minded intellectuals and social activists who would utter a word of caution and hoist the 'go slow' signal in order to achieve productive social results. This approach is informed by the experience of world history and the knowledge that crude homogenization is not the best solution. This caution must not, however, be equated with acceptance of the status-quo nor treated as a call for inaction.[1]

The current research is guided by a similar concern.

1.2 The Scope of the Research

The study is an attempt to map the issue of gender and law reform upon a broad canvas of history and politics and explore strategies which could safeguard women's rights within a sphere of complex social and political boundaries. While the aim of this research is not to formulate a complex code reflective of this plurality, it is hoped that the thumbnail sketch of the origin and development of family laws in India, along with an exploration of the state interventions at various strategic points in history, will provide the necessary backdrop, against which the demand for gender equality can be reformulated.

The under-currents beneath the rhetoric of women's rights are examined here. Since property and its regulation forms the basis of all civil laws, the legal systems located within feudal and capitalistic patriarchal moulds would necessarily be based upon anti-women stipulations to varying degrees. But within this universe of sexist biases, it is interesting to observe that at particular historical junctures, certain biases of a particular system are either over-emphasized or undermined.

The quote from Manu that a woman must be protected by

her father in childhood, by her husband in youth and by her sons in her old age, and that she is not entitled to freedom is common knowledge. But it is less well-known that Manu laid down comprehensive principles concerning women's separate property approximately two thousand years before the English legal system accepted this in principle, and issued the warning; 'Friends or relations of a woman, who, out of folly or avarice, live upon the property belonging to her, or the wicked ones who deprive her of the enjoyment of her own belongings go to hell'[2], or that Narada dictated that the husband must give one-third of his property to the first wife at his second marriage.[3] These positive dictates are shrouded by an over-emphasis on practices, which are not contained in the *smriti* texts, just as the universally accepted principles of Hindu law—widow immolations and infant marriages—are not. These projections which rendered the Hindu society barbaric, provided the moral justification for colonial rule and its reformist scheme. During the corresponding period, undermining the issue of meagre economic rights of English women, within an indissoluble marital bondage under the tenets of feudal Christianity then becomes a political mission.

To cite another example, the Muslim husband's right to polygamy and triple *talaq* is known to the common man in every street corner. But the awareness that Islam introduced the revolutionary concept of contractual marriage and provided the wife with a unique right of *mehr,* as a restraint upon the husband's power of arbitrary divorce and further, that the Muslim law protects female heirs by restraining the male power of testamentary succession is confined to academic echelons. In this sphere of selective knowledge, the polygamy of a Muslim male, which would lead to an increase in the Muslim population and threaten Hindu society, would provide the basis for the enactment of a Uniform Civil Code, within a culture of aggressive majoritarianism. This political agenda can then be conveniently crouched under an avowed concern for the protection of Muslim women's rights. The codified Hindu law has to be then held up as a model of reform, glossing over the fact that this codification has not been able to arrest the trend of increasing violence towards and even murder of young Hindu brides in their matrimonial homes, to curb Hindu bigamy nor to protect Hindu wives from poverty and destitution.

Similarly, in the political controversy over the UCC, which is locked within the binaries of Hindu majority and Muslim minority, the claims of other religious minorities to a separate personal law, as a marker of their cultural identity, can be conveniently undermined.

The issue is shrouded with other riddles. Why are Christians, whose parent statute revolutionalized the matrimonial laws of all other communities in India, still saddled with archaic provisions which deny them the basic right of divorce? Why does a numerically insignificant religious community like the Parsis, warrant a separate personal law or, even more pertinently, why does an important secular statute like *the Indian Succession Act* divide the secular Indian population into two basic categories: 'Parsis' and 'non-Parsis'? If this is the norm, then why are the reformist and breakaway religions like the Buddhists, Jains, Sikhs (and also the Arya Samajis, Brahmos and the Prarthana Samajis), who are numerically more significant and whose basic tenets differ from Hinduism, and from each other, clubbed together under legal Hinduism?

How was it possible to codify Hindu law despite strong opposition from the various sects and the *sanathan* religious leaders, while even a stray whisper of opposition suffices to stall minority reforms? Then again, if stalling minority reform is the norm, how was a hastily formulated bill constraining the rights of divorced Muslim women hurriedly enacted despite opposition from secular forces?

Probing the answers to these riddles, which lie not in legal edifices but within political vagaries, is the starting point of this book. To achieve this, it was essential to cross the boundaries of popular presumptions and examine the lesser known aspects of family law. The first task was to examine whether, within the constrained sphere of patriarchal norms, there were spaces within religious laws and customary practices of Hindus and Muslims, which women could negotiate to protect their economic rights. The second task was to explore whether the statutory interventions during colonial and post-colonial periods, which were set within the adversarial adjudicative fora introduced by the British, have led to the widening of this constrained sphere. This political grounding of women's rights is essential for evolving strategies which will effectively safeguard women's rights in a communally vitiated political climate.

1.3 The Scheme of the Chapters

The study is divided into four parts. Part One deals with the pre-colonial and colonial legal systems. Chapters 2 and 3 set out the scriptural mandates and customary practices which governed family relationships of various communities in the pre-colonial societies of ancient India. Within the broad scheme of legal principles, the safeguards provided for securing women's rights form the nucleus. The following two chapters, 4 and 5, examine the transformations brought about within these systems through colonial interventions. Since the present legal system in India was introduced by the British, changes brought about during nearly three centuries of colonial rule in the administrative structure of the courts and in the realm of personal laws, both by statutory reforms, as well as judicial interpretations, are important markers. The politicization of women's rights within the realm of family law is inextricably woven into the history of this period.

Part Two of the study examines the Post-independence developments. The Constitution enacted in 1950, became the touchstone against which women's claims to gender equality were to be tested. In Chapter 6, the Hindu law reforms of the 1950s and the implications of this for women are examined in the context of the constitutional guarantee of equality and non-discrimination. Chapter 7 examines whether, in the subsequent decades, the state adhered to its promise of moving towards uniformity and gender equality, or whether there has been a reverse trend, consolidating communal identities. The implications of two significant judicial decisions which invoked wide media publicity and altered the parameters of the discourse on family law reforms—the Tilhari judgement invalidating triple talaq, and the Supreme Court directive for the enactment of a Uniform Civil Code in the context of conversion and bigamy by Hindu males—are analysed in Chapter 8.

In Part Three, the political questions which shroud reforms within non-Muslim minorities (the Parsis and the Christians) are explored. Since the legal systems governing these communities do not figure prominently in the discourse on the Uniform Civil Code, the legislative history contextualized within the social and political terrains is set out in detail, starkly revealing the intricate links between political issues and women's rights.

The concluding section, Part Four, addresses current debates. The issue of the Uniform Civil Code has dominated the gender discourse during the last decade. The communally vitiated atmosphere has brought two constitutional guarantees—minority rights and gender equality—into direct conflict, which has resulted in a political stalemate. To circumvent this problem, legal scholars and women's organizations have been compelled to reformulate their earlier demand for a compulsory Uniform Civil Code. Various alternative measures, both long-term and interim, are being explored by the legal academia, women's groups, and official fora, as well as the Muslim intelligentsia. These efforts are summarized in the concluding chapters. The relevance and implications of the various formulations and strategies to women's economic rights, both within marriage and after its dissolution, are critically assessed. Some suggestions for strengthening the economic rights of women are made which are, at best, tentative. The objective is to bring the focus of the debate to the central issue, that of arresting the trend of destitution and consequential impoverishment of women.

1.4 Research Methodology

The research is grounded within the contemporary women's movement and addresses itself to the trends and currents within it. The analysis of legal texts is undertaken within the framework of feminist jurisprudence. Although the study is primarily a legal exploration, the legal discourse is located within historical developments and contemporary political events and therefore acquires an interdisciplinary flavour.

The research is based on published material, such as legal texts, law journals, reported and unreported judgements; Constituent Assembly and Parliamentary debates, official documents, drafts and bills prepared by legal academicians, women's groups and the official fora; papers presented during conferences and seminars, informal presentations and discussions at legal workshops, and media reportage.

An examination of the strengths and weaknesses of the model drafts formulated in recent years is an important feature of this research. This will hopefully aid the process of arriving at the level of minimum consensus among the progressive and secular lobbies concerned with women's welfare which is a basic pre-condition for reform in the realm of family laws. Even if the first step of this process is facilitated by this work, the attempt would be well worth while.

Notes

1. Mishra, V.C. (ed.), 'Special Issue on Uniform Civil Code', *Indian Bar Review* XVIII/3–4 (1991) p.vi–vii.
2. Manu's dictate is reaffirmed by later *smritikars* such as Katyayana.
3. Narada's dictate is based on Manu who says: 'To a woman whose husband marries a second wife, let him give an equal sum as a compensation for the supersession, provided no stridhana has been bestowed on her but if she has been allotted let him allot half', (*Manusmriti* III: 52).

PART ONE:

PRE-COLONIAL AND COLONIAL LEGAL STRUCTURES

2

Plurality of Hindu Law and Women's Rights Under it

Introduction

It is generally believed that the 'pristine' Hindu law was particularly harsh towards women and denied them sexual and economic freedom. These two freedoms, in fact, are co-ordinate. The Hindu joint family structure based on male coparcenary, was the institution through which sexual control was effected by denying women the right to own property. In this realm of patriarchal domination, women were treated as chattels and upon marriage dominion over them was transferred from the father to the husband within the confines of perpetual tutelage. In support of this premise, it is emphasized that Manu, the arch law giver of the Hindu religion stipulated: 'A woman must be dependent upon her father in childhood, upon her husband in youth and upon her sons in old age. She should never be free.' The strict sexual control was also effected through ordeals. Sita's ordeal by fire is set out as an example. It is also believed that the modernity ushered in during the colonial rule and post-independence period helped to loosen out this strict sexual control by granting women the right of divorce and property ownership.

While not negating in their entirety the above premises, this chapter sets out to explore whether, within these strict dictates, the Hindu law permitted any space for negotiating women's rights. In addition, whether the Indian society of the pre-colonial era was uniformly governed by a singular set of laws and if not, whether the diversity within customary practices situated women's rights on a varying scale. In order to probe the answers to these queries, the following areas are explored: (i) the diverse sources of Hindu law; (ii) women's right to property under the orthodox scriptural law; (iii) the various regional and local customs which granted women rights; (iv) the heterogeneous characteristics of the Indian society governed by the Hindu law.

2.1 The Diverse Sources of Hindu Law

Plurality of laws and customs and non-state legal structure were the essential characteristics of the ancient Indian communities. The original texts were of Aryan origin but the assimilation between Aryan and non-Aryan tribes led to diverse customs and practices.

The scriptural law, like most ancient legal systems, traces its origin to divine revelations. During the early period, there was no distinction between religion, law and morality. They were cumulatively referred to as *dharma*. The three sources of dharma are *shruti* (the divine revelations or utterances, primarily the *Vedas*), *smriti* (the memorized word—the *dharmasutras* and the *dharmashastras*) and *sadachara* (good custom).[1] Although the Vedas were treated as the fountainhead of Hindu law by jurists, they do not contain positive law (or lawyer's law).[2] Hence the codified laws governing Hindu marriage and family relationships derive their roots from the smritis and *nibandhas* (commentaries and digests).[3]

From about eight century BC to fifth century AD elaborate guidelines governing all aspects of social relations were laid down in the smritis—the dharmasutras and the dharmashastras. The *smritikars* were neither kings, religious heads nor legislators.[4] They were philosophers, social thinkers and teachers. They preached dharma, a code of conduct governing all aspects of life from the spiritual to the temporal. The dharmashastra literature is a complete science and covers all aspects of law, ethics and morality. These were works of encyclopaedic scope and covered a wide range of topics—social obligations and duties of the various castes and of individuals in different stages of life; the rules of governance, principles of punishment and warfare for kings and officials; codes of social behaviour between men and women of different castes, as well as between husbands and wives, fathers and sons and family members within the domestic sphere; rules of exogamy and endogamy, sonship and punishments for sexual improprieties; rituals of birth, death, marriage, worship and sacrifice; the philosophy of karma and rebirth; civil or financial matters like rules of contracts, property devolution and interest rates etc. While some rules were mandatory, others were indicatory and hence were not binding and could be treated as mere guidelines. The religious and moral precepts were *achara* and the legal business or positive law was *vyavahara*.

These were not written texts and the knowledge was passed down by an oral tradition from generation to generation through the institution of Brahminical priesthood or *guru-shishya parampara*. So each generation could have re-interpreted the guidelines incorporating their contemporary contexts. In this tradition, the same smriti could have been evolved by several philosophers and at different historical times. Hence it is not surprising to find contradictory statements regarding a controversial issue attributed to the same smritikar.

The nibandhas which were detailed commentaries upon the earlier smritis, were of a later period (fifth to eighteenth century AD). Here too, the authors had sufficient scope to re-interpret the original precepts as per the social organizations of their times. Many a times, while laying down a new principle, the commentators used the ploy of interpretation or explanation of an old dictum for greater validity.

Despite the claim of divine origin, the smritis were based on local and well-established customs.[5] The general agreement among the smritikars was that the time-honoured and accepted customs have greater validity than the scriptures. Since each smriti was influenced by local customs of its region, the eighty-odd known smritis differed a great deal from each other.

The two distinct and dominant schools, validated under the Anglo-Hindu law (a colonial construction), were *Mitakshara* of Vijnaneshwar (eleventh century) and Dayabhaga of Jimmutavahana (twelfth century). While the latter was the leading authority in Bengal, the former was recognized as an authority in the rest of the British India. But there were also several regional deviations, which were categorized as sub-schools of Mitakshara. Significant among these were Mithila, Benares, Bombay and the Dravida schools.[6]

The smritis regarded marriage as an essential *sanskar*. Marriage was mandatory, to discharge the debt to one's ancestors, the debt of begetting offsprings. It was also essential for performance of religious and spiritual duties. So a wife was not just a *patni* or *grihapatni* but a *dharmapatni*. Since progeny was the most important factor, a husband could procure numerous wives for this purpose and could also appropriate the children born to these wives out of other alliances through the institution of sonship, to fulfil spiritual obligations or for temporal objectives such as property devolution. Children could also be begotten through concubines, slaves and other informal alliances and these children were conferred recognition under a legal premise called *dasiputra*.

Although marriages were deemed indissoluble, under certain exceptional situations, the wife or the husband were permitted to dissolve the matrimonial union. Narada (who relied upon an earlier version of *Manusmriti)* laid down five situations in which a woman could take another husband—her first husband having perished, died naturally, gone abroad, impotent or lost caste.[7] Kautilya's *Arthashastra* also stipulated certain situations in which either the husband or the wife could divorce each other—mutual enmity, apprehension of danger and desertion for justifiable reasons. According to scholars, the stipulation in *Manusmriti* against remarriage of wives and widows appears to be a later insertion.[8]

2.2 Concept of Stridhana in Smritis[9]

The smritis and commentaries, with their roots in a feudal society of agrarian landholdings,[10] prescribed a patriarchal family structure, within which women's right to property was constrained. Under the Mitakshara law, the property of a Hindu male devolved through survivorship jointly upon four generations of male heirs. The ownership was by birth and not by succession. Upon his birth, the male member acquired the right to property.

Although the male members owned property, this ownership cannot be equated with the modern notion of ownership which essentially confers the right of alienation. The basic characteristic of the joint property was its inalienability. The property could not be easily disposed of by way of sale, gift or will. Hence the joint ownership, of males was more notional than actual. The property was managed by the head of the family or *karta* for the benefit of the entire family including its female members. So, in effect, until the property was partitioned, the right of male members was essentially the right of maintenance. Even after partition, the property in the hands of each of the coparcenars, continued to be joint property, held in trust along with his male progeny for the benefit of the next line of descendants.

Since women did not form part of the coparcenary, they did not have even the notional right of joint ownership, hence they could not demand partition. After partition, a sonless widow had the right to inherit the share of her deceased husband.[11] Women had the right to be maintained from the joint property and this right included the right of residence. Since divorce was not commonly prevalent, after marriage, women could not easily be deprived of their right of residence and maintenance in their husband's house.

The husband was bound to maintain the wife despite all her faults including quarrelsome nature, neglect of household, barrenness and adultery, though the scale at which she had to be maintained would go down as per the severity of her faults. He could marry again, but he was under the legal obligation to continue to maintain the first wife. In addition, the wife was entitled to 'supersession fee' an equal share of the property, which the husband gifted to the new wife. Women also had the right to claim marriage expenses from the joint property in their natal house.

In order to partially set off the disability suffered under the notion of joint ownership by male members, the smritikars assigned a special category of property to women they termed as *stridhana*. The first mention of this term is found in the Gautama Dharmasutra. He provided not only for the woman's separate property but also distinct and separate rules for its succession.[12] From this period to the next millennium, the scope of stridhana was gradually expanded to include almost every category of property.

Continuing the tradition set by Gautama, Manu laid down six forms of stridhana consisting of gifts by relatives on various occasions : (i) gifts before the nuptial fire (*adhyagni*); (ii) gifts during bridal procession, while the bride is being led from her natal residence to her husband's house (*adhyavahanika*); (iii) gifts of love from father-in-law and mother-in-law (*pritidatta*) and gifts made at the time of obeisance at the feet of elders (*padavandanika*); (iv) gifts made by father; (v) gifts made by mother; and (vi) gifts made by brother. A dictate of Manu[13] which empowered a righteous king to punish as thieves, the relatives, who appropriated the property of a woman, is quoted in all the later smritis with approval.

Vishnu, a later smritikar, added four more categories to this enumeration—gifts by the husband to his wife on supersession, that is, on the occasion of his taking another wife (*adhivedanika*); (ii) gifts subsequent, that is, gifts made after marriage by husband's relatives or the wife's parents (*anwadheyaka*); (iii) *sulka* a marriage fee or a gratuity; and (iv) gifts from sons and relatives. The later sages, Yagnavalkya, Katyayana, Narada, Devala etc. widened the concept further. Yagnavalkya (around second century AD) expanded the scope of stridhana by adding the word *adhya* ('and the rest') to the enumerations of Manu and Vishnu.

The Katyayana Smriti lays great emphasis on stridhana and discusses the concept elaborately. Katyayana classified the stridhana property as *saudayika* and *asaudayika* and explained the concept as follows: What is obtained by a married woman or by a maiden, in the house of her husband or her father, from her brother, husband and parents is saudayika stridhana. The saudayika stridhana could include immovable property. He emphasized the exclusive ownership both in terms of sale and gift and laid down: Neither the husband, nor the son, nor the father, nor the brother have authority over stridhana to take it or to give it away. This injunction is almost in the nature of a warning to male members to lay their hands off the woman's property.[14] If the husband borrowed saudayika money, he was under a legal obligation to repay it with interest.

The wealth which was earned through mechanical arts or through gifts from strangers during the subsistence of marriage was categorized as asaudayika stridhana and only these were made subject to the husband's control. This is not to deny that these were also a woman's separate property or her stridhana which she could use according to her will. The stipulation was merely that a woman had to obtain her husband's consent before disposing off the property of this category during the subsistence of her marriage. There also seems to have been a usage that property upto the limit of two thousand *panas* should be given annually to a married woman by the father, mother, husband, brother or kindred (relatives) for her personal use.[15]

Sir Henry Maine in his '*Early History of Institutions*, while describing the institution of stridhana comments, 'It is certainly remarkable that the institution seems to have been developed among the Hindus at a period relatively much earlier than among the Romans.' But he seems to be under the erroneous impression that it gradually deteriorated to an insignificant position. There is no historical basis for this premise, if the later commentaries are the indicators.[16]

The *Mitakshara* (Vijnaneshwar, eleventh century AD), the most widely recognized source of the Anglo-Hindu law, expanded the scope of the term *adhya* mentioned by Yagnavalkya and laid that property obtained by a woman through inheritance, purchase, partition, seizure (adverse possession), and finding is her stridhana. Through this expansion, every category of property was brought under the scope of stridhana and the woman was granted exclusive ownership over it. While this was endorsed by many of the later commentators, *Vyavahara Mayuka* (of Nilakantha Bhatta, seventeenth century, Bombay school), further expanded the scope.[17]

The *Dayabhaga*, the accepted authority of the Bengal school, did not adopt the notion of joint male ownership or coparcenary. Upon the death of the head of the family, the property was partitioned equally between the legal heirs. Women as widows, daughters and mothers were conferred a share in the family property. Despite this, even the Dayabhaga school recognized the concept of a woman's specific property. But in the absence of a ccparcenary spreading over four generations, the need to prescribe a wide interpretation to the term was absent here. So under the Dayabhaga system, stridhana was restricted to gifts and movables. Under all other schools, stridhana included movable, as well as immovable property. Property acquired by a woman by her own exertions was her stridhana according to the Bombay, Benares and Dravida schools.[18]

As can be observed, a system of property ownership by women seems to have been an integral and significant part of the ancient moral, ethical, and legal social norms. Due weightage was granted to this subject in Sanskrit scriptures. It does appear that patriarchal collusions constantly undermined the scriptural dictates of the dharma of stridhana. At each time the smritikars, with great effort, brought the emphasis back to women's ownership of property and in the process also expanded its scope. There seems to be a constant tussle between the smriti dictates and patriarchal subversions within the family. The task of the smritikars seems to have been challenging, as can be observed from the comments of Jimutavahana, the author of Dayabhaga, on completion of his chapter on stridhana. Thus has been explained the most difficult subject of succession to a childless woman's stridhana.[19]

The most distinguishing feature of stridhana property was its line of descent. Under *Mitakshara*, after the woman's death, it devolved firstly on the unmarried daughter, then on the married daughter who is not provided for, followed by the married daughter who is provided for. Next in line was the daughter's daughter followed by the daughter's son. The woman's own son could inherit it only in the absence of heirs in the female line.[20]

2.3 Women's Rights Under Customary Law

As already mentioned, custom was an important source of law. Two points need to be stressed regarding this source—(i) its validity under the smriti law; and (ii) its relevancy to castes and tribes who were not governed by the smriti law.

Local customs were held in high esteem and were acknowledged as an important source of law under the smritis. The widely used smriti terms, *achara, sadachara, shishtachara, loksangraha* etc. denote custom. Gautama, Manu and Brihaspati granted special recognition to custom.[21] Narada went further and proclaimed that custom overrides the sacred law. The local customs varied from region to region with the southern states granting women greater rights. Incidentally, it is believed that both Yagnavalkya and Vijnaneshwar, who had expanded the parameters of women's right to property, hail from the southern (*Dakshina*) region.[22]

The southern and predominantly Dravidian regions followed various pro-women practices of property inheritance even under smriti law. The liberal construction of stridhana under the Bombay and Madras schools is an indication. There were also several other lesser known local customs and practices prevalent in this region. For instance, there are many references to women and their use of property in inscriptions in Tamil Nadu which can be traced back to the thirteenth to fourteenth century AD during the reign of the Cholas, Pandyas and Pallavas. The inscriptions indicate that the ownership rights of women included the power of alienation through gifts and sales.[23]

Some recent studies indicate the prevalence of such a custom in various parts of southern India. A custom of handing over a piece of land to the daughter at the time of her marriage prevailed within the Madras Presidency. The income from this land was meant for the woman's exclusive use. This was her stridhana and devolved on the female heirs and passed from mother to daughter. Known as *manjal kani*, the land was perhaps meant to provide an independent income to the daughter which would be sufficient to provide for her personal expenses—manjal (turmeric) and kumkum (vermilion) while in her husband's house.[24] A similar custom of providing a piece of land for the daughter's personal expenses also prevailed in the Maratha region of Bombay Presidency by the name *bangdi choli* (which literally means bangles and blouse).[25] A woman's right to one-third of the property upon her husband's remarriage was also recognized within certain lower castes of Madras Presidency and was termed as *patnibhagam*.

Carol Upadhya[26] in her study of the coastal Andhra region has recorded a practice of giving land to the daughter at the time of her marriage which was known as *katnam*. As per her observation, this land owned by the woman was very distinct from the land owned by the husband's family and also distinct from the present day north Indian practice of dowry. Even after marriage, traditionally, women continued to exercise control over this land.

In another study of Virasaiva women from the Karnataka region, it was observed that twelve per cent women inherited property in the form of land from their mother and this property customarily passed on only to daughters, even when boys did not inherit from their fathers.[27] The Lingayat women of Dharwar region, who were categorized as sudras in various judicial pronouncements, also had rights of divorce, remarriage and property ownership. An illegitimate son was recognized as an heir, which is a marker of the status enjoyed by women in informal alliances. The Buddhist literature also indicates that women could own and gift property in their own right.[28]

The Brahminical-Aryan customs followed by the upper castes of north India exercised a strict control over women and their sexuality and the status of women among them was low, as compared to women from the lower castes and the Dravidian regions. Brahminical norms such as pre-puberty marriage, restraint on widow remarriage and divorce, the ceremony of *kanyadan* (the ritual of gifting away a bedecked bride to a scholarly groom), the theory of the *kshetra and beeja* (soil and seed symbolizing that the woman was a mere carrier of the children who actually belonged to the man), are an indication of the lower status of women among the north Indian higher castes.

The main aim of these rituals was to maintain the caste purity through a very strict control over women and their sexuality. Since the women of the lower castes were relatively free from these notions of purity and pollution, they were governed by a relatively lax code of sexual morality and women held a slightly higher social status. The lower castes or sudras were considered to be out of the varna system and hence they were not governed by the code of the smritis. The code was applicable only to dwijas or the twice born (upper castes) who had the sanction to study the sacred texts.[29]

The women from the lower castes worked and contributed to the household and hence were not totally dependent upon their men. Most lower castes practised the custom of bride price, (*kanya sulka*), where the father of the girl had to be compensated for the loss he suffered by the marriage of his daughter. Although the smritis shunned this practice, as it amounted to sale of a daughter, the fact that it is mentioned in most smritis and commentaries indicates its wide acceptance by the various castes including the Brahmins.[30] It continued to be followed by several castes in the southern region, northern Himalayan regions and various tribes right up to the pre-independent period.[31]

Marriages among the various lower castes were less sacramental and more contractual. The ritual of *saptapadi* (seven steps round the sacrificial fire, which is essentially a Brahminical ritual) or kanyadan did not prevail among these communities. Child marriages were not the norm. The contractual marriages were based on consent of adult women and the rituals and ceremonies reflected this element of consent and contract. The rituals of remarriage of widows and divorcees varied from those of virgin brides. Steele, while recording the customs of the Deccan region mentions an interesting phenomenon. Remarriages of women whose husbands had been absent for a long time was permitted. If the first husband eventually returned, the woman had a choice to live with either the first or the second husband, but the husband who was deserted had to be reimbursed his marriage expenses.[32]

A careful scrutiny of the contemporary customs of the various castes reveals the different customary forms of divorce and remarriage prevailing within these communities even to the present day. In the Deccan (Maratha) and Gujarat region, such practices are termed as *kadi mod* (literally, breaking of a twig symbolizing the termination of the relationship) or *chor chittee* (deed of divorcement drawn up by community or family elders after breaking the wife's neck ornaments). If the process is initiated by the woman, either she or her father would have to return the bride price and also a part of the marriage expenses.[33] Normally, the mother is given the custody of her younger children, while the father retains the custody over older children and is under an obligation to bear their marriage expenses. The practice of maintenance after divorce is not prevalent among these communities. This is perhaps because the women are gainfully employed and the husbands do not possess property, resources or a steady income upon which the women can lay their claim to maintenance. Also divorced women are accepted within the natal family and a subsequent remarriage or an informal alliance is not unusual.

The custom of divorce and remarriage was also prevalent among Lingayats of Karnataka, Kapus of Telengana, the Jats of Punjab and Ajmer, certain castes among the Maravars, Namo-sudras of Bengal and the Banias of Bihar. In northern parts of Bihar, Orissa, Chota Nagpur and Assam all castes and tribes except the Brahmins, Kayasthas, Banias and Rajputs permitted remarriage. It was also accepted as a universal custom in the Darjeeling and Manipur regions.[34] The prohibition to divorce and remarriages of widows and divorcees existed only among communities, who emulated the Brahmins in order to rise in social scale. As a community progressed economically, it took on Brahminical practices and exercised a stricter sexual control upon its women.

Among various castes and tribes, along the Malabar coast, there were female-headed joint family households and matrilineal inheritance patterns.[35] Of these the Marumakkathayam and Aliyasanthana received judicial recognition during the British period. The female-headed joint families were called Tarwad and Tavazi and the line of descendants was traced through the female line. These systems were in existence until recently and were brought to an end through specific state intervention in the form of legislations in the post-independence period.[36] Under these systems, the women contracted loose marriage alliances which were called *sambandham*, which could be easily terminated with the consent of both the parties.[37] Since property devolved along the female line, there was no premium on the sexual purity of these women.

From the above discussion it is evident that even a casual glance at the customs of the lower castes is sufficient to indicate an absence of a strict sexual code and correspondingly, a wider scope for negotiating women's rights of divorce, remarriage and property ownership among them.

2.4 'Hindu'—An Amorphous Society

If communities practised such diverse norms of marriage, divorce, remarriage, property ownership, notions of legitimacy and illegitimacy then, for the purpose of administering the Hindu law, who is a Hindu becomes a central issue. The question has baffled the judiciary for well over a century and has continued to be illusive to the present day. Is it a question of affiliation to a religious institution as the European Christians understood the term or a far more complex phenomenon?

While contextualizing the Hindu law and its diverse practices, it is necessary to highlight that the term 'Hindu' is not located within the smritis.[38] It is derived from 'Indoi', a term used by Greeks to denote the inhabitants of the Indus valley.[39] The first known use of the term to denote a community was in 1424, by Krishnadevaraya II in a plate Satyamangala, to distinguish themselves from the Muslim rulers.[40] The Portuguese referred to the 'natives' as Gentoos which is derived from the word gentiles indicating non-believers. The initial Regulations of the East India Company also used the same term to denote non-Muslim natives.

In the pre-colonial era, diverse local customs were administered by family or caste councils or village panchayats, which were termed as *kula* (family or tribe), *shreni* (artisan's guilds) and *puga* or *gana* (assembly or association).[41] These local panchayats which were non-state legal fora regulated civil life and family relationships. These local councils co-existed along with the royal courts *sabhas* and *samitis* where the king (or his appointees) administered justice according to the school or authority accepted in the area with the help of Brahmin Pundits. It was an accepted norm that territorial conquest did not lead to tempering of local customs. During the Moghul rule, although the Muslim rulers introduced the Islamic criminal courts, they did not interfere with the local customs and civil laws. Hence, during this period civil laws continued to be regulated by local customs and usages.

At various historical points, when the Brahminical hold over the scriptures became oppressive, several religious and social reform movements challenged the Vedic orthodoxy and Brahminical hegemony and formed various religions and sects i.e. Buddhism, Jainism and Sikhism, Virashaivism, the Bhakti movements, the social reform movements during the nationalist struggle etc. A common thread which runs through all these reformist religions is their revolt against the dominance of rituals, the supremacy of Brahmins and the Sanskrit language. In retaliation, the reformers preached in the language of the common people (the lower castes). Like the smritis, their preachings were also codes governing social relationships, i.e. denouncement of the caste hierarchies and concepts of purity and pollution laid down by smritis, simple forms of marriage, divorce and re-marriage, an elevated status for women and the lower castes as preachers, peaceful co-existence based on the principle of non-violence etc. Some sects like the Sikhs preached monotheism and some even atheism. But conversion did not necessarily entail a change in property regulations. The institution of property and religious affiliation were not co-ordinate. So although people converted to different religions, faiths and sects, they continued to follow the local customs and usages regarding property devolution.

As far as property was concerned, the law of the land was binding. Laws and customs applied to people locally, regionally and along family, tribe (or caste) and trade divisions. Hence, it is not surprising that there was greater similarity between customs and usages (as well as language and traditions) of people from a region irrespective of their religious faiths and affiliations, rather than between followers of a religion living in far flung regions. The Malabar region and the north-eastern tribal belts provide concrete examples of this. On the Malabar coast, not only the Nairs, but also the predominantly Muslim population of the Lakshadweep Islands of around 99 per cent, follow the matrilineal system of Marumakkathayam.[42] The Khasi, Jaintia and Garo tribes of north-east region who converted to Christianity continue to follow the matrilineal inheritance. The Khojas, Cutchi Memons, the Bohras and the Halai Memons, who were converts from the trading communities of Gujarat, followed the Hindu custom of joint family property, based on male coparcenary.[43]

The system of dividing the communities on the basis of their religion and applying to them their own 'divine law' disregarding their caste, tribe and race differences is of recent origin, introduced by the British. The British administrators tried to introduce a concept of institutionalized religion with clear affiliations along the lines of Christian church fellowships and subordinated the institution of property to it. The Indian subcontinental trend for well over 2000 years, right from Buddha and Mahavir around 500 BC had been to gravitate away from the structure of Brahminical superiority and Sanskrit orthodoxy. But the new colonial structure reversed the trend and subjected communities to the dominance of the smriti rules.

Since there were sharp differences in the customs and practices of Aryan and non-Aryan communities, the British system of deciding cases on the basis of a 'divine and ancient Hindu law' caused a lot of confusion and hardship. Whether Dravidians and other non-Aryan races should be brought into the pale of Hinduism through the application of the shastric law of Aryan origin was a highly contested issue. Whether the reformist sects, who had protested against Brahminical orthodoxy, ought to be governed by the same Vedic law which they had renounced was another disputed question. Several aboriginal tribes also challenged the application of shastric Hindu law to them. It is through this process of litigation over property disputes that the sharply defined community of Hindus governed by the present day Hindu code was constructed during the colonial regime.[44] The diversity of the communities to whom the Hindu law was made applicable led Derrett to comment as follows: 'The Hindus are as diverse in race, psychology, habitat, employment and way of life as any collection of human beings that might be gathered from the ends of earth.'[45]

The Brahminical smriti rules of marriage and property ownership were applied to people who could hardly be called Hindus and conversely, since the Hindu law was applied to them, these communities were termed as Hindus. Although, the ground for the construction of a Hindu community was laid during the colonial rule, this perceived homogeneous religious community of the Hindus was given the final seal of statutory recognition only in the recent past, when the 'Hindu Law' was codified in the post-independence period. By then the dilatory measures adopted by the courts had reached such a scale that it was easier to indicate a Hindu negatively, i.e. a person who is not a Muslim, Christian, Parsi or Jew.[46]

A precise meaning of the word 'Hindu' has defied all efforts at definition through statutes or judicial pronouncements. An attempt to define the term was made in 1966 by the Supreme Court in *Shastri Yagnapurushadasji v Muldas Vaishya*:[47]

> Acceptance of the Vedas with reverence, recognition of the fact that the means of ways to salvation are diverse and realisation of the truth that number of gods to be worshipped is large is the distinguishing features of Hindu religion.

Relying upon this definition, the court held that the Satsanghis are Hindus. The issue before the court was one of social justice, i.e. entry of Harijans to a temple belonging to the Satsanghis of Swaminarayan *sampradaya* (sect). The Satsanghis pleaded that they were not Hindus and hence were not governed by the pre-constitution temple entry legislation of the Bombay Presidency through which Harijans were granted the right to worship in a Hindu temple. By the time the judgement was pronounced, the courts were under the Constitutional mandate of equality, non-discrimination and social justice. And hence the question, whether the Satsanghis are Hindus had become irrelevant and was only of academic interest.

In the broad context in which the terms 'Hindu' and 'Hindu law' are used, the definition of the Supreme Court is highly inadequate. According to Paras Diwan, instead of a religious sect, had it been argued that *chamars* were not Hindus, the court would have faced an uphill task.[48] It would be problematic to define a community like the chamars, who apparently know little of Hindu religion and less of Hindu philosophy, as Hindus.

Under the present day statutes governing Hindus, any definition of Hindu in terms of religion will be inadequate. A person who practices or professes it, is a Hindu. But a person does not cease to be a Hindu, nor become less of a Hindu only because he/she does not have faith in Hindu religion/philosophy or does not practice or profess it. Even when a Hindu starts practicing, professing or having faith in a non-Hindu religion, he will not cease to be a Hindu unless it is conclusively established that he has formally converted to that faith. Even an atheist does not cease to be a Hindu.

So, the present day 'Hindu' community governed by the 'Hindu laws' with their Brahminical tilt and an Anglo-Saxon base, is more a legal fiction than a religious entity or a social reality. In effect, it was an attempt to impose an alien and higher caste system of law upon a pluralistic society.[49]

Notes

1. Desai, S.T., (ed.), *Mulla's Principles of Hindu Law,* Bombay: N.M. Tripathi (1994) (16th edn.) p.3.
2. Sarkar Shastri, G.C., *A Treatise on Hindu Law,* Calcutta: B. Banerjee & Co. (1933) (7th edn.) p.12.
3. Bhattacharjee has argued that nibandhas had already replaced the smritis at the time of colonial intervention and hence smritis could no longer be considered as the 'source' of Hindu law. See Bhattacharjee, A.M., *Hindu Law and the Constitution,* Calcutta: Eastern Law House (1994) (2nd edn.) p.17 n.4.
4. Ibid. p.19.
5. Bhattacharjee has emphasized that smritis and commentaries were mere recordings of existing customs. Ibid. pp.12–39.
6. Raghavachariar provides a comprehensive list of various schools and the relevant authorities. See Raghavachariar, N.R., *Hindu Law: Principles and Precedents,* Madras: The Madras Law Journal Office (1980) (7th edn.), VOL. p.5.
7. Narada Smriti, XII 106–110.
8. See Alladi, K. (ed.), *Mayne's Treatise on Hindu Law & Usage,* New Delhi: Bharat Law House (1993) (13th edn.) p.146.
9. Desai, S.T. (ed.) *Principles of Hindu Law,* pp.157–63.
10. By the time the initial smritis were written roughly around 800–300 BC the pastoral and nomadic Aryans of the early Vedic period had settled into agriculture and feudal land relationships had been well established. The period of the early smritis coincides with the Mauryan period, the Magadha and Kosala kingdoms and early Buddhism. This is the period when agriculture was revolutionalized by the use of the iron plough. See Chapters VI and VII of Sharma, R.S., *Material Culture & Social Formations in Ancient India,* Madras: Macmillan India Ltd. (1983), pp.89–134.
11. Under Dayabhaga school a woman had a right even to the undivided property of her deceased husband, while under Mitakshara the right was limited to the divided property.
12. The relevant passage is found in Gautama Dharmasutra, XXVIII, pp.24-6. The reference to this is made by Dr Jolly, J., *'Hindu Law'* Tagore Law Lecture Series Publication (TLLS 1883) p.228. See Alladi, Mayne's *Treatise on Hindu Law and Usage,* p.874. Some scholars believe that the concept is rooted in the tradition of bride price.

13. *Manusmriti*, VIII : p.29.
14. Gill, K., *Hindu Women's Right to Property in India*, Delhi: Deep & Deep Publications (1986) p.301. Also see Mayne's *Treatise on Hindu Law & Usage*, p.877.
15. *Alladi*, p.875.
16. Ibid., p.875 fn.5.
17. According to him every category of property belonging to a woman was her stridhana.
18. Desai (ed.), *Principles of Hindu Low*, pp.163–9.
19. Banerjee, G., 'Hindu Law of Marriage and Stridhana' (TLLS-1878), Calcutta: S.K. Lahiri & Co. (1923) (5th edn.) p.290.
20. Desai (ed.), *Principles of Hindu Law*, pp.172–3.
21. The famous quote of Brihaspati, '*Deshe deshe ya acharah paramparayakramagateh; Sa shastrarthabalavanaiva langhaniyah kadhachava*', which exhorts local, tribal and family usages. The principle was given judicial recognition by the landmark decision of the Privy Council in *Collector of Madura v Moottoo Ramalinga* (1868) 12 MIA 397, which laid down, 'clear proof of usage will outweigh the written text of law'. According to Mulla, the importance attached to the law-creating efficacy of custom in Hindu jurisprudence was so great that the exponents of law were unanimous in accepting custom as a constituent part of law. Desai (ed.), *Principles of Hindu Law*, p.2.
22. Mukund, K., 'Turmeric Land—Women's Property Rights in Tamil Society since Medieval Times', *Economic & Political Weekly*, XXVII/17 (1992), p.WS-2.
23. Ibid., p.WS-3.
24. Ibid., p.WS-5.
25. See the decision in *Yadeorao Jogeshwar v Vithal Shamaji* AIR 1952 Nag 55, where a reference to this custom is made.
26. Upadhya, C., 'Dowry and women's property in coastal Andhra Pradesh' (1990), in *Contributions to Indian Sociology*, New Delhi: Sage Publications(n.s.) 24, 1 (1990), p.29.
27. Mullati, L., *The Bhakti Movement and the Status of Women: A Case Study of Virasaivism*, New Delhi: Abhinav Publications (1986), p. 106.
28. Talim, M., *Women in Early Buddhist Literature*, Bombay: Popular Prakashan (1972).
29. Srinivas, M.N., *Caste in Modern India and Other Essays*, Bombay: Media Promoters & Publishers (1962) (Rpt. 1986) p. 55.
30. Ibid., p. 54.
31. Ibid., p. 44, 'A note on Sanskritisation and Westernisation.'
32. Ibid., p.44 Also K. Alladi *Mayne's Treatise on Hindu Law and Usage*, p.147.
33. The recording of customs of the Deccan and Gujarat region by Steele and Borradaile during the period 1820–1830 provides an ample proof of these practices. The fact that these customs still prevail among the lower castes was confirmed during various legal workshops in the Padra, Vagoria and Daboi districts of Baroda region organized by the Mahila Samakhya, Gujarat which were co-ordinated by the author

during the years 1996 and 1997. Women from various lower castes, Vankar, Baria, Vasava, Ratodia, Chamar and Rohit, participated in the workshops.

34. See Alladi, K., *Mayne's Treatise on Hindu Law and Usage*, p.147.
35. According to Mayne, The Marummakkathayam was practised by Warriers, Unnis, Padvals, Chakkiars, Thiyas, Nambiars (Brahmin) and Mopillas (Muslim). The Aliyasanthana was prevalent in south Kanara among the Billavas, Bunts, Maraveers etc. See Alladi, K., *Mayne's, Treatise on Hindu Law & Usage*, p.1209.
36. The Hindu Succession Act, 1956; The Kerala Joint Hindu Family System (Abolition) Act 1975.
37. Through the Malabar Marriage Act of 1896 the Sambandham marriages were granted legal recognition
38. The term used in the smritis is Arya.
39. Diwan, P., *Hindu Law,* Allahabad: Wadhwa & Company (1995), p.4.
40. Discussion with Prof. Sukumari Bhattacharji, author of *Women and Society in Ancient India,* Calcutta: Sasumati Corporation Ltd. (1994).
41. Desai (ed.), *Principles of Hindu Law,* pp.34–5.
42. Dube, L., 'Conflict and Compromise Devolution and Disposal of Property in Matrilineal Muslim Society', in *Economic & Political Weekly* (1994) XXIX/21, p. 1273.
43. Alladi, K., *Mayne's Treatise on Hindu Law and Usage*, p.63.
44. See Chapter 4 for a further discussion of this process.
45. Derrett, J.D.M., *Hindu Law Past and Present*, Calcutta: Mukherjee & Co. (1957), p.1.
46. S2 (c) of the Hindu Marriage Act, 1955. The same explanation is also found in the other Hindu Acts. The scheduled tribes are exempted from the application of these Acts.
47. AIR 1966 SC 1119
48. Diwan, *Hindu Law.*
49. It is relevant to note that the Brahmins constitute only around 5 per cent of the population. The upper castes who could have been governed by the smriti law could not, at any point, have been more than 20 per cent of the total Indian population. See *Table 1* for a caste-wise composition of the population.

3

Evolution of Islamic Law and Women's Spaces Within It

The Islamic law is of later origin than the smritis and also lays greater claim to divinity. Despite this claim, its evolution is not through a process of continuous revelations but through a rational method of interpretations.[1] A similarity can be traced between the smriti law and the Islamic law regarding the various schools and sects which flow from the original text which have led to plurality of practices. In this chapter, the origin and development of Islamic Law, its entry into the Indian subcontinent, women's rights under the Islamic jurisprudence as well as the later reforms are briefly sketched.

3.1 Origin and Development of Islamic Law

Islam means peace and submission.[2] The *Shariat* is the central core of Islam and is an infallible guide to ethics.[3] But this is not law in the modern sense. The jurisprudential law is called *Fiqh*. According to Fyzee, this is the name given to the whole science of jurisprudence. It is the knowledge and obligation derived from the four sources of Islamic law,[4] — the Koran, Sunna, Ijma and Qiyas.[5] The Koran which is the divine revelation (the word of God), is the highest source. Compiled from memory after the Prophet's death from the version of Osman, the third Caliph, it contains about six thousand verses but not more than two hundred verses deal with legal principles and only eighty verses deal with law of personal status. The Caliphs, as the Prophet's successors, took up the responsibility of adjudication of disputes among the people and while drawing upon the Koran, they continued the application of the ancient Arab system of arbitration and customary law.

The second source of Islamic law is *Sunna* or tradition. The word 'Sunna' means trodden path, Initially, the term was applied to the custom and practice of pre-Islamic tribes and the early

Muslims of seventh century AD. But later the word denoted the practice and precedents of the Prophet—Hadis. As a source of law, Hadis is as binding as the principles of the Koran. By the eighth century, Sunna became the ideal and established doctrine of the ancient schools, expounded by its representatives. Hence, in the present context, Sunna could either mean the living tradition of the schools or the traditions of the Prophet.

The third and equally binding source is Ijma, which is an agreement among legal scholars of any generation. This was supported by the Hanafi doctrine that the provisions of law must change with the changing times and of the Maliki doctrine that new facts require new decisions. In developing Islamic law by consensus, the doctrine of Ijtihad was developed. Ijtihad means one's own reasoning to deduce a rule of Shariat law. With the passage of time, liberty to reason was restricted and by ninth century Ijtihad was considered as the privilege of great scholars of the past.

The last source of Islamic Law is Qiyas which is reasoning by analogy. It does not involve laying down new principles but is merely a rule of interpretation. A principle laid down in the text can be applied to another situation, if it can be demonstrated that the rule laid down in the text governs the situation at hand by applying logic or reasoning, though the language of the text and the situation at hand are not strictly the same. It became a source of law as a sort of compromise by the Shafii and Maliki school. The Fatawas (legal opinions of scholars and judges), though not a source of law, have been instrumental in the development and enrichment of legal principles.[6]

There are two broad sects of Islam, the Sunnis and the Shias. The four recognized schools of Sunni Law are Hanafi, Maliki, Shafii and Hanbali. The Hanafi school founded by Abu Hanifa (699- 767 AD), has a wide following. The school is also known as Kufa school. Originating in Iraq, the doctrine spread to Syria, Afghanistan, Turkish Central Asia and the Indian subcontinent.

The founder of Shia school is Imam Jafar. The most important among the Shia schools of law are Ithna Ashari and Ismaili. The Ismaili sect of Shia school is the dominant majority in Persia. Elsewhere, they are generally in a minority. In India, the Bohras and Khojas (Agha Khani) are Shias belonging to the Ismaili sect.

The main difference between the Shia and Sunni sects is the

doctrine of *Imamat*.[7] According to the Sunnis, the leader of Muslims is Khalifa, the successor of the Prophet, who is a temporal and political ruler rather than a religious chief. For religious matters they must follow the Shariat. The institution of the Khalifat was abolished in 1924. According to the Shias, the Imam is the final interpreter of the law on earth. He is a leader not by the suffrage of the people but by divine right as descendant of the Prophet. Some Shia sects like the Dawoodi Bohras originated as an outcome of a rebellion against the oppressive Sunni theology in around eighth century BC and were considered to be reformative and emancipatory.

The laws of the two main sects and their sub-sects vary a great deal from each other. Among the various schools, the Maliki school is the most favourable to women and the Shafii school comes next. North Africa follows mainly the Maliki law and women enjoy greater rights. Under this doctrine, a wife has an option to dissolve her marriage on the following grounds: cruelty; non-payment of maintenance; absence of husband; insanity; leprosy; castration and sexual malformation.[8]

3.2 Introduction of Shariat Law in India

Islam came to India through the trade routes of the Arabs via the Arabian sea. Some of these traders settled down along the Malabar coast in eighth century and adopted the local customs and practices (Mopillas of Kerala). They did not follow the Shariat law.[9]

The Shariat was first introduced to the Sultanates of Afghan and Turkish rulers and entered India around the twelfth to the thirteenth century AD. The Muslim Sultans who invaded India were Hanafis. They relied upon the Ullamas to be the religious and legal arbitrators. The new Sultanates followed the basic law of Islam, the Shariat, as interpreted by the Ullama in the royal courts. The Moghul emperors were Hanafis and the Qazis appointed by them administered the Hanafi law. It is through this channel that the Shariat was established in India. The text books of Hanafi law are based on Fatawa Alamgiri, which is a collection of Fatawas compiled during Aurangzeb's regime and the Hedaya (the guide).[10]

The Muslim society as it evolved in India fell into three broad categories, the nobility, the peasantry and the artisans. The

Muslim population of the towns consisted of artisans and traders. Among the artisan classes, there was great assimilation between Hindu and Muslim rituals, ceremonies and customs.

There were many instances of the converted Muslims following their earlier non-Islamic norms and practices (for instance, the caste system or the joint family property system—coparcenary).[11] The Islamic law of pre-emption crept into Hindu customs and practices and came to be accepted as part of Hindu law. The population in the villages, both Hindus as well as Muslims, followed their own local laws and customs. The Bhakti and the Sufi movements of the fourteenth to sixteenth century, which were based on egalitarian principles of equality and love in opposition to the stronghold of religious orthodoxy and caste hierarchy, helped to bring further assimilation between the lower strata of Hindu and Muslim communities.[12] At the advent of colonial rule there were several amphibious communities which could not clearly be distinguished as either wholly Hindu or wholly Muslim due to the intermingling of their laws, customs and practices. The case of the Khojas, Cutchi Memons and other converted Muslim trading communities of Gujarat who followed the Hindu joint family system of property devolution and the matrilineal practices of the Mopilla community of the Malabar coast has already been mentioned in the preceding chapter. There were several other communities like the Meos of Rajasthan and the Satpanthis of Madhya Pradesh whose legal identity raised difficult questions of law. The Satpanthis and Pirpanthis of Gujarat, Cutch and Khandesh were by caste Matia Kunbis. They followed the *Atharva Veda* and worshipped the tombs of Muslim saints. They observed some Islamic practices like fasting during the holy month of Ramadan and repeated the Kalima. They buried their dead both with Hindu and Muslim prayers.[13]

In a rather recent case, the disputed issue was the right of females to inherit property. In an effort to deny females the right, it was pleaded that Meos follow Hindu family law and hence women have no right to inherit property. Over-riding this premise the court held that the Meo Mewati community is Muslim and is governed by Mohammedan law. Hence, daughters cannot be denied a right in the property in the absence of a conclusive proof of a custom to the contrary.[14] A curious trend in the litigation of the pre-independence period was for the females to plead the cover of the Mohammedan law while the opposing patriarchal subversive forces could be aided by a plea of customary Hindu practice of property devolution.[15]

According to R. H. Hutton, such an interesting illustration of the commixture of Hinduism and Islam was not restricted only to western India. He observed that at times great difficulty existed in deciding whether a particular body of people is Muslim or Hindu. Other such illustrations provided by him are those of the Naayitas of Malwa, the Kuvachandas of Sind, the Hussaini Brahmins and the Malkanas of Uttar Pradesh, the Bhagwanias or Satyadharmis of Bengal and the Chuhras of Punjab.[16]

3.3 Rights of Women Under Islam

It is important to contextualize the principles of Shariat law within tribal Arabia. The Arabs were traders and had mastered the law of contract.[17] The basic principle of contract was applied to other social relationships including marriage. Although the Shariat is premised upon a patriarchal familial structure, it is not based on a feudal economic structure. The matrimonial principles differ from the principles evolved within European feudalism reflected in the Canon law. The principal of indissolubility of marriage, which is intrinsically linked to inalienability of feudal land, did not govern Islamic law of marriage and divorce. The principles governing marriage transactions were similar to trade contracts—offer, acceptance and consideration—forming its base. The principles of a contractual marriage provided a better scope for defining women's rights than the status marriages under the Christian laws of feudal Europe during the corresponding period.

The Prophet converted the custom of bride price of tribal Arabia to mehr which would be a future security to a married woman.[18] In an era of unlimited polygamy, the Prophet restricted the number of wives to four with an injunction that each wife be treated with equal dignity and affection. Islam was also the first legal system to grant women the right of inheritance. Some positive provisions of the Islamic law of marriage and succession are listed below:

Marriage is a civil and dissoluble contract: This is in sharp contrast to the principles of Christianity and Hinduism where marriage was traditionally viewed as an indissoluble sacrament. Later at the advent of nineteenth century when Europe made a shift from feudalism to capitalism, the marriage was transformed from status to contract. This concept was later introduced into the Anglo-Saxon law and subsequently incorporated into the codified Hindu law in 1955.

The right to stipulated mehr: Stipulation of mehr at the time of marriage is an important aspect of a Muslim marriage. This is meant as a safeguard to the woman. Under the Shariat law, the woman has a charge over her husband's property for the payment of her mehr, even after his death. The high amount of mehr stipulated in the *nikahnama* (marriage agreement) was meant to act as a deterrent to unilateral divorce.[19]

The right to enter into a pre-marriage agreement (kabein nama): These agreements relate mainly to two aspects, (i) regulation of matrimonial life, and (ii) stipulations regarding dissolution of marriage. This can be an effective way of controlling polygamy. The woman can stipulate that in the event of the husband entering into a second marriage he should provide her with a separate residence. If the husband violates the agreement, the wife is entitled to divorce herself without the intervention of the Court.[20]

According to Ameer Ali, the renowned Islamic scholar, the following agreements can be enforced in a court of law.[21]

- the husband will not contract a second marriage during the subsistence of the first;
- the husband will not remove the wife from the conjugal domicile (matrimonial home) without her consent;
- the husband will not absent himself from the conjugal domicile beyond a certain period;
- the husband and wife will live in a specified place;
- certain amount of dower will be payable immediately after marriage or within a stated period;
- the husband will pay the wife a fixed sum of maintenance;
- the husband will maintain the children of the wife from her former husband; and
- the husband will not prevent her from receiving visits from her relations whenever she likes.[22]

The one third rule regarding testamentary succession:[23] As per this rule, a Muslim cannot will away more than one-third of his property. Wills also cannot be made in favour of legal heirs. The heirs have to inherit according to the rules of succession as laid down in the Shariat. Women are granted defined shares under the scheme of succession.[24]

The woman's share, under the Islamic law of inheritance, is not equal to that of her male counterpart. She is entitled to half the share of the male counterpart.[25] Although the stipulation falls short of the present concept of gender equality, it was a radical measure for its time and was based on a principle of equity. The man had to provide the mehr for the wife and bear the marriage expenses of unmarried daughters and sisters from his share of inheritance. The women were excluded from such encumbrances.

It is interesting to note that at the time of independence, women's rights under Muslim law were far superior to both the Hindu as well as the Christian laws. The subversion of women's rights by the constant pleadings of patriarchal interests for the application of Hindu personal laws on the basis of custom has already been discussed. Another interesting case decided by the Privy Council in 1898, *Skinner v Skinner*[26] reveals that the succession rights of a Muslim widow were even superior to those granted under the *Indian Succession Act*. The case concerned a couple who were Muslims but who had, at the time of their marriage converted to Christianity and performed the wedding ceremonies as per Christian rights. Subsequently thereafter, they reconverted to Islam and performed a nikah ceremony. An amount of Rs 50,000 was settled as mehr at the time of the nikah ceremony. Within a few years, the couple was estranged and the parties lived with other partners. The husband, prior to his death drew up a will and disinherited the wife of her rightful share in property and bestowed the property upon the children from the subsequent alliance.

After the death of her husband, the widow claimed her mehr and her share in the property and challenged the validity of the will under the Muslim law. The issue before the court was whether the couple was governed by the Indian Succession Act or the Islamic law. If the couple was governed by the Indian Succession Act, disinheritance through a will was valid. But the wife pleaded that she had never been divorced and both the parties were followers of Islam until the death of her husband and hence were governed by the Muslim law of succession. The trial court as well as the appellate courts, including the Privy Council, held that since a valid divorce could not be proved, and the parties had continued to follow Islam, the Islamic law would apply and the widow could not be disinherited of her rightful share in property through a will.

Although the Muslim law contains several positive provisions which would safeguard women's rights, these provisions have deteriorated due to socio-cultural reasons and patriarchal subversions of a later period. Practices like seclusion (*purdah*) and child marriage have rendered women vulnerable and dependent on their male relatives. Poverty and illiteracy have further contributed to the subordination of women. The amount of *mehr* which is fixed at the time of marriage has been reduced to a mere token and has ceased to be a safeguard against arbitrary divorce. The Brahminical custom of dowry has crept into most lower castes and Muslim communities. Recent studies indicate that among several Muslim communities the amount of dowry is substantially higher than the amount of mehr.[27]

A scrutiny of reported judgements would reveal that the amount of mehr was substantial during the pre-independence period and could function as an effective deterrent upon arbitrary and capricious divorce. But there is a marked decline on the reported cases on this issue in the post-independence period. Perhaps this is reflective of the lowered economic status of Muslims in post-partition India. So, for positive case law on this issue, one has to refer to Pakistani law journals.

The courts in Pakistan have consolidated the right of mehr through the following judgements:[28]:

(i) Various amounts paid by the husband to the wife during the marriage should not be presumed to be in lieu of dower;

(ii) Dower can be fixed or raised by the husband at any point during the continuance of the marriage. A declaration by him to this effect is sufficient;

(iii) Even after consummation has taken place, the wife may refuse to live with her husband unless he pays her prompt dower. Non-payment of mehr is a complete defense to a suit for restitution of conjugal rights and the wife is competent to refuse herself to her husband;

(iv) A woman can claim dower upon divorce if none had been fixed initially. This is applicable even in case of Muslim male and Christian female contracting a registered marriage abroad.

3.4 Reform Within Islam

Although the Islamic law is stated to be theocratic, several countries (Islamic as well as others) have modified the law to meet the demand of the changing social conditions and values. Furqan Ahmad maintains that the major portions of the statutory personal law enacted in most Muslim countries represent a mere codification of the traditional law and at best unification of divergent legal principles. But it cannot be denied that these changes have brought about significant reform in the classical Islamic law. The reforms have been either approved by the *Ullamas* or have been modified according to their suggestions.[29]

The process of change within the Muslim world has not been linear. The countries where Islam is the state or the predominant religion (particularly in the Arab world) have continued to preserve the uncodified Muslim law as locally followed. At the other end, countries like Turkey and Albania have opted for a complete abandonment of the traditional Islamic family law and replaced it with secular systems. Lebanon and Israel have incorporated the provisions of the Turkish family code and have made them applicable to the Muslim population.[30]

Many countries have adopted a moderate course—retaining the fundamental structure of the traditional family law of Islam but adapting its various locally prevalent versions to the contemporary social requirements. Around twenty countries have enacted either substantive or regulatory reforms to change the matrimonial law either partly or wholly, by relying upon the principle of Ijtihad within the broad framework of Islam itself.[31] Crossing the barriers of the officially adopted or dominant schools, laws have been codified on the basis of a selection of legal rules derived from the various schools of Islamic law.

For example, although the dominant school in India and Pakistan is Hanafi, the Dissolution of Muslim Marriages Act, 1939 incorporated the principles of Maliki law.[32] Similarly, on the basis of a doctrine of the Hanbali school of Islamic law, several countries have granted women the right to stipulate a restraint against bigamous marriages of their husbands.

Several countries have also regulated the husband's right to polygamy through statutory and regulatory provisions. Turkey and Tunisia have abolished polygamy altogether. In many countries, prior permission of the court is required for a bigamous marriage. Indonesia, Sri Lanka and Pakistan have imposed various restrictions on polygamy.[33] For instance during the regime of Ayub Khan, the *Muslim Family Laws Ordinance of 1961* was promulgated in Pakistan. Through this Ordinance, the husband's right to bigamy was regulated. It became mandatory for the husband to obtain prior permission of an Arbitration Council. These reforms are meant to mould the classical Islamic law according to the changing social needs.

Notes

1. Schacht, J., *An Introduction to Islamic Law*, New Delhi: Oxford University Press (1964) (Rpt 1975), p.1.
2. In its religious sense, it denotes submission to the Will of God and in its secular sense, the establishment of peace. In English, the word 'Muslim' is used both as a noun and as an adjective and denotes both the person professing the faith and something specific to Muslims such as law, culture, art etc. See Hidayatullah M. & A. Hidayatullah (ed.), *Mulla's Principles of Mohammedan Law*, Bombay: N.M. Tripathi (1981) (18th edn.), p. XIX.
3. Fyzee, A.A.A., *Outlines of Muslim Law*, New Delhi: Oxford University Press (1974) (4th edn.), p.16.
4. Ibid., pp.17-18.
5. For the explanation of the four sources, I am relying upon *Mulla's Principles of Mohammedan Law*, pp. XIX-XXIV.
6. Ibid., at p. XXIV.
7. Fyzee, A.A.A., *Outlines of Muslim Law*, pp.39-40.
8. Ibid., p.169.
9. See Chapter 2 ns.35 & 42.
10. The original texts were translated into English during the early phase of colonial rule and became the basis of Anglo-Mohammedan law in India. In Chapter 4, this issue is further discussed.
11. There were several cases concerning Bohras, Khojas, Cutchi Memons of Gujarat and Muslim Ghirasias of Bharuch, where during litigation the Hindu law of coparcenary was applied.
12. Thapar, R., *A History of India*, Delhi: Penguin (1992), Vol. I pp.298-312.
13. See Derrett, J.D.M., *Religion, Law and the State in India*, New York: The Free Press (1968), p.49, n.1; Also Fyzee *Outlines of Mohammadan Law*, p.65.
14. *Hooriya v Munna* AIR (1956) Madh Bh 556.
15. The *Khojas & Memons Case* decided by Lord Erskine Perry in 1847 (POC 1853 p.110), which is discussed in detail in the following chapter provides a concrete example of this trend.
16. See Fyzee, *Outlines of Muslim Law*, p.65.
17. According to Paras Diwan, Hindus perfected the concept of (gift) *dan* and applied it to marriage alliances, i.e. kanyadan. The Muslims perfected the concept of sale and found it convenient to express many transactions including marriage in the language of sale. Diwan, P.,

Muslim Law in Modern India, Allahabad: Allahabad Law Agency (1993) (6th edn.), p.52-3.

18. The concept of mehr was latent in pre-Islamic Arabia. A gift is called Sadaq and the wife is called Sadaqi or woman friend. The Prophet released marriage from the bride purchase notion of Sadaq. Mehr became part of a marriage settlement to be paid to the wife. See Diwan, P., *Muslim Law in Modern India*, Allahabad: Allahabad Law Agency (1993).
19. No other legal system known to the Indian matrimonial jurisprudence subscribes to this concept. Both Hindu and English systems rely upon the concept of maintenance to safeguard women's economic right within marriage. Maintenance presumes a state of dependency. The concept of stipulating mehr is based on the more noble principle (a mark of respect for the woman) than maintenance and eternal dependency. Further, under all matrimonial laws, maintenance is linked to a woman's chastity and hence becomes a way of controlling the woman's sexuality. An unchaste woman is not entitled to maintenance either during the subsistence of marriage or after its dissolution.
20. Before the enactment of the Dissolution of Muslim Marriages Act, a Muslim reformist, Mrs Hamida Ali, on behalf of some of the leading women's organizations in India, had prepared a specimen form of such an agreement which was published in the *Bombay Law Journal* in the year 1936. See Fyzee A.A.A. The Muslim Wife's Right of Dissolving her Marriage in (1936) B.LR, p. 113.
21. Diwan, P., *Law of Marriage and Divorce*, Allahabad: Wadhwa & Company (1988), p.62.
22. The right to enter into a pre-marriage agreement is not available under any other matrimonial statute (except under the Goan law modelled on the French code). Since marriage under the Anglo-Saxon law was indissoluble, pre-marriage and post-marriage contracts stipulating conditions are held to be against public policy under the English law.
23. Hidayatullah & Hidayatullah (ed.), *Mulla's Principles of Mohammadan Law*, p.104.
24. Under the Indian Succession Act and the Hindu Succession Act there is no restraint regarding testamentary succession and a person can will away all the property and disinherit his legal heirs.
25. Although there are wide differences in the laws of various sects and sub-sects, the inheritance rights of women under the Islamic law can be broadly categorized as follows:
    ** the daughter inherits half the share inherited by the son, e.g. when there are no other heirs, the daughter inherits one third and the son inherits two thirds of the property.
    ** the mother inherits one sixth of the property while the father inherits one third.
    ** the wife (or if there is more than one wife then all of them jointly) inherits one eight of the husband's property [Hidayatullah & Hidayatullah (ed.), *Mulla's Principles of Mohammadan Law*, pp. 48-62].
26. *Skinner v Skinner* (1898) ILR 25 Cal 537 PC.

27. In a recent study of Muslim women conducted by Women's Research and Action Group, Bombay (WRAG) during 1994-6, most communities confirmed that they still follow the custom of mehr but it has been reduced to a mere token. The communities have now adopted the practice of dowry. They further confirmed that the amount of dowry is always higher than mehr. The final report of the study is yet to be published. I am relying upon the various newsletters brought out by WRAG during 1994 and 1995, where some of the preliminary reports of the research from Maharashtra, Gujarat, Kerala, Tamil Nadu, West Bengal and Assam have been published. See the following issues: I/2 (September, 1994); II/1 (February, 1995); II/2-3 (August, 1995) and II/4 (October, 1995).
28. See Balchin, C. (ed.), *A Handbook on Family Law in Pakistan*, Lahore: Shirkat Gah (1994) (2nd edn.), p.52.
29. Ahmad, F., *Triple Talaq: An Analytical Study*, New Delhi: Regency Publications (1994), p.113.
30. Mahmood, T., *Family Law Reform in the Muslim World*, Bombay: N.M. Tripathi (1972), p.3.
31. For a detailed discussion regarding reform in Muslim family law in various Islamic countries, see *Mahmood, T., Family Law Reform in the Muslim World*, pp.270-2.
32. According to Hanafi authorities, rules of other Sunni schools may be applied by command of the sovereign power. Through this principle, in 1931, the ruler of Bhopal enacted a code, *Dabita Tahaffuzi Huquqai Zawjain* (Law for the Protection of Rights of Spouses) incorporating Maliki rules. This principle was later incorporated into the *Dissolution of Muslim Marriages Act* of 1939, to grant Muslim women in British India the right of divorce. See Fyzee A.A.A., Outlines of Muslim Law.
33. Ahmad, F., *Triple Talaq: An Analytical Study.*

4

Colonial Rule and Subversion of Rights

Introduction

In order to study the judicial structure of modern India, a study of the process of colonization in the Presidencies of Calcutta, Bombay and Madras during the eighteenth and nineteenth century is essential. The Calcutta Presidency of the Bengal region, in particular, had felt the presence of the British through the establishment of the East India Company from the early eighteenth century. Here, what began as trading relations expanded into political domination. It is at this starting point that we will have to locate the routes of the present legal structure.[1]

With the advent of colonialism there was a substantial change in the legal structure of the newly established Presidencies. The non-state arbitration fora were transformed into state-regulated and state-controlled adjudicative systems. The transformation was at two levels: (i) through the introduction of a legal structure modelled on English courts, (i.e. Anglo-Saxon jurisprudence); and (ii) through principles of substantive law which were evolved and administered in these courts, (i.e. Anglo-Hindu and Anglo-Mohammedan laws). This set in motion a gradual process of homogenizing the local customs and practices which could be regulated through the state machinery.

During the initial period of the colonial rule, two different models of adjudication were adopted in the Presidencies of Calcutta and Bombay. While the Calcutta Presidency, under the administration of Hastings, adopted the Roman model of differentiating between the Canon and Civil law, the Bombay Presidency under the administration of Elphinstone, adopted the English model of King's law and Common law which provided greater scope for validating customary law. But gradually the

Bengal model was adopted for the centralized administration of British India. The adaptation of the canonical mould overriding the common law norm, curtailed women's customary rights which did not have a textual base. As the pluralistic communities became characterized as 'Hindu', the women's right to property ownership became curtailed. In addition, as already stated, the Bengal school followed the Dayabhaga principle of strict construction of stridhana. Gradually, this notion of a constrained and limited stridhana became the accepted principle of Hindu law for the whole of British India (with a few concessions granted to the Bombay Presidency). The transformation of the legal structure and its effects on women's rights is traced in this chapter.

4.1 Company Jurisdiction Over Natives

At the advent of the colonial rule, the Moghul power was on the decline and the law and order situation was at its lowest ebb. Although the Moghul courts arbitrated in family disputes, towards the end of the Moghul reign, the arbitration mechanisms had collapsed both in the Moghul Empire, as well as in the independent princely states. The Company officers, who were engaged in setting up trading establishments were often called upon to adjudicate over family and civil disputes in these areas.

The first seed of the Anglo-Saxon jurisprudence was sown at this juncture. Since the Company officers did not have a legal background, they relied either upon the local *qazis* and *pundits* or upon the principles of English law in an *ad hoc* manner. To provide legal validity to such arbitrations, after the Company established its rule, various charters of the British Parliament bestowed upon the Company, the jurisdiction over the natives and also deputed lawyers to adjudicate over these disputes.[2]

The initial charter, the Charter of Charles II in 1661, was the first in a series of charters, which authorized the East India Company judicial powers in India. The Charter of George I in 1726, authorized the establishment of Mayor's Courts (courts of the King of England) in Calcutta, Bombay and Madras. This Act was silent regarding jurisdiction over native inhabitants. The Warren Hastings' Plan of 1772, provided for the establishment of civil and criminal courts in each district (mofussil courts). This plan granted the Company jurisdiction over the natives. The plan explicitly protected the right of Hindus and Muslims to apply their own personal laws in civil matters concerning inheritance, marriage, caste etc.[3]

In 1774, the Mayor's Court of Calcutta was converted into a Supreme Court and in 1781, it was granted express jurisdiction over natives. It was laid down that in matters of inheritance, succession, land rent, goods and all matters of contract, the respective customary laws should be applied. In case the laws of the parties differed, the laws applicable to the defendant were to be applied. The practice of saving the personal laws of the natives which started at this juncture continued through all subsequent British Regulations. But the charters were not clear whether the native laws of Hindus and Muslims referred to their religious laws or to the customary usages or to both. Article XXIII of the Hastings' plan stated, *'the laws of Koran with respect to the Mohammedans and those of the shastras with respect to the 'Gentoos'*[4] S.17 of the Act of 1781 again stipulated that *laws of Gentoos* and *laws of Mohammedans* were to be applied.

The communities were categorized on the basis of their religion. The customs and laws, which the English administrators had decided to save, were in turn deemed to be religious. This created a legal fiction that the laws of Hindus and Muslims are rooted in their respective scriptures and further that Hindus and Muslims are homogeneous communities following uniform laws. There was also a presumption that the dividing line between the communities is their religion, over-riding other factors such as caste, sect, occupation, language or regionality. This legal fiction provided no space for validating the role of customary law which has no scriptural basis and is evolved at the local level transgressing boundaries of religious identities.

4.2 Anglicization of Scriptures

Since scriptures were unequivocally accepted as the source of both Hindu and Muslim family laws, the English administrations set the task of translating the ancient texts as an essential precondition to good governance. Translation of scriptures became the first priority for the political scheme of English administrators. The process of codifying the Hindu and Mohammedan laws was initiated by Hastings in eighteenth century and was facilitated by Jones, Halhed, Colebrooke and Macnaghten.

As discussed in the preceding chapters, till the advent of the colonial rule, civil law was enforced primarily by local and non-state legal fora applying the norms of customary law and adaptations of the smriti or quranic injunctions to suit local conditions. But when the Company officers stepped in to arbitrate in civil and criminal disputes, due to their limited understanding of local traditions and customs, they relied upon Hindu pundits and Muslim qazis to ascertain their respective laws. This set in motion the process of Brahminization and Islamization of laws.

The local systems of arbitration were a source of constant irritant to the colonial administrators due to various factors such as lack of regularity in procedures, delays, decisions based on maxims which were beyond the comprehension of the administrators etc. The plurality of customs often led to the pundits expressing contradictory opinions. The wide range of customs which had no shastric authority met with the disapproval of the administrators. They distrusted the pundits and felt that their opinions were biased and favoured the interest of their own caste. The administrators were of the opinion that if the original texts were made available, they could rule directly, without the help of partisan and corrupt pundits. So in their desire to be independent of the local clergy, they took upon themselves the task of translating the ancient texts. These translated texts became the basis of Anglo-Hindu and Anglo-Mohammedan law in India.

The activity of translation of the texts was based primarily in the Bengal region. In 1772, Hastings hired a group of eleven pundits for the purpose of creating a digest of Hindu law, which brought a heavy Anglo-Brahminical bias into the law. This was translated into Persian and then later into English and was published in 1776 under the title, *A Code of Gentoo Laws or Ordinations of Pundits*. The subsequent work of William Jones, has been compared with the Justanian *Corpus Juris*.[5] The code prepared by him had a strong bias in favour of the Bengal school. He then went on to translate *Manusmriti* which became one of the most favoured texts of the British. It influenced oriental studies far more profoundly than it had ever influenced the administration of law in pre-British India.[6] Colebrooke's translation of Dayabhaga and Mitakshara, became the two most frequently quoted sources of Hindu law in court judgements.

Jones also translated *Al Sirajiyyah,* the Mohammedan law of inheritance. In 1791, under directions from Hastings, Charles

Hamilton, translated the Arabic text, the *Hedaya* (the Guide) into English. But Muslim law proved to be too complex and the translation process had to be abandoned halfway.[7]

During this time, several Sanskrit scholars wrote treatises to meet with the British demand. But the work of European authors came to be trusted and used in preference even to the genuine shastric works.[8] The translated codes, backed by the authority of British courts, began to make alterations in custom. In their attempt to make the shastric injunctions precise and definite, to suit the structure of the Anglicized courts, the British forced it towards a straight-jacketed mould which led to a loss of complexities and localized contexts and also provided the scope for the biases of the English scholars to creep into the translated texts.

The administrators of Bengal, in their fervour to trace the correct and 'original' sources, totally disregarded local customs. But the Bombay Presidency Regulations of the same period, especially the 1799 Regulation (under John Duncan), did not follow the legal scheme devised by Hastings in Bengal. Here the English distinction between King's law and Common law was applied rather than the Roman categorization of Canon Law and Civil Law[9] and custom was granted due recognition as an important source of law.

From 1803 to 1827, through treaties with Gaikwad and the defeat of the Peshwa, the territories under the Bombay Presidency were expanded to Deccan. This resulted in a major reorganization of the legal and judicial administration. Mountstuart Elphinstone presided over this early organization of Company administration, first as Commissioner of the Deccan (1818–19) and then as Governor of Bombay Presidency (1819–27). The recorder's court of Bombay was replaced with a Supreme Court in 1823. Influenced by the English jurist Bentham, Elphinstone was of the opinion that the Bengal model of categorizing laws as 'Canon' and 'Civil' would not work in the Bombay Presidency. In his scheme, codification of Common Law was essential to guide the European judges in their administration of the native law to the natives. The Common Law had to be based on customary practices of the people rather than the archaic religious texts. This need for the compilation of common practices stemmed from two presumptions, a desire to preserve for the natives their way of ruling, which was combined with an unwillingness to allow the natives to manage their own affairs. To concretize this scheme, he set up a Regulation Committee and brought about the Regulation Code 1827 (also known as Elphinstone code). Two officers appointed by Elphinstone, Harry Borradaile and Arthur Steele, were assigned the task of recording the customs of the Deccan and Gujarat region.[10] Although the recordings were not systematic, the compilations provide some useful insights into the customs and practices of the various castes in the region.

4.3 Subversion of Women's Rights

The establishment of courts based on the model of English courts with English rules and procedures and a clear hierarchy of courts was meant to make the arbitration fora certain and definite. The English principles of justice, equity and good conscience were used as direct channels for introducing English laws and customs into areas reserved as personal laws.[11] These notions which crept into the Hindu and Muslim laws transformed the local traditions and usages in unforeseen directions.

Despite the initial policy of non–interference in 'personal' matters, as the British rule gained acceptance and stability, there was a gradual process of tampering with the established local customs through various means. The legal structure was seen by the administrators as an important forte of its civilizing mission.

At this stage, the process of evolving laws at the local level through commentaries, which incorporated within them the local customs, was arrested. The British interpretations of the ancient texts became binding and made the law certain, rigid and uniform. This clear marker of modernity was welcomed by the newly evolving English-educated middle class of Bengal and provided the British a moral justification for ruling India as harbingers of enlightenment.[12] Through their interventions the Hindu society could rid itself of its 'barbarism' and enter an era of 'civilization'. An image of the cruel and superstitious natives who needed Christian salvation was deliberately constructed by the Evangelists. The entry of Hindu social reformers into the campaign against Sati at the advent of nineteenth century strengthened the process of interventions not only by judicial decisions but also by legislative reforms.

The much-acclaimed *Sati Regulation Act of 1829* was followed by other legislations such as the *Widow Remarriage Act 1856*, the

Age of Consent Act of 1860, and the *Prohibition of Female Infanticide Act of 1872*. These legislations, focusing on the 'barbaric' customs of the natives, convey an impression that the exceptions to the rule of non-interference in the realm of 'personal' laws were for the benefit of women. There is a presumption that by incorporating the concepts of modernity into the native jurisprudence, the status of women in India was alleviated. But recent scholarship has questioned this premise.[13]

The British intervention did not stop at the level of welfare legislation for women but extended into two other spheres which have not yet received due attention. One set of legislations carved out a space for men's individual property rights into a system based on joint family property and rigid caste affiliations and laid the ground for the introduction of the capital mode of production in an urban setting.[14]

But the other area is even more disturbing for our purpose here. Simultaneously, through a series of judicial decisions the scope of women's rights was constrained beyond all recognition. As already discussed in Chapter 2, the Mitakshara had expanded the scope of stridhana to include property acquired by woman through every source, including inheritance and partition. But the judicial decisions changed this concept and laid down that inherited property is not stridhana. A new legal principle was gradually introduced through court decisions that whether the property is inherited by a woman through her male relatives (father, son, husband) or through her female relatives (mother, mother's mother, daughter), it is not her stridhana and that it would devolve on the heirs of her husband or father. The women lost the right to will or gift away their stridhana and it acquired the character of a limited estate. Any transaction by a widow in respect of the property inherited by her had to be justified on two grounds, legal necessity or religious or charitable purpose. Upon the widow's death, the property reverted back to the husband's male relatives. The introduction of this concept of 'reversioners' which is basically a legal principle under the English law, bestowed upon the male relatives the right to challenge all property dealings by Hindu widows.

To provide concrete examples of this trend, some decisions of the newly evolving legal machinery of British India are discussed below. These judgements have several commonalities. The litigations against the widows were initiated by the husband's heirs. In a significant number of cases, following local customs, the lower courts upheld the women's rights. The lower court decisions were reversed by the higher judiciary and then became binding principles of law. Significantly, in all the cases discussed below, the decisions were from property disputes within the Bengal Presidency but under the consolidated scheme of the hierarchy of courts, they became the binding principles of law for other Presidencies.

In 1868, in *Srinath Gangopadhya v Sarbamangala Debi,*[15] the Calcutta High Court held, that as per the Benares School, once a stridhana property devolves upon an heir, it loses its character as stridhana and devolves as per ordinary rules of Hindu law.

In another landmark case around this time, the Privy Council held that the property inherited by the widow from her husband was not her stridhana. The Privy Council reversed the judgment of the lower court and proclaimed:

> Under the law of the Benares School, notwithstanding the ambiguous passage in the *Mitakshara,* no part of her husband's estate whether movable or immovable to which a Hindu woman succeeds by inheritance, forms part of her Stridhana[16] (emphasis added).

The legal precedents set by the Privy Council became the binding rule of law and dealt a lethal blow to the property rights of Hindu widows, as the decisions of the various High Courts in the subsequent decade reveal.

This principle was followed by the Calcutta High Court in 1874 in *Gonda Kooer v Kooer Gody Singh.*[17] The widow had purchased property out of the accumulated income from her stridhana and pleaded that it should be considered as her stridhana. But following the rule laid down by the Privy Council, the Calcutta High Court held that the property was not stridhana and hence she does not have the right to dispose it off by will and upon her death it would devolve on her husband's heirs.

The courts also ruled that the property inherited by a daughter from her father is not stridhana.[18] This principle was then extended to the property inherited by an unmarried daughter from her mother[19] and later stretched to include the property inherited from all female relatives, thus sealing all avenues for the continuation of property devolution in the female line.

The substantial case law on this issue made it impossible to retreat from this position. In 1879, while holding that the property inherited from the father is not stridhana, the Privy Council expressly stated that since this rule has been established by a series of decisions in Bengal and Madras, a different interpretation of the old and obscure texts cannot be followed. The Privy Council further stated that the courts ought not to unsettle a rule of inheritance affirmed by a long course of decisions, unless it is manifestly opposed to law and reason. The Privy Council explained that the rule has been laid down by Sir William Macnaghten in his *Treatise on Hindu Law* , as follows: 'Under no circumstances can a daughter's son, daughter, husband or other descendants inherit the property which devolved on her at her father's death. Such property is not stridhana and will devolve on her father's heirs.' The court further held that this rule is not opposed to the spirit and principles of Mitakshara.[20] It is interesting to note that while during the early years of administration, contemporary practices were discarded in favour of ancient and 'obscure texts', during the later period, after the establishment of Anglicized courts, the court decisions and translated texts were granted greater validity than the written texts which now came to be discarded as 'old and obscure'.

The facts of two more cases on the issue of women's property are set out in detail. In the first case, *Mussammat Thakoor Deyhee v Rai Baluk Ram*[21], a childless widow Choteh Babee, gifted the property she inherited from her husband to her niece. It is reported in the judgment that Choteh Babee, despite being a *purdah nishin,* was an excellent business woman who managed her property well.

The husband's heirs challenged the deed, *inter alia,* on the ground that it was fraudulent and that she had no power of alienation over immovable property inherited from her husband. Sudder Ameen of Benares held that the widow was competent to gift the property. Sudder Dewaney Adawlut of Agra reversed the decision on the ground that the deed of gift was a forged document. At this point the right of the widow to gift her property was not a disputed issue before the court. The court only examined whether the gift deed was an authentic or a forged document. In appeal, the Privy Council ruled: 'The widow has no power to dispose immovable property inherited from her husband, whether ancestral or acquired.'

The second case decided by the Privy Council in 1903, *Sheo Shankar v Debi Sahai,*[22] provides yet another illustration of the judicial trend. The woman had inherited the property from her mother. After her death, her sons claimed the property as heirs of the mother and grandmother and deprived their sister. The subordinate judge of Gorakhpur, on 7 December 1897 held that the property inherited through the female line was the woman's stridhana and hence her sons had no right over it. On appeal, the Allahabad High Court reversed the decision. This resulted in an appeal to the Privy Council. In February, 1903, the Privy Council upheld the decision of the High Court and laid down that the property inherited by a woman from her mother is not her stridhana and hence it will not devolve on her daughter who is her stridhana heir, but will devolve upon her son.

Only the Bombay School which relied upon the local authority, Vyavahar Mayuka of Nilakantha Bhatta, which validated local customary practices of the region, provided a better scope for women's rights. The cases decided between the period 1862–5 and reported in the first issue of *Bombay High Court Reporter* are illustrative of this trend.[23]

In one of the cases, *Navalram Atmaram v Nand Kishore Shivnarayan*[24] the woman inherited property from her father. She died leaving a daughter and daughter's sons. Upon her death, her husband's brother took charge of the property. In a suit to reclaim the property, the trial court (Sudder Ameen) declared in favour of the daughter's son. On appeal, Assistant Judge reversed the decree. On second appeal, the Bombay High Court held that according to the usage of the caste and in accordance with Hindu law as interpreted by the authorities in the Bombay Presidency, the daughter was an absolute heir to the property which the woman had inherited from her father.

Ironically, while Hindu women were better protected by invoking the local customs in the Bombay region, the Muslim women's textual right to inherit property was defeated by upholding Hindu customs and usages. The Muslim trading communities of Gujarat, the Khojas and Cutchi Memons, followed the local custom of coparcenary or joint family property.[25] The male-headed coparcenaries denied women their right to a stipulated share in the property as per the Shariat. (As already discussed in the preceding chapter, under the rules of Shariat coparcenary is not recognized).

On 11 October 1847, by a common judgment, Justice Erskine Perry decided three cases filed by women claiming inheritance right to parental property.[26] In the first case, two daughters of a rich merchant Mir Ali, who did not leave behind a male heir, filed a suit to claim their father's property worth three lakhs. On their behalf, it was argued that the Hindu custom of disinheriting daughters, which has been adopted by Mohammedans, is most unreasonable. Hence public policy would dictate the adoption of the wiser rule laid down by the Koran by which daughters are awarded a fixed share. A contrast was drawn between the relative position which females held in Hindu and Muslim systems. On behalf of the woman, it was further argued that since the Muslim system was more beneficial to women, in larger interest of women's welfare, it was the duty of the court to give it effect when the two diverse practices are examined.

The comments of Lord Erskine Perry while disallowing the woman's claim make interesting reading:

> A custom for females to take no share in the inheritance is not unreasonable in the eyes of the English law for it accords in great part with the universal custom, as to real estates where there are any male issues and with some local customs mentioned by Blackstone through which in certain manors females are excluded in all cases.[27]

The judge commented further that since the attempt of the young women to disturb the course of succession, which has prevailed among their ancestors for many hundreds of years, has failed, they must now pay the price of this unsuccessful experiment by paying the cost to the defendants.[28]

While at one level the smriti law was distorted, at the other, this distorted law was applied to a wide range of communities following diverse customs. As the above case reveals, an interesting phenomenon during litigation seems to be for women to plead a non-Hindu status in order to protect their rights and for the men within the family to implore the protection of the distorted smriti law. If the courts could be convinced that the community was ruled by either the Muslim law, the *Indian Succession Act* or the customary law (by claiming a sudra status) the rights of women could be saved. If the courts bestowed a Hindu status upon the communities (or validated the application of the Hindu law as in the above case), women's right would be curtailed. Most of these were borderline cases where the pendulum would swing from one end to the other. But when the issue was finally decided by the Privy Council or the respective High Court as the case may be, the religious status of the community (and thereby the fate of its women and illegitimate children) would be sealed for all future litigations.

To provide some illustrations, in several litigations the widows from various Jain sects pleaded their right to adopt a son to their deceased husband under a separate law or a local custom. But the custom could not be proved to the level of legal validity and women lost their right of adoption as smriti law was applied to them. It is through these disputes that Jains became categorized as a Hindu sect. Another illustration is the *Asura* (or an unapproved) form of marriage. If a custom to this effect could be proved, the property could be saved from the 'reversioners'. Yet other examples are the disputes between widows and illegitimate sons within the Lingayat community. Since the existence could be proved of the custom of remarriages of divorcees and widows, the community was categorized as sudra and hence the illegitimate sons were declared as heirs to the father's property. The dispute could be confined between widows and illegitimate sons rather than its extension to reversioners.[29]

The period between 1850 and 1930 witnessed the elimination of a wide range of customs which diverged from the Anglo-Hindu law as the standard of proof required was very high. Unless it could be proved that the custom was ancient, certain, obligatory, reasonable and not against public policy, it had a very slim chance of survival. Derrett comments that in this manner, the Anglo-Hindu law with its Dharmashastra background was spread more widely than it had ever been before. The only customs which were saved from the crushing effects of the British courts were the customs of the agricultural classes in the Punjab and matrilineal practices of the Malabar region.[30] The tendency of both the British courts and of the urban Hindu middle class was to ignore the diversities and to impose a legal Hinduism upon these communities. Contrary to popular belief, many of the customs which were crushed were those in favour of women.

4.4 The Status of Women Under English Law During the Corresponding Period

During litigation, the courts often relied upon the principles of justice, equity and good conscience, while ascertaining women's rights. Since the Law Lords' notions of justice, equity and good conscience were the clinching factors, it would be relevant to glean over the decisions of English courts during the corresponding period, and assess the judicial notions of justice and equity regarding women.

The leading decisions indicate that the concept of modernity upon which the Anglo-Saxon jurisprudence rested did not encompass within its scope, the notion of women's rights. Since disinheriting women was not unreasonable or immoral as per the established legal precepts, the judges could, with ease, incorporate them into the Indian legal system.

Until the twentieth century, women in Britain could not vote. Married women did not have a right of disposal over their separate property. The husband could transact all property dealings on her behalf in respect of her separate property. Even worse, married women did not have a legal existence. As soon as a woman got married she lost her legal identity. Her identity merged with that of her husband. She could not even enter into a contract because she could not sue anyone nor be sued against. Since the husband was the woman's guardian he had a right to chastize her. Under the English common law, the husband had a right to whip the wife provided he used a switch not thicker than his thumb for correctional purposes under a legally accepted notion called thumb rule.[31]

At the social level, there are several judicial decisions which held that the women could not enter universities, that they could not hold elected posts, that they could not be enrolled to the bar and beyond this, that they are not even persons and further that the term 'he' does not include 'she'.[32] These 'persons cases,' as they came to be called, were launched by feminists in the hope of legally establishing the fact that an individual gender was irrelevant to his or her factual or legal capacity and that females were obviously to be included in the word 'person.' But what was self-evident truth to feminists, however, seemed an absurdity to the judges.[33] After a prolonged and sustained campaign by the suffragettes, finally in 1929, the courts granted women the right to be persons.[34] As a result of a sustained campaign, the women in Britain obtained the right to own property through a legislation in 1882[35] and the right to vote in 1918.[36]

But despite the near subordination of women in Britain, in order to rationalize the colonial rule, it was often projected in the colonies that the honour and respect in which women were held in Britain was one of the glories of British civilization and blessed fruits of Christianity.[37] The position of the English woman was extolled throughout the commonwealth as being without compare. This mystical sentiment served not only to obscure the true position of the great majority of women in Britain, but also to suggest a false status for English women when compared with that of women in the colonies.

While it was relatively easy to pose as 'rescuers' of Indian women from the clutches of 'barbaric' customs like Sati and infant marriages, it was indeed not easy to conciliate with the notions of civil right of property ownership which was a contentious issue in Britain at the time. The antagonism and hostility towards the women suffragettes demanding equality seems to have influenced the Law Lords of the Privy Council, while sitting in judgment over the appeal cases from the Commonwealth. The prolonged legal battles of English women for equality are an indication of the status-quoist attitude of the jurists who were modelled along Blackstonian notions of women's rights. These notions were adopted into the Indian system, even while posturing to liberate Indian women from the barbaric customs through legislative reforms.

An analysis of the legal cases of women's right to property reveals that with the benevolence of the English jurists, (who were aided by the subversion of women's rights in England) and the worst distortions of Brahminical smriti texts, the patriarchal modernity of India was ushered in.

Notes

1. Radha Kumar argues that this intimacy with the British later resulted in most social movements of the nineteenth century also being located in these two states. See Kumar, R., *The History of Doing —An Illustrated Account of Movements for Women's Rights and Feminism in India 1800 — 1990*, New Delhi: Kali for Women (1993), p.7.
2. Jain, M.P., *Outlines of Indian Legal History* , Bombay: N.M. Tripathi (1966), p.24.
3. Parashar, A., *Women and Family Law Reform in India* , New Delhi : Sage Publications (1992), pp. 61–9.
4. 'Gentoos' was the Portuguese term for Hindus. The term has its origin in the Biblical term 'Gentiles' meaning heathens or non-believers.
5. He set out to give his subjects their law in a similar fashion as Justanian guaranteed his Roman and Greek subjects their laws.
6. Derrett, D.J.M., *Religion, Law and the State in India,* New York: The Free Press (1968), p. 225.

7. Chhachhi, A., 'Identity Politics, Secularism and Women: A South Asian perspective,' in Zoya Hasan (ed.), *Forging Identities: Gender, Communities and the State*, New Delhi: Kali for Women (1994), p.82.
8. Kishwar, M., 'Codified Hindu Law: Myth and Reality,' *Economic and Political Weekly*, XXIX/33 (1994), p. 2145.
9. Amrita Shodhan has recorded how Macnaghten's *Principles and Precedents of Hindu Law*, written in 1827, relied only upon the works of Jones and Colebrooke and some Sanskrit texts. Cases brought before the courts were treated only as illustration of how the textual law was treated in the European court. He did not examine *Bebasthas* given by pundits and recorded only those cases adjudicated in British courts. See Shodhan, A., 'Legal Representations of Khojas and Pushtimarga Vaishnavas : The Aga Khan Case and the Maharaj Libel Case in Mid-nineteenth Century Bombay,' unpublished Doctorate dissertation, submitted to the Department of South Asian Languages and Civilizations, Chicago, Illinois (1995).
10. See Borradaile's *Report of Civil Cases 1820–1824*, and Arthur Steele, *Hindu Caste, Their Law, Religion and Customs*, Bombay: Courier Press (1827). Since most of the territory of the Bombay Presidency was newly acquired, perhaps it was felt necessary to record their customs.
11. This principle was laid down in a case of guardianship, *Waghela Rajsanji v Shekh Masluddin* (1887) 14 IA 89.
12. Kumar, R., *The History of Doing*, p. 9.
13. I am relying upon the work of Lata Mani and Uma Chakravarty on Sati and of Lucy Carrol on Widow Remarriage. Regarding the discourse on Sati for example, Lata Mani has commented that women were not the central concern of this debate. But rather, women were the site upon which the discourse on culture and identity was debated and women's rights did not figure in this debate. See Mani, L., 'Contentious Traditions: The Debate on Sati in Colonial India' (1989), in Sangari, K. and S. Vaid (ed.), *Recasting Women, Essays in Colonial History*, New Delhi: Kali for Women (1989), p. 88.
14. These legislations included:
    * The Caste Disabilities Removal Act 1850 set aside the provisions of Hindu Law which penalized the renunciation of religion by depriving a convert of his right in the joint family property.
    * The Hindu Inheritance (Removal of Disabilities) Act, 1928 prohibited the exclusion from inheritance of certain disqualified heirs.
    * The Hindu Gains of Learning Act 1930 stipulated that all gains of learning (income earned through professional qualifications) would be the exclusive and separate property of a Hindu male even if he had been supported to acquire professional qualifications from the funds of the joint family.
15. (1868) 10 WR 488.
16. *Bhugwandeen Doobey v Myna Baee* (1867) 11 MIA 487.
17. (1874) 14 BLR 159.
18. *Deo Parshad v Lujoo Roy* (1873) 20 WR 102.

19. *Dowlut Kooer v Burma Deo Sahoy* (1874) 22 WR 54.
20. *Chotay Lal v Chunno Lall* ILR (1879) 4 Cal 744.
21. (1886) 11 MIA 139.
22. (1903) 30 IA 202.
23. *Venayak Anandrav v Lakshmi Bai* (1861) 1 BHCR 117 and *Pranjivandas Tulsidas v Devkuvarbai* (1861) 1 BHCR 130.
24. (1861) 1 BHCR 209.
25. The Cutchis are originally from Sindh or Cutch and speak Cutchi language. They are believed to have been converted to Islam by Sadr Din. Although they practise Islam, their manners and customs continued to be Hindu. They believe in the ten incarnations of Lord Vishnu and during the period of litigation, as per the comments of the judge, not a single person knew Arabic or Persian.
26. The first two cases concerned Khoja women, *Hirbae v Sonbae* and *Gungbae v Sonabae*. The third case was by a Cutchi Memon, *Rahimatbae v Hadji Jussa & Ors.*
27. *Hirbae v Sonbae* POC (1853), p. 110 (also referred to as the Khoja's and Memon's case).
28. Ibid., p.121.
29. See Alladi, K. (ed.), *Mayne's Treatise on Hindu Law & Usage*, New Delhi: Bharat Law House (1993) (13th edn.), p.63-5, where some of these cases are cited.
30. Derrett, J.D.M., *Hindu Law Past and Present*, Calcutta: Mukherjee & Co. (1957), p.78.
31. See Martin, D., *Battered Wives*, New York: Pocket Books (1976), p.30-2. Also see Davis, E.G., *The First Sex*, New York: Putnam (1971), pp.254-5.
32. For the status of British women in nineteenth and early twentieth century, see the following cases:
    1869—Manchester Voters case—*Chorlton v Lings* declared that common law disability prevents women from voting.
    1873—Edinburgh Medical Students case—*Jex-Blake v Senatus*—Women's expulsion from University upheld.
    1889—London County Council cases—Lady Sandhurst case exclusion of women elected to the county council upheld.
    1903—Refusal by the Bar to enrol Bertha Cave upheld by the judges.
    1908—Scottish University Voters case—*Nairn v Scottish Universities*—House of Lords, upheld trend to exclude women from public functions and voting.
    1914—Women Solicitors case—*Beeb v Law Society*, refusal by Law Society to enrol a woman upheld by the courts.
    1923—The Lady Rhondda case—House of Lords refused to seat Lady Rhondda.
    1925—The Marriage Bar case—*Price v. Rhondda UDC*—judges upheld a requirement that only women (and not men) teachers resign on marriage as 'not unreasonable'.
    The above list of cases is cited from Sachs, A. and J.H. Wilson, *Sexism and the Law*, Oxford: Law in Society Series, Martine Robertson (1967), p.227.

33. Ibid., p.6.
34. 1929—Canadian Senators case—*Edwards v. Attorney General*—the Privy Council finally acknowledged that women are included within the term 'Person'. Ibid., p.227.
35. *The Married Women's Property Rights Act of 1882.*
36. In 1918, the vote was granted to women aged thirty years and above. A decade later this right was extended to all adult women. In 1919, the *Sex Disqualification Removal Act* revoked all disabilities suffered by women in respect of holding public office and exercising public functions.
37. Alladi, K., (ed.), *Mayne's Treatise on Hindu Law & Usage,* p.139-140.

5

Politicization of Women's Rights

Introduction

The period of ninety years—1857–1947—which mark the nation's struggle for independence are also the years in which the edifice of personal laws was erected. Hence, the edifice is rife with the political undercurrents of the period. The struggle for women's rights within the realm of family laws is entrenched within these undercurrents and has become an integral and inseparable part of this discourse.

The process was initiated with the codification of laws after the administration of India was transferred from the Company to the British Crown. At this time a distinction was made between the laws of the 'personal' and 'public' spheres. The personal laws, to a large extent, were left uncodified to be governed by native jurisprudence. Despite this restraint, the legal structure of the personal laws, as we understand the term today, was shaped during the period 1860 to 1950. While women's welfare was the stated agenda, the political undercurrents played a crucial role in moulding this structure.

With the introduction of matrimonial statutes for Christians and Parsis and certain statutes of common application, English legal principles were introduced within the Indian jurisprudence. These principles gradually influenced even the uncodified 'personal laws' of Hindus and Muslims and remoulded them along the lines of English statutes to suit the requirements of an adversarial court system. The English principles of matrimonial jurisprudence could now be read into the native laws and customs. The anti-women bias and English norms of Victorian prudity could now be elevated into rigid legal principles of Indian family laws.

Towards the end of the nineteenth century, women's rights became a highly contested issue within the discourse of national identity and the plea of the reformers met with a great deal of hostility from the conservatives. The growing antagonism between Hindu and Muslim communities within the nationalist movement also rendered the project of evolving uniform family laws an impossibility.

Later, during the 1920s, in response to Gandhi's call, a large number of women entered the political arena. At their insistence, the question of women's rights was once again placed within the political sphere of the nationalist discourse. This resulted in the enactment of some statutes in the 1930s, which secured Hindu and Muslim women certain significant rights. In the years immediately preceding independence, during the debate in the Constitutional Assembly, the mandate on equality provided the necessary backdrop for formulating women's rights. But at this stage, the issue of women's rights was coloured by political concerns of an emerging nation. While laying the foundation of a modern democracy, the rights of citizens had to be defined. Here, the conflicting pulls between the rights of minorities to a cultural and religious identity and the concern for an integrated nation within clearly defined territorial boundaries, became the context within which the issue of women's rights had to be renegotiated. The legislative history of Hindu and Muslim family laws during the politically significant ninety years preceding independence is traced in this chapter.

5.1 Power from the Company to the Crown

After the political upheaval of 1857, when the administration of India shifted from the Company to the British Crown, a reassurance of non-interference in religious beliefs and practices became imperative. In her historic proclamation, Queen Victoria promised equal protection of the law for all religions and restrained the administrators from interference in the realm of personal beliefs and practices of the natives by declaring: 'We do strictly charge and enjoin all those who may be in authority under us that they abstain from all interference with the religious belief or worship of any subjects on pain of our highest displeasure.'[1] Since the British administrators had already concluded that practices governing family relationships are 'religious', this proclamation could be construed to protect the family laws from any interference from the administrators.

The *Government of India Act of 1858*, transformed every aspect of Indian administration. The legal structure went through a major change. The Supreme Courts in the Presidency towns of Calcutta, Bombay and Madras which operated with relative autonomy were replaced by integrated High Courts with the Privy Council as the final Court of Appeal. The Presidencies lost their autonomy and were joined into a unified imperial rule. The features of the administration as developed in Bengal were made the basis for new forms of unified administration for all the three Presidencies. The Bombay Presidency's treatment of self-governing groups and its acceptance of customary law gave way to the practice in Bengal Presidency of viewing all groups as possessing of a unified Hindu and Muslim legal entity.[2]

While the realm of the 'personal' was largely left untouched as per the proclamation, the new legal structure based on the model of the English courts necessitated the enactment of statute to regulate the 'public domain'. The extent of codification can be gauged by the fact that from 1861 to 1869, under Henry Maine, Member of Governor General's Legislative Council, 211 enactments were formulated, out of which 30 were major.[3]

The cornerstones of this new legal edifice were the Indian Penal Code and the Indian Contract Act, which facilitated smooth administration by laying down uniform laws regulating crime and punishment and commercial transactions. These two statutes formed the core of the criminal (penal) and civil (economic) legal principles in India. *The Indian Penal Code of (1860)* (along with the *Indian Evidence Act of 1872* and the *Criminal Procedure Act of 1898)* replaced the Islamic criminal system. *The Indian Contract Act of 1860* (along with the *Specific Relief Act of 1877*, the *Negotiable Instruments Act of 1881* and the *Transfer of Property Act of 1882)* laid down uniform laws to facilitate smooth economic transaction for the corporate world.[4]

As already discussed in Chapter 2, the Hindu notion of dharma differed a great deal from the British notion of law and justice. The term 'dharma' was broad and inclusive and could be applied to all aspects of life. Manu's categorization of 18 heads of law included both civil and criminal issues. The Islamic law also dealt with civil and criminal aspects. But the process of legislation adopted by the British was selective and affected only some aspects of civil and criminal law while a large area which was termed as 'religious' was left out of its purview, to be regulated by the natives as per their religious doctrines. But the categorization of matters to be dealt under personal laws was fluid, to be determined by the needs of the rising colonial empire. For instance, the initial charters had listed 'contract' as an issue left for the application of customary law. But since contract was essential to lay the foundation of a capitalist economy, it was taken out of the realm of 'religious' personal laws and was legislated upon. By treating only some aspects of these laws as religious, the British jurists were applying to them the Roman categorization of ecclesiastical and temporal (canon and civil) laws. Further, all issues concerning 'personal' matters were deemed 'religious' rather than customary. Over a period, the terms 'religious laws' and 'personal laws' were used as synonymous and interchangeable.[5] The First Law Commission's recommendation to codify personal laws was rejected on the ground that these laws are religious and since British legislature cannot regulate Mohammedan or Hindu religion, it also cannot (or shall not) legislate for Mohammedans or Hindus.[6]

But under the new system of adjudication, case law or judicial interpretation became an important new source of law entrusted with greater validity and binding force than the scriptures themselves. Through this source, inroads were made into the realm of personal laws. *The Indian Law Reports Act of 1875* strengthened the already established practice of relying upon the rulings of other courts. The subversion of women's rights through this process of case law has already been discussed in the preceding chapter. By the end of the nineteenth century the realm of uncodified 'personal law' was reduced primarily to case law reported in law journals.[7]

5.2 State Enacted Religious Laws

The restraint upon legislating in the realm of personal matters was applicable only to the Hindus and Muslims. The other religious communities, the Christians and the Parsis were not placed under this restraint. Hence statutes could be enacted to govern the matrimonial relationships of these communities.

The first few enactments in the realm of matrimonial laws were meant mainly for European Christians and Christian converts.[8] Significant among these is the *Indian Divorce Act* of 1869, which was modelled on the *Matrimonial Causes Act of 1857* of England. This statute was a milestone in the history of English matrimonial law as it transferred matrimonial jurisdiction from ecclesiastical courts to the civil courts in England and provided for the dissolution of Christian marriages.

Even prior to the enactment of the Indian Divorce Act in 1869, the British legal principles of morality, equity and good conscience could be effectively used as channels for incorporating the Anglo-Saxon jurisprudence into the Indian legal system. But in 1869, through a statutory process, the principles of English matrimonial law were firmly established within the Indian jurisprudence.

While some matrimonial remedies had already entered India through English lawyers practising in the Indian courts and by the application of the Civil Procedure Code,[9] the Indian Divorce Act gave a statutory recognition to the matrimonial reliefs like restitution of conjugal rights, judicial separation and annulment, which did not have any scriptural or customary basis in the Indian setting. It is significant to note that at this historical juncture, the laws and customs regulating most lower caste Hindus and the Muslim communities provided for the dissolution of marriages. These dissolutions could be effected through community-based arbitration fora by fulfilling certain minimum conditions and without engaging in lengthy legal battles nor incurring phenomenal costs. The relevant point to note is that these dissolutions were not effected through adversarial processes but through community arbitrations and with the consent of the parties or their families after returning the gifts received from the other spouse. In most cases, the party seeking dissolution had to pay back the marriage expenses and at times was called upon to pay a compensation to the other party. In communities practising the custom of bride price, if the wife was seeking dissolution, she herself, or on her behalf, her father or her future husband, would have to return the bride price. Among Muslim communities, if the wife was seeking dissolution, she would have to forego her mehr amount which was stipulated by the husband at the time of marriage.

But under the Christian view, marriage was deemed as an eternal and indissoluble sacrament. The *Matrimonial Causes Act of 1857* made some dent into the concept of indissoluble marital bondage by providing for the dissolution of marriage under certain stringent grounds. But divorce was a 'relief' available only to an innocent spouse, if a matrimonial fault could be proved against the guilty partner. The spouse could also obtain a lesser relief of judicial separation and keep intact the matrimonial tie and thus deny the guilty spouse the option of remarriage. The parties could also enforce conjugality through judicial proceedings and compel a deserted spouse to return to the matrimonial dwelling under threat of imprisonment or confiscation of his/her property, a concept unheard of in the Indian setting. Overall, the Christian concept treated matrimony as a state of eternal bondage and the 1857 Act was meant to provide marginal respite from these archaic and anti-women notions. The aim of the *Indian Divorce Act of 1869* was to extend the progressive provisions for European Christians and British subjects residing in India. But gradually, these English notions of marriage and matrimonial 'reliefs', (e.g. restitution of conjugal rights, judicial separation and annulment of marriage) were incorporated into the personal laws of other communities either through judicial precedents or legislative enactments.

The Parsis who were governed by customary laws, demanded for a separate enactment to govern their marriage and succession. In response to this demand, a statute was enacted to govern Parsi marriages and the principles of English matrimonial law were incorporated into this statute.[10]

Although the statutes governing Christians and Parsis were state enactments, since they governed family relationships they came to be viewed as 'religious laws'. The implications of these statutes to Christian and Parsi women are addressed in Part Three of this book.

5.3 Remoulding of Indian Family Law Within a Western Model

The statutes governing Christian and Parsi communities set the trend of matrimonial adjudications for Hindus and Muslims. Within the new legal structure founded on adversarial principles of English civil law, family relationships of Hindus and Muslims came to be contested. The matrimonial rights and obligations were reinterpreted within the paradigm of the matrimonial remedies introduced by the new statutes.[11]

It is not intended to negate the fact that the customary

practices, as well as the doctrinal precepts of the pre-colonial Indian society contained several anti-women stipulations. But the scriptures were not statutes and contained several contradictions and ambiguities both internally within each authority, as well as between the different authorities within a region. Further, the language and the context of these texts was open to several interpretations leading to diverse customs within a pluralistic society. Hence, it would be logical to infer that the customs and interpretations were not uniformly anti-women and that there were spaces for negotiating women's rights.

The English translations of the original texts had already subverted the context and meaning of these precepts. The anti-women biases and the orientalist approaches of the translators would also have coloured the translations. Within the new litigation fora, the coloured opinions expressed in these translated texts became definite legal principles of universal application. Published in law journals and relied upon in subsequent litigations, the most negative aspects of Hindu and Muslim laws were highlighted and over a period of time became the settled infallible principles of Hindu and Muslim family law.

Many a times, the ancient texts were used mainly to co-opt the anti-women provisions of English matrimonial statutes. The application of the medieval European (Christian) remedy of restitution of conjugal rights (which was incorporated in the English matrimonial statutes in 1857), to both Muslims and Hindus in India by re-interpreting their ancient legal texts is one concrete example of this new trend.[12] Subversion of women's economic rights upon marriage, i.e. the Hindu woman's right to stridhana and the Muslim woman's right to mehr (both of which could include immovable properties) to the English concept of maintenance provides another example. The introduction of the English principle of widow's limited estate and the concept of 'reversioner' (to whom the property would revert back upon the death of the widow) is a third example of this trend.

Ironically, while the British used the issue of the status of Indian women to rationalize the political subjugation of India as a civilizing project, the Hindu revivalists tried to re-locate these principles into their ancient texts, armed by the orientalists approach of a shared distant Aryan past. The concern of reformers for changing the status of women became trapped within the binaries of a superior Hindu culture projected by the revivalists and the civilizing project of the British administrators. But the rigid Victorian morality was the parameter set by all factions for determining the status of women.[13]

During the last phase of nineteenth century, Hindu conjugality became the main battleground for the revivalist struggle for national identity and any reform within personal laws came to be viewed by this faction with extreme hostility. The issue was foregrounded in the controversy regarding the Age of Consent (and restraint upon child marriage) both in Bombay and Bengal.[14] The controversy was galvanized by the decision of the Bombay High Court in the case of Rukmabai, who was married in childhood and whose marriage had not been consummated.[15] The court had declined to pass a decree of restitution of conjugal rights in favour of the husband. The revivalists interpreted this judgement as an interference in the sacrosanct arena of Hindu conjugality by the British courts (and a breach of the assurance on non-interference). For the reformers, the intervention of the English courts was an armour in their campaign against the upper caste Hindu custom of child marriage.

The litigation, the judgement and the controversy which followed were all laden with ironies. The husband's case was trumpeted by the revivalists and it is with their support he had approached the English courts, rather than the caste panchayat, for the remedy of restoring his Hindu conjugality. As already stated, within the customary law, the relief of restoring conjugality was non-existent and the husband could not obtain any relief in this sphere. Conjugality has not been instituted and hence the question of 'restoring conjugality' an European Christian remedy did not apply to this case.[16] Also, the parties belonged to the lower caste among whom the custom of the caste recognized the right of the wife to dissolve her marriage. And most important, Justice Pinhey, who presided over the matter, had declined the relief on the ground that it was an outdated medieval Christian remedy under the English law and further that the Hindu law did not recognize such a barbaric custom.[17] But in the highly politicized climate, these subtle legal points were lost. The debate was confined within the binaries of the barbaric Hindu custom of child marriage by the reformers and the audacity of an English judge to intervene in the sacred realm of Hindu conjugality by the revivalists.

5.4 Option of Secular and Civil Statutes

During this period, certain uniform and secular statutes governing family relationships were also enacted. The *Indian Succession Act* of 1865 (re-enacted in 1925), the *Special Marriage Act* of 1872 (re-enacted in 1954) and the *Guardians and Wards Act* of 1890. Modelled on the principle of separation of the canon and the civil, which was gradually being accepted under the Anglo-Saxon law, these were purely civil enactments. There was no camouflage of religiosity here as in the enactments governing Christian and the Parsi communities.

The *Special Marriage Act* was a response to the demand raised by the Brahmo Samajis, as part of their campaign against Brahminical rituals and idol worship within the Bengal Presidency, for a law enabling registration of simple, non-ritualistic civil marriages. The Act was passed despite opposition from orthodox sections and provided the opportunity for Indians to contract a marriage, devoid of any religious trappings, in a civil registry. But it was mandatory for the parties contracting the marriage to declare that they had renounced their religion. The stipulation of renouncing religion narrowed the scope of the Act. In 1912, a demand was raised for the deletion of this provision, but was not conceded. But later, through an amendment in 1923, this clause was deleted. This facilitated the registration of civil marriages without the accompanying encumbrance of religious renouncement. After the marriage, for matters of property inheritance, the couple would be governed by the provisions of the *Indian Succession Act*.

The *Indian Succession Act* contained separate sections for Parsis and non-Parsis. The provisions governing Parsis granted daughters a share in the family property but followed the Islamic principle of granting them half the share of their male counterparts. The general section was more egalitarian. Daughters were granted equal right of inheritance along with their brothers. But the statute also simultaneously validated the English notion of testamentary succession. The individual acquired an absolute right in the property and there were no restraints upon alienation either by transfer or bequest. This concentration of rights upon an individual was contrary to the prevailing norms governing both Hindu and Muslim property inheritance.

Although applicable primarily to Christians, this statute could be deemed a residuary law since it was also applicable to persons contracting civil marriages.

The *Guardians and Wards Act* of 1890 which authorized the courts to appoint guardians for minors was also applicable uniformly. Despite the limitation, the *Special Marriage Act*, the *Indian Succession Act and the Guardians and Wards Act*, provided secular and civil options to persons who did not want to be governed by religious enactments. These could have gradually developed into a comprehensive family code. But the growing resentment against the British rule and their policy of constituting Hindus and Muslims as separate, homogeneous and antagonistic communities restricted the scope for developing uniform family laws.

5.5 Sectarian Reforms Within Communalized Communities

The events at the turn of the century brought in a sharp cleavage between the two distinct political constituencies of Hindus and Muslims. The division of Bengal, the communal riots at the close of the century and the separate electorates introduced by the Morley-Minto reforms collapsed the space for any further enactments of uniform applicability in the realm of family law.[18]

But when women entered the political arena in response to the call given by Gandhi in the twenties, the issue of women's rights and family law reform gained limelight. Women leaders of the nationalist movement raised the demand for a comprehensive code regulating marriage, divorce and inheritance. Kamaladevi Chattopadhyay, Sarojinidevi Naidu, Muthulaxmi Reddy, Begam Shah Nawaz and other prominent members of the All India Women's Conference (AIWC) were the most vocal protagonists of this demand.

Lamenting over the plight of women, Captain Laxmi, a protagonist of women's rights, stated at the 1933 AIWC meet: 'The members of the Legislative Assembly who are men will not help us in bringing any drastic changes which will benefit women.' At the urging of Renuka Ray, another vocal member, 24th November 1934 was declared as a Legal Disabilities Day. The AIWC also initiated a comparative study of the family laws of different communities with a view to evolving uniform family laws.[19]

The pressure from women leaders led to the Indian National Congress ratifying the demand for a uniform code during its conventions. But when the Congress leaders acquired the power to legislate through the *Government of India Act* of 1935, the law reforms initiated by them were not only limited and short-sighted but also widened the gulf between the Hindu and Muslim family laws.

The Government of India Act of 1935, provided an opportunity for nationalist leaders to legislate and regulate family relations. Using this opportunity, both the Hindu and Muslim leaders pressed for law reform within their respective personal laws ostensibly to elevate the status of women. The issues addressed by the reforms, their impact on women's rights and the political motive beneath the reforms make interesting study.

The Hindu Women's Right to Property Act, 1937: The aim of the *Hindu Women's Right to Property Bill*, introduced by Dr G.V. Deshmukh, was to set right the problems created by the judicial decisions of the English courts which had constrained the scope of stridhana, during the later phase of the nineteenth century.[20]

While introducing the Bill in the Legislative Assembly on 4 February 1937, Deshmukh stated:

> The British concepts like 'reversioner' 'surrender' etc. had caused a great loss to women's right to property. The word 'reversioner' reflected an English notion peculiar to their own country. From that moment, the widow began to be infested by those pests called 'reversioners'. In fact, a majority of the litigation in connection with the property of widows was by and on account of the reversioners. The reversioner could harass the widow by challenging every act of hers in dealing with the property.[21]

Deshmukh added that due to the prevailing social conditions, the English judges had arrived at an erroneous conclusion that the temperament of the Hindu society was such that it did not want Hindu women to have an absolute right in the property.[21]

Through this Bill, Deshmukh hoped to achieve equality between Hindu men and women in respect of their property. Clause 3 of the Bill stipulated that no person should be excluded from inheritance and partition on the basis of sex. Regarding the devolution of the property of a Hindu dying intestate, Clause 4 of the bill specifically provided that it would devolve upon the wife, mother, daughter and wife of a predeceased son along with the sons and all would have equal share in the property. Clause 5 equated the status of women to that of men and made them absolute owners of the property.[22]

The Bill met with a great deal of hostility and Deshmukh was ridiculed for introducing this bill. After much debate, a watered down version of the original Bill was finally enacted. The provisions of the Bill granting women absolute right to property were mutilated and widows were granted only a limited right of inheritance through a concept called 'widow's estate'. The provision granting daughters a share in the parental property was excluded. The right of married women to separate property under the scriptural notion of stridhana, which the Bill originally set to restore was subverted. The women's right to property was confined within the limited sphere of inheritance rights of widows.

Reform within Islam (1937 and 1939): Using the same opportunity, the Muslim religio-political leaders enacted two important legislations which had far-reaching effect upon the Muslim communities. As mentioned earlier many communities which had converted to Islam continued their customary practices of property inheritance. The Muslim League with the support of the religious leaders, the Ullamas, initiated a legislation through which all Muslims would be mandatorily governed by the Shariat law.[23] The second statute[24] conferred on the Muslim women a statutory right of divorce under certain specific conditions.[25]

The arguments in favour of the Application of Shariat Act 1937 were that the customary laws of inheritance based on the concept of joint family property were discriminatory against women and that application of the Shariat would raise their status. M.H.M. Abdullah, who introduced the Bill in the central legislature spelt out the objectives of the Bill as follows:

> ...the bill aims at securing uniformity of law among Muslims in all their social and personal relations. By doing so it also recognises and does justice to the claims of women for inheriting family property who, under customary law, are debarred from succeeding to the same. If Shariat law is applied they will automatically be entitled to inherit the same.[26]

Another Muslim member Sir Mohammad Yamin Khan stressed that Muslim women had been lobbying for the passage of the bill and pointed out that

> ... being Muslim why (women) not get the benefit of Islamic law and why should they be deprived of their genuine right of inheritance on account of the customary law which gives to a man a much bigger share than what he is entitled to...(A Muslim woman) does not enjoy only the limited right of maintenance but she becomes the full owner of her property.... she is under no obligation to give the property to her husband .... not even have it managed by her husband ...human society must live on the right principles of equity....[27]

The Bill had the support of all Muslim legislators and women members. G.V. Deshmukh was another supporter of the Bill. The stated aim of the legislation was to declare that in matters relating to marriage, divorce and inheritance all Muslims would be mandatorily governed by the Shariat, (which is more progressive and pro-women) to the exclusion of other laws and customs, throughout British India. But beneath the stated objective, the Bill also had a deeper political agenda, of unifying Muslims and strengthening the political base, as well the religious hold over the community.[28] This was the period when the two nation theory was being formulated and within the nationalist movement there was a sharp divide between Hindu and Muslim leaders. A uniform law was viewed by the Muslim League as an important step towards unifying the community. Since unification of Muslims was the primary aim, customs of matrilineal inheritance were opposed as vehemently as those which denied women property rights. To achieve the crucial political motive beneath the Bill, an attempt had to be made to pacify the feudal landowners who were opposed to the Bill. As a conciliatory move, M.A. Jinnah introduced an amendment to keep agrarian landholdings out of the purview of the Bill. Despite the tall claim of empowering women, women's rights were subverted to the political agenda.[29]

The second legislation during this period was the *Dissolution of Muslim Marriages Act*, 1939. As per the Shariat, on apostasy a Muslim marriage stood dissolved. Muslim women who felt trapped within oppressive marriages used the provision to dissolve their marital ties. The Act sought to arrest this trend by providing Muslim women a statutory right to divorce within their religious boundaries and thus retain them within the Islamic fold.

The Act was based on a book entitled, *Al-Hilat al-Nazjizalil Halilat al-Ajizah* (a lawful divorce) published in 1932 by the renowned Islamic jurist Maulana Ashraf Ali Thanavi. In defence of women's rights, he had enumerated the principles of the Maliki law by which a court could dissolve a Muslim woman's marriage under specified conditions.[30] Based on his recommendations, a Bill was introduced in the Central Legislature by Muhammed Ahmad Kazimi in 1936.[31]

The Islamic jurists, Asif Ali Fyzee and Maulana Thanavi actively campaigned for its enactment. The Bill was supported by several non-Muslim members. But some Hindu legislators cautioned that while they would support a bill granting divorce to Muslim women, they would oppose any move to confer a similar right on Hindu women.

The statement of objects and reasons mentioned that the aim of the Bill was to alleviate the unspeakable misery caused to Muslim women. The Act was applicable only to women. The Muslim men's right to unilateral divorce was not affected by the reform. Again, beneath the profound objective of women's welfare lay a deeper political motive of strengthening Islam. But despite the hidden agenda, it was a landmark reform in the history of Islamic (predominantly Hanafi) law in India.

5.6 Debate Within the Constitutional Assembly

The years immediately preceding independence were the years marked by the controversy around the Hindu Code Bill. Compared to their Muslim counterparts, the caste Hindu women lagged far behind. They had neither a right to divorce nor an absolute right of inheritance as widows and daughters. The consistent campaign by women leaders compelled the Congress to prioritize this issue. But although two separate committees were set up during the forties to explore the scope of reform within the customary Hindu law and these committees submitted detailed reports, the political developments necessitated the shelving of this issue until independence.[32]

It is interesting to observe that while laying the foundation of a new nation, the scheme of women's liberation had to be relocated within the master scheme of national integration and became subservient to it in all later developments, both legislative and judicial.

The issue of personal laws was debated primarily in the Constituent Assembly in the context of rights of minorities within the new nation. The trauma of partition had brought in its wake an insecure and defensive Muslim minority who had to be reassured of their right to religious and cultural freedom within the new democracy, which would be governed by majority concerns. The political impediments which necessitated this assurance bear resemblance to Queen Victoria's Proclamation after the Sepoy Mutiny almost a century earlier.

Within these political constraints, the debate around the Uniform Civil Code in the Constituent Assembly centered on the 'nation' and 'national integration'. The issue of gender and women's rights did not figure in this debate. It was deemed necessary that the integrated nation should be governed by a uniform set of family laws to facilitate national unity and smooth governance. The Indian leaders had inherited the British scheme of making laws certain, uniform and rigid for easy administration and carried a similar contemptuous approach towards plurality of laws and non-state legal systems which were deemed as pre-modern. But, the flip side of this objective of smooth governance was an assurance to minorities of their separate religious and cultural identity symbolized by the continuance of their personal laws.

The clause on the Uniform Civil Code became a highly contested issue and only after the rights were divided into two segments, i.e. Fundamental and Enforceable Rights (Part III of the Constitution), and Directive Principles of State Policy, which were non-enforceable (Part IV of the Constitution) that the Muslim members consented to placing this clause under Part IV of the Constitution. This move was opposed by liberals within the Constituent Assembly, M.R. Masani, Hansa Mehta, Rajkumari Amrit Kaur, K.M. Munshi, Alladi Krishnaswami Ayyar etc. in the context of evolving a new nationhood and ushering India into modernity and did not address the issue of women's rights. M.R. Masani, Hansa Mehta and Rajkumari Amrit Kaur voiced their notes of dissent on the ground:

> One of the factors that has kept India back from advancing to nationhood has been the existence of personal laws based on religion which keep the nation divided into watertight compartments in many aspects. [According to K.M. Munshi, the important point was whether] We are going to consolidate and unify our personal law in such a way that the way of life of the whole country may in course of time be unified and (become) secular. ...After all we are an advancing society. We are in a stage where we must unify and consolidate the nation by every means ... [Alladi Krishnaswami Ayyar added,] Are we helping those factors which help the welding together into a single nation, or is this country

to be kept up always as a series of competing communities?[33]

But withstanding this opposition, Dr Ambedkar pointed out that the Muslim members probably had read rather too much into this provision which merely proposes that the state shall endeavour to secure a civil code for the citizens of the country. It does not say that after the uniform code is framed, the state shall enforce it upon all citizens merely because they are citizens. It is perfectly possible that future parliaments may provide for an optional code.[34] Guided by these assurances, Article 44 of the Constitution is worded as follows: The State shall endeavour to secure for the citizens a *Uniform Civil Code* throughout the territory of India.

Notes

1. Desika Char, S.V., *Readings in the Constitutional History of India 1757–1947*, New Delhi: Oxford University Press (1983), p. 294.
2. I am grateful to Amrita Shodhan for sharing with me her unpublished doctoral thesis where she has dealt with this point elaborately. For reference, see Chapter 4, n.9.
3. Rankin, G.C., *Background to India Law*, Cambridge: Cambridge University Press (1946).
4. While enacting the *Indian Contract Act*, the fact that contract was initially treated as part of personal law was conveniently overlooked and it was transformed into territorial law uniformly applicable to all British subjects.
5. While a large part of the personal laws relates to family matters, the term also applies to issues like management of Hindu religious and charitable institutions and Muslim *wakfs*, as well as the Muslim law of pre-emption and the Hindu law of Damdupat.
6. Rankin, G.C., *Background to India Law*, p.67.
7. See Cohn, B.S., 'Anthropological Note on Disputes and Law in India' in Nader, L. (ed.), *The Ethnography of Law* (American Anthropological Association) (1965), pp.112-13.
8. The *Native Converts Marriage Dissolution Act*, 1866, the *Indian Divorce Act*, 1869 and *Indian Christian Marriage Act*, 1872 are illustrative of this trend.
9. See *Peerozeboye v Ardaseer Cursetjee* (1853) POC 57.
10. The *Parsi Marriage and Divorce Act* of 1865. The history of this legislation is discussed in detail in Chapter 9.
11. According to Bhattacharjee, with their bulk, alien appearance, exotic trappings and Westminsterish logomachy, the law of the country became alienated from the people. See Bhattacharjee, A.M., *Hindu Law and the Constitution*, Calcutta: Eastern Law House (1994) (2nd edn.), p.11.

12. See *Gatha Ram Mistree v Moohito Kochin Domoonee* (1875) 14 BLR 298 and *Moonshee Buzloor Ruheem v Shumsoonissa Begum* (1867) 2 MIA 551.
13. See Banerjee, S., 'Marginalization of Women's Popular Culture in Nineteenth Century Bengal' (1989), in Sangari, K. & S. Vaid (ed.), *Recasting Women, Essays in Colonial History*, New Delhi: Kali for Women (1989), p.127.
14. Sarkar, T., 'Rhetoric Against Age of Consent,' in *Economic and Political Weekly*, XXVIII/36, (1983) p.1870.
15. Chandra, S., 'Rukmabai: Debate over Woman's Right to Her Person,' in *Economic and Political Weekly*, XXXI/44 (1996), p.2927.
16. Among most lower castes which practised child marriage, the right of conjugality would commence not from the date of marriage but only after the performance of a second ceremony after attaining puberty.
17. *Dadaji Bhikaji v Rukmabai* (1885) ILR 9 Bom 529.
18. Sarkar, S., *Modern India 1885–1947*, Madras: Macmillan (1993).
19. Basu, A. and B. Rai, *A History of the AIWC 1927–1990*, Delhi: Manohar (1992), pp.46-7.
20. Gill, K., *Hindu Women's Right to Property*, New Delhi: Deep & Deep Publications (1986), p.485.
21. Ibid., p.104.
22. Ibid., pp.105-7.
23. The *Application of Shariat Act*, 1937.
24. The *Dissolution of Muslim Marriages Act*, 1939.
25. It is relevant to record that Hindu women were granted corresponding rights almost two decades later. The right to divorce was conferred on the Hindu women through the *Hindu Marriage Act*, 1955 and the absolute right of inheritance was conferred through the *Hindu Succession Act* 1956.
26. Lateef, S., 'Defining Women through Legislation,' in Hasan, Z. (ed.), *Forging Identities : Gender, Communities and the State*, New Delhi: Kali for Women (1994), p.43.
27. Ibid., p.45.
28. Parashar, A., *Women and Family Law Reform*, New Delhi: Sage Publications (1992), p.150.
29. Ibid., p.149.
30. Ibid., p.151.
31. Ahmad, F., 'Fatwa needed to make talaq revocable,' in *The Pioneer*, Delhi 17.V.94.
32. See the following chapter for a detailed account of the process of Hindu law reforms.
33. Dhagamwar, V., *Towards the Uniform Civil Code*, Bombay: N.M. Tripathi (1989), pp.2-3.
34. Ibid., p.4.

PART TWO:

POST-INDEPENDENCE DEVELOPMENTS

6

Hindu Law Reforms—Stilted Efforts at Gender Justice

Introduction

Constitution is rightly the most significant touchstone for determining the scope of women's rights in the post-independence period. The provisions of adult franchise, non-discrimination on the basis of sex and positive discrimination (or affirmative action) in favour of women and children placed Indian women far ahead of many of their western counterparts.[1] Equality and non-discrimination became fundamental and enforceable legal rights. The scope of Article 21, could be expanded to read into it issues of social and economic justice.[2] It is against this backdrop that we examine the major law reform of the post-independence period.

Although the reformed Hindu law is projected as the ideal piece of legislation which liberated Hindu women, the underlying motive of the reform was consolidating the powers of the state and building an integrated nation. This crucial objective could be achieved only by diluting women's rights to arrive at a level of minimum consensus so that the agenda of reform could be effected without much opposition. Several customary rights were sacrificed to arrive at uniformity. The statutes that were finally enacted were merely ornamental instead of being markers of genuine and concrete efforts at rectifying the gender discrimination written into the Hindu law. Some of the anomalies within the reformed laws, as well as the complex and labourious process of the reform is examined here.

In the years that followed, several discriminatory aspects of the personal laws came up for judicial scrutiny under the constitutional mandate of equality and non-discrimination. But the courts, in most cases, stopped short of declaring the discriminatory aspects as unconstitutional. Over the years, the courts have held that the discrimination under the personal laws of various communities is based on reasonable classification. This has thrown further stumbling blocks in the path of gender equality.

6.1 Concerns Governing the Reforms

The history of Hindu Law reform spans a period of fifteen years from 1941 to 1956. It was discussed in three Parliaments of historical significance i.e. the Federal Parliament, the Provisional Parliament and the first Parliament of the newly independent nation. At each stage, it went through a dilution of rights till finally, the political interests of the ruling party became the primary consideration. But the rhetoric continued to be 'liberation of women'.

The Hindu Law Committee, set up in 1941 to look into the anomalies of the 1937 Act, recommended a comprehensive code of marriage and succession, which led to the setting up of the second Hindu Law Committee in 1944. After soliciting opinions of jurists and the public, the Committee submitted its report to the Federal Parliament in April, 1947. The recommendations were debated in the Provincial Parliament between 1948 and 1951 and again from 1951 to 1954. Finally, a diluted version, in the form of four separate Acts could be passed only in 1955-6.

The three important factors which need to be examined in the context of the Hindu law reform are, (i) the opposition to it within the Congress leadership, (ii) the political impediments which necessitated the reform, and (iii) the veracity of its dual claim of being a code and of liberating women.

Opposition from Conservative Forces: Several provisions including the provisions of monogamy, divorce, abolition of coparcenary and inheritance to daughters were opposed. It was felt that the Hindu society will receive a moral setback if women were granted the right to divorce along with a right to inherit property. The reforms were opposed by the then President and Constitutional head, Dr Rajendra Prasad, senior Congressmen like Pattabhi Sitaramayya and the architect of the united Indian nation, Sardar Patel, the President of the ruling Congress, P.D. Tandon among others.[3]

The representatives of Hindu fundamentalist parties termed

it as 'anti-Hindu' and 'anti-Indian' and raised the demand for a uniform code as a delaying tactic. At this point, the women parliamentarians who had initially propagated a uniform code, reversed their position and supported the Hindu law reform. This is a significant political move, since an uncompromising demand for a uniform code would have meant an alliance with the most reactionary and anti-women lobby and would have caused a further setback to women's rights.[4]

Political impediments which necessitated the reform: The concerns which were instrumental in bringing about reform in Muslim Law, i.e. of homogenizing a community by uniting them under one law, were also the driving force for the Hindu law reform. The integration of Hindus from three different political regimes, i.e. British India, the princely states and the tribal regions into one nation could best be done by bringing them under one law. Hence, the primary concern was to define the term 'Hindu' in its widest sense and encompass all sects and castes and religious denominations within it. The Hindu Law Committee had defined 'Hindu' as anyone professing the Hindu religion. But later the word 'professes' was deleted to broaden its scope.[5]

Examining the motive for Hindu law reform, Archana Parashar[6] argues, that the hidden agenda was unification of the nation through uniformity in law. National integration was of paramount importance. Establishing the supremacy of the state over religious institutions was another important consideration. This could be best achieved by re-defining the rights given to women. Through the re-orientation of female roles the state could replace the claim of religion and religious institutions over people's lives. While bringing in reforms the state relied upon two conflicting claims of tradition and modernity. While professing that it was bound by the Constitution, the state projected the image of a continuity with the past (by preserving the provisions from the ancient sacred law) to bring in selective reforms.

For the state, the unifying potential of the common code became more important than its potential for ensuring legal equality for women. Hence, several customary rights of women, particularly from the lower castes and the southern regions, were sacrificed in the interest of uniformity. Local customs of matrilineal inheritance and other customary safeguards were not incorporated into the new code.

For instance, most lower castes had a right of divorce and remarriage under the customary law with consent of the parties. Through the *Marumakkattayam Act* of 1933, (applicable to the Malabar region) the right of divorce by executing a registered instrument of dissolution by the concerned parties was granted statutory recognition. Further, under the scriptural law as well as customary law, the right of females as stridhana heirs was superior to their male counterparts and that of parents was superior to in-laws. But under S.15 of the *Hindu Succession Act*, 1956, sons and daughters were granted equal rights. Further, under the provisions of the *Hindu Succession Act*, the property of a childless woman devolves upon the husband's heirs and only in their absence would it devolve upon the woman's own parents. A further and inexplicable distinction was made between the heirs of the father and those of the mother of a female and the mother's heirs were placed in an inferior category.[7] Despite the wide diversity under the Hindu law the reforms relied upon one school irrespective of its provisions favouring women.

The Congress party was dominated by lawyers trained in British law or those who studied law in England and consequently imbibed all the colonial biases regarding the functioning of Indian society, as well as the changes that were supposedly needed to modernize it. There was a fascination among social reformers with uniformity as a vehicle of national unity. The notion of the state as an instrument of social reform to be imposed upon the people without creating a social consensus derives essentially from the norms of functioning inherent in the colonialist state machinery and ideology. The English-educated elite had faithfully imbibed the colonial state's ideology, projecting itself as the most progressive instrument of social reform.[8]

The reforms did not introduce any principle which had not already existed somewhere in India. Despite this, the reforms were projected as a vehicle for ushering in western modernity. There were, however, several liberal customary practices which were discarded by the Hindu code for the sake of uniformity. In their stated determination to put an end to the growth of custom, the reformers were in fact putting an end to the essence of

Hindu law, and ironically, persisted in calling the codification 'Hindu'.[9]

Claims of liberating women: There is a general presumption that the Hindus are governed by a secular, egalitarian and gender-just code and that this code should now be extended to Muslims to liberate Muslim women. The judiciary has contributed to this myth by reiterating that Hindus have forsaken their personal laws and are governed by a common code.[10] This misconception forms the basis of the demand for the Uniform Civil Code. Hence, the veracity of this demand needs to be closely scrutinized.

Since the political impediment to reform Hindu law was grave, several balancing acts had to be performed by the state while reforming the Hindu law. Crucial provisions empowering women had to be constantly watered down to reach the level of minimum consensus. While projecting to be pro-women, male privileges had to be protected. While introducing modernity, archaic Brahminical rituals had to be retained.[11] While usurping the power exercised by religious heads, needs of emerging capitalism had to be safeguarded. Only through such balancing acts, the agenda of law reform could be achieved.

Unfortunately, the anomalies and anti-women bias within the Hindu code were not discussed widely in public forum. They remained hidden in statute books and legal manuals. There seemed to be almost a conspiracy of silence beneath which these inadequacies were crouched. This led to a fiction that the Hindu Code is sufficiently modernized and hence it is the perfect family code which ought to be extended to other religious denominations in order to liberate women.

The Acts were neither Hindu in character nor based on modern principles of equality but reflected the worst tendencies of both. Inheritance rights of daughters, the right of divorce for women and the imposition of monogamy upon Hindu males were the issues which were severely contended. Some aspects of these issues are examined here.

6.2 Illusory Inheritance Rights

The extent of opposition within the Congress to daughters inheriting property, was such that the then Law Minister C. C. Biswas, in 1954, on the floor of the house, publicly expressed his disagreement with this provision.[12] Due to severe opposition, coparcenary system had to be maintained, which resulted in the denial of rights to women in the ancestral home and property. When compared to the position of the brother, the sister's share was dismal.[13] Since the earlier safeguard provided by the ancient law givers to women by way of stridhana, a necessary concomitance to male coparacenary, had been corroded due to judicial decisions,[14] denial of equal rights to daughters only served to widen the gulf between the gender divide.

The daughters had equal rights only in the separate or self-acquired property of their father. But daughters could be denied a share even in this separate property by throwing the property back into the common stock using the doctrine of blending or by forming new coparcenaries. An incentive for such a move was provided by the state by conferring tax reliefs for coparcenaries under the *Income Tax Act*.[15]

While at one level coparcenary was retained, all the safeguards for protection of women's rights were abrogated. The main feature of the traditional Hindu joint family was its inalienability. But the new right granted to the male members to will away the property, further weakened the position of female members.[16] In this context, the daughters' right to be maintained from the family property or to claim marriage expenses out of this became illusory. The property inherited by the son from the father now became his separate property and the female members could not lay any claims to it.[17] While the English concept of alienation through testamentary succession was incorporated into the *Hindu Succession Act*, the protection granted to the family members under the English law did not find a mention here.[18] So individual men could will away both their share in the joint family property as well as the whole of their separate property with absolute abandonment. During Parliamentary debates, these loopholes were specifically pointed out to the members who were opposing the provision granting property rights to daughters to indicate how they could circumvent the provisions of the Act.[19]

While there were no safeguards to protect the right of daughters in their natal family, the capitalist, consumerist forces transformed the ancient custom of stridhana into a modern distortion called dowry.[20] Under its modern guise, the daughters lost control upon this property, which was presumably given on her behalf, to secure her happiness in her matrimonial home. In the subsequent years, the demand for dowry became an instrument of violence and subjugation of the newly married brides.

6.3 Implications of Formal Equality

The Hindu Marriage Act of 1955 was based on a formal concept of equality where the spouses were deemed equal and had equal rights and obligations towards each other. Both men and women were granted equal rights to matrimonial remedies and ancillary reliefs.

So, while a basic inequality between men and women persisted within the scheme of inheritance rights,[21] under the perverse logic of equality the Hindu woman was under a legal obligation to maintain her husband.[22] The concept did not exist under any prevalent notion of marriage in the Indian context—Hindu law, either scriptural or customary, or the Muslim law or even in the modern and secular *Special Marriage Act,* enacted in 1954. The concept was introduced for the first time under the *Hindu Marriage Act* and was based on the western notion of formal equality.[23]

It is pertinent to note that the enactment of 1955 did not grant Hindu women the right of divorce by mutual consent which had already been introduced under the *Special Marriage Act* in 1954 as it was considered too radical for the conservative Hindu Society.[24] And yet women from such conservative societies were deemed to be sufficiently progressive, liberated and economically advanced so as to provide maintenance to their husbands. While a boy of 18 years was not entitled to claim maintenance from his father on the ground that he had reached the age of majority and hence is capable of earning his own livelihood, an adult male was granted the privilege of exercising a choice of remaining unemployed and claiming maintenance from his employed wife. This, despite the social reality that a large number of women are engaged in unpaid domestic work and among those who are engaged in wage labour, a significant percentage are in low paying jobs or in the unorganized sector.[25]

Ironically, while women were burdened with the responsibility of maintaining the husband under a modern concept of equality, the courts continued to undermine a woman's right to retain her job against her husband's wishes under the ancient notion of the

Lord and Master and granted them the privilege of determining the choice of matrimonial home. If the woman was employed at a place away from the matrimonial home, the husband could claim restitution of conjugal rights against the wives.[26]

For decades after the enactment, in a series of decisions, the courts held that Hindu marriage is a sacrament and it is the sacred duty of the wife to follow her husband and reside with him wherever he chooses to reside. In all the cases, the women were working and supporting the family. The husbands had approached the courts for restoring conjugality just to spite the women. The courts upheld the husband's rights and granted them a decree of restitution. The decisions are summarized below:

- In 1958 in *Ram Prakash v Savitri Devi*[27] the court held: According to Hindu Law, marriage is a holy union for the performance of marital duties with her husband where he may choose to reside and to fulfil her duties in her husband's home.
- In *Tirath Kaur v Kirpal Singh*,[28] the wife pleaded that she was willing to carry on with the marriage but was not prepared to give up the job. But the court disallowed her plea and ruled in favour of the husband as follows: The wife's refusal to give up the job amounts to desertion. This would entitle the husband for a decree of restitution of conjugal rights.
- In 1966, the Madhya Pradesh High Court held: A wife's first duty to her husband is to submit herself obediently to his authority and to remain under his roof and protection.[29]
- In 1973, in *Surinder Kaur v Gardeep Singh*[30] it was held: The Hindu law imposes on the wife the duty of attendance, obedience to and veneration for the husband to live with him wherever he chooses to reside.
- In 1977, the issue came up before the Full Bench of the Punjab and Haryana High Court in the case of *Kailash Wati v Ayodhia Parkash*.[31] The wife was employed prior to the marriage. Seven years after the marriage, the husband asked the wife to resign her job and on her refusal to do so, filed for restitution of conjugal rights. The wife stated that she was prepared to honour her matrimonial obligations but was not prepared to resign her job. The Full Bench of Punjab and Haryana High Court held: According to Hindu Law marriage is a holy union for the performance of marital duties with her husband where

he may choose to reside and to fulfil, her duties in her husband's home. The court reaffirmed that the wife's refusal to resign her job amounts to withdrawal from the husband's society, and granted the decree in favour of the husband.

So while under the modern concept of equality, the husbands had the right to be maintained by their wives, under the concept of a sacramental marriage, they could restrain them from gainful employment. The right was based on a plea that it was the sacred duty of a Hindu wife to reside under the care and protection of her husband, her lord and master. While the husbands' plea is not surprising, the judicial affirmation of this plea under a modern statute is disturbing.

It is only around 1975 that the courts began to recognize the woman's right to hold on to a job away from her husband's residence. Three important judgements of this time, secured for women their constitutional right of holding a job away from their husband's residence. The Gujarat High Court[32] while denying the husband the relief declared:

> In the modern outlook, the husband and wife are equally free to take up a job and retain it. Since there had been a mutual arrangement, it was not a case where it could be said that the wife had withdrawn from the society of the husband.

Similarly, the Madras High Court, in a case where the wife's income was used to sustain herself and her child, ruled: 'Under the modern law, the concept of the wife's obedience to her husband and her duty to live under his roof under all circumstances does not apply'.[33] In another significant development, the Delhi High court in 1978, in *Swaraj Garg v R.M. Garg*[34] dissented from the Full Bench decision in *Kailash Wati* and held that in the absence of a pre-marital agreement between the parties, it cannot be said that the wife who had a permanent job with a good income had to live at a place determined by the husband when the husband did not earn enough to maintain the family. Providing constitutional validity to the wife's right to hold on to the job, Justice Deshpande ruled that an exclusive right to the husband to decide the matrimonial home would be violative of the equality of sexes clause under Article 14 of the Constitution. In all the cases, the fact that the wives were earning more than their husbands and were substantially contributing towards household expenditure seems to have influenced the judges while denying husbands the decree of restitution of conjugal rights.

6.4 Consequences of Monogamy

The Hindu Marriage Act introduced the Christian concept of monogamy into the Hindu marriage and this provision seems to have caused a great deal of resentment among Hindus. The popular support for the demand for a Uniform Civil Code is rooted in the resentment that while the sexual tendencies of Hindu males are curbed by the introduction of monogamy, the Muslim males are left free to enjoy the privileges of bigamous marriages. The provision of monogamy was introduced ostensibly to elevate the status of Hindu women and it was a demand raised by women in the nationalist movement. Hence it would indeed be interesting to observe how the provision of monogamy under the Hindu Marriage Act has affected women.

Although it was claimed during Parliamentary debates that Hinduism is not a religion but a conglomeration of culture and the Act transformed the Hindu marriage from status to a dissoluble contract, the form of solemnizing the contract remained Brahminical and scriptural with saptapadi (seven steps round the sacred fire) and vivaha homa (the sacred fire) as its essential features. But within a pluralistic society, the Act also had to validate diverse customary practices.[35] But the notion of a valid custom remained ancient and that of time immemorial, as stipulated under the English law. This mingling of Brahminical rituals at one end, customary practices at the other, with English principles thrown in for good measure, has resulted in absurd and ridiculous rulings regarding the validity of Hindu marriages and women have been the worst sufferers of these legal absurdities.

In the process of urbanization, most customary forms have been modified and urban communities living in close proximity have adopted a synthesis of marriage rituals. The forms range from exchange of garlands to applying *sindoor* (vermilion) on the bride's forehead, declaring themselves married by signing on a stamp paper in a lawyers chamber or performing some rituals before a deity in a particular temple (for instance, marriages contracted at the Kalighat temple in Calcutta). The media and more particularly the Hindi films have contributed to the confusion by projecting these practices as valid forms of Hindu marriage.

This ambiguity regarding the valid form of marriage is not to be found under any law governing minority communities. Under the laws of minority communities, the formalities of solemnizing marriage are strictly prescribed and the officiating priest has to provide the necessary document by way of a marriage certificate or he is required to register the marriage with the Registrar of Births, Deaths and Marriages. Since Muslim, Christian and Parsi religions are more institutionalized, their rules and procedures for contracting marriage are definite and unambiguous and are strictly controlled by the religious hierarchies. But Hindu marriages (as well as the Hindu law) which were based more on community practices are relatively less institutionalized and hence their legality is more ambiguous. Due to the breakdown of traditional communities within which these marriages were performed, the situation has further deteriorated.

This ambiguity has provided a Hindu male ample scope to contract bigamous marriages. Since the law recognizes only monogamous marriages, the women in polygamous relationships are placed in a vulnerable situation. In the absence of any clear proof, the man has the choice of admitting either the first or his subsequent relationship as a valid marriage and escape from financial responsibility towards the other woman. When the man refuses to validate the marriage, the woman loses not only her right to maintenance but also faces humiliation and social stigma as a mistress. So much is at stake for the woman that it is not an uncommon sight for two women who are vying with each other for the status of a wife to come to blows during the court proceedings.

A random glance at law journals would reveal how widely prevalent is the ploy of refusing to validate the marriage in maintenance proceedings by Hindu husbands.[36]

The flip side of this predicament in maintenance proceedings is the dilemma faced by women in criminal proceedings in cases of bigamy. Here, years of litigation failed to end in conviction for the errant male due to the courts adopting a rigid view that Saptapadi, Vivaha homa and Kanyadan etc. are essential for solemnizing a Hindu marriage. If these ceremonies could not be proved by the first wife in respect of her husband's second marriage, the husband could wriggle out of conviction even though he had cohabited with the second wife, the community had accepted the man and the second wife as husband and wife or even if he had fathered children through the second wife.[37]

Later studies revealed that in spite of the provision of monogamy under the reformed Hindu law, the percentage of polygamy among Hindus is greater than polygamy among Muslims.[38] So the progressive sounding provision of monogamy not only turned out to be a mockery but in fact even more detrimental to women than the uncodified Hindu law which recognized rights of wives in polygamous marriages. For instance, in a case for maintenance where the husband pleaded that since the woman was his second wife he was not entitled to pay her maintenance, the court took recourse to the uncodified Hindu law and held that since the couple is governed by the ancient Hindu Law (which permits bigamy) and not by the reformed code, the second wife is entitled to maintenance.[39] This judgement speaks much for a law which was ushered in with great fanfare as an instrument of empowering Hindu women.

6.5 Constitutional Challenges

It is not surprising that the first challenge to the constitutional provision of equality, came from the Hindu male challenging the provision of monogamy. A petition was filed in the Bombay High Court challenging the monogamy imposed by the *Bombay Hindu Marriage Act*. In its eagerness to uphold the principle of monogamy among the Hindus, the Bombay High Court in *State of Bombay v Narasu Appa Mali* [40] held that the personal laws are not 'laws in force' and hence they are not void even when they come into conflict with the provision of equality under the Constitution.

In a subsequent case, *Srinivasa Aiyar v Saraswati Ammal*[41] it was argued that prohibiting polygamy denied Hindu men equality before the law and equal protection of law and further that it discriminated against Hindu men on the grounds of religion as it restricted the right to freely profess, practice and propagate religion. The Madras High Court did not address the issue whether the term 'laws in force' includes personal laws but held that even assuming that the term 'laws in force' includes personal laws, the Act does not offend Article 15 which stipulates non-discrimination on the basis of sex.

The judgments ruled that discriminatory personal laws do not violate the constitutional provision of equality. For obtaining the short-term gain of defending the provision of monogamy for

Hindu males, the judiciary erected an unsurmountable obstacle for gender equality within personal laws, by providing a legal basis for the continuation of discriminatory personal laws. However, in a recent judgment, *C. Masilamani Mudaliar v Idol of Sri Swaminathaswami Thirukoil*[42], the Supreme Court, while not referring specifically to the principle laid down in *Narasu Appa Mali*, has implicitly overruled the same. The Court held as follows:

> The personal laws conferring inferior status on women is anathema to equality. Personal laws are derived not from the Constitution but from the religious scriptures. The laws thus derived must be consistent with the Constitution lest they become void under Article 13 if they violate fundamental rights... .

The second issue which came up for judicial scrutiny was the provision of Restitution of Conjugal Rights under Section 9 of the *Hindu Marriage Act*. Justice Chowdhary of Andhra Pradesh in July 1983, struck down this provision as unconstitutional on the ground that it constitutes the grossest form of violation of an individual's right to privacy.[43] The court held that it denies the woman her free choice whether, when and how her body is to become the vehicle for the procreation of another human being and hence is violative of the right to privacy guaranteed by Article 21 of the Constitution.

Although S. 9 of the *Hindu Marriage Act* is based on formal equality and there is no distinction between the rights of husband and wife the court held that equality of treatment regardless of equality of the unequal situation is neither just nor equal. By treating husband and wife who are inherently unequal as equal, the judge held that this section offends the rule of equal protection under the laws ensured by Art.14 of the Constitution. He further added that in actual fact, the remedy works only for the benefit of husbands and is oppressive to women.

But later in the same year, the Delhi High Court took a totally different position and maintained that S. 9 of the *Hindu Marriage Act* is not violative of Art. 14 and 21 of the Constitution. The court held that the object of the restitution decree is to bring about cohabitation between the estranged parties so that they can live together in the matrimonial home in amity. According to the judge, it is a two-in-one provision. On the one hand, it enables the court to coax and cajole the parties to resume marital life and is designed to encourage reconciliation.

The court ruled further: 'Introduction of constitutional law in the home is most inappropriate. It is like pushing a bull into a china shop. It will prove to be a ruthless destroyer of the marriage institution and all that it stands for. In the privacy of the home and the married life, neither Art. 21 nor Art. 14 have any place'.[44]

Subsequently, the Supreme Court upheld this judgment in *Saroj Rani v Sudarshan Kumar Chaddha*[45] and stated the provisions of restitution of conjugal rights serves a social purpose and overruled the judgment of the Andhra Pradesh High Court. The main objective of this provision has always been to ensure conjugality through coercive measures. Whether the constitutionality of a legal provision can be tested by attributing to it a laudable social purpose for which it was never meant for, is a debatable question.[46]

So while the codification has brought some gains to Hindu women by granting a right to absolute ownership of property, monogamy and the right of divorce, these rights are more conceptual than actual. While attempting to resolve some issues, the codification has foregrounded others which have yet to find a satisfactory solution.

Notes

1. In contrast, the Canadian women were granted the right of equality in 1982, the Swiss women were granted the right to vote in 1972 and the United States has not yet endorsed the Equal Remuneration Act.
2. Art 21 of the Constitution ensures Protection of life and personal liberty. In recent years, the Supreme Court has read various socio-economic measures into this right to life. For instance in *People's Union of Democratic Rights v Union of India* (1982) 3 SCC 235, the Supreme Court read the right to minimum wages into Art 21. In *Olga Tellis v Bombay Municipal Corporation* (1985) 3 SCC 545 it was held that the right to life includes the right to livelihood. In *Mohini Jain & Ors v State of Karnataka* (1992) 3 SCC 666 and *Unnikrishnan J.P. & Ors v State of AP* (1993) 1 SCC 645, it was held that the right to education is a fundamental right.
3. Lateef S., 'Defining Women through Legislation,' in Hasan, Z. (ed.) *Forging Identities: Gender, Communities and the State*, New Delhi: Kali for Women (1994), p.51.
4. Karat, B., 'Step by Step Approach—Equal Rights, Equal laws,' in *Women's Equality* V/1, p. 20.
5. Parashar, A., *Women and Family Law Reform in India*, New Delhi: Sage Publications (1992), p.103.

6. Ibid., p.140.
7. S.15 (1)(d) and (e) of *Hindu Succession Act*, 1956.
8. Kishwar, M., 'Codified Hindu Law : Myth and Reality,' *Economic and Political Weekly*, XXIX/33 (1994), p.2145.
9. Ibid.
10. See the comments made by the Supreme Court in a recent judgment, *Sarla Mudgal v Union of India & Ors.* (1995) 3 SCC 635.
11. S.7 (2) of the *Hindu Marriage Act*, specifically mentions saptapadi which is a Brahminical ritual. Most lower castes were not permitted the ritual of saptapadi. Among some castes five steps were permitted and among others only four. Further, the ritual for the marriage of virgin brides differed from that of the second marriage of widows and divorcees.
12. Kishwar, M., 'Codified Hindu Law: Myth and Reality', p.2154.
13. For instance, as per the provisions of S.6 of the *Hindu Succession Act*, 1956, in a family where there are two sons and one daughter, upon the death of the father each of the sons would inherit one-third of the property as coparcenars. The remaining one third, is the father's separate property which would be divided in four parts, one for the wife, one for the daughter and one each for the sons. So while the sons would be entitled to one-third plus one-twelfth, the daughter's share would only be one-twelfth of the property. This dismal share is projected as gender equality.
14. See Chapter 4.
15. Under S.10.2 of the *Income Tax Act* an exemption is granted to income from the Hindu Undivided Family (HUF). Under SS.20 & 20A of the *Wealth Tax Act*, certain tax concessions are granted to members of HUF at the time of partition.
16. Under S.29(2) of the *Hindu Succession Act*, a power was granted to individuals to will away their property and in subsequent years this provision was used mainly to deprive the daughters their share in their parental property.
17. See the decisions in *Commissioner of Wealth Tax v Chandra Sen* ILR 1986 370 and *Yudhishter v Ashok Kumar* AIR 1987 SC 558, where the court held that the property inherited by the son is his separate property.
18. The English statute, *Inheritance (Family Provision) Act* of 1938 provided for a legal remedy, if the husband failed to make reasonable provisions for his wife and children. The right of a former wife who is entitled to receive maintenance was protected through the *Matrimonial Causes (Property and Maintenance) Act* of 1958 (subsequently re-enacted in the *Matrimonial Causes Act* 1965). Since this enactment placed a divorced wife in a superior position relative to the surviving spouse, a further statute was enacted entitled, *Inheritance (Provision for Family and Dependents) Act* 1975 through which the surviving spouse could claim not only maintenance but also a share in the capital.
19. Kishwar, M., 'Codified Hindu Law: Myth and Reality', p.2155.
20. M.N. Srinivas has argued that modern dowry is entirely the product of the forces let loose by British rule such as monetization, education

and the introduction of the 'organised sector'. To equate it with dakshina is only an attempt to legitimize a modern monstrosity by linking it up with an ancient and respected custom. See Srinivas, M.N. *Some Reflections on Dowry*, New Delhi: Oxford University Press (1984), p.11-13.

21. *Hindu Succession Act*, note 13.
22. SS. 24 and 25 of the *Hindu Marriage Act*, 1955. Also see S. Khanna, 'Padmasini's Quest for Justice,' in *The Lawyers* VII/2 (1992), p.25.
23. This concept has subsequently been incorporated into the Parsi Marriage & Divorce Act, 1936 by the 1988 amendments (SS.39 and 40 of the Act).
24. The remedy of divorce by mutual consent was introduced into the *Hindu Marriage Act* in 1976 through S.13 B of the Act. Cruelty and desertion as grounds of divorce were also introduced in 1976.
25. As per the *Report of the Committee on the Status of Women, Towards Equality* in the year 1971 only 11.86% of women were employed and they constituted only 17.35% of the total labour force (p.153) and women constituted only 10.9% of the labour force in the organized sector (p.184).
26. S.9 of the *Hindu Marriage Act*.
27. AIR 1958 Punj 87.
28. AIR 1964 Punj 28.
29. *Gaya Prasad v Bhagwat* AIR 1966 MP 212.
30. AIR 1973 P&H 134.
31. ILR (1977) 1 P&H 642 FB.
32. *Praveenben v Sureshbhai* AIR 1975 Guj 69.
33. *N.R. Radhakrishna v Dhanalakshmi* AIR 1975 Mad 331.
34. AIR 1978 Del 296.
35. S. 7 (1) & (2) of *Hindu Marriage Act*, 1955.
36. In *Divorce and Matrimonial Cases* (1994), Volume I reported cases where validity of marriages was an issue while claiming maintenance, were as follows:
    Reported cases relating to maintenance: 40–100%
    Cases where validity of marriage was an issue: 9–36%
    Cases where the Husband's plea was upheld: 4–16%
    Admittedly Polygamous Marriages: 6–24%
37. For a detailed discussion on this issue, see Agnes, F., 'Hindu Men, Monogamy and the Uniform Civil Code,' in *Economic and Political Weekly*, XXX/50 (1995), p.3238.
38. Report of the Committee on Status of Women *Towards Equality*, pp.66-7.
39. *Anupama Pradhan v Sultan Pradhan* 1991 Cri.LJ 3216 Ori.
40. AIR 1952 Bom 84.
41. AIR 1952 Mad 193.
42. (1996) 8 SCC 525, decided by Justices K. Ramaswamy, S. Saghir Ahmad and G.B. Pattanaik.
43. *T. Sareetha v T. Venkatasubbiah* AIR 1983 AP 356.

44. *Harvinder Kaur v Harminder Singh* AIR 1084 Del 66.
45. AIR 1984 SC 1562.
46. See Bhattacharjee, A.M., *Matrimonial Laws and the Constitution*, Calcutta: Eastern Law House (1996), p.19.

7

Erosion of Secular Principles

Introduction

Under Art. 44, the state is bound by a constitutional mandate to secularize and homogenize the family laws. The enactment of a uniform code was a goal to be achieved through a gradual process.[1] This was a directive principle of governance. In this chapter, the extent to which the state adhered to this principle is examined.

The first departure from the declared objective was the codification of the Hindu family laws. Within the first decade after the adaptation of the new and revolutionary Constitution, the state enacted special laws for its 'Hindu' citizens. By validating diverse customary practices and rituals as 'Hindu', by grouping various castes and sects under the banner of a 'legal Hinduism' and by naming the attempts at modernizing family laws as 'Hindu' reforms, the state departed from its declared goal of secularizing the family law. Through these enactments, Hindus were not subject to the application of some statutes, which had hitherto been uniformly applicable to all citizens. For instance, the scope of the *Caste Disabilities Removal Act* of 1850, which prohibited loss of rights upon conversion was constrained, as apostasy constituted a matrimonial offence.[2] The non-Hindu spouse was not entitled to maintenance from the Hindu spouse either while living together or separately.[3]

The converted parent lost the right to be the natural guardian of a minor child.[4] Children born to a Hindu after conversion were disqualified from inheriting the property of a Hindu relative.[5] The scope of another secular provision, the *Guardians and Wards Act*, 1890, was restricted by the *Hindu Adoption and Maintenance Act*, 1956. Hindus were taken out of this secular and uniform provision and were placed under the new statute, which validated adoptions through the Brahminical Hindu ritual of giving and taking in adoption,[6] while the customs and practices of lower castes, which were more fluid and secular were disallowed.[7] By stipulating a special provision under S.18 (a) of the *Hindu Marriage Act*, Hindus were taken out of the general provisions of the *Child Marriage Restraint Act* of 1929 and were liable for lesser punishment for the same offence. In addition, while such marriages performed under other matrimonial statutes (for instance the *Parsi Marriage and Divorce Act*, 1936 and the Special Marriage Act of 1954), were held to be void, marriages performed in violation of the stipulations regarding child marriage were deemed valid under the *Hindu Marriage Act*.[8] Certain tax benefits were conferred upon Hindu coparcenaries within taxation laws.[9] These enactments violated the constitutional mandate under Art. 14 (equality) and Art. 15 (non-discrimination on the basis of religion) as the 'Hindu religion' was the sole criteria for the classifications.[10]

During the decades that followed, the state moved further away from its declared objective of a uniform and secular family law. In several instances, the vested, patriarchal and community interests of the influential sections superseded the rights of women and children.

The issue was further problematized by the erosion of secular principles within the polity. A steady decline of secular values can be traced through the debates on the enactment of the *Special Marriage Act* in the fifties, the fate of the Adoption Bill in the seventies and the controversy around the Muslim Women's Bill in the eighties. The policy on secularism had changed from the Nehruvian concept of maintaining equidistance from all religions to the increasingly instrumental use of religion for political gains during the Rajiv Gandhi rule in the eighties. Rather than maintaining a distance from all religious groups, the state became increasingly entangled with the communal factions. If the state granted one concession to one communal group, to set the balance right, it was compelled to grant another concession to another group. *The Muslim Women's Act*[11] was a direct outcome of this political jugglery. The economic interests of Muslim women were sacrificed by the state in this balancing act. The gradual erosion of secular principles is traced in this chapter.

7.1 Constraining the Scope of Civil Marriage Law

The enactment of the *Special Marriage Act* in 1954 is the only significant move in the post-independence period to secularize family laws.[12] In 1952, while introducing the Bill, the Law Minister C.C. Biswas had described it as the first step towards the attainment of the objective of a Uniform Civil Code contemplated in Art. 44 of the Constitution.[13] The Act provided for a civil marriage of two Indians, without the necessity of renouncing their respective religions.

The Act contained several redeeming features. It introduced the concept of 'breakdown theory'[14] or a divorce by mutual consent. The Act also provided for the re-registration of marriages solemnized in accordance with the customs or rituals of the spouses.[15] This provision of subsequent registration enabled parties to avail of secular and uniform remedies despite the solemnization of the marriage through the performance of religious ceremonies.[16]

Since a marriage under this Act is a secular and civil contract, conversion or apostasy of the spouse is not a ground for divorce. The marriage is contracted at the civil registry in the presence of a marriage officer appointed by the state and a certificate is issued to the parties which constitutes a clear proof of a valid marriage having been performed for all future litigation purposes. This serves as a restraint against husbands contracting subsequent bigamous marriages.[17] Once the parties opt for a secular form of marriage, in matters of succession they are governed by the *Indian Succession Act*, 1925 (which is more egalitarian and gender-just), and not by the provisions of their respective personal laws.[18] This was a concrete step towards gradual unification of family laws.

Conservative Hindu, Muslim and Christian opinion was strongly opposed to the Act. Although the concept of contractual marriage was closest to the Islamic concept of marriage, during parliamentary debates a demand was raised by a section of Muslims that the Muslim community should be exempted from its purview, as the persons marrying under it would not be governed by the Shariat. But this demand was not conceded. Prime Minister, Jawaharlal Nehru pointed out that the constitutional provision which guarantees the freedom to practise religion also includes the freedom not to practise a religion. He emphasized that since it is a facilitating legislation, no one was compulsorily bound by it and the state would not come in the way of any one opting for its provisions.[19]

The Act had the potentiality of being developed further into a comprehensive code of marriage and divorce which could incorporate adequate safeguards for women, without invoking the controversy of freedom of religion. The premise that the Act is merely a facilitating measure which would apply only to consenting couples had already been accepted both politically as well as legally. Hence equitable principles of gender justice could easily have been incorporated into this Act. But unfortunately, the Act has not been well publicized and there seems to be a manipulation to subvert its provisions.[20]

Despite its secular credentials, the Act leaned towards the dominant Hindu upper caste practices, which prohibit marriages between first cousins and close family relatives. Such prohibitions are not found in the customary practices of several lower castes, as well as among the practices of Muslims, Christians, Parsis and Jews. Among several south Indian communities marriages between uncles and nieces and first cousins are a norm. Similarly, marriages among first cousins are a norm among the Muslims.

In order to rectify this lacuna and widen the scope of the Act, in 1963, an amendment was introduced, which subordinated the Act to customary practices.[21] During the debate, the amendment was criticized as a retrograde measure by several members of the Parliament.[22] Prior to this Act, the *Special Marriage Act* subordinated the personal laws to its provisions. The amendment on the other hand introduced the pernicious principle of reversing this principle and subordinating the Act to the personal laws. The stated reasons for the amendment were the practices of south Indian communities which permit marriages between uncle and neice and first cousins.[23] The objective was to co-ordinate the Act with the provisions of the *Hindu Marriage Act* which validated customary practices. Its relevance to minority communities was not in context during the debate. This placed the Act further away from its objective of a secular code.

In 1976, major amendments were introduced within the *Hindu Marriage Act* by incorporating additional grounds of divorce and by introducing divorce by mutual consent. So superficially, it appeared that the *Hindu Marriage Act* and the *Special Marriage Act* are synonymous and provide similar reliefs. But the anomalies of the *Hindu Marriage Act* regarding proof of valid ceremonies were not addressed during these reforms and Hindu marriage continued to be an illusory legal incident.

At the other level, amendments introduced to the *Special Marriage Act* in 1976[24] conferred concessions to Hindus marrying under the Act, which led to an undermining of the secular provisions of the statute. If a Hindu couple married under the Act, they were taken out of the purview of the *Indian Succession Act* of 1925 and were permitted to be governed by the *Hindu Succession Act*. This move was to ensure that coparcenaries (and male privileges within it) are not dissolved by the contracting of a civil marriage by means of the Act. The interests of a Hindu male who contracted a civil marriage were protected so long as he married a woman within the broad Hindu fold (which would include inter-caste and inter-regional marriages, as well as marriages with women from Boudha, Jaina and Sikh religions and also Brahmos, Prarthana Samajis and Arya Samajis or even atheists).

At one level, it gave a further lease to coparcenaries, which, in any case, are anti-women. But the move was deemed progressive because it protected the interests of a Hindu male contracting a civil marriage. Even if one concedes to this reasoning, why a similar benefit was not conferred upon a Hindu male contracting an inter-religious civil marriage remains unexplained. In effect, the amendment was a deterrent to a Hindu male wishing to marry a woman from any minority religious communities, i.e., Parsi, Muslim and Christian. Such an event would result in the dissolution of coparcenary. The reasoning that the broad Hindu fold is only a legal fiction and that the idea of a sudra or a neo-Buddhist woman entering the household would be as abhorrent to an orthodox Hindu as of a Muslim or a Christian woman entering the household, seems to have escaped the law makers. The provision was clearly unconstitutional as the basis of discrimination was religion. Further, progressive Hindus who married under a secular Act were not given a choice to be governed by a uniform and secular law of succession.

This clear violation of the mandate towards uniformity and secularization of family laws did not warrant a public debate. The benefits conferred on a Hindu male contracting a civil marriage, were deemed a progressive step for the Hindu community. Hence the deterrent it would pose to marriages of

Hindu males with minority women and to the secular principle of the nation, did not figure in the public debate. The criticism against this amendment remained within the confines of legal academia[25] and did not result in a media furore.

7.2 Efforts at Introducing an Adoption Bill

The next attempt at uniformity was the Adoption Bill, which was introduced in the Rajya Sabha in 1972[26] and was referred to the Joint Committee of the Parliament.[27] The Joint Select Committee held public hearings. At these hearings, the representatives of Muslims and Scheduled Tribes expressed their desire to be excluded from its application.[28] The demand made by the Scheduled Tribes was conceded by the Committee and it recommended that the Bill should be uniformly applicable to all Indians except the Scheduled Tribes. The three Muslim members of the Committee, in their note of dissent, pressed for the exclusion of the Muslim community from its application.[29] The Joint Select Committee submitted its report to the Parliament in August, 1976. But in order to avoid any politically costly controversy over this issue, the Bill was not presented till the Parliament was dissolved in March 1977 and consequently, the Bill lapsed. The Janata government which was voted to power after the election, introduced a new bill but withdrew it following opposition from a section of the Muslims.[30]

In 1980 when the Congress party regained power, the government re-introduced the Bill in a modified version and paid heed to the Muslim demand for exclusion. This time the Bill was referred to the Minorities Commission. At this juncture, the Parsi community demanded exemption from it application.[31] Thereafter, the Bill was abandoned.

Although the opposition to the Bill was based on various factors, the economic motive was the most dominant. The adoption would affect the inheritance rights of other heirs or make inroads within the common property of the community. These were the two major concerns expressed by the voices of dissent.

The tribal communities opposed adoption of children from outside the tribe, as this could lead to the inheritance of the tribal property by non-tribal children who may be adopted. They also opposed the provision of registering the adoptions as it would pose technical difficulties. The change of name after adoption was also against the tribal custom.

The Parsis did not want their charitable trust funds and their fire temples to be thrown open to non-Parsi children. They had no objection to inter-religious adoption if the rights of the non-Parsi child were restricted to inheritance of private property and would not extend to community resources.

The Muslim religious leadership argued that the Bill would be against the tenets of Islam. Adoption would create prohibited degrees of relationships in matrimonial alliances (with the adopted parents) which would violate Islamic principles. But most important, the adopted child would become an heir to the property of the adopting parents and the shares of the natural heirs would be altered. This would amount to an interference with the scheme of succession under the Shariat.

Although the conservative segment of the Muslim religious leadership opposed the bill, it received the support of several prominent Muslim scholars and jurists.[32] Some scholars suggested modification to the bill which would make it more acceptable to the Muslim community. Justice Hameedullah Beg suggested that instead of excluding Muslims, the Bill should contain a provision to declare that adoption is not contrary to their religious beliefs and added that the Constitution gives every individual his or her religious freedom.[33]

A certain shift in the government's stand can be discerned in this debate. In 1954, while enacting the *Special Marriage Act*, the government had not accepted the claim that it would encourage Muslims to leave the fold of Islam. But two decades later, while debating the Adoption Bill the government accepted the religio-political leaders as the spokespersons for the entire community and conceded to their posture that no Muslim would have the opportunity of rejecting Islamic law through a State enactment.

7.3 The Shah Bano Controversy and the Muslim Women's Bill

The political events which followed the Supreme Court judgement in the Shah Bano case[34] eventually resulted in the enactment of the *Muslim Women (Protection of rights on Divorce)* Act in 1986. (Hereinafter, the *Muslim Women's Act*) But the issue of maintenance to divorced Muslim women which marked the controversy had a long and turbulent history, which is reflective of a collusion between two different legal systems.

As already discussed, the Muslim law evolved within the context of trading communities of Arabia and regulated their marriages in the language of their trade contracts. A sum of mehr was stipulated at the time of marriage as a future security. Since marriage was a dissoluble contract, and women had a right of remarriage, the legal system did not provide for any recurring liability after the termination of the contract. After the dissolution of the matrimonial bond, the wife was not entitled to any further reliefs such as maintenance.[35] But despite these restraints, the Holy Quran contained a provision, 'For divorced women, maintenance should be provided on a reasonable scale'. (*Surah* III *Aiyat* 241).

Under the English and Indian legal systems, marriage constituted an indissoluble bond and the husband was entrusted with a legal obligation of maintaining the wife for life. Later, the Islamic concept of marriage as a dissoluble contract was accepted by the English law in the nineteenth century and by the Hindu law in the twentieth century,[36] but under these legal systems, the husband's obligation to maintain his wife continued even after the dissolution of marriage. Only the wife's remarriage or unchastity would redeem the husband of his obligation.

During the debate on the *Dissolution of Muslim Marriages Act* in 1939, the primary concern of the reformers was the absence of women's right to divorce in contrast to the husband's right of arbitrary divorce. And perhaps due to the fact, that as the economic rights conferred upon women by the Islamic law were superior to the rights granted to women under other legal systems, the reformers did not address the issue of economic rights of divorced women. The Act did not contain any provision of ancillary reliefs found in other matrimonial statutes based on English law.

Within the cultural ethos, where the pro-women stipulations of a minority community can easily be subverted by aping the majority practices (and at the same time, anti-women practices can be strictly adhered to on the premise of preserving the cultural identity) stipulations of mehr have been reduced to a token amount and the custom of dowry has been adapted among most Muslim communities. Within this social reality, a divorced Muslim woman was left with no economic options to escape from destitution upon divorce. As a corrective measure, in 1973, S.125 of Cr.PC, which granted the deserted or destitute wife the right to claim a maximum amount of Rs 500 as maintenance from her husband, was extended to a divorced wife by expanding the scope of the term wife to include ex-wife (or divorced wife).[37]

The amendment came after an acrimonious debate on the Muslim woman's customary right of mehr. Conceding the demand raised by Muslim leaders, the government included a clause that if a woman had received the customary settlement, the amount of maintenance due to her would be set off against the amount she had already received.[38]

Although this had constrained the scope of the Muslim woman's right to maintenance, two significant decisions of the Supreme Court delivered by Justice Krishna Iyer in 1979 and 1980 respectively had placed the divorced Muslim woman's right to maintenance on a secure footing without arousing a political controversy around this issue.[39] These decisions examined the right of Muslim women from a humanitarian context of social justice.

But the controversial Shah Bano judgement delivered by Chief Justice Y.V. Chandrachud (for the Full Bench comprising of five judges) in 1985, apart from affirming the right of a divorced Muslim woman, also commented upon Islam and interpreted the Muslim Personal Law while deciding a right under a secular and uniform statute. The call for a UCC and the comments on the Quran evoked a communal backlash.

Relenting to the pressure exerted by the Muslim orthodoxy, the government introduced a Bill in Parliament titled, *The Muslim Women (Protection of Rights on Divorce) Bill* to exclude divorced Muslim women from the purview of S.125 Cr.PC. This move met with severe opposition from women's organizations and progressive sections.

As the debate progressed, the media projected two insular and mutually exclusive positions, i.e. those who opposed the Bill and supported the demand for a UCC as modern, secular and rational, while those in support of the Bill and opposing the demand for a UCC as fundamentalist, orthodox, male chauvinist, communal and obscurantist. To be progressive, modern and secular was also to be a nationalist. By the same logic, the opposing camp was projected as against national integration and hence anti-national. There was hardly any public space left for arguments which pleaded for conciliation or compromise.[40]

As the controversy over the judgement escalated, the 'Muslim' was defined as the 'Other', both of the nation and of the Hindus. Muslims all over India, in turn could be mobilized to view this as yet another threat to their tenuous security. The communal turn to the event finally, led to Shah Bano herself withdrawing her claim to maintenance. This strengthened the popular misconception that to maintain the religiosity in Islam, women's economic rights have to be subordinated and further the Islamic religion is opposed to granting women economic rights.

The rigid approach of the Muslim leadership provided further fuel to the Hindu right wing forces in their anti-Muslim propaganda. This placed the secular groups in a precarious position. In order to distinguish their position from that advocated by Hindu right-wing forces, opposition to the Bill had to be withdrawn.

For the first time, the women's movement was constrained to address the complexities of the demand for a UCC.[41] The issue could no longer be addressed within the binaries of a gender divide. The political sub-text beneath the apparent gender concerns warranted a more complex framework.

Analysing the political developments around this period, Zoya Hasan argues that the compromise of surrendering women's rights has to be viewed from the perspective of a communalized polity.[42] It was an outcome of a rightward shift in politics and the economy in the 1980s, resulting in a close interaction of politics and religion marked by a decline in the commitment to secularism, equal opportunities, and social welfare benefits for the under-privileged and the disadvantaged.

The Congress faced defeat in several state assembly elections in 1985–6 as the Muslim vote, angered by the Shah Bano verdict, tipped the balance in favour of opposition parties. The Congress responded to the crisis by a shift in strategy, highlighted by the appropriation of pro-Hindutva themes which were gaining popularity in north India. This won the support of some Hindu factions but further alienated Muslims, the traditional supporters of Congress, who were dissatisfied with the party's failure to alleviate their long-standing grievances. Their disenchantment was further aggravated by the Ram Janmabhumi movement for the liberation of the Ram temple in Ayodhya started by Vishwa Hindu Parishad in 1984.

Against this background of declining political support, the Congress government decided to open the locks of the disputed Babri Masjid in February 1986 and simultaneously, enact the Muslim Women's Bill. Together, these two decisions, i.e. the introduction of the Muslim Women's Bill and the reopening of the disputed shrine in Ayodhya were part of a 'grand' Congress strategy of using religious issues and sentiments to regain its hold over Hindu and Muslim votes.

The Muslim Women's Act was thus an effort to pacify Muslim sentiments which were ruffled over the reopening of the disputed site. The Congress government exaggerated the strength of the conservative opposition, manipulated by a politically ambitious Muslim leadership. The Congress viewed the All India Muslim Personal Law Board (AIMPLB) as the sole arbiter of Muslim interests. Opposition from liberal and progressive groups was ignored, allowing the Ullama to appropriate the task of defining the overarching concerns and interests of Muslims.

7.4 The Unpredictable Turn of Events

Only after the dust raised by the controversial Act had settled down, could the various contradictory implications of the enactment to Muslim women, Muslim Personal Law and the Muslim community be examined. Thus:

(i) Despite the claim of divine origin and the consequential claim that a secular Indian State does not have the right to legislate upon Muslim law, through this legislation, the Muslim religious leaders conceded to the state the right to modify the Shariat. The Act imposed obligations on Waqf board and family members which were not imposed by the Shariat and to this extent modified the rules of the Shariat and overruled the theory of its immutability.

(ii) Despite the mobilization of a large number of Muslim women against the judgement and in support of the Bill, a significant number of divorced Muslim women continued to approach the courts for claiming their right to maintenance, as the cases filed by Muslim women indicate. Hence the claim of religious leaders that Muslim women are opposed to accepting maintenance from their ex-husbands after divorce has not been substantiated. The divorced Muslim women were able to separate their religiosity from their temporal needs of economic survival.

(iii) The judicial decisions in the period immediately following the enactment of the Bill proved contrary to the fears expressed by women's organizations that the Act would snuff out the economic rights of divorced Muslim women. In a few cases, judges used the provision of the new Act to award substantial amounts as lump sum divorce settlements.[43] The Act seemed to provide a better remedy than the meagre amount which a Muslim woman could claim under S.125 Cr.PC prior to this Act.

These judgments interpreted the scope of S.3 (1) (a) of the Act to mean that the husband must pay a reasonable and fair provision for the future during the *iddat* period. For throwing light on the ambiguities contained in S.3 of the Act, the courts relied upon the preamble which proclaimed that the aim of the Act is to protect the rights of Muslim women.[44]

(iv) Although there were instances where Muslim women could be granted maintenance by a progressive interpretation of the provisions of the Act, Muslim men are constantly being advised by their advocates that they no longer need to pay maintenance to their wives and it is their religion that says so. Studies revealed that even when the lower courts granted maintenance to wives, the husbands, upon advice by their lawyers, filed appeals against orders of settlements, by relying upon the provisions of the Act, thus making the litigation processes far more cumbersome and ambiguous for Muslim women.[45] In response to the generous interpretations of the Act, Syed Shahabuddin (Janata Dal) moved a Private Member's Bill (Bill No. 155 of 1992) in Parliament in August 1992. The aim was to amend the Act and restrict its scope in clear terms to maintenance only for and during the iddat period.

(v) The Act has been used by court officials to express a general anti-Muslim bias. The general attitude within court rooms is that Muslim marriages are unstable, Muslim women remarry and Muslim men are polygamous. In a study of maintenance cases filed in the magistrate's courts at Calcutta, Maitrayee Mukhopadhyay recorded the following comments:

> When a Muslim comes to our court we are already biased; their 3–4 marriages are repugnant to us. ...For them (Muslims) marriage is nothing. They get married, have a few children and then they leave their wives. ...Muslim marriages are unstable because of easy divorces and Muslim women are no better than prostitutes because they remarry; ...Muslim women are worse off than the household dog. ...We are Hindus, we do

> not like this law and it is repugnant ...but we have to give judgments according to this new law.[46]

As per the study, the magistrates declined from awarding maintenance even for the duration of the marriage or for the period before the act came into force.

Did the new Act protect Muslim women better than the earlier provisions under S. 125 Cr.PC, which entitles women to a paltry maintenance dole of Rs 500 per month? Could the controversy have been used to consolidate the traditional right of mehr (which has been corroded in recent years and has given way to the Hindu practice of dowry) and negotiate lump sum divorce settlements? These questions have now become redundant in the political climate which followed the enactment. The *Muslim Women's Act* has been projected as the most glaring instance of the defeat of the principle of gender justice for the Indian women, as well as the defeat of secular principles within the Indian polity. The Act has led to the further strengthening of the Muslim appeasement theory in judicial discourse and in popular media.[47]

For the women's movement, the Shah Bano judgement and the *Muslim Women's Act* was a watershed. From this point onwards, the gender discourse became far more complex. Identity politics and gender equality could no longer be placed as two mutually exclusive and hostile terrains. While gender equality continued to be the desired goal, the demand had to be reformulated within the context of cultural diversity and rights of marginalized sections.

Notes

1. See the assurance given by Dr Ambedkar to Muslim members of the Constituent Assembly (VII CAD, 23 November 1948 pp.550–1).
2. S.13 (1) (ii) of the *Hindu Marriage Act* 1955.
3. As per Hindu law, conversion results in the legal death of a Hindu. Hence, the Hindu husband is not under obligation to maintain his converted wife. In *Sundarambal v Subbaiah Pillai* AIR 1961 Mad 323, the courts went even further and held that an order for maintenance obtained prior to the conversion cannot even be enforced after the conversion.
4. A change of religion by the mother will disentitle her to the custody of her child as under Hindu law, since the father is the natural guardian, it is presumed that the child will automatically be following his religion.

5. Although the bar on conversion or change of caste was removed by the *Caste Disabilities Removal Act*, 1850 and the convert cannot be denied rights in the ancestral property, under the modern statute, the children of a converted parent cannot inherit property of a Hindu relative unless at the time when the succession opens, the child is a Hindu (S.26 of the *Hindu Succession Act*).
6. See S.11 (vi) of the Hindu Adoption and Maintenance Act, 1956.
7. Kishwar, M., 'Codified Hindu Law: Myth and Reality,' in *Economic and Political Weekly*, XXIX/33 (1994), p. 2145.
8. See Bhattacharjee, A.M., *Matrimonial Laws and the Constitution*, Calcutta: Eastern Law House (1996), pp.11-14.
9. See Note 15 of Chapter 6.
10. For a more detailed discussion on the constitutionality of the *Hindu Marriage Act*, see Bhattacharjee, A.M., *Matrimonial Laws and the Constitution*, pp.10-27.
11. The *Muslim Women (Protection of Rights on Divorce) Act*, 1986, which was enacted after the Shah Bano controversy.
12. This was a re-enactment of the 1872 Act, discussed in Chapter 5.
13. Law Minister's statement on the Bill made in the Rajya Sabha on 28.7.1952.
14. This is a later and more progressive doctrine of English law, than the earlier 'fault theory' where one spouse is required to prove a matrimonial fault against the other.
15. S.16 of *Special Marriage Act*, 1954. Prior to this, the remedy was available only under the Muslim law.
16. Since the provision of divorce by mutual consent was not available under the *Hindu Marriage Act*, until 1976, parties wishing to avail of the provision could re-register their marriage under the *Special Marriage Act* and then subsequently obtain the divorce. Since the *Indian Divorce Act*, 1869 governing Christian marriages does not provide for divorce by consent even today, a Christian couple can use this provision to re-register their marriage under this Act, prior to initiating court proceedings. But unfortunately, this provision has not been much publicized and the progressive option offered by the Act has remained mainly on paper. See Table 2A in this context.
17. In contrast, the Hindu marriage is an illusory legal entity. The ambiguity and laxity provided by the Act in respect of customary practices is manipulated by legal practioners to 'perform' hasty, fraudulent and at times invalid 'court marriages'. The lawyers resort to this practice to overcome the more stringent provisions such as the mandatory one month notice period. A public-interest petition, demanding rectification of the legal lacunae, filed by a centre providing legal advocacy to women, *Majlis Manch v State of Maharashtra* WP 1842 of 1996, has addressed this issue before the Bombay High Court.
18. S. 21 of the *Special Marriage Act*, 1954. The provision was meant to further secularize inheritance laws. *The Indian Succession Act* grants better rights of inheritance to daughters than the *Hindu Succession Act* of 1956 which continued to recognize male coparcenary.

19. Parashar, A., *Women and Family Law Reform in India,* New Delhi: Sage Publications (1992) p.161.
20. The gross under-utilization of this provision is indicated in Table 2B.
21. The *Special Marriage (Amendment) Act* of 1963 (Act 32 of 1963) added the following proviso to S.4 clause (d): Provided that where a custom governing at least one of the parties permits of a marriage between them, such marriage may be solemnized notwithstanding that they are within the prohibited degrees of relationship.
22. See the comments of U.M. Trivedi, L.M. Singhvi etc. Lok Sabha Debates XX No.12, Col. 3234 and 3250. 1962
23. Speech by Deputy Minister Bibhudhendra Mishra, *LSD,* XX No.12, Col.3228. 1962
24. The Law Commission of India, *Fifty Ninth Report* (1974), p.98.
25. See B.Sivaramayya, 'The Special Marriage Act, 1954 Goes Awry', in V. Bagga (ed.), *Studies in the Hindu Marriage and the Special Marriage Acts,* Bombay: N.M. Tripathi (1978), p.310.
26. *Gazette of India,* Part II, 1972, pp.601–10.
27. *LSD,* 26.viii.1972.
28. Joint Select Committee, *Evidence on Adoption Bill* Vol. II 1972 p. 111.
29. Ibid. Minutes of Dissent, IX-XI.
30. Baig, T. A., 'Urgency of Adoption Law,' in *Mainstream,* 15 November, 1980, pp.9-10.
31. *Fourth Annual Report,* the Minorities Commission (1983).
32. Justices Chagla, Hidayatullah and Beg and jurists Asaf Ali Fyzee, Daniel Latifi to name a few. Parashar, A., *Women and Family Law Reform in India,* p.171.
33. Ibid.
34. *Mohd. Ahmed Khan v Shah Bano Begam* AIR 1985 SC 945.
35. The various legal workshops conducted with rural women's groups reveals that a similar legal provision prevailed among communities which permitted divorce and re-marriage of women in Maharashtra and Gujarat region. The only difference was that the custom of bride price was prevalent and if a divorce was obtained at the initiation of the woman, she (or her father) was required to return the bride price.
36. The English women were granted the right of divorce through the *Matrimonial Causes Act* of 1857 and the upper caste Hindu women acquired this right under the *Hindu Marriage Act* of 1955.
37. Explanation (b) to S.125 of Cr.PC stipulates that wife includes ex-wife.
38. S.127 (3) (b) of Cr.PC provides as follows:

    > (if) the woman has been divorced by her husband and (if) she has received, whether before or after the date of the said order, the whole of the sum which, under any customary or personal law applicable to the parties, was payable on such divorce (the magistrate) may cancel such order.

    The wordings do not specifically mention the right of mehr under Islamic law but the amendment was effected at the instance of Muslim legislators in the context of the Muslim women's right to mehr. *Supra* n.19, pp.164-8.

39. *Bai Tahira v Ali Hussain Fideali Chotthea* AIR 1979 SC 362 and *Fuzlunbi v K.Khadil Vali* AIR 1980 SC 1730.
40. Fazalbuoy, N., 'The Debate on Muslim Personal Law,' Paper presented at the Third National Conference on Women's Studies, Chandigarh, 1986. Also see Mukhopadhyay, M., 'Between Community and State: The question of women's right and personal laws,' in Z. Hasan (ed.), *Forging Identities: Gender, Communities and the State,* New Delhi: Kali for Women (1994), p.109.
41. Pathak Z. and R. S. Rajan, 'Shah Bano' *Signs* XIV/3 (1989); Kishwar, M. 'Pro-Women or Anti Minority? The Shah Bano Controversy,' in *Manushi* VI/2 (1986), p.4.
42. Hasan, Z. (ed.), : *Forging Identities: Gender, Communities and the State,* New Delhi: Kali for Women (1994), pp.67-8.
43. One of the judgments which received publicity was passed on 6 January 1988 by a woman judicial magistrate at Lucknow's Diwani Kacheri. A divorced woman, Fahima Sardar was awarded Rs 85,000 as mehr maintenance and fair and reasonable provision. See Gandhi, N. & N. Shah, *Issues at Stake,* New Delhi: Kali for Women (1991), p.242. In 1992, in a judgement of the Kerala High Court (*P.K. Saro v P.A. Halim,* Cri.MC 1331 of 1991), against which a challenge is pending in the Supreme Court, the High Court endorsed the session court's order which awarded Rs 3,00,000 towards reasonable and fair provision and Rs 7,500 per month as maintenance for the period of iddat. Case cited from Singh, K., 'The Constitution and the Muslim Personal Law,' in Hasan, Z. (ed.), *Forging Identities: Gender, Communities and the State,* New Delhi: Kali for Women (1994), p.96.
44. S.1 (a) of the Act which was meant to restrict maintenance to the iddat period states as follows:
    'Notwithstanding anything contained in any other law for the time being in force, a divorced woman shall be entitled to (a) a reasonable and fair provision and maintenance to be made and paid to her within the iddat period by her former husband.' For clarifying the ambiguity of the words `reasonable and fair provision and maintenance' the courts relied upon the preamble of the Act, which states that the aim of the Act is to protect Muslim women. See the decisions in *A.A. Abdulla v A. B. Mohmuna Sayedbhai,* AIR 1988 Guj 141; *Ali v Sufaira* 1988 (3) Crimes 147; *Mohd. Tajuddin v Quomarunnisa Begam & Ors.* 2 (1989) DMC 204 AP; and *Ahmed v Aysha* 2 (1990) DMC 110 Ker.
45. Maitrayee Mukhopadhyay has argued that the issue is not whether S.125 Cr.PC is more advantageous than S.3 of MWA since neither really protects women's claims to a share in their husband's property, here the claim that Muslim men need not maintain their wives once they have divorced them is being legitimized. The provisions are being interpreted to mean that Muslim men, by resorting to this section, have greater ability to deny their wives' claims for maintenance. The legal sanction to do so derives authority from the evocation of tradition, a term which is interchangeable with religion and culture. Mukhopadhyay, M., 'Between Community and State: The question of

women's right and personal laws', in Hasan Z. (ed.), *Forging Identities: Gender, Communities and the State*, New Delhi: Kali for Women (1994), p.109.

46. Ibid., p. 126.
47. Sathe, S.P., 'Uniform Civil Code. Why? What? and How?' (1995), in *Towards Secular India*, I/4 Bombay: Centre for Study of Society and Secularism (1995), p.31.

8

Communal Undertones Within Recent Judicial Decisions

Introduction

The fifth decade of independence witnessed a further erosion of secular principles. The events escalated to an extent that led inevitably to the demolition of the Babri Masjid at Ayodhya on 6 December 1992. The demolitions and the riots that followed are indicators of an aggressive majoritarianism. The gulf between the Hindu and Muslim communities widened. Along with the demolition of the ancient monument, the hopes that had been expressed by the Constituent Assembly, that after the independent nation settled down into political stability, the time would be ripe for the enactment of a Uniform Civil Code, came crumbling down. Ironically, the demand which was meant to be a symbol of India's claim to modernity, became a weapon in the hands of regressive and communal forces to beat down the minorities.

Along with these political developments, the judicial trends set by the Shah Bano judgement, echoing communal undertones, consolidated during this period. The wide media coverage which followed these judgements resulted in a further collapse of the parameters of the gender discourse.

Ironically, the judicial fervour of the nineties to reform Muslim personal law was not supported by individual Muslim women during the litigation process. But the judiciary seemed undaunted in its modernizing mission. One cannot help but strike parallels between the contemporary judicial zeal to modernize and civilize the Muslim community by abolishing polygamy and triple talaq, with the colonial zeal to reform the Hindu society through regulations on sati and child marriage in the last century.

The judgements were portrayed by the media as serving the cause of women's empowerment. But if they are stripped of this veneer of gender justice, they stand exposed in the garb of their communal hue. Beneath the rhetoric, they do not even further the cause of women's rights in actual terms. The implications of the judgements for gender discourse as well as identity politics are examined in this chapter.

8.1 Judgement of Justice Tilhari Invalidating Triple Talaq

The judgement invalidating triple talaq was delivered by Justice Hari Nath Tilhari of Allahabad High Court (Lucknow Bench) on 15 April 1994.[1] 'Since the practice of triple talaq denigrates women it is violative of the Constitution' the judgement proclaimed.

Apparently, the cause of Muslim women was served and the judgement was hailed as bold and progressive.[2] The response of Muslim religious leadership was predictable.[3] The comments by the *amicus curie* during the proceedings that knowledge of Arabic is essential for commenting upon the provisions of the Quran and the Hadis (which constitute the Shariat), provided further fuel to the communal myth that Muslims do not owe allegiance to the sovereign Indian state and that they are not governed by the state enacted legal system.[4]

The judgement caused concern to progressive scholars who, while criticizing the inertia of the All India Muslim Personal Law Board (AIMPLB) to declare the practice as invalid, apprehended that the judgement might hamper the process of reform from within the community.[5] Legal scholars also questioned whether a retrospective judgement of a single judge, in a land ceiling dispute, was the proper forum to examine the validity of triple talaq.[6] Several Muslim scholars and leaders who had supported the Supreme Court judgement in the *Shah Bano*[7] case and had opposed the Muslim Women's Bill in 1986, were critical of the Tilhari judgement and expressed their resentment about the sensationalization of the issue by the media.[8]

The media reportage led to a misconception that the High court had upheld a Muslim woman's petition challenging triple talaq and had protected her rights and consequently, the rights of all Muslim women. The implications of the judgement upon the woman concerned received least media attention.[9]

The press reports drew a comparison between the Shah Bano controversy and the triple talaq judgement.[10] However, the comparison was based on a warped understanding of the issue.

The only common denominator between the two judgements was the judicial interpretation of the Shariat. While Shah Bano herself had approached the court and had gained personally from the judgement, the judgement of Justice Tilhari had in fact deprived the woman concerned of her right to property.

Briefly stated, the facts of the case are as follows: When a notice was issued to Rahmatullah in 1974 under the U.P. Land Ceiling Act,[11] he pleaded that he had divorced his wife Khatoon Nisa in 1969 and that the land belonging to her was erroneously added to his assets. The judicial process which was initiated in 1974 had a long history and went through several stages and was examined by several state authorities. Finally, the issue before the court in two separate Writ Petitions filed by Khatoon Nisa and Rahmatullah was whether the plea of divorce was genuine or was resorted to only to defraud the state.

Initially, Khatoon Nisa was not a party to the case. But in 1980 she deposed before the concerned authority that she had been divorced eleven years ago. Under the Land Ceiling Act, a woman who is married relinquishes her right to hold separate property. However, the Act recognizes the right of a divorced or judicially separated woman to separate property. In such a situation, the property of the spouses is not clubbed together.[12] Hence the second issue before the court was whether a woman who is divorced as per the rules of her personal law is entitled to similar benefits as a woman who is separated or divorced through a court decree.[13]

The woman concerned did not dispute the fact of the divorce nor challenged the constitutional validity of oral and unilateral divorce (triple talaq). The opposing party was not her husband but the state authorities. Initially, the wife was not even a party to the case. It is pertinent to note that not just the advocates representing the parties and the *amicus curie* assisting the court, but even the advocate general appearing for the state (the opposing party) had pointed out to the judge that validity of triple talaq was not an issue before the court. But overriding these objections Justice Tilhari hastily pronounced the judgement after he received his transfer orders. When the advocate general questioned the constitutionality of such a move, rather curiously, the Avadh Bar Association passed a resolution to suspend him.[14]

The sum effect of the judgement for the concerned woman was that through a court decree her marriage which was dissolved twenty five years earlier was held to be valid and subsisting even against her own wishes and depositions and consequently, the land belonging to her was held to be surplus for the purpose of acquisition by the state under the Land Ceiling Act.

The judgement examined the serious issue of invalidating triple talaq in a flippant manner and relied upon a couplet written by an Urdu poet:

Talaq de rahe ho bare gharur ke saath;
Mere shabaab bhi lautaa do mere mehr ke saath

(you divorce me with such pride
give me back my youth along with my mehr).

The romantic poem cannot be treated as an authority to be relied upon in a judicial decision. While dealing with an issue of such magnitude, quoting a romantic couplet does not seem appropriate. The stanza had no relevance to a case where the wife herself affirmed her divorce.[15]

The rambling judgement of over a hundred and fifty pages lamented the position of Muslim women under their personal law and relied upon not just legal arguments but prose and poetry to prove the point. But the preoccupation with gender justice seems to be limited to the issue of Muslim women and triple talaq and does not extend to issues of gender discrimination under the Land Ceiling Act. The provision of clubbing the married woman's property with that of her husband is blatantly anti-women and smacks of European medievalism. It is based on the premise that the husband and wife are one unit (and that unit is the husband) and the unit is of a permanent nature. Under this concept, upon marriage, the woman lost her right over her individual assets and the husband acquired the power not only to manage it but even to alienate it. Incidentally, the Muslim law does not recognize the concept of the merging of the wife's assets with that of her husband.[16]

This blatantly discriminatory aspect of the Land Ceiling Act has been declared as constitutionally valid in an earlier judgement.[17] The Land Ceiling Act also provides for two additional hectares of land for each adult son but no such benefits are provided for adult daughters who form part of the domestic unit. The Act presumes that either women are not capable of owning and administering property or property is of no concern to adult females. So neither as unmarried daughters nor as married wives do they have an additional entitlement and their status is confined to that of dependents. The Tilhari judgement which claims to address the issues of gender equality, does not concern itself with this aspect.

One curious edge to the judgement is that while in this case the court went out of its way to declare the discriminatory aspect of personal laws as unconstitutional although the issue was not challenged before the court, in several instances when the discriminatory aspects of personal laws was an issue directly before the courts, the courts have upheld the constitutional validity of these discriminatory provisions.[18]

Even presuming that there was an intention to gain monetary advantage by defrauding the state through the misappropriation of the provision of oral and arbitrary talaq, such misappropriations and manipulations are not unique to this case. The right to form Hindu coparcenaries which grants tax benefits are routinely used for monetary gains. Several Hindu couples have also obtained collusive decrees for saving their land from the provisions of the Land Ceiling Acts.[19] Here the collusive factor had not led to invalidation of the decree of divorce.

In another instance, when the issue of collusive decrees was examined by the High Court of Bombay, the court specifically ruled that so long as the necessary conditions have been met, it is not up to the court to examine the motive for a divorce by consent. The question had arisen because the Family Court had refused to grant a divorce by consent on the ground that the Petition was based on an ulterior motive of defrauding creditors.[20]

Viewed within this broader context, there is reason to infer that the motive for the judgement lay elsewhere. Gautam Navalakha[21] has pointed out the communal tendencies underlying the judgements and has also pointed out other instances where a communal motive can be attributed. Immediately after the demolition of the Babri Masjid, when the issue of public worship of the idols of Ram in the newly erected temple was before the court, the judge permitted public worship on the site on the ground that Lord Ram is a constitutional identity. He based his logic on the fact that a picture of Ram appears on the copy of the constitution given to him by his father. In another judgement, while granting custody of a minor child born of a Christian mother and a Hindu father, the judge held that the father would be a better guardian as he is a Hindu.[22]

In his press interviews following the judgement on triple talaq, Justice Tilhari reaffirmed that he is a firm Hindu and that he believes that everyone born in Hindustan is a Hindu as this is his motherland. The language of motherland and cultural Hinduism of all Indians bears close resemblance to the propaganda by the communal Hindu factions in their anti-Muslim agenda.[23]

8.2 Supreme Court Directive to Implement a Uniform Civil Code

The second significant development in the debate on Muslim personal law and Uniform Civil Code is the decision of the Supreme Court in a case concerning polygamy of Hindu men after conversion to Islam.[24] While the issue before the court was bigamy of Hindu men and validity of their marriage contracted prior to conversion, the court primarily addressed the issue of Uniform Civil Code in the context of nation, national integration and minority identity.

In the much publicized judgement delivered by Justice Kuldip Singh (with a concurring judgement by Justice R.M. Sahai), the Court commented:

> Since Hindus along with Sikhs, Buddhists and Jains have forsaken their sentiments in the cause of the national unity and integration, some other communities would not, though the Constitution enjoins the establishment of a common civil code for the whole of India. ...Those who preferred to remain in India after the partition, fully knew that the Indian leaders did not believe in two-nation or three-nation theory and that in the Indian Republic there was to be only one Nation, the Indian Nation and no community could claim to remain a separate entity on the basis of religion. In this view of the matter no community can oppose the introduction of common civil code for all citizens in the territory of India.[25]

The obvious reference to Partition and to the choice to remain in India are targeted towards the Muslim minority as Parsis and Christians did not have any choice in the matter. The discourse of choosing to remain in India after Partition has long been a warning to Indian Muslims from the Hindu Right. The reference to 'civilized' and 'human' in relation to the Uniform Civil Code suggests that those who oppose the code (read Muslims) are barbaric and uncivilized. The comments seem to suggest that Hindu family laws are entirely secularized and gender just and further that Muslim community is the uncivilized enemy to national integrity.

Ratna Kapur and Brenda Cossman have argued that the language of the judgement in deflecting attention away from the continuing religious and discriminatory aspects of Hindu personal law and in attacking the Muslim community is disturbingly similar to the political rhetoric of the Hindu Right. In this view, all religious communities must be treated the same and it is the dominant Hindu community which is to be the norm against which equality is judged. [26]

But the norm of monogamy of the Hindu society, which was the issue under scrutiny before the apex court, escaped all public debate. The spotlight was turned on polygamy of Muslim men and the plight of Muslim women and solution offered to curb polygamy was the immediate enforcement of a Uniform Civil Code. There was a presumption that the uniform code would render Hindu marriages more stable by curbing the bigamous tendencies of Hindu men. A reading of the judgement seemed to indicate that the only breach of monogamy among Hindus was by conversion to Islam. To quote from the judgement, '...there is an open inducement to a Hindu husband, who wants to enter into a second marriage to become a Muslim...'.

The norm of Hindu monogamy presumed by the judgement needs further scrutiny. Monogamy was introduced among the Hindus through the *Hindu Marriage Act* in 1955. Prior to this, Hindu men were absolved of the criminal consequences of bigamy under S.494 of IPC. After 1955, a Hindu wife could divorce her husband on the ground of bigamy and also prosecute him under the penal law.

The right to dissolve the marriage on the ground of bigamy is also available, to a certain extent, to a Muslim wife under the *Dissolution of Muslim Marriages Act*.[27] The additional relief that the Hindu wife can avail of is criminal prosecution for bigamy. But since only the first wife can initiate prosecution, a popular notion prevails that a Hindu husband can remarry with the consent of his wife and at a practical level, this notion is not far from the truth. So although on paper the position of a Hindu wife appeared slightly better than a Muslim wife, in respect of her husband's bigamy, the statistics of bigamous marriages among Hindus and Muslims are comparable.[28] By declaring that the earlier marriage was valid, the only legal remedy (apart from a petition for divorce on the ground of bigamy) that the litigating women are entitled to is a prosecution for bigamy.

It is in this context that judicial attitude towards bigamy by Hindu men has to be posed as the central issue. The judgement seemed to indicate that the judiciary has dealt severely with all breaches of monogamy among the Hindus and the only loophole through which a husband can escape is conversion. But an examination of the decisions of the Supreme Court and the various High Courts reveal that bigamy of the Hindu male persists despite statutory restraints and the judicial attitude has been extremely lax towards Hindu bigamy.

Ten years after the provision of monogamy was introduced, the Supreme Court dealt with the case of Bhaurao Lokhande.[29] The errant husband was convicted by the lower courts. But the apex court acquitted the husband on the ground that essential ceremonies for a valid Hindu marriage, i.e *vivaha homa* and saptapadi (invocation before the sacred fire and seven steps round it) had not been performed in the second marriage. The court ruled that the bare fact of a man and a woman living as husband and wife does not give them the status of husband and wife unless valid ceremonies of a marriage have been performed and hence such cohabitation would not warrant conviction under S.494 of IPC.

This principle was followed by the Supreme Court in 1966, in Kanwal Ram's case and in 1971 in Priya Bala's case.[30] While acquitting the errant husbands, the Supreme Court reaffirmed that proof of essential ceremonies is a precondition for conviction. The court further ruled that this condition must be met even when the husband and the second wife admit the marriage or the fact of cohabitation.

In the intervening period of 30 years from Bhaurao in 1965 to Sarla Mudgal in 1995, the various High Courts not only followed the trend set by the Supreme Court, but in their zeal, advanced the logic to absurd ends, stamping out all hopes of justice and fairness in criminal prosecutions. Ceremonies performed in a temple, registration with the caste panchayats or temple authorities or even with a civil registrar fell short of the degree of clinching proof which the first wife was expected to produce. The paternity of the child of a second marriage if proved could only amount to its bastardization and not proof of bigamy by its father. The complainant wife could also lay herself open to the risk of invalidating her existing marriage.[31]

The decisions ignored the reality of a pluralistic Hindu society and thrust upon it an absurd notion of uniformity. The second marriages of lower castes were judged by the yardstick which can only be applied to marriages of upper caste virgin brides. The lower castes did not follow the Brahminical rituals and also permitted divorce and remarriage prior to the *Hindu Marriage Act* and followed distinct ceremonies to distinguish the first and the second marriage. Hence a remarriage of a lower caste person could never meet the high judicial standards set by the courts in co-ordination with the provisions of the *Hindu Marriage Act*.

A discernible pattern emerging from prosecution for bigamy is conviction by the lower judiciary and leniency by the apex court. The higher judiciary rescued the errant husbands by applying the standards of Brahminical rituals of homa, saptapadi and kanyadan. The complexities of bigamous Hindu marriages and the afflictions of both the first and the second wife were addressed neither by the courts nor by the media while the focus continued to remain on Muslim bigamy.

8.3 Implications for Identity Politics

The gains of the much publicized judgments for gender justice amounted to naught. The single judge decision invalidating triple talaq has been stayed by the Supreme Court. In the second judgement, the direction of the court to the legislature was criticized by legal scholars.[32] The then Prime Minister, P.V. Narasimha Rao, declared in a press statement that the government will not interfere with the personal laws of minorities. Within the stipulated period of one year the Parliamentary elections brought a change in government. The United Front which assumed power was a broad-based coalition of non-Congress, non-communal parties. Some of these parties had opposed the communal demand of UCC in its election campaigns.

At the expiry of the one year period, the government filed an affidavit in the Supreme Court expressing its inability to enact such a code.[33] A review petition filed against the judgement has been admitted. The Supreme Court has subsequently observed that its direction to the Union government to take necessary steps was only *obiter dicta* (not binding in law).[34]

The welcome change from the Shah Bano controversy to the triple talaq judgement was that in the post Babri Masjid political scenario, the triple talaq judgement could not polarize the issue within the binaries of progressive and secular Hindus and obscurantist and fundamentalist Muslims. The judgements met with criticism from several women's organizations and human rights activists for their communal undertones.[35]

The reactions of the AIMPLB were more subdued in comparison to the communal frenzy whipped up after the Shah Bano judgement. In a press release issued after the Tilhari judgement, the AIMPLB appealed to the community to restrain from taking the battle to the streets and assured them that the Board would approach the Supreme Court for redress.[36] In its meeting held at Lucknow on 1 May 1994, the Board assured the community that it would initiate the process of codifying sections of the Muslim law.

But the judgement provided a boost for the rhetoric of the Hindu Right. In Maharashtra, with the BJP-Shiv Sena in power since 1993, the judgement provided the impetus to fulfil its election manifesto of enforcing a Uniform Civil Code (which in effect, is confined to abolishing Muslim polygamy).[37] A hurriedly formulated Bill abolishing polygamy was rushed through both Houses without any public debate and was submitted for the President's assent. Since no effort is made to plug the loopholes within the *Hindu Marriage Act* or to protect women's rights, the only aim of the Bill seems to be to bring Muslim men under the penal provisions of S.494 IPC.[38] With a change in the government at the centre, the Bill seems to have lapsed.

So while the gains for the gender discourse have been nil, the judgements have dealt a severe blow to identity politics. The judgements have led even legal scholars, who had earlier advocated Uniform Civil Code, to re-examine their position. They have severely constrained the scope of gender discourse and have forced human rights activists and women's rights advocates to take a more restrained and cautious position in order to clearly distinguish their demand from that of the right wing communal forces.

Notes

1. *Rahmat Ullah v State of U.P.*, Writ Petition no.45 of 1993 and *Khatoon Nisa v State of U.P.*, Writ Petition no.57 of 1993 (unreported).
2. 'Triple Talaq Again', *The Times of India*, 19 April 1994; 'The practice is contrary to the spirit of Islam'. *Indian Express*, 25 April 1994; 'Muslim women welcome court verdict on talaq'. *The Statesman*, 22 April 1994, Anjana Basu, 'Behind the Four Walls The Veil.' *The Statesman*, 30 April 1994.
3. 'Muslims resent talaq verdict.' *The Times of India*, 18 April 1994; 'Divorced From Reality.' *The Pioneer* 25 April 1994.
4. Ahmad, F., *Triple Talaq—An Analytical Study*, New Delhi: Regency Publications (1994), p.104.
5. See comments by Tahir Mohammed quoted in, 'Beyond the law: The Strange case of Justice Tilhari,' *Frontline* 20 May 1994, p. 35.
6. Ibid. Also Advocate Daniel Latifi, who had represented Shah Bano in the controversial case criticized the Tilhari judgement in his article 'Verdict on talaq', in *Hindustan Times* 5 May 1994.
7. AIR 1985 SC 945.
8. Arif Mohammed Khan, the Congress Minister who had resigned in protest against the Muslim Women's Bill criticized the judgement in an interview with Neena Vyas, 'Much more at stake than triple talaq,' in *The Hindu*, 1 May 1994. In another article by Ajaz Ashraf titled 'A cap and a beard: Is that all to Muslims,' *The Pioneer*, 1 May 1994, several scholars expressed their resentment about the media coverage. Historian Harbans Mukhiya drew a parallel between the way the West covers India and the response of the media to Muslim issues. Mushirul Hasan opined that the media and the Muslim tend to stereotype each other.
9. Agnes, F. 'Triple Talaq Judgement Do Women Really Benefit,' *Economic and Political Weekly*, XXIX/20 (1994), p. 1169.
10. The report which appeared in *The Times of India*, 25 April 1994 was entitled, 'Another Shah Bano in the Making'. Several articles while commenting on the judgement carried a picture of Shah Bano. See for instance, 'Fear Behind the Purdah,' *Blitz*, 21 May 1994; 'One Nation, One Law', *Sunday*, 17 May 1994.
11. The U.P. Imposition of Ceiling on Land Holding (Amendment) Act 1972 (U.P. Act No.13 of 1972).
12. S.3 (7) and (17) provided for wives who were legally separated and divorced through a court decree to hold separate property.
13. Triple talaq under the Shariat law has statutory recognition under S. 2 of the *Application of Shariat Act*. 1937 Further talaq either in one sitting or in three consecutive months is the only remedy available for a Muslim man to divorce his wife. A Muslim man cannot approach a

court for a divorce either by consent or on fault ground. *The Dissolution of Muslim Marriages Act* of 1939 is applicable only to women. The matrimonial relief of judicial separation is of western origin and is not recognized under the Muslim law. The fact that an orally divorced wife's right to hold separate property does not figure in the provisions of the Act while a legally separated wife's rights are recognized is an indicator of the state's blinkers towards the specificity of minority practices, while enacting legislations. In *Sita Devi v Additional Commissioner, Agra* AIR 1996 All 75, the court upheld the plea that the property of a judicially separated Hindu wife cannot be clubbed with that of her husband. If this is the legal position there, was no basis for holding that an orally divorced wife is not entitled to hold separate property.

14. 'Avadh Bar to Suspend Advocate General,' *Times of India*, 19 April 1994. The interest of the Bar Association of Avadh is another curious aspect of the case. Perhaps it is relevant to note that the advocates of the Avadh Bar led a demonstration to Ayodhya demanding public worship of Ram idols installed at the newly constructed temple after the demolition of Babri Masjid in December, 1992.
15. Ahmad, F., *Triple Talaq—An Analytical Study*, p.108.
16. The press note issued by the AIMPLB on 1 May 1994, from Lucknow, stressed that Muslim law is more progressive than the Land Ceiling Act in this respect. But ironically, the AIMPLB had not opposed this provision of clubbing together the properties of the spouses, by raising the plea of religious dictates, prior to this judgement.
17. *Ambika Prasad Mishra v State of U.P.* 1980 (3) SCC 719.
18. See *Dwarakabai v Prof. Mainam Mathews* AIR 1953 Mad 792 *Harvinder Kaur v Harminder Singh* AIR 1984 Delhi 66, *Krishna Singh v Mathura Ahir* AIR 1980 SC 707.
19. Mali, A., 'Uniformity among equals,' in *Hindustan Times*, 8 May 1994 and Kannabiran, K.G., 'Outlawing Oral Divorce,' in *Economic and Political Weekly*, XXIX/25 (1994), p. 1509.
20. *Leela Mahadeo Joshi v Mahadeo Sitaram Joshi* AIR 1991 Bom 105.
21. Navlakha, G., 'Triple talaq: Posturing at Women's Expense,' *Economic and Political Weekly*, XXIX/21 (1994), p.1264.
22. The judgement of Justice Tilhari in the case of *Indumati Koorichh v Yogendra Pal Koorichh* W.P. no. 325 of 1993 dated 29 July 1993. See Bindra, A., 'Child Custody for Hindus only,' in *The Lawyers* IX/2 (1994), p.11. Also see 'Beyond the law—The strange case of Justice Tilhari,' *Frontline*, 20 May 1994, p. 35.
23. Basu, T. et al., *Khaki Shorts Saffron Flags*, New Delhi: Orient Longman (1993).
24. *Sarla Mudgal v Union of India & Ors* (1995) 3 SCC 635.
25. Ibid., para 34 and 35.
26. Kapur R. and B. Cossman, *Subversive Sites*, New Delhi: Sage Publications (1995), p.260.
27. S.2 (viii) (f) of the *Dissolution of Muslim Marriages Act*, 1939. Under this section, if the husband does not treat both wives equitably, the woman

has a right of dissolution of marriage. A similar right also exists if the husband associates with women of ill repute.

28. As per the Census report 1961, incidences of polygamous marriages for the decade 1951–60 are as follows: Tribal—17.98per cent; Hindus—5.06 per cent Muslim—4.31 per cent. According to another study, the incidence of polygamy is as follows: among tribals—15.25 per cent, Buddhists—7.97 per cent, Jains—6.72 per cent, Hindus—5.8 per cent and Muslims 5.7 per cent. (*Towards Equality*, pp.66-7; 104) Since Buddhists and Jains are also governed by Hindu law, the statistics for Hindus collectively would be 6.83 per cent as compared to 5.7 per cent for Muslims. See Table 3.
29. *Bhaurao Shanker Lokhande v State of Maharashtra* AIR 1965 SC 1564.
30. *Kanwal Ram & Ors v The H.P. Administration* AIR 1966 SC 614; and *Priya Bala Ghosh v Suresh Chandra Ghosh* AIR 1971 SC 1153.
31. For a further discussion on this issue see Agnes, F., 'Hindu Men, Monogamy and the Uniform Civil Code,' in *Economic and Political Weekly*, XXX/50 (1995), p. 3238.
32. Seervai, H.M., 'Judiciary oversteps its Brief', *The Times of India*, 5 July 1995.
33. 'No change in Muslim personal law, says P.M.,' *The Times of India*, 28 July 1995.
34. 'Suggestion on civil code not binding says Court,' *Asian Age* , 12 August 1995.
35. Punwani, J., 'Women veto a common civil code,' *The Sunday Review*, 23 July 1995; Sathe, S.P., 'Uniform Civil Code Implications of the Supreme Court Judgement,' in *Economic and Political Weekly*, XXX/35 (1995), p. 2165; Also see Kannabiran, Ahmad, F., *Triple Talaq*.
36. See note 16.
37. Bill No. XXXII of 1995 introduced by Liladhar Dake, Minister for Law and Judiciary on 7 August 1995.
38. Gangoli, G., 'Anti-Bigamy Bill in Maharashtra,' *Economic and Political Weekly*, XXXI/29 (1996), p. 1919.

PART THREE:

DEVELOPMENTS IN THE PERSONAL LAWS OF NON-MUSLIM MINORITIES

9

Legal Significance of the Parsi Community

Introduction

The history of law reform of minority communities, Muslims, Parsis and Christians, can broadly be categorized into three phases: (i) the reforms during the initial phases when the administration was transferred from the Company to the Crown; (ii) the reforms initiated when the Indian legislators, under the *Government of India Act*, assumed the power to legislate; (iii) reform measures initiated during the eighties when the issue of gender was foregrounded by the women's movement and legislative reform became an important arena of women's rights discourse. It is significant to note that during the first decade after independence, during the process of nation building, when major rehauling of the Hindu legal system was undertaken, there were no attempts to reform laws governing minorities.

The legislative history of Muslim minorities has been discussed in the preceding chapters. In this and the following chapter, an attempt is made to trace the legislative history of Parsi and Christian communities. Although the recent debate on Uniform Civil Code has posed the problem within the narrow confines of Hindu majority and Muslim minority, the issue also has implications for other minorities, Parsis and Christians. Hence it would be relevant to trace the history of personal laws among these communities and examine the strategies adopted by them to bring in reform.

The initiatives by the Parsi and Christian communities, during the recent phase of reforms, have met with diagonally opposite ends. While the Parsi community has been reasonably successful in bringing about legislative reforms, the initiatives by the Christian community have met with hostility and procrastination. The fate of reform among the two communities indicates that, even when the process is initiated from within the community, the official response is coloured with extraneous considerations and political undercurrents. To trace the linkages between political undercurrents and legal reform, it is necessary to locate the two communities within the context of the colonial and post-colonial political power structures.

9.1 The Ancient Civilization and the Transition to a New Land

The Parsis are a small and well-knit community. Numerically they are so insignificant that in the census report, under the classification, 'religious communities', they do not even merit a separate listing and are clubbed together under the head 'other communities'. The Parsi population in India is roughly around 1,00,000.[1] Since it was not a proselytizing religion, there was no significant increase in the population and the community continued to be homogenized. In 1851, the world population of the Parsis, including Persia, was around 1,50,000 out of which around 1,10,544 were in India.[2] As per a recent study, in 1986 the Parsi population of the world was around 2,50,800.[3]

The Parsis originate from Iran (abode of Aryans). The Greek writers called this land 'Persis' and the people Persians, hence the land acquired the name Persia. The country was divided into two parts, Media, the north-western region and Pars, the south-western region. The inhabitants of Pars were called Parsees (or Parsis).[4]

In AD 636, when the Arabs invaded Persia and Caliph Omar defeated the Parsi king Yezdezind, to escape persecution, they sailed off in boats in search of a new land, carrying with them their sacred fire. After a great ordeal at sea, the boat landed twenty-five miles south of Daman.[5] The head of the group implored the local king, Jadao Rane, to give them refuge with a promise that they would enrich his land. The history of India bears testimony to the fact that they kept this promise.

The king laid down five conditions: (i) the Parsis should adopt the local language; (ii) they should translate their holy texts into the local language; (iii) their women must change their dress and wear the local saree; (iv) their marriage ceremony should include the local rite of tying of the sacred knot; and (v) they should surrender their arms.[6] They consented to all the five terms and in return the king granted them permission to build their fire temples[7] and allotted to them a stretch of undeveloped country, near Diew (Diu). They renamed the place as Navsari[8], settled down to agriculture (some were also weavers and craftsmen) and lived amicably with the local Hindu community. Navsari became the centre of learning of the Parsi community. Due to the rigid caste system of the Hindus, assimilation was not possible and hence they were able to maintain their separate and distinct identity. But they adopted many local customs.[9]

Within this integrated community there are two sects Shensoys (or Shuhursaees) and Kudmis. The Kudmis are a breakaway sect formed in 1746 and consists of only around 10,000 Parsis. The difference between the two sects is not as major as among the Shias and the Sunnis in the Muslim community or the Catholics and the Protestants amongst the Christians.

The fortunes of this community seem to have transformed when they were touched by the magic wand of colonization. They were able to gain the maximum advantages of the economic and political transformation taking place during the colonial rule. Within the Bombay Presidency, they were the first to adapt to English education, new trading patterns, and later to commerce and industry. They fitted in well with the new colonial administrative structure and also played an important role in the nationalist politics. The contribution of the Parsi community to building the city of Bombay, after the English take-over, is particularly significant. It is through their close interaction with the British, that the community, though numerically insignificant in the post-colonial political map, evolved as an important economic and political force during the colonial regime and were able to negotiate for themselves a separate set of personal laws.

The records indicate that during the time of Portuguese rule, there was only one Parsi in Bombay, Dorabjee Nanabhoy.[10] After the island of Bombay was gifted over to the King of England by the Portuguese, the Parsis started trickling in and were able to obtain various commercial contracts from the British for building the new commerical centre of the British empire.[11] This helped the community to acquire a new economic and political status within the Bombay Presidency. The prosperity of Bombay attracted other Parsis who found life in famine-stricken Gujarat difficult. Over a period, 70 per cent of the Parsis in India began to live in Bombay. The more prosperous among them built hospitals, gardens, schools and housing schemes and were also significant contenders in the field of commerce, industry, science and art.[12]

9.2 Development of Parsi Laws of Marriage and Succession

The development of the Parsi legal system must be viewed within the context of the above mentioned role played by the Parsis within the colonial scheme. As already mentioned, after settling down, the Parsis adopted the local language and customs, while maintaining a distinct and separate identity. The adaptation of the institution of local panchayats for administration of their affairs is an important indicator of this adaptation.

During the initial phase of the Company rule, the various British charters explicitly saved the customs and usages of Hindus and Muslims in civil matters as they were deemed religious. But no such saving provision was granted to other communities like Parsis, Christians, Jews, Portuguese, Armenians and Europeans. The Presidency towns applied English law and in the Provinces, the law and custom of the parties (or the law of the defendant) was applied. In exercise of the discretion granted to the judges, English principles of justice, equity and good conscience were also applied as a residuary rule of law.[13] Under this legal scheme, English laws were applied to Parsis in all civil matters except marriage and bigamy.[14]

In 1778, after the Parsis petitioned William Hornby, the Bombay Parsi Panchayat was granted recognition and a lawfully constructed Panchayat came into effect from 1 January 1787.[15] This fitted in well with the legal scheme devised subsequently by Elphinstone of granting recognition to customary usages.

In 1835, a suit was filed by a son to appropriate the whole of the father's property through the application of the English principle of primogeniture (through which the eldest son inherits the whole property). Since this was not the custom followed by Parsis, the community was alarmed and pressed for a separate legislation. In their submission to the government, they pleaded that they were subjected to serious disadvantages in the absence of a fixed written code.

In response to this appeal, an Act was passed in June 1837,[16] which relieved the Parsis of Bombay from the operation of the English law of primogeniture. Through this statute, widows were granted a share in the property and the residue was divided equally amongst the children and their descendants. But English principles continued to be applied to them in all other respects.

In the case of the mofussil Provinces, it was almost impossible to ascertain with precision the Parsi customs because on many points the Parsis of Surat, Broach, Poona and Ahmedabad differed from each other and all of them differed from the Parsi in Bombay. So in November 1838, the Parsis forwarded to the Legislative Council a petition along with the answers which they had prepared to Borradaile's queries[17] and prayed that a regulation might be framed on the basis of those answers 'as embracing the rights of inheritance and succession that are acknowledged by the Parsi nation.'

The Parsis wanted to be protected from two primary principles of English law: (i) the English Statute of Distribution in case of intestacy; and (ii) from the English common law relating to husband and wife which denied married women independent control over their property during coverture.[18] But there was no further development on this issue. In a subsequent litigation, the Chief Justice of the Supreme Court of Bombay held that the ecclesiastical relief of restitution of conjugal rights applies to Parsi marriages.[19] At this juncture, the community renewed the demand for separate legislations to govern Parsi Marriage, Divorce and Succession. But the Third Law Commission rejected this demand as it felt that the demand was not substantiated. This left the community highly dissatisfied.

So on 20 August 1855, a meeting of the Parsis of Bombay was convened at central hall of the main fire temple to campaign for a separate law. The meeting was attended by 3,000 Parsis. A committee was appointed 'to prepare a draft Code of Laws adapted to the Parsi nation and to petition the Legislative Council of India for the enactment thereof.'

On 5 December 1859 the Managing Committee of the Parsee Law Association settled and adopted a body of rules titled a Draft Code of Inheritance, Succession and other matter. On 31 March 1860, this Draft Code was presented to the Legislative Council and was referred to a Select Committee. On 10 August 1861, the Select Committee of the Legislative Council presented their report and recommended that the Government of Bombay may appoint a Commission to make a preliminary inquiry into the usages recognized as laws by the Parsi community of India.

On 26 December 1861, the Government of Bombay appointed the commission, who recorded the evidence, both written and oral of the community representatives. As regards inheritance, succession and property between husband and wife, the mofussil Parsis objected to the rights of females to inherit the family property upon the death of a male Parsi dying intestate and to the right of married women during coverture to hold or dispose of their separate property. The mofussil Parsis, however, agreed with the Bombay Parsis that the English Law of Inheritance and Succession was unsuited to the requirement of the Parsi community. The commission submitted its report on 13 October 1862 and disallowed the contention that there should be two separate Inheritance Laws, one for the Parsis of Bombay and another for the Parsis of the mofussil towns.

As a next step, in 1864, the Parsi Law Commission was appointed and based on its report, in February 1865, two bills were introduced, Parsi Marriage and Divorce Bill and Succession and Inheritance (Parsis) Bill. They were referred to the Select Committee which presented its report on 31 March 1865.[20] Based on this report the two Bills were enacted, i.e. The Parsi Intestate Succession Act, 1865 and The Parsi Marriage and Divorce Act of 1865. Thus due to their perseverance, finally, the Parsis succeeded in securing a separate law for themselves.

The Parsi marriage and divorce law incorporated the provisions of the English matrimonial statute[21] which transformed the Christian marriage status to a dissoluble contract. Following the Christian model, the Parsi marriages were made monogamous and adultery was made into a ground of divorce.[22]

Through these statutes, the Parsis also secured legal recognition for their customary arbitration forum of the panchayat. Under the Act, a jury system consisting of seven representatives of the community was introduced. Through this process, the community obtained a hold over matters of marriage and divorce within the Anglo-Saxon court structure. In the process of emulating the English statutes, certain biases against women crept into the matrimonial laws. Despite the enactments, in matters not covered by the statute, either the English common law or principles of justice, equity and good conscience continued to be applied to Parsis.[23]

Like other communities the characteristics of the Parsi community also were 'fixed' in the process of litigation over property disputes. In an important case decided in 1908, the courts ruled that there is no conversion among the Parsis. The issue arose due to a dispute between the head of the Parsi Anjuman of Bombay, Sir Dinsha Petit and the Sir Jamsetji Jeejeebhoy, the industrialist. The issue before the court was the creation of private trusts and the relegation of huge properties to it by the industrialist. The Parsi Anjuman objected to the creation of such private trusts. But the issue which was foregrounded during litigation was that of conversion. The Parsi Anjuman pleaded that Juddins (converts) to whom the Navjot (initiation ceremony) is performed and are given the *sudra* and *kusti* become Parsis. In a lengthy judgement of around a hundred pages, a two member bench consisting of one Parsi (Justice Davar) and one English judge ruled in favour of Jamsetji and validated the creation of private trusts. In the process, they also invalidated conversions among Parsis. Adopting a rather curious logic, the court explained that while Zorastrianism is a religion, Parsis are a race and there cannot be conversion to a race. Just like a person cannot convert and 'become' an Englishman or a Frenchman, in a similar manner no one can convert and 'become' a Parsi the court explained.[24]

In order to prevent the Parsi trust property and fire temples from withering away from the Parsi fold, in another decision it was ruled that converts to Zorastrianism and children born to a Parsi woman, who is married to a non-Parsi are not Parsis.[25] The children of a Parsi father and a non-Parsi mother are deemed Parsis. Interestingly, the issue before the court did not concern the rights of children born to a Parsi woman through her non-Parsi husband. The case concerned a Goan Christian girl Bella, who was adopted and raised as a Parsi by a Parsi benefactor settled in Rangoon. Attracted to Zorastrianism, she expressed a desire to convert and was initiated into the faith through a ceremony of initiation by a Parsi priest. But when she started attending worship at the fire temple, the community elders raised an objection and filed a suit for an injunction restraining her entry into the fire temple in Rangoon. They pleaded that her presence in the fire temple caused distraction and prevented the Parsis from offering worship. Ironically, the land upon which the fire temple was built was a state endowment for religious worship, to the Parsis. The two lower courts held that since Bella had converted to Zorastrianism, her entry cannot be prevented and she was entitled to worship in the fire temple. But the Privy Council relying upon the Bombay High Court decision in *Dinsha Petit v Jamsetji Jeejeebhoy* held that the double requirements of religion and race are essential to worship in the fire temple, despite the fact that the legal deeds were drawn specifically in the context of religion. Through these two significant decisions, the avenues for conversion and adoption among the Parsis were sealed.

In 1925, when the *Indian Succession Act* was enacted, (which governs mainly Christian succession) the *Parsi Intestate Succession Act* was verbatim incorporated in Chapter III of this Act. Interestingly, during the years 1870 to 1925, considerable progress was made in the realm of married women's property rights under the English statutes and the concept of equality between men and women regarding inheritance had been accepted. Based on these developments, the *Indian Succession Act* did not discriminate between male and female heirs. But the Parsi inheritance laws, continued to maintain the discrimination and females continued to inherit half the share of their male counterparts.[26] This is a rather surprising development, given the context that the demand for a separate law for the Parsis originated with their resentment against the anti-women provisions of the English statutes being inadvertently applied to them.

9.3 A Wave of Reforms During the Thirties

When reforms were initiated in the family laws of Hindus and Muslims, the Parsis also initiated a process of reform. In 1933, the Council of the Parsi Central Association submitted a Draft Bill for the opinion of the Parsi public to amend the Parsi law of succession. The main objective was to improve the position of the widow and daughter under the statute and allotment of share to parents. The changes were incorporated into the *Indian Succession Act* in 1939.[27]

During the period 1865 to 1930, the status of women in England was radically transformed through various statutes and great strides were made in the English family laws. Against this backdrop, the *Parsi Marriage and Divorce Act* of 1865 had become outdated. So the Parsi Central Association took up the question of reforms in 1923 and a sub-committee was appointed to suggest suitable changes. The Parsee Laws Revision sub-committee submitted its report in 1927. The Parsi Central Association sent copies of this report to various trustees of the Parsi Panchayats, Parsi Associations, Parsi Anjumans, the delegates of the Parsi Chief Matrimonial court and to Parsi jurists all over India, as well as to Parsi Associations in China and Persia.[28] The report was also published in the press.

The Parsi Central Association made some modifications to the Bill after which it was circulated for public opinion. A conference was arranged under the auspices of the Parsi Panchayat. Twenty-five Parsi associations participated in this process and twenty-one associations approved the modifications.[29] Based on the various views expressed, a draft of the proposed Act was prepared and circulated which had the approval of leading members of the Parsi community including Sir Dinshaw E. Wacha and Right Hon'ble Dinshaw F. Mulla.

A Bill was introduced into the Council of State in 1935, by Sir Pheroze Sethna. It was circulated for opinion and a Joint Select Committee was appointed to consider the Bill. The Select Committee reported to the Council of State in the same year and the Bill was passed on 13 March 1936. The Federal Assembly considered the Bill in April 1936. Sir Cowasji Jehangir who moved the Bill, explained that an overwhelming majority of the Parsi community held progressive views and were anxious to modify the provisions of their archaic laws to suit the modern conditions.[30] The reforms expanded the scope of dissolving the marriage by introducing several new grounds— non-consummation of marriage, insanity, pre-marriage pregnancy, grievous hurt and desertion.

9.4 Reforms During the Eighties

The eighties witnessed the emergence of a new women's movement in India. Reform in personal laws was an important demand of this movement. There were significant reforms in various laws concerning women, rape, dowry prohibition, domestic violence etc. The controversy around the Shah Bano judgment and the Muslim Women's Bill also focused attention on discriminatory aspects of various personal laws. At this stage, the Parsi community again initiated reforms to modernize their laws.

The reforms were based on the recommendations of the Law

Commission's *110th report*. The process was initiated by the Board of trustees of the Bombay Parsi Panchayat. It submitted the recommendations to the government. The then Law Minister, Dhiraj Goswamy introduced two Bills for reforming the personal laws of the Parsis. While the amendment to marriage laws was passed in 1988, the amendment to succession laws had to be shelved and was enacted in 1991, during the Congress rule.

The *Parsi Marriage and Divorce (Amendment) Bill* was introduced in the Rajya Sabha on 24 November 1986. It was passed by both the houses in the following year, received President's assent on 25 March 1988 and came into force in April 1988.[31]

The provisions of marriage and divorce were modified along the lines of the *Hindu Marriage Act*. Grounds of divorce were further liberalized and divorce by mutual consent was introduced.[32] The disparity between the rights of legitimate and illegitimate children was abolished. In 1991, by amending the succession laws, the discrimination between female and male descendants was abolished.

The following aspects need to be highlighted in the context of Parsi law reforms:

i. At each juncture, the process of reforms was initiated from within the community and a broad consensus was reached before the Bills were introduced. So finally, when the Bills were presented to the legislature they were passed unanimously without much debate.

ii. Women from the community were conspicuously absent from the discourse. Although the community is liberal and holds a progressive stand on women's issues, women's names do not figure in any phase of the reform. The process seems to have been initiated at the instance of a few liberal male members. They interacted both with the community institutions at one level, and with the state institutions at the other.

iii. Although gender justice was the stated agenda, the motive of reform seems to be dual: (i) maintaining a separate community identity and once this is achieved (ii) ensuring that the laws do not lag far behind the dominant ideology, i.e. in the pre-independence period the British statutes and in the post-independence period, the *Hindu Marriage Act*. Since the *Hindu Marriage Act* grants the husband a right to maintenance, the same was also introduced in the Parsi laws. Under the *Special Marriage Act* of 1954, husbands do not have a similar right. It is significant to note that the reform followed the provisions of Hindu law rather than the *Special Marriage Act*, which is a secular legislation and more beneficial to women than the *Hindu Marriage Act*.

iv. The premise that gender equity was not the primary object is substantiated by the retention of certain outdated discriminatory notions inherited from the British statutes in 1865. The law provides for settling the property of an adulterous woman in favour of the children(S.50). The statute also treats women as legal minors and provides for a trust to be set up in respect of the maintenance allowance with the power to restrain women's access to the maintenance (S.41).

v. Even while modernizing the statutes, the community has maintained its hold over the matrimonial matters by retaining the jury system introduced in 1865. The jury system has been abolished under other Indian statutes. Constituting a special Parsi Matrimonial Court causes severe hardships and delays to the litigants. In the Bombay High Court, the Parsi Matrimonial Court is constituted twice a year and functions for about a week during each term. Even in the interest of uniformity or modernity, this system has not been abolished. This clause did not meet with any criticism during the legislative debate.

vi. The debate in the Parliament when the Bills were enacted has been cursory.[33] The members did not concern themselves with the implications of the Bill for Parsi women. The debate was confined to two spheres: (i) now that the Parsis have willingly modified their laws, it is time to enact a Uniform Civil Code; (ii) praises to the Parsi community that they are an enlightened and progressive community and thereby insinuating that other communities (more specifically the Muslims) are backward and reactionary. The fact that the Parsi community had also opposed the imposition of a Uniform Civil Code and the Adoption Bill, that they had retained the jury system in matrimonial adjudication and the relief of divorce by consent was introduced as late as in 1988, did not even figure in the debates. The Act also retained the sexist provision under S.50 of the Act, which empowers the court to settle a wife's property for the benefit of the children in case a ground of adultery is proved against her in a petition filed by her husband.

In conclusion, it is obvious that only through its political and economic significance during the colonial rule, the Parsi community could negotiate for a separate law, where none existed. The liberal leaders of the community, during each phase of reform, have ensured that the law does not lag far behind the dominant social norms, i.e. of the British, during the colonial rule and of the Hindu in the post-colonial rule. Although their initial demand for a separate law was premised on protecting the rights of women from the vagaries of the British legal principles, in the process of codification and reform, the community incorporated the biases inherent in the dominant system, both of the British and of the Hindu, which aided and reaffirmed the biases inherent within the customary practices. Hence their claim for a separate law to safeguard women's rights cannot be substantiated. But the existence of a separate law has substantially aided the numerically insignificant community to retain its own separate identity within the legal arena and granted statutory recognition to community interventions in judicial processes.

Notes

1. See Table 4.
2. Framjee, D., *The Parsees—Their History, Manners, Custom and Religion*, London: Smith Elder & Co. (1858), p. 52.
3. Cabinetmaker, P.H., 'Parsis and Marriage', Pune: International Institute of Population Studies (Mimeo) (1991), pp.2-3.
4. The Parsis are followers of Zarathushtra, the prophet of ancient Iran, born 1,500 years before Christ, who preached that life is a struggle between good and evil, with the ultimate triumph of good over evil. They worship the Supreme Being Hormuzd, the sun and five elements. Their ancient kingdom lays claims to many markers of civilization. In its hey day, the Persian kingdom extended from Egypt to Sind and from the Mediterranean to the Arabian Sea. Cyrus and Darius are the two illustrious Persian kings.
5. Framjee, D., *The Parsees*, p.10.
6. Cabinetmaker, P.H., 'Parsis and Marriage'.
7. The first fire kindled when they landed is preserved in the holiest of the holy shrines Imamshah at Udwada near Navsari.
8. New Sari, as it reminded them of a place they had left behind in Persia which was called Sari.
9. For instance, washing the toes of the bridegroom with milk during marriage rituals, offering *pan-sopari* on auspicious occasions, sprinkling of rose water etc. Framjee, D., *The Parsees*, p.84.
10. Framjee, D., *The Parsees*, p.26.
11. In 1735, when the British started building the Bombay dockyard, a

Parsi from Surat, Lowjeee Wadia was granted the contract of ship building (ship wright). Rustom Patel, another Parsi, helped the British to stall the Moppila attack. Rustomjee Cursetjee wrote the first book in English in 1780, called *Bombay Calendar*. On 1 July 1822, Mobed Fardoonje Marzben started the first newspaper in Gujarati, *the Bombay Samachar*. When the British started building the railways, the contract of laying the tracks was granted to Jamsetjee Dorabjee. In 1857, Rustomjee Byramjee, obtained a commission as a surgeon.

12. For a numerically insignificant community, the list of dignitaries in every field is endless. Sir Jamsetjee Jeejeebhoy, the first Baronet, Sir Nes Wadia, Dinshaw Jamsetjee Petit, the philanthropists, Sir Cowasjee Jehangir, the Patron of Art, Jamsetjee Tata, Homi Mody and Godrej, the industrialists, Behram Malabari, the social reformer, Homi Bhabha, the scientist, Sir Phirozshah Mehta, Sir Dadabhai Naoroji, Sir Dinshaw Wacha, Madam Bhicaji Cama, the nationalist leaders, Sir Dinshaw Mulla, the legal luminary and member of the judicial committee of the Privy Council and so on.
13. Jain, M.P., *Outlines of Indian Legal History*, Bombay: N.M. Tripathi (1966) (2nd edn.), p.59.
14. As shown by a case decided on 16 December 1817 by the Court of Appeal of Surat Adawlut, *Kaoosjee Roostumjee v. Mt. Awan Baee*, the matters concerning marriage and control over women's sexuality were regulated by Modees, Dustoors and members of the Parsi *unjoomun* and bigamous marriages were permitted under certain conditions. The case is discussed in *Mihirwanjee Nuoshirwanjee v Awan Baee*, Borradaile's Reports SDA Vol.I 1800–1824, pp.231–8.
15. Framjee, D., *The Parsees*, p.99.
16. Succession to *Parsees Immovable Property Act*, 1837, Act IX of 1837.
17. In 1828, a questionnaire was administered to the Parsis of Surat by Borradaile, who was assigned the task of recording the customs of various castes in the Gujarat region. The Surat Parsis did not respond to the questionnaire. So the Bombay Parsi Panchayat published it in 1832 and obtained the response of the Bombay Parsis to these queries. Framjee, D., *The Parsees*, p.120.
18. The history of Parsi law reform is based on the report in Roy Chowdhury, S.K. and H.D. Saharay Paruck's *The Indian Succession Act*, Bombay: N.M. Tripathi (1988) (7th edn.), p.73.
19. *Ardeseer Cursetjee v Peerozebai* 6 MIA 348.
20. Roy Chowdhury, S.K. and H.D. Saharay Paruck's *The Indian Succession Act*, p.74.
21. *Matrimonial Causes Act, 1857.*
22. With this, the penal provisions of bigamy under the Penal Code were made applicable to Parsis. But the Act did not have any retrospective effect and marriages contracted prior to the enactment could not be governed by the penal provisions. See Manchanda, S., *Parsi Law in India*, Allahabad: The Law Book Co. (1991) (5th edn.), p.14.
23. See the decisions in *Manchersha v Kamirunissa Begum* 5 BHCR 109 and *Mithibai v Limji N. Banaji* ILR 5 Bom 506.

24. *Dinsha Petit (Sir) v Jamsetji Jeejeebhoy (Sir)* (1909) ILR 33 Bom 509.
25. *Saklat v Bella* 1925 ILR 53 The court held that in a marriage between a Parsi woman and a non-Parsi man, there is a presumption that the wife will have to accept the religious faith of her husband. So it would follow that the children will be brought up according to the religion of the father.
26. This principle was borrowed from the then progressive Islamic law in 1865.
27. The Amending Act XVII of 1939.
28. Mentioned in the Statement of Objects and Reasons of the Act (Gazette of India, 1934, Part V p.221).
29. The non-concurrence of the rest of the associations was explained by Sir Phiroze Sethna as, 'This opposition chiefly comes from a small section who are ultra conservative in their views and do not, as a rule, approve of any changes in keeping with the changing times.'
30. *LAD* IV 1935, pp. 3246-7; *LAD* V, 1936, pp. 4149-53. Also see Parashar, A., *Women and Family Law Reform in India,* New Delhi: Sage Publications (1992), pp. 192-3.
31. The *Parsi Marriage and Divorce (Amendment) Act* 1988 (Act No.5 of 1988).
32. S. 32 (a), (b), (c), (e) and (g) of the Act.
33. For a discussion on the Inheritance laws, see *LSD* 10th Series, VI/10 4 December 1991, pp.662–7; 5 December 1991 pp.442–51.

10

Political Reformulation of Christian Personal Law

Introduction

The process of tracing the developments within the Christian personal law is far more complex than that of other religious communities, i.e. Hindus, Muslims and Parsis discussed in the preceding chapters. At one level the Christians are governed by the pioneering statutes which revolutionalized the scheme of personal laws in India and set the parameters of reform for all communities. At the other, these statutes have remained static for well over a century, while the other communities have made some attempts to keep abreast with the changing trends in matrimonial laws in the western world. Hence the statutes have now become archaic and redundant. This dichotomy is enmeshed within the political events which reduced Christianity from its hallowed position of being the religion of the colonial masters to the religion of an insignificant minority in the post-colonial phase.

Apart from this, two other factors of historical significance have also contributed to the complexity; (i) The laws governing Christians are shaped by two distinct colonial influences, the Anglo-Saxon jurisprudence introduced by the British and the continental system introduced by the French and the Portuguese within their respective territories (ii) The post-independence attempts of reform are marked by the conflict between the conservative Roman Catholic doctrine and the reformist Protestant theology which has its roots within European politics.

The concept of marriage as a permanent bond has gone through a full cycle, with the early churches of Orthodox traditions permitting customary forms of marriage and divorce; the medieval church of Latin rites evolving the doctrine of sacramental indissolubility, with the medieval European church moving in to regulate marriages through canon law and ecclesiastical courts[1] and the reformist Protestant traditions reformulating marriages as civil and dissoluble contracts to be regulated by state enactments.[2]

Keeping the above mentioned global trends in view, in this chapter an attempt is made to trace the complex legal history of the Indian Christian community, the attempts at reform in the post-independence period and recent judicial interventions.

10.1 Christianity in India and its Diverse Origins

While homogeneity is the characteristic of the Parsis, the Christian community is marked by its diversity. As per the 1991 census, Christians constitute 2.32 per cent of the total Indian population. Christians in India belong to three different traditions: (i) the Orthodox churches of west Asian traditions, i.e. Syro Malabar, Syro Malankara, the Mar Thoma Church etc.; (ii) the Roman Catholic Church of Latin rites and (iii) the various reformist churches of Protestant traditions now consolidated into the Church of South India (CSI) and the Church of North India (CNI).[3] There also exists a large population of Christians among various tribes, particularly in the north-east region. These tribes are granted protection under the constitution in respect of their culture, tradition, customs and laws[4] and hence are not governed by the Christian personal laws.

It is believed that Christianity was first brought into India by a disciple of Jesus Christ, Saint Thomas, soon after the crucifixion in the first century. As per the oral history, Saint Thomas landed on the Malabar coast. A church in Quilon is believed to have been built by the saint.[5] The Christianity of this period was affiliated to the orthodox traditions of west Asia, i.e. Syria, Armenia, Antiochia and also Constantinople.

The Indian Christian community of this early period, concentrated along the south-western coastland, was loosely structured and was assimilated with the local communities. The Christian priests were invited to participate in local rituals like *chattam* and *sradhas* and the non-Christians joined the Christians in their annual pilgrimage to the tomb of Saint Thomas.[6] The priests were not governed by a separate dress code or celibacy and Christian marriages were not indissoluble unions. Hence divorce and remarriage was accepted.

The second phase of conversion was carried out in the sixteenth century after the Portuguese established the trade routes and conquered a few Indian territories. As the popular saying goes, the white man landed on the Indian shores with a sword in one hand and a cross in the other. The conquests of this period were concentrated along the western (Konkan) coast. In 1550, the Pope (the Patriarch of the Church of Rome) entered into a pact with the Portuguese king to evangelize the newly acquired territories and in return granted the king a voice in the appointment of bishops in these territories.[7] The popular saint of this period, Saint Francis Xavier, landed in Goa in May 1542[8] and travelled along the western coast and instituted the Roman Catholic church in India.[9] The evangelists were engaged not only in proselytizing but in Latinizing the Thomas Christians of west Asian traditions.[10]

The third phase of Christianity is the Protestantism and the theology of enlightenment brought in by the missionaries of various European and American churches during the nineteenth and twentieth centuries.[11]

While being shaped by the European philosophies of the conservative and highly institutionalized Roman Catholic Church and the liberal and loosely structured Protestant theology, the indigenous Christian community also incorporated the local customs, traditions and languages resulting in wide regional diversities. The converted Christians also retained their pre-conversion caste hierarchies.[12]

10.2 Family Laws Governing Christian Communities

The laws governing the Christian communities have three distinct sources, i.e. the statutes enacted by the British in the nineteenth century; the Civil Code introduced by the Portuguese and the French within their colonies and the local customary laws. In addition, the Roman Catholics are governed by a dual system of civil law and canon law. Since the Roman Catholic church does not recognize divorce, to deal with the practical aspect of breakdown of marriages, it provides for liberal grounds of annulment under a legal fiction that marriages which are annulled were not valid marriages in the first place. This legal fiction enables the church to hold on to its dogma of indissolubility *vis-à-vis* the Protestant doctrine and at the same time provide for dissolution of broken marriages. Since Protestants are not saddled with the doctrine of sacramental indissolubility, a civil dissolution of the contract of marriage is recognized by the Protestants as valid.[13]

Until the nineteenth century, the converted Christians followed the local customary practices of pre-conversion traditions in respect of property inheritance and marriage rituals. The concept of a distinct Christian personal law evolved much later, i.e. only during the later half of the nineteenth century with statutory enactments introduced by the British and the Portuguese.

The two initial statutes enacted by the British were meant only to aid the process of proselytization. The *Caste Disabilities Removal Act* (or the Freedom of Religion Act) of 1850, was aimed at protecting the Christian converts from disinheritance from their respective families.[14] The *Native Converts Marriage Dissolution Act* of 1866 provided for the dissolution of the converts' marriages contracted prior to conversion.

Later, two more statutes were enacted to regulate Christian marriages. The *Indian Divorce Act* (IDA) of 1869 was modelled on the British matrimonial statute, the *Matrimonial Causes Act of 1857*[15] and provided for adultery as the sole matrimonial offence (which, as far as the wife was concerned, had to be coupled with either cruelty, desertion, incest or bestiality). The later enactment, the *Indian Christian Marriage Act* (ICMA) of 1872, provided for the solemnization and regulation of Christian marriages. The primary aim was to extend to the British and other Europeans the beneficial provisions of the English statute. The inclusions of indigenous Christians was only incidental, as a careful reading of the ICMA reveals.[16]

The subsequent British enactments liberalized divorce and by 1937, adultery, cruelty, desertion and insanity were made into independent grounds of divorce in England. Attempts were made to incorporate these liberal grounds into the laws governing Parsis, Muslims and Hindus in subsequent years through the enactment of *Parsi Marriage and Divorce Act* of 1936, the *Dissolution of Muslim Marriages Act* of 1939 and the *Hindu Marriage Act* of 1955. Ironically, during the period 1935–1955, when the three religious communities went through a process of remoulding their laws along the Anglo-Saxon matrimonial principles, there were no attempts to modernize the Christian family laws.

Two diverse factors, one political and the other legal, could have led to this stalemate. The political factor being that perhaps the nationalist leaders viewed the Christian religion (and laws) as the religion of the colonial masters, which would not warrant any reform through nationalist interventions. Absence of an Indian Christian political leader of repute within the nationalist movement, perhaps resulted in the invisibility of issues concerning indigenous Christians.

The legal factor being that the *Indian Divorce Act* of 1869 (modelled on the English statute of 1857) was so structured as to automatically incorporate the developments in the English matrimonial statutes within its scheme.[17] The comments of the Full Bench ruling of the Madras High Court in 1936 are revealing. While interpreting S.7 of IDA, the court held:

> The Indian courts have to keep pace with the practices in England and to note changes that are made in the principles and rules of the English divorce law from time to time since the English statute is the parent law.[18]

Hence, the necessity of statutory reform may not have arisen.

After independence, the changes in the political structure brought about a new status for indigenous Christians who were now reduced to the status of a politically insignificant minority. But the community continued to be governed by archaic and unreformed British statutes of the Victorian era.

Another significant development of the post-independence reformulation was that the dominant Protestant ideology with which the Christian community in British India was governed during the colonial rule, was replaced by the Roman Catholic Church, which became politically the most powerful among all the constituents of the Church in India. The Victorian ideology of indissolubility of marriage fitted in well with the Roman Catholic doctrine and the Catholic Church became an ardent supporter of a statute enacted by the British (Protestant) government and resisted any attempt of reform.

The Civil Code of Goa: Roughly around the time of British reforms, the Portuguese colonies of Goa, Daman and Diu also introduced a comprehensive civil code in 1867 in keeping with the European trend of separation of church and state.[19] Based on the French Civil Code (also known as the Napoleon Code), it contained, among other civil matters, provisions regulating marriage and succession.

The French code was evolved in reaction to the Roman law of pre-industrial Europe which advocated the doctrine of dissolubility of marriage and also deprived married women of their right to own property. Hence, granting married women the right over property became a predominant feature of the French code. Under this code, the principles of common matrimonial property and pre-marriage agreements in respect of the separate property of the spouses were granted legal recognition. These were revolutionary principles which secured married women crucial economic rights.

The Portuguese code introduced in Goa is based on similar principles. Validation of ante-nuptial (pre-marriage) agreements in respect of the separate property of the spouses[20], protection of a woman's separate property by way of gifts and inheritance.[21] and joint ownership of matrimonial property[22] are significant features of the Goan Code which are not found in any matrimonial statutes founded on English common law traditions. Since the wife is deemed as the joint owner, the property cannot be disposed off without her consent.[23] The restraint upon testamentary disposition is another important provision. Within the scheme of joint ownership, the husband can dispose off only half of his property by a will.[24] The widow also has a right to retain possession of property until it is partitioned and a share is allotted to her.[25]

While these are positive, pro-women stipulations, the code also contains several discriminatory aspects. The power of managing all the properties of the conjugal society is vested on the husband and only in his absence is the wife empowered to manage it. But even in these circumstances, she cannot alienate any immovable property without the authorization of the family council.[26] The husband cannot be deprived of his right of administering the family properties including those which belong to the wife through an ante-nuptial agreement.[27] The initial code also contained a provision restraining the wife from publishing her writings without the consent of her husband.[28] But these provisions must be viewed within the context of the nineteenth century European traditions.

While the initial code provided only for legal separation, in

1911, the right of divorce both by contest and consent was granted statutory recognition.[29] Under Article 2 of the Law of Marriage enacted in 1911, marriages were rendered as civil contracts which had to be compulsorily registered.[30]

In the debate on UCC, the Goan Code is projected as the model of uniformity for the rest of India.[31] This projection is based on an erroneous understanding of the Goan code which, in fact, grants recognition to various customary practices including Hindu polygamy.[32] The situation in Goa is unique as compared to the rest of the country. Here Hindus are granted the customary right of polygamy, while Muslims are governed by the principle of monogamy. Neither a nikah nor a talaq is recognized and Muslim marriages and divorces are regulated by the code. The fact that this situation has not led to any political controversy can be attributed to the non-politicization of the issues concerning Muslim minorities, who in any case are numerically insignificant (as per 1971 census, 3.76 per cent).[33]

The code also grants certain concessions to Catholics who were the dominant segment. While marriages of other communities have to be performed in the office of the Registrar, a Catholic marriage is valid only when solemnized before a minister of church in accordance with canon law. Hence the sacramental aspect of only a Catholic marriage is granted statutory recognition.[34] An annulment granted by an ecclesiastical tribunal is also granted automatic recognition.[35] Hence, the Catholics in Goa do not have to go through a dual process of obtaining a civil divorce and a canonical annulment as the Catholics in the rest of India. After the liberation in 1961, Goa, Daman and Diu were incorporated into the Indian nation as union territories. But at this time, the Hindu Code Bill or the personal laws of other religious communities were not made applicable to these territories and the laws which were in force were allowed to be retained.[36]

While the Goan Code would provide useful guidelines regarding the concept of community of property, its claim to a model of uniformity cannot be substantiated. The positive and the negative aspects of the code cannot be isolated from the context of the Continental legal system, as well as the colonial policies of the Portuguese within which it is located. The legal system, which worked well for a small and homogenized territory under the rule of assimilation cannot be applied to a vast and pluralistic nation which was governed for about two hundred years by the British policy of divide and rule.[37]

Customary Laws of Succession: In matters of succession, the Christian subjects of British India were governed by the provisions of *Indian Succession Act* of 1865 (re-enacted in 1925). The *Indian Succession Act* of 1925 is a progressive piece of legislation which grants equal rights to daughters and sons in the parental property. The concept of ancestral property or coparcenary is also not recognized by this Act. Hence it granted better rights to women than the Hindu legal system (including the *Hindu Succession Act* of 1956), as well as the Muslim and Parsi (until it was amended in 1991) legal systems. But this legislation seemed to apply mainly to Europeans and other foreigners than to Indian Christians, as large sections of the Christian community governed by customary laws were excluded from the application of this Act.[38]

As already mentioned, even after conversion, communities continued to follow the pre-conversion laws regarding succession. Most Christian communities followed the rule of coparcenary or joint Hindu family property. The leading case on this issue is *Abraham v Abraham*[39] decided by the Privy Council in 1863. The case concerned the issue of succession to the property of a Roman Catholic who had subsequently converted to the Protestant religion. The dispute was between the widow and her husband's brother. The brother pleaded that although they had converted to Christianity they continued to follow the Hindu law of coparcenary. While holding that the property is joint, the Privy Council laid down the rule regarding conversion as follows:

> The profession of Christianity releases the convert from the trammels of the Hindoo law but it does not of necessity involve any change of the rights or relations of the convert in matters with which Christianity has no concern such as his rights and interests in and his powers over property.

But subsequently, the *Indian Succession Act* came into force and when the issue came up before the court again in 1886, the Madras High Court, in *Tellis v Saldanha*[40] held, that after the enactment of the *Indian Succession Act*, the Christian converts are governed by the provisions of the *Indian Succession Act*. The case concerned Roman Catholics of Mangalore who had converted several centuries ago. While the widow pleaded the application of the *Indian Succession Act*, the brother of the deceased pleaded that they are converts from a Brahmin sect and are governed by the Mitakshara law of coparcenary. But a subsequent decision of the Bombay High Court in the year 1907, dissented from the view expressed in *Tellis v Saldanha* and held that Christians are governed by the Hindu law of coparcenary.[41] The customs were also granted validity under S.5 of the *Punjab Laws Act* 1872.

Despite the enactment of the *Hindu Succession Act* of 1956 which improved the situation of Hindu women and granted daughters and wives a share in the parental property (but not in the ancestral property), Christians continued to be governed by the discriminatory provisions of the uncodified Hindu law, which denied daughters a share in the parental property.[42] In 1957, the Cochin and Travancore High Courts affirmed that Christians in the region are not governed by the *Indian Succession Act* and the discriminatory statutes enacted by the princely states apply to them.[43]

In 1974, a single judge of the Madras High Court adopted a progressive stand and ruled that the *Travancore Succession Act* stood repealed after independence and Christians in the region are not governed by this discriminatory statute but by the *Indian Succession Act*.[44] But this decision was overruled in 1978 by the Full Bench of the Madras High Court which reaffirmed that Christians in the state are governed neither by the progressive provisions of the *Indian Succession Act* nor by the *Hindu Succession Act* but by the uncodified Hindu customary law and under this law, the brother is the sole heir to the father's property to the exclusion of the daughter.[45] The controversy was finally resolved in a ruling given by the Supreme Court in Mary Roy's case.[46] The court struck down the discriminatory provisions on a technical ground that after independence the laws enacted by the erstwhile princely states, which were not expressly saved have been repealed. While the repeal was welcome and overdue, the court restrained itself from examining the provision under the constitutional mandate of equality and non-discrimination on the ground of sex under Articles 14 and 15 of the Constitution which could have set the precedent for examining gender discrimination under other personal laws.[47]

10.3 Law Commission Recommendations and Community Based Initiatives

Amongst the several discriminatory provisions of their personal laws, the narrow and constrained ground of divorce has caused the greatest hardships to Christian women. Cruelty and desertion do not constitute independent grounds of divorce. Under S.10 of the *Indian Divorce Act*, the husband's grounds of divorce are also constrained but he can obtain a divorce on the ground of adultery *simpliciter*, whereas the wife has to prove an additional ground either of cruelty or desertion. Since adultery is extremely difficult to prove, and not all husbands who treat their wives with cruelty or desert them also commit adultery, Christian women face great hardships and are discriminated against both *vis-à-vis* Christian men and *vis-à-vis* women governed by other matrimonial statutes. Though subsequently, cruelty to wives has become an offence under the penal code, such cruelty does not entail the Christian wife to a divorce.[48] The hindrance to reform has been caused by the Catholic dogma and the Protestant women have been the worst sufferers as their religion does not even subscribe to the theory of stringent divorce. Christian women (and more specifically, the Protestant women) set the task of reforming the archaic divorce laws as their first priority. These attempts have had a long and checkered history.

To initiate the process of reform, private member's bills were introduced in Parliament in 1958–1959 and in response, the matter was referred to the Law Commission (LC).[49] A draft bill titled, *The Christian Marriage and Matrimonial Causes Bill, 1960* was circulated by the LC to religious leaders and community organizations. The representatives of the Roman Catholic Church raised the plea that in adherence to the canonical doctrine, the Catholic community should be exempted from its application. The LC overruled these objections on the basis that the provision of divorce exists since 1869 and the Church had not raised any objection to this relief. The proposed bill was merely widening the scope of the existing provision and was not providing for any new reliefs.[50] After ascertaining the views of representatives of the community, a comprehensive report (*Fifteenth Report*) was prepared and submitted to the Ministry of Law by the LC on 19 August 1960. Due to the resentment expressed by the Catholic church hierarchy to the proposed Bill, the government returned the Bill with a request to further elicit public opinion.[51] Some of the clauses in the proposed Bill were re-examined and a Report (Twenty-Second Report) was submitted to the Law Ministry in December 1961. Following the recommendations of the LC, the government introduced the Christian Marriage and Matrimonial Causes Bill (Bill LXII B of 1962) in the Lok Sabha.[52] But the Bill was not debated and lapsed in 1971.

In 1983, in response to the letters received from Christian women, under the Chairmanship of Justice K.K. Mathew, the LC again took up the limited question of amending S. 10 of IDA.[53] After considering various options, the LC made a strong recommendation for amending the discriminatory provision as follows:

> If the Parliament does not remove the discrimination, the Courts in exercise of their jurisdiction to remedy violations of fundamental rights, are bound some day, to declare the section as void .... The Ninetieth Report of the LC was submitted to the Law Ministry in May 1983, but despite the recommendations, the government did not introduce the amendments in Parliament.[54]

This set in motion a chain reaction within the community which culminated in the Marriage Bill of 1994. Jyotsna Chatterjee, Director of Joint Women's Programme (JWP), a branch of the Christian (Protestant) institute for the Study of Religion and Society, mobilized community support and a memorandum signed by around ten thousand people, was sent to the Union Law Minister demanding changes in the personal laws.[55]

In February, 1986, members of various Women's Fellowships of the Churches in Delhi, representing the opinion of a wide cross-section of the Christian community, presented a memorandum to the Prime Minister of India.[56] It seemed that without the approval of the religious hierarchy, the government would not respond. So Jyotsna Chatterjee, with the backing of Church of North India (CNI) drafted a bill titled *'Christian Marriages and Matrimonial Causes Bill,* 1988' (CMMC), which was sent to the representatives of various churches.[57] At a Conference organized by CNI at Delhi, which was attended by representatives of various churches, as well as representatives of the Law Commission and Minorities Commission, a broad consensus among the various churches was arrived at. The Catholic church supported the recommendation to repeal the IDA, the provision of automatic recognition of church annulments by civil courts as in Goa but instead of a new Bill providing for divorce, suggested a *via media* that provisions of the *Special Marriage Act*, 1954 should apply to all marriages solemnized under ICMA.[58] This was a tactical and face-saving move which would save the church embarrassment that may be caused even by a tacit acquiescence to a Bill liberalizing divorce.[59] The rigid stand of the Catholic clergy was resented by the Catholic laity and several Catholic organizations extended their support to the proposed Bill.[60] Due to pressure from these organizations, finally, the Catholic church relented from its rigid and orthodox stand and withdrew its opposition to the proposed Bill. Following this, a broad forum titled, 'Ecumenical Committee for Changes in Christian Personal Laws' was formed, consisting of representatives of various churches, as well as secular organizations. The Committee finalized three draft Bills dealing with (i) marriage, divorce, custody, maintenance and right to matrimonial property; (ii) succession; and (iii) adoption. The Catholic Bishops Conference of India (CBCI), 27 Member Churches of the National Council of Churches in India (NCCI) and some other independent churches of west Asian traditions extended their support to the draft bills.[61]

Despite these sustained, systematic and marathon efforts, the government did not introduce the Bills. When a question regarding the status of these Bills was raised in Parliament, the government gave an evasive reply to the effect that the Joint Women's Programme, a women's organization had submitted certain draft legislations relating to marriage, divorce, adoption, maintenance and succession. Further, that since the policy of the government had been not to interfere with the personal laws of the minority communities, unless the necessary initiative came from the community concerned it would not be possible to bring in reform. The government also assured the house that the matter was being referred to the Minorities Commission.[62] These comments undermined the decade-long efforts initiated by community leaders and women's organizations to arrive at a consensus within the community to present a united front to the government. With this statement, the ball was thrown back to the religious hierarchy to reaffirm its commitment to Law Reform and women's concerns were once again made subject to the vagaries of the religious dogmas. This was a cause of concern for the community, as the response of the religious clergy to this new challenge could be highly unpredictable.

Through a stroke of luck, the bills endorsed by NCCI and CBCI were submitted to the government through the Minority Commission on 27 October 1997.[63] But while the community was awaiting eagerly for the presentation of the Bills to the Parliament, the government lost its majority and mid-term polls were declared. This political development has again delayed the process of reform. During the last round of deliberations, for reasons best known to the leaders, the consolidated Bill for marriage and divorce has been shelved and two separate Bills titled, *The Christian Marriage Bill* and *The Indian Divorce Bill* have been submitted along the lines of the current statutes. The provisions of matrimonial remedies have been brought on par with the *Hindu Marriage Act* and the *Special Marriage Act* with the additional provision of community of property or joint matrimonial property.

The thwarted efforts of Christian reforms, in comparison to the successive efforts of the Parsi reforms, reveal that in this political game, there is more to reform than a mere initiative from within the community as is publicly propagated. Perhaps there are extraneous considerations which have a bearing on the issue which can only be hinted at:

i. Except in pockets like Kerala, Goa and the north-east India, the community has neither the numerical weightage of the Muslims nor the economic clout of the Parsis. Hence, issues concerning women from this insignificant minority do not warrant serious political debate and can safely be rendered invisible.

ii. The Christian reforms were not initiated by the Church hierarchy of male leaders. Initiatives by women met with hostility from the conservative church leadership. Since the women's groups which supported the initiatives were mainly of an autonomous nature, they could not create the required political pressure to bring in legislative reforms. The government did not take a serious note of the initiatives by women as compared to the Parsi reforms initiated by the liberal male community leadership.

iii. The diverse viewpoints hindered the process of reforms. The community could not present a unified view to the government, as was the case with Parsi reforms. The government did not want to antagonize the conservative and politically powerful Catholic church.

iv. By the time the Catholic church withdrew its opposition and a unanimous front could be presented to the government in 1994, (in the post-Babri Masjid phase), the political climate had deteriorated as compared to the period when the reforms in Parsi law were enacted. The Hindu communal forces made the demand for a UCC an important political plank. Introduction of the Bill reforming Christian law would give an opportunity for the Hindu communal forces to rake the controversy and cause embarrassment to the ruling government. The minority Congress government led by the Rao ministry or the subsequent coalition government of the United Front could not afford this political impediment or to antagonize its Muslim supporters. What is the fate of this Bill in the hands of the new government is yet to be seen?

10.4 Constitutional Validity of Discriminatory Provisions

Confronted with this intricate political maze, the courts became the only avenue left for the community to bring in marginal respite. The constitutional validity of the discriminatory provisions of S.10 of IDA was first challenged before the Madras High Court in Dwarakabai's case. Adopting an extremely *anti*-women posture, the court ruled that the discrimination is based on a sensible and reasonable classification, after taking into consideration the ability of men and women and the results of their acts and hence it is not arbitrary. The court explained this logic further as follows:

> Adultery by a man is different from adultery by wife. A husband cannot bear a child and make it legitimate to be maintained by the wife. But if the wife bears a child the husband is bound to maintain it.[64]

Later judgments departed from this extremely sexist premise, but the courts refrained from striking down the offensive provisions as unconstitutional. In 1968, the Madras High Court held that the *Indian Divorce Act* is wholly out of date.[65] In 1989, a special bench of the Calcutta High Court in *Swapna Ghose v Sadananda Ghosh*[66] ruled that the offensive provision 'smacks of sex-discrimination.' The judgment also quoted with approval the recommendations of the *Ninetieth Report* of the Law Commission while it observed that if Parliament did not amend the offensive provision, the courts would be compelled to strike it down as unconstitutional. It however, stopped short of striking down the section as unconstitutional.

In 1990, in an interim application, in Mary Sonia Zachariah's case, the Kerala High court, set a time limit and directed the Government of India to give effect to the recommendations of the Law Commission within six months of the order.[67] But the government at the centre ignored these directions. So in February, 1995, in a landmark judgment, the Full Bench of the Kerala High Court stuck down the offensive provisions of S.10 of the IDA as arbitrary and violative of Articles 14 and 21 of Constitution.[68]

The court held:

> The legal effects of the provisions of S. 10 is to compel the wife who is deserted or cruelly treated to continue a life as the wife of a man she hates. Such a life will be a sub-human life without dignity and personal liberty. It will be humiliating and oppressive without the freedom to remarry and enjoy life in the normal course. Such a life can legitimately be treated only as a life imposed by a tyrannical or authoritarian law on a helpless deserted or cruelly treated Christian wife quite against her will and will be a life without dignity and liberty ensured by the constitution. Hence the provisions which require the Christian wives to prove adultery along with desertion and cruelty are violative of Article 21 of the Constitution of India.[69]

The community's eagerness to reform their laws can be judged by the number of interveners to the Petition. Protestant churches belonging to CSI, Bishops of the Eastern Orthodox Church, Christian institutions and women's organizations filed affidavits to be included as interveners in support of the petitioners.[70]

Since it was a High Court ruling, its effects were confined only to the State of Kerala. So in the years 1995–96, Christian women filed similar petitions in the Bombay High Court and by a judgment of the Full Bench delivered on 6 April 1997, the Bombay High Court also struck down the discriminatory provisions.[71] Whether Christians in other parts of the country will have to file similar proceedings, or whether the benefits can now be extended to the whole of India through a clarification by the Supreme Court is yet to be seen.

The Christians are also constrained by the denial of the remedy of divorce by mutual consent. The consenting couple has to take the circuitous route of first re-registering their marriage under the provisions of the *Special Marriage Act* and then filing a joint petition for divorce by mutual consent.

When this issue came up for scrutiny before the Supreme

Court, the Court commented that there was no point or purpose to be served by the continuance of a marriage which has so completely and signally broken down and recommended legislative intervention to remedy the situation.[72] But it held that even while adopting a policy of social engineering, the judiciary cannot introduce a new remedy into the matrimonial statutes.[73]

10.5 Judicial Responses to Challenges Posed to the Sovereignty of the Indian State

It is interesting to observe the manner in which the post-independence state established its sovereignty over its Christian subjects *vis-à-vis* two different sources of power, i.e. the statutes enacted by the British Parliament which was deemed as the parent law and the religious hierarchy of the Roman Catholic Ecclesiastical Tribunal.

As already mentioned, under S.7 of the IDA, the principles and rules of English Divorce Courts were to be automatically applied to matrimonial litigations by Christians in British India. The issue before the Madras High Court was whether after declaration of the country as a Republic, it was prudent for a free country, in the administration of justice, to adhere to the principle that the laws and regulations of its colonial masters should continue to be automatically adapted. In 1955, the Full Bench of the Madras High Court held that as per the provisions of the enactment of the *Laws Order Act* of 1950, English laws and procedures should be applied and it directed that the courts must follow the law and practice of the English matrimonial courts.[74]

In 1970, the special bench of the Madras High Court reversed this position and held that S. 7 cannot be read to incorporate the statute of a foreign country as part of the law of the land. But instead of striking down S.7, the court provided an explanation that practices and principles of the English matrimonial courts should be subjected to the scheme of IDA.[75]

In 1995, the Supreme Court in another significant judgment undermined the authority of Ecclesiastical Tribunal by holding that annulments granted by the Tribunal are not valid under the civil law and a couple who has gone through such annulment cannot contract a valid remarriage.[76]

Although Christian marriages are solemnized in church, they are simultaneously registered with a civil authority, i.e. the

Registrar of Births, Deaths and Marriages.[77] This transforms them into civil contracts and these contracts can only be dissolved through a court decree under the provisions of the IDA.[78] But most Christians are unaware of this dual procedure and believe that an annulment granted by the Tribunal qualifies them for remarriage. Since the church will not remarry the couple without a canonical annulment, generally a couple facing problems is encouraged to file a petition with the Tribunal and Christian couples are under the misconception that the annulment granted by the Tribunal constitutes a final dissolution of their marriage.

In the case before the Supreme Court, the woman had remarried after a church annulment. When marital discord arose, the husband approached the court for annulment on two grounds, i.e. i) the wife is insane, and ii) the annulment granted by the church in her earlier marriage is not valid under the civil law and hence her subsequent marriage to him is not valid.

In the proceedings before the trial court, the wife admitted her previous marriage and pleaded that it was annulled by Ecclesiastical Tribunal and this fact was known to the husband. Based on her admission of the earlier marriage, and disregarding her plea of the church annulment, the trial court granted a decree in husband's favour. The woman approached the High Court and not satisfied with its ruling, approached the Supreme Court. Dismissing her appeal, the Supreme Court declared:

> A marriage cannot be dissolved by a declaration granted by the Ecclesiastical Tribunal. Such annulments are not binding on the District Court or the High Court. The Ecclesiastical Tribunal cannot exercise a power parallel to the power which has been vested in the District Court or the High Court by the provisions of the Indian Divorce Act. The Church Authorities would continue to be under disability to perform or solemnize a second marriage for any of the parties until the marriage is dissolved or annulled in accordance with the statutory law in force.[79]

Through these decisions, the state has established its sovereignty over its Christian subjects subordinating the procedures laid down by the colonial state, as well as the religious hierarchy to its laws. This could be interpreted as a welcome move, but these decisions rendered the Christian marriages even more stringent and blocked all avenues of any progressive interventions.

In the case decided in 1955, the lower court had reduced the mandatory period between granting of a decree and its confirmation to six weeks from six months, following the developments under the English matrimonial statutes. But the 1970 judgment reversed this position and restored the period to six months, blocking the process of relaxing the stringent stipulations prescribed in 1869.[80]

In the second instance, the woman had taken recourse to the liberal grounds of annulments under the canon law, as is the common practice. As already mentioned, Christians to a large extent are unaware of the dual procedures. Due to its rigid stand on divorce, information about a civil decree of divorce is not easily forthcoming.[81] By subsequently holding such marriage as invalid, the stranglehold round Christian married women seems to have been tightened.

This judgement also raises other issues of legal ethics. In a situation of limited grounds of divorce, advocates are bound to exploit all possible legal loopholes to aid their clients. A common tactic adopted by advocates who specialize in Christian divorces is to advise their clients to file for a civil decree of annulment on the grounds either of relative impotency, insanity or fraud. It does seem that the legal strategy to question the validity of the marriage was formulated in the lawyer's chamber as can be seen from the two grounds pleaded by the husband: (i) insanity of the wife; and (ii) a technical ground of invalidity of marriage due to inadequate annulment.

As pleaded by the wife, the second husband had married the woman with the full knowledge of her previous marriage and its annulment by the church. So his act of entering into a marriage with her would amount to collusion and connivance. Matrimonial statutes specifically bar parties from taking advantage of their own wrongs while claiming reliefs. Since the remarriage was performed by the church with full knowledge of the previous annulment, it would seem that by the act of solemnizing her second marriage, the church led the woman into believing that the annulment, as well as the remarriage are legally valid and binding.[82] But finally, exploiting the procedural lapses, the husband was able to turn the situation in his favour, while rendering the woman a convenient scapegoat of a complicated legal maze. The Supreme Court seems to have aided this manipulation on the part of the husband and his advocate.

The judgement is a stark reminder that reforms cannot be confined to statutes but must extend to coherent and simple drafting style, easily comprehensible procedures and adequate dissemination of legal information regarding crucial issues like solemnization of marriages, their validity, women's rights within invalid marriages, their rights to custody and maintenance etc. Acknowledging the fact that literacy levels, in any given social strata, are lower for women and further, women would find it more difficult to access legal information under the prevailing socio-economic conditions, an additional responsibility is cast on the state by Art. 15 (3) of the Constitution to protect the rights of women and children. The state must ensure that the naive and the unassuming do not become victims of manipulative tactics adopted by legal practitioners. But it appears that the Supreme Court did not concern itself with this constitutional mandate while delivering this judgement invalidating an existing marriage. The only fault on the part of the woman seems to be her inadequate knowledge of the complicated and archaic law which governs her life.

In conclusion, it must be emphasized that to unravel the legal maze within which the Christian family laws are ensnared, a whole range of legal reforms are necessary and imperative. Unfortunately, even though the community is ready and willing, the political will to legislate for them is sadly lacking.

Notes

1. By the twelfth century the Western Church began to enact legislations for marriages of Christians. Pope Alexander III clarified the principle of indissolubility, declaring that once a Christian sacramental marriage was consummated no power on earth could dissolve it. Monterio, R., 'Belief, Law, and Justice for Women,' in *Economic and Political Weekly*, XXVII/43 & 44 (1992), pp., WS-74, 77.
2. In 1800, under the French Civil Code the power to regulate marriages shifted from the church to the state and thereafter the concept of contractual dissolubility was introduced. Gradually, the doctrine of separation of state and church and marriages as dissoluble contracts spread throughout Europe and later to the colonies.
3. Formation of these federations is a post-independence phenomenon. The Church of South India (CSI) was formed on 7 September 1947, within a month of India attaining independence. See note 11, p.73. The formation of Church of North India (CNI) is a more recent development of the seventies.
4. Article 371 A (Nagaland), 371 B (Assam) and 371 C (Manipur) of the Constitution of India.

5. It is believed that the trade routes between south India and west Asia were in existence from the tenth century BC during the time of King Solomon and Queen Sheba. See Mundadan, A.M., *History of Christianity in India Upto Sixteenth Century*, Bangalore: The Church History Association of India (1982), Vol.I p.20. Major religions of west Asia, i.e. Judaism, Christianity, Islam and Zorastrianism entered India through this trade route.
6. Thekkedath, J., *History of Christianity in India—1542–1700*, Bangalore : The Church History Association of India (1982), Vol.II, p.27.
7. Ibid., p.5.
8. Ibid., p.1.
9. Various religious orders, i.e. Franciscans, Jesuits, Augustinians and Dominicans set up their institutions in the coastal regions of Goa, Konkan and Bassein. Ibid., p.6.
10. Of particular significance is the Synod of Diamper which was held in 1599, through the initiatives by Archbishop Menezes. Ibid., p.28.
11. The Methodist Church, Anglican Church Mission, Church of Scotland Mission, Danish Missionary Society, Leipzig Evangelical Lutheran Mission, Free Church Mission, American Madurai Mission etc. See Grafe, H. *History of Christianity in India: Tamil Nadu in the Nineteenth and Twentieth Centuries*, Bangalore: The Church History Association of India (1982), Vol.IV (Part 2), p.24–34.
12. Ibid., p.98, Thekkedath, J., History of Christianity in India—1542–1700, p.23.
13. One of the fundamental differences between Roman Catholic and Protestant doctrines in the West is their diagonally opposite view on divorce. The Council of Trent rejected the opinion propounded by Luther and other reformers that marriage should be made into a civil contract and should be brought under the jurisdiction of civil courts. See Diwan, P., *Law of Marriage and Divorce*, Allahabad: Wadhwa & Company (1988), p.17.
14. Apart from Christians, the Act also protected persons converted to reformist sects like Brahmos and Arya Samajis who suffered loss of caste. The principle was first introduced through S.9 of the Regulation VII of 1832 of the Bengal Code. In 1850, the principle contained in the Bengal Code was made applicable throughout British India. It was a very brief Act consisting of only one section.
15. Under the provisions of this Act, the matrimonial jurisdiction was transferred from the ecclesiastical courts to the civil courts and the remedy of divorce was provided on a narrow and stringent ground of adultery (coupled with other offences). Prior to this a divorce could only be obtained through an Act of Parliament, a procedure which was extremely expensive. This statute rendered divorces within the reach of commoners.
16. For instance, Part IV of the ICMA lays down special procedure for registering the marriages of native Christians.
17. S.7 of IDA provides as follows: Court to act on principles of English Divorce Court.

18. *Sumathi Ammal v D. Paul* AIR 1936 Mad 324 FB.
19. The code became enforceable in the colonies w.e.f. 1 July 1870.
20. Art.1096. The ante-nuptial agreements could not be revoked after marriage (Art.1105), thus providing further security to women.
21. Arts. 1134–77.
22. Arts. 1130–33.
23. Art. 1119.
24. Art. 1766.
25. Art. 1122.
26. Arts. 1189 & 1190.
27. Art. 1104.
28. Art. 1187.
29. Ch. I, II & III of the *Decree of Divorce* promulgated on 3 November 1910. The enactment came into force w.e.f. 26 May 1911.
30. Art. 3 of the Family Law No. 1 promulgated on 25 December 1910.
31. Vargo N. and R. Goldfaden, 'The Goa Uniform Civil Code—Alive and Kicking,' *The Lawyers* X/7 (1995), p.21.
32. Art. 3 of *Usages & Custom of Gentile Hindus of Goa.* Identical statutes were enacted also for Daman and Diu.
33. The Portuguese did not resort to the divide and rule policy of the British which led to the constitution of Hindus and Muslims as distinct and mutually hostile communities. The Portuguese policy was one of assimilation and codification to facilitate smooth administration and hence various castes within their colonies were listed and their customs and usages were codified. But Muslims in Goa have lived on the periphery of social and political activity and there does not seem to be any categorization of their customs and usages under Portuguese rule.
34. Art. 1069. Also see Chadha, K., 'The Law that breaks the Constitution,' in *The Hindustan Times,* 8 August 1993.
35. Hence the Catholic community in Goa does not have to go through the rigours of a civil divorce, as is the situation in the rest of India under the IDA.
36. S.5 of the *Goa Daman and Diu (Administration) Act,* 1962.
37. In this context, also see the note of caution in the 'Foreword' by Chief Justice Sabyasachi Mukherji to Usgaocar's very useful translation of the Goan Family Code. Usgaocar, M.S., *Family Laws of Goa, Daman and Diu,* Panaji: Vela Associates (1988) Vol II.
38. S.29(2) of the *Indian Succession Act,* 1925.
39. *Abraham v Abraham* (1863) 9 MIA 195.
40. *Tellis v Saldanha* (1986) ILR 10 Mad 69.
41. *Francis Ghosal v Gabri Ghosal* (1907) 31 Bom 25.
42. In *Premchand & Anr v Lilavathi Shanti & Anr* AIR 1956 HP 17, while validating a custom which grants sons the right of inheritance to the exclusion of daughters, the court held that Christians are governed by S. 5 of the *Punjab Laws Act* of 1872 and not by *Indian Succession Act* which grants equal inheritance rights to daughters.
43. *Kurian Augusty v Devassy Alley* AIR 1957 Tra-Co 1.
44. *Solomon v Muthiah* (1974) 1 MLJ 53.

45. *D. Chelliah Nadar & Anr v. Lalitha Bai* AIR 1978 Mad 66.
46. *Mary Roy v State of Kerala* AIR 1986 SC 1011. Under the *Travancore Christian Succession Act*, the right of daughter was limited to a quarter of the share of the son or Rs 5000 whichever is less. Under the Cochin *Christian Succession Act* 1922, the share of daughter was one third of the son or Rs 5000, whichever is less.
47. Part B *States (Laws) Act*, 1951.
48. S.498(A) of IPC which was introduced in 1983, makes cruelty to wives and dowry harassment a criminal offence.
49. Fifteenth Report of the Law Commission, p.1.
50. Ibid., p. 26.
51. *Twenty-Second Report of the Law Commission*, p.1.
52. *Gazette of India*, Extraordinary, Part II, S.2, 22 June 62.
53. *Ninetieth Report of the Law Commission*, p.1.
54. Ibid., p.17.
55. I am relying upon a comment made by Archana Parashar to this effect. See Parashar, A., *Women and Family Law Reform in India*, New Delhi: Sage Publications (1992), p.190.
56. Ibid.
57. Two more Bills were also drafted at this time, i.e. Indian Succession Bill 1988 and Indian Christian Adoption Bill 1988.
58. Circular from the Catholic Bishops' Conference of India (CBCI), 90/cir-17, Sub-Christian Marriage Law II, 6 June 90.
59. See note 1.
60. The organizations include: All India Council of Christian Women (AICCW), All India Catholic Union (AICU); Satyashodhak, Bombay; United Christian Women's Association (Prerana), Pune; Justice and Peace Commission, Bombay etc.
61. This fact was brought to the notice of the court by the pleader for the state in *Ammini E.J. v Union of India & Ors* AIR 1995 Ker. 252 FB, p.258.
62. Unstarred question No.752 raised by Shrimati Susheela Gopalan answered on 6 March 1996.
63. A letter from the Secretary, NCCI to the author dated 7 November 1998.
64. *Dwarakabai v Prof. Mainam Mathews* AIR 1953 Mad 792.
65. *Solomon Devasahayam v Chandirah Mary* 1968 MLJ 289.
66. AIR 1989 Cal 1 SB. Also see, *Ramish Francis Toppo v Violet Francis Toppo* 1 (1989) DMC 322 (Cal).
67. *Mary Sonia Zachariah v Union of India & Ors* 1990 (1) KLT 130.
68. *Ammini E.J. v Union of India & Ors* AIR 1995 Ker 252 FB (Also reported as *Mary Sonia Zachariah v Union of India & Ors* 2 (1995) DMC 27 FB.
69. Ibid., head note (B) also para 31.
70. Ibid. para 3.
71. *Pragati Verghese & Ors v Cyril George Verghese & Ors* 1 (1998) DMC 375 (FB).
72. *Jorden Deigdeh v S.S. Chopra* AIR 1985 SC 935.
73. Ibid. Also see the Supreme Court directives in *Reynold Rajamani & Anr v Union of India* AIR 1982 SC 1261.

74. *George Swamidoss Joseph v Harriett Sundari Edward* AIR 1955 Mad 341 FB.
75. *T. M. Bashiam v M. Victor* AIR 1970 Mad 12 SB.
76. *Molly Joseph & Anr v George Sebastian & Anr* 1996 AIR, SCW 4267.
77. Under the provisions of Ss.36, 55 and 62 of the *Indian Christian Marriage Act*, 1872, every person authroized to solemnize Christian marriages is bound to send a copy of all the marriage certificates of the marriages solemnized by him to the Registrar General of Births, Deaths and Marriages at monthly or periodical intervals. Any marriage which is not solemnized as per the provisions of the Act is void as per S.4 of the Act.
78. Here it is necessary to emphasize that although Christian marriages are solemnized in the church they are governed by purely civil statutes, the *Indian Christian Marriage Act*, 1872 and the *Indian Divorce Act*, 1869.
79. See note 72, paras 3 and 5.
80. Several judgements have commented that the statutory waiting period of six months under S.17 of the IDA constitutes procedural unreasonableness. See *Neena v John Pormer* AIR 1985 MP 85 SB; *Swapna Ghosh v Sadananda Ghosh* AIR 1989 Cal 1 SB and *Ramish Francis Toppo v Violet Francis Toppo* 1 (1989) DMC 322 Cal.
81. The Metropolitan Tribunal of the Archbishop of Bombay has clarified the legal position through a pamphlet, '*Questions People Ask About Annulments.*' But the functioning of smaller tribunals is rather haphazard and the legal position ambiguous. See note 1.
82. Under the Goan code, annulments granted by the church are granted recognition by the civil court and the parties do not have to initiate separate proceedings. The proposed reforms include the suggestion of civil ratification of church annulments.

PART FOUR:

CURRENT DEBATES

11

Model Drafts and Legal Doctrines

Introduction

The diverse sources of personal laws, the uneven developments within different communities, politicization of women's rights during colonial rule and the aggressive majoritarianism of recent times provide the backdrop against which an ideal family code will have to be assessed. Although the contemporary debate is more a political rhetoric, there have been some attempts at formulating model drafts during the decade following the Shah Bano judgement. These attempts can broadly be grouped into three categories, i.e. drafts by legal scholars, women's organizations and the official fora. The legal doctrines on which the various recommendations are premised are examined in this chapter in the context of their implications to women's rights and their claim to modernity. The positive and negative features of these drafts, as well as their contradictions and internal inconsistencies are also highlighted.

The drafts are tentative and their aim is to initiate a debate and arrive at a consensus. While some drafts are comprehensive and deal with the entire gamut of personal laws, others address primarily the issues of marriage and matrimonial reliefs. The discussion in this chapter is confined to marriage, divorce, rights upon marriage and its dissolution, with a focus on economic rights of women. While the drafts by legal scholars and the official fora are fully formulated bills, the recommendations from women's organizations are principles and strategies which have yet to be formulated as legal drafts.

The drafts attempt to modernize and bring uniformity into the diverse family laws. The governing principles upon which the provisions rest are equality between the sexes, respect for the status of women and improvement in the conditions of children. Despite the common goal, the measures prescribed for improving the rights of women vary and at times even contradict each other. This is due to the fact that the drafts are premised on two different concepts of equality, the formal and the substantive.[1]

The formal approach to equality is based on equal treatment doctrine, viz. treating likes alike. As per this premise those who are the same or similarly situated must be treated in the same manner. When matrimonial reliefs are based on this approach, a gender neutral term 'spouse' is used while determining the rights of the parties within the matrimonial relationships. This doctrine equalizes the responsibilities and obligations of the husband and the wife who, within the prevailing socio-cultural and economic structures are unequally situated. This approach of treating the unequal partners of a marriage contract, with the mantle of equality will only serve to widen the gender divide.

Conversely, the doctrine of substantive equality directs attention to the question of historic and systemic disadvantage and the actual impact of reform upon the disadvantaged group. The objective of substantive equality is the elimination of the root structure of inequality in society.[2] This approach is not based on equal treatment of the law but addresses the actual impact of the law upon the concerned group. The two approaches to equality would inadvertently result in two different sets of rights and obligations within marriage.

11.1 Drafts by Legal Scholars

The two drafts discussed in this section were formulated during the period immediately following the Shah Bano controversy. During the debate on the *Muslim Women's Bill*, the then Prime Minister, Rajiv Gandhi, proclaimed that the enactment was the first step towards a Uniform Civil Code. This comment seems to have provided the impetus for these formulations.[3] According to the initiators, the drafts are based on the constitutional values of equality, social justice and secularism and incorporate the doctrine of legal pluralism. There is also an assurance that the code would not interfere with the right to religion or the freedom of minorities.[4]

Draft by the Bar Council of India (1986) (Hereafter referred to as the Bar Council draft). There seems to be an immediate response from the Bar Council of India to the Prime Minister's assurance regarding enforcement of a comprehensive family code. At their behest several legal luminaries concerned themselves with the task of drafting the various sections of an entire code. The whole gamut of personal laws, marriage, divorce, maintenance, custody and guardianship of children, adoption, legitimacy, inheritance, succession, implementation machinery and procedures were addressed. The tentative draft was discussed at a three-day National Convention organized by the Bar Council of India at Delhi in October 1986. The convention was attended by judges, lawyers, jurists, law ministers, legislators, law officers and law teachers from all over the country. This seems to be the most broad-based and comprehensive attempt at drafting a code. The recommendations of the convention were submitted to the Prime Minister. But the interest of the Bar Council of India in this issue seems to be one-time, as the Convention did not lead to any public debate or other follow-up measures.

The controversy of compulsory versus optional code seems to have dominated the convention. The initial draft proposed an optional code.[5] There was considerable opposition to this proposal from a section of the participants. The final recommendations have been in favour of a compulsory code with other options built into it[6]. The possibility of exempting certain communities from the application of part of the code or the entire code for a particular period or its implementation in phases has been examined. There was a consensus that sufficient time should lapse after the enactment of the code before it is brought into force. It was also felt that it might be more feasible to introduce reforms within small and specific aspects of personal laws by generating sufficient pressure within communities. There is a note of caution that though the enforcement of a new and progressive code from above may seem as a quick solution, this kind of crude homogenization may not be the best solution[7].

A concern was expressed regarding the style of legislative drafting. The Continental style renders itself to translation more easily and facilitates effective dissemination. It was recommended that this style should be adopted if the message has to permeate to the lower strata of society, than the present British style which is formal and meant mainly for lawyers.[8] But a uniform guideline regarding drafting style was lacking and this experiment seems to have been carried out only in a small portion of the code.

The draft prescribes compulsory registration of marriages and stipulates that a marriage certificate is essential for claiming maintenance.[9] This stipulation would adversely affect the rights of women and children.

A new section, i.e. effect of marriage which could have spelt out concrete matrimonial rights, deals only with irrelevancies like change of surname after marriage, a provision which is not found in any matrimonial statute and is based only on custom and tradition with wide regional variations. As per the stipulations of the draft, a change of surname after marriage seems to be mandatory and the claim to women's liberation lies in an absurd notion of granting the spouses the freedom to use the surname of either of them.[10]

While the draft retains the conventional matrimonial reliefs, the provisions regarding permanent alimony and maintenance during litigation are absent. Instead S.125 Cr.PC has been incorporated to provide for maintenance of wives and children during the subsistence of marriage and after its dissolution. The existing ceiling of Rs 500 per month has been abolished.

The draft protects the children's interests by recognizing them as an independent party during matrimonial litigation and stipulates that unless adequate arrangements are made for protecting children's interests, the matrimonial court should not pass a decree. The property of both parents should be settled in favour of the children so that the welfare of the children is not jeopardized due to paucity of funds.[11] These are positive provisions which would safeguard children's rights.

The draft introduces the concept of joint ownership of matrimonial property.[12] Under this concept all property acquired after marriage is deemed to be the joint property of the spouses. The concept of joint ownership of property was introduced by the French Code (Continental system) and has been subsequently adopted by several legal systems based on principles of English law (Commonwealth systems). Curiously, this right is placed in the section on inheritance rather than as a matrimonial right. Upon breakdown of marriage, the spouses would be entitled to half the share each. Upon death, the surviving spouse will inherit half the property while the other half devolves by testamentary or intestate succession. Property acquired by the spouses prior to marriage is deemed to be their separate property. This includes the customary gifts received by a woman, i.e. stridhana, mehr etc. Introduction of the concept of joint ownership of matrimonial property is a significant development in the realm of women's rights.

Draft by ILS Law College, Pune (1986) (Hereafter referred to as the ILS draft). A Bill titled 'The Indian Marriage and Matrimonial Act of', was presented at a public meeting in Pune in 1986, by ILS Law College. Thereafter, it was discussed at various seminars in Pune, Bombay and other places.[13] The authors cautioned:

The Bill provides for the repeal of all existing matrimonial statutes and to this extent prescribes a compulsory code. But elsewhere the authors have examined possibilities of an optional code or reform within personal laws in keeping with the federal structure of the Indian state.[14] The authors cautioned:

> There is great danger in enforcing a compulsory code in a sudden fashion as it might result in the alienation of the minorities which is not wise from the point of view of national integration. Even the most authoritarian State would avoid doing so. Any enactment of a uniform code must be preceded by a well conceived programme of public education.[15]

Viewed in the context of this concern, the provision of repeal of all existing laws seems to be a contradiction.

In addition to the prevailing matrimonial reliefs, the draft incorporates provisions of maintenance under S. 125 Cr.PC, conviction for bigamy under Ss. 494, 495 and 496 of IPC (which deal with matrimonial offence of bigamy) and punishment for non-payment of maintenance.[16]

The draft provides for compulsory registration of marriages and invalidates non-registered marriages. Not withstanding this stipulation, it seeks to marginally protect the rights of women and children in void marriages by conferring on them the right to maintenance.[17]

Adopting the formal equality model (reflected in the *Hindu Marriage Act*) it provides for maintenance to husbands,[18] a concept which is not prevalent in other statutes, the *Indian Divorce Act*, the Muslim Personal Law and the *Special Marriage Act*) and S.125 of Cr.PC.

Regarding rights to matrimonial property, a vague and confusing provision of the *Hindu Marriage Act*, which confers on the court, jurisdiction over property presented jointly to the parties at the time of marriage is incorporated.[19] Here there is no mention of any other property acquired by the spouses during the subsistence of the marriage, customary gifts, monetary security made to the bride at the time of marriage or the property of either of the spouses acquired prior to the marriage. Perhaps the concept of joint ownership of property is included in a separate bill dealing with inheritance and succession.

11.2 A Critique of the Proposed Drafts

There is no radical departure from the reliefs under the existing matrimonial statutes, The *Hindu Marriage Act*, 1955, the *Special Marriage Act*, 1954 and the *Parsi Marriage and Divorce Act*, 1936, and hence the claim to modernity cannot be sustained. The drafts have retained the conventional matrimonial remedies which were adopted from the English family law principles including the archaic remedy of restitution of conjugal rights, although the same has now been abolished under the English matrimonial statutes.[20]

Leprosy as a matrimonial offence which is a relic of biblical Christianity is retained, despite advances in the field of medicine which have helped to reduce the stigma attached to it. Archaic remedies such as bestiality, sodomy and unnatural sex have been retained. The term 'sodomy' also carries with it a biblical flavour.

Rather surprisingly, the ILS draft has also retained conversion as a matrimonial offence, under a purely civil statute and to this extent undermined the existing provision of the *Special Marriage Act*. The stipulation of conversion as a matrimonial offence had a rationality under religious laws which provided for marriages between persons professing the same religion. Since the draft provides for the solemnization of marriages of two persons belonging to two different religions, it is difficult to comprehend how change of religion can be a matrimonial offence. In any case, grounds such as leprosy, conversion, bestiality, sodomy and unnatural sex are hardly used in the normal course as grounds of divorce and would have more academic than practical use.

The drafts do not provide for maintenance as an ancillary matrimonial relief in matrimonial proceedings and the provisions of S.125 Cr.PC seem to have been substituted for this relief. The drafts recommend the abolition of the ceiling of Rs 500 prescribed under S.125 Cr.PC. While the stipulation for abolishing the ceiling is welcome, such a recommendation has also been made by the Law Commission in its *132nd Report*.[21] But it is not clear whether the right of maintenance will be shifted to a district court from the magistrate's court, where the proceedings are of a summary nature. Also under the prevailing matrimonial statutes, the courts can order lump sum maintenance and settlements. The proposed drafts do not seem to include this very useful provision. The procedures for enforcing an order of a criminal court are more stringent that those of the civil court and hence the provisions of S.125 Cr.PC will provide a better scope for enforcing maintenance orders. But the drafts have not addressed these deeper implications.

The ILS draft has retained the clause linking maintenance to sexual purity. It would be useful to compare the existing provisions regarding this stipulation. Clause (4) of S.125 Cr.PC stipulates that if the woman is living in adultery she is not entitled to maintenance; Clause (5) stipulates that if subsequent to the order, the woman is living in adultery, the husband can move the court to vary the order. In contrast, S.17 (6) of the ILS draft modifies the position and stipulates as under:

> If the Court is satisfied that the party in whose favour an order has been made under this section has had sexual intercourse with any person other than the spouse, it may, at the instance of the other party, vary, modify or rescind any such order in such manner as it may deem just.

Under the prevailing stipulations, the courts have ruled that the words 'living in adultery' used in clauses (4) and (5) of S.125 Cr.PC indicate that isolated instances of adultery are not sufficient to deny the wife maintenance. The husband must prove that the woman is living with another man and that other man is now maintaining the wife. Even when a husband has succeeded in obtaining divorce on the ground of wife's adultery, the wife cannot be denied maintenance.[22] By substituting the words, 'sexual intercourse' to the prevailing phrase, 'living in adultery' the draft narrows the scope of maintenance and renders the situation far worse for women than the prevailing stipulation.

Although an attempt to justify this stipulation can be made by pointing out that a similar restraint is also placed upon husbands, one cannot loose sight of the social reality that the norms of sexual morality applicable to women are very different from those which apply to men. Further, the stipulation would apply only to women in the normal course, as maintenance to husbands would only be under exceptional circumstances.

The draft renders maintenance a premium to chastity not only during the subsistence of marriage but even after the marital bond is dissolved through a decree of divorce. Since this provision is often used by husbands to embarrass women in court proceedings, the Law Commission in its *132nd Report* had recommended its abolition.[23] To this extent the stipulation in the ILS draft lags far behind and is even more regressive and anti-women than the prevailing legal position.

The stipulation by the Bar Council that maintenance would be granted only on the production of a marriage certificate will also adversely affect the rights of women and children and falls below the existing stipulation under matrimonial statutes and S.125 Cr.PC. In addition, proceedings under S.125 Cr.PC are of a summary nature and a woman is not required to prove the marriage. Women approaching the courts for maintenance are protected by the presumption regarding valid marriage laid down under S.50 of the *Indian Evidence Act*.

It is rather alarming to observe that the stipulations for maintenance contained in both the drafts are inconsistent with their objective, i.e. improving the rights of women and children. The drafting authors seem to have lost sight of this objective somewhere along the way.

The claim to modernity rests on the stipulation of monogamy and compulsory registration of marriages. The provision of registration exists under the Parsi, Christian and Special Marriage Acts and also, to a limited extent, under the Muslim law (where marriages are performed through written contracts, nikahnamas, and are registered with the office of the qazi.) S. 8 of the *Hindu Marriage Act* provides for registration of Hindu Marriages. But keeping in view the plurality of Hindu society, its loose social and religious organizations and non state regulatory structures, the Act has specifically laid down that non-registration cannot invalidate an existing marriage. The stipulations of compulsory registration seek to modify the existing legal position under the Hindu law to the detriment of women's rights. The provision seems to stem from a concern to curb bigamy by providing for valid proof of marriage and to this extent is defended as beneficial to women. But in reality, the suggestion is extremely short-sighted. The fact that a far greater number of women are likely to approach the courts for maintenance than for a criminal prosecution in cases of bigamy and maintenance is of far more crucial importance to women than penal provision of bigamy is something that seem to have escaped the notice of the drafters.

The recommendations are also confusing and contradictory. For instance, the Bar Council draft provides for registration of two types of marriages, i.e. civil and traditional.[24] The recommended procedure for registering a civil marriage is a verbatim repetition of the provision under the present *Special Marriage Act*. The procedure for registering a traditional marriage is complex. After solemnization of a marriage in the traditional form, a declaration signed by the parties and three witnesses must be sent to the registrar, which is treated as a mere notice. After the expiry of one month and after the Registrar satisfies himself that the requirements of a valid marriage have been complied with, the parties will have to present themselves before the Registrar along with three witnesses for completing the formalities of registration.

The marriage becomes valid and binding only after a certificate of marriage is issued by the Registrar. Hence, a section which elaborately lays down various traditional forms of marriage under different religions and some customs (S.21) seems redundant and illusory and a mere token gesture to provide for legal plurality. This will lead to unnecessary ambiguities and legal complexities. Traditional marriage is a social event with customary rituals and ceremonies which include the ritual of consummation. It is rather absurd to presume that a mandatory refrain from consummation under a statute, will prevent a couple from consummating the marriage performed traditionally until a certificate is obtained from the Registrar after a month. The implications of consummating a marriage performed in a traditional form before a certificate is obtained from the registrar are not addressed.

In this context, the ILS draft is more direct and provides greater clarity. While civil registration is mandatory, the parties are free to perform religious ceremonies of their choice. This provision is projected as incorporating legal plurality.[25] The marriage becomes legal and binding only upon a civil registration. But the draft stipulates that the parties are free to celebrate their marriage in the traditional manner. Since in any case, social events are celebrated with traditional rituals and ceremonies and sanction of the state is not necessary for these celebrations, providing for them within a statute would still amount to a gesture of mere tokenism and may lead to ambiguities which are best avoided.

The stipulations loose sight of the fact that civil registration of marriages is an alien concept under the Hindu law. If this stipulation has to meet with a measure of success, it is essential that the procedures are simple, inexpensive and decentralized. The drafts do not provide for this. The statutory notice of one month stipulated under the *Special Marriage Act* of 1954 is mechanically retained. The fact that this has proved to be the greatest deterrent against registering marriages under the *Special Marriage Act* has not been examined. The stringent stipulations have led to the mushrooming of several *vivaha karyalayas*, where registration of marriages has become a lucrative business. In Mumbai and other cities of Maharashtra and Gujarat, forced, fraudulent and invalid marriages can be registered for a premium within a matter of minutes, by manipulating the provisions of an outdated statute, *Bombay Marriage Registration Act, 1953* (BMRA) (which provides for the registration of a mere document and not of the marriage.)[26] Unscrupulous lawyers have successfully misled naive, unassuming, young couples, who wish to marry despite parental opposition, into registering invalid marriages in this manner. This could be done only because the procedures for registering a marriage under the *Special Marriage Act* are stringent and cumbersome and information about correct procedures is scarce. Hence there is an urgent need to simplify and decentralize the procedures of registration and reduce the existing notice period of one month. The drafts do not concern themselves with these current social realities.

The ILS draft starts off with rigid stipulation regarding registration of marriages, but the rigidity is relaxed in a subsequent section which grants women in void marriages the right of maintenance. If a woman can prove a customary marriage and subsequent cohabitation, despite the fact that the marriage is bigamous, she will be entitled to maintenance. While this is a positive suggestion which will be beneficial to women who are tricked into bigamous marriages, it leads to an internal inconsistency within the draft and reduces registration to a mere facilitating measure. This in any case is the present legal position. Hence while the Bill may rake a controversy over abolition of bigamy and compulsory registration of marriage, on closer scrutiny, the Bill would not drastically change the existing situation.

While granting women in void marriages a right to maintenance is beneficial, the provision of granting husbands a similar right of maintenance under the concept of formal equality would open up new avenues of harassment in matrimonial litigation and will saddle women with unwarranted encumbrances.

The prescribed ceremony of solemnizing the marriage under both the drafts is a marriage oath, rooted in Christianity, i.e. 'I take thee (name of the spouse) as my lawful husband/wife'. Most Indian women are under cultural constraints regarding pronouncing their husband's name. It is rather ironical that while Indian Christians have, in recent years, sanskritized their marriage ceremonies and other religious rituals, the framers of the draft have not paid due attention to evolve a solemnization which would reflect the tradition and culture of a pluralistic and predominantly rural Indian society.[27]

The failure to provide for the right of residence in the matrimonial house as a right flowing from the contract of marriage and for civil injunctions restraining the dispossessing of the wife from the matrimonial home seems to be another major drawback of both the drafts. Perhaps this provision is sought to be included under the section dealing with succession and inheritance. But the right to reside in the matrimonial home and the right to a share of matrimonial assets need to be clearly stipulated as matrimonial rights flowing from the contract of marriage. Further, since there is a lot of ambiguity regarding the matrimonial home in judicial discourse there is an urgent need to define the matrimonial home within the statute. The drafts have failed to respond to this pressing need.

So overall, despite their stated objective, the primary concern of the drafts seems to be with uniformity and regulation of sexuality than a genuine concern for protecting the rights of women and children.

11.3 Recommendations by Women's Organizations

The new phase of the women's movement which gained recognition during the early eighties has focused primarily on issues of violence against women—rape, dowry harassment and domestic violence. As a response to the growing need, several women's groups set up counselling and legal aid centres. In this process the groups have had to grapple with the failure of the legal system to protect the economic rights of women in matrimonial relationships. The recommendations of the women's organizations stem from this grassroot level experience. The recommendations discussed here are not fully formulated drafts but are principles upon which a bill could eventually be formulated.

Confronted with the problems of desertion leading to destitution, dilatory and manipulative tactics adopted by husbands to evade economic responsibilities and complex, cumbersome and expensive litigation processes, the concern of the recommendations is to plug existing loopholes within the legal system. The recommendations are clearly and unambiguously based on the substantive model of equality. The two drafts discussed in this section are rooted in two different streams within the women's movement, the autonomous groups and party affiliated women's organizations.

Women's organizations had been advocating a compulsory Uniform Civil Code till 1985.[28] But the Shah Bano judgment seems to be the turning point. Due to the distinct communal tone of the demand in recent times, there has been a gradual shift within the women's movement to an optional code and reform within personal laws.[29] So while a reading of the recommendations may seem like a brief for a compulsory code, these have to be contextualized within the shift towards an optional code and other possible strategies of reform.[30]

Recommendations by Vimochana and Lawyers Collective (1988): These recommendations were evolved at a workshop organized by Vimochana, a counselling and support group based in Bangalore along with *Lawyers Collective*, in May 1988 at Bangalore.[31] Protection of economic rights of women within marriage is a major concern of this draft. The draft proposes joint ownership of property acquired after marriage and grants women the right to reside in the matrimonial home. The husband is restrained from selling the matrimonial home or relinquishing the tenancy of the house without the consent of the wife.

Departing from the outdated 'fault' theory of divorce where one spouse has to prove a matrimonial fault (adultery, cruelty, desertion, insanity etc.) against the other, the 'breakdown' theory is based on incompatibility between the spouses and is borrowed from the principles of English matrimonial statutes of recent times.[32] With this, the archaic provision of restitution of conjugal rights is automatically abolished. To grant additional protection to women, it is proposed that a divorce demanded by the husband on the ground of irretrievable breakdown of marriage, should be granted only after he makes adequate economic provision for the wife. The draft stipulates that if the wife is in possession of the matrimonial home, her right of residence should not be extinguished upon divorce.

Since enforcement of maintenance orders is one of the major hurdles faced by women, the draft suggests that the husband should be required to make a voluntary disclosure of his assets and income immediately after a petition for divorce is filed by either of the spouses. Thereafter, he must deposit three months' maintenance for the wife and children. The amount must be calculated by dividing the income in equal shares between the husband, wife and minor children. The draft also stipulates that matrimonial courts should have the power to award lump sum maintenance, property settlements and salary attachments. Criminal and civil remedies to prevent violence against women including ouster injunctions are also proposed to provide protection to women within marriage.

The concept of father as the natural guardian of the child is sought to be abolished. The draft specifically protects the mother's rights to custody by stipulating that custody should be given to the parent who has taken the responsibility of looking after the child in the past. The draft also suggests that the lack of earning capacity of the mother or the fact that she has no dwelling should not disentitle her to the custody of the children and further, factors like alcoholism, violence towards the mother or the children should be considered while determining the best interest of the child in custody petitions.

The recommendations provide for compulsory registration of marriages but grant rights to women in informal relationships. Further, it is clarified that for the purpose of conviction for bigamy, cohabitation should be deemed as marriage. It recommends abolition of the offence of adultery under S.497 IPC.

The contradiction between providing for compulsory registration of marriages, granting recognition to informal marriages and providing for the rights of cohabittees, abolishing the punishment for adultery and broadening the base of conviction for bigamy (from formal marriages to informal relationships) has not been addressed in the recommendations. This seems to be its major drawback. If the rights of cohabittees are on par with the rights of spouses then registration serves no purpose at all and there would be no compulsion to register a marriage in a society where marriages are viewed more as social functions than legal contracts. Also if marriages and informal cohabitations are granted similar weightage and are deemed as offences then the whole premise upon which conviction for bigamy is based collapses. Here the existing law makes a clear distinction between solemn marriages and illegitimate and informal alliances where the ceremony of solemnization and permanency of the relationship is of greatest relevance. The widening of the scope would render adultery an offence rather than bigamy. But in the same stroke, it is recommended that adultery ought not to be deemed as an offence. So there is an ambiguity about whether the focus of the reform is curbing sexual immorality by a penal provision or protecting women's economic rights through widening the scope of maintenance to include women in informal alliances.

The recommendations introduce the remedy of irretrievable breakdown of marriage. This was proposed by the Law Commission in its *71st Report*.[33] But due to opposition from various women's organizations, the issue was abandoned. The opposition from the women's organizations was based on the fact that the remedy may not suit the Indian cultural ethos and women will be worse affected by it. It will provide an avenue for husbands, after years of marriage, to opt out on flimsy grounds and leave the wife and children in the lurch. While the opposition is valid, it is premised on an abstract theoretic basis since at the practical level, the remedy has already made a back door entry into the matrimonial statutes. Firstly, the ground of mental cruelty is used by the parties almost on the same footing as irretrievable breakdown of marriage.[34] Further by the 1976 amendment, several new grounds of divorce have been introduced in the *Hindu Marriage Act* and the *Special Marriage Act* which amount to irretrievable breakdown of marriage.[35] So the opposition does not have a legal basis. The proposed recommendations are an improvement on the current legal position as well as the Law Commission recommendations. As far as the husbands are concerned, the remedy is linked to economic settlements in favour of wives. But if the litigations for maintenance are an indication, the husbands will find myriad ways to wriggle out of their economic responsibilities.

Recommendations by the All India Democratic Women's Association (AIDWA) (1995): The AIDWA is affiliated to CPI (M) and has been active in the campaign for women's rights in the post-independence period. Its campaign against the enactment of the Muslim Women's Bill is particularly significant.[36] While initially the group endorsed the demand for a UCC, in its more recent convention, it has opposed this demand and has suggested alternate recommendations.

While concern for strengthening women's rights is the governing principle, the focus of the recommendations is upon the strategies of reform. At its national convention held at Delhi on 9–10 December 1995 titled Equal Rights, Equal Laws, AIDWA has proposed a step by step approach to bring in reform.[37] The convention rejected implementation of a comprehensive code, whether compulsory or optional, and instead has advocated legislation on specific issues and reform within existing personal laws as dual strategies of achieving the goal of gender justice.

An umbrella legislation would require the complete overhauling of all existing laws. This may pose obstacles in the path of immediate reform. Before implementing a comprehensive code, the foundation of equality between men and women would have to be laid. Secular legislation in specific areas of crucial concern will be an important step in this direction. The three specific areas of legislative reform proposed by the convention are: (i) right to matrimonial property; (ii) protection against domestic violence; and (iii) marriage registration facilities.

A legislation on joint matrimonial property would grant recognition to women's contribution to the household by way of unpaid labour and reduce the incidents of destitution which are common to women of all communities. A Domestic Violence Act could provide for both civil and criminal remedies. The demand for a law on registration of marriages clarified that there should be no interference in the nature of rituals and ceremonies of marriages. A decentralized machinery should be provided for registering marriages at the village levels and local panchayats could be granted the power of registration. Such registration could be of great help to women by providing documentary proof of a valid marriage in the event of dispute.

The convention acknowledged that the task of reform is not easy and it cannot be achieved without a sustained and broad based political struggle, campaigns and awareness programmes. Although there have been discussions within smaller groups in recent times, lack of widespread movements for changes within personal laws have been the major constraints. The convention resolved that campaigns within communities are important strategies for reform in personal laws.

Both the drafts discussed in this section are based on ground realities of helping women in distress situations and hence are aimed at seeking practical solutions to the problem despite some minor inconsistencies. If translated into specific acts, they would provide some relief to the economic problems faced by women.

11.4 Official Drafts and Parliamentary Trends

The four drafts discussed above reflect the concern of social organizations and legal academia. But unless these concerns are reflected in official state discourse, the process of law reform will not even get off the ground. Hence it is relevant to examine the position reflected in official drafts in recent times.

The recommendations made by the Law Commission from time to time have already been mentioned during the course of the discussion. But since the setting up of the National Commission for Women in 1990, law reform for women will have to be steered through this body. Hence the drafts formulated by them are important indicators of the direction of reform. In addition, there has been some debate on women's economic rights through the Private Members Bills introduced in the Parliament. One such Bill which was discussed at length in Parliament is also examined here to assess the response of Parliamentarians, for in the ultimate analysis, the legislative power to usher in reforms rests with them exclusively.

Bills formulated by the National Commission for Women (1994): It is rather disconcerting to observe that while the recommendations by women's organizations are cautious and practical, a Bill formulated by the National Commission for Women titled, 'The Marriage Bill 1994',[38] makes sweeping and unrealistic recommendations, throwing all caution to the winds.

The primary concern of the Bill seems to be abolition of

polygamy by ensuring compulsory registration of marriages. But instead of a facilitating measure (of providing proof in case of dispute), registration becomes an end in itself.[39]

The Bill stipulates that a declaration of marriage must be sent to the Registrar of marriages within three days of its performance. A fine of Rs 100 per day is levied for default for a period of one month and thereafter the marriage is deemed void.[40]

While prescribing such stringent measures of compulsory registration, the fact that the government has not been able to provide bare necessities like clean drinking water, primary education and basic health facilities to a large section of its people has been overlooked. The Bill does not spell out the measures through which the government will make it possible for people to register their marriages within three days of its performance.

While many countries in the south Asian region stipulate compulsory registration, no country has extended this logic so far as to invalidate an existing marriage with its adverse implications to women and children. In fact, the modern trend is towards granting rights and benefits to people in informal relationships. But the official trend in India seems to be tilting towards greater regimentation in family relationships.

The Bill abolishes the concept of restitution of conjugal rights. While this could be interpreted as a positive measure, it leaves no legal avenue for a deserted woman to apply to the courts for remedies of maintenance, custody of children, right of residence in the matrimonial home etc. unless she is willing to dissolve the marriage either by divorce or annulment. These crucial rights are incorporated only as ancillary reliefs in petitions for divorce and annulments. The Bill does not confer a statutory right of residence in the matrimonial house during the subsistence of marriage.

While stipulating stringent measures for registration of marriages, divorce is made easy by introducing the ground of incompatibility or irretrievable breakdown of marriage.[41] The statutory period of separation for a divorce by mutual consent is reduced from one year to three months.[42] The rationality behind rendering the bond of marriage so transient at one level and prescribing such stringent measures for its registration at the other are difficult to comprehend.

While the Bill deals elaborately with the issue of registration, only one section collectively deals with the economic rights of maintenance and residence, both during the subsistence of marriage and after its dissolution.[43] Here, adopting the model of formal equality, the Bill grants husbands and wives similar rights of maintenance and residence in the matrimonial home as ancillary measures.[44]

Another Bill drafted by the Women's Commission titled, The Domestic Violence to Women (Prevention) Bill (1994)[45], seems to offer a more practical solution to the problems faced by women and is based on the substantive model of equality. While the term 'domestic violence' is gender neutral, the Bill recognizes that the IPC already provides for violence of a generic category and concerns itself only with the specificity of violence faced by women in domestic situation.[46] The wide definition of violence includes not only any conduct amounting to cruelty, but also acts which violate the dignity of women. To make justice more accessible the term 'court' includes, family court, civil court and mahila court (which can consist of three women members of a gram panchayat). To avoid delays, a time frame of six months is prescribed for disposing off cases filed under its provisions. The Bill also provides for urgent *ex-parte* injunctions.

The most important aspect of this Bill is the stipulation to provide safe shelter to the woman either within the matrimonial home or alternatively, where feasible, in a separate residence. While the provision of a separate accommodation may not be viable in most cases, granting women the right to reside within the matrimonial home and securing their safety through protective orders is a very useful recommendation which will help a large number of women who are victims of domestic violence. As it is well established, the problem of domestic violence transcends class, caste and religious denominations.[47]

Private Member's Bill (1994): This bill was introduced by a Congress member, Veena Verma, in the Rajya Sabha in May 1994 and is titled, *The Married Women's (Protection of Rights) Bill* 1994.[48] It is in the nature of specific enactments like *Dowry Prohibition Act, Medical Termination of Pregnancy Act* and punishment for cruelty to wives (S.498(A) IPC) etc. Although these enactments altered the provisions of personal laws, they were not situated within the political controversy of Uniform Civil Code versus personal laws.

This Bill is significant for a number of reasons: (i) it provides for a new remedy which is non-existent in any matrimonial statute; (ii) it subscribes to the step by step approach; (iii) it is premised on the model of substantive equality; and (iv) the debate in Parliament provides insights into legislative responses to protecting women's economic rights.

While the drafts discussed earlier, grant women rights over property acquired after marriage (and also grant husbands reciprocatory rights over wives' property) this Bill grants rights to women over all the property of the husband and does not confer similar rights to husbands. Whether these provisions will be within the scope of protective discrimination under Art. 15 (3) of the Constitution is yet to be ascertained. But if they withstand this test, they will indeed be beneficial stipulations.

In its 'Statement of Objects and Reasons' the Bill highlights the exploitation faced by women:

> ...Although we are going to cross over to the 21st Century, our attitude towards women is still that of the feudal lords. Even today we are not prepared to grant the same liberty to women which men themselves are enjoying dauntlessly. ...The real cause of the exploitation of a woman by her husband is that she has no right in the house of her husband. ...Our laws confer the right of property on a woman only after the death of her husband. ...If a woman's right in the property of her husband is recognised she will start feeling secure and she will overcome her sense of helplessness and economic insecurity... .

The term property is defined broadly and is inclusive of movables and immovables whether ancestral or self-acquired, whether held jointly with other members of the family and includes contributions to provident fund and public saving schemes, bank deposits, shares, ornaments, land and dwelling house.[49]

The Bill grants the wife the right to live in the house of her husband, whether owned by him or by members of his joint family, the right to food, clothing and other facilities; the right to an equal share in the property of her husband and the right to be consulted in matters of family business and other financial transactions regarding the husband's property.[50]

The Bill was debated in the Rajya Sabha during three sessions, 12 August 1994, 9 December 1994 and 31 March 1995. The 23 members who commented on the Bill, barring stray adverse comments, unanimously supported the Bill. The adverse comments were made by Mr S. S. Ahluwalia (Congress) on the following presumptions: (i) In Indian society women are treated as Devis and hence would not need any such protective law based on western concepts. The Bill will cause chaos and confusion and is against the norms of Indian (read Hindu) culture and tradition. (ii) Since most people do not own property the Bill would benefit only a few educated, urban women who do not wish to fulfil their role as dutiful wives and want to while away their time in kitty parties.[51]

The Minister of State for Law, Justice and Company Affairs, Mr H.R. Bhardwaj endorsed these views and commented:

> We cannot insist that a husband must give fifty per cent of his property to his wife. The women's movement in India is different from the west. We cannot really think that women will be better only by making legal provisions. ...We will also have to see how the question of property can be settled under diverse personal laws...There was a suggestion to examine whether a flat allocated to a man under government schemes should be in joint names of husband and wife. But Income Tax regulations and other problems crop up. ...[52]

The problem of diverse personal laws was raised by the minister and not by any Muslim member of Parliament. It is also interesting to note that the reluctance to enact the Bill was not based only on diverse laws of succession but also on taxation laws. When reforms cause a dent in the economics of patriarchy, perhaps it is easier to stall them off by communalizing the issue. Due to the overwhelming support, the minister was constrained to assure the house that it will be re-introduced as a government Bill. But the government did not keep to this assurance, and after elections when the new United Front government assumed power there was no further development on this issue.

11.5 Salient Points Emerging from the Model Drafts

A summary of the salient points which emerge from the various model drafts may help to focus the debate upon the various and at times contradictory premises, examine their theoretical base and prioritize the reform measures.

1. Starting from the premise of a compulsory Uniform Civil Code, a consensus seems to be steadily, albeit gradually, emerging that the process of family law reform has to be cautious. Enforcing a compulsory Uniform Civil Code from above may not be the best solution. Campaign and education are essential strategies for initiating reform in the realm of personal law. This reality

seems to be permeating through the suggested reforms in the wake of the current political climate of majoritarianism.

2. If the goal is to improve the rights of women and children, the recommendations have to be based on the substantive model of equality. The use of the term 'spouse' while determining the rights and obligations of the parties to a marriage will result in further deterioration of women's rights. While concern for women's welfare is universal, the concern cannot be expressed in rhetorics. A greater clarity regarding the theoretical framework upon which the remedies are based needs to be evolved, particularly where the legal academia is concerned.

3. Abolishing polygamy through compulsory registration of marriages seem to form the core of the controversy over Uniform Civil Code. Although this concern is reflected in all the drafts (except the Private Member's Bill) the drafts have not been able to recommend viable solutions to resolve the issue. This is due to the two opposing concerns which are manifested in the issue (i) prescribing stringent measures (both civil and criminal) as deterrents to (male) bigamy; and (ii) providing for the rights of women in informal relationships. A tilt towards the first option will increase state control over people's lives and will drastically affect the rights of women and children. A tilt towards the second option will render inconsequential the provisions of monogamy and compulsory registration of marriages. The drafts have not paid due attention to this internal contradiction of the demand. The consensus seems to be governed more from a sense of middle-class morality and the Christian framework of marriage adopted by the liberals in India than a genuine concern for women's rights, as the recommendations seem to indicate.

4. A shift away from—marriage as a sexual contract to control/ regulate sexuality—to marriage as an economic contract where weaker partners need additional statutory protection (as in labour legislations) is visible in the drafts by women's organizations. There is an increasing realization regarding the link between divorce/desertion and destitution of women in development discourse. This has led to the coinage of a new term feminization of poverty. Some of the drafts reflect an urgency regarding this issue. Women's right to shelter in their matrimonial home and the right to a share of matrimonial property upon divorce are emerging as concrete strategies of tackling the issue at hand.

5. Since women's rights are integrally linked to the political developments, at this juncture of communally vitiated political climate, a step by step approach seems to be more feasible than a comprehensive code, either compulsory or optional. Some bills which have already been formulated, i.e. the Private Member's Bill on women's right to matrimonial property, the Bill by the Women's Commission on domestic violence which provides for urgent injunction and secures women's right to shelter and the recommendations of the *132nd report* of the Law Commission (abolishing the ceiling of Rs 500 per month maintenance under s.125 Cr.PC) can be the starting points of a campaign.

6. There seems to be one lacuna which runs through all the drafts which have been examined. The drafts are based on either of the two premises: (i) Women as a class are non-working spouses and their only contribution is unpaid domestic labour; or (ii) Men and women are equal partners and hence their rights, duties and responsibilities are equal and of a similar nature. A third category of women, who are the sole providers of their families, are invisible in this debate. The recommendations do not protect these women who shoulder the double burden as wage earners and home makers. The implications of introducing the concept of joint family property and equal right to matrimonial home and maintenance etc. using a gender neutral term spouse would be detrimental to the rights of these women, most of whom belong to the marginalized sections of society. The concerns of this large category of women are not reflected in any of the drafts.

In conclusion, while there have been some concrete efforts at evolving drafts which would protect women's rights, a sustained campaign around specific issues to pressurize the government to bring in reform is lacking. The fact that despite the media publicity on women's rights, no pressure could be exerted even to remove the ceiling of Rs 500 set in 1955, as recommended by the Law Commission, is an indication of the lack of a concentrated campaign. Women's rights seem to be lost in the larger controversy around Uniform Civil Code which today, has become a political question. Only through a step by step approach to bring in small and specific reform through concentrated campaigns can the rights of women be salvaged from the political entangle within which they are currently enmeshed.

Notes

1. The substantive model of equality is governed by Art. 15 (3) of the Constitution while the formal equality is based on Art. 14 and 15 (1) of the Constitution.
2. Kapur, R. and B. Cossman, *Subversive Sites*, New Delhi: Sage Publications (1995), p.175-80.
3. *The Times of India* 17 July 1986; Also see Mishra, V.C. (ed.), 'Special Issue on Uniform Civil Code' *Indian Bar Review* XVIII/3-4 (1991), p.293-4.
4. Mishra, V.C. Ibid and also See S.P. Sathe, 'Uniform Civil Code—Why? What? and How?', in *Towards Secular India* I/4 Bombay: Centre for Study of Society and Secularism (1995), p.31.
5. Mishra, V.C. p.65. The initial draft proposed that Muslims and scheduled tribes be exempted from its application. An individual Muslim could opt to be governed by it. The tribal communities could be governed by it only by a notification in the Government Gazette. S.1 (a) and (b) of the proposed draft.
6. Mishra, V.C. See note 3, p.iv.
7. Ibid., p.vii.
8. Ibid.
9. S. 26, Ibid., p.65.
10. Ss. 36 & 37. Ibid., p.100.
11. Ibid., p.121.
12. Ibid., p.238.
13. The presentation at the Seminar on Personal Laws and Gender Justice organized by the Centre for Study of Society and Secularism, Bombay on 19–20 February 1994.
14. Dr S.P. Sathe has emphasized that federalism is not only a geographical phenomenon but also cultural and ethnic, that the need to be different is not anti-national and that nationalism does not require regimentation. See Sathe, S.P., 'Uniform Civil Code Implications of the Supreme Court Judgement,' in *Economic and Political Weekly*, XXX/35 (1995), p.2165.
15. Ibid. Also see note 4.
16. Ss. 17 & 33 of the proposed Bill.
17. S.18 of the Act r/w S.3(a) and S.9 of the proposed Bill.
18. S.17 of the proposed Bill.
19. S.27 of the *Hindu Marriage Act*, 1955.
20. S.20 of the *Matrimonial Proceedings and Property Act*, 1970.
21. The report brought out under the Chairmanship of M.P. Thakkar was submitted to the government in April 1989.
22. *Mahalingam Pillai v Amsavalli* (1956) 2 MLJ 289 DB; *Gulab Jagduse Kakwani v Kamla Gulab Kakwani* AIR 1985 Bom 88; *Khem Chand v State & Anr* 1 (1990) DMC 38 All; *T. Raja Rao v T. Neelamma* 1990 Cri.LJ 2430 AP; *Vijay Shankar Prasad v Manika Roy* 2 (1990) DMC 457 Pat etc.
23. Point 7 of the *132nd Law Commission Report* suggested that Sub-section (4) and (5) of S.125 depriving a wife from claiming maintenance on the ground that she is living in adultery should be deleted as it is by and large invoked to embarrass and harass the wife.

24. See Chapter III, sections 15 to 24, p.86-8.
25. See note 14 and 15.
26. Agnes, F., 'In the Dock,' *Humanscape*, Bombay August 1996, p.26.
27. See Table 5 for the urban-rural distribution of the population.
28. *Report of the Committee on the Status of Women*, (1974), 'Towards Equality,' p.142. Further, at two successive national conferences of women activists held at Bombay in 1980 and 1985 passed resolutions demanding a Uniform Civil Code. See resolutions passed during the two conferences.
29. Kishwar, M., 'Pro Women or Anti Muslim; the Shah Bano Controversy,' *Manushi* VI/2 (1986), p.4. Agnes F., *State, Gender, and the Rhetoric of Law Reform* (Bombay), Research Unit on Women's Studies, S.N.D.T.University (1995), pp.204-9; Gandhi, N. & N. Shah, *Issues at Stake*, New Delhi: Kali for Women (1991), pp.252-9; The Forum Against Oppression of Women, (1995) *Views on the Uniform Civil Code* presented at a public meeting held on 22 July 1995 (unpublished document available with the group); Anveshi Law Committee, 'Is Gender Justice Only a Legal Issue— Political Stakes in UCC Debate,' *Economic and Political Weekly*, XXXII/9-10 (1997), p. 453.
30. Vimochana, The Quest for a Uniform Civil Code: Some Dilemmas', some issues (1988) (unpublished document available with the group).
31. 'Recommendations of the Lawyers Collective Bangalore Law School,' *The Lawyers* III/7 (1988), p.20.
32. The remedy is based on a similar provision under the English law under S.2 of the *Matrimonial Causes Act* 1973. See Jackson, J. (ed.), *Raydens's Law and Practice in Divorce and Family Matters*, London: Butterworths (1983), p.2499–501.
33. The report was brought out in 1980 and was circulated to various women's organizations in 1981.
34. A scrutiny of the reported cases indicates that husbands file petitions on the ground of mental cruelty making frivolous allegations like refusal to cook food, asking the husband to clear the dining table in the presence of friends, not following specific instructions about taking care of his mother, quarrelsome nature of the wife, arrogance due to higher educational qualifications, pressurizing the husband to set up a separate house etc.
35. S.13 (1A) of the *Hindu Marriage Act* and S.27 (ii) of the *Special Marriage Act* stipulate that if after one year of obtaining a decree of restitution of conjugal rights or judicial separation the cohabitation is not resumed, either of the parties can approach the courts for a divorce. In actual effect, if the wife has obtained a decree of restitution of conjugal rights and the husband thereafter has refused to comply with the decree, one year later he can obtain decree of divorce. See the decision in *Saroj Rani v Sudarshan Kumar Chaddha* AIR 1984 SC 1562 in this respect. This provision was introduced in the *Parsi Marriage and Divorce Act* in 1988 by adding S.32(A).
36. Memorandum dated 17 April 1986 to the President of India by Susheela Gopalan, General Secretary, AIDWA and *Susheela Gopalan & Ors v Union of India*, No.1055, dated 24 July 1986.

37. Karat, B., 'Uniformity vs equality: The Concept of uniform civil code,' *Frontline* 17 November 1995, p.82, Singh, K. 'Combating Communalism,' *Seminar*, n.441 (1996), p.55.
38. The draft was approved by the Expert Committee on Laws in its meeting held on 18–19 August 1994. The bill is unpublished. For various provisions of the bill see Tiwari, B., 'Marriage Laws Revamped,' in *The Lawyers*, X/5 (1995), p.28.
39. The Statement of Object and Reason declares, 'A Bill to consolidate and amend the law relating to marriages in India and to provide for their compulsory registration.'
40. S.17 proviso of the draft Bill.
41. S.7 (2) of the draft Bill.
42. S.11 (i) of the draft Bill.
43. S.10 of the draft Bill.
44. S.14 of the draft Bill.
45. This bill seems to be debated along with the Marriage Bill, see Karat, B., 'Uniformity vs equality' n.38. For text see Appendix I.
46. The problem is grave as the statistics reveal. See Table 6 for the number of women who have died in unnatural situations in the city of Mumbai.
47. See Table 7 for a religion-wise distribution of cases filed in Mumbai under S.498(A) IPC (cruelty to wives) for the period 1990-1995.
48. Bill No.XXV of 1994 introduced by Veena Verma in the Rajya Sabha on 13 May 1994. For text see Appendix II.
49. S.2 (c) of the Bill.
50. S.3 of the Bill.
51. RSD dated 12 August 1994 p. 824–6 (unpublished).
52. Ibid., p. 836–8.

12

Strategies of Reform

12.1 Implications of the Shift in the Focus of UCC from Gender Justice to National Integration

The genesis of the demand for uniform family laws is situated within the women's movement of the pre-independence era within the larger context of the nationalist struggle. The All India Women's Conference (AIWC) was an active protagonist of this demand and placed the issue of gender within the political agenda. This led to some enactments during the thirties securing women's rights within marriage.

In 1940, the National Planning Committee, while focusing upon the economic dimension of women's rights, resolved that in a planned society, women's place shall be equal to that of men and to achieve this recommended the enactment of a Uniform Civil Code.[1] During the initial phase, the UCC was to be an optional code which could gradually replace the different personal laws followed by various religious communities. This position seems to have continued till the draft for the UCC was presented at the Convention held by the Bar Council in 1986 (discussed in the preceding chapter).

Later, during the Constituent Assembly debates, the focus shifted from gender equality to national integration. The demand for UCC was seen as a corrective measure for the divisive colonial policies. Integration of communities in the modern state was sought to be achieved through uniformity of personal laws. While pressing for setting a timeframe for the enactment of a UCC M.R. Masani, Hansa Mehta and Rajkumari Amrit Kaur bemoaned the continuance of personal laws as keeping India back from advancing to nationhood.[2] The proceedings of the Constituent Assembly show a marked absence of discussion about the significance of a UCC for women. The issue of women's rights seems to have been subsumed beneath graver political concerns of building a modern state.[3] There was also a presumption that a modern state would automatically ensure gender justice.

In the years immediately following independence, the issue of Uniform Civil Code, either for reasons of ensuring gender equality or to further the cause of national integration, did not figure in any important national debate. But a passing reference to this demand was made by conservative sections while opposing the Hindu law reforms.[4] In 1974, the report of the committee on the status of women shifted the focus and situated gender justice at the centre of the core of the demand for a UCC, but did not quite distance itself from the premise of national integration.[5]

During the subsequent decades, the issue was further problemetized by judicial comments. While examining gender bias within the Muslim personal law, the courts have explicitly commented that oneness of the nation as well as loyalty to it would be at stake if different minority groups follow different family laws.[6] It is a matter of debate whether a Uniform Civil Code will ensure national integration and communal harmony.[7] But the comments have enabled the communal forces to appropriate the demand. This appropriation has posed insurmountable obstacles in the path of family law reform from the perspective of gender justice. To counter the communal propaganda, some scholars, in recent times, have differentiated between a uniform civil code and a common civil code and held that the demand for a uniform code is premised upon modernity and gender justice, whereas the common code would only ensure commonality of oppression.[8] But this differentiation between the words 'common' and 'uniform' appears to be rather stretched.

The root of the communal propaganda is centered around the growth in the Muslim population. As per this premise, non-implementation of Art. 44 of the Constitution has resulted in a growth of the Muslim population and this constitutes a danger to the majority community. The image of a polygamous Muslim has been constructed to serve this propaganda.[9] It is in this context that monogamy imposed by a compulsory code becomes the need of the hour.[10] The gains to the gender concerns by the imposition of monogamy seems to be only incidental. Muslim scholars have countered this with statistical data and focused upon sociological factors such as poor socio-economic conditions and low level of education among the Muslims which are the root causes of a slight increase in Muslim population and pointed out that a UCC will not resolve this problem.[11] But the doctrine of monogamy (which is the basic tenet of Christianity) also draws the unquestioning support of liberals moulded in the western ethos. Here bigamy is reflective of pre-modern barbarism and monogamy symbolizes civilization, enlightenment, modernity and progress.[12]

Within the context of identity politics, a support to the demand of a Uniform Civil Code is being construed almost as a betrayal of the community not only by the religious leadership but also by secular and progressive sections of the community. The shift in the trend can be gauged by the responses to the Tilhari judgment on triple talaq and the Supreme Court verdict on conversion and bigamy discussed in Chapter 8. The obvious reference to Muslims in respect of partition and two nation theory in the case concerning Hindu bigamy have also evoked critical comments. The secular Muslim response to these comments has been: 'Those who stayed in India had a right to remain here as they were citizens of this country. This does not grant the state the power to deny Muslims a right to a separate cultural identity.'[13]

It is within this restricted sphere of communalized ambience that reforms from within assume significance. This course upholds the principle imperative to a democratic polity, that culturally distinct communities must be granted a degree of autonomy to exist alongside a majority nation. The trends within non-Muslim minorities in this direction have already been discussed in the preceding chapters. But since the issue of UCC is locked within the binaries of Muslim minority and Hindu majority, the efforts by Muslim intelligentsia and pro-reform organizations become important markers in this discourse.

12.2 Scope of Reform from Within

There is unanimity among the Muslim social reform organizations regarding the need to bring in changes in the Muslim law. A rejection of the demand for UCC cannot be construed as a negation of women's rights. There is a consensus that obstinate opposition to reform will worsen the situation and substantiate the communal propaganda that Muslims are a backward community, hostile to any change that favours women. A community which is already the victim of prejudice can ill-afford to have its negative image reinforced.[14] Since the fundamentalist religious clergy and self-serving politicians are content to preserve the status quo, the mantle of reform must now fall upon the Muslim intelligentsia.

The progressive groups have identified certain specific issues which need immediate modification. Regulation of polygamy and arbitrary divorce, delegated right of the wife to divorce herself, right to matrimonial property and provision for a reasonable and fair settlement upon divorce are being listed as areas which need immediate intervention. The suggested strategies for reform range from codification/modification of the entire realm of Muslim personal law to small, specific and focused interventions.

Codification of Muslim personal law in accordance with the needs of a modern society, through community-based initiative has been suggested by several scholars as a possible strategy. Citing the experience of enacting the *Dissolution of Muslim Marriages Act*, 1939, a positive note has been expressed by many scholars that it would be possible to create a broad forum of legal scholars and ullamas to lay the ground for eventual codification.[15] Syed Shahabuddin whose reactionary stand has often been criticized by reformers, also has endorsed the need for codification.[16]

But the process of codification can be initiated only through an institutional framework. The setting up of such institutions can be facilitated by the state. Alternatively, if the interventions by the state are viewed as an encroachment upon the autonomous space of the minorities, the concerned sections would first have to create an institutional structure for rationalization and/or reform and then dialogue with the different segments of the community to work out a consensus.[17]

Another variation of the same module is the suggestion to set up a commission comprising of Muslim women, judges, lawyers and ullamas to elicit Muslim public opinion on specific issues with the view of bringing in certain modification in the Muslim law.[18] The suggestion is based on the model adopted by Pakistan to bring in reform. In 1955, the Pakistani government set up the Rashid Commission to look into the reforms within Muslim personal law in response to the demand raised by women's groups. During Ayub Khan's regime a seven member commission was appointed to frame a questionnaire to seek the referendum of the people on the issue of family law reform. Based on the recommendations, the *Family Law Ordinance* of 1961 was enacted which regulated polygamy, provided for compulsory registration of marriages, set up arbitration councils to oversee divorce proceedings and granted women the right of delegated divorce.[19]

The criticism against this suggestion has rightly been that what was possible in a Muslim majority country may not suit the socio-political conditions of minority Muslims in India. The pro-reform voice within the community is weak and the reformers lack the institutional support available to the fundamentalist religious leaders to influence public opinion.[20]

While the task is difficult, it may not be unsurmountable as the developments in Bihar indicate. A progressive forum has drafted a Bill titled, The Muslim Family Council Bill.[21] The aim is to set up a Muslim Family Council consisting of a former Muslim High Court judge and six members to regulate the process of Muslim marriage and divorce. The Bill provides for compulsory registration of marriages. The Council is granted the power to regulate polygamy and arbitrary divorce. Women are granted the right of delegated divorce (talaq-e-tafwiz). The suggested reforms have the scope of introducing significant advancement in the rights of Muslim women.

Another course is to work towards piecemeal reform of the practices which violate the provisions of the constitution on a priority basis. This could be a small beginning which could lead to the eventual codification of the entire corpus of Muslim personal law. Since arbitrary and unilateral triple talaq has been one of the most controversial issues, this practice needs to be declared un-Islamic. The practice is prevalent mainly among Sunni Hanafis. But Pakistan and Jordan which are Sunni majority countries have abolished the practice and it would not be difficult to follow this course in India.

12.3 Reform through Judicial Interventions

While the various strategies are being debated within the Muslim intellectual fora, the resentment among women who are victims of arbitrary divorce is growing. At the time of the enactment of the Muslim Women's Bill several Muslim wor en joined the campaign against the Bill, voiced their protest and endorsed the demand for a Uniform Civil Code. In this regard, the efforts by the Muslim Satyashodhak Mandal based in Maharashtra are particularly significant. The organization has been addressing the problems of women victims of arbitrary divorce and raising the demand for a UCC to safeguard the rights of Muslim women for well over a decade.[22]

The resentment of women is manifest in delegations to the government and petitions to the Supreme Court. In 1983, Shehanaz Sheikh, a 24-year-old Muslim woman divorced by her husband through oral talaq, filed a petition in the Supreme Court challenging the constitutional validity of the various provisions of the Muslim law and pleaded for the enactment of a Uniform Civil Code.[23] The petition evoked wide publicity and the support of various women's organizations in the country. But subsequently, the petition was withdrawn, due to the apprehension in the post Shah Bano phase, that it could provide fuel in the hands of communal elements.[24]

A decade later, in 1995 the Supreme Court admitted a Writ Petition filed by Zenat Fatima Rashid, a divorced Muslim woman challenging the adverse provisions of Muslim personal law. She has demanded a common civil code to ensure justice to Muslim women who are victims of triple talaq.[25]

The petition seems to have originated from individual effort. In a recent interview, Zenat has remarked that no organization has extended support to her cause.[26] Individual efforts by women cannot be sustained without adequate institutional and organizational support. The process of reform cannot be confined to a single petition as it involves issues affecting the whole community. The Supreme Court would keep this factor in view while bringing in legal reform through litigation as the process of family law reform among the Parsis and Christians indicates.

While the Petition filed by Zenat is pending, the Supreme Court gave a ruling on the interventionist role of the judiciary. A public interest petition filed by an Ahmedabad-based women's organization, the Ahmedabad Women Action Group had challenged the various discriminatory aspects of Muslim law including polygamy and triple talaq. While dismissing this petition (and other similar petitions challenging the discriminatory aspects of Hindu and Christian law) without examining the merits of the contentions, the apex court ruled that it is not within the jurisdiction of the courts to make laws for social change. The court observed that the petitions raised issues of state policy and it is the function of the legislature to lay down these policies of social change. With this ruling, the scope of reform through judicial interventions has been curtailed.[27]

12.4 Standard Nikahnama and Pre-Marriage Agreements

Since reform through legislative and litigation process has met with severe obstacles, attempts are now being directed towards mechanisms of change which are built in within the personal laws. Here, while anti-women practices of unilateral talaq, a token amount of mehr etc. have gained popularity in recent times, through a nexus between qazis, lawyers and husbands, several protective measures provided by the Islamic law have become obscure.

A powerful weapon provided by Islam to the protection of women is the right to enter into pre-marriage agreements (Kabein nama) and stipulate conditions in the marriage deed.[28] A Muslim woman also has the additional protection of mehr which forms an essential ingredient of a marriage contract (without such stipulation the formality of marriage cannot be complete) But these safety measures have been corroded and anti-women practices have become the norm. The judicial recognition granted to these anti-women practices and the media sensationalization of these events have reinforced their validity and these are now viewed as the norm, rather than aberrations of community practices.

Rather curiously, even in the 'best of all laws' theory adopted by some model drafts[29] there is no mention of the positive stipulations of the Muslim law. This is perhaps due to the fact that the basis of the reform is a comparative study of the statutory provisions of different matrimonial laws and popular misconceptions and misappropriation of the Muslim law. Hence these model drafts also subscribe to the communal presumption that Muslim personal law is least favourable to women. A scrutiny of these provisions is essential, if the 'reform from within' strategy has to yield some positive results.

From the earliest times, Islam gave due recognition to the fact that women, being weak and unequal partners in a marriage, must be provided with additional protection. Since marriages are contracts between consenting individuals, the woman has the option of laying down detailed conditions of marriage including provision of a separate house for her use and the right to abstain from cooking food or performing other domestic chores.

Conditions could be included in the nikahnama prohibiting the husband from taking a second wife or constraining him to make it subject to her consent. The wife can also spell out terms of fair and kind treatment and prescribe the terms of divorce. Through this stipulation the husband can be committed to the *ahsan* mode of talaq and also provide for a machinery for reconciliation. She can also set out the detailed terms of a divorce, including *mattan-bilmaroof*, i.e. reasonable and fair provision. The agreement can also contain a clause assigning to the wife her right of delegated divorce, i.e. talaq-e-tawfiz. The contract may also include agreement on the proportion of share of the divorced wife in the movable and immovable property acquired during the subsistence of marriage.[30]

More than half a century ago, Maulana Ashraf Ali Thanavi, the renowned Islamic, Jurist of Hanafi Sunni school, drew up a model contract called Kabein Nama providing for delegation of right of divorce to wife or any third party which may be enforced in the event of the violation of any of the terms and conditions. Even prior to this, in 1929, Iqbal, the philosopher-poet and jurist of Islam had strongly recommended that conditions including monogamy and delegated divorce are to be included in the nikahnama.[31]

Iqbal Ansari has argued that inclusion of such provisions in the marriage contract will not need any modernization of Islamic laws through ijtihad as it is already provided for in the traditional schools of Muslim jurisprudence. Courts in India have recognized and enforced the conditions in a marriage contract or a pre-marriage contract including the right of talaq-i-tawfiz.[32]

Though theoretically, the choice to enter into a marriage agreement lies with every woman (or her parents as the case may be), the social situation of Muslim women renders it extremely difficult to implement these provisions while negotiating a marriage proposal.[33] The educational backwardness of Muslims especially of Muslim women and the low status that the Indian ethos accord to women do not leave much scope for any conditions to be stipulated in a marriage contract.

The obstacle can be overcome only if the Muslim Personal Law Board issues a direction that a standard nikahnama, with all protective provisions written into it, must be used for solemnizing all Muslim marriages in India. To facilitate the process, a group of Muslims led by a few women have prepared a model nikahnama ensuring the conditions that favour women.[34] One important suggestion is that the amount of mehr must be stipulated in gold coins, valuables, bank securities or immovable property rather than in currency to meet with the inflation and currency devaluation.

The draft evolved by the group has been forwarded to the All India Muslim Personal Law Board (AIMPLB) and the group has had preliminary discussions with the members of the Board. But sustained pressure has to be maintained through community-based organizations until the AIMPLB accepts the recommendations and issues the necessary directions.

Unfortunately, the efforts of 'reform from within' have remained sporadic and the secular voice muffled, with Muslim and Hindu fundamentalists being projected as the arch players in this tug of war. The debate is located within the paradigm of politics with gender concerns, the most popular scapegoat used by all factions for their vested interests.

Notes

1. Lateef S., 'Defining Women through Legislation,' in Hasan, Z. (ed.) *Forging Identities: Gender, Communities and the State*, New Delhi: Kali for Women (1994), p.48.
2. The note of dissent attached to the Draft Report of 14 April 1947 of the sub-committee on Fundamental Rights and the note of dissent attached to the Draft Report of 17-20 April 1947. See Shiva Rao, B., *The Framing of India's Constitution*, New Delhi: The Indian Institute of Public Administration (1968), Vol.II, p.162, 177.
3. See sub-sec. 5.6. of Chapter 5.
4. The opponents of the Hindu law reform used the occasion to remind the government of the constitutional directive to enact a UCC for all communities. Some members of Parliament argued that if a constitution could be enacted on the principles of equality and equity for the entire country, then similar laws could be made for the whole country. This was a tactic adopted by the conservatives to forestall Hindu law reforms (Vidyavachaspati, 5 February 1951, pp.2387, 2389–90; Sarwate, Ibid. pp. 2374–5; Deshmukh, Ibid. p.2399).

5. The report stated that the absence of a UCC in the last quarter of the twentieth century, twenty-seven years after independence is an incongruity that cannot be justified with all the emphasis that is placed on secularism, science and modernism (p.142).
6. See Chapters 7 and 8.
7. See Kamila Tayabji quoted in Mahmood, T., *An Indian Civil Code and Islamic Law,* Bombay : N.M. Tripathi (1976), p.29 and Aggarwal, R., 'Uniform Civil Code—a formula not a solution' in Mahmood T. (ed.) *Family Law and Social Change,* Bombay : N.M. Tripathi (1975) pp. 110–44. Also see Bhattacharjee, A.M., *Matrimonial Laws and the Constitution,* Calcutta: Eastern Law House (1996), Preface [9].
8. Dhagamwar, V., *Towards the Uniform Civil Code,* Bombay: N.M. Tripathi (1989), p.71.
9. 'Since Muslims are allowed to marry four wives, the Muslim population is growing at a faster rate', is the communal propaganda. See Table 8 for the actual rate of increase in Muslim population.
10. The hastily passed Maharashtra bill on abolition of polygamy is a case in point.
11. Badshah, H., 'Uniform Civil Code—Chasing a Mirage,' *The Hindu,* 24 December 1995.
12. While not holding a brief for male bigamy, one is only questioning whether sexuality can be controlled through state regulations when the economic restraints that were rooted in European feudalism (bastardization of children from informal alliances and denying them the right of property inheritance) have broken down. The modern tendency is towards laxity in marriage contracts, conferring rights to spouses in informal relationships and dissolving the differences between legitimate and illegitimate children.
13. Zafar, J., 'Begin by Codifying Muslim Family Law,' *The Times of India,* 29 August 1995.
14. Anand, J., 'Uniform Civil Code: Case for a Supreme Court Judgment,' *The Asian Age,* 8 June 1995.
15. Ahmad, F., 'Fatwa needed to make talaq revocable,' The Pioneer, 17 May 1994; Engineer, A.A. 'Personal Law and Gender Justice,' The *Times of India,* 10 June 1995.
16. Shahabuddin, S., 'A Mountain is being made out of a molehill,' *The Hindustan Times,* 28 May 1995.
17. Ahmed, I., 'Personal Laws: Promoting Reform from Within,' *Economic and Political Weekly,* XXX/45 (1995), p. 2851.
18. Engineer, A.A., 'A Model for Change in Personal Law,' *The Times of India,* 25 July 1995.
19. *Muslim Family Law Ordinance,* 1961 (Ordinance No.VIII of 1961) S.5 of this Ordinance provides for registration of marriage; S.6 provides for regulated polygamy with the permission of the Arbitration Council; S.7 stipulates that talaq will be valid only after 90 days of its pronouncement and provides for efforts of reconciliation during this period; S.8 grants the wife delegated right of divorce and S.10 stipulates that mehr should be paid to the wife on demand. Further, Clause 18 of

the prescribed nikahnama provides for the wife's delegated right of divorce if the query is answered in the affirmative. For text see Appendix III.

20. Anand, J., 'Only hope for gender justice rests with Supreme Court,' *The Times of India*, 10 August 1995.
21. Engineer, A.A., 'Muslim reformists draft new legislation on marriage and divorce,' *The Times of India*, 10 April 1996.
22. Muslim Satyashodhak, an organization based in Pune has been demanding changes in law through judicial and legislative interventions. See Shikhare D., 'Talaq Mukti Morcha in Maharashtra,' *Manushi* Vol. VI n.2 (1986), p.23. A report of a recent protest march and delegation to the government to enact a UCC organized by the group appeared in *The Times of India*, 11 May 1997.
23. For details of the petition see a report titled, 'Abusing Religion to Oppress Women,' in *Manushi* IV/4 (1984), p.9.
24. Comments based on a personal interview with Shehanaz Sheikh.
25. Bhatnagar, R., 'Muslim Woman moves Court on Talaq,' report by *The Times of India*, 31 January 1995.
26. Hussain, W., 'I am a believer in Islam but can't accept discrimination,' *The Asian Age*, 13 April 1997.
27. *Ahmedabad Women Action Group (AWAG) & Ors v Union of India* JT 1997 (3) SC 171. But in this connection also see *C. Masilamani Mudaliar & Ors v Idol of Sri Swaminathaswami Thirukoil & Ors* (1996) 8 SCC 525, where the Supreme Court, held that: 'The personal laws must be consistent with the Constitution and can be struck down if they violate fundamental rights.'
28. As already discussed in Chapter 3, only a Muslim woman has the power to stipulate conditions by way of such agreements. Such agreements are void under the English law as well as all Indian matrimonial statutes which are derived from the English law.
29. For the salient features of these drafts see Chapter 11.
30. Ansari, I., 'Muslim Women's Rights: Goals and Strategy of Reform,' in *Economic and Political Weekly* XXVI/17 (1991), p.1095.
31. Ibid.
32. Ibid.
33. Translated into ground reality, this can be compared to the right of a Hindu bride not to give dowry at the time of her marriage. In both cases, the parents of the bride can exercise this choice only at the risk of marring the chances of marriage of their daughters, a risk very few parents would take in the prevailing social milieu of both urban and rural India across caste, religion and cultural divide.
34. Engineer, A.A., 'A Model for Change in Personal Law'.

Conclusions

While examining the evolution of family laws situated within a patriarchal social structure, discrimination against women is a foregone conclusion. Caste, class and clan purities are maintained through a strict sexual control. Punitive deterrent measures and denial of economic rights are the means through which this control is exercised.

This study set out to explore whether traditionally, within this constrained sphere, there were spaces through which women's rights to property could be negotiated. And also, whether the statutory interventions during colonial and post-colonial phases have led to the widening of this constrained sphere. This historical exploration was undertaken to gauge the nature and scope of law reform which is imperative to reverse the current trend of poverty and destitution among women. In this context, whether the models of a uniform code which have evolved in recent times would provide a solution to the problem at hand has also been examined.

The study reveals that the history of women's rights is not linear with the religious and customary laws forming one extreme end of the scale and the statutory reforms slowly and steadily progressing towards the other end, as it is popularly believed. The history is complex with various interactive forces constantly at play. Women's rights are not only constrained by a uniform set of patriarchal norms but are also shaped and moulded by several social, economic and political currents. So more accurately, within this complex framework, it has been a case of 'gain some, lose some'.

While examining the patriarchy located within the parameters of Indian feudalism of the smriti and post-smriti period, it is evident that despite the negative dictates, there were certain protective measures built into laws and customs, which granted women certain significant rights over property. While these rights do not meet the modern concept of equality, they were governed by a notion of equity. The Hindu woman's rights over ornaments, valuables and movable and immovable property under a specific category called stridhana are indicative of this protectionist approach. These measures were meant to provide some respite to women who were outside the sphere of coparcenary rights bestowed upon a Hindu male.

A social structure determined by caste hierarchies, necessitates relocation of women's rights within this hierarchy. The women situated in the higher strata of the caste structure were governed by a strict code of sexual control to maintain caste purity and secure property devolution through legitimate children. The women of the lower castes were out of the varna system prescribed by Manu and hence, the smriti code of sexual morality did not apply to them. As wage earners women contributed to the household. The patriarchal control of men in matrimonial relationships was lax and women had greater freedom of divorce and remarriage. The labour powers and sexuality of these women, as well as the labour powers of their men, were at the disposal of the higher castes and the seat of oppression was located within this structure. Most marginalized communities did not own property and hence the issue of being maintained from the family property and resources was not relevant. The concept of maintenance envisages a non-working dependent woman. The working class woman did not fit this description.

The Islamic jurisprudence of the pre-colonial period sought to protect women's economic rights within the concept of contractual marriages. Since the Arabs were primarily traders, they regulated all economic and social transactions through the concept of contracts. The marriage alliance was also defined in a similar fashion with certain additional measures built into the contract for the protection of women, the weaker partners. The women were granted the power to enter into pre-marriage agreements and lay down conditions within the marriage contract. In addition, the stipulation of a fixed amount which could provide future security to the wife was an essential ingredient of a Muslim marriage. Since marriage was a dissoluble contract, stipulation of high mehr amounts was meant to act as an economic deterrent upon the husband's power of arbitrary divorce.

While this was the textual position of Hindu and Islamic

jurisprudence, the colonial interventions must be contextualized within the customary, caste based, non-state arbitration fora prevalent at the advent of the colonial rule. As already mentioned, all legal systems, i.e. the Hindu, Islamic, as well as the Roman, contained several discriminatory provisions. During the colonial and post-colonial period, the discriminatory measures within the Hindu and Islamic legal systems were highlighted with a political motive. While the portrayal of a barbaric Hindu provided the justification for the colonial interventions in the pre-independence period, the image of a backward, pre-modern and polygamous Muslim served the Hindu communal forces in the post-independence period. The negative aspects of these systems were reinforced through judicial decisions and sensationalized media reportage. The protective measures built into these systems were allowed to become obscure and redundant. Stripped off the balancing counter measures, the traditional systems became severe and harsh towards women.

It is generally believed that the interventions by the colonial state in the realm of family law were meant primarily for the liberation of Indian woman from the barbaric customs of sati, female infanticide and marital rape of infant brides. It is also believed that women's right to property is a western concept introduced by the British during its modernizing mission. But this premise overlooks the fact that the Roman law, as well as the English common law contained several stringent anti-women biases. These biases crept into India through the Anglo-Saxon jurisprudence and subverted the traditional legal systems which provided women with a certain measure of economic security. The traditional systems were remoulded into linear, formal and stringent structures, which exercised greater patriarchal control over women and their right to property.

The colonial interventions also facilitated the construction of distinct and mutually hostile religious communities of Hindus and Muslims, to be governed by their respective personal laws along the model of the canon law. The basis of the legal system were the ancient scriptures translated with a western mind set. These scriptures were never meant to be used as rigid legal principles of an adversarial legal system. The translated texts drastically changed the nature and character of the customary and scriptural Hindu law and the Hindu woman's right to property suffered a severe set back. In the process of streamlining the pluralistic society several customary rights of women were crushed as they could not meet the legal requirement set by the British courts to prove a custom. Ironically, in this process the character of the communities was fixed and the mutually exclusive communities of Hindus and Muslims were constructed through litigation over property disputes.

The restructuring of the easily accessible non-state judicial fora dispensing quick redressals through community-based interventions, into an alien model of English courts rendered justice adversarial, expensive and dilatory. Within a system of hierarchy of courts, the decisions of the Privy Council became binding principles of law and the process of evolving laws at the local level to suit the needs of local communities was arrested. Concepts of justice, equity and good conscience became the direct channels of introducing English laws, principles and puritanical notions of morality into India.

During the nationalistic struggle, there were attempts to restore women's rights. The primary aim of the two legislations enacted in 1937, The *Hindu Married Women's Right to Property* and the *Application of Shariat Act* was to restore the property rights subverted through the legal precedents set by the Privy Council. But within a changed socio-economic and political context these legislations brought in only marginal respite.

The Constitution with its mandate of equality brought in visions of gender justice. Restructuring of the feudal family laws to suit the needs of women within a modern democracy was the challenge before the newly independent state. But the much trumpeted Hindu law reforms of the post-independence period were concerned more with homogenizing the culturally diverse Hindu community through a uniform set of state regulated enactments than widening the sphere of women's rights. Hence crucial women's rights located within customary laws were compromised. The enactments turned out to be a curious mixture of the English law and the shastric law with the worst biases of both written into them.

To cite one example, although the *Hindu Marriage Act* introduced divorce, the Act did not provide for any economic security for divorced women except the right of meagre maintenance. The concept of maintenance could provide safety only within a feudal property structure where property is inalienable and marriages are indissoluble. The large-scale destitution of Hindu women after divorce in the post-reform phase seemed as though Hindu women had bartered the right of residence and economic security, to the right of divorce and consequent destitution.

Traditionally, the Hindu woman had a distinct economic right called stridhana. The definition of stridhana, its changing character during various phases of a woman's life, the woman's power of disposal over it etc. had been the subject of elaborate discussion under the smriti law. The commentators of the post-smriti period were engaged in widening its scope and strengthening its base. And yet, while restructuring the traditional sacramental form of marriage into a dissoluble contract and bestowing upon the Hindu woman a new status of a divorcee, the character of her stridhana and control over it during this new phase of life did not find a mention in the *Hindu Marriage Act*. This is perhaps due to the fact that most nationalist leaders were advocates trained in English law which they held as a model for reform and had imbibed the colonial contempt for the traditional system of law. So the *Hindu Marriage Act* turned out to be a poor imitation of the *English Matrimonial Causes Act*. Based on the concept of formal equality, the Hindu law was stripped of all its protective measures. Even the traditional right of maintenance was now extended to husbands, a concept unheard of under either the scriptural or customary Hindu law.

The principle of monogamy, which was modelled on the western and Christian doctrine was not suited to the cultural conditions of a custom-ridden, pluralistic Hindu society. So at one level the law was ineffective in curbing monogamy, but conversely it strengthened the patriarchal base by depriving women in informal relationships of their customary rights.

The much proclaimed right of inheritance was subverted by surreptitiously granting Hindu men the right to will away the property. The protective restraint against bequests under the Islamic law to safeguard women's rights, did not find a place in the codified Hindu law, since the Hindu law was remoulded on the English model of exclusive and absolute rights to the individual. To facilitate the transformation of the economic system from feudalism to capitalism, it was crucial that property be alienable in the hands of individual men. The inalienable and immovable property could now be converted into liquid and negotiable capital. Within this new economic structure, women's rights of maintenance and inheritance became transient and illusory.

Despite these limitations, the enactments were projected as proof of India's claim to modernity. During the following decades, the discourse on family law reform, targeted the Muslim personal law as the object. This criticism can be extended not only to Hindu communal forces but also to the judiciary, legal academia and the media. Polygamy and arbitrary divorce were projected as the major problems affecting women. Although at one level, statistics for wife murder and suicide by young brides signalled a phenomenal increase in family violence among Hindus and the soaring number of the destitute reflected the inadequacy of the reformed Hindu law, the discourse on the Uniform Civil Code continued to project the codified Hindu law as a model for women's liberation and empowerment. The correlation between increasing rates of suicides, murder and destitution of Hindu women and the reformed Hindu laws was not examined by the protagonists of the UCC. This led to the demand for this code acquiring a distinct communal hue.

Although uniformity was the aspiration, during the decades that followed, inroads were made into uniform laws to protect the patriarchal interests of Hindu and Muslim men. The Hinduization of the *Special Marriage Act* in 1976 and the denial of rights to divorced Muslim women through the enactment of the *Muslim Women's Act* in 1986, following the Shah Bano controversy are two concrete examples of this trend. But while the *Muslim Women's Act* has been projected as the worst instance of communal appeasement by the ruling government, the Hinduization of the *Special Marriage Act*, a decade prior to this enactment went unnoticed by scholars and the media except for a few stray protests.

The adverse comments by the judiciary while deciding issues of gender during the last decade reinforced popular communal misconceptions and served to widen the communal gulf. These comments and the adverse publicity that followed led to the alienation of even progressive segments within the Muslim community. Within the communalized politics of the post-Babri Masjid phase, support to the demand of a Uniform Civil Code came to be construed as a betrayal of the cause of identity politics and minority rights. These developments have rendered the task of family law reform extremely complex.

The issue of women's rights is also ridden with other complexities. Located within an adversarial, dilatory, formidable and expensive court structure, even the limited rights granted by the statutes have become illusory and beyond the reach of most women. Hence they could not provide any respite or tilt the balance in women's favour. In the clamour for reforms, the impact of existing legal provisions upon individual women at a micro level or on the broad category of women at a macro level has not been adequately assessed. The adversarial system modelled on the notion of formal equality has become ineffective. Unless the statutory measures are re-located within informal, inexpensive and easily accessible legal systems which are governed by an interventionist approach, the most ideal and gender just statutes will, in effect, be redundant.

The new economic order ushered in during the nineties which resulted in opening of the Indian markets has led to a widening of the gap between the rich and the poor, the urban and rural, the haves and the have nots. It is logical that in this era of increasing inequalities, the gender gulf would also widen. If the joint family structure was the norm of a feudal society and the nuclear family, the norm of a capitalist society, single women families are fast becoming the norm of the post-capitalist society. Statistics reveal that one-third of all Indian households are women headed and a large segment of these live below the poverty line.

Any suggestion for reform in family laws which sets out to redefine gender relations within marriage and the family, would have to take into consideration the above social, political, legal and economic realities. But the drafts for the enactment of a Uniform Civil Code framed by the legal academia, do not seem to have contextualized women's rights within these diverse complexities. The model for reform is the *Hindu Marriage Act* which in turn is based on archaic English principles. Since all statutory matrimonial laws in India, except the Muslim law, are based on English laws of marriage, the primary aim of the suggested reforms seems to be to streamline the 'pre-modern' or 'medieval' Islamic family law along 'modern' principles. Since a medieval Christian remedy of restitution of conjugal rights located within European feudalism is retained in these drafts, the attempt to modernize the family law appears to be confined only to the Muslim law.

Although gender justice is the stated goal of these reforms, the predominant concern seems to be with uniformity. In judicial decisions, as well as in popular projections, the demand for uniformity is linked to national integration and homogenization of religious communities through a common family law. While the demand is raised primarily in the context of Muslim personal law, there have been no attempts to examine whether such uniformity would suit the culturally diverse and unevenly modernized Hindu society. The fact that the *Hindu Marriage Act* has validated diverse customary forms of marriage and divorce, seems to have been overlooked by the zealous reformers. Although the *Hindu Marriage Act* set out to 'reform' Hindu law and bring it under the state control and regulations, sufficient scope was provided for Hindu customs and practices. Hence under the present statute, a Hindu need never approach a state functionary or a religious institution either for solemnization of his/her marriage or for its dissolution.

The *Hindu Succession Act* also contains ample examples of regional diversities. The central statute enacted in 1956, retained Hindu male coparcenaries or joint family property holdings. This concept deprived women of the right of inheritance in ancestral property. Their right to equal inheritance was limited only to self-acquired property of a Hindu male. In 1976, in the state of Kerala under the leftist scheme of land reforms, the concept of joint family holdings was abolished. In 1984, women in Andhra Pradesh were granted the right of coparcenary through a state amendment. The states of Tamil Nadu and Karnataka introduced the provisions of the Andhra Pradesh amendments in 1990 and 1994, respectively. Under a women's policy introduced in Maharashtra in 1994, women in Maharashtra were granted the right to be recognized as coparcenars.

Since the southern states had a culture of granting women rights to property under customary law, the state amendments did not cause a major stir. In contrast, none of the northern states have enacted such a provision nor has there been a central amendment to this effect. At the other extreme, the state of Haryana unanimously passed an amendment in 1987 for the abolition of Hindu women's rights in the self-acquired property of a Hindu male under the plea that it leads to fragmentation of agricultural land. The bill could not be enacted because it did not receive the President's assent. This is just one example of the cultural diversity reflected within the codified Hindu law. Once the state acquired the power to legislate for its Hindu citizens and established its superiority to the religious heads, the diversity reflected in the Hindu family law did not seem to have caused any concern to the state.

The Indian Constitution contains an internal inconsistency regarding family laws. While Art. 44 directs the state to enact a Uniform Civil Code, the power to legislate in the realm of family law is situated in the concurrent list (Entry 5, List III of the Seventh Schedule) which indicates that the power is granted to both central and state legislatures. Since the constitution provides for a federal structure with clearly defined legislative powers, depriving the states of this power through the enactment of one set of rigid and uniform family laws would lead to the dominance of the centre over the states. While this would affect the centre-state relationships in all the states, it would cause a serious dent in relationships with the north-eastern states which are further protected through specific constitutional guarantees.

The scheme of this study has been to place women's rights within the political developments of the nation. The study reflects that women's rights is not a primary concern of the dominant forces but the rhetoric can conveniently be brought into the public arena in support of other hidden political objectives. In this context, it is necessary to emphasize that when a previously colonized state achieves independence, and sets out to redefine its authority over other prevailing power structures through statutory reforms, in the fervour of constituting the infrastructure of a new state, it is relatively easy to push the agenda of women's rights and enact a comprehensive family code. But the Indian independence was marked by a bloody partition. Hence within the new democracy, it became imperative to assure the minorities of their right to a cultural identity, to ensure political stability. The continuance of the personal laws was a marker of this assurance. Hence the family law reforms undertaken by the independent Indian nation in the fervour of the newly acquired independence were confined to the majority community. Even this limited task was undertaken only after the ruling Congress party, under the leadership of Pundit Nehru, the most popular prime minister of independent India, was returned to power with an overwhelming majority in the first elections held in 1952.

Regarding law reform for minorities, it was hoped that in the years that followed, the ruffled feathers would smoothen and the political stability would facilitate the enactment of a uniform family law. But the decades that followed witnessed not only the widening of the communal gulf but formations of precariously perched minority and coalition governments. In this climate of increasing electoral insecurity, no government would risk forcing a uniform code upon unwilling constituencies or rake up controversies which could become politically costly. The government's approach towards Christian law reforms is an indication of this political apathy.

In this vitiated atmosphere, the process of reform would have to be carefully carved out and systematically followed up through sustained campaigns. Within a democratic political structure with an assurance of the protection of the cultural identity of the minorities, the law reform for minorities would essentially have to be initiated from within the communities and endorsed by its leaders. The efforts of non-Muslim minorities in this direction have been discussed in detail. The strategies adopted by the Parsi community are particularly relevant. The community has been able to preserve its specific cultural identity while modernizing the family laws. The attempts by the Christian community have been more laborious and are marked by tensions between liberal Protestants and conservative Catholics at one end and the Catholic clergy and the laity at the other, with the government's posture of inaction supporting the status-quoists. It is only through a balancing act that the community has been able to inch its way towards reform.

Community-based initiatives are particularly lacking among the Muslims. Although the progressive Muslim intelligentsia has expressed concern over the discriminatory provisions within the personal laws, the suggestions for reform lack the institutional support which is essential to organize sustained campaigns. One concrete suggestion which could lead to redefining gender equations within the framework of Islamic jurisprudence is the formulation of a standard nikahnama and the setting up of arbitration councils to regulate marriages and divorces. The standard nikahnama could contain provisions of monogamy, curtail the power of arbitrary and unilateral divorce, grant the wife delegated power of divorce and provide for the future security of the wife by stipulating securities, conceding valuable or immovable property as mehr in lieu of token cash amounts, in accordance with the economic status of the parties. If the

Muslim Personal Law Board acts upon the suggestions made by progressive groups, the Muslim personal law would be more equitable towards women while retaining its specific characteristics without invoking a major political controversy. But this can be achieved only when the progressive elements within the community are able to exert pressure on the Muslim Personal Law Board which is not the case at present.

Another important political strategy at this juncture is to disassociate concerns of gender from the context of identity politics within which the demand for a Uniform Civil Code is currently located. The legislative history of last fifty years reveals that it is possible to enact uniform legislations in specific areas of family law without invoking the controversy of majority-minority politics. *The Dowry Prohibition Act,* 1961, the Medical *Termination of Pregnancy Act,* 1971, introduction of new offence of cruelty to wives under S.498(A) *IPC* in 1983 and the *Family Courts Act,* 1984 are indicative of this possibility. In a phased out scheme of reform, least controversial aspects could be prioritized. Concrete suggestions for specific enactments made by some women's organizations have already been discussed. In this context the Private Member's Bill to secure the rights of married women is of special significance.

The suggestions for widening the base of women's economic rights would have to be backed by campaigns. During the eighties, women's organizations were successful in bringing about changes in laws concerning rape and dowry after sustained, nationwide campaigns. But in the realm of economic rights such campaigns are particularly lacking. Even the recommendations by the Law Commission in its *132nd Report* in 1989 to abolish the ceiling of Rs 500 maintenance under S.125 of the Cr.PC has not been backed by a public campaign. Similarly although there has been a demand for the enactment of a Domestic Violence Act with powers of granting restraining injunctions and the Law Commission has also formulated a Bill in this regard, so far a Bill on this issue has not been introduced in Parliament. Focused and sustained campaigns around specific issues might prove more effective than following the mirage of an all-encompassing, ideal Uniform Civil Code.

The suggestions by women's organizations which bring economic rights at the centre of matrimonial reforms are indicative of a shift in the women's rights discourse. While this is positive, a theoretical framework regarding the nature of matrimonial rights under different economic systems has not yet evolved.

Currently, the matrimonial statutes revolve around the concept of marital conjugality and exclusive sexual access/control. The reformist concept of contractual marriages with the right to terminate the contract of conjugality was ushered in as a liberating and empowering weapon which would relieve women of the sacramental bond of sexual servitude. But this definition of marriage as primarily a sexual or conjugal contract overlooks a historical reality of marriage as an institution of economic regulation of property relationships. Sexual control within marriage served primarily to regulate property relationships. If this is the basic framework, then the sexual liberation ushered in through the concept of contractual and dissoluble marriages would be a hollow relief if it is not simultaneously linked to a redefinition of property relationships. This intrinsic link between the right of divorce and access to property is apparent in the evolution of English matrimonial statutes but is sadly lacking in the Indian statutes. Although based on English principles, Indian matrimonial statutes have failed to incorporate the more recent developments regarding matrimonial property under the English law on a perfunctory premise that marriage is a holy and sacrosanct union under the Indian setting and hence it cannot be reduced to a contract of property regulations.

Since the institution of marriage is integrally linked to the institution of property, then any change in the character of property under different economic systems would necessarily bring in changes in the nature of matrimonial property and its access. The economic rights which flow from a marriage contract under the Indian matrimonial statutes are presently defined within archaic laws which originated in a feudal society of agrarian landholdings which were inalienable and immovable. The concepts of the permanency of marriage and inalienability of land were coordinate. The members of the joint family were maintained by the produce of the land. In the event of lapses, the property could be charged for maintenance of its members and this right could be traced to the subsequent buyer. It is within this economic structure that the right to maintenance had evolved and had a specific significance for women. When the economic structure changed from feudalism to capitalism and the organization of the society changed from agrarian-rural to industrialized-urban the land became alienable and property was rendered movable and transient. Simultaneously, the western woman's rights to property also underwent a change. Concepts such as married women's right to separate property, joint matrimonial property with equal rights to both spouses, right of residence in the matrimonial home after the dissolution of the marriage, the spousal claim to a share of matrimonial property in the event of it being willed away depriving her/him of her/his rights etc. have become important principles of matrimonial law.

But in India the rights of married women and divorcees have continued to be confined to a right of maintenance. The implication of this right to women from propertyless, wage earning sections of societies has not been examined. The right is also defined in the context of a dependent woman who is treated under the matrimonial statutes as a ward of her husband. The concept of maintenance also envisages a sexually pure woman, both within marriage and after divorce and renders maintenance a premium to sexual purity.

These are complex questions which need to be addressed in the discourse on family law reform. Unless a theoretical framework is evolved which situates marriages centrally within the context of economic structures, women's right to economic security in matrimonial relationships will continue to be illusive.

In this study, while discussing the political context of women's rights, a passing reference to the economic systems under which these rights evolved, has been made. But the issue of property was not the central focus of this study. There is a need to locate property at the centre of matrimonial law reform, if adequate solutions to the trend of poverty and destitution of women have to be evolved. Since patriarchy is reinforced through economic structures, be they of feudalism, capitalism or post-capitalism, a solution to the oppression and destitution of women would have to be found primarily in the context of the economic structures and the state responsibility towards women within these structures. It is towards these directions that efforts of family law reform need to be forged.

Appendix I

THE DOMESTIC VIOLENCE TO WOMEN (PREVENTION) BILL, 1994*

A BILL to provide for the prevention of domestic violence to women and for matters connected therewith or incidental thereto BE it enacted by Parliament in the Forty-fifth Year of the Republic of India as follows:

1. Short title, extent and commencement

(1) This Act may be called the *Domestic Violence to Women (Prevention) Act*, 1994.

(2) It extends to the whole of India.

(3) It shall come into force on the 1st day of January, 1995.

2. Definitions

In this Act, unless the context otherwise requires:-

(a) 'Court' means, in any area for which there is a Family Court established under the provisions of the *Family Courts Act*, 1984, that Court, and in any other area, the principal civil court of original jurisdiction, and includes any civil court or a Mahila Panchayat consisting of three women members of a Gram Panchayat which the State Government may, by notification, specify as the court competent to deal with all or any of the matters specified in this Act.

(b) 'Domestic violence' means any of the following acts committed on a woman by her husband or any of his or her relatives, namely;

(i) any willful conduct which,

- is of such a nature as is likely to drive the woman out

*As Approved by the Expert Committee on laws in its meeting held on 18-19 August 1994 of the house or to commit suicide or to injure herself, or

- causes injury or danger to the life, limb or health (whether mental or physical) of the woman; or

(ii) harassment which causes distress to a woman; or

(iii) any act which compels the woman to have sexual intercourse against her will either with the husband or any of his relatives or with any other person; or

(iv) any act which is unbecoming of the dignity of the woman; or

(v) any other act of omission or commission which is likely to cause mental torture or mental agony to the woman.

(c) 'Notification' means a notification published in the Official Gazette.

(d) 'Prescribed' means prescribed by rules made under this act.

(e) 'Protection Officer' means an officer appointed by the State Government in relation to or for the purposes of this Act and includes any institution or organization designated by the Government to perform the functions of a Protection Officer under this Act, in relation to an area.

(f) 'Protection Order' means an order made under this Act for the protection of a woman subject to domestic violence and for such other provisions like separate stay, maintenance and the prevention of further domestic violence.

(g) 'Relative' includes any person related by blood, marriage or adoption.

3. Act Not in Derogation of Any Other Law

The provisions of this Act shall be in addition to, and not in derogation of the provisions of any other law, for the time being in force.

4. Presentation of Petition to Court

(1) Any woman subject to domestic violence or any other person on her behalf or a Protection Officer may, without prejudice to the provisions of this Act, or of any other law for the time being in force, present a petition to the court for the passing of a Protection Order.

(2) A petition presented under sub-section (1) shall, among other things, contain the following particulars, namely:

(a) the name and particulars of the woman subject to domestic violence or if the petition is presented by any other person, the particulars also of such other person;
(b) the name and address of the husband or the relative who has committed domestic violence;
(c) the nature of domestic violence;
(d) all other particulars which would be necessary for the issue of a Protection Order.

(3) On receipt of a petition under sub-section (1), and on consideration of the statements made therein, and the evidence produced, if the Court is satisfied that a Protection Order may properly be made forthwith, it may make such order *ex-parte*, and shall fix a date for further consideration of the petition.

(4) If, on consideration of the petition under sub-section (3) the Court is not so satisfied, it shall fix a date for further consideration of the petition without making any Protection Order.

(5) The notice of the date fixed under sub-section (3) or sub-section (4), which shall not be more than seven days from the date of issue of such notice, shall be given to the petitioner, or if the petitioner is not the woman subject to violence, to the woman and the Protection Officer, her husband or the relative who has been committing domestic violence and to any other person to whom, in the opinion of the Court, such notice shall be given.

(6) A notice given under sub-section (3) or sub-section (4), shall be served on all the persons to whom it is intended, sufficiently in advance of the date of hearing, and if it is not possible for any reason to serve such notice on any of the parties, it shall be pasted on the main door of the premises in which the person to whom the notice is intended is known to have last resided or worked for gain, in accordance with the provisions specified in the *Code of Civil Procedure*, 1908 for such service, and any notice so served shall be deemed to have been validly served on the party, to whom it is intended to be served and shall not be called in question in any court on the ground that the notice had not been validly served.

(7) On the date fixed under sub-section (3) or sub-section (4) or on such date or dates to which the hearing may be adjourned and after hearing the parties, the Court is satisfied that the woman is subjected to domestic violence, it may pass a Protection Order, and if it is not so satisfied, it shall dismiss the petition setting forth the reasons for such dismissal:

Provided that the Court may extend any Protection Order issued under sub-section (3) with or without any alteration or modification or where no such order is issued, it may issue such order, pending disposal of the petition.

(8) Every endeavour shall be made by the Court hearing the petition under this Act to dispose off it expeditiously and in any case not later than three months from the date of presentation of the petition.

(9) Where any of the parties to the petition so desire, the Court shall on an application made by such party, conduct the proceedings in camera.

(10) A copy of the Protection Order shall be forwarded to the Protection Office and to all the parties concerned.

(11) A Protection Order made under this section shall be in force for such period not exceeding four years as the Court may fix.

5. Contents of Protection Order

The Protection Order shall contain, among other things, the following matters, namely:

(a) directing the husband or the relative to desist from committing any domestic violence;

(b) directing in all cases that the wife live separately from her husband, along with the children, if any, and the matrimonial home be given to the wife for her separate living.

Explanation: For the purpose of this clause, 'matrimonial home' means the accommodation in which the husband and the wife lived together immediately before the presentation of the petition, and if such accommodation happens to be rented or belonging to a joint family in which the husband is a member, that house or part of the house.

(c) Where the women subject to domestic violence is unmarried, widow, divorcee or deserted, directing that separate accommodation be provided for her living along with the children, if any;

(d) directing that the expenses of such separate living be borne by the husband or relative;

(e) directing the husband or relative to pay such maintenance to the wife or any children staying with her;

(f) such other matters as may be considered necessary.

Explanation: For the removal of doubts, it is hereby declared that in the cases covered under clause (e), no maintenance will be provided under any other law for the time being in force.

6. Duties of the Protection Officer

(1) It shall be the duty of the Protection Officer to make himself aware of all the domestic violence being committed in the area for which he is appointed and try to settle it peacefully and amicably between the parties.
(2) Without prejudice to sub-section (1), it shall be within the competence of the Protection Officer,
On an application presented to him by the woman subject to domestic violence or any other person on her behalf to arrive at a mutual settlement or on the failure of the parties to arrive at any settlement, to file a petition to the Court under this Act.
(3) It shall also be the duty of the Protection Officer to see that the provisions of the Protection Order are complied with.

7. Protection Officer to be a Public Servant

The Protection Officer shall be deemed to be a public servant within the meaning of Section 21 of the *Indian Penal Code*.

8. Power to Call for Information or Document

The Protection Officer may, for the purposes of efficient performance of his duties specified in Section 6, require any person or authority to furnish any information or document and it shall be the duty of such person or authority to furnish such information or document.

9. Consequential Amendment to the *Indian Penal Code* and the *Code of Criminal Procedure* 1973

(1) In Chapter XX-A of the Indian Penal Code, 1860, after section 498-A, the following section shall be inserted, namely:
498-B. Husband or relative of husband or of the woman subjecting her to domestic violence: Whoever, being the husband or the relative of the husband or of the woman, subjects such woman to domestic violence shall be punished with imprisonment for a term which may extend to three years and shall also be liable to fine.
Explanation: For the purposes of this section, 'relative' and

'domestic' violence shall have the same meanings as in the *Domestic Violence to Women (Prevention) Act,* 1994.

(2) In the *First Schedule to the Code of Criminal Procedure* 1973, in the entries relating to 'Chapter XX-A—Of cruelty by husband or relative of husband', after the entries relating to section 498-A, the following entries shall be inserted, namely:-

498 (B) Punishment for subjecting a woman to domestic violence.	Imprisonment for three years and fine.	Cognizable if information relating to the commission of the offence is given to an officer incharge of a police station by any person aggrieved by the offence or by any person related to her by blood, marriage or adoption, or if there is no such relative, the Protection Officer appointed under the Domestic Violence to Women (Prevention) Act, 1994, or such other officer as may be notified by the State Government in this behalf.	Non-bailable.	Magistrate 1st Class

10. Power to Make Rules

The State Government may by notification make rules to carry out the provisions of this Act.

Background

The Committee of Experts considered aspects pertaining to domestic violence with a view to providing legal remedies to the distressed victims, taking note of the Indian conditions. It recommends the accompanying Draft Bill, titled 'The *Domestic Violence of Women (Prevention) Bill'* for adoption. The background relating to domestic violence and the salient features of the Draft Bill are given below:

The term domestic violence is wide and encompasses in its scope all types of violence resorted to within the precincts of a home whether by male or female members of a family. But the overwhelming majority of victims of domestic violence are women. To be sure all such acts are punishable under the provisions of the *Indian Penal Code,* 1861. Nonetheless resort to the general law of the land is very seldom made by the women-victims of domestic violence owing to a variety of factors. Some of these factors are : a) close familial relationship; b) dependency, financial or otherwise; c) lack of legal literacy; and d) helplessness of the victims. Most of these cases go unreported and give rise to serious human problem.

Studies have pointed out that family violence is cyclic and is apt to pass from one generation to another; that children who had experienced violence are more likely to be violent towards wife and children in their adult life, and that in order to reduce societal violence, it is necessary to reduce violence within the family.

A prominent type of domestic violence in India is dowry-related domestic violence. In recent years considerable number of legislations were enacted and amendments to legislation were made to curb the evil. The *Criminal Law (Second Amendment) Act,* 1983 introduced the new offence of cruelty under Section 498-A; Section 174 of the *Criminal Procedure Code* was amended to secure post-mortem in case of death or suicide of a married girl; section 113-A was inserted in the *Indian Evidence Act;* and new Section 304-B relating to 'Dowry death' was incorporated in the *Indian Penal Code.* In view of these specific legislative provisions, the Draft Bill limits itself to other forms of domestic violence against women.

Domestic violence has been given a wide definition. It includes not only conduct which amounts to cruelty but also includes any act which is unbecoming of the dignity of the woman. Clause 3 of the Draft Bill states that the provisions of the *Domestic Violence to Women (Prevention) Act* are in addition to and not in derogation of any other law.

The Committee considered the 'Model Law Against Domestic Violence' of the *Lawyers Collective* sent by Ms. Indira Jaising. The Draft sent by her is heavily based on Lisa G. Lerman's 'A Model State Act: Remedies for Domestic Abuse' published in *Harvard Journal of Legislation.* This Model State Act does not at all take into consideration the social milieu and conditions in India. For this reason the Model State Law was found to be unsuitable.

The other foreign legislation noticed by the Committee was the *Domestic Violence and Matrimonial Proceedings Act,* 1976 of the U.K. Under this, a party to a marriage is entitled to get an injunction from a Country court restraining the other party from molesting the applicant or a child living with the applicant. Their injunction may also contain a provision excluding the other party from the matrimonial home or any part of it. Further, if the judge is satisfied that actual bodily harm has been caused to the party to a marriage or a child of the spouse, it may attach a power of arrest to the injunction for its breach; thereby a constable is empowered to arrest a person committing the breach of the injunction without a warrant.

Some of the factors which inhibit or discourage women-victims from seeking the available legal remedies have been mentioned before. The approach of the Draft Bill to meet these problems may be pointed out.

One of the major difficulties faced by victims of domestic violence is their inability to approach the courts for relief as they (courts) are located in urban centres. This is specially so in case of victims drawn from rural areas. The Draft defines a 'court' in wide terms as including a Family Court, a Civil Court and a Mahila Panchayat consisting of three women members of a Gram Panchayat, if so declared by a State Government. The creation of Mahila Panchayats as courts takes note of the socio-cultural context that prevails in rural areas and will help in rendering speedy justice in cases of domestic violence.

The existing delays in getting a legal remedy in cases of domestic violence discourage a victim, or a relation of the victim or a social worker who wants to aid the victim from seeking relief. Therefore, Clause 4 of the Draft Bill proposes a time-frame in the matter of disposal of the petitions. First, if the court is satisfied on a consideration of the statement made in the petition, it can forthwith make a Protection Order, even *ex-parte,* and fix a date for further consideration of the petition. Second, in case it is not satisfied with the statement made in the petition, it will fix a date without making an order; but the date so fixed should not be more than seven days from the date of issue of notice to the concerned persons. Sub clause 8 of Clause 4 of the Draft envisages that the court should dispose of the petition expeditiously and not later than 3 months from the date of filing of the petition.

Experience shows that lack of living accommodation primarily makes a woman suffer silently the battering given by the husband or other male relative. To meet this difficulty Clause 5 of the Draft Bill says that the Protection Order direct that the woman shall live separately from her husband and the matrimonial home be given to the wife for her separate living. The term 'matrimonial home' includes accommodation that is rented as well as belonging to the joint family. The Draft also envisages that in case the battered woman is unmarried or widow or divorcee, the Protection Order will direct separate living accommodation be provided for her living. Lack of financial support and fear of losing the custody of children force victims of violence to lead a captive existence. To overcome this the Clause 5 empowers the court to grant maintenance to the wife and children living with her, and give directions with respect to 'such other matters as may be considered necessary'.

The Draft envisages a key-role to Protection Officers. The term Protection Officer covers not only an officer appointed by the State Government but also any institution or organization designated by the State Government to perform the function of a Protection Officer in relation to an area. Thus it envisages a role to non-governmental organizations in combating the problem of domestic violence. If the helpless condition of a woman does not permit her to file a petition for Protection Order, any person on her behalf or a Protection Officer can file a petition for securing the remedies.

Sd/-

Professor B. Sivaramayya

Appendix II

The Married Women (Protection of Rights) Bill 1994 (Bill No. XXV of 1994) (R.S. 13-5-94)

A BILL to protect the rights of a married woman and for matters connected therewith.
BE it enacted by Parliament in the Forty-fifth Year of the Republic of India as follows:

1. Short Title

This Act may be called the *Married Women (Protection of Rights) Act,* 1994.

2. Definition

In this Act unless the context otherwise requires:
(a) 'appropriate government' means the Central or the State Government under whose employment the husband of the widow was at the time of his death;
(b) 'prescribed' means prescribed by rules made under this Act;
(c) 'property' means movable and immovable property whether ancestral or not, or whether acquired jointly with other members of the family or by way of accretion to any ancestral property of the husband of a married woman, and includes deposits of the husband in provident fund, banks, shares, any public saving schemes, ornaments, land and house.

3. Rights of a Married Woman

A married woman shall be entitled to the following rights, namely:-
(1) she shall have a right to live in the house of her husband whether owned by him or by his joint family without seeking

judicial separation or divorce from her husband;
(2) she shall without seeking judicial separation be entitled to have food, clothing and other facilities and maintenance and support for herself form her husband;
(3) she shall be entitled to have an equal share in the property of her husband from the date of her marriage and shall also be entitled to dispose off her share in the property by way of sale, gift, mortgage, will or in any other manner whatsoever;
(4) she shall have a right of free access till her life to the children born out of the wedlock if they remain in the custody of her husband irrespective of the dissolution of marriage;
(5) she shall have an option to bring up the children separately, have their custody, maintenance and education consistently by remaining in the family of her husband;
(6) she shall be consulted by her husband in matters of family business and other financial transactions made out of the property of her husband or of the joint family.

4. Rights of a Widow

A widow shall be entitled to the following rights, namely:
(1) she shall, if eligible, be entitled to get suitable employment in the event of the death of her husband who happened to be an employee in a given Department;
(2) she shall be entitled to pension at such rates and on such conditions as the appropriate Government may have prescribed;
(3) she shall have the first claim and absolute right on the property of her deceased husband.

5. Enforceability of Rights

(1) The rights conferred by this Act shall be enforceable in a court of law or in a Lok Adalat.
(2) Any transaction or business entered into in violation of subsection (6) of Section 3 shall be null and void.

6. Act to Have Overriding Effect

The provisions of this Act shall have effect notwithstanding anything inconsistent therewith contained in any other law for the time being in force or in any instrument having effect by virtue of any law other than this Act or in any decree or order of any court, tribunal or other authority.

7. Power to Make Rules

The appropriate Government may, by notification, make rules for carrying out the provisions of this Act.

Statements of Objects and Reasons

In the wake of independence, the Indian woman has not only been able to recognize her status but has also made man recognize it. Nevertheless, the status of a woman is still far from being dignified and safe in the Indian society. Although we are going to cross over to the twenty-first century from the twentieth century, our attitude towards women is still that of the middle-aged feudal lords. Even today we are not prepared to grant the same liberty to women which men themselves are enjoying dauntlessly.

Today, the real cause of the exploitation of a woman by her husband is that she has got no right in the house of her husband; she has got no right on the property of the husband. Even our laws confer the right of property on a woman only after the death of her husband and not during her coverture.

If a woman's right in the property of her husband is recognized the moment she marries, she will start feeling secure and will overcome her sense of helplessness and economic insecurity. This will minimize if not eliminate to a great extent the cases of separation and divorce whose basic reason is economic in many cases. What she will get on divorce, society should grant her during the subsistence of marriage. It is the most glaring injustice and indignity to woman that while she is a partner of the husband, the latter does not even think it necessary to inform her about his financial and family transactions, leave alone consultation with her.

The Bill seeks to achieve the above objectives by granting women certain rights.

VEENA VERMA

Appendix III

A: The Muslim Family Law Ordinance, 1961

[Ordinance No. VIII of 1961]

[15th July, 1961]

Preamble, WHEREAS it is expedient to give effect to certain recommendations of the Commission on Marriage and Family Laws:

NOW, THEREFORE, in pursuance of the Proclamation of the seventh day of October 1958, and in exercise of all powers enabling him in that behalf, the President is pleased to make and promulgate the following Ordinance:

1. Short Title, Extent, Application and Commencement

(1) This Ordinance may be called the *Muslim Family Laws Ordinance,* 1961.

(2) It extends to the whole of Pakistan, and applies to all Muslim citizens of Pakistan, wherever they may be.

(3) It shall come into force on such date as the Central Government may, by notification in the official Gazette, appoint in this behalf.

2. Definitions

In this Ordinance, unless there is anything repugnant in the subject or context:

(a) 'Arbitration Council' means a body consisting of the Chairman and a representative of each of the parties to a matter dealt with in this Ordinance:

Provided that where any party fails to nominate a representative within the prescribed time, the body formed without such representative shall be the Arbitration Council;

(b) 'Chairman' means the Chairman of the Union Council or a person appointed by the [Central Government in the Cantonment areas or by the Provincial Government in other areas] or by an officer authorized in that behalf by any such Government, to discharge the functions of Chairman under this Ordinance:
Provided that where the Chairman of the Union Council is a non-Muslim or he himself wished to make an application to the Arbitration Council, or is owing to illness or any other reason, unable to discharge the functions of Chairman, the Council shall elect one of its Muslim members as Chairman for the purpose of this Ordinance;
(c) 'Prescribed' means prescribed by rules made under section 11;
(d) 'Union Council' means the Union Council or the Town Union Committee constituted under the Basic Democracies Order, 1959 (P.O. No. 18 of 1959), and having jurisdiction in the matter as prescribed,
(e) 'Ward' means a ward within a Union or Town as defined in the aforesaid Order.

3. Ordinance to Override Other Laws, etc.

(1) The provisions of this Ordinance shall have effect notwithstanding any law, custom or usage, and the registration of Muslim marriages shall take place only in accordance with these provisions.
(2) For the removal of doubt, it is hereby declared that the provisions of the *Arbitration Act,* 1940 (X of 1940), the *Code of Civil Procedures* 1908 (Act V of 1908), and any other law regulating the procedures of Courts shall not apply to any Arbitration Council.

4. Succession

In the event of the death of any son or daughter of the propositus before the opening of succession, the children of such son or daughter, if any, living at the time the succession opens, shall per stripes receive a share equivalent to the share which such son or daughter, as the case may be, would have received if alive.

5. Registration of Marriages

(1) Every marriage solemnized under Muslim Law shall be

registered in accordance with the prevision of this Ordinance.
(2) For the purpose of registration of marriages under this Ordinance, the Union Council shall grant licenses to one or more persons, to be called Nikah Registrars, but in no case shall more than one Nikah Registrar be licensed for any one Ward.
(3) Every marriage not solemnized by the Nikah Registrar shall, for the purpose of registration under this Ordinance be reported to him by the person who has solemnized such marriage.
(4) Whoever contravenes the provision of sub-section (3) shall be punishable with simple imprisonment for a term which may extend to three months, or with fine which may extend to one thousand rupees, or with both.
(5) The form of nikahnama, the registers to be maintained by Nikah Registrars, the records to be preserved by Union Councils, the manner in which marriages shall be registered and copies of nikahnama shall be supplied to the parties, and the fees to be charged thereof, shall be such as may be prescribed.
(6) Any person may, on payment of the prescribed fee, if any, inspect at the office of the Union Council the record prescribed under sub-section (5), or obtain a copy of any entry therein.

6. Polygamy

(1) No man, during the subsistence of an existing marriage, shall except with the previous permission in writing of the Arbitration Council, contract another marriage, nor shall any such marriage contracted without such permission be registered under this Ordinance.
(2) An application for permission under sub-section (1) shall be submitted to the Chairman in the prescribed manner together with the prescribed fee, and shall state reasons for the proposed marriage, and whether the consent of existing wife or wives has been obtained thereto.
(3) On receipt of the application under sub-section (3), Chairman shall ask the applicant and his existing wife or wives each to nominate a representative, and the Arbitration Council so constituted may, if satisfied that the proposed marriage is necessary and just, grant, subject to such condition if any, as may be deemed fit, the permission applied for.
(4) In deciding the application the Arbitration Council shall record its reasons for the decision and any party may, in the prescribed

manner, within the prescribed period, and on payment of the prescribed fee, prefer an application for revision, in the case of West Pakistan to the Collector and, in the case of East Pakistan, to the Sub-Divisional Officer concerned and his decision shall be final and shall not be called in question in any Court.
(5) Any man who contracts another marriage without the permission of the Arbitration Council shall:
(a) pay immediately the entire amount of the dower whether prompt or deferred, due to the existing wife or wives, which amount, if not so paid, shall be recoverable as arrears of land revenue; and
(b) on conviction upon complaint be punishable with simple imprisonment which may extend to one year, or with fine which may extend to five thousand rupees, or with both.

7. Talaq

(1) Any man who wishes to divorce his wife, shall, as soon as may be after the pronouncement of talaq in any form whatsoever, give the Chairman a notice in writing of his having done so, and shall supply a copy thereof to the wife.
(2) Whoever contravenes the provision of sub-section (1) shall be punishable with simple imprisonment for a term which may extend to one year, or with fine which may extend to five thousand rupees, or with both.
(3) Save as provided in sub-section (5) talaq, unless revoked earlier, expressly or otherwise, shall not be effective until the expiration of ninety days from the day on which notice under sub-section (1) is delivered to the Chairman.
(4) Within thirty days of the receipt of notice under sub-section (1), the Chairman shall constitute an Arbitration Council for the purpose of bringing about a reconciliation between the parties, and the Arbitration Council shall take all steps necessary to bring about such reconciliation.
(5) If the wife be pregnant at the time talaq is pronounced, talaq shall not be effective until the period mentioned in sub-section (3) or the pregnancy, whichever later, ends.
(6) Nothing shall debar a wife whose marriage has been terminated by talaq effective under this Section from remarrying the same husband, without an intervening marriage with a third person, unless such termination is for the third time so effective.

8. Dissolution of Marriage Otherwise Than by Talaq

Where the right to divorce has been duly delegated to the wife and she wishes to exercise that right, or where any of the parties to a marriage wishes to dissolve the marriage otherwise than by talaq the provisions of section 7 shall, mutatis mutandis and so far as applicable, apply.

9. Maintenance

(1) If any husband fails to maintain his wife adequately, or where there are more wives than one, fails to maintain them equitably, the wife, or all or any of the wives, may in addition to seeking any other legal remedy available, apply to the Chairman who shall constitute an Arbitration Council to determine the matter, and the Arbitration Council may issue a certificate specifying the amount which shall be paid as maintenance by the husband.
(2) A husband or wife may, in the prescribed manner, within the prescribed period, and on payment of the prescribed fee, prefer an application for revision of the certificate, in the case of West Pakistan to the Collector and, in the case of East Pakistan to the Sub-Divisional Officer concerned and his decision shall be final and shall not be called in question in any Court.[1]
(3) Any amount payable under sub-section (1) or, (2) if not paid in the due time, shall be recoverable as arrears of land revenue.

10. Dower

When no details about the mode of payment of dower are specified in the nikahnama or the marriage contract, the entire amount of the dower shall be presumed to be payable on demand.

1. Under the *Punjab Amendment Punjab Act* XI of 1975 Section 9 of Ordinance VIII of 1961 was amended thus: In Section 9, sub-section (2), the full stop occurring at the end shall be replaced by a colon and thereafter the following provision shall be added, namely:-
'Provided that the Commissioner of a Division may, on an application made in this behalf and for reasons to be recorded, transfer an application for revision of the certificate from a Collector to any other Collector, or to a Director, Local Government, or to an Additional Commissioner in his Division.'

11. Power to Make Rules

(1) [The Central Government[2] in respect of cantonment areas and the provincial Government in respect of other areas] may make rules to carry into effect the purposes of this Ordinance.
(2) In making rules under this section such Government may provide that a breach of any of the rules shall be punishable with simple imprisonment which may extend to one month, or with fine which may extend to two hundred rupees, or with both.
(3) Rules made under this section shall be published in the Official Gazette and shall thereupon have effect as if enacted in this Ordinance.

12. Amendment of Child Marriage Restraint Act, 1929 (XIX of 1929).[3]

13. Amendment of the *Dissolution of Muslim Marriages Act*, 1939 (VIII of 1939)[4].

2. Substituted by PO No.1 of 1964.
3. Omitted by Ordinance XXVII of 1981.
4. Omitted by Ordinance XXVII of 1981.

Bibliography

BOOKS

Agnes, F., *State, Gender, and the Rhetoric of Law Reform*, Bombay: Research Unit on Women's Studies, S.N.D.T. University (1995).

Ahmad, F., *Triple Talaq: An Analytical Study*, New Delhi: Regency Publications (1994)

Alladi, K., (ed.), *Mayne's Treatise on Hindu Law & Usage*, New Delhi: Bharat Law House (1993) (13th edn.).

Balchin, C. (ed.), *A Handbook on Family Law in Pakistan*, Lahore: Shirkat Gah (1994) (2nd edn.).

Banerjee, G., *Hindu Law of Marriage and Stridhana* (TLLS-1878), Calcutta: S.K. Lahiri & Co. (1923) (5th edn.).

Basu, A. & B. Rai B., *A History of the AIWC 1927–1990*, Delhi: Manohar (1992).

Basu, T. *et al.*, *Khaki Shorts Saffron Flags*, New Delhi: Orient Longman (1993).

Bhattacharjee, A.M., *Hindu Law and the Constitution*, Calcutta: Eastern Law House (1994) (2nd edn.).

————, *Muslim Law and the Constitution*, Calcutta: Eastern Law House (1994) (2nd edn.).

————, *Matrimonial Laws and the Constitution* Calcutta: Eastern Law House (1996).

Bhattacharji, S., *Women and Society in Ancient India*, Calcutta: Sasumati Corporation Ltd. (1994).

Borradaile's, *Report of Civil Cases 1820 - 1824*, Bombay Sudder Adaulat Folio 1825 Bombay: Education Society's Press (1825) (Rpt. 1862).

Bromley, P.M., *Family Law*, London: Butterworths (1976) (5th edn.).

Cabinetmaker, P.H., 'Parsis and Marriage,' Pune: International Institute of Population Studies (Mimeograph) (1991).

Cassandra, B. (ed.), *Muslim Law in Modern India*, Allahabad:

Allahabad Law Agency (1993) (6th edn.) p.62.

Dadachanji, F.K., *Parsis—Ancient and Modern*, Karachi: (1980).

Desai, S.T., *Mulla's Principles of Hindu Law*, Bombay: N.M. Tripathi (1994) (16th edn.).

Diwan, P., *Law of Marriage and Divorce*, Allahabad: Wadhwa & Company (1988).

————, *Muslim Law in Modern India*, Allahabad: Allahabad Law Agency (1993) (6th edn.).

————, *Hindu Law*, Allahabad: Wadhwa & Company (1995).

Derrett, D.J.M., *Hindu Law Past and Present*, Calcutta: Mukherjee & Co. (1957).

————, *Religion Law and the State in India*, New York: The Free Press (1968).

Davis, E.G., *The First Sex*, New York: Putnam (1971).

Desika Char, S.V., *Readings in the Constitutional History of India 1757–1947*, Delhi: Oxford University Press (1983).

Dhagamwar, V., *Towards the Uniform Civil Code*, Bombay: N.M. Tripathi (1989).

Dube, L., *Matriliny and Islam Religion and Society in the Laccadives*, Delhi: National Publishing House (1969).

Framjee, D., *The Parsees, Their History, Manners, Custom and Religion*, London: Smith Elder & Co. (1858).

Fyzee, A.A.A., *Outlines of Mohammadan Law*, 4th Edn. New Delhi: Oxford University Press (1974).

Gandhi, N. & N. Shah, *Issues at Stake*, New Delhi: Kali for Women (1991).

Gill, K., *Hindu Women's Right to Property in India*, Delhi: Deep & Deep Publications (1986).

Grafe, H., *History of Christianity in India—Tamil-Nadu in the Nineteenth and Twentieth Centuries*, Bangalore: The Church History Association of India (1982), Vol.IV (Part 2).

Hasan, Z. (ed.), *Forging Identities: Gender, Communities and the State*, New Delhi: Kali for Women (1994).

Hidayatullah, M. & A. Hidaytulla *Mulla's Principles of Mahomedan Law*, Bombay: N.M. Tripathi (1990) (19th edn.).

Jackson, J. (ed.), *Raydens's Law and Practice in Divorce and Family Matters*, London: Butterworths (1983).

Jain, M.P., *Outlines of Indian Legal History*, Bombay: N.M. Tripathi (1966) (2nd edn.).

Jolly, J., *Hindu Law*, Tagore Law Lecture Series (TLLS) (1883).

Kapur, R. and B. Cossman, *Subversive Sites*, New Delhi: Sage Publications (1995).

Kumar, R., *The History of Doing An Illustrated Account of Movements for Women's Rights and Feminism in India 1800–1990*. New Delhi: Kali for Women (1993).

Mahmood, T., *Family Law Reform in the Muslim World*, Bombay: N.M. Tripàthi. (1972).

——————, *An Indian Civil Code and Islamic Law*, Bombay: N.M. Tripathi (1976).

——————, *Civil Marriage Law*, Bombay: N.M. Tripathi (1978).

Manchanda, S., *Parsi Law in India*, Allahabad: The Law Book Co. (1991) (V edn.).

Martin, D., *Battered Wives*, New York: Pocket Books (1976).

Mishra, V.C., (ed.), 'Special Issue on Uniform Civil Code', *Indian Bar Review*, XVIII/3-4 (1991).

Mullati, L., *The Bhakti Movement and the Status of Women: A case study of Virasaivism*, Abhinav Publications (1989).

Mundadan, A.M., *History of Christianity in India Upto Sixteenth Century*, Bangalore: The Church History Association of India (1982) Vol.I.

Parashar, A., *Women and Family Law Reform in India*, New Delhi: Sage Publications (1992).

Raghavachariar, N.R., *Hindu Law: Principles and Precedents*, Madras: The Madras Law Journal Office (1980) (7th edn.) Vol I & II.

Rankin, G.C., *Background to India Law*, Cambridge: Cambridge University Press (1946).

Roy Chowdhury, S.K. and H.D. Saharay (ed.), *Paruck's The Indian Succession Act*, Bombay: N.M. Tripathi (1988) (7th edn.).

Sachs, A. and J. H. Wilson, *Sexism and the Law—A Study of Male Beliefs and Judicial Bias*, Oxford: Law in Society Series, Martine Robertson (1978).

Sangari, K. & S. Vaid (ed.), *Recasting Women, Essays in Colonial History*, New Delhi : Kali for Women (1989).

Sarkar Shastri, G.C., *A Treatise on Hindu Law*, Calcutta (1933) (7th edn.).

Schacht, J., *An Introduction to Islamic Law*, Delhi: Oxford University Press (1964) (Rpt. 1975).

Sarkar, S., *Modern India 1885–1947*, Madras: Macmillan India Ltd. (1983).

Sharma, R.S., *Material Culture & Social Formations in Ancient India*, Madras: Macmillan India Ltd. (1983).

Shiva Rao, B., *The Framing of India's Constitution* New Delhi: The Indian Institute of Public Administration (1968) Vol.I & II.

Shodhan, A., *Legal Representations of Khojas and Pushtimarga Vaishnavas : The Aga Khan Case and the Maharaj Libel Case in Mid-nineteenth Century Bombay'* (unpublished Doctorate Dissertation submitted to the faculty of the Division of the Humanities), Department of South Asian Languages and Civilizations. Chicago, Illinois (1995).

Srinivas, M.N., *Caste in Modern India And Other Essays*, Bombay: Media Promoters & Publishers (1962) (Rpt. 1986).

————, *Some Reflections on Dowry*. New Delhi: Oxford University Press (1984).

Steele, A., *Hindu Caste, Their Law, Religion and Customs*, Bombay: Courier Press (1827).

Talim, M., *Women in Early Buddhist Literature*, Bombay: Popular Prakashan (1972)

Thapar, R., *A History of India*, Delhi: Penguin (1992) Vol. I.

Thekkedath, J., *History of Christianity in India 1542–1700*, Bangalore: The Church History Association of India (1982) Vol.II.

Usgaocar, M.S., *Family Laws of Goa, Daman and Diu*, Vaso Da Gama: Devi Shreevani Education Society (1980) Vol I.

————, *Family Laws of Goa, Daman and Diu*, Panaji: Vela Associates (1988), Vol. II.

ARTICLES

'Abusing Religion to Oppress Women', in *Manushi* IV/4 (1984), p.9.

'Recommendations of the Lawyers Collective Bangalore Law School', in *The Lawyers*, III/7 (1988), p.20.

'A Christian Woman Demands Equal Succession Rights', in *Manushi* No.25 (V/1) (1984), p.7.

'Hazir Hai—Mary Roy', in *The Lawyers* I/11–12 (1986), pp.33-5.

Agnes, F., 'Protecting Women Against Violence—Review of Decade of Legislation', in *Economic and Political Weekly*, XXVII/17 (1992), p.WS-19.

————, 'Triple Talaq Judgment Do Women Really Benefit', in *Economic and Political Weekly* XXIX/20 (1994), p. 1169.

———, 'Hindu Men, Monogamy and the Uniform Civil Code', in *Economic and Political Weekly,* XXX/50 (1995), p.3238.

———, 'Economic Rights of Muslim Women', in *Economic and Political Weekly,* XXXI/41–42 (1996), p.2832.

———, 'The Politics of Women's Rights', *Seminar* no.441 (1996), p. 62.

———, 'In the Dock', in *Humanscape* August 1996, p.26.

Aggarwal, R., 'Uniform Civil Code—a formula not a solution', in *Family Law and Social Change* (ed.) Mahmood T. Bombay : N.M. Tripathi (1975), pp. 110–44.

Ahmed, I., 'Personal Laws: Promoting Reform from Within', in *Economic and Political Weekly,* XXX/45 (1995), p. 2851.

Ansari, I., 'Muslim Women's Rights: Goals and Strategy of Reform', *Economic and Political Weekly,* XXVI/17 (1991), p.1095.

Anweshi Law Committee 'Is Gender Justice Only a Legal Issue—Political Stakes in UCC Debate', in *Economic and Political Weekly,* XXXII/9–10 (1997), p. 453.

Banerjee, S., 'Marginalization of Women's Popular Culture in Nineteenth Century Bengal', in Sangari, K. & S. Vaid (ed.), *Recasting Women, Essays in Colonial History,* New Delhi : Kali for Women (1989), p.127.

Bindra, A., 'Child Custody for Hindus only', *The Lawyers* IX/2 (1994), p.11.

Carroll, L., 'Law, Custom and Statutory Social Reform: The Hindu Widow's Remarriage Act of 1856', *Indian Economic and Social History Review,* Vol. XX/4 (Oct–Dec) (1983), pp. 363-88.

———, 'Law, Custom and Statutory Social Reforms The Hindu Widow Remarriage Act, 1856', J Krishnamurthi (ed.), *Women in Colonial India : Essays on Survival Work and State,* Delhi: Oxford University Press (1989).

Chandra, S., 'Rukmabai: Debate over Woman's Right to Her Person', in *Economic and Political Weekly,* XXXI/44 (1996), p.2927.

Chhachhi, A., 'Identity Politics, Secularism and Women: A South Asian perspective', (1994) in Zoya Hasan (ed.), *Forging Identities: Gender, Communities and the State,* New Delhi: Kali for Women (1994) p.82.

Circular from the Catholic Bishops' Conference of India (CBCI) 90/ckir-17, Sub-Christian Marriage Law II, 6 June 1990.

Cohn, B.S., 'Anthropological Note on Disputes and Law in India', in L Nader (ed.), *The Ethnography of Law* (American Anthropological Association) (1965), p.112.

Dube, L., 'Conflict and Compromise Devolution and Disposal of Property in Matrilineal Muslim Society', in *Economic and Political Weekly*, XXIX/21 (1994), p. 1273.

Fazalbuoy, N., 'The Debate on Muslim Personal Law', Paper presented at the Third National Conference on Women's Studies, Chandigarh (1986).

Fyzee, A.A.A., 'The Muslim Wife's Right of Dissolving her Marriage', in (1936) 38 Bom.LR, p. 113.

Gangoli, G., 'Anti-Bigamy Bill in Maharashtra', in *Economic and Political Weekly*, XXXI/29 (1996), p. 1919.

Hasan, M., 'Indian Muslims since Independence: In search of Integration and Identity', in *Third World Quarterly*, April, 1988.

Hasan, Z., 'Minority Identity, State Policy and the Political Process' (1994), in Hasan, Z. (ed.), *Forging Identities: Gender, Communities and the State*, New Delhi: Kali for Women (1994), p.59.

Karat, B., 'Step by Step Approach: Equal Rights, Equal laws', in *Women's Equality* V/1 (1993), p.5.

Khanna, S., 'Padmasini's Quest for Justice', in *The Lawyers* VII/2 (1992), p.25.

Kannabiran, K.G., 'Outlawing Oral Divorce' in *Economic and Political Weekly*, XXIX/25 (1994), p. 1509.

Kishwar, M., 'Pro-Women or Anti Minority? the Shahbano Controversy', in *Manushi* VI/2 (1986), p.4.

————, 'Codified Hindu Law: Myth and Reality', in *Economic and Political Weekly*, XXIX/33 (1994), p. 2145.

Lateef, S., 'Defining Women through Legislation' (1994), in Hasan, Z. (ed.), *Forging Identities: Gender, Communities and the State*, New Delhi: Kali for Women (1994), p.38.

Mani, L., 'Contentious Traditions: The Debate on Sati in Colonial India' (1989), in Sangari K. & S. Vaid (ed.), *Recasting Women, Essays in Colonial History*, New Delhi : Kali for Women (1989), p. 88.

Monterio, R., 'Belief, Law, and Justice for Women', in *Economical and Political Weekly*, XVII/43& 44 (1992), WS-74.

Mukhopadhyay, M., 'Between Community and State: The question of women's right and personal laws' (1994), in Hasan, Z. (ed.), *Forging Identities: Gender, Communities and the*

State, New Delhi: Kali for Women (1994), p.109.

Mukund, K. 'Turmeric Land—Women's Property Rights in Tamil Society since Medieval Times', in *Economic & Political Weekly*, XXVII/17 (1992), p.WS-2.

Nag, A., 'The Many faces of Sati in the Early Nineteenth Century', *Manushi* 42–3 (1987), p.26.

Navlakha, G., 'Triple talaq: Posturing at Women's Expense', in *Economic and Political Weekly*, XXIX/21 (1994), p. 1264.

Pathak, Z. and R.S. Rajan, 'Shah Bano', *Signs*, Vol. 14, n.3 (1989).

Sarkar, T., 'Rhetoric Against Age of Consent', *Economic and Political Weekly*, XXVIII/36, (1993) p.1869.

Sathe, S.P., 'Uniform Civil Code Why? What? and How?' (1995), in *Towards Secular India*, I/4, Bombay: Centre for Study of Society and Secularism (1995), p.31.

——————, 'Uniform Civil Code Implications of the Supreme Court Judgement', *Economic and Political Weekly*, XXX/35, (1995), p.2165.

Shikhare D. , 'Talaq Mukti Morcha in Maharashtra', in *Manushi*, VI/2 (1986), p.23.

Singh, K., 'The Constitution and the Muslim Personal Law' (1994), in Hasan, Z. (ed.), *Forging Identities: Gender, Communities and the State*, New Delhi: Kali for Women (1994), p.96.

——————, 'Combating Communalism', *Seminar*, N.441 (1996), p.55.

Sivaramayya, B., 'The Special Marriage Act, 1954 Goes Awry', in V. Bagga (ed.), *Studies in the Hindu Marriage and the Special Marriage Acts*, Bombay: N.M. Tripathi (1978), p.310.

Tiwari, B., 'Marriage Laws Revamped', *The Lawyers* X/5 (1995), p.28.

The Forum Against Oppression of Women Views on the Uniform Civil Code' (1995), unpublished document available with the group.

Upadhya, C., 'Dowry and women's property in coastal Andhra Pradesh' (1990), in *Contributions to Indian Sociology*, Delhi: Sage Publications (n.s.) 24, 1 (1990) p.29.

Vargo, N. and R. Goldfaden, 'The Goa Uniform Civil Code—Alive and Kicking', in *The Lawyers* X/7 (1995), p.21.

Vimochana, 'The Quest for a Uniform Civil Code: Some Dilemmas, some issues' (1988), unpublished document available with the group.

NEWSPAPER REPORTS/ARTICLES

'Muslims resent talaq verdict', *The Times of India*, 18 April 1994.

'Triple Talaq Again', *The Times of India*, 19 April 1994.

'Muslim women welcome court verdict on talaq', *The Statesman*, 22 April 1994.

'Divorced From Reality', *The Pioneer*, 25 April 1994.

'The practice is contrary to the spirit of Islam', *Indian Express*, 25 April 1994.

'Another Shah Bano in the Making', *The Times of India*, 25 April 1994.

'One Nation, One Law', *Sunday* 1-7 May 1994.

'Beyond the law—The Strange Case of Justice Tilhari', *Frontline*, 20 May 1994.

'Fear Behind the Purdah', *Blitz*, 21 May 1994.

'Avadh Bar to Suspend Advocate General', *The Times of India*, 19 May 1994.

'No change in Muslim personal law, says P.M.', *The Times of India*, 28 July 1995.

'Suggestion on civil code not binding says Court', *The Asian Age*, 12 August 1995.

The Times of India, 11 May 1997.

Ahmed, F., 'Fatwa needed to make talaq revocable', *The Pioneer*, 17 May 1994.

Anand, J., 'Uniform Civil Code: Case for a Supreme Judgment', *The Asian Age*, 8 June 1995.

———, 'Only hope for gender justice rests with Supreme Court', *The Times of India*, 10 August 1995.

Ashraf, A., 'A cap and a beard: Is that all to Muslims', *The Pioneer*, 1 May 1994.

Badshah, H., 'Uniform Civil Code—Chasing a Mirage', *The Hindu*, 24 December 1995.

Basu, A., 'Behind the Four Walls The Veil', *The Statesman*, 30 Aprii 1994.

Bhatnagar, R., 'Muslim Woman moves Court on Talaq', *The Times of India*, 31 January 1995.

Chadha, K., 'The Law that breaks the Constitution', *The Hindustan Times*, 8 August 1993.

Engineer, A.A., 'Personal Law and Gender Justice', *The Times of India*, 10 June 1995.

—————, 'Muslim reformists draft new legislation on marriage and divorce', *The Times of India*, 10 April 1996.

—————, 'A Model for Change in Personal Law', *The Times of India*, 25 July 1995.

Hussain, W., 'I am a believer in Islam but can't accept discriminination', *The Asian Age*, 13 April 1997.

Jung, Z., 'Begin by Codifying Muslim Family Law', *The Times of India*, 29 July 1995.

Karat, B., 'Uniformity vs Equality: The Concept of uniform civil code', *Frontline* 17 November 1995.

Latifi, D., 'Verdict on talaq', *The Hindustan Times*, 5 May 1994.

Mali, A., 'Uniformity among equals', *The Hindustan Times*, 8 May 1994.

Punwani, J., 'Women veto a common civil code', *The Sunday Review*, 23 July 1995.

Seervai, H.M., 'Judiciary oversteps its Brief', *The Times of India*, 5 July 1995.

Shahabuddin, S., 'A Mountain is being made out of a molehill', *The Hindustan Times*, 28 May 1995.

Venkataramanan, S., 'Devaluation of rupee: Past and present', *The Sunday Times of India*, 10 August 1997.

Vyas, N., 'Much more at stake than triple talaq', *The Hindu*, 1 May 1994.

OFFICIAL DOCUMENTS

Constituent Assembly Debates

Gazette of India, (Extraordinary, Part II, S. 2, 22 June 1962)

Joint Select Committee Report *Evidence on Adoption Bill*

Law Commission Reports

Parliamentary Debates

Rajya Sabha Debates

Report of the Commmittee on Status of Women

Towards Equality (1974)

Tables

Table 1: Caste-wise Composition of the Population

A:	SCHEDULED CASTES AND TRIBES:	22.65
	SCHEDULED CASTES	15.05
	SCHEDULED TRIBES	7.51
B:	NON HINDU COMMUNITIES AND RELIGIOUS GROUPS:	16.16*
	MUSLIMS	11.19
	CHRISTIANS	2.16
	SIKHS	1.67
	BUDDHISTS (OTHER THAN SC)	0.47
C:	FORWARD HINDU CASTES AND COMMUNITIES:	17.58
	BRAHMINS	5.52
	RAJPUTS	3.90
	JATS	1.00
	MARATHAS	2.21
	VAISHNAVAS	1.58
	KAYASTHA	1.02
	OTHER FORWARD CASTES	2.00
D.	OTHER BACKWARD CASTES (OBC) (DERIVED): 100 - (A+B+C)	43.70
	*AN ESTIMATED 52% UNDER B ARE ALSO OBC:	8.40
	TOTAL OTHER BACKWARD CASTES (43.70 + 8.40)	52.10

Note : Cast-wise ennumeration of population began in 1881, stopped in 1931, therefore culled out from 1931 by the Mandal Commission.

Source : Report of the Backward Class Commission, 1980, Government of India.

Table 2A: Marriages Registered Under the Special Marriage Act (SMA) in Mumbai. 1968–72

MARRIAGES REGISTERED UNDER SMA AND THOSE PERFORMED IN OTHER FORMS AND SUBSEQUENTLY REGISTERED UNDER SMA

Year	Org. Reg.	Sub. Reg
1968	601	19
1969	621	18
1970	766	43
1971	705	36
1972	816	26

Source: Towards Equality, p.114.

Table 2B: Marriages Registered under the Special Marriage Act (SMA) in Mumbai. 1986–96

	City		Suburbs		Total	
Year	BMRA	SMA	BMRA	SMA	BMRA	SMA
1986	14,300	755	5,885	787	20,185	1,542
1987	16,460	777	6,625	929	23,085	1,706
1988	15,572	693	7,005	790	22,577	1,483
1989	19,133	773	7,126	956	26,259	1,729
1990	18,200	719	9,657	901	27,857	1,620
1991	15,100	764	10,697	958	25,797	1,722
1992	12,423	634	16,075	937	28,498	1,571
1993	11,316	672	16,415	962	27,731	1,634
1994	11,581	606	17,962	1,113	29,543	1,719
1995	12,516	602	19,925	1,101	32,441	1,703
1996	11,380	577	18,264	1,325	29,644	1,902

SMA - *Special Marriage Act,* 1954
BMRA - *Bombay Marriage Registration Act,* 1953

Source: Office of the Registrar of Marriages Bombay City and Suburbs.

Table 3: Community-wise Incidences of Polygamous Marriages

A: INCIDENCES OF POLYGAMOUS MARRIAGES 1951–1960		
Tribal	-	17.98%
Hindus	-	5.06%
Muslim	-	4.31%

Source: Towards Equality, p.67

B: INCIDENCES OF POLYGAMY		
Tribals	-	15.25%,
Buddhists	-	7.97%,
Jains	-	6.72%,
Hindus	-	5.8%
Muslims	-	5.7%.

Source : Towards Equality, p.104.
Note : Since Buddhists and Jains are also governed by Hindu law, the statistics for Hindus collectively would be 6.83% as compared to 5.7% for Muslims.

Table 4: Parsi Population in India 1901–1961

1901	—	94, 190
1911	—	100, 096
1921	—	101, 778
1931	—	101, 778
1941	—	109, 752
1951	—	114, 890
1961	—	100, 772

Source : Cabinetmaker, P.H. (1991), *Parsis and Marriage,* Pune: International Institute of Population Studies, p.1-2.

Table 5: Population of India : Urban–Rural Distribution

Total Population of India	:	843,930,861
Urban Population of India	:	25.7%
Rural Population of India	:	74.3%

Source : Census Report—1991.

Table 6: Reported Cases of Unnatural Deaths of Married Women in Mumbai

Year	1990	1991	1992	1993	1994	1995	1996
Dowry Murder	7	3	12	8	9	43	11
Dowry Death	14	21	13	8	21	-	16
Dowry Suicide	21	8	18	21	34	18	59
Total	42	42	43	37	64	61	86

Source : Commissioner of Police, Bombay.

Table 7: Religion-wise Distribution of Cases Filed under S. 498(A) IPC 1990–95

	No.	Percentage
Hindus	737	69.1%
Sikhs	28	2.6%
Buddhists	63	5.9%
Jains	2	0.2%
Total Hindus governed by Hindu law	**830**	**77.8%**
Muslims	204	19.2%
Christians	25	2.3%
Parsis	4	0.4%
Religion not Known	3	0.3%
Total	1066	100%

Source : Research conducted by Tata Institute of Social Science, 1996 (unpublished).

Table 8: Population of India—Religion-wise Distribution 1961–91

RELIG ION	PERCENTAGE TO THE TOTAL			
	1961	1971	1981	1991
Hindus	83.5	82.7	82.6	82.41
Sikhs	1.4	1.9	2.0	1.99
Buddhists	0.7	0.7	0.7	0.77
Jains	0.5	0.5	0.5	0.41
Total Hindus governed by Hindu law	**86.1**	**85.8**	**85.8**	**85.58**
Muslims	10.7	11.2	11.4	11.67
Christians	2.4	2.6	2.4	2.32
Others	0.4	0.4	0.4	0.43

Source : Census Reports.

Index

ENSLAVED DAUGHTERS

ENSLAVED DAUGHTERS

Colonialism, Law and Women's Rights

Sudhir Chandra

For
Geetanjali Shree

Preface

The making of a book is a transformative experience. This one has been particularly so for me. I ran into its subject some twenty years ago. Planning a paper for the Indian National Social Conference, I was browsing through Malabari's *Indian Spectator* when I saw a report about a young woman of twenty-five who told a British Indian High Court in 1887 that she would willingly endure the maximum punishment it would accord to her but would not obey its command to go to a husband whom she disliked. The Social Conference was forgotten. From the *Indian Spectator's* portrayal of Rukhmabai—that was the young woman's name—as a martyr to the cause of Indian women, I moved on to learn more about her from other sources. The chance discovery of her defiance initiated a convergence of academic and existential compulsions that rendered this monograph a virtual necessity.

From the surprise and awe occasioned by the discovery, to the completion of this book, has meant a good deal of learning and, hopefully, some understanding of women's perspective(s). This text may not indicate how much that experience has fashioned my position, but I hope it will reveal at least some signs of my struggle with myself to overcome entrenched prejudices and easy solutions. The questioning of colleagues and the insightfulness of so much new writing in this area have greatly helped in my attempts at rethinking. Particularly corrosive of my inherited 'male' stance (even a 'liberated' male stance) has been the anamnesis set off by Rukhmabai's story, which released unsettling parallels from the world in which I had grown up: parallels, the significance of which slowly unfolded as I progressed through different stages of work on this book.

Much that I have learnt in this process about our own times must remain unelaborated in what pretends to be a historical monograph. What must not remain unstated are the debts I have incurred on account of the material, moral and intellectual sustenance provided by a large number of institutions and individuals. Most of the material for this monograph was collected in Delhi at the Nehru Memorial Museum and Library and the National Archives of India, and in London at the India Office Library, the British Museum, and Collindale Library. My thanks to the authorities and staff of these libraries, and personally to Mr Richard Bingle, K.S. Talwar, Mr Sharma, and Mina. I also thank the authorities and staff of the Supreme Court of India Library, the Bombay Asiatic Society Library, Bombay University Library, the Maharashtra State Archives, the *Kesari* Office, and the Regenstein Library of Chicago University where I found useful additional material. I am particularly thankful to Mr Khudalkar of the Maharashtra State Archives and to Rusheed Wadia who, despite the brittleness of the paper, managed to get me a xerox copy of Rukhmabai's 'Reply' to her husband which appears here as Appendix D.

The Indian Council of Historical Research and the Charles Wallace (India) Trust provided most of the money required for research on this book in India and England. To these organizations, and to Prof Irfan Habib and Mr R.E. Cavaliero, I am much obliged.

As always, the Maison des Sciences de l'Homme offered me a chance to consult its rich library, meet French scholars, and work on successive drafts of this monograph. I deeply appreciate the readiness of this grand institution and its chief, Prof Maurice Aymard, to aid my research endeavours.

I am indebted to the Rockefeller Foundation: first, for the opportunity to write a draft of the fourth chapter at that unique institution, the Bellagio Study and Conference Center; then, for a Rockefeller Foundation Fellowship at the Institute on Culture and Consciousness in South Asia, University of Chicago, which allowed more than two months of uninterrupted writing.

The Indian Institute of Advanced Study granted me a Visiting Professorship and the chance to present my work in a series of lectures. My heartfelt thanks to the Institute and its Director, Prof Mrinal Miri, and to Prof Sujata Miri, Prof Sundararajan, and Jyotirmaya Sharma for their critical comments.

I have also benefited from discussions at other academic institutions where portions of this work were presented in early stages: the Centre for Historical Studies, Jawaharlal Nehru University; Departments of History and Sociology of the Bombay

University; the ILS Law College, Pune; the Department of History at the University of Texas in Austin; the Institute on Culture and Consciousness in South Asia at the Chicago University; the Research Centre for Religion and Society at the University of Amsterdam; and the South Asia Institute at Heidelberg University. To these institutions, and especially to Professors K.N. Panikkar, J.V. Naik, A.R. Momin, Gail Minault, Patrick Olivelle, Susanne Rudolph, Peter van der Veer, Dietmar Rothermund, and Dieter Conrad I express my gratitude.

Work on the final draft was facilitated by the combined generosity of the Japan Society for the Promotion of Science and the Institute for the Study of Languages and Cultures of Asia and Africa at the Tokyo University of Foreign Studies. I am obliged to both institutions, and especially to Prof Masao Naito who was the perfect host scientist. I also wish to thank Ms K. Tanikawa for her courtesy and efficiency.

There are many other individuals whose contribution I must mention. Of these, Gabriel who casually asked me how the Rukhmabai book was doing, should be the first. I was baffled by his question; for I had by then just written a short paper on the subject. He had copyedited the volume containing that paper, and he felt the subject deserved a whole book. This book is not exactly self-sown, and to Gabriel must go the credit of having tended the seed.

Gyan Pandey, with his uncanny ability to abstract larger significance from concrete details has all along offered me valuable advice and support. The text has also gained considerably from his editorial skill. For all this, and more, I owe him 'yet another drink'.

In Delhi Anuradha Kapur, Suresh and Deepa Sharma, and in Bombay, Jayanti and Atul have been the warmest of friends and the most welcoming of hosts and critics.

In London, David Page and Sanjay Suri provided me with similar warm hospitality. David did more. With his own training as a historian, he encouraged me to discuss my daily 'findings' with him, and helped to clarify much through his enthusiastic questions and comments.

Rajeev Dhavan liberally gave his time to discuss and plan my study, and arranged for photocopies of important English and British Indian judgments in suits relating to restitution of conjugal rights. His friendship is one of the gains of this study.

Ram Bapat introduced me to the nuances of the *Kesari's* insinuations and diatribes against Rukhmabai, and of Narayan Bapuji Kanitkar's *Tarunishikshan Natika*, an anti-Rukhmabai play in Marathi that was released while her case was still pending. That apart, his learning and sensitivity have influenced this book in ways that his self-effacing generosity will not even recognise.

Alok Bhalla edited and extensively commented on the penultimate draft. He also encouraged me by publishing an earlier version of the first chapter in his *Yatra*. Rustom Bharucha and Tanika Sarkar, too, kindly read an earlier draft and offered valuable comments. Kapil Raj went through parts of the work and ensured that the first chapter was substantially rewritten. Prof T.N. Madan made some very important suggestions for rewriting the 'Prologue'. Vasudha Dalmiya, who included part of this research in *Representing Hinduism*, which she co-edited with Henry Stietencron, alerted me to some ambiguities in my narrative. Others whose comments and criticism have helped me are Amrita Shodhan, Justice D.A. Desai, Uma Chakravarty, Flavia Agnes, Paramjeet Singh Judge, Achyut Yajnik, late Bhagirath Shah, Arjun Patel, E.V. Ramakrishnan, and Professors Lotika Sarkar, Namvar Singh, A.N. Pandeya and Ram Swarup Chaturvedi.

But for what Dhirubhai Sheth and Ravinder Kumar did, work on this book would have been badly hampered, if not discontinued. To them, and to Prof N.R. Sheth, I am grateful for keeping it going.

In preparing the final text I have gratefully benefited from the criticism and suggestions of the anonymous reader of the Oxford University Press; as also from the editing within the Oxford University Press.

Martin Fuchs very kindly prepared a long note for me on the changing pattern of the law relating to restitution of conjugal rights in nineteenth-century Germany. Christophe Jaffrelot was equally kind. He introduced me to scholars in Paris who had worked on the French law relating to *l'abandonne du domicile conjugale*, and also helped me with translation of relevant material in French. Aniket Jaaware and Urmila Bhirdikar read for me and translated much precious material from Marathi. Biswaroop Das kindly translated a long article in the Bengali monthly, *Prachar*, which Indira Chowdhury Sengupta had the generosity to pass on to me. Veena Naregal, Gopal Guru, Lakshman Dewani and Shrungi Shah also helped me obtain much-needed material.

Vimal Trivedi, Margit van Wessel, Rakesh, and Hiroshi Kobayashi-san helped with their technical expertise and facilities.

Those in charge of the library, typing, and xeroxing at the Centre for Social Studies, Surat—Mrs Mac, K.M. Bhavsar, Dayanandan, Nitin Patel, Nikhil Vyas, Hina Jardosh, V.P. Betkar, and Ashok Pawar—were ungrudging in their help. But for them, the making of this book could not have been so smooth. I recall here with deep sadness the premature death of Mrs Mac in a road accident. Without her as its librarian, the Surat Centre will be so much the poorer.

Readers will realize the delicacy of writing on issues of the kind raised by the Rukhmabai case. How does one do justice to the individual or individuals living out their lives at the centre of historical controversies that seize our attention? In this regard, I have incurred one exceptional debt. That is to Dr Bimla Chaturvedi who, having shown all her life the courage of a Rukhmabai, taught me to empathise with the vulnerability of those, especially women, who possess the strength to resist entrenched authority.

Finally, do dedications express even a small part of what we wish to express through them?

S.C.

4 February 1997

The scriptures forbid the sacrifice of female animals, but in the case of human beings sacrificing females gives the greatest satisfaction.

Rabindranath Tagore, *Chaturanga*

So they have a law by which they would not mind surrendering girls of ten to the brutal embrace of their husbands.

Behramji Malabari

Contents

Prologue

In terms roughly understood, misunderstood, and beyond
my comprehension, the world continuously imagines
new versions of itself in my head...

Tony Connor

A unique event in colonial India forms the subject of this monograph. In an inspired gesture of defiance, a girl of twenty-two—Rukhmabai—refused to be obligated to a marriage solemnized when she was only eleven. She would not, she said, offer her person to one for whom, during the eleven years of their unconsummated marriage and separate living, she had grown to develop a strong dislike. Wedded at an age at which she was incapable of giving intelligent consent, she argued that she was not bound to go to that man. For asserting her right over her person, as a woman, she was dragged into a trying litigation (1884–8) as her husband moved the Bombay High Court for the restitution of his conjugal rights. This further steeled her resolve to resist the combined tyranny of indigenous social authority and colonial legal dispensation.

Unique for its times, and not just for colonial India, Rukhmabai's resistance inevitably produced a 'social drama'.[1] The drama featured a fierce and fascinating debate about reshaping modern Indian society in which individuals, ideas, and institutions were interlocked in complex relationships of compromise and antagonism. In the unique was encapsulated the normal.

The case was filed in early 1884. But the public drama began in September the following year with the first of a series of judgments in the case. Overnight Rukhmabai was thrown into the limelight, and pictured in sharply divergent ways. Some turned her into an icon; a martyr to suffering sisterhood. Others saw personified in her their worst fears about 'modernized' women subverting family and society. Her defiance provoked a clash of fears and hopes—of contending conceptions of the desired social order. It gave the women's question and the embattled generalities of the debate on social reform an immediacy and a passion all the more charged because on its outcome hung, for once, the fate of someone in real flesh and blood.

On the triumph or defeat of the young rebel also seemed to hang the fate of a pervasive domestic-social order which rested on parentally arranged child marriages, especially among sections of the Hindus for whom marriage was a *sanskar*. Sacrosanct and indissoluble, the sanskar was generally believed not to require the spouses' consent—certainly not the bride's who, being the subject of a gift, was not a party to the marriage transaction.[2]

To the extent that marriage was, besides its other regulatory functions, an instrument of female subordination, Rukhmabai's defiance was all the more disturbing for coming from a woman. Besides threatening the sanctity of marriage and family, it posed a risk to male domination, since she, as a contemporary observed, was rejecting 'the preconceived idea of woman's inferiority'.[3] Questioning what was assumed to be natural, she offered a subversive model of assertion by women of their desire, as individuals, in a domain dominated by the family, community and men. True, though she was only asserting her right not to be forced into the arms of a man who repelled her, without claiming the freedom to remarry (a freedom that belonged to the man), that logical extension was implicit in her rejection of a woman's inferiority. If not Rukhmabai now, others inspired by her transgressive act could, in future, demand just that.

Impinging disturbingly upon the nebulous world comprising women, marriage and family, Rukhmabai's case stirred up passions that ranged from the cultural to the psychic. This was a nebulous world in that it constituted the 'private' world over which many among the subject people seemed desperate to retain a reassuring sense of autonomy. But this was also a 'public' world over which the semiotic war—a 'war in discussion' as a contemporary described it[4]—occasioned by the case was fought. Ironically, those most vocal in opposing the extension of colonial authority into their socio-religious affairs were the keenest, in this 'war', to utilize the colonial legal system and its alien practices.

This was not simply a 'civil war' involving different groups within the Indian society. It was also, necessarily in a colonial ambience, a war between the rulers and the ruled in which exceptions apart—the two sought to distinguish their respective institutions, ideals and values with regard to women, marriage and family in order to claim superiority over the other.

Because marital litigation had sparked off the trouble, the issue of law and justice also figured prominently in the ensuing controversy. This, too, deepened the civilizational encounter between the ruled and the rulers. Who was responsible for the young woman's tragic predicament? Those who professed that they would brook no interference with their venerable laws and usages? Or the intrusive colonial masters with their alien socio- legal notions and practices who insisted on mediating in the familial affairs of the ruled? In what ways did the guiding ethico-legal assumptions of the two vary with regard to women as persons and within marriage, the family and society?

In the unfolding of these larger questions were revealed conflicting normative and empirical claims with regard to the society and culture of the rulers and the ruled. As passions were aroused and partisan positions taken, this critical moment revealed the ideas, illusions and contradictions of various segments of the subject and the ruling peoples. That which usually operated subterraneously in the life of the society was brought to the surface. The macrocosm, so it appears in retrospect, was frozen in the micro.

The battle lines in this war of discussion were not sharply drawn. Rather, it, brought together in a shifting pattern of confrontation and alliance what may be distinguished as three separate discourses, each marked by its own internal variations and contradictions: the orthodox/reactionary, the imperialist, and the reformist. The first two were relatively entrenched discourses of authority, while the third was struggling to emerge as an alternative voice.

Although this discursive categorization appears neat, it ill matches the shifting patterns of social consciousness. This neatness reflects the methodological inability of 'academic' prose to name a social phenomenon and at the same time suggest that it could also be the reverse of what the nomenclature denotes. Though used in my narrative for their obvious functional utility, these categories will not connote three fixed and unambiguous sets of ideas, attitudes and beliefs, each segregated from the other two. Instead, the narrative will assume, and occasionally demonstrate, that even when they operate as distinct and rival entities, the three discourses betray varying degrees of unsuspected commonality.

Take, by way of illustration, what I have designated here, in keeping with an accepted semantic convention, as the orthodox/reactionary in contradistinction to the reformist discourse. There were, as we shall see, some remarkable orthodox Hindus who radicalized orthodoxy and contributed in a major way to the reformist discourse. On the other hand, there were Hindus who assumed a reformist stance and ended up giving an anti-reformist twist to their arguments. As a whole, however, the reformist discourse, its compromises notwithstanding, maintained a degree of internal consistency. The imperialist discourse almost always sounded the most aggressively humanitarian and claimed, particularly on the women's issue, to have set afoot an irreversible process of emancipation among the colonized. But it betrayed androcentric assumptions that, taking women's inferiority for granted, underlay the ideological as well as institutional sexism of Victorian England.

Ostensibly, however, both the orthodox and the imperialist discourses made a show of reverence and concern for women, and employed stratagems to avoid being pinned down to the actualization of that reverence and concern. These stratagems covered a wide range from reliance on a scapegoat—but for so-and-so things could have been changed—and pragmatism—the time for change was not yet—to bizarre interpretative moves that extracted from a proposition meanings that did not belong to it. (During the height of the controversy over Rukhmabai's case, however, many Hindus broke into brazen outbursts against women.)

The two entrenched discourses rested on a contrariety that permitted them to wield a charming rhetoric and effect the opposite of it. Many may have been naively seduced by the rhetoric. But there were many more who, with their own consciousness deeply divided by one of these discourses, were addicted precisely to this contrariety. It must, indeed, have been intoxicating to be an imperialist with the burden of a civilizing mission, or reactionary with the make-believe of reformism.

The power of the word was magnified by other modes of social control. The rhetorical resources of the orthodox and imperialist discourses, much more than those of the fledgling reformist discourse, were strengthened by the varieties of non-discursive powers wielded by both organized social authority and the colonial dispensation. Indeed, these two, for all their acerbic differences, also operated in tandem. As in the Rukhmabai case, the coercive power of the colonial law court and prison could be added to the customary disciplinary mechanisms employed by organized social authority against recalcitrance.

The two further acted in concert as they settled down to argue, even as they felt shaken, that the Rukhmabai case disclosed nothing wrong with either Hindu society or colonial law. 'Hard cases make bad laws' was the legal maxim they invoked to suggest that the case was an aberration which called for no tampering with the legal or social system that had caused it.

It was, indeed, a hard case in the sense that Rukhmabai was exceptional in her defiance. Nothing like her personal courage and the radicality of her defense had arisen before. The chances were that in the foreseeable future, too, her case would remain exceptional. Given the state of Hindu/Indian society, Rukhmabai's example was unlikely to inspire other women, who may have suffered much worse circumstances than she, into similar defiance.

For this reason, the exceptionality of the case was a measure of the commonality of women's oppression. But those who needed the 'hard case' doctrine to feel reassured about the health of Hindu conjugality and colonial law would not see this. Pandita Ramabai, the crusader, did. Her searing comment was:[5]

> Many women put an end to their earthly sufferings by committing suicide.[6] [Yet] Suits at law between husbands and wife are remarkable for their rarity in the British Courts in India, owing to the ever submissive conduct of women who suffer silently, knowing that the gods and justice always favour the men.

A radical understanding such as Ramabai's is what this monograph seeks. In a way, indeed, this understanding suggests itself through the kind of microscopic view attempted here.[7] The inconsistencies, ruses, and falsehoods which, together with its charming rhetoric, constitute the reality of a given discourse, barely escape detection when viewed so closely. But, then, illusions do not necessarily vanish with their objective stripping. Their reality resides, also, in our mode of perceiving them. That is where the attempt to see things from Ramabai's vantage point—'the vantage point of women'[8]—helps. It unravels the underlying opposite that was subserved behind the professed concern of the dominant discourses/ideologies for women's welfare.

Despite their oppositional stance, however, neither the then emerging vantage point of women as represented by rebels like Ramabai and Rukhmabai nor the alternative reformist discourse was free from the hold of the two discourses of authority. This was particularly true of the imperialist discourse which, all said and done, was assumed—and still is—to be an emancipatory force. Even Ramabai's outburst against justice had something rhetorical about it. It was an invocation of the very justice—British justice of which it was an indictment. Whatever she may have felt, as an apostate, about the gods—Hindu gods—so far as justice was concerned, she retained her faith in the providentiality of British rule. So pervasive was this paradox that Rukhmabai herself, in the moment of her defiance and ever after, viewed legislation by the colonial government as the best hope for women in India.

Nothing should have been more plain during the Rukhmabai case than the implication of the highest colonial judiciary in upholding social practices and relations that were inequitous to women. The judiciary, even at the higher levels, was run on principles and by people that assumed the inferiority of women. The Rukhmabai case, in fact, shot into limelight with a demonstration of such an assumption in Justice Pinhey's brilliant but abortive judgment in favour of Rukhmabai. Yet, the criticism voiced during the case neither lost nor weakened faith in the progressive character of the colonial legal mediation.[9]

Sustaining faith in the liberal humanitarian conception of its jurisprudence was, perhaps, the colonial dispensation's most impressive, and abiding, hegemonic achievement. Winning most reformers' hearts, that conception privileged a unified legal system with uniform laws. Projected as a superior alternative to the traditional plurality of laws, the system invoked the idea of justice and claimed for itself freedom from the corrupting touch of personal intervention which, it claimed, inevitably rendered the working of the customary laws capricious.[10]

Justice was inscribed as the supreme touchstone of law in the imperialist discourse around the third quarter of the nineteenth century. Defining it as universal, this idealized notion of justice promised a thrilling justification to a people whose duty it was to wield power, and wield it without being corrupted by it. The point was made by Cardinal Manning with the force of an epigram: 'Our power is the measure of our duty.' This, pertinently, was said in the context of the imperial duty to legislate for the elimination of social evils in India.[11] Even this duty, as the aftermath of the Rukhmabai case illustrated, they were keen to evade, but without deviating from their imperious moralism. They, rather, held back, democrats that they were, because of conservative Indian opposition.

Justice, forming with equity and good conscience an irresistible trinity, harmonized with high imperialism. As late as in the 1860s, though, it had inspired suspicion,[12] inducing the Privy Council to direct courts in India to beware of the trinity, lest Indians should become victims of English judges' ethnocentric application of what they believed were universal values. The fear was not unfounded. The trinity actually did mean English law, and by the 1880s—the time of the Rukhmabai case—this could openly be recommended for possible application in India.[13]

Justice universalized gave the imperialist discourse a new moral authority. Their laws were instruments of, if not actually the same as, justice. But, as during the Rukhmabai case, there could be no guarantee against injustice flowing from the selfsame laws. On such occasions the maxim about hard cases making bad laws came in handy. Nevertheless they brought to light an unresolved tension between justice and law. A law that, conceived as an instrument of justice, also produced injustice was the opposite of justice. More so when injustice was seen to stem from judges who, even when they knew what in a particular case justice required them to do, felt hemmed in by a technical legal requirement. The Rukhmabai case was but one illustration of the inescapability of injustice as law took precedence over justice.

That the system implied a fundamental subordination of the end of justice to the means of law is not how the imperialists saw it. They did not realize that an aporia lay at the heart of any jurisprudence that invoked justice as the supreme value and nursed a fundamental suspicion of the human agency. Justice required that each case be treated as unique, and judges not be obliged to give decisions they knew were unjust.

The aporia was not noticed even in the reformist and orthodox discourses which, between them, spanned the emerging Indian thought on the nature of law and its socio-political functions. Cast as it was in the liberal-rational image of the West, the reformist discourse could not possibly have sensed the systemic reversal of priorities between justice and law. But the failure of even the orthodox discourse to sense this reflected the speed with which Indians were coming round to the western assumptions about universal justice and uniform laws. Their defense of traditional laws and customs, and wailing over the consequences of colonial legal mediation, indicated more and more a surrender to, rather than a critque of, the imperialist discourse. Even as they regretted the loss of the elasticity of customary laws and panchayat courts, the reformers and the reactionaries alike planned to make the Hindu law, both substantively and procedurally, rigidly homogenized. So decisive, within the continuing ambivalence, was the lure of the new assumptions that some of the best Hindu minds, irrespective of their ideological persuasions, ended up suggesting changes calculated to make the Hindu law unrecognizably rigid and arbitrary.[14] The process, it is true, was assisted by the political urge towards communal solidarity. But it need not have meant surrender to the imperialist discourse.

The surrender is now complete.[15] Justice as a supreme normative notion no longer inspires any reservations, and more often than not the State is accepted as the supreme arbiter. Plurality of laws is anathema, and uniformity of laws an axiomatic virtue. The suspicion of human mediation as an invitation to uncertainty and arbitrary exercise of power is firmly entrenched. Faith in the administration of laws through an impersonal machinery has been shaken. But that is at the level of everyday experience; the principle remains inviolate. This, ironically, is believed even by people who, in other contexts, advocate decentralization and the revival of the community as a necessary check on the all-powerful modern State.[16]

These observations may today be criticized as obscurantist, and citing Gandhi's *Hind Swaraj* in defense may aggravate matters. But obscurantism could not in the 1860s have been responsible for the Privy Council's anxiety that justice and equity could offer English judges in India an illusory justification for thrusting their parochial ideas and values upon an alien populace. This realism about justice, as Derrida has so effectively reminded us, had a respectable lineage in Europe. Pascal, following Montaigne, had seen that custom alone provided justice with 'the mystical foundation of its authority': 'Whoever traces it to its source annihilates it'.[17] The arrogance of high imperialism had no use for such realism. Bent, under the same impulse, on banishing whatever remains of custom within the kingdom of law—with nothing but justice for its normative base—we dread today to critique the mystique of justice.[18]

Why, however, have these observations been made here? This book, initially was meant to focus on a critical moment in the making of our society. I have since discovered the persistence of that moment over the last hundred years and more. On the women's question an unsuspected attitudinal and institutional continuity has marked a century of change that, in certain respects, seems to have been dramatic. The debate that erupted with Rukhmabai's defiance, the 'Epilogue' will show, has not yet dated. A stance like hers still remains transgressive. 'Mere dislike', the term that hostile public opinion and judicial authorities then used, obliterating from view the reasons of the [mere] dislike, still prompts judicial verdicts in favour of husbands their wives *do not like*.

A continuity such as this calls, as a point of departure, for a questioning of the practice and founding assumptions of the reigning system of jurisprudence. As a movement and as an academic enterprise, feminism has advanced impressively since the 1880s. From subtly discursive/ideological to brutally coercive social/political, it has laid bare many modes of exercising power. It could, perhaps, generally and in specific contexts, aspire to so unmask the mystical foundations of law as to annihilate its authority. What the point of arrival will then be is a premature question or a rhetorical one because, historically, there never really are points of arrival.

To aspire to that radical-feminist stance is not to achieve it. Not only because there never is a fixed stance, but also because one is never fully self-aware. Privileged with hindsight, we may have relatively less difficulty in discerning the constraints within which, unbeknown to them, the consciousness of our great forerunners like Ramabai and Rukhmabai operated. Can we be similarly self-aware of our hidden constraints and of the full posssibilities of our positions? With all my limitations and consequent failures, of some of which I am acutely aware, I could not have written this book from any other perspective. Not the least so because of what it has meant to me to be in the presence of Rukhmabai.

I take heart from the following strangely moving observation of Deirdre David at the end of her *Intellectual Women and Victorian Patriarchy*:[19]

> I would like to think a male critic could have written this book, or perhaps should say would have wanted to do so. For me, the desire of female and male critics to write from a feminist perspective about writers of both sexes signifies an end to the patriarchal attitudes resisted in one way or another, by Martineau, Barrett Browning, and Eliot.

One more word of confession. In what began as a polite

conversation at a formal dinner, a Black American feminist got seriously interested in the drama of Rukhmabai, asked many searching questions about its protagonist—recognizing in her a 'shero' for contemporary feminism the world over—and said at the end: 'Colleague, do you realize the importance of her story?' I do not remember having shown due diffidence then. Now I must, in this 'Prologue', where the beginning and the conclusion of my narrative converge.

The story possesses more hermeneutic possibilities than I have followed in this monograph, or am even aware of. Rukhmabai, to cite what may seem a striking lacuna, could have been a more pervasive and direct presence. Closer attention to biographical details could have revealed the psycho-social factors that gave her the strength to rebel where most women submitted to or chose less defiant ways of negotiating a similar suffering. Such an understanding would no doubt yield important insights. For my purpose, though, it has been important to follow the point that while Rukhmabai's kind of resistance was *possible* as a grand act of defiance towards the turn of the last century, it could not herald a common struggle.

None of the other possibilities are, however, foreclosed. My failure must act as a provocation to explore them.

NOTES

1. Readers may recall the notion of 'social drama' to appreciate the advantages of focusing on a suit that shot into a *cause celebre* and excited socio-political passions in India and England.
2. Consider the following from a brilliant contemporary synthesis of Hindu laws and usages relating to marriage: '... a woman is not regarded in Hindu law as an active party in marriage. In fact, she is hardly regarded as a party at all. Marriage is viewed as a gift of the bride by her father or other guardian to the bridegroom: the bride, therefore, is regarded more as the subject of the gift than as a party to the transaction.' Further, 'exceptional cases' of *swayamvara* notwithstanding: 'The early age at which a girl is enjoined to be married, makes her unfit to act as a party to the nuptial contract, and throws upon her guardian the sole responsibility of negotiating a proper match for her. ...Minors are not only eligible for marriage, but are the fittest to be taken in marriage.' Gooroo Dass Banerjee, *Hindu Law of Marriage and Stridhan,* Calcutta, 1879, pp. 45–6. This, as we shall see in the context of the debate on the Rukhmabai case, was not an uncontested view of shastric Hindu marriage.

3. *Indian Spectator,* 13 Mar. 1887.
4. *Native Opinion,* 11 Apr. 1885.
5. Pundita Ramabai Sarasvati, *The High-Caste Hindu Woman,* Philadelphia, 1888 (reprinted in 1984), p. 64.
6. Immured in her solitude, one wonders, how many times would Rukhmabai have contemplated such an end to her miseries.
7. The fluid interplay of various forces revealed in the moment of Rukhmabai's defiance lends itself to the kind of microscopic view suggested by Michel Foucault when he writes: 'At the moment, people are returning increasingly to the monograph form, but no longer so much in terms of studying a particular object as of rendering apparent the point at which certain type of discourse is produced and formed... What one would thus try to reconstitute would be the enmeshing of a discourse in the historical process... ' Further, stressing the importance of 'making all these discourses visible in their strategic connections than in constituting them as unities, to the exclusion of all other forms of discourse', he remarks: 'But in thinking of the mechanisms of power, I am thinking rather of its capillary forms of existence, the point where power reaches into the very grain of individuals, touches their bodies and inserts itself into their actions and attitudes, their discourses, learning processes and everyday lives.' Michel Foucault, *Power/Knowledge: Selected Interviews and Other Writings 1972–77,* Colin Gordon (ed.), Brighton, 1980, pp. 37–9. One may also recall that in 1927 Jayashankar Prasad, struck by the easy sway of injustice, had a woman character in one of his historical plays, *Dhruvaswamini,* say about women's acceptance of subjection: 'Something like a tradition of dependence has for so long wormed its way into their very veins, their consciousness.' Ratnashankar Prasad, (ed.), *Prasad Granthavali,* Allahabad, 1985, vol. II, p. 776.
8. For a discussion of feminism as a 'vantage point', as a 'perspective on social reality', besides being a social movement, see Joan Kelly, *Women, History & Theory,* Chicago, 1984.
9. While presenting aspects of this work at seminars in India, I have at times met with criticism from some scholars, especially legalists, who insist that Hindu law and usage were responsible for Rukhmabai's predicament.
10. The colonial Indian achievement was contrasted with the inadequate realization of the ideal in the parent country itself. In a panegyric, which was also a self-laudation, one of the nineteenth century 'makers' of Hindu law could not avoid the 'sacrilege' of suggesting that the 'unknown' legislators of British India had achieved what the British parliament had vainly struggled to effect. John D. Mayne, 'The Anglo-Indian Codes', *The Asiatic Quarterly Review,* Oct. 1887, pp. 334–53. An unsigned article on 'The Development of India' in the liberal-radical *Westminster Review* asserted: 'Since the introduction of the Queen's Government criminal justice has been entirely reformed, and its principles and procedures have been rendered uniform... Everywhere through British India the courts— assuming that men are likely to speak truth than to lie—have

adopted a national procedure... The *Zeitgeist* of modern Europe is inspiring a society that still loves the ways of the ancient world.' Mar. 1888, pp. 342–51. In keeping with the reigning shibboleth of evolutionism, progress towards uniform laws across geographical and cultural frontiers had emerged as a cherished ideal. See Charles Stuart Wells, *The New Marriage and Other Uniform Laws*, London, 1887.

11. Cardinal Manning, 'Indian Child Marriages', *The New Review*, Nov. 1890, pp. 447–48.
12. See M.C. Setalvad, *The Common Law in India*, Bombay, 1970, pp. 19–25.
13. Within two decades of this the Privy Council was overtaken by a different mood, and Lord Hobhouse could plainly say in 1887 that 'justice, equity and good conscience' were 'generally interpreted to mean the rules of English law if found applicable to Indian society and circumstances'. Ibid., p. 25.
14. Dewan R. Raghunath Rao and V.N. Mandlik, both of whom we shall meet frequently in the following narrative, illustrate the growing hold of the imperialist discourse. Raghunath Rao, who gladly donned the description 'revivalist of the Hindu law' as he sought to radicalize tradition, favoured the elasticity of panchayat courts as against the impersonal, procedure-bound courts established by the British. *Pall Mall Gazette*, 24 Mar. 1887. Yet, he wanted the government to introduce a bill, the draft of which he and some other reformers had prepared. The implications of the proposed bill, of which these reformers seem to have been oblivious, can be imagined from the following clauses:
    'Marriages contracted between Hindus shall become so complete after sexual intercourse has taken place, that all civil rights of inheritance, maintenance, and the like, shall thenceforward recur to either of the contracting couple, and not before.' 'The contracting parties, who may complete their marriage by consummation, as aforesaid, shall within fifteen days from the date of nuptials, sign their names, either personally or by a duly authorized agent, in a book to be kept for the purpose in the office of a Sub-Registrar of Assurance, or where there is no Sub-Registrar, in that of the Local Village Munsiff, in evidence of the fact of the completion of their marriage.' *Asiatic Quarterly Review*, Jan. 1888. Mandlik, opposed in his social views to Raghunath Rao, was for years ambivalent with regard to the plurality of Hindu law. See his English translation of *The Vyavahar Mayukha*, Bombay, 1880, Introduction and Appendix IV. He, too, was converted to the idea of a uniform Hindu law by the time of the Rukhmabai controversy.
15. Though the starkness of its expression may hit many as neo-imperialistic, the process is realistically summed up when A. Gledhill thus explains the uninterrupted 'reception' of English jurisprudence in India: 'Unless one is a confirmed believer in the view that the Law of England is the "true embodiment of everything that's excellent" it may be a matter of surprise that India, now mistress of her own destinies, should be willing to retain the law, the legal system, and the institutions which Britain

imposed upon her.' *The Republic of India*, London, 1964, p. 147.

16. It is difficult not to mention, in this context, the recent Supreme Court directive to the Government of India to expedite the framing of a uniform civil code for the whole country. It is, in such a situation, heartening that an Indian feminist should warn against unquestioning reliance on the State, legislative reformism and a uniform civil code. See Madhu Kishwar, 'Codified Hindu Law: Myth and Reality', *Economic and Political Weekly*, XXIX, 33, 13 Aug. 1994, pp. 2145–61.
17. See Jacques Derrida, 'Force of Law: The "Mystical Foundation of Authority"', *Cardoza Law Review*, July–Aug. 1990.
18. We may also recall, in this context, the teaser: '... by what criteria are we to judge the justice of custom... ?' John Rawls, *A Theory of Justice*, London, 1978, p. 35.
19. Dierdre David, *Intellectual Women and Victorian Patriarchy: Harriet Martineau, Elizabeth Barrett Browning, George Eliot*, London, 1987, p. 231.

1

Rukhmabai and Her Case

Rukhmabai was the daughter of Jayantibai from her first husband, Janardan Pandurang. When she was two and a half and her mother merely seventeen, Janardan died. He left behind some property and willed it to his young widow. After six years of her husband's demise, Jayantibai married Dr Sakharam Arjun, a widower. Remarriage of widows was permitted among the *suthars*—carpenters—the caste to which the couple belonged. Before marrying Sakharam, Jayantibai transferred her property to Rukhmabai, then a minor of eight and a half.

Two and a half years later, when she was eleven,[1] Rukhmabai was married to Dadaji Bhikaji, a poor cousin of Sakharam Arjun. It was agreed that, deviating from the patriarchal norm, Dadaji would stay as a *gharjawai* with Rukhmabai's family and be fully provided for by them. It was hoped, Rukhmabai tells us about the arrangement, that he would in due course acquire education and 'become a good man'.[2]

Within seven months of the marriage, Rukhmabai reached puberty. The event, customarily, heralded *garbhadhan,* the ritual consummation of marriage. But Dr Sakharam Arjun, an eminent medical man known for his reformist predisposition, would not permit early consummation.[3] The denial did not please Dadaji who, at twenty, was keen to partake in the pleasures of marriage. He also resented the regimen prescribed by the family to make him a 'good man'. What particularly distressed him, with his proven aversion for education, was the compulsion to go to the sixth standard of school at an age when he should have been at the university.

Meanwhile Dadaji lost his mother who, to ensure her none too promising son a decent life, had along with Sakharam Arjun agreed to this particular marital arrangement. In the absence of her restraining influence Dadaji's waywardness became inexorable. He left school, fell into bad company, began defying Sakharam Arjun, and started living with his maternal uncle, Narayan Dhurmaji. This uncle, a man of some means, had internalized the ethos which permitted men to treat women, especially their wives, as simply means of domestic labour and carnal pleasure. He kept a mistress—a *Kamatee* labourer named Chinamma whom he had picked up from a lime factory. This, at this time, was socially accepted male behaviour. But Narayan Dhurmaji did worse. He brought the mistress to live in the same house as the rest of his family, an arrangement that once drove his harassed wife to attempt suicide by jumping into a well.[4]

The change in Narayan Dhurmaji's surroundings suited Dadaji. With this commenced a phase of life that, in Rukhmabai's description, carried Dadaji 'through every course of dissipation' into 'ways which a woman's lips cannot utter'. He—we only know what the woman could mention—was 'attacked with consumption, confined to his bed for three years, in such a state that he was not expected to live another season'. 'But', Rukhmabai's account continues, 'by God's grace he recovered a little day by day'.[5]

The recovery was confined to bodily ailments alone. Dadaji continued to slide deeper into indolence and an irresponsible existence, dependence on others, and consequent loss of self-respect. He began to accumulate debts and received most of his loans from Narayan Dhurmaji. With his sight trained on the property that would accompany Rukhmabai into his house, the uncle encouraged the nephew's dependence and indebtedness so as to be able to manipulate him later. He was the prime instigator of the suit against Rukhmabai.[6]

In contrast to Dadaji's waywardness, Rukhmabai evolved during the same years into an intelligent and cultured young woman. Sakharam Arjun, her stepfather, had contacts with social and religious reformers, including Vishnu Shastri Pandit, perhaps the most committed supporter, in his day, of women's cause in western India. These contacts along with association with Europeans, both men and women, exposed young Rukhmabai to liberal reformism. Sakharam Arjun, in fact, rejoiced that there was, among the middle and higher classes, hardly a family that did not 'gladly avail itself of the girls' school'.[7]

Even among such families, however, a girl's marriage resulted in, almost automatically, the termination of her schooling. Even if she was young enough to continue to stay on in her natal home after marriage, she needed the permission of her in-laws or, when he was mature and independent, of her husband to continue with her school. Only rarely was the permission forthcoming. It was unlikely to come from Dadaji and Narayan Dhurmaji, both of whom had their reasons to desire an early commencement of this marriage. If anything, Rukhmabai's continued schooling was likely to provoke them to demand that she be sent to live with Dadaji. The prudent way to avoid an early consummation of Rukhmabai's marriage was not to precipitate matters.

That, however, did not make the denial of education bearable for young Rukhmabai.[8] Eleven years after her 'great liking for study' was abruptly interrupted in her nuptial year, she wrote:[9]

> I am one of those unfortunate Hindu women whose hard lot it is to suffer the unnameable miseries entailed by the custom of early marriage. This wicked practice has destroyed the happiness of my life. It comes between me and the thing which I prize above all others—study and mental cultivation. Without the least fault of mine I am doomed to seclusion; every aspiration of mine to rise above my ignorant sisters is looked down upon with suspicion and is interpreted in the most uncharitable manner.

This anguished cry constituted the only confessional moment in a long pseudonymous letter Rukhmabai sent to the *Times of India* on the ills of infant marriage. The letter was not an exercise in cold, controlled reasoning. It was written with a passion which, if at all, was restrained by a melancholy born of the writer's own tragic situation which she could translate to the lot of women in general. That she broke into the autobiographic only on this point shows how acutely she felt about the correlation between early marriage and denial of education to women.

Rukhmabai, however, did not give up. She began a process of self-learning. But in her day, as she soon realized, it was 'very hard for women to study at home'. The realization was rendered all the more piquant by the refusal of her pro-female-education stepfather to support her efforts.[10] Slow and painful, at times overtaxing even those she turned to for help, her education, as she described it, proceeded as follows: 'I used to ask a number of pronunciations and meanings of English words at a time whenever my European lady friends happened to call.' Cloistered in a home at once liberating and claustrophobic, young Rukhmabai moved from one word to the next—intonating them, dwelling on their meanings, making sense of them in the light of her own experience and vice versa—on to a widening perspective:[11]

> Day by day my love for education and social reform increased... I began seriously to consider the former and present condition of our Hindu women, and wished to do something, if in my power, to ameliorate our present sufferings.

She even began writing on the subject of social reform.[12] Alive to the injustice of her suffering, the future rebel was able to discern in personal tragedy the predicament of her sisterhood. Self-suffering was leading to an awareness of a cheerless womanhood: Hindu/ Indian womanhood. (Later, in England, she would discover a yet larger cross-cultural feminist identity.)[13] This saved her from consuming self-pity. She could see fellow-victims all around. The personal and the general—the existential and the political—coalesced.[14] She talked of the 'daughters of India'. This was not merely a rhetorical expression for her. It was a tragic reality. Her sufferings were also 'our' sufferings, and her fight was a larger fight.

It was this girl who saw her spouse go from bad to worse. Over a period of five or six years, as Dadaji sank deeper into his 'wild reckless life style', Rukhmabai's 'aversion for him became firmly settled'. So was her 'natural distaste for married life' which —she rationalized—she had felt from childhood. Finally, realizing that he was 'irreclaimably lost', she decided to wash her 'hands of him for ever'.

The decision was, in some measure, strengthened by the sinister figure of Narayan Dhurmaji. After the first year of her marriage, when she occasionally visited Narayan's house, Rukhmabai never went there again. Then aged twelve (fourteen according to Dadaji), she must have grasped, with a vague sense of fear, the bizarre goings-on in that household. But a vague sense of fear alone could hardly have occasioned a resolve so drastic as to never set foot in that house. Something more traumatizing, it appears, transpired.

The resolve, perhaps, resulted from a sexual advance made upon young Rukhmabai by the concupiscent uncle. Sexual abuse of their young wards' wives by guardians was not an uncommon phenomenon. This even, at times, prompted marriages of very young boys with older girls so that the boys' guardians could have at hand objects for their own illicit gratification. The evil was sufficiently widespread to induce reformers like Malabari to campaign against it. Even Rukhmabai insisted that 'under no circumstances' should a girl be married to a boy younger than her.[15] Narayan Dhurmaji was unlikely to be above such a failing. True, Dadaji was not a child. But in deepening Dadaji's dependence on himself, the scheming uncle may well have desired the attractive niece-in-law, in addition to her property.[16]

Eleven years thus elapsed and the couple was yet to cohabit. At twenty-two Rukhmabai was no longer too young for conjugal relations; her husband had touched thirty. For far too long had Sakharam Arjun warded off, on one pretext or another, the attempts made by, and on behalf of, Dadaji to have his wife with him. Unless the husband was inclined to write off this relationship and chance another marriage, he was unlikely to leave matters as they were.

Dadaji was anything but so inclined, especially since Rukhmabai owned property worth twenty-five thousand rupees. Substantial for those times, the property must have lured Dadaji irresistibly, living as he was on favours from relatives and friends. As 'her lawful husband' he believed, characteristically enough, that the custody of his wife's person and property was his 'as a right'.[17] So, after years of informal initiatives had yielded mere evasion, Dadaji embarked in March 1884 on a course that led to litigation.

On 19 March he sent through his solicitors—Messrs Chalk and Walker—a letter to Sakharam Arjun, asking that 'my wife might be allowed to come and live with me, as I thought the probation period had lasted long enough'. To compound the threat of legal action with pressure from the community, a number of anonymous letters were sent to Sakharam, chastising him for 'harbouring' Rukhmabai against her husband's wishes. Despite his protestations to the contrary, presumptive evidence points towards Dadaji and his close associates in directing this epistolary orchestration.

Sakharam had been Dadaji's benefactor. Besides treating him during several prolonged illnesses, one of which had been near fatal, he had offered the security of his roof to Dadaji and his brothers. Consequently, even when litigation loomed as a certainty, Sakharam hoped he could shame Dadaji into submission. He sent for his son-in-law and old ward, and asked him to sign a letter to the effect that there was no truth in the anonymous epistles. The meeting ended in frayed tempers.

Realizing that a legal showdown was in the offing, and obliged to respond to Dadaji's solicitors before there was time to devise a definitive strategy, Sakharam wrote back on 22 March:[18]

> Gentlemen,—In reply to yours of the 19th instant, I have to inform you that Rukhmabai, mentioned therein, has not been detained at my house against the wishes or demands of your client, Mr Dadaji Bhikaji. Her stay at my house hitherto has been by the consent of the relatives on both sides, because of the unfortunate circumstances of your client.
>
> I have not the slightest wish to detain her even now, and I shall be rather glad if your client provides her with a suitable house and takes her away, which is however his own look out. He is at liberty, so far as I am concerned, to take her away at any time.

The ambiguity of the reply was both a preparation for the imminent legal battle and an attempt to avert it. On the face of it, the letter conveyed a simple message to Dadaji. If he did not want his wife to stay on with her parents he could take her away at any time. There was, for all they knew, a half chance of Dadaji being induced to try informal negotiations yet again. Also, if the family decided to avoid a legal tangle, Sakharam could send Rukhmabai to her husband without much loss of face. Should it, however, be necessary to take up the gauntlet, the message was qualified enough not to be annulled. At the very least, the decision was postponed.

Dadaji's side, conveniently, read the reply as an offer to send back Rukhmabai. A day later, on 25 March, a party was sent to bring her to Dadaji. Besides Narayan Dhurmaji, the party included Damodar Bhikaji, an elder brother of Dadaji, and, significantly, Ganpatrao Raoji, a clerk from the firm of Dadaji's solicitors. Rukhmabai refused to accompany them on the ground that Dadaji was not in a position to provide her with a suitable house and maintenance. A letter was sent the following day on behalf of Dadaji. It asked Rukhmabai 'to join him forthwith' and assured her, with cool ambiguity, that he would 'give her suitable maintenance and lodging *according to his rank and position*'. (Italics added.)

The stage was set for litigation. The middlemen of colonial law had taken charge of affairs on both sides. Acting through her solicitors—Messrs Payne, Gilbert, and Sayani—Rukhmabai now introduced a new ground for her refusal to live with Dadaji. Besides reiterating that he was unable 'to provide her lodging, maintenance and clothing'—the last item appearing along with lodging and maintenance as part of a ritualized legal drafting—her reply added that Dadaji was 'in such a state of health' that she could not 'safely live with him'.

This was the beginning of escalating of charges and counter-charges that frequently mark legal proceedings. Dadaji, while filing the actual suit, similarly extended the range of charges by implicating Rukhmabai's mother and maternal grandfather as well. 'The true reason' why Rukhmabai 'refused to live with him', he now alleged, was the pressure exerted upon her 'by her mother, Jaentibai, and her mother's father, Harrichand Yadowji'. The two feared that once Rukhmabai started living with her husband, she would 'assert her right to the property of her deceased father, Janardhan Pandoorang'.[19]

This was said in the plaint to the High Court. Later, offering the public his view of the case in April 1887, Dadaji was more forthright. Estimating the property's value to be 'upwards of Rs. 25,000', he maintained: 'In this little history of property lies the whole secret of the world-wide case of Dadaji vs. Rakhmabai.' Or, apropos of Harichand Yadowji—this time making him the sole covetous villain and omitting the name of Jayantibai: 'If the name Harichand is substituted for the name Rakhmabai in this case, its realities will be better understood but its poetry will be gone'.[20]

Dadaji's charge was not implausible. Rukhmabai, however, dismissed it as 'entirely false' and as an attempt 'to divert the public mind from the real issues in the matter'. She contended that the property was 'not worth half the sum' suggested by Dadaji; that, far from being covetous, her mother had transferred the property 'purely due to her affection for me'; that although Harichand Yadowji collected the rents 'for a long time... he submitted the accounts to me, and I checked them myself'; and that since 1882, 'long before Mr Dadaji filed his present suit', she had operated an account with the Bank of Bombay in her own name. She also accused Dadaji of having 'conveniently' omitted a few words from the text of her father's will so as to mislead the public about its contents.[21]

Charges relating to property usually make messy business, rendering it difficult to sift the contradictory evidence of rival litigants. But, considering that the Hindu Widows' Remarriage Act (1856) had damaged a remarrying widow's entitlement to the property of her deceased husband—even where customary law permitted unprejudiced inheritance[22]—Rukhmabai possibly over stated the role of maternal affection in the transfer of Janardan Pandurang's property to her.[23]

Indeed, her very marriage with Dadaji was influenced by considerations of property. True, the arrangement was justified by the hope that living under Sakharam's roof and supervision would make Dadaji a 'good man'. But the hope also camouflaged a design to control Rukhmabai's property. As he heard the appeal against the first judgment in the Rukhmabai case—the only one in her favour—Sargent, the Chief Justice, wondered how 'this very attractive lady' came to get 'married to this man'.

Latham, Rukhmabai's counsel, explained how Sakharam Arjun had 'hoped to educate the boy' who 'turned out to be a blockhead with whom you could do nothing'; and how this had made Sakharam 'very averse to the marriage before he died'. However, even Latham felt that Sakharam had 'acted rather in the interests of his own family than that of the girl'.[24] No wonder that Dr K.R. Kirtikar, a hostile witness who had once been a protegé of Rukhmabai's stepfather, insisted that the young lady's ruin was achieved by 'her new father... in order to retain her property in his house'.[25]

In fact, Rukhmabai's own account confirms, more than it removes, the suspicion that her guardians' conduct was not quite above board. It combined petty material calculations with affection and solicitude for their hapless ward. They may have liked to control her finances, but without unduly compromising themselves. They may even have believed that control to be vital for her welfare. But they did not conspire to keep the couple apart for the sake of property.

There is no necessary correlation between covetousness and material circumstances. Yet, their relative prosperity seems to have shielded Rukhmabai's guardians from obtrusive scheming. Harichand Yadowji was a well-to-do man whom the government had, following years of service, rewarded with a title and a personal allowance in addition to his pension. Dr Sakharam Arjun was a self-made man who had earned enough by the time of his death in April 1885 to leave Jayantibai and his children from her better provided than Rukhmabai was.

It is Dadaji's own conduct, and his uncle's, that made property central to the suit he had filed to obtain his conjugal rights. We may situate this in the context of Sir J. Hannen's generalization that suits for restitution of conjugal rights are 'far from being in truth and in fact what theoretically they purport to be', i.e. proceedings 'for the purpose of insisting on the fulfilment of the obligation of married persons to live together.' Delivering an important judgment in *Marshall v. Marshall* (1879), the eminent Victorian authority on matrimonial causes remarked: 'I have never known an instance in which it has appeared that the suit was instituted for any other purpose than to enforce a money demand.'[26]

Hannen, of course, generalised about motives behind the filing of restitution suits, not about defence therein. Rukhmabai made sure that what Dadaji called 'poetry' was not blotted out by property from the heart of the matter. Her defense, and resolve to be a martyr for the principles enunciated therein, converted the suit into a historic fight for a new conception of and deal for Indian women. Such was her sense of mission that, while she could afford it, she refused public funds to prosecute her case. When in 1886 the *Bombay Gazette* opened a subscription list to defray her legal expenses, she had it closed at once.

The first intimations of high principles, relating to the general condition of women, appeared in Rukhmabai's written statement before the High Court in answer to Dadaji's plaint. Earlier, when Dadaji's men had gone to bring her, her mundane reply had been that 'she would not live with him unless he rented another place, and took her there'.[27] To this was added the ground of his unsafe health. These were contingent objections which, if removed, implied readiness for cohabitation.

But Rukhmabai introduced a radical repudiation in her answer to Dadaji's plaint. Because, she averred, she had not 'arrived at years of discretion' at the time of her marriage, she could not be bound to it. This entailed a fundamental proposition. A marriage—even a Hindu marriage—ought not to be binding on a spouse who had not consented to it. The proposition would become central to the case and be hotly debated within as well as outside the court. As the case progressed, Rukhmabai's defence came to rest exclusively on general principles of this nature.

Moving from the basic principle to specific merits, Rukhmabai's statement explicated what Sakharam, in his letter to Dadaji's solicitors, had vaguely referred to as 'the unfortunate circum-stances' owing to which Rukhmabai had not joined Dadaji. These related to 'the character of the persons, under whose protection' he lived and 'expected her to join him'. At stake here was the larger question of the right of a Hindu woman to choose not to live in a joint family of which, by virtue of being her husband's wife, she compulsorily became an inseparable part. This implied a challenge to the sanctity and integrity of the joint family as an essential unit of Hindu social organization. More immediately, however, the dark hint at Narayan Dhurmaji's liaison with Chinamma, his *Kamatee* mistress, to be partially uncovered during evidence in the case, posed greater peril to Dadaji.

These circumstances, Rukhmabai submitted at the end of her statement, constituted 'the only true reasons for her refusing to live with the plaintiff'. She prayed that the suit be 'dismissed, and that her costs be provided for'.[28]

II

Rukhmabai and Sakharam had finally decided to fight the legal battle. As she recalled the events—in a private letter of 17 February 1887 and in her public 'Reply', four months later, to Dadaji's public 'Exposition' of the case—Rukhmabai claimed to have resolved, on her own and long before Dadaji precipitated matters, 'to wash my hands of him for ever'. She also claimed to have felt from early childhood 'a great disgust for married life'.

Rukhmabai's recall carries the impress of its circumstances. Her 'truth of the narrated past' was coloured by an exceptionally charged 'narrative instant'.[29] This was the instant of her martyrdom when, in a glorious gesture of defiance, she had told the judge that rather than accept his verdict and go to her husband, she would submit herself to the maximum penalty admissible under the law. She believed herself to have been destined for sacrifice to a higher cause. Her misogamy, reserved disposition and love of study seemed to constitute a 'natural' justification for, and lead inexorably to, her defiance.

However, misogamy does not seem to have turned Rukhmabai against Dadaji. Her resolve to be done with him 'once for all' took shape over the years as she realized the irreversibility of his degeneration. This turned into a revulsion for married life; and the revulsion acquired a higher justification as she pondered over the inequity that marriage entailed for women in India. Once the resolve was made and the battle waged, the recall of events from childhood to the great drama of 1887 turned teleological.

It is difficult to document the development of Rukhmabai's thought process and to know when they began to acquire their subversive edge. But these reflections could not possibly have been as focussed, or acquired as early, as she retrospectively suggested. The desire to stay away from her husband, and the realization that she could act accordingly, must have come from a prolonged and painful 'internal polylogue',[30] of which only traces are available in her *Times of India* letters and some other scanty personal testimony. Beyond the suggestion of a lonely and unhappy childhood, there are no details to substantiate possible speculations regarding her fears and reveries as she oscillated between the melancholy of her reality and wondrous dreams of escape and freedom.[31] She must have struggled endlessly with the thought that she could leave her husband before it acquired in her mind the visage of a practical possibility.

However, irrespective of when she reached it, Rukhmabai's resolve not to go to Dadaji was her own. She had little interaction with her stepfather,[32] the only guardian who would not have dismissed as insane the thought of not fulfilling her marital obligations. It is doubtful, though, if she could have alone carried through the explosive resolve to the bitter end. She was lucky that her stepfather realized the enormity of sending her to the man he had chosen as her husband.[33] She recalled with gratitude—in contrast to her discreet silence about him in the context of her self-cultivation—that on his own her 'father', 'considering his [Dadaji's] constitution, habits, and unfitness for any work, resolved not to send me to his house to live as his wife'.[34]

It was not an easy decision for Sakharam. He had to face the hostility of his wife and father-in-law who were determined to send Rukhmabai to Dadaji. They pressed him for a whole year after the suit had been filed, until his death in April 1885, to settle the matter out of court. He also worried that his refusal to send Rukhmabai to her husband could confirm suspicions that he had designs on her property. Indeed, the suit itself was intended to be a neat little operation to blackmail Sakharam into submission because, as Rukhmabai wrote, 'to have a suit of this kind in a Court is considered a [sic] greatest disgrace among us Hindoos'. That he risked the disgrace was some penitence for his original lapse.

Once litigation had begun, Rukhmabai set about neutralizing the conception her mother and grandfather had of their *dharma* and family honour which required that she be sent to Dadaji.

This proved a difficult and arduous task. In the event, they were converted less by her pleadings than by the way Dadaji repulsed the overtures made by Sakharam on their insistence. There could be no trusting a man so ungrateful—albeit instigated by 'evil counsellors'—as could spurn a beneficiary like Sakharam who, as Rukhmabai put it, 'had heartily fed and clothed him and his brothers for years'. Their conversion came in time for Rukhmabai not to feel stranded when Sakharam died months before the case came up for hearing.

That she would not be without powerful support was also ensured by the espousal of her cause by Behramji M. Malabari (1853–1912). Wise beyond his years, and compassionate, he had dedicated himself to the service of his country and the regeneration of his society. A consummate publicist, he used his English weekly, the *Indian Spectator*, to promote causes that as a patriot and social reformer he considered important.

Malabari was an extraordinary man. What was, perhaps, most unique about him deserves special mention in the context of his interest in Rukhmabai's case. Sensitive in his own life to the need for convergence between precept and practice, and between ends and means, he was among the first in colonial India to propose personal sacrifice—martyrdom—as an instrument of social action. He shared and projected Rukhmabai's vision of her case that sublimated it far above her personal matrimonial dispute. When the expensive expedient of an appeal to the Privy Council seemed necessary, Malabari proposed the formation of a fund to defend Rukhmabai. Though not rich, he was among the first and highest contributors to the fund.[35]

Around the time Dadaji filed the suit, Malabari was working on his historic 'Notes' on 'Infant Marriage in India' and 'Enforced Widowhood'. He visited Simla in the summer of 1884 and discussed the 'Notes' with the highest officials, including Viceroy Ripon and his Law Member, Ilbert. Satisfied of 'their readiness to do everything in their power, on proper representation', he sent out the 'Notes' to a large number of government officials and a cross section of Indians. This was intended to initiate a public discussion that might facilitate governmental action.[36]

Malabari soon received a letter from Auckland Colvin, the Finance Member, suggesting the advisability of 'obtaining test decisions' from the law courts on matters taken up in the 'Notes'. A similar suggestion was made by G.E. Ward, the collector of

Jhansi.[37] It made sense to test the limits of existing laws to know if legislation was needed to improve women's position. The Rukhmabai case, with its unmistakable social significance, offered just that chance.[38]

Rukhmabai saw Malabari's 'Notes' when she was 'almost giving way to despair'. Sakharam Arjun was dead. The moral boost she would receive from the transformation of the suit into a *cause celebre* lay in the future. For the present was only the terror of judicial uncertainty. The 'Notes' lifted her spirits up: 'I felt that fortune was about to smile on the unhappy daughters of India'.[39]

Another influential person to support Rukhmabai during those difficult days of anonymity was Henry Curwen (1845–92), the editor of the *Times of India.* A grandson of Wordsworth, Curwen had made some name as a novelist before coming out to India in 1876. Quick to grasp the personal and public dimensions of her case, he decided to promote the young woman's cause. Lest the orthodoxy be prematurely stirred into organized action, it seemed prudent to him not to push Rukhmabai into the limelight at this stage. Instead, in an inspired tactical move, she was projected as a mysterious figure. Her mystique even travelled to England and, through coverage in the London *Times,* engaged the attention of such English women and men as were interested in Indian affairs or cared for the cause of women.

Under the pseudonym 'A Hindu Lady', Rukhmabai contributed two letters to the *Times of India.* At a time when middle and upper class Hindu women were but little visible, the pseudonym alone could be trusted to exercise a spell; and the effect was facilitated by the power and pathos of the letters, and by the illusion of a personal *rapport* with the author that the epistolary genre tended to create. There was an air of expectancy about the identity of the mysterious 'Lady', though there also were insinuations that the pseudonym hid behind it a man. The insinuations obliged the *Times of India,* while carrying the second letter, to admonish the sceptics: 'this letter is exactly what it professes to be, the genuine and spontaneous production of a "Hindu Lady".'[40] In any case, a space was created in the public mind for the mysterious lady. Whenever necessary, the pseudonym could be unveiled and the space utilized to promote Rukhmabai's cause.

The appearance of the two letters was brilliantly timed. Published on 26 June 1885 as a preparation for the controversy the suit was bound to occasion, the first letter lent a feminist perspective to 'the question of the social status of Hindu women'.[41] The second letter was published on 19 September 1885, the day Rukhmabai's case first came up for hearing before Justice Pinhey. The judge must have read the letter over his morning tea or breakfast—the daily routine of Anglo-Indian officials making it a reliable conjecture—and hours later the proceedings in the case would have confirmed the impression made by the morning's reading. No wonder Hindu orthodoxy looked back upon the letters of 'A Hindu Lady' as a conspiracy to bring pressure on the High Court.[42]

The effect of the letters, including their readership, was maximized by the *Times of India* through an uncommon move. It carried an editorial on each occasion to strongly recommend the letters to its readers. They provided, according to the 26 June editorial, a 'feminine emphasis' to the discussion that had begun with Malabari's 'Notes' about the status of Hindu women and their relations with the other sex. The editorial exhorted Indians to carry to its fruition the 'genuine and unprompted' protest of 'A Hindu Lady' against men's unjust laws for women.[43]

In its editorial on the day of the hearing, the *Times of India* impressed upon its readers the exceptional qualifications of 'A Hindu Lady', qualifications that would soon be used to present a contrast between Rukhmabai, the supremely accomplished woman, and Dadaji, her good-for-nothing husband. A 'high-spirited woman of refinement, culture and intellectual superiority', she was 'well versed in Western as well as Eastern literature, and intimately acquainted with the position of her sisters in Europe'. She had disposed of 'the stock arguments of the Shastris' that had for centuries kept Indian women in servitude.[44]

In her pseudonymous letters, which were on the theme of Malabari's 'Notes'—infant marriage and enforced widowhood—Rukhmabai acknowledged the 'debt of gratitude' that 'all Indian women' owed him. Moreover, with disarming modesty she admitted that, not 'being much accustomed to write in English', she had her letters corrected by a friend who felt 'genuine sympathy… for our condition'. It was just as well. The admission sustained her credibility later when, during the controversy that raged around her case, imputations were made about her literary competence.

Indicting Hindu social customs for victimizing women the most, Rukhmabai showed that the 'wicked institutions' of infant marriage and enforced widowhood did not 'entail on men half the difficulties which they entail upon women':

> Marriage does not interpose any insuperable obstacle in the course of their [men's] studies. They can marry not only a second wife, on the death of the first, but have the right of marrying any number of wives at one and the same time, or any time they please. If married early they are not called upon to go to the house and to submit to the tender mercies of a mother-in-law; nor is any restraint put upon their action because of their marriage.

The reverse happened in the case of women. If a girl was married at eight (as most girls were), and lucky to have enlightened parents, she could go to school till she was ten. Her schooling thereafter depended on 'the express permission' of her mother-in-law. But not even in Bombay, 'the chief centre of civilization', did many mothers-in-law allow their daughters-in-law to continue their education. Girls, thus, were taken out of school just when they were 'beginning to appreciate education'. Even those given an exceptional reprieve did not enjoy it long. Early maternity (usually around fourteen, the age when Jayantibai gave birth to Rukhmabai) obliged them to 'give up the dream of mental cultivation and face the hard realities of life'. Higher female education was not possible while 'infant or rather early marriage' persisted.

Rukhmabai's attack on early as well as infant marriage was radical for the time. The contemporary debate on social reform invested considerable passion in the distinction between infant and early marriage. There were many who condemned infant marriage, but considered early marriage shastric and essential to the Hindu domestic economy. Even Malabari was constrained to propose twelve as the minimum age of consent for girls.[45] Rukhmabai, in contrast, wanted no marriage to be 'legal unless the bride is fifteen and the bridegroom is twenty years old'. Even fifteen did not ensure women a decent schooling. But twelve was absurd. She stuck to fifteen as a reasonable compromise.[46] This she did while making a few suggestions to alleviate the sufferings of her sisterhood, although she realized the difficulty of outlining 'a law calculated to affect the whole of this vast country'.

Rukhmabai, then, described the young bride's domestication within her husband's family. Subjected to 'inhuman treatment' and worse off than the servants (who, at least, had 'the option of refusing to work'), she was deprived of 'mental and physical freedom'. A 'torrent of abuse, often followed by direct or indirect corporal chastisement', made the girl 'as docile as a beast'. If, perchance, it did not, the mother-in-law could employ 'her last weapon' and 'turn the girl out of [the] door'. No wise girl could ever wish for this. After marriage she could not expect refuge in her natal home, which she was told—as she still is—ceased to be *her* home after marriage. Nor could she turn for support to her husband:

> The poor fellow, hardly out of his teens, is saddled with a wife and a family of two or three children. He is entirely dependent on his parents for his barest necessities, and, by taking the side of his wife it would be hard for him to keep his body and soul together... if he has the will he has not the power to help his wife out of misery... Even in the case of an educated boy husband there is not much happiness in store for the girl wife... If he dislikes his parents for their harsh treatment of his wife, he despises his wife for her ignorance.

Women, Rukhmabai's penetrating description continued, became 'timid, languid, melancholy, sickly, devoid of cheerfulness and therefore incapable of communicating to others'. Their subordination was sealed by the life long indoctrination that they were innately inferior to men, so that 'we have naturally come to look down upon ourselves'. Women were handed over their gloomy destiny by the shastric law-givers who:

> being men have painted themselves... noble and pure, and have laid every conceivable sin and impurity at our door. If these worthies are to be trusted, we are a set of unclean animals, created by god for the special service and gratification of man who by divine right can treat or maltreat us at his sweet will.

Rukhmabai stayed awhile with men's incomprehension of women's suffering. Quoting a Marathi proverb to the effect that 'we can philosophically (i.e. coolly) bear the misfortunes of our neighbours', she commented: 'Men cannot, in the least, understand the wretchedness which we Hindu women have to endure'. But this did not belie women's desires: 'Because you cannot enter our feelings, do not think that we are satisfied with the life of drudgery that we live, and that we have no taste for and aspiration after a higher life'.

This identity of women *as* women rested on men's injustice towards them. It brought Rukhmabai to the point of sounding a warning—'do not think'—but left her uncertain about what to do if the warning went unheeded. However strong its will to defiance, in the existing state of women's consciousness and organization, the identity belonged in the region of aspiration and could at best lead to symbolic resistance. The 'bitterness of (her) heart', in having to acquiesce in men's injustice, encapsulated the predicament of Rukhmabai and the mute sisterhood for whom 'A Hindu Lady' spoke:

> I entreat my countrymen to judge the miseries of widows by transferring the same penalties to men... I ask would my countrymen not have long since revolted against such inhuman treatment?... however unhappy a widow's lot might be, it would have been capable of defence had it been based on any principle of equity or justice. But in the eyes of our law-makers men and women belonged to quite different species of humanity...

A familiar mode of entreaty by the weak, this hypothesized revolt of men against gendered injustice was also an intimation, somewhat wistful, of similar behaviour by women some day. The present offered little hope. The progress made 'in the direction of reform' following 'the advent of the English' had affected individuals and not transformed families. This created stress within the domestic world, estranging educated husbands from their 'illiterate and superstitious' wives.

Coming from Rukhmabai, this perceptive observation carried an ironic poignancy. As a woman she had experienced, from the position of superiority, usual for men, the disruption of conjugality by disparity in the couple's upbringing. But it had not brought her the strength that accrued to men in similar circumstances. The prevailing socio-legal mores rendered her vulnerable nonetheless. Her superiority was viewed, generally, as if it was something she ought to feel guilty about; or else as an aberration for which her guardians were answerable. No less than the Chief Justice of the Bombay High Court blamed those 'well-meaning but ill-advised people' who 'not only educated but impreganted' Rukhmabai, *after she had been married*, 'with English ideas on the subject of matrimony so as to render her entirely unfit to discharge the duties of marriage'. No more girls, His Lordship hoped, would be so handicapped by education.[47]

Rukhmabai's own ironic vulnerability confirmed her remark that progress required the schooling of families (and indeed of communities), as socially operating units, and not of just so many individuals. It epitomized her prime indictment that, even if it scarred men, the prevailing system crushed women far more.

Taught by experience to be wary of the beneficiaries of English education, Rukhmabai rather turned to legislation to do away with women's 'grinding thraldom'. If educated men, she asked:

> who fully admit the existence of the evils, have neither the pluck nor the strong sense of duty to fight them, need we wonder at the indifference of the uneducated masses? In a state of society where the educated, or the 'upper ten', are indifferent and the uneducated ignorant, is it rash to invoke government aid for the redress of these crying grievances?

Rukhmabai regretted that opinion in the country, as reflected in the 'specious' objections to Malabari's 'Notes', was opposed to legislation. She, however, hoped that the English—governing India by God's grace—would not flinch.[48] Her faith in the providentiality of British rule was not the political naïvety of a cloistered girl. The myth of divine dispensation was part of social consciousness in later nineteenth century India.[49] Similarly, faith in legislation as an instrument of social reform, besides having respectable political philosophical antecedents, was subscribed to by some of Rukhmabai's illustrious contemporaries as well.[50]

What is more, she did not let the indefensibility of social injustice close her mind. For example, as 'A Hindu Lady' she had accused shastric law of making the widow 'a leper of society', 'unbeloved of God and despised of man—a social pariah and domestic drudge'.[51] But when some supporters faulted her understanding of shastric law, she was not inattentive to their criticism.

Among these supporters were some radical exponents of Hindu orthodoxy, persons steeped in the *shastras* and not innocent of western learning. Thus, not knowing that they were but one person, Dewan Bahadur Raghunath Rao lent in quick succession the weight of his impassioned erudition to both 'A Hindu Lady' and Rukhmabai. But he appealed to 'A Hindu Lady':[52]

> to find out whether our Rishies were really as cruel as they have been made to appear… they fully sympathised with you and shared all your views. They say that the family in which the softer sex is not happy brings ruin upon itself. This saying has been fulfilled.

A similar stance of critical sympathy was assumed by some 'progressive' reformers as well. The *Indu Prakash*, an Anglo-Marathi weekly from Bombay, could appreciate why 'A Hindu Lady' should have given expression to 'vituperation and sarcastic abuse directed against the devoted heads of the poor old Rishis'. After all, the oppressive system was all too often justified 'on the authority of those old law-givers'. Yet, the weekly protested, the rishis were 'no more to blame for the hard lot of the modern Hindu widow than the poor widow herself'.[53]

Rukhmabai subsequently modified her position. Less than three years later, in a letter that recapitulated much of what she had said as 'A Hindu Lady', she wrote about shastric law: '...these good laws have ceased to be observed and other pernicious customs have taken their place, the results of which lie before us in many horrible forms...'[54]

The force of what 'A Hindu Lady' wrote flowed from an understanding born of personal suffering. On the question of enforced widowhood, however, she, perhaps carried away by her enthusiasm for Malabari, treated compulsory widowhood as a universal Hindu custom. This led the *Bombay Gazette*, an Anglo-Indian daily that would later support Rukhmabai to the hilt, to accuse 'A Hindu Lady' of exaggeration. Did she, it asked, 'ever look into the vernacular papers?' The question bore reference to the advertisements—'by no means few and far between'—that harassed wives issued through these papers, warning their 'absent or erring husbands' that 'if they did not, by a given date, signify their resolve to turn a new leaf, the marriage would stand dissolved, and the wives would marry again'.[55] True, these notices possessed 'no legal validity whatever'. But they were accepted 'by the lower castes, that is, by the bulk of the community in the mofussil'. 'The Punchayets', the *Gazette* continued, 'acquiesce in the repudiation of the husbands, when they are considered to be unworthy of their position, and what is still more remarkable, marriage with another man is regarded as valid'.[56]

Women of 'this stamp' were unlikely to 'readily resign themselves to the role of the weeping widow'. It was, therefore, 'a great mistake to represent the average woman of India as a mild, spiritless creature, totally unequal to the duty of protecting her own rights and interests'. Having accused 'A Hindu Lady' of exaggeration, the *Bombay Gazette* concluded with a dash of hyperbole: 'In the great masses of the people a practical recognition of woman's rights has been obtained by the force of circumstances, helped out by feminine self-assertion, which on some points might make an American lady of the newer and freer States die of envy.'[57] Had it known the identity of 'A Hindu Lady', the *Gazette* would have relished reminding her of her own mother's remarriage.

Yet the truth in Rukhmabai's complaint of injustice against her sex shone through her exaggerations. Indeed, as Malabari argued, the exaggerations emanated from the selfsame injustice:[58]

> It is a sin to talk of exaggeration in the case of a woman who has become

> frenzied by the cruel injustice which has blighted her life. She writes strongly because she feels strongly. Here is a language of exaggeration only so far as it is the language of acute suffering.

The letters of 'A Hindu Lady' were embellished with an appropriate Victorian flourish by the 'friend' to whom they were submitted for 'correction'. Even Malabari admitted that there was 'something palpably artificial throughout the epistles'. But the artificiality related only to 'the outward form'; their spirit was 'quite genuine, all too convincing'.[59] That spirit was Rukhmabai's own—and, through her, of women's struggle for their rights.

Such was the person Dadaji expected to overwhelm into capitulation. Modest but inquisitive, determined to rise above the vulnerability of her person and her kind, she had awakened to a sense of mission as she grasped the relationship between the personal and the social/political. What she stood for brought to her, early enough, supporters like Malabari and Curwen, and their numbers kept mounting.

She was represented, for the same reason, by three eminent lawyers—F.L. Latham, K.T. Telang and J.D. Inverarity—who were alive to the larger purpose and principles of law. A liberal in his politics, Latham was then Advocate-General of Bombay. D.E. Wacha, the nationalist leader, said of him: 'No counsel was more conscientious.' About Inverarity, 'the prince of counsel', Wacha remarked: 'But it would be gilding refined gold to say aught about Mr Inverarity who is to-day head and shoulders above the generality of counsel of the day.'[60]

Telang (1850–93), as a nationalist, social reformer and admirer of George Eliot's fiction, had a greater stake in defending Rukhmabai. Familiar with English jurisprudence, he was, along with his senior and rival interpreter, V.N. Mandlik (1833–89), the leading authority in western India on Hindu law. As a lawyer and, later, as a judge of the Bombay High Court, Telang sought to develop the dynamic potential of shastric and customary law without neglecting its conservative role. Taking his cue from the traditional law-givers themselves, he believed that what custom had made, custom could also ameliorate.[61] Interpretation for him was an instrument for making Hindu law responsive to the complexities and needs of modern life. An English judge of the Bombay High Court observed about Telang:[62]

> ... it was refreshing sometimes to hear him arguing for 'modernisation', while on the other side an English advocate, to whom the whole Hindu

> system must have seemed more or less grotesque, contended for the most rigorous construction of some antique rule.

Rukhmabai's counsel decided, therefore, that Telang argue the part of her defence that involved an exegesis of the Hindu law on the question of conjugal rights. Outside the court room as well, his intervention in the controversy over the Rukhmabai case was marked by sophistication and responsiveness to the politico-cultural complexities of an old and now colonized society.

For the defence counsel, then, this was not just another brief. They had grasped its wider import. Consequently, they stuck to the principles of the case even after it became clear that the decision in the British Indian courts would be on its merits. They hoped, eventually, to have the principles settled in appeal to the Privy Council. This, as we shall see, did not happen. But before that we must turn to Pinhey's 'revolutionary judgment'.

III

In keeping with their reliance on basic principles, the first of the three issues raised by Rukhmabai's counsel, when the case came up for hearing on 19 September 1885, was: 'Whether the plaintiff was entitled to maintain the suit?' The issue arose from the submission in her written statement of July 1884 that she had not arrived at years of discretion at the time of her marriage. In July 1884, it may be noted, the fact was stated but the issue was not framed. The second issue—'Whether the plaintiff was in a position to provide for the lodging and maintenance of the defendant?'—related to the merits of the case. Latham declined to raise any issue on the allegations relating to Dadaji's health and to the character of the person under whose protection he was living. But he expressed his intention to avail of these allegations—if proved—under the general issue. From these issues a third one arose: 'Whether the plaintiff was entitled to the relief claimed, or any part thereof?'

Dadaji's counsel—Vicaji and Mankar—challenged the veracity of the allegations against him. More important, they raised the counter-issue whether—even if true—these allegations constituted, in Hindu law, sufficient justification to refuse conjugal rights. They then argued that since marriage between the two parties had been admitted, 'the onus is on the defendant to prove that she is legally justified in resisting the husband's suit for enforcing his marital rights'. As for consent, they contended on the strength of Mayne's *Hindu Law* that want of consent due to infancy was immaterial. Marriage among Hindus was 'not a contract strictly so called, but a religious duty'.

Anticipating, rightly, a possible difficulty about the meaning of 'restitution', they made a pre-emptive move, and asked, 'in the alternative, for a restitution or institution of conjugal rights'. If, taking a rigorous view, emphasis was laid on the question of cohabitation or the consummation of the marriage—Rukhmabai and Dadaji, we may remind ourselves, had never lived together—the 'suit would, strictly speaking, be one for the institution of conjugal rights'. But if it was seen that the defendant, after attaining her maturity, was staying with her stepfather only because her husband had permitted the arrangement, the suit would be 'one for the restitution of his conjugal rights'. These rights, Dadaji's counsel stressed, had never been 'disputed since the marriage until within a month before the suit'. Still relying on Mayne, they argued:

> From the moment of marriage the Hindu husband is his wife's legal guardian, even though she be an infant, and has an immediate right to require her to live with him in the same house as soon as she has attained puberty; her home is necessarily her husband's home... Dr Sakharam's house, where the plaintiff frequently visited her, was constructively the husband's place of abode, or, at least, it was a place appointed by him for the purpose of her residence.

In taking care of the distinction between restitution and institution, Dadaji's counsel dealt with more than the ground—marriage before the age of discretion—on which maintainability of the suit had been challenged. They apprehended, again rightly, that the issue could be further enlarged to question the very admissibility by a law court of suits for restitution of conjugal rights wherein the parties involved were Hindus. They, therefore, contended that there was 'the authority of law texts and the decisions of Courts for holding that a suit for restitution of conjugal rights does lie among the Hindus'. They also drew the court's attention to the fact that the issue of maintainability was not raised in the statement originally filed by the defendant.

Besides pleading that the onus of proof rested on the defendant, Dadaji's counsel disposed, in principle, of the issue of the husband's means to provide for his wife:

> The poverty of the husband does not constitute a matrimonial offence so as to operate as a legal bar to the husband's right to seek his wife's society and assistance.

Pinhey, accepting neither their plea nor the authority cited by them, ruled:

> I don't agree with Mr Mayne's position,[63] which seems to me to be too broadly laid down by him, and to go much beyond the decisions of the Courts... the plaintiff must prove his case, and is, therefore, bound to begin.

Evidence for the plaintiff then followed. The witnesses included Dadaji himself, his brother, his uncle Narayan, and two doctors. The doctors testified that they had found no symptoms of asthma or consumption in Dadaji. The other evidence disclosed that Dadaji, with his uncle's aid, made from thirty to forty rupees a month, though there were months when he earned nothing. To allay suspicions arising from the Chinamma connection, it was stressed that Narayan Durmaji had his wife and daughters living with him.

Latham got up at this stage. It was Monday and the proceedings had been resumed after adjournment on Saturday. Before Latham could utter a word, the judge said:

> Mr Advocate-General, unless you are particularly anxious to make some remarks for the assistance of the Court, I think I need not trouble you as I am prepared to dispose of the case at once.

This was an unorthodox move, the more astonishing for coming from someone known to be a weak judge. Due to retire in three weeks, Robert Hill Pinhey had found the occasion for his swan-song. A memorable judgment would be his farewell to the city of his birth.[64] Having read the letter of 'A Hindu Lady' on Saturday morning and, later in his court room, seen the character of the men who claimed Rukhmabai among their midst, he had spent an agonizing Sunday. The whole case was clear. The plaintiff had done himself in. The real anxiety was to find a legal way out of what, if done, would be reprehensible. So powerful was the case's impact on Pinhey that even from his retirement in England, where he espoused the lost cause of pacifism, he manfully defended Rukhmabai and his own decision in her favour when the High Court ordered her to go to her husband.

The Advocate-General, naturally, evincing no anxiety to assist the court, the judge began with his verdict. Ever since the case came up before him on Saturday, he had been thinking about it and 'looking into the authorities'. He had 'arrived at the opinion that the plaintiff cannot maintain this action'. The verdict given straightaway, he proceeded to elaborate the grounds thereof.

It was 'a misnomer', Pinhey explicated, 'to call this a suit for the restitution of conjugal rights'. According to the practice in England and British India, a suit for restitution of conjugal rights was one that, in the event of separation and living apart after cohabitation, either spouse could bring against the other. The suit filed by Dadaji was not of that character. In a narrative reflective of his axiomatics, Pinhey observed:

> The parties to the present suit went through the religious ceremony of marriage eleven years ago when the defendant was a child of eleven years of age. They have never cohabited. And now that the defendant is a woman of twenty-two, the plaintiff asks the Court to compel her to go to his house, that he may complete his contract with her by consummating the marriage. The defendant, being now of full age, objects to allowing him to consummate the marriage, objects to ratifying and completing the contract entered into on her behalf by her guardians while she was yet of tender age.

Having shown his sympathies, Pinhey unburdened his shocked sensibility in a morally charged diction:

> It seems to me that it would be a barbarous, a cruel, a revolting thing to do to compel a young lady under those circumstances to go to a man whom she dislikes, in order that he may cohabit with her against her will...

It was, however, on legal grounds that Pinhey avoided what seemed to him barbarous, cruel, and revolting. Going over the case law he was persuaded that no court had ever ordered 'a woman, who had gone through the religious ceremony of marriage with a man, to allow that man to consummate the marriage against her will'. Neither the law nor the practice of the courts in England and India would, therefore, justify him in 'making such an order', or Dadaji in 'maintaining the present suit'.

Pinhey realized the futility of expecting an English precedent that would be 'on all fours' with the suit before him. For, unlike infant and early marriages in India, marriages in England were generally between persons of mature age; the marriage and consummation were not normally separated much in time. He regretted the transplantation into India of 'the practice of allowing suits for the restitution of conjugal rights' which had 'originated in England under peculiar circumstances'. It had 'no foundation in Hindu law—the religious law of the parties to the suit'. 'Under the Hindu law', he emphasized, 'such a suit would not be cognizable by a Civil Court'. Indeed, for 'many years' after he came to India—in 1851—the courts did not admit such suits. They began doing so only in the wake of the post-1857 judicial and legal reconstruction that brought about the amalgamation of the Supreme and Sadar Courts into the High Courts.

Pinhey's regret regarding the transplantation in India of the English practice was heightened by the fact that it had been discredited in England. Crystallized in Sir James Hannen's judgment in *Weldon vs. Weldon*,[65] English opinion against the practice had resulted in the Matrimonial Causes Act—Stat. 47 & 48 Vic., cap. 68—of August 1884. The Act removed the penal provisions of the law which subjected to imprisonment and/or attachment of property a spouse who disregarded the court's directive to resume cohabitation.[66] The Act had, in fact, rendered 'almost inoperative' the practice of allowing such suits.[67]

However, whatever his regrets, Pinhey was bound by the unregenerated English law that still obtained in India. All he could do was to refuse to enlarge its application to include *institution* within the meaning of *restitution*. Legally not incumbent, such an enlargement would be morally outrageous. In his impassioned words, he was not bound:

> to carry the practice further than I find support for in the English authorities, especially when the granting of the relief prayed would produce consequences revolting not only to civilized persons, but even to untutored human beings possessed of ordinary delicacy of feeling... I am certainly not disposed to make a precedent, or to extend the practice of the Court in respect of suits of this nature beyond the point for which I find authority.

Obliged by 'neither precedent nor authority' to subsume institution within restitution, Pinhey rejected the interpretation attempted by Dadaji's counsel while asking 'in the alternative, for a restitution or institution of conjugal rights'. Secure in the belief that he had devised a legal way out of a moral dilemma, he was 'glad' that:

> in the view of the law which I take, I am not obliged to grant the plaintiff the relief which he seeks, and to compel this young lady of twenty-two to go to the house of the plaintiff in order that he may consummate the marriage arranged for her during her helpless infancy.

The moral exuberance of Pinhey's oration belonged in the tradition of those trenchant judicial pronouncements—a classic example being Justice Maule's speech in *Regina vs. Hall* (1845), exposing the inequitousness of English matrimonial laws[68]—which stirred the conscience of Victorian England and facilitated many an important legislative intervention. However, the anxiety to provide his moralism with the cover of law led Pinhey to explain not only the 'why' but also the 'why not' of his verdict. Worried lest his sympathy for the 'enlightened and cultivated' lady be misunderstood, he took pains to clarify that he had not accepted her entire defence. For example, he was in no doubt that Dadaji was very poor and had given 'much false evidence' about his pecuniary position; and that his uncle had on the same point given, 'if possible, evidence less credible still'. But poverty was 'not one of the reasons' for the rejection of Dadaji's claim. 'A poor man,' Pinhey reassured, 'has as much right to claim his wife as a rich man to claim his'.[69]

If his cautious concluding remarks were meant to offset the flamboyance of his judgment, the effect was neutralized by an outburst from Pinhey moments after the conclusion of his judgment. The sheer force of that outburst made it inseparable from the morally charged judgment, of which formally it was not a part. Sticking longer in popular remembrance than the judgment proper, the outburst was sparked off when Dadaji's counsel, Vicaji, took exception to the award of costs to Rukhmabai. Referring to Pinhey's ruling that in Dadaji's case a suit did not lie for the restitution of conjugal rights, Vicaji pleaded:

> I submit to your lordship that this is not a case in which the plaintiff should be ordered to pay costs. He has been acting under advice of counsel who considered the suit would lie.

Pinhey saw this as the last straw after the inconsistencies and lies in the evidence for Dadaji. He had done well, in the judgment, to limit his displeasure about the plaintiff and his collaborators to their false evidence. But he was ill-prepared for an appeal in the name of the plaintiff's innocence. It brought forth the wrath that had been welling up since the week-end:[70]

> When the plaintiff found that the young lady was unwilling to share his home, he should not have tried to recover her person, as if she had been a horse or a bullock.

The outburst was used to support the charge that Pinhey was moved by sentiment rather than law. The charge came from a variety of quarters, from Pinhey's peers sitting in judgment on his verdict to reactionary elements within the Hindu society.[71]

Compared, for example, to Maule's *exposé* in *Regina vs. Hall*, which paved the way for judicial divorce in England, or to Hannen's judgment in *Weldon vs. Weldon*, which resulted in the Matrimonial Causes Act of 1884, Pinhey's critique of the law he was obliged to administer was a failure. His verdict was set aside within six months. With it also fell an alternative and less aggressive conception of colonial law and legal procedure, a conception which was pregnant with profound politico-cultural possibilities.

However, Pinhey succeeded in drawing attention to the vexed question of the relationship between morality and law, and in embedding the case within a broader legal-humanitarian framework. In doing this, and in refusing to be bothered about its details, Pinhey imparted a more compelling moral dimension to the case than had been envisaged even by Rukhmabai's own counsel. His verdict made the case inseparable from the women's cause. There was now no chance for those who sought to make it a private matrimonial dispute.

NOTES

1. Dadaji, however, maintained that Rukhmabai was thirteen at the time of their marriage. This may well have been intended to weaken the effect of Rukhmabai's contention that, married at eleven, she was incapable of giving intelligent consent to the arrangement. Thirteen during those days, it may be noted, was not considered very young. Early in the following decade even Malabari would agree to have the age of consent fixed at twelve for girls. Rukhmabai, however, maintained that they were eleven and nineteen at the time of their marriage. See Dadaji Bhikaji, *An Exposition of Some of the Facts of the Case Dadaji vs. Rakhmabai*, Bombay, 1887, p.1 (hereafter referred to as *Exposition*, it is reproduced as Appendix C); 'Rukhmabai's Reply to Dadaji's Exposition', *Bombay Gazette*, 29 June 1887. (Hereafter referred to as 'Rukhmabai's Reply'. See Appendix D for the text of this reply.) Earlier also, in her letter of 17 Feb. 1887, which found its way through the Bishop of Carlisle in the London *Times* of 9 April 1887, Rukhmabai mentioned the same ages. So also in her reply to Dadaji's plaint in the Bombay High Court. See *The Indian Law Reports*, Bombay Series, vol. IX, p. 529. Dadaji's counsel maintained that she was thirteen. Ibid., p.530. In the *Times* letter Rukhmabai says that she was married in 1876. This could not have been true because she had been married for ten or eleven years when the case was filed in 1884.
2. Rukhmabai's letter of 17 Feb. 1887, *Times*, 9 Apr. 1887.
3. Dadaji's own description of this says: 'The marriage was not at once consummated because Dr Sakharam Arjun volunteered the opinion that an early consummation would result in the issue of a weak progeny,

and he told me this in a friendly way, while I accepted his advice in the same friendly spirit.' Dadaji Bhikaji, *An Exposition of Some of the Facts of the Case of Dadaji vs. Rukhmabai*, Bombay, 1887, p. 2. Hereafter referred to as *Exposition.*

4. The suicide bid made by his wife was the subject of a detailed discussion and cross-examination in the libel suit filed by Narayan Dhurmaji against Rukhmabai, her maternal grandfather and Grattan Geary, editor of the *Bombay Gazette*. For the bizarre details of this aspect of the case, see *Bombay Gazette*, 20, 30 July 1887.
5. *Times*, 9 Apr. 1887.
6. *Times of India*, 4 Mar. 1887. Rukhmabai had Narayan Dhurmaji uppermost in her mind when she told the High Court that 'certain evil-minded persons' had instigated Dadaji into litigation 'for their own sinister purposes'. He had filed the suit, she asserted, 'not because he was really desirous that she should live with him'. The others Rukhmabai had in mind were some caste leaders whom Sakharam Arjun had annoyed.
7. Ibid., 14 Aug. 1884.
8. People like Dr K.R. Kirtikar, who knew him and his family well, accused Sakharam Arjun of indifference towards Rukhmabai. But these accusations were brushed aside by Rukhmabai. Mentioning, in her letter of 17 Feb. 1887, the marriage of her mother to 'a celebrated doctor in Bombay', she said that he 'proved an unusually kind stepfather to me', and 'protected and loved me as his own child throughout his life'. *Times*, 9 Apr. 1887. See also Rukhmabai's 'Reply' for a bristling attack on Kirtikar. Kirtikar appeared for Narayan Dhurmaji in the libel case that the latter filed in July 1887 against Rukhmabai and her grandfather. Kirtikar's evidence in this case, and the angry contempt shown towards him by Rukhmabai's lawyer, Jardine, would make interesting reading. *Bombay Gazette*, 8 Sep. 1887.
9. Ibid., 26 June 1885.
10. The few letters in which Rukhmabai discussed her predicament are discreetly silent about the role of Sakharam Arjun in relation to her efforts at self-education. Yet, the inference seems hard to resist that she had him, too, in mind while complaining, in her pseudonymous letters to the *Times of India*, that her educational endeavours were uncharitably misconstrued. Considering her warm acknowledgment of his support during the decision to resist Dadaji's claims, this silence is suggestive. See her 'Reply' to Dadaji's 'Exposition', Appendix D. There is also the direct evidence of Dr K.R. Kirtikar. A hostile witness, Kirtikar seemed to be telling the truth, for once, when he accused Sakharam of neglecting his stepdaughter's education.
11. *Times*, 9 Apr. 1887. There is but one lukewarm mention by Rukhmabai of her stepfather in the context of her education. See Appendix D.
12. Rukhmabai claimed that she had begun writing on the question of social reform 'long before' Malabari did. Taking her 'long before' with a pinch of salt, we may assume that she had started writing about social reform

quite early. *Bombay Gazette*, 29 June 1887.

13. For the 'assertion of women's common sisterhood in oppression' in the development of feminism, see Caroline Ramazanoglu, *Feminism and the Contradictions of Oppression*, London, 1989.
14. For a discussion of the relationship between what they call the experiential and the ideological, see the editors' 'Introduction' to Kumkum Sangari and Sudesh Vaid, (eds.), *Recasting Women: Essays in Colonial History*, New Delhi, 1989, p. 20.
15. The speculation about Rukhmabai having been subjected to a sexual advance was first suggested to me by my sociologist friend, Paramjit Singh. His academic training and the experience of growing up in rural Punjab suggested this as the only plausible reason why after the first year of her marriage, Rukhmabai never went to Narayan Dhurmaji's house. Later I found this described as an actual occurrence in a fictional account of Rukhmabai's life. See Sarojini Sharangapani, *Male Ha Lagna Manya Nahi* (Marathi), Pune, 1983, pp. 33 ff.
16. When litigation seemed imminent, it may be noted, the last-minute condition proposed by Sakharam was that Dadaji should arrange to live with Rukhmabai in a house other than Narayan Dhurmaji's. Considering that Sakharam was as yet undecided about getting embroiled in a legal tangle, and that there could be a chance of Dadaji accepting the proferred arrangement, it is important that Sakharam laid such stress on ensuring that Rukhmabai did not have to live in Narayan's house.
17. *Exposition*, p. 11.
18. Ibid., p. 3.
19. History of the case as recapitulated by Dadaji's counsel before Mr Justice Farran on 3 Mar. 1887. *Times of India*, 4 Mar. 1887; *Madras Mail*, 8 Mar. 1887.
20. *Exposition*, pp. 2, 8.
21. 'Rukhmabai's Reply', *Bombay Gazette*, 29 June 1887.
22. Lucy Carroll, 'Law, Custom, and Statutory Social Reform: The Hindu Widows' Remarriage Act of 1856', in J. Krishnamurty, ed., *Women in Colonial India: Essays on Survival, Work and the State*, Delhi, 1989, pp. 1–26, has dealt with the conflicting judicial interpretations in British India of section 2 of the Act. She argues that the conservative and, for the remarrying widows, harsh view of this section, viz., that taken by the Bombay High Court, constricted the rights of even those widows whose caste, tribe or sect customarily sanctioned their remarriage. The constriction, to the extent it actually occurred, was marginal. For, given the hold of patriarchy even in social groups that permitted a degree of latitude to their women, it was 'generally' found, as Gooroo Dass Banerjee pointed out, that 'wherever remarriage of widows is allowed by custom, their rights to the estate of their deceased husbands are taken away by the same custom'. *The Hindu Law of Marriage and Stridhan*, p. 269. For a comprehensive listing of the conflicting decisions given on this question by various high and chief courts in British India, and for the draft of the Hindu Widows' Re-

marriage Act (1856), see S.V. Gupte and G.M. Divekar, *Hindu Law of Marriage*, Bombay, 1976, pp. 67–73.

23. Rukhmabai argued, with some strain on the readers' credulity, that her mother, before marrying Sakharam Arjun, could have, if she so wished, disposed of the way she liked the property that she had been willed by her first husband and Rukhmabai's natural father. 'Rukhmabai's Reply', *Bombay Gazette*, 29 June 1887.
24. This was on the first day of the hearing before the Appellate Bench on 12 March. Sargent came back to the point during the second hearing a week later. See *Times of India*, 13 and 19 Mar. 1886. When Marpherson, Dadaji's lawyer, tried to object that nothing had been proved about his client's poverty, the Chief Justice pre-emptively referred to Dadaji's own evidence earlier when the case was heard by Justice Pinhey. It may be recalled that in his judgment Pinhey had observed about this portion of Dadaji's and Narayann Dhurmaji's evidence: 'The plaintiff gave much false evidence as to his pecuniary position; and his uncle, who was examined on plaintiff's behalf on the same point, gave, if possible, evidence less credible still.' *The Indian Law Reports*, Bombay Series, vol. IX, p. 535.
25. Kirtikar said this in a public lecture, a detailed report of which was published in *Kesari*, 19 Apr. 1887.
26. *Probate Division*, vol. V, p. 23. For a demonstration of the validity of Hannen's generalization, see J.D.M. Derrett, *Religion, Law and the State in India*, London, 1968, pp. 352–99.
27. Narayan Dhurmaji's evidence in the libel case. *Bombay Gazette*, 29 July 1887.
28. *Times of India*, 4 Mar. 1887.
29. For a short discussion of the 'narrative instant' and the 'screen between the truth of the narrated past and the present of the narrative situation', see Jean Starobinski, 'The Style of Autobiography', in Seymour Chatman (ed.), *Literary Style: A Symposium*, Oxford, 1971, pp.74 ff.
30. I borrow this phrase from Jacques Derrida, *Acts of Literature*, London, 1992, p. 34.
31. Of relevance, in this context, is the pattern of simultaneously experienced enclosure and escape on which Sandra M. Gilbert and Susan Gubar have founded their pioneering work, *The Madwoman in the Attic: The Woman Writer and the Nineteenth-Century Literary Imagination*, London, 1984.
32. A close reading of Rukhmabai's own testimony confirms the assertion made by Dr Kirtikar, that he never saw Sakharam Arjun talk to Rukhmabai.
33. Pique at Dadaji's ingratitude may also have contributed to Sakharam's decision. It is difficult to isolate such considerations from anxiety about Rukhmabai after being convinced of Dadaji's irredeemable ways.
34. Rukhmabai's letter of 17 Feb., *Times*, 9 Apr. 1887. This was a private letter written by Rukhmabai to Miss Goodwin whose father, Bishop Carlisle, passed it on to the *Times*. See Appendix A.

35. It is tempting to recall Malabari's wry humour as he wrote about young Sayajirao assuming charge of his kingdom after years of tutelage: 'I do not envy Maharaja Siajirao, though I should like to have a fraction of his pocket money, now and then, for a hundred deserving objects.' *Gujarat and the Gujaratis*, Delhi, 1983 (reprint), p. 62.
36. See *Infant Marriage and Enforced Widowhood in India: Being a Collection of Opinions For and Against, Recorded by Mr. Behramji M. Malabari from Representative Hindu Gentlemen and Official and Other Authorities*, Bombay, 1887.
37. Ibid., pp. 17, 62.
38. Telling his critics that he had 'nothing to do with the case personally' and that Dadaji 'is as much a brother to me as Rukhmabai is a sister', Malabari wrote: 'It is a mere accident that has thrust the case upon my notice. I find it to be a test case, and am anxious to make the most of it in what I take to be the general interests of the public. I have also to guide myself by the result of this suit at law.' *Indian Spectator*, 20 Mar. 1887.
39. *Times of India*, 26 June 1885.
40. Ibid., 19 Sep. 1885.
41. Ibid., 26 June 1885; *Times*, 6 July, 28 Sep. 1885.
42. See N.C. Kelkar, *Lo Tilak Yanche Charitra*, Pune, 1923, vol. I, p.186.
43. 'We have done what we could,' the editorial wrote, 'in giving unusual prominence to her appeal, to bring it to the notice of the Viceroy and Government. But the social reformers of India must... be Hindu and not English.' *Times of India*, 26 June 1885. The editorial on the second letter began: 'The "Hindu Lady", whose letter to us on "Infant Marriage" went the round of the world and evoked a very unusual amount of sympathy, sends us another contribution to-day upon "Enforced Widowhood". Again she writes out of the fulness and bitterness of her heart. Countless generations of silent sufferers have found an eloquent exponent at last; and it is impossible to read her letter without being struck with the really lofty tone of her invective, with the virility of her arguments, and, above all, with the indignant scorn she showers upon those who hold that Hindu women have no reason for complaint.' Ibid., 19 Sep. 1885.
44. Ibid.
45. When the *Westminster Review* reported Malabari as favouring sixteen as the minimum marriageable age for girls, the great reformer disclaimed: 'I have not been able to see my way beyond 12.' Adding: 'And even that I would not see enforced on the people.' *Indian Spectator*, 17 July 1887.
46. After sympathy for her was built in England, the only practical step Rukhmabai wished the English people to support was the insertion of the following 'mere sentence into our law books': 'Marriages performed before the respective ages of 20 in boys and 15 in girls shall not be considered legal in the eyes of the law if brought before the Court.' *Times*, 9 Apr. 1887.

47. Two years after he had given a verdict that was adverse to Rukhmabai, the Chief Justice wrote in response to the official query about the need to change the existing law on restitution of conjugal rights following the embarrassment caused by the Rukhmabai case: 'The circumstances of that case are very peculiar and are a good illustration of the folly of putting new wine in old bottles. We may hope that it will not happen again that a Hindu girl should be brought up as Hindu maidens usually are and married when 11 or 12 years of age as prescribed by the Hindu law and custom should then straightaway and before she has joined her husband be taken in hand by well-meaning but ill-advised people and not only educated but impregnated with English ideas on the subject of matrimony so as to render her entirely unfit to discharge the duties of the marriage she has already contracted; but in any case I presume that the law should be determined with regard to the interests and wishes of the general community and not so as to meet the special circumstances of a particular case.' *Home Department, Judicial Proceedings, May 1890, nos. 410–715* (National Archives of India).
48. The whole of this discussion is based on A Hindu Lady's letter in *The Times of India*, 26 June 1885. This and her second letter are reproduced in Mohini Varde, *Dr Rukhmabai: Ek Aarta* (in Marathi), Bombay, 1982, pp. 190-208.
49. I have discussed this in *The Oppressive Present: Literature and Social Consciousness in Colonial India*, New Delhi, 1992.
50. See *Infant Marriage and Enforced Widowhood in India.*
51. *Times of India*, 19 Sep. 1887.
52. Ibid., 3 Oct. 1885.
53. *Indu Prakash*, 21 Sep. 1885.
54. These 'good laws', as now explicated by Rukhmabai, included the command that girls 'should be allowed to marry when they become of age and with their own liking'. *Times*, 9 Apr. 1887. She took a similar position in her 'Indian Child Marriages: An Appeal to the British Government', *The New Review*, No. 16, Sep. 1890, pp. 263–9. Launched in the preceding year by Archibald Grove, a liberal, as a sixpence monthly, the *Review* was conceived as a counter to the older and more expensive journals like the *Edinburgh Review, Quarterly Review* and *Westminster Review*. Covering a wide variety of subjects, and offering an open platform veering slightly to the left, *The New Review* occasionally carried articles and stories by stalwarts like Henry James, Cardinal Manning, Max Mueller, Tolstoy, Walter Pater and Saintsbury.
55. Here is one of the specimens given by the *Bombay Gazette*:

NOTICE

To Sakharam *bin* Bapu Chambhar, residing at Mouje Varvod, Taluka Bhimthud, District Poona.

I, the undersigned, hereby give notice that I am your lawful wife, having been married to you about seventeen or eighteen years since.

During this period I lived with you altogether for about a year, sometimes for a month, and sometimes for a fortnight. A portion of this total period of one year was passed when I was under age, while the remaining was passed after I had attained the age of puberty. In this latter portion, however, you slighted me, owing to your having in the meantime entered into a second matrimonial alliance with a widow; you treated me as though you were not my husband. Accordingly I returned to the house of my parents, and have by this time incurred a debt of Rs. 350 for maintaining myself. I now hereby require you, within a period of eight days from the date of this notice, to come to my parents' house, and to take me to your house, after having paid me the amount of the debt incurred by me, and after having assured me of your regard for me, and after having given security that I should be well treated in future. Should you fail to do this within the prescribed period, I shall marry another person.

Be this known to you.

(Sd.) Bhagu *kom* Sakharam Chambhar.

September 2nd 1885.

The care taken in these notices to affect the phraseology of colonial law and the use made of the print media indicate the utilization of precisely the forces that were also corrosive of traditional ways of life for buttressing custom.

56. *Bombay Gazette*, 24 and 29 Sep., 7 Oct. 1885. It is indicative of the recognition of the *Gazette* as a supporter of reform that, even while joining issue with it on the question of 'enforced widowhood', the *Indian Spectator* described it as 'our best friend'. 1 Nov. 1885.

57. Ibid., 24 Sep. 1885. The *Bombay Gazette* realized the legal invalidity of the customary provisions that gave the 'average Indian woman' her freedom. But, significantly enough, it failed to mark the erosion of that freedom by the rigid moralism of colonial judicial mediation. That process had already struck Gooroo Dass Banerjee: 'And even where there is a custom among the lower castes for a wife to contract a second marriage, called a *natra* or *pat*, during the lifetime of the husband, on permission obtained from a *punchayat* of her own caste, the Courts of British India have refused to recognize such custom, on account of its being immoral and opposed to the spirit of the Hindu law, and have held the parties to such marriage liable to punishment under the Indian Penal Code, as guilty of offences relating to marriage.' *The Hindu Law of Marriage and Stridhan*, p. 134. See also pp. 185–6, 244.

58. *Indian Spectator*, 1 Nov. 1885. Malabari added with characteristic sarcasm: '"A Hindu Lady" does not belong to that class of reformers who plume themselves upon their scientific accuracy and exactitude, entering upon the decimal fractions of social diseases, with a philosophic calm which can never lead to action.' Reverting to a serious tone, he further remarked: 'It is these virtuous, these moderate reformers who are the greatest obstruction in the path of progress. They are so plausible

that the stranger is sure to be taken by their airs of impartiality. But it is to this warmth of expression (exaggeration, if you like) and not the trick of concealing one half and explaining away the other half that we owe all important reforms.'

59. Ibid., 4 Oct. 1885. Ascribing the 'cry' of 'A Hindu Lady' to 'a weary heart yearning after that perfect womanhood which is her natural heritage and of which she has been despoiled by selfish man—the maker and enforcer of law', Malabari wrote: 'She is writhing in the agony of despair, and is, therefore, more violent than is seemly... It is a hopeful sign, this daughter of India rising to plead for her sex, to plead for the motherhood of the nation. May her appeal move the (un)natural leaders of society.'
60. D.E. Wacha, *Shells from the Sands of Bombay: Being My Recollections and Reminiscences*, 1860–1875, Bombay, 1920, pp. 736–7, 739.
61. 'Indeed he went so far as to say and maintain that British rule had stopped the natural and progressive development of Hindu civilization and had fossilized the law, which but for that would have developed naturally.' *Kashinath Trimbak Telang 1850–1893*, Bombay, 1951, p. 49.
62. Sir Raymond West, 'K.T. Telang', in V.N. Naik, ed., *Select Writings and Speeches* [of K.T. Telang], Bombay, n.d., vol. II, Appendix 'A', p. 536. Calling Telang the '*facile princeps* of the Bombay Bar', West wrote: 'He was, when not retained as Counsel, on several occasions consulted by the Judges as to the right interpretation of those enigmatic texts which having been framed under archaic influences lend themselves with almost equal inexactness to antagonistic applications in the affairs of modern life.' Telang succeeded in creating an influential following around him. For example, N.G. Chandavarkar (1855–1923) who, as editor of the *Indu Prakash* at the time of the Rukhmabai case controversy, wrote week after week in favour of the young lady, believed as a result of Telang's influence: 'But our very shastras have given us a free hand in changing with the times, by agreeing upon one point more than upon anything else—that is, by pronouncing without any hesitation that custom or usage can supersede the injunctions of the shastras... The shastras have been more liberal than we care to be, by giving us a free hand to deviate from them when necessary.' L.V. Kaikini (ed.), *The Speeches and Writings of Sir Narayan G. Chandawarkar, Kt. Judge of the Bombay High Court and Vice Chancellor of the Bombay University*, Bombay, 1911, p. 65.
63. Mayne's position was as follows: 'When the marriage is once completed, if either party refuses to live with the other, the cause is no longer one for specific performance of a contract, but for restitution of conjugal rights. It has long since been settled that such a suit would lie between Hindus, but there was much conflict of authority as to the mode in which the decree was to be enforced. The point has now been settled by s. 260 of the Civil Procedure Code (1877)... *Prima facie* the husband is the legal guardian of his wife, and is entitled to require her to live in his house, from the moment of the marriage, however young she may

be. But this right does not exist, where by custom or agreement the wife is to remain in her parents' home, until puberty is established.' John D. Mayne, *A Treatise on Hindu Law and Usage*, Madras, 1878, p. 80. See also pp. 371–73.

64. Son of Robert Pinhey and Elizabeth Barclay, Robert Hill Pinhey was born on 22 Nov. 1831 in Bombay. His father was a surgeon in the Bombay Medical Service. Pinhey was eighteen when, after five and a half years of schooling at Manor House, Finchley, under Rev. Charles Norsley, he was nominated to the East India College, Haileybury, by an uncle, Sir Charles Jenkins, who was a Director of the East India Company. See J/1/77, India Office Library, London.
65. 57 L.J. 9 P. & D.
66. Douglas M. Ford, *Matrimonial Law and the Guardianship of Infants*, London, 1888, pp. 53–6.
67. Because, in comparison to men, it was more difficult for women in England to obtain divorce under the Divorce Act of 1857, they were tempted to use the Matrimonial Causes Act of 1884 as a less cumbersome route to separation and/or divorce. See Olive M. Stone, *Family Law: An Account of the Law of Domestic Relations in England and Wales*, London, 1977, p. 122.
68. See Lawrence Stone, *Road to Divorce: England 1530–1987*, Oxford, 1992, pp. 366–9.
69. For the judgment and the proceedings in the case, see *The Indian Law Reports*, Bombay Series, vol. IX, pp. 529–35.
70. *Times of India*, 25 Sep. 1885.
71. The metaphor of the horse—the image conveyed was that of an animal—as indicative of the strong disapproval of what coverture implied for women had been in circulation for sometime. In a landmark judgment (1866), one that twenty-eight years later Malabari quoted with some relish to support the proposed amendment of the law relating to restitution of conjugal rights, Justice Jackson gave expression to his puckish humour while refusing to issue a restitution decree: 'A wife cannot be looked upon as property, moveable or immoveable, which passively undergoes transfer from one person to another. If she could be so dealt with, it would have to be determined whether she was moveable or immoveable, and some curious questions of limitation might arise; and if the wife were property, she could not, obviously, be a party to the suit, as she is in this, and always must be in suits of this nature. And further, it seems to be repugnant to the principles of civilized society, whether European or British Indian, that an adult human being, wife or otherwise, should be delivered over as a horse or other brute animal might be.' Quoted in *Indian Spectator*, 23 Dec. 1894. This judgment also figured in the confidential governmental discussion, sparked off by the Rukhmabai case, about the possibility of changing the existing law. See Home, *Judicial Proceedings*, June 1887, nos. 189–92 (National Archives of India).

2

A Disputed Charter

Pinhey's judgment immediately aroused diametrically opposed reactions. It was for some a bold declaration of the rights of Indian women to personal freedom and dignity. For others it was an assault on the sanctity and integrity of Hindu marriage and family that threatened to turn the whole society upside down. The latter realized the urgency of challenging the judgment to seek its reversal. The prospect of appeal worried the former lest Pinhey's charter to Indian women be aborted.

The *Dadaji Bhikaji v. Rukhmabai* suit was now the subject of a contentious debate. No longer two anonymous litigants, the wife and husband now emblematized two opposing socio-cultural positions which their private dispute had helped sharpen.[1] Henceforth these opposing forces, as much as the individual litigants, would be concerned to obtain a resolution favourable from their point of view, no matter how prolonged or expensive the litigation became.[2]

I

Among the first to comment on Pinhey's verdict, the *Times of India* described it as 'the embodiment of righteousness and common sense'. The flattering editorial referred to Pinhey, with transparent exaggeration, as a judge whose 'prestige' had been 'growing steadily year by year and month by month', and whose 'knowledge of native life and of native ways of thinking is probably unrivalled in India'. Having established the credentials of the judge, it offered a touching account of Rukhmabai's tragic life. Confident that its readers would remember the woes narrated by 'A Hindu Lady', the second of whose letters had appeared just three days earlier—and guarding the mystery of the pseudonym—it wrote:

> "The Hindu Lady", whose letters have won universal sympathy, never dreamt of a harder case than this when she told us that the evil custom of infant marriage had destroyed the whole happiness of her own life in a pitiable manner.

Happily, Mr Justice Pinhey 'declined to allow the law to be made an instrument of torture'. 'He showed that a suit of this kind was a creation of the English law, which was intended to refer only to persons of mature age, who accepted the responsibilities of marriage with their eyes open.' 'There was,' moreover, 'no authority in English law to support a case like this, and his lordship did not wish to extend the law further.' He also said that there was 'nothing more barbarous than to compel a young lady to go to a person whom she disliked'.

The judgment, the *Times of India* exulted, was 'a shrewd blow at the whole system of infant marriage' that would 'have a most wholesome influence in the direction of reform':[3]

> With the use of a little firmness and common sense. Mr Justice Pinhey has, in the course of a morning's work, probably done more for the amelioration of the wretched condition of Indian womanhood than has ever yet been accomplished.

The exultation overpitched the moral righteousness of Pinhey's judgment. Indeed, the judge had reason to guard himself from being misunderstood. But he guarded himself rather inadequately. The foundation in law that he sought for his decision, as also his firm disclaimer with regard to the plaintiff's poverty, were offset by the resounding moralism of his exposition.

Given the cultural arrogance of the average Englishman and woman in India and England, moreover, Pinhey's observations about the discredited English practice of allowing suits for restitution of conjugal rights tended to fall within the zone of their cognitive blindness. As if Pinhey had expressed no anguish over still being bound to that discredited practice, the *Times of India* supported the practice on the ground of having been designed for mature men and women who accepted marital obligations with open eyes. Similarly, despite Pinhey's observation that restitution suits were alien to Hindu law, it called Hindu marriage laws 'as unjust as they are unnatural'.[4]

Defense of the imported English legal practice and denunciation of Hindu law—both in the face of contrary pronouncements by Pinhey—led to a representation of his verdict that denuded it of all legality:[5]

> Mr Justice Pinhey has decided that a young girl married in her twelfth year, and without any consent of her own to a man unable to maintain her and in a feeble state of health could not ten years afterwards, when she had arrived at years of discretion, be forced to live with him.

The Anglo-Indian understanding of this momentous event, which the *Times of India* typified, was generous in acknowledging the role of the brave Indian girl. She was, however, assumed to have been inspired by English ideas and example, but for which she would have, like other Indian women, been resigned to her fate. Now that, so inspired, she had struck for 'the rights of Indian womanhood', the Bombay daily exhorted Indian reformers to utilize the case to produce 'very far-reaching consequences'. Their responsibility was particularly grave, as rumours were afloat of Dadaji's intention to appeal.[6]

The *Times of India's* coverage of the case was widely used by other Anglo-Indian papers all over the country, thereby revealing an overall similarity in their stance. Thus, the *Bombay Guardian* reacted to the case in a manner indistinguishable from that of the *Times of India*. It claimed, unjustifiably, to have for years been 'singular' in advocating that the government should 'recognize nothing as marriage in which the marrying parties were not of marriageable age, and in which they did not voluntarily make the compact'. Someone was needed to 'break the ice', and Pinhey had done just that. Of course, what had made this possible was Rukhmabai's refusal 'to be sacrificed'. She had 'very ably fought the battle, not merely for herself, but also for millions of her sisters'.[7]

In Allahabad the *Pioneer* was quick to grasp that the problem lay in 'the awkward grafting of our English marriage laws upon a Hindu marriage system to which they were never intended to apply'. But, following the common Anglo-Indian failure to recognize that Pinhey's had impugned not the Hindu law but the imported English law, it lamented that the unfortunate grafting had forced English judges in India to 'give legal sanction to some of the glaring iniquities of Hindu customs'. Pinhey's 'far-reaching and most salutary decision' had shown them a way out. It had 'legally' established that 'a girl whose marriage has gone no further than a formal ceremony in her infancy cannot in after-years be compelled against her will to accept the position of a wife'.

The *Pioneer*, advising Indian reformers to build on Pinhey's verdict, worked out a strategy for them:

> The next step would be to establish the argument that a woman who cannot be compelled by law to accept the position of a wife is not a wife in the legal sense, and that, therefore, should her so-called husband die, she cannot become a widow. This position, once established by law, would have enormous effect upon the evils of Hindu womanhood. The force of the baneful custom is almost entirely owing to the claims which infant marriages give to family property. But, unless the law recognizes the marriage, the claims to property would be valueless, and thus the one great incentive to infant marriages would be removed.

Trusting that the reformers would not 'overlook the importance of this simple argument'—the simplicity of the argument we shall soon see—the *Pioneer* advised them to 'take every means to secure that Mr. Justice Pinhey's decision shall be upheld, and subsequently carried to its logical conclusion'.[8]

Coming from the powerful Anglo-Indian press, especially the *Pioneer* with its access to the corridors of power, the advice to Indian reformers was more a display of the rhetoric of moral-cultural superiority. With all their eagerness to take advantage of Pinhey's judgment, the reformers were no better equipped than their Anglo-Indian declaimants to prevent its reversal in appeal. As Malabari wrote:[9]

> It is lucky for Rukhmabai that she has counsel like Messrs. Inverarity and Telang. The latter, who has his whole heart in the business, may be trusted to do all he can for her. But it is hard to see what can be done, unless the final Court of Appeal refuse to recognize unconsummated infant marriages.

Farther off in Lahore, brimming with imperial pride, the *Civil and Military Gazette* saw eye to eye with the *Times of India* almost to the point of plagiarizing. Displaying the other side of English humour—especially visible in the Anglo-Indian denunciation of India and Indians—the Lahore daily employed exaggeration more than understatement:

> Whatever may be Mr Justice Pinhey's shortcomings, in the matter of jealous Hindoos who bite off the noses of their mistresses, it cannot be denied that he has most notably helped forward the cause of social reform...

Describing how the stepdaughter of a 'well known native doctor in Bombay was married, at the mature age of eleven years, to a man suffering from symptoms of consumption, and unable to support her', the paper averred:[10]

> The idea of establishing any comparison between the marriage of an English man and woman of mature years, and two native *children of nineteen* and eleven, would strike most people as preposterous. (Emphasis added.)

From the Lahore *Gazette* to the *Indian Daily News* of Calcutta is a considerable geographical leap and a jump from jingoism to moderation. But the sober Calcutta daily, too, found Pinhey's verdict 'thoroughly' in accord with 'European notions of justice and equity'. Unlike its Anglo-Indian contemporaries, however, the *News* felt that even the husband had a 'grievance' in this case:[11]

> He is saddled with a wife who is not a wife... not in the sense that she is a burden upon him... but in the sense that she is still legally his wife. Mr Justice Pinhey's judgment, though it debars him from access to his wife, does not sever the marriage tie. So if the young wife is a victim of the unfortunate marriage custom of the country, the husband is only a degree less a victim.

The Anglo-Indian celebration of Pinhey's verdict, without appreciating his criticism of the British Indian legal mediation, squared with their belief in the superiority of English over 'native' sensibilities. It also necessitated, as a counterpoint to the 'common European sympathy', a supplementary belief in a common Indian/Hindu reaction of hostility to the verdict. The *Civil and Military Gazette*, for example, was convinced that the hostile Hindu response, to which we shall turn in the following section, reflected 'the native mind'.[12] The *Bombay Gazette*, likewise, believed that the 'native papers unanimously disapprove of the judgment of Mr Justice Pinhey in the case of Rukhmabai and her poor illiterate husband'.[13]

The evidence of Indian/Hindu support to Rukhmabai and approval of Pinhey's verdict did little to upset this belief. More than in the reality of Indian reaction, the belief was lodged in Anglo-Indian/English perceptions. There was, perhaps, something in the judgment itself that evoked a self-congratulatory impulse among the English. Pinhey's moral recoil from a barbarous act, and the support he found in 'the English authorities', could seem the quintessential assertion of English spirit and principles over minds with a certain kind of cultural predisposition; all evidence of a contradictory tendency notwithstanding. It would be misleading, however, to locate this response primarily in Pinhey's declamation. For, as we shall see, the response remained unaffected even when his verdict was reversed.

In the midst of the *a priori* Anglo-Indian assumption of Indian opposition to the verdict, the *Bombay Chronicle* was exceptional in anticipating a 'battle' that, it believed, 'will be one of tremendous consequences to the social institution of the Hindus, and will attract to the arena of the fight some of the best intellects of the race'.[14]

There did ensue a battle which continued intermittently as the case passed through various judicial stages. The battle—like most social battles—was not entirely fought between sharply defined rival forces whose positions and followings were very clear. It also involved people who, though drawn into the contest, betrayed varying degrees of ambivalence towards the claims and objectives of the rival sides. The battle—again like most social battles—was an 'internal' one as well. It was fought out *within* the minds of many of the individuals drawn into it.

II

What the *Pioneer* saw as a 'simple argument' for ending the 'evils of Hindu womanhood' was for large sections of Hindus/Indians a serious threat to their domestic and social order. (While the main opposition to Pinhey's verdict came from among the Hindus and Sikhs, the Muslims and Parsis were not indifferent to it.) Indeed, what led to the Anglo-Indian celebration of the verdict—and the celebration itself—caused the Hindu/Indian anxiety about it. The anxiety was so overriding that it inspired distrust of even Pinhey's ruling that suits for restitution of conjugal rights were unknown to Hindu law. There was a Hindu parallel to the Anglo-Indian blindness towards Pinhey's judgment. Contentious interpretations of the judgment also flourished because it had left unsettled some of the issues relating to the merits of the case. The only exception was the issue of the husband's poverty, but even that was deployed differently by the supporters and detractors of Pinhey.

The earliest and, perhaps, the best argued critique appeared in the *Native Opinion.* This Anglo-Marathi weekly from Bombay was controlled by Vishwanath Narayan Mandlik, a leading authority on traditional and Anglo-Hindu law.[15] Although he stood solidly behind Dadaji, Mandlik was not entirely opposed to social reform. Living in a subject country, he, however, advocated the primacy of political reform.[16] Narayan Chandavarkar, who as editor of the progressive Anglo-Marathi weekly *Indu Prakash* often entered into heated debate with Mandlik, believed him to be a supporter of social reform 'from within'.[17] But Malabari's description of Mandlik as 'devoid of every liberal sentiment'[18] seemed to be, during the Rukhmabai–case controversy, more accurate.

The *Native Opinion* assailed Pinhey's judgment as 'a revolution' that was 'entirely subversive of the principles that have governed society for ages', and of the British commitment to uphold those principles. 'Any Hindu wife' could now 'any day refuse to go to her husband'; it was 'enough if she says that she dislikes him'.[19] Pinhey, 'mistaking his functions', had legislated and not interpreted the existing law:

> and when a judge attempts to do so then there is an end to all stability. The single decision of Mr. Justice Pinhey will convulse the whole community. Husbands and wives would be deprived of all their rights under the Hindu Law...

The weekly disputed Pinhey's propositions—calling them 'serious inaccuracies'—'that a suit of this kind was a creature of English law, and that there was no decision on this point'. It cited 'Indian decisions' which 'conclusively' showed that suits for restitution of conjugal rights were 'founded upon the Hindu and the Muhamadan Laws'; and that the kind of relief prayed for by Rukhmabai's husband had been given in the past. These decisions, the *Opinion* added, had come from 'Messrs Justice Couch, Melvill, West, and Mitter, men who, it must be allowed, know Hindu Law and custom at least as well, if not better than the Hon'ble Mr Justice Pinhey'.

The *Native Opinion* capped its appeal to case law with a reference to the Privy Council judgment in *Moonshee Buzloor Ruheem v. Shumsoonnissa Begum*, which proved decisive for Dadaji at the appellate stage. This was a Muslim case in which a man had inveigled a rich widow with five children into marrying him six months after the death of her first husband. They lived together for some years, during which time the man managed to defraud his wife of a great part of her fortune. He then commenced to ill-treat her, virtually making her a prisoner in the house. Following magisterial intervention, she left her husband's house, with only the clothes on her back, and took up separate residence. Meanwhile she obtained a decree of five lakh rupees against the man. At this stage he brought a case of restitution of conjugal rights against her. His pleader argued that the case must be decided according to Muslim law, which did not permit a wife to separate from her husband, except upon a divorce, adding that cruelty was no ground for the court to set aside the provisions of Muslim law.

The *Native Opinion*, significantly, omitted these crucial details and only quoted briefly from the Calcutta High Court judgment against which the Privy Council had been moved. Because of the pivotal role of this case in the disposal of the issue raised by Pinhey, and also because it helps us locate him within a certain juridic genealogy, we may follow the Calcutta High Court verdict in greater detail. The judges, C. Steer and W. S. Seton-Karr, observed:[20]

> Are we to compel the Defendant to return to her Husband, convinced as we are that she should not be forced to return? If under the Mahomedan Law no Wife can separate herself from her Husband under any circumstances whatsoever, the law is clearly repugnant to natural justice... The Mahomedan Law giving no relief to a Wife, be the conduct of the Husband ever so bad, it is a case to be disposed of by equity, and good conscience. And on these principles, we have no hesitation in saying, that the grounds upon which the Defendant has separated from her Husband justify her in that step, and that we should be making the Court the engine of a grievous injustice, if we gave the Plaintiff free power and control over the person of the Defendant, by ordering her to return to him.

The *Native Opinion* argued that, in overruling this verdict, the Privy Council had enunciated the 'policy of the law in British India'. It forbade the disposal of certain categories of cases in accordance with equity and good conscience: 'i.e., according to what the Judge may think the principles of natural justice require to be done in the particular case'. Instead, the Privy Council directed that:

> in suits regarding marriage and caste, and all religious usages and institutions, the Mahomedan Laws with respect to the Mahomedans and the Hindu Laws with regard to the Hindus are to be considered as the general rules by which Judges are to form their decisions...

The *Native Opinion* quoted with relish the Privy Council's strictures against the Calcutta High Court on the ground that nothing was:

> more likely to give just alarm to the Mahomedan community than to learn by a judicial decision that their law, the application of which has

> thus been secured to them, is to be overridden upon a question which so materially concerns their domestic relations.

'We can safely say,' the paper gravely added, 'that the decision of Mr. Justice Pinhey is calculated to do what the Privy Council have so solemnly deprecated.'

Colonial case law apart, claims for restitution of conjugal rights were recognized by Hindu law authorities even 'when there were no courts like the present'. To these authorities, which consisted of caste heads, deserted 'Hindu husbands always carried their complaints', and the 'authorities always compelled the wives to go and live with their husbands'. (It is notable that husbands alone are mentioned in this context).

On the question of how the traditional authorities enforced their decisions, however, the Hindu weekly became vague. Instead of specifying the penalties, it wrote that these were 'at least as effectual in their effects as imprisonment'. The quaint tautology of 'effectual in their effects' apart, the invocation of traditional legal procedure implied a disapproval of the penalty of imprisonment which the British had brought to India. This suggestion of a favourable comparison of traditional penalties—whatever they were—with the provision of imprisonment anticipated the transference, as we shall see later, of the charge of barbarity from Hindu laws and usages on to English legal practice.

Pressing home the subversive potential of the verdict, the *Native Opinion* assumed that Pinhey, 'swayed by the fact' that Rukhmabai was married when a minor, must have considered her marriage with Dadaji invalid. The question it asked was: 'granting that the defendant was a minor when married, as all Hindu wives are, was it a valid marriage or not?' The answer was plain: 'If it was a valid marriage, and according to Hindu Law it indisputably was, the right of the husband in this case admits of no dispute.'

The *Native Opinion* claimed to speak specifically for the Hindu orthodoxy as well as for the whole of society and in its larger long-term interests. It spread its concern from 'men' to 'women' as well. Invalidating marriages contracted in nonage, it warned, would render null and void 'the right of maintenance of wives and widows'. That might not appear 'sufficiently alarming' to 'certain persons'. The taunt was meant to marginalize reformers and, like Pinhey, dismiss them as being irresponsible. It ended thus: 'But a judge must deal with the whole country and its people and not with a few people who may perhaps not be afraid to see the fabric of their society turned topsy turvy all at once.' The orthodox were, thus, shown to care for 'the whole country and its people', not just for 'men' or 'Hindus'.

The *Native Opinion* shrewdly garbled the facts of the case to contend—even as it pretended to clear Pinhey of the accusation—that his verdict was influenced by considerations other than judicial.[21] In addition, it mocked Pinhey's sense of moral outrage so as to deny him even the credit of having defied the law for justice and conscience.[22]

The *Native Opinion* spelt out the alarmist implications of Pinhey's verdict in a way that would deepen Hindu fears and stress the need for collective resistance. It did so with a quiet pride in the order that the verdict had threatened. What, moreover, was important for dealing with a judicial pronouncement, it showed an aggressive confidence vis-a-vis Pinhey. His verdict, the *Opinion* assured its readers, would not survive an appeal. This confidence gave the *Native Opinion* a degree of consistency unmatched in other hostile orthodox responses. But it could not altogether avert the inherent contradictions of a defense that was necessarily deferential towards women and also justified their subordination.

This Janus-facedness at times found extravagant manifestations. As it did in the *Mahratta*, an Anglo-Marathi weekly that appeared from Poona under the guidance of Balgangadhar Tilak (1856–1920) who, on the question of social reform, showed an ambivalence deeper than Mandlik's. The *Mahratta* was pleased that the verdict had not 'commended itself to the majority of our Hindu brethren'. Then, in one unbroken sentence, it appreciated the 'humanity' of the verdict 'on social and religious grounds' and also felt 'forced to condemn' the verdict. 'Mr Justice Pinhey', it rationalized, 'has not understood the spirit of Hindu Laws'. He had sought to introduce reforms 'by violent means', and endeared himself to 'a certain set of reformers'—obviously the kind reviled by the *Native Opinion.*

The *Mahratta* ascribed to Pinhey the view that 'among Hindus the performance of the marriage ceremony is merely a contract which might be set aside before consummation'. Ignoring that a Hindu marriage, 'once entered, can never be dissolved', he had consulted 'merely a principle of the English law, English custom'.

What Pinhey had done was to refuse to extend the application of an English legal practice. If anything, he had regretted the supersession of Hindu law in matters relating to the restitution of conjugal rights. Bafflingly enough, after accusing Pinhey of not recognizing the irrevocability of Hindu marriage, the *Mahratta* ruled on its own: 'The wife, then, may refuse to live with her husband, but for all that she is debarred from marrying another.'

What else had Pinhey done? His verdict, as the *Indian Daily News* commented, was premised on the indissolubility of the marriage between Dadaji and Rukhmabai. Rukhmabai herself never presumed that a court verdict in her favour would entitle her to marry again. That entitlement, she knew, belonged to the husband alone whether or not restitution was ordered:[23]

> ... a man can marry any number of wives at a time, or whenever he chooses to do so, keeping all of them with him, or driving away those for whom he does not care much; while a woman is wedded once for all. She cannot remarry even after the death of her first husband,[24] nor can she deny to live with him even on reasonable grounds... Is it not inhuman that our Hindu men should have every liberty while women are tied on every hand for ever?

Hindu orthodoxy refused to be embarrassed by the question. It deflected the charge of inequity onto Pinhey's verdict and staked its own claim to be humane. The interests of a whole class of hapless Hindu females, those who had been married before the years of discretion and whose marriage had remained unconsummated, were put in jeopardy. The *Native Opinion* had already made the point. The *Mahratta* sharpened it by quoting the *Indian Nation* of Calcutta: 'Where a man possessed of property has married a girl of eight or nine, and died before consummation of marriage, it would be dangerous to hold that the infant widow was not entitled to her husband's property, because the marriage-contract had not been completed'.

Further, the Poona weekly accused Pinhey of ignoring yet another distinguishing feature of Hindu marriage. It was arranged by the parents or senior family members. Serving to curb the egoism of the spouses, the arrangement was essential for that linchpin of Hindu social organization, the joint family, which of necessity placed 'certain restraints upon the social liberty' of its individual members.[25] Pinhey had given 'no consideration' to the fact that Rukhmabai's guardians 'had entered into the contract for her and in her behalf'.

After the idealization of sacramental Hindu marriage, this was no absent-minded use of the word 'contract'. The *Mahratta* developed the logic of contract, of material loss and gain, in the context of *sanskaric* marriage to argue that Dadaji's family had incurred on the marriage what in 'their poor circumstances' was 'a heavy expenditure'. Non-restoration of his conjugal rights meant that:[26]

> so much money becomes a dead loss to him. Can he file a suit against the legal or natural guardians of his wife for compensation? If they are dead, are heirs made liable? If they are not, who is to reimburse him for the pecuniary loss which he has suffered?

The dissimulation behind this relentless logic, of its concern for both men and women, is betrayed by the extra satisfaction it claimed for the husband. Taking off from a perceived loss of money to one of the spouses—the husband—it reeled off various possibilities of material recompense, not one of which was available in this particular case. The logic, then, moved inexorably—to be fixated there—to a recompense that was not material. It bound the other spouse—the wife—for life, and bound her body and soul. All questions of law and ethics were at this point exhausted for the proponents of this logic. If the spouse complaining of the loss had been a wife, the logic would have stopped at material recompense, i.e., maintenance. That is why, though the remedy was theoretically available to both husbands and wives, the *Native Opinion*, typically, mentioned only husbands in the context of the restitution of conjugal rights.

It may be tempting to see in these arguments evidence of the hypocrisy of orthodoxy. But, more than that, they reflect the limits within which the orthodox, by and large, thought and within which their humanitarianism operated. These limits were further constricted by the fear of domestic-social erosion following Pinhey's refusal to send Rukhmabai to her husband.

The critics of Pinhey and Rukhmabai were also disconcerted by the disclosure that the rebellious girl was the much acclaimed 'A Hindu Lady'.[27] They feared that extra public sympathy would be generated for the victim if she was known to be an accomplished young woman. Their reaction, as often happens in such situations, was to deny the fact. The man who did it for them on the strength of first-hand knowledge was no other than Dr K.R. Kirtikar whom we have already met in the last chapter. He avowed that, 'as far as I know' (and he professed to know a great deal), Pinhey's decision, 'legal or illegal, safe or dangerous', had 'no connection whatever' with the 'Hindu Lady'.[28]

III

Among the most determined Indian supporters of Pinhey's judgment was Malabari's *Indian Spectator.* However, owing to Malabari's absence from Bombay when Pinhey unexpectedly cut short the proceedings in the case to deliver his judgment, the first write-up in the *Indian Spectator* turned out to be an exercise in vacillation, rather than a defence of the verdict. The writer, signing himself 'K', drew attention to the 'unconventional tone' of the judgment which was sure to receive 'admiring plaudits' from 'our youthful reformers'. It would, moreover, be 'consecrated by the Hindu girls of the period as their charter of emancipation from the thraldom of matrimonial slavery'. For the orthodox, however, it would be 'a matter of very grave reflection'.

This was an accurate assessment which 'K' failed to maintain in his explication of the judgment. His appreciation of reformist efforts and women's pain was eclipsed by his orthodox sympathies. 'K' argued that if the marriage between Dadaji and Rukhmabai was considered not consummated, that was so 'according to the English notion of that act'. 'If the husband had died the next year, the girl would have been pronounced a widow by the Hindu and English law, and would have all her rights and privileges secured to her'. Consummation—completion—of a Hindu marriage was not dependent on sexuality.

'K' used this to mount a cultural-moral offensive against the rulers. He alluded to Smollett's *Memoirs of a Lady of Quality* in which the husband consummates a 'stolen' marriage post-haste with his fifteen-year old wife lest her father disturb their plan.[29] Poor illiterate Dadaji had no chance to learn from such an example; and his own culture had not taught him to treat a physical act as the validating moment of something so sacrosanct as marriage. 'In plain English,' 'K' chided, 'the husband [Dadaji] had not perpetrated "a legalized rape" on his Hindu wife, and therefore an English Judge finds it in his wisdom to cut asunder the solemn connection of a holy wedlock.'

The judge pronounced that a Hindu marriage—'a solemn compact' to which the spouses pledged 'their faith before God and man'—could be legally broken. He did that simply 'because the wife was an enlightened woman and the husband an illiterate man'.

The verdict, 'K' commented, did 'infinite credit to the Judge's heart', but not to his 'legal acumen'. A judge was 'always supposed to base his decisions on law'.

'K' admitted that Pinhey's was a humanitarian verdict. He also commended Rukhmabai's will to 'emancipate herself from the prevailing ignorance, which is the badge of her sisterhood'. But his commendation of Rukhmabai was couched in a sarcastic tone that conveyed a contrary impression as well.[30]

For all that, 'K' would not allow that the verdict was valid. He rested his argument on a decision by Justice Tucker in a case filed by a Parsi woman for the restitution of her conjugal rights.[31] The husband, a government doctor who had studied medicine in England, 'demurred to the claim, on the ground, amongst others, that ... he was moving in a respectable educated society, for which his wife was not a fit companion'. The woman lost the case on the ground of domicile; she lived in Bombay and the husband in the mofussil. But, 'K' drove home the point, the judge rejected the plea of educational incompatibility and told the husband that 'he was bringing education into discredit and disgrace by availing himself of such an excuse for putting away his legally married wife'.

The inference was clear. Rukhmabai and her supporters were misusing the fact that she was educated. 'K' was disturbed by another fact too. In the case cited by him, it was a *Parsi*—a *man*—who had pleaded educational incompatibility:[32]

> But in the present instance it is a *Hindu wife* who alleges the plea, and the benevolent quixotry of another Judge allows its validity. (Italics added.)

It was bad enough for a man, and a non-Hindu, to be swayed from marital obligations under the effect of western education. But for a Hindu woman to do that spelt the very subversion of civilized life.

This was a candid expression of a confusion felt by many others with varying degrees of self-awareness. Fear of social instability influenced circles much wider than those categorically opposed to Pinhey's verdict. Even those who realized its emancipatory potential could feel anxious about its subversive effect on domestic and social relations. They were torn between concern for and fear of women's emancipation. To offer a somewhat glaring example, the *Kaiser-i-Hind*, a Gujarati weekly from Bombay, was happy that Pinhey's judgment had dealt a severe blow to the objectionable Hindu practice of infant marriage. But it also worried that, 'swayed by personal motives', millions of Hindu girls married in their infancy 'may with impunity break the sacred matrimonial bond'.[33]

Those living with such unresolved tension, perhaps, constituted a majority of the Hindus/Indians who cared about the issues thrown up by the Rukhmabai case. Their response belied the Anglo-Indian contention that disapproval was the sole Indian reaction to Pinhey's verdict. There was also a more emphatic repudiation of that contention. It came from Indians who matched the support and surpassed the understanding that the verdict received from those who claimed to represent English/European 'sensibility'.

Despite the accident of the write-up by 'K', the *Indian Spectator* led the Indian defence of Pinhey's judgment. Malabari urgently despatched a signed note—a rarity—which appeared in the very next issue of his weekly. Recording his 'entire' disagreement with 'K', and calling him a 'correspondent' in an effort to dissociate the *Indian Spectator* from his views, Malabari described the judgment as 'sound in equity and not inconsistent with common sense'.

This obviously was lukewarm. But from Punjab, where he did not have access to the judgment, Malabari could not have sent forth an informed defense. Despite the handicap, however, he tried to create an effect by assailing the restitution of conjugal rights as a 'mode of hunting down an unwilling wife'. Even if feasible for adult marriages, its application in case of unconsummated infant marriages was indefensible. In the absence of the spouses' consent and of consummation, these 'nominal' marriages were 'not binding even according to the Shastras'. The campaigner against infant marriage and enforced widowhood pressed this shastric argument to question the validity of widowhood 'on the death of the nominal husband'. He ended with the 'devout' prayer 'that the judgment might be upheld on appeal, so as to remain a worthy precedent'.[34]

Malabari was, as a practical reformer, particularly sensitive to the efficacy of exegetics in a predominantly traditional society. He sought to sanctify Pinhey's verdict by coupling it with shastric arguments. In a very different spirit, Malabari drew from the verdict implications as radical as those obtained by the Anglo-Indian endeavour to humanize it. This did not endear him to the hard-core orthodox. But it promised the reformers' cause some hearing among those torn between contrary inclinations.

The way it appeared in the *Indian Spectator*, Malabari's hurried despatch carried an error that reflects the depth to which faith in English justice had been internalized. After his own description of it as a 'mode of hunting down an unwilling wife', Malabari had followed Pinhey to call the restitution of conjugal rights an English practice. But the published version called it 'un-English'. The compositor, we can imagine, could not possibly believe Malabari to mean 'English' in a context like this. Believing it to be an inadvertent slip, and not doing his thankless job mindlessly, the compositor appears to have decided to save his master the embarrassment of a misprint that could have smacked of disloyalty. Malabari had to clarify in the following week's issue:[35]

> In my paragraph on the Hindu lady's case, please read English for un-English. What I mean is that a barbaric relic of English law should not influence the administration of Indian laws.

The clarification exuded a confidence that was missing in the previous week's misprinted reference to English law. Still without the text of Pinhey's judgment, Malabari had in the meanwhile received a comforting opinion from an Englishman who had spent 'nearly twenty years in India, both as Judge of a Presidency High Court, as well as a legal practitioner'. The judgment, this expert had opined, was 'sound and irreversible morally as well as legally', although it was not as exhaustive from the legal point of view as it might have been.

As against Malabari, who nervously prayed that the judgment be upheld, his English correspondent was confident that the appeal would 'undoubtedly be dismissed on the ground that it is not, in fact or in law, a suit for restitution of conjugal rights, but a suit for specific performance of a marriage contract'. For, unlike a mercantile or other contract, a marriage contract was a contract *sui generis* which could not be 'enforced specifically'. 'Such is the invariable law,' the Englishman asserted, 'of England, British India, America—in short, of every civilized nation.'[36]

Armed with such expert opinion, Malabari sharpened his polemics. He declared, for instance, that Rukhmabai was less Dadaji's wife 'than I am his first cousin'. He advised his 'conservative friends' to describe the connection between Rukhmabai and Dadaji as one of 'slave and slave-owner'. They could then insist on her 'being driven home to the owner, or rather the owner's uncle, to be suffocated, dismembered and offered up on the altar of Custom'. Malabari's rage seemed to overflow:

> Just fancy the little rebel delivered into the hands of Dadaji Bhikhaji, his uncles, aunts, sisters and cousins. It makes one's blood curdle only to

> think of the outrage. If I had a child in that predicament, I would far rather she died before my eyes.

This was no polemicist's hyperbole. His experience, since his own sad childhood, of the cheerlessness of daughters-in-law in joint families made Malabari fear for the 'little rebel'.[37] The fear was aggravated by what he knew of Narayen Dhurmaji and his household wherein Rukhmabai would be required to live.[38]

Malabari was a man of faith, and not irreverent towards traditional ideals. A Parsi, he had an intelligent and sympathetic, almost deferential, understanding of Hindu traditions. He claimed to represent not only reformist Hindu opinion but also the best of Hindu orthodoxy. His claim had some justification, even *apropos* of the Rukhmabai case. He joined issue, for example, with a 'usually sensible and impartial' writer who had waxed eloquent on 'the wifely sacrifices' of Damayanti and advised Rukhmabai to follow the example of her famed mythological progenitor. Malabari admired Damayanti and believed her story to be true. 'But,' he countered, 'we cannot expect every Hindu girl to be a Damayanti in this Kaliyuga.' He did not, in saying this, derogate the Hindu women of his day.[39] Rather, he turned the argument against the orthodox and the system they upheld:

> For, they are never tired of assuring us that Manu and the other wise law-makers ordained the present rigid injustice against women, because they knew women would be dangerous enemies of society in the Kaliyuga, if treated like human beings.

The quality of womanhood had not declined since. But systemic injustice had produced contrary results:

> Damayanti accepted the husband of her choice, when she was old enough to exercise her judgment. Rukhmabai never lived with her husband since the sham marriage, did not know him, had no opportunity of studying his character... Rukhmabai's nominal husband is said to have gone to the bad, ruining his mind and body for ever...

'What right have we, as honest observers, to ask Rukhmabai to follow the example of Damayanti?' No law or authority could 'make Damayantis of nominal Hindu wives', Malabari warned at the end of his stirring reversal of this venerable story.

He even denied that these 'conservative friends' cared for tradition. They were actually agitated by the threat to their domination over women. What they could not take in the Rukhmabai case was that, for once, it was the wife who had the best of the bargain. She, not her husband, was educated and endowed with a little fortune. They had to rein her in. Dadaji's predicament hit them as 'exceptional' because he was a man. Such a predicament was normal for women. Employing a favourite device of the reformers, one that Rukhmabai had used in the letters of 'A Hindu Lady', Malabari invited his readers to suppose that, instead of Dadaji, Rukhmabai 'herself had turned out incurably diseased and unacceptable', and completed the scenario:

> What would the husband and his friends have done? Why, they would have discarded the wife like a burnt stick, and supplanted her with one or more new wives.

This system was deadly enough with its conventional sanctions and means of socialization. Rukhmabai's adversaries wanted to place at its disposal the authority of the law as well. Malabari hoped that the English would not permit that. 'At any rate,' he wrote wishfully, 'no Englishman will be guilty of betraying the poor lamb into what may prove worse than a slaughter-house.'[40]

It was Dewan Bahadur Raghunath Rao, the orthodox Hindu we met briefly in the last chapter, who radicalized the very conception of Hindu marriage as he explicated Pinhey's assertion that a suit for the restitution of conjugal rights did not lie in Hindu law. In fact, the Dewan Bahadur had done something similar even before the Rukhmabai case hit the headlines and attracted his notice. Using the ancient legend of *vriddha kanya*, he had shown that the spouses' consent and consummation were essential for a Hindu marriage to be valid.[41] Always on the alert for arguments that strengthened the reformist position, Malabari was quick to use this in defense of Rukhmabai. But the argument carried an extra force for coming from an orthodox Hindu rather than a Parsi who could be admonished, as Malabari often was, to reform his own community and not meddle with the affairs of the Hindus.

Raghunath Rao was no ordinary orthodox Hindu. Shastras impregnating his thought practice, his interpretations could not be dismissed as mere tactical moves. He had the learning, and the courage, to officiate as the priest at a publicly organized widow marriage. But he would not join in the feast that followed. Similarly, going by steamer from Madras for the Calcutta Congress (1886), he went without regular food during the five days of the journey rather than share the food cooked by a Brahman engaged by his fellow delegates.[42] Enthusiasm for the country's regeneration and fidelity to what he knew to be tradition enabled Raghunath

Rao to be simultaneously radical and orthodox.[43]

'As in all contracts, so in Hindu marriage contract,' Raghunath Rao affirmed, 'consent and consummation are the requisite elements.' Hindu law, he contended, prohibited consummation during the first three days of the marriage. The bride became of the bridegroom's *gotra, pinda* and *sutaka*—this being the decisive evidence—after 'actual personal consummation on the fourth night or thereafter'.[44] Here was a counter to the charge that, in imagining consummation as essential to the institution of conjugal rights, Pinhey had disregarded the fact that the rights of the Hindu husband and wife were complete the moment the marriage ceremony was performed.

Against this background of sharp, even passionate, division over the issues involved in the case was the appeal against Pinhey's verdict argued before and decided by the Bombay High Court.

NOTES

1. While Rukhmabai was from the outset conscious of the larger issues in this case, Dadaji needed the outburst against Pinhey's verdict to realize that he could project himself as a martyr: 'If religious pledges are to go for nothing, then where does morality begin? It is both a precept and a divine law to the Hindus that it is a wicked and an undutiful act on the part of girls or women to form matrimonial connections without the consent of their parents or relatives… Non-Hindus do not understand this matter; it has formed no part of their religious training; but to a Hindu it is at once conscience, reason, and religion… The true Hindu will suffer martyrdom for it. I appeal with boldness to all my co-religionists, for they alone can understand my feelings and the power of the doctrine which I have endeavoured to explain.' *'Exposition'*, p.10.
2. The 'orthodox party' in Bombay collected funds and offered considerable assistance to Dadaji soon after Pinhey's judgment so that he could appeal against it. This move was master-minded by V.N. Mandlik who secured a one-line appeal for funds from Dadaji and circulated it among his circle of friends. See Ganesh Ramkrishna Havaldar, *Rao Saheb Vishwanath Narayan Mandlik Yanche Charitra*, Mumbai, 1927, vol. II, pp. 860–1.
3. *Times of India*, 22 Sep. 1885.
4. It got so carried away as to add, unmindful of the criticism implicit in the following italicized phrase, that with Pinhey's verdict the law in British India had, '*for the first time*, refused 'to be made the instrument of this personal degradation'. Ibid.
5. Ibid. The *Civil and Military Gazette*, similarly missing the legal basis of Pinhey's verdict, commented: 'From the evidence it appeared that the

present plaintiff was not able to maintain his wife; and a decree was accordingly given for the defendant with costs.' 30 Sep. 1885.

6. Ibid., 25 Sep. 1885.
7. *Bombay Guardian*, excerpted in *Times of India*, 28 Sep. 1885 and in *Civil and Military Gazette*, 12 Oct. 1885.
8. *Pioneer*, reproduced in *Civil and Military Gazette*, 2 Oct. 1885.
9. *Indian Spectator*, 6 Mar. 1887.
10. *Civil and Military Gazette*, 28 Sep. 1885.
11. *Indian Daily News*, 29 Sep. 1885, reproduced in *Times of India*, 2 Oct. 1885.
12. *Civil and Military Gazette*, 28 Sep. 1885.
13. *Bombay Gazette*, 5 Oct. 1885.
14. Excerpted in *Times of India*, 28 Sep. 1885.
15. Mandlik's translation, with its introduction and appendices, of the *Vyavahar Mayukha* bears witness to his understanding of both shastric and customary laws. See V.N. Mandlik, *Vyavahar Mayukha Or Hindu-Law*, Bombay, 1880, part ii. After a brief spell of government service, Mandlik joined the Bombay bar, was appointed government pleader in 1884, and in the same year was nominated to the Viceroy's legislative council. Earlier he had been for eight years a member of the Bombay legislative council. He founded the *Native Opinion* in 1864 and continued to edit it until 1871. His influence over the weekly, which actually never waned, was particularly marked during the Rukhmabai case controversy.
16. Noticing Telang's now famous lecture, 'Must Social Reform Precede Political Reform', Mandlik noted with satisfaction: '... the learned lecturer tried to show that though reform may be necessary in social matters as well as in our political situation, it is the political reform to which our energies should be directed in the first instance.' And further: '... the lecturer's conclusion is the one which we had arrived at when this journal was started and which was adopted and has been adhered to as the governing policy of this paper.' *Native Opinion*, 28 Feb. 1886.
17. Ganesh L. Chandavarkar, *A Wrestling Soul: Story of the Life of Sir Narayan Chandavarkar*, Bombay, n.d., pp.79–80.
18. *Indian Spectator*, 18 Dec. 1887. Referring to the Madhavbag meeting where, under Mandlik's chairmanship, a rabidly anti-social reform position was taken, and even the sober Telang was shouted down, the *Spectator* wrote: 'The sin of the Madhavbag meeting will stick to this aged pleader, and he will have to account for it to a higher tribunal than to the public of Bombay. We would never have said a word against him even in this connection had he acted from conviction; but we must decline to believe that a man of Mr Mandlik's intelligence could conscientiously favour the views emitted at that meeting of illiterate Banias and Bhattias.'
19. *Native Opinion*, 27 Sep. 1885. The fear of subversion is further reflected in the *Opinion*'s angry outburst, in its issue of 11 Oct. 1885, against the *Sind Times* for taking a favourable view of Pinhey's judgment: 'Why

not seek to establish a system of divorce instead?'

20. See Edmund F. Moore, *Reports of Cases Heard and Determined by the Judicial Committee and the Lords of Her Majesty's Most Honourable Privy Council, on Appeal from the Sudder Dewanny Adawlut and High Courts of Judicature in the East Indies*, Bangalore, n.d., vol. XI, pp. 558–61. *Moore's Indian Appeals*, hereafter.
21. It wrote: 'Now as to the allegation of the husband's ability to maintain, we are glad the Judge does not hold that the poverty of the husband was a good answer to resist his claim. The inability to maintain is a relative term and can be used in almost every case. What may be competence to one may be poverty to another, and if such an indefinite definition were held good in such suits society would be sorely disarranged. With regard to dislike we may remark that there is only one case in which a wife can resist her husband's claim to conjugal rights and that is in the case of cruelty which involved danger or fear of danger to her person by the violence of the husband… We think the learned Judge completely misunderstood the law on the subject, like or dislike having nothing to do with the matter… we cannot but think that Pinhey J. was influenced by considerations other than judicial.' *Native Opinion*, 27 Sep. 1885.
22. Ibid.
23. *Times*, 9 Apr. 1887.
24. Here Rukhmabai is getting carried away, if she is not making a polemical point. She could not possibly have forgotten the marriage of her own mother after she became a widow.
25. Letter by an anonymous Hindu correspondent to a Bombay daily, reproduced in *Civil and Military Gazette*, 6 Oct. 1885.
26. *Mahratta*, 11 Oct. 1885.
27. The disclosure about the identity of 'A Hindu Lady' first appeared in the *Bombay Guardian*'s comment on Pinhey's judgment. However, for tactical reasons, the *Times of India*, which alone was supposed to know, evaded the issue. 'Whoever she may be,' it said, the 'Lady' wanted her name to be kept secret. For the moment, consequently, the *Bombay Guardian*'s disclosure was no more than a rumour. *Times of India*, 25 Sep. 1885. Given the certainty of an appeal against Pinhey's judgment, it may have seemed prudent to reveal her identity, and harness possible public sympathy, when Rukhmabai was faced with defeat rather than in the moment of her uncertain triumph.
28. *Bombay Gazette*, 6 Oct. 1885.
29. 'K' seems to have mixed some details of the story. He mentioned the second husband of a wayward lady, whereas it was her first husband and she herself was then an innocent wench of fifteen. 'K' was, however, right about the substantive point, which is thus described by the protagonist-narrator: '... the bridegroom gave me to understand that, there was a necessity for our being bedded immediately, in order to render the marriage binding, lest my father should discover and part us before consummation. I pleaded hard for a respite till the evening,

objecting to the indecency of going to bed before noon; but he found means to invalidate all my arguments...' Tobias Smollett, ***The Adventures** of Peregrine Pickle*, London, 1930, vol. II, p. 41.

30. Returning to Rukhmabai after introducing the hypothetical scenario in which the young wife loses her husband in the year following her marriage to be pronounced a widow by Hindu as well as English law, 'K' wrote: 'But the Fates reserved a better destiny for the fortunate girl, and, being well-connected and well-befriended, she ventured to take advantage of the general advancement of the time and emancipate herself from the prevailing ignorance, which is the badge of her sisterhood, by seeking the protection of the High Court against the suit filed by her husband to compel her to live with him.'
31. It is a noticeable fact, one worth examining, that whereas among Hindus and Muslims it was almost exclusively husbands who brought in cases of restitution of conjugal rights, Parsi women made considerable use of it.
32. *Indian Spectator*, 27 Sep. 1885.
33. *The Times of India*, 28 Sep. 1885. *Gujarati*, an Anglo-Gujarati weekly started in 1880 to champion the cause of Hindu orthodoxy, observed that Pinhey's 'revolutionary' judgment was a double-edged weapon. Ibid.
34. *Indian Spectator*, 4 Oct. 1885.
35. Ibid., 4, 11 Oct. 1885.
36. Ibid., 11 Oct. 1885.
37. Here is a random reading list for those who wish to be acquainted with contemporary accounts of the existential reality within the Hindu joint family. The list includes fiction, diary and reminiscences. G.M. Tripathi, *Sarasvatichandra* (the four volumes of this first major novel in Gujarati came out between 1887 and 1901), Mumbai, 1985; Kantilal C. Pandya and others, eds., *Govardhanram Madhavaram Tripathi's Scrap Book*, Bombay, 3 vols. 1957, 1959; *Ranade: His Wife's Reminiscences*, English translation (from Marathi) by Kusumavati Deshpande, New Delhi, 1969; Hari Narayan Apte, *Pan Lakshyant Kon Gheto* (Marathi novel which appeared in 1890), Hindi translation, entitled *Kaun Dhyan Deta Hai* by Srinivas Kochkar, New Delhi, 1961. I have discussed the question of joint family in my *The Oppressive Present*, pp.74–82.
38. Possessing intimate knowledge of the dispute and the actants therein, Malabari let it be known to his readers that the prime villain in this murky drama was an 'uncle' whom Rukhmabai 'naturally dreads with a mortal dread'.
39. Malabari is exceptional in the turn he gave to the argument about Kali-yuga. Usually the argument rested on an initial admission of the degeneration that had come about in the character of women, as of men, so that they were no longer capable of living upto the ideals of old. For example, even the most committed advocates of widow marriage argued that since Hindu women were unable to lead a life of austerity and celibacy after losing their husbands, and often fell into evil ways, causing such problems as foeticide and infanticide, it was much better

to let them have the option of remarriage. This is precisely why *Parashar Samhita*, with its less rigorous expectations, is considered the authoritative *sambita* for *Kali-yuga*.

40. *Indian Spectator*, 1 Nov. 1885. Despatched from Amritsar, this too was a signed write-up.
41. See *A Letter Addressed to the Honorable W.W. Hunter, L.L.D., C.I.E., on the Subject of Hindu Re-Marriage by Dewan Bahadur R. Ragoonath Row*, Madras, 1885. Illustrating through the legend of the vriddha kanya the indispensability of the spouses' consent and of consummation of marriage, Raghunath Rao wrote: 'The legend is that there was a daughter of a Brahmin. She was well read. She was not disposed to be a devotee and desirous of final beatitude, but was looking after a husband. The bridegrooms who were willing to marry her and to whom her father was prepared to give her, proved her inferiors. Following Manu's view, viz., rather than marry an unequal partner, it is better to die a virgin, she continued a virgin till she grew very old. As she was going to commit suicide, Narada asked her what Lokas are secure for unmarried women. She then gave her hand to a Rishi, and, having had sexual intercourse with him (as without it, there was no marriage) she died and went to heaven.' p.5.
42. See K. Subba Rao, *Revived Memories*, Madras, 1934, pp. 140–1, 202–5.
43. Representing the younger generation of social reformers, Subba Rao describes how they looked upon Raghunath Rao as a 'venerable guru', valued his association with the reformist cause, and yet felt constrained to criticize him for what seemed to them 'his glaring inconsistency between precept and practice'. Subba Rao also records Raghunath Rao's 'spirit of frequent fight in public regarding ideals and methods without any diminution in the slightest degree in personal esteem and in personal attachment'. Ibid., pp. 140, 204–5.
44. *Indu Prakash*, 26 Oct. 1885.

3

The Law on Trial

Reflecting the paradoxical structure of the larger imperialist exercise, a contradiction was inherent in the British Indian judicial practice. Driven by an expansionist urge for unquestioned jurisdiction over the affairs of the ruled, it was, simultaneously, obliged by the force of indigenous laws and usages into a self-limiting minimalist conception of its mediation. A shift occurred after 1857 in the way this paradox worked. The minimalist conception, though still part of the imperialist rhetoric, began to yield to the expansionist urge.[1] The massive restructuring intended to negotiate the mutually irreconcilable needs and strategies dictated by the experience of 1857 had introduced a new stress in the structural ambivalence of the colonial dispensation. The reversal of Pinhey's verdict shows this ambivalence at play in a particularly sensitive context.

The appeal against Pinhey's judgment came up for hearing on 12 and 18 March, and the judgment was given on 2 April 1886. Dadaji hired a third lawyer, Macpherson, while Rukhmabai decided to make do without Inverarity. Latham explicated the principles and significance of Pinhey's verdict in a theoretical and historical perspective. Telang expounded the issue of the non-maintainability of a suit for the restitution of conjugal rights in Hindu law. Dadaji's hiring of Macpherson, we shall see, proved decisive.

The Appellate Bench comprised the two senior most judges of the Bombay High Court, Chief Justice Sir Charles Sargent (1821–1900) and Sir Lyttleton Holyoake Bayley (1827–1910). Educated at King's College and Trinity College, Sargent was called to the bar at Lincoln's Inn. Before coming to India he had been a member of the Supreme Council of Justice of the Ionian Islands and also its Chief Justice for six years. He joined the Bombay High Court as a judge in 1866, and had a long innings as Chief Justice from 1882 until his retirement in 1895. He was considered a strong judge.

Son of a baronet, Bayley was sent to Eton. He qualified for the bar from the Middle Temple, and went to New South Wales as Attorney-General and member of the Legislative Council (later entering the Legislative Assembly). The year Sargent joined the High Court, Bayley came to Bombay as Advocate-General and member of the Legislative Council. Appointed to the Bench three years later, in 1869, he retired, along with Sargent, in 1895 and acted as Chief Justice on five occasions.

In contrast to Sargent and Bayley, Pinhey had risen from the second class of the civil service and roughed it out in the *mofussil* for twenty-five years before his elevation to the High Court in 1875. Bayley had by then been six years on the Bench. We know little about their relations during the ten years that they were colleagues. But the appellate proceedings indicate more than a touch of superciliousness in Bayley's attitude towards Pinhey. This superciliousness was matched by a contempt for Hindu laws and customs that betrayed both inadequate knowledge thereof and, perhaps, a certain want of mental acuity.

Beginning the proceedings, Macpherson highlighted what he described as the sentimental dimension of Pinhey's judgment and questioned its legality. He was soon interrupted by an impatient Bayley: 'I don't quite understand on what ground the suit was dismissed, although I have read the judgment more than once.' Bayley's understanding of the judgment—no matter how many times he read it—had little to distinguish it from the prejudiced popular reactions we noticed in the last chapter. Believing the judgment to rest on Rukhmabai's dislike of Dadaji—an understanding itself suggestive of gender bias—he remarked: 'According to Mr Justice Pinhey's view, if a lady takes, rightly or wrongly, a dislike to a man, there is an end of the matter.'[2]

Gratified with the interruption, Macpherson sought to confirm the impression that 'the suit was dismissed more on sentiment than on law' by fusing together Pinhey's moral outburst and legal reasoning: 'Mr Justice Pinhey said he did not like the idea of compelling this young lady to go to her husband as the marriage had not been consummated.'

To this Macpherson added the graver charge that the verdict

rested 'on fallacies'. The 'fundamental fallacy' was that consummation was essential for the completion of a Hindu marriage. This obliged Sargent to query: 'Where does he say that?' The pat reply, 'In his judgment,' failed to convince the Chief Justice, who observed: 'Mr Justice Pinhey only seems to have thought that a suit for institution would have been more appropriate.' But that was precisely Macpherson's point. The issue of 'institution' arose only if the marriage was construed as incomplete 'without consummation'. 'If a marriage is completed without consummation'—as indeed, he contended, a Hindu marriage was—'the rights accrue as soon as the marriage ceremony is completed'. He pressed home the argument:

> The marriage is admitted. The rights of the parties are complete when the marriage ceremony is performed... Consummation is not necessary to effectuate marriage. The husband has a right to the society of his wife, and the Court is bound to enforce the right... The Civil Procedure Code (XIV of 1882), sec. 260, recognizes the right, and provides a means of enforcing it.

'Thus we have the right admitted,' Macpherson maintained, 'and the remedy provided.' Anticipating that even after the right was admitted, the provision of the remedy could be disputed in the case of Hindus, he interrogated: 'If the right and its incidents be the same among Christians, Mahomedans, Parsis and Hindus, why should the remedy be denied to Hindus?' His answer was meant to be a key move in his strategy. 'The Court,' he asserted, 'has no discretion.'

Latham led the argument for Rukhmabai. 'The marriage is admitted' had been Macpherson's confident opening. Latham chose to be less certain in the matter. 'It is not disputed', he argued, 'but at the same time I shall submit that according to the principles laid down, there's not sufficient proof of that.' When Macpherson insisted that no such issue was involved, Latham added: 'It has been laid down in the courts at home, that if even both parties admit the marriage, there must be proof of it.'[3]

Latham's real defence, however, hinged on the two legal arguments which had figured in Pinhey's judgment. First, 'that a suit for restitution of conjugal rights does not lie between Hindus'. Second, 'that the present case is one without precedent, being a suit to enforce rights not yet enjoyed', and there being 'no English authority for enforcing the commencement of cohabitation'.

As a question of principle the first point mattered the most.

He would be 'most pleased', Latham told the judges, if they upheld Pinhey's judgment on the ground that such a suit did not lie among Hindus. This, he knew, would require them 'to decide contrary to a series of cases between Hindus' which the courts had entertained previously. Yet, it would involve 'no new departure' because all those cases were 'of a very recent date'. None was earlier than ten years ago. Only after the Privy Council decision in *Buzloor Ruheem v. Shumsoonnissa Begum* had these cases 'followed one another like a flock of sheep'. When Sargent recalled that such cases had come up before the *Sadar Diwani Adalat*, Latham remarked: 'They were Mahomedan cases, and by Mahomedan law a woman is treated more completely like a chattel.'

Related to this was an argument far more important than the recency of admission of Hindu cases of restitution of conjugal rights by British Indian courts. Two judgments of the Privy Council were ritually cited—Macpherson, too, had invoked them—to justify the admission of such cases. Besides the Buzloor Ruheem case, with which we are already acquainted, the other was *Ardaseer Cursetjee v. Perozebye* (1856). Latham questioned the applicability of these judgments, neither of which had considered the Hindu law on the subject.

As a matter of fact, the observations made in the Buzloor Ruheem judgment 'were not intended to apply to cases between Hindus'. In maintaining that 'a suit for restitution of conjugal rights will lie in the Civil Court', the Privy Council had referred to yet another Muslim case, *Maulvi Abdul Wahab v. Mussumat Hingu*, which the Sadar Diwani Adalat had tried. It had, moreover, directed that in suits relating to marriage, caste and religious usages and institutions, judges should administer to Hindu and Muslim litigants their respective laws.[4] This refuted Macpherson's contention that if the right and its incidents were the same among Christians, Muslims and Parsis as among Hindus, the same remedy should be available to all:

> It does not follow that such a suit lies between Hindus according to their law, because it lies between Mahomedans according to Mahomedan law.

If Muslim law was not applicable to Hindus, ecclesiastical law applied only in suits involving Christians. And the English law with respect to restitution of conjugal rights was ecclesiastical law, not a part of common law or equity. It was, therefore, pointless for Dadaji's counsel to refer to English authorities.[5] This reasoning was based on the Privy Council ruling in *Ardaseer Cursetjee v. Perozebye*:

> The Civil Court in India can bend their administration of justice to the laws of the various suitors who seek their aid. They can administer Mahomedan law to Mahomedans, Hindoo law to Hindoos; but the Ecclesiastical law has no such flexibility. Change it in its essential character, and it ceases to be Ecclesiastical law altogether.

Though it ruled out the application of ecclesiastical law, the Privy Council did not envisage the British abdication of their obligation to administer justice in such disputes among their native subjects. A shift in the conception of this role from an obligation to a right marked a change in judicial practice in British India. We shall see that the conception of this role as a right lay behind the reversal of Pinhey's verdict by the Appellate Bench. But for the present we may follow the Privy Council's enunciation of the role as an obligation. It went on to say after the comment quoted above:[6]

> But we should much regret if there were no Court and no law whereby a remedy could be administered to the evils which must be incidental to married life amongst them. We do not pretend to know what may be the duties and obligations attending upon the matrimonial union between Parsees, nor what remedies may exist for the violation of them, but we conceive that there must be some laws, or some customs having the effect of law, which apply to the married state of persons of this description... Such remedies we conceive that the Supreme Court on the civil side [as against its ecclesiastical side] might administer, or at least remedies as nearly approaching them as circumstances would allow.

Latham submitted that the Appellate Court must 'have regard only to the law and usages of the people of this country'. That being the case, it could not admit Dadaji's appeal insofar as the remedy he asked for was unknown to Hindu law. However, if the principles of ecclesiastical law needed to be applied at all, 'they should be applied in their integrity' (or else cease to be part of ecclesiastical law). That, he stressed, would require proof of free consent in Rukhmabai's marriage with Dadaji.

Neither the Privy Council nor, following its two landmark judgments, the High Courts admitting restitution suits in cases involving Hindu parties, had actually established such admissibility. Initially admitted on the illusion of authority in the two Privy Council judgments, each one of these dubiously admitted cases became authoritative in its own right.

This set in motion a self-perpetuating legal fiction which became more and more complex with the passage of time. Judgments in these cases were ascribed meanings they did not possess, and even explicitly disavowed. For example, no decree was awarded in *Gatha Ram Mistree v. Moohita Kochin Atteah.* Yet Latham had to refute Macpherson's interpretation of that case. He had also to refute the authority of two other suits—*Yamunabai v. Narayan Moreshvar* and *Jogendonundini Dossee v. Hurry Doss*—for the admission of which *Gatha Ram Mistree v. Moohita Kochin Atteah* had been cited as an authority.

Perhaps the most probing pronouncement, prior to Pinhey's, on the law relating to the restitution of conjugal rights was Markby's supplementary judgment in the Gatha Ram Mistree case. It inspired, within two years, an unrealized official proposal to make restitution decrees merely declaratory.[8] (The proposal, if accepted, would have anticipated the reformed English Matrimonial Causes Act of 1884, and pre-empted the Rukhmabai case controversy).

Arguments in the Rukhmabai appeal turned on Markby's judgment as Sargent asked Macpherson if there was 'any case in which a decree for restitution of conjugal rights was made in recent times'.[9] Certain that there was no such case, Sargent reinforced the drift of his question by adding that Markby had opposed 'granting the decree at all'. Macpherson demurred. Markby, he contended, 'saw reasons why a decree should not be granted for restoring the wife to the husband's protection', but realized that the law bound him to act differently. Sargent was obliged to change his view of what Markby had done: 'He showed a very strong objection to make a decree of that sort and at the same time made it.' 'Yes,' Macpherson pressed home the advantage, 'the only difference between Mr Justice Pinhey and him is that Mr Pinhey acted upon his conviction, while Mr Justice Markby did not.'

Macpherson's correction, though effective, violated the constitutive spirit of Markby's judgment. Latham captured it as he summarized the judgment: 'The decree that Markby, J., was prepared to make was apparently not a declaration for restitution of conjugal rights, but a declaration that conjugal rights existed.' Markby's judgment, therefore, was 'no authority for the decree asked for' by Dadaji. This also answered the charge—the source of widespread alarm—that Pinhey had denied the validity of the marriage between Dadaji and Rukhmabai.

Latham's accurate summary suggests nothing of the comparative perspective of Markby's understanding of Hindu law and society, which it will be helpful for us to follow. Gatha Ram Mistree, the plaintiff, had sued for the restitution of his conjugal rights. The defendants, the alleged wife and her mother, denied the marriage. The first court found that the marriage had been solemnized according to the custom of the caste to which the parties belonged. This consisted of a feast given to the caste folks. The Deputy Commissioner reversed this decision on grounds which Justices Markby and Mitter found arbitrary. They ordered him to retry the appeal.

Alongside this short joint judgment, Markby separately made 'some observations upon the form of the decree and the nature of the proceedings which may be taken upon it'. He believed that whenever the law recognized that the relation of husband and wife existed, it also recognized that the two were bound to live together. If that obligation was denied by either party, 'Courts ought certainly to declare the rights to exist'. Up to this point there was 'neither doubt nor difficulty'. The problem arose when one of the spouses refused to perform the conjugal duties after the matrimonial relationship had been ascertained.

Markby referred to the belief that, in India, 'the duty of cohabitation should be enforced by seizing and making over the recreant party bodily to the claimant'. Cases were reported of recalcitrant wives having been thus restored to their husbands. No husband, however, was known to have ever been so returned to his wife. That could be explained in terms of an almost universal notion that 'the husband purchases the wife at marriage, and that she thereby becomes an article of his property'.

But that notion, Markby affirmed, was 'wholly abhorrent to the Hindu law'. The problem, therefore, was: 'In what way then is the decree to be enforced?' Only one recent case, *Jhotun Beebee v. Ameer Chand*, pertained directly to this point. Seton-Karr, one of the two judges in this case, thought that the wife could be delivered bodily to the husband in execution of the restitution decree. The other judge, Macpherson, thought that the person of the wife could not be taken in execution. He said that if the wife refused to obey, the decree could be enforced by her imprisonment or the attachment of her property, or both.[10]

Markby favoured neither mode of executing the decree. But—unlike most people then and now—he appreciated the force of Seton-Karr's reasoning that:

> if you are to compel the woman to cohabit at all, then the direct way of

> doing so, by delivering her person to her husband, is not more inhuman, and [is] infinitely more effectual, than throwing her into prison…

This led Markby to what he saw as the core of a restitution decree. The decree could not be 'for the performance of a particular act', although Justice Macpherson had said so in *Jhotun Beebee v. Ameer Chand*. The word 'particular' here had to be given a specific meaning; and it 'clearly could not be said that such a decree would be obeyed simply by a return to the husband's house only'. (Hence the distinction between returning to the husband's house and returning to his arms). The courts could not 'declare specific performance of continuous duties' which they had 'no means to enforce except by repeated infliction of fine and imprisonment.' Marriage was a contract—Markby was 'not unwilling' to so view it—that no court 'would be wise to undertake specifically to enforce'. Even the Privy Council judgment in *Moonshee Buzloor Ruheem v. Shumsoonnissa Begum* had declared only the admissibility of a suit for the restitution of conjugal rights. It had 'carefully' abstained from 'laying down any final proposition of law upon the exact form of decree, or exact mode of enforcing the decree'.

A restitution decree, Markby inferred, must be a 'bare declaration of the existence of the relation'. Such a declaration, 'even if not a "relief" in the technical sense of the term', could be 'of the greatest value and assistance' to the concerned parties. Markby agreed that 'in order to be logically consistent', the courts must 'follow up this declaration with all the powers which they possess'. But they could not be 'hemmed in by any such absolute necessity'. He argued:

> The simplest and most direct and indeed only really effectual mode of enforcing the obligation, and, therefore, the one to be adopted, if the Courts have no discretion in the exercise of their powers, is to bring the parties together by force. But this has been universally repudiated, not only in India… but in every other country, as shocking to our feelings of humanity.

Markby supported this assertion with the results of an 'anxious inquiry' he had undertaken into different European and American laws on the subject. In Europe 'the right of both the husband and of the wife to cohabitation (in the etymological sense)' was 'considered as altogether beyond dispute'. But the enforcement of this duty by compulsion had been 'abandoned or very nearly so'. A similar tendency was at work in England. Considered in terms of 'forms and words only', English law gave the impression of 'almost unbounded exercise of judicial power in this direction'. But the extremities provided in law were 'very rarely proceeded to'. During the eighteen years since the abolition of the ecclesiastical courts' jurisdiction in matrimonial matters in 1857, writs were issued only in three cases; and in two of them the recusant party had fled England.[11]

Markby's final example came from the U.S.A. So 'repugnant' did that country find the idea of enforcing 'the performance of conjugal duties by compulsion' that it did away altogether with that provision even while patterning its marriage laws generally after the English law.

The conclusion was irresistible:

> ... if we were to hold that a Court could enforce the continuous performance of conjugal duties by unlimited fine and imprisonment, we should place the law of this country in opposition to the law of the whole civilized world, except the ecclesiastical law of England.

The Hindu law was no 'less humane in this matter than that of other civilized countries'. Nor did India need any 'severer remedies' than had been effective elsewhere. There was no need to bring in the English law.[12]

The discussion of Markby's judgment, naturally, brought up the question of the mode of enforcing the decree in case it was given against Rukhmabai. Macpherson's first impulse was chivalrous: 'Of course, I am not asking for an execution of the decree. But, it seems, the character of those who had hired him flashed across his mind, and he promptly added: 'and, perhaps, we will never do so.' Later in the day Macpherson was even more evasive: 'I don't know what the views of those who instruct me are as to enforcing the decree.'[13] Still later, when the issue of enforcing the decree took an inconvenient turn, Macpherson simply demanded a decision according to the law. As to what happened thereafter, he asked: 'But are your lordships concerned with that in any way?' The chilling question was his answer to an observation by Sargent:

> If the wife and husband won't live together, he can, of course, be made to support her; but there is no way of enforcing such a decree as you ask for.

The Chief Justice persisted in his humane protestations. 'No woman,' he remarked on the second day of the hearing, 'who has not entered the married state with her free consent should be ordered to go to her husband if she does not like it.' Latham could not have asked for more. If the Court accepted this position, he would press no 'additional circumstances'. For, 'no poverty or sickness', proven in Dadaji's case, could be compared to 'such matrimonial hardship.'

Sargent, however, wanted to know if other circumstances existed to 'induce the Court to exercise its discretion'. Having already mentioned poverty and sickness, in addition to want of consent, Latham became more specific. Dadaji, he pointed out, had 'absolutely no house to take her to'. This, Sargent demurred, had not been proved. Latham cited Dadaji's own testimony before Pinhey. Poor and indebted, the man lived in a room in his uncle's home. When Macpherson said that Dadaji was prepared to take a house, Latham taunted with a laugh: 'Yes; he might say he is prepared to take Windsor Castle.' And to Bayley's counter that Dadaji had enough money to engage three lawyers, Latham retorted: 'I don't think he will pay a penny of that himself.'

Sargent was uncertain if, as a judge, he possessed the discretion to do what in this case he considered desirable. He was probing the limits of the Court's powers and the rationale of a decree that could not be enforced except by a moral declaration. Such a decree could hardly help Dadaji if Rukhmabai was determined not to live with him. In a muffled echo of Pinhey, who had censured Dadaji for filing the case at all, Sargent wondered if the relief was not 'one which had better not now be sought, because it cannot virtually be enforced'; and also, if the near impossibility of enforcement would not justify the court in refusing the relief.[14]

However encouraging Sargent's remarks, Latham knew that he had to establish the court's discretion in the matter.[15] He had already argued that the case law cited by Macpherson was not binding on the court in a case involving Hindu parties; that the critical Privy Council rulings possessed a very different meaning. Now he even elicited from the English case law—cited by Macpherson to them in the court—a justification for the court to exercise discretion. Even ecclesiastical courts, he showed, had ceased to be 'so absolutely rigid' as Macpherson wished the Appellate Court to be. Latham cited *Molony v. Molony* as an example. This case involved neither adultery nor cruelty—grounds that could then form a defence against a plea for the restitution of conjugal rights—or anything to justify a judicial separation. Rather, the wife had resisted the husband's plea on the ground that his place of residence, Dublin, did not suit her health. Like Macpherson in the present case—Latham underlined the comparison—the husband's counsel in *Molony v. Molony* had vainly opposed the admission of the wife's defence, arguing that, even if proved, the point about her health would not justify the court in declining to order the restitution prayed for by the husband.[16]

This liberal trend, Latham continued,[17] gained further momentum from the reform of the English marriage law in 1857, which served as the point of a new departure. Henceforth, as in *Marshall v. Marshall*, pleas began to be allowed on equitable grounds, something the old courts would 'never' have done. Caroline Marshall, who had filed this suit after twenty years of separate living, was held to be bound by a deed of separation which contained a covenant not to sue her husband for restitution of conjugal rights. Such a deed would have in earlier times been dismissed as an invitation to immorality. Instead, dismissing Caroline Marshall's petition, Justice Hannen exposed the ulterior motives that generally lay behind suits for the restitution of conjugal rights. These suits, he observed, were instituted for no other purpose than to enforce a money demand.[18]

Latham advanced the iniquity of Rukhmabai's hardship as another reason why the Court should exercise discretion. She was revolted by the idea of cohabitation with someone like Dadaji. But, as a Hindu wife, she could only choose 'the inconveniences of a solitary life'. Her husband was not so bound. Sargent, anxious to test the rival counsel, searched Latham: 'But is it not a hardship on the man?' 'Nothing to compare with the hardship inflicted on the other side,' shot back Latham; sending Rukhmabai to Dadaji 'would be the greatest hardship to inflict on a human being'.[19] He asked the Court to examine her and see for itself:

> She is a most intellectual person, as educated as an English lady, while this man is little better than a coolie. It is no secret that the defendant is a writer of some eminence; and it is altogether revolting to one's sense of decency to think that she should give up her person to such a man as this.

Latham had obviously got carried away, prompting Bayley to remark: 'That's putting it rather strong.' Macpherson took the cue and protested: 'I might as well talk about my learned friend's client's head being turned by over-education. It won't strengthen his case by calling my client a coolie.'

But even they had to admit the substantive fact of greater hardship for Rukhmabai, although Bayley, characteristically, was somewhat tardy. Both Rukhmabai and Dadaji, he said, were 'tied for life'. As Latham decided to be content with a laconic, 'No;

they are not', it was Macpherson, for once unable to play the chorus to Bayley, who explained: 'The plaintiff can take another wife.' Sargent, too, saw the point.[20] His bafflement about Rukhmabai having been married off to Dadaji was itself a recognition of her iniquitous hardship.

Latham related the issues of discretion and hardship to what he reckoned was the 'strongest argument' in his favour: the matter was 'entirely devoid of precedent'. The argument contained two parts that, as he put it, worked 'one into the other'. First, assuming that such a suit lay among Hindus, in the present instance no court would order that 'such a suit could lie' because it was for the commencement, and not resumption, of cohabitation. Secondly, because cohabitation had not begun, the court had the discretion to refuse to make the order prayed for.

Latham showed that Pinhey had been modest in assuming that, since marriages in England were generally consummated soon after the wedding, it was futile to expect an English case that would be similar to the Rukhmabai case. Conditions in England once resembled those obtaining among Hindus in the nineteenth century, and it was 'by no means impossible that there could have been a precedent in regard to this matter'. Early marriages, especially among the aristocracy, were not unknown prior to Lord Hardwicke's Act (1753).[21] Yet, never during 'the whole of the centuries' was a decree 'made for the commencement of cohabitation'. When the court resumed the hearing a week later, Sargent asked Macpherson if he had discovered such a decree. Even as Macpherson replied, 'No, my lord,' Latham asseverated: 'My learned friend has never heard of such a suit; and I am sure none of us ever have.' 'The very title of the suit in England,' he stressed, 'shows that it lies only where the wife has already granted conjugal rights.'

Having given Pinhey's ruling an unsuspected temporal and cross-cultural depth, Latham resonated the judgment he was asking the Appellate Court to uphold: 'A suit like this I may call a discredited suit, and the court will not step one inch beyond what previous courts have done.'[22] There being no precedent, he hoped, the Court 'would be very slow' to create one.

Latham created a dilemma for the judges. Whatever they decided, they would be exercising discretion. If, concluding that the court had no discretion, they gave a decree on the basis of the authorities cited by Macpherson, they would have used their discretion to pronounce the applicability of those authorities to a case that was *sui generis*. To accept his view of the court's powers would be an overt exercise of discretion. The courts, Latham argued, not only possessed discretion, but had in the past actually exercised it. For, granting a decree too meant exercising a 'large discretion'.[23] To this dilemma, moreover, Latham gave a normative edge by pointing to the discredited nature of restitution suits.

Here, for us, is an *exposé* of the fiction on which rested the powerful mystique of a transcendental legal system unvitiated by personal factors. The fiction that judges simply administered the existing laws, exercising discretion only where it was explicitly provided, underlined the Victorian conception of judicial objectivity. The conception was especially suited to a colonial situation. It enabled the ruling power to claim a high stance of neutrality for its judicial mediation. For the fiction to be effective, those administering the system and those administered by it needed to not see it for what it was. Hence Sargent's anxiety to fix the discretion available to the Court without a commensurate realization that judicial judgments ever so subtly, but constantly, modified even what were supposed to be settled laws. Hence also, more importantly, Latham's unawareness of the radical implications of his own argument about the inescapability of discretion.[24]

Latham's point about discretion would not, however, necessarily help his client. The Appellate Court could decide to use its discretion in favour of Dadaji. This seemed a distinct risk as Sargent, for all his humanitarianism, thus defined what he called 'the principle of the thing':

> If by Hindoo law the marriage is perfectly valid, quite independent of any consent as we understand the word—for she has been given away by her parents, and they have a right to do so—can the court refuse to grant the relief?

Unimpressed by Latham's reply—'I say yes'—Sargent pressed further: 'If she had been an adult at the time she was married, could the court then refuse to grant the relief?'

Latham was getting into deep waters. Two absences were crucial for Rukhmabai's defence: absence of consent, and absence of a precedent decreeing commencement of cohabitation. Shown together in the life of a real human subject, they cried for redressal. That is how Latham liked to have it. Separated and seen in terms of an abstracted 'principle of the thing', the absences lost their cutting edge. That is how Sargent preferred them.

Just before posing the hypothetical question about Rukhmabai having been married as an adult, Sargent had caught Latham off guard with a variation of the same question. 'If a married woman were to run away from her husband immediately after the wedding,' he had asked, 'could the husband sue for restitution of conjugal rights?' Latham's answer in the negative had been countered by Macpherson: 'I argue to the contrary.' This time Latham was more discreet. Instead of proffering a 'yes' or 'no' in answer, he suggested that in a suit involving a woman married as an adult, 'the existing hardship' should influence the court's decision.

Sargent remained unimpressed. He would, rather, consider refusing the relief only on the ground of specific performance: 'We can regard it from no other point.' Latham was willing to have it so regarded. In response to a remark from Sargent, in fact, he had already brought in the issue of specific performance in conjunction with the notion of imperfect obligation. That remark, along with several others that came from Sargent and Bayley during the proceedings, betrays the kind of dominant mentality that influenced the working of what was supposed to be an impressive rule-bound legal system. That mentality assumed as axiomatic, and even idealized, the subordination of the wife/woman to the husband/man, and sought to regulate marital/social relations correspondingly.

Sargent's remark was: 'I should have thought it scarcely worth while citing authorities to show that, according to Hindoo law, a wife's proper place is her husband's house.' Though made in the context of Hindu law, the remark was one that as an average Christian Englishman—as an 'average westerner', perhaps I should say—the Chief Justice believed to be universally valid. He subscribed to 'the general view of marriage' which laid down the simple rule: 'Women *obey* your husbands, and husbands *love* your wives.' (Italics added.) Also revelatory of a cross-cultural attitudinal similarity between the rulers and the ruled with respect to women was Sargent's question: 'Does not a Hindoo wife undertake to enter the condition of matrimony for better or worse, for richer or poorer?' (Latham, who had already questioned the universality of the assumption, reiterated that Sargent was 'rather thinking of the obligation of an English wife', and added, on Telang's testimony, that the Hindu wife did not so enter matrimony.)

Such was the power of the assumption about the wife's place that Sargent, after asserting it, confidently added: 'I don't think

Mr Latham is going to contend that it is not.' The seemingly unexceptionable remark gave Latham the chance to introduce the interrelated notions of imperfect obligation and specific performance. It was, he admitted, the duty of a wife to live with her husband who, as a corollary, was entitled to her society. But the duty was 'under certain circumstances of imperfect obligation', and the entitlement did not vest in the husband 'an objective right to a suit'. Very few rights arising from family relations could be enforced by law. These rights—such as those between husband and wife, and between father and child—were rights of imperfect relationship:

> With reference to the duty enjoined on a wife to love, honour and obey her husband, those rights are left by the law to the sphere to which they belong, that of morality and religion. And so it is the collateral duty of a husband to love and cherish his wife, but that is a duty absolutely incapable of being enforced by law.

Drawing upon Justice Melvill's summary of 'the law of the civilized world',[25] which was similar to Markby's, Latham contended: 'The experience of the world is against such suits being entertainable.' Informing the Court that Telang would later demonstrate how such a suit was unknown to Hindu law, he submitted: 'A complaint like this is to be regulated by social penalties, and the caste has the power to pronounce them.'

When Sargent intervened that the High Courts had dealt with such cases, Latham tersely insisted: 'There is no authority.' (He had already shown that in none of those cases had the Hindu law on the subject been established.) Sargent, unaware that he was actually supporting Latham, then countered with cases where 'the punchayat ordered a woman to go back to her husband, and where the husband was ordered to take his wife back, refusal being met with excommunication.' Latham rejoined with irrepressible relish that excommunication was not a legal penalty:

> I know of a case in which there was a spiritual penalty, such as being a worm for ten thousand years [a laugh]; and I said that my client was quite willing to take his chance of that. [Laughter].

He supported his argument by citing an illustration mentioned in section 21 of the Specific Relief Act (I of 1877) which said that a contract of marriage could not be enforced.[26] No law court could enforce the specific duties that would necessarily follow the completion of the contract to marry. These duties depended for their discharge upon the volition of the contracting parties. The same logic ought to apply in a suit of restitution of conjugal rights insofar as it implied the specific performance 'not of the marriage contract, but of the obligations arising out of that contract':

> With regard to the connective relation between husband and wife, the court will never enforce a specific performance. This is the one isolated instance. Even if it is a contract of service, the court will not enforce a specific performance, otherwise it would create an infinite amount of mischief.

The courts could award pecuniary compensation, Latham conceded. But that was not what Dadaji had asked for.

It was incumbent on the court to exercise discretion in a suit involving specific performance. Using the very authorities cited by Dadaji's counsel, Latham showed that in one instance a decree was issued subject to the condition that 'the house which the husband provided should be in every way fit for the reception of a virtuous and respectable wife'. He supplemented this with the latest case on the subject. The March 1886 issue of the *Allahabad Reports*—the month of the hearing in the Appellate Court—reported a decree which stipulated that 'the husband should first secure his re-admission into the caste'.

The courts had, thus, exercised discretion in deciding the conditions under which, in a specific case, they could feasibly issue a decree for the restitution of conjugal rights. No such feasibility, Latham submitted, existed in Rukhmabai's case.

The issue of specific performance was also related to the fact of early marriage. Although the status of husband and wife was created in early marriages, specific performance depended on the contractual relation, not on the marital bond. Between Rukhmabai and Dadaji the contractual relation did not exist. Sargent, disinclined to accept such hair-splitting arguments, corrected Latham: 'Contractual relation according to Hindoo law. The parents or guardians may contract for them.' Latham accepted the correction, and asked Sargent, who had said more than once that he was testing the case, to test it as follows:

> We find that a suit for breach of a contract of marriage is not brought against the marrying parties, where there is an infant marriage, but against the persons who gave them in marriage. That shows that those who contract the marriage are not the infants.

Sargent would not test it that way. His concern, he said, was the 'duty of the parents or guardians to give the children in marriage'. The children exercised no volition. That is precisely what Latham's argument was. Because they exercised no volition, they could not have a suit brought against them. Sargent resisted the implied introduction of 'the English idea'. Latham was unapologetic: 'When you have a specific performance, you might introduce the English idea. It is impossible not to.'

Latham supported his reasoning with a ruling by Justice Westropp in the case of a wife who had sued her husband for maintenance. They were married as infants, and it was difficult to affirm that they had themselves ratified the marriage subse-quently. The wife maintained that the suit arose out of an implied contract. Westropp said it did not. If the suit was for a breach of contract, the person to be sued was the father or mother and not the husband or wife.

Another powerful argument Latham employed related to section 260 of the Indian Civil Procedure Code (xvi of 1882) which provided for the restitution of conjugal rights. Macpherson, naturally, had laid great stress on the section, and the judges, too, would feel bound by it. The section, Latham submitted, implied that it would apply where suits for the restitution of conjugal rights were maintainable, as they were between Christians, Muslims and others in India. But it did not follow that such suits were maintainable between Hindus.

Combining scholarship with logic, wit and moral concern, Latham concluded his plea for maintaining Pinhey's verdict with an appeal to the judges' sentiments. Referring to Macpherson's derogatory description of the case as 'a question of sentiment', he observed: '"Sentiment" is a word we are apt to use as a "bad sentiment", a "foolish sentiment", and so on.' But there was also 'a sentiment of feeling'. Rukhmabai's case was in that sense truly a question of sentiment. Latham tried to give his appeal a human touch: 'Supposing, my lords, this woman was your own daughter ...' His sentence was cut short by laughter in the court and by Sargent's comment: 'Oh, you are going into another matter altogether.' Another round of laughter ensued, and Latham left it at that. But he did make a final appeal, a different kind of appeal, before giving the floor to Telang:

> Well, I ask your lordships to affirm the decree of Mr Justice Pinhey on all the grounds I have urged, and more specially on the ground which is fully open to the court, and that is that it has a discretion which it can exercise.

Latham was expansive. Telang, in contrast, was spare. His logic was stern, also subtle, as he unfolded the Hindu law on the issue under dispute. He occasionally heightened the effect of his erudition with an impassive humour.

Telang's assigned role was to demonstrate that a suit for the restitution of conjugal rights was alien to Hindu law. It possessed a subversive potential. The argument about the distinction between institution and restitution of conjugal rights, if accepted, would cover only cases of unconsummated marriages. Inadmissibility of restitution suits carried far-reaching consequences for a society where early marriage was the norm.

However impressive their arguments. Latham and Telang laboured under the suspicion that the Appellate Court would defer to the recent case law, no matter how dubious it was jurisprudentially. Their defense was, for all practical purposes, a preparation for another occasion. Should the Appellate Bench decide, as they suspected it would, that it possessed no discretion, their plan was to have the principles of the matter settled by the Privy Council. Latham had even apprised the court quite early during the hearing of their 'full intention to take this case before the Privy Council'.[27] The presentation of the case at this stage would decide its fate before the Privy Council.

Though Hindu law books prescribed the duties of husband and wife, Telang began, they said very little about the mode of enforcing these duties. The little that was said was relevant only for a husband who had forsaken his wife, not vice versa. 'That,' Telang inferred, 'is a strong argument, showing that the right for restitution by suit either by the husband or the wife was not constituted.'

A short section in the *Vyavahar Mayukha* laid down the duties of a wife and husband. It required a man who had forsaken his wife to pay her a third part of his income; if poor, he was to provide for her maintenance. There was nothing in this section, or in other books, by way of an 'express provision as to how a wife is to be punished for deserting her husband'. Hindu law, Telang emphasized, did not provide what Mrs Weldon could obtain in England.

Mrs Weldon, who had obtained a decree for restitution of conjugal rights, was provided with a suitable establishment and sufficient income by her husband. Realizing that it was impossible for them to live together harmoniously, the husband, William H. Weldon, wrote to her: '... as we have now been living apart for many years it must surely be possible to come to some agreement to continue to do so, as our living together again could only entail certain misery on both of us… I am quite willing, as I have always been, to settle a proper allowance upon you, when you might continue to pursue your own objects in life unfettered by me, which you never could do if we lived together.' Mrs Weldon, however, insisted that the court's decree bound her husband to live under the same roof with her, and won her point in a judgment delivered by Justice Hannen on 27 November 1883.[28]

This was real restitution of conjugal rights. The *Mayukha*, the lone Hindu law text to consider the enforcement of conjugal duties, merely enabled a deserted wife to 'go before the king, not to obtain restitution, but one-third of the husband's income'. The *Mayukha* also enumerated sixteen kinds of altercations between man and wife, but, again, it made no provision for the enforcement of these duties by the king 'except by fine'.

Asked by Sargent if no other conjugal duties were mentioned in Hindu law books, Telang mentioned the *Institutes of Manu* which specified that the first duty of a wife was to live in harmony with her husband. But, he added, 'the question is whether it is not a duty of imperfect obligation'. It was 'a religious duty to be enforced by religious machinery'. The whole section on the duties of the woman in Manu dealt with them as religious duties. Probed by Sargent if there was 'nothing to show how a violation of such duties' was to be punished, Telang answered puckishly: 'Well, as is stated here, she is punished by going to hell.' (Laughter)

'Oh, that's not worth much here,' quickly added Bayley to renew the laughter. Having shown his humour, Bayley flaunted his knowledge. Had not Vishnu, too, said that a deserted wife was to seek justice from the king? Telang held his ground: no other authority but the *Mayukha* provided for an appeal to the king. Bayley thereupon remarked that a great deal of the directions of Vishnu were not obligatory. Telang, holding that these were imperfect obligations, had no reason to disagree. Bayley, out to impress and oblivious that he was supporting Telang, continued his fatuous comment about Vishnu: 'It is directed here that you are not to marry one with a broken limb or one whose hair is decidedly red [laughter] and so on.'

Bayley had earlier betrayed a similar combination of incomprehension and an avidity to show off. When Latham referred to infant marriages in England before Hardwicke's Act, Bayley had commented rather pruriently: 'There were those Gretna Green marriages which we knew of in our younger days.' Latham had to point out to the judge that 'those were with the consent of the marrying parties and without the consent of the parents or guardians.'[29]

Before Telang could turn to Bayley, Sargent came up with a question that had been nagging him and that seemed to affect the heart of the matter. He had earlier directed it at Latham whose reply, with its unsettling implications, had done little to put Sargent's mind at rest. He now asked Telang: 'Do you mean to say that the duty of a wife to live with her husband is an imperfect obligation?' Telang put the question in perspective: 'Yes, an imperfect obligation that cannot be enforced by this manner.' Having elicited an answer similar to the one Latham had earlier given, Sargent questioned Telang's evidence: 'Who can say what kings did in former times?' 'Yes,' Telang moved from the empirical to the prescriptive, 'but we can say what they ought to have done.'

The positions were becoming rigid. Pushing Telang further, Sargent persisted:

> If you are going to say that the obligation of a woman to live with her husband is not one of the highest order, then I think one would be doing violence to Hindoo views.

Sufficiently self-assured not to bristle or go on the defensive as a 'Hindu', Telang replied sternly: 'Yes, but that does not decide the question.' Sargent was obliged to clarify: 'I don't say we can make her do it.' This gave Telang a chance to bring back the question of imperfect obligation. The courts, he asserted, had decided not to interfere 'with a certain class of relations'. Sargent accepted this, but not in the absolute sense in which Telang had made the statement. The courts, Sargent admitted, had taken this view. Yet they had enforced a duty that stemmed from such relations when they found it 'of such importance as to be a duty beyond that of an imperfect obligation'.

Sargent assumed that the courts would enforce relations that were of overriding social importance, as, indeed, conjugal relations were. Telang questioned the courts' authority to transgress, in the name of society's welfare, the spirit and principles of Hindu—and by implication any indigenous—law. The courts, he submitted, had to judge the importance of conjugal relations and duties 'by the manner in which the Hindoo law points it out'.

Sargent dismissed that as 'very imperfect', and reminded Telang of the provision in Hindu law that 'the wife should be in obedience to her husband'. As Telang admitted her subordinate position, Bayley added with his usual lack of restraint: 'She is always in dependence'. Earlier also, Bayley had remarked: 'According to the Hindu notion, a wife is always under subjection of her husband.' Telang, who had already conceded what his understanding of Hindu law obliged him to, countered that, though dependent on her husband, the Hindu wife 'is not entirely subservient to him, and she has her rights'. In any case, Telang reiterated, 'there was no law which could force a Hindu to perform the duties in question by suit'.

This did not convince Sargent who had all along struggled to appreciate—even as he resisted it—the view that Hindu law did not admit a suit for the restitution of conjugal rights. He repeated—making the point for the third time—that the caste could excommunicate the offending party in such a case. Telang, like Latham before him, admitted that the caste could, and did, decide such cases. 'A good deal of that machinery is still available to either of the parties.' But this did not authorize the civil courts to try these cases. For, what had devolved upon the courts was 'the authority which belonged to the king when the Hindu law books were written', and not the functions exercised by the caste.[30]

In contemplating a wife's desertion of her husband, Hindu law did not provide that 'the king shall order her to go back'. Even the *Vyavastha Chandrika*, of which much was made in support of Dadaji's claim, contained no provision for restitution. However, in the absence of any 'provision at all for the case of a wife separating from her husband', Telang was prepared to concede that 'the same remedy or punishment' to which an offending husband was liable, i.e. fine, could be applied to an erring wife as well.

Telang's argument that the civil courts were entitled only to the authority enjoyed by the king and not to the functions of the caste, implied a serious constriction of the powers of the colonial state. Sargent would not let that pass. Caste, he observed, was not an ecclesiastical body, and there was no reason why its functions should not be assumed by the civil courts. This brought out at its subtlest Telang's understanding of the indigenous view of caste and its functions:

> I should say it is an ecclesiastical body from a Hindoo point of view. Of course, your lordships may not treat this as a religious question; but the

> caste will not treat it as a question not religious. They will not recognize the distinction between a social and religious question. They often excommunicate for reasons which the courts themselves have over and over again said they could not enforce.

The caste excommunicated a Hindu for going to England. 'Will your lordships,' Telang asked, 'hold that to be good?' 'The caste,' he continued, 'can order that the husband or wife, as the case may be, should go back; but what can the caste do if the order is disobeyed?' Sargent interrupted that the court could put the woman—unlike Telang, he thought only of the wife in this context—in jail for six months. This prompted Telang to ask: 'Why should the court assume to itself the functions which belong to the caste, and which the caste can exercise if it pleases?' When Sargent remarked that the court could in a case such as this deal with property, Telang introduced the idea of a 'divided jurisdiction': 'The caste would deal with the religious duty and the court deal with the property.'

Telang ended with an invocation of the Privy Council judgment in *Moonshee Buzloor Ruheem v. Shumsoonnissa Begum.* Like Latham, he recalled the ruling 'that in India the rights and duties resulting from the contract of marriage can only be ascertained by reference to the particular law of the contracting parties'. Acting on this principle, the Privy Council had based its decision in the case on Muslim law. Going by the same principle, Telang contended, 'as the Hindu law does not provide for such a suit as the present... it does not lie'. The court, therefore, 'ought to uphold' Pinhey's decree.

Winding up the arguments in the case, Macpherson stuck to his strategy of denying the court discretion in the matter. He had not, he said, dealt with the point about the inadmissibility of a suit of this nature between a Hindu couple because he wanted, in the first instance, to rely on the authority of previous judicial decisions. What, he now asked, was the other party's position on that point? First, that the suit was a discredited one; and secondly, that it was not recognized by Hindu law.

The argument about the suit being discredited possessed 'no weight whatever'. The Matrimonial Causes Act of 1884 had taken the sting out of such suits in England. That it was not so in India was 'a matter for the Legislature, and not for this Court'. Moreover, 'at all events', such suits were still recognized in England and in British India.

The point about a suit for the restitution of conjugal rights not lying in Hindu law, Macpherson admitted, went 'much more to the root of the thing'. He confessed that 'if it could be established that this suit is out of harmony altogether with Hindoo law, I daresay it would be very difficult indeed to say that the suit would lie'. So couched, Macpherson's confession was a cunning semantic manoeuvre to get around the impossibility of demonstrating that such a suit lay in Hindu law. What, instead, now needed to be shown was that a suit of this kind was not *altogether* out of harmony with Hindu law. Macpherson had turned the issue of inapplicability into one of inconsistency. He could now argue: 'As to the provision of Hindu law, while admitting there may be no direct authority for the suit in Hindu law we deny that the suit is inconsistent with Hindu law.' He clinched the argument as follows: 'That law contains nothing forbidding it.'[31]

Macpherson carried the day as he backed this flourish of negative logic with an audacious counter-attack. Having himself made the most of the absence of authority, he turned the tables upon Telang and Latham who, he charged, had not cited 'any express text' to show 'that this suit is out of accord altogether with the whole system of Hindu law'. (Macpherson's stress on 'altogether' was important and, as it turned out, effective.)

Besides dismissing as non-injunctive the entire array of Telang's citations, Macpherson upturned his adversary's argument with regard to the *Vyavahar Mayukha* permitting the king to try husbands who deserted their wives. Howsoever constricted, once the king's authority in matrimonial disputes was recognized, the nature of remedy or punishment was a matter of mere detail. 'Surely,' he counter-argued, 'if the king had the power to inflict a fine, then your lordships stand in the shoes of the king and would have the power to order a restitution of conjugal rights.'

About the Privy Council judgment in *Moonshee Buzloor Ruheem v. Shumsoonissa Begum*, Macpherson repeated his earlier argument that 'as regards the principle of the thing, there is no distinction whatever between the Hindus and the Mahomedans'. The Hindu law on the subject was 'established beyond all controversy'. Dadaji possessed under it the right Pinhey had denied him.

II

The Appellate Court reversed Pinhey's verdict. 'The immediate question', the judges observed, 'which presents itself for our determination is, whether a suit for institution or restitution of conjugal rights will lie under the circumstances alleged in the plaint.' In determining that it would, they relied on the Privy Council ruling in *Ardaseer Cursetjee v. Peerozebye* that the civil courts in India 'should afford remedies for the evils incidental to married life'. This ruling had commenced frequent admission of restitution suits 'in the case of natives, whether Hindus or Mahomedans'. Indeed, as Justice Melvill had observed, the courts had 'no discretion in the matter' unless their jurisdiction was taken away by legislation. And legislation in India, contrary to Markby's 'wish' to make restitution decrees merely declaratory and the English reforms of 1884, had 'done its best to provide means to enforce the decree' under section 260 of the Civil Code.

They could not 'with propriety' entertain an objection that went 'to the root of the jurisdiction'; more so as no Hindu legal text had been cited 'forbidding or deprecating compulsion'. The British having established in India 'a systematic administration of justice', 'the Civil Courts would properly and almost necessarily assume to themselves the jurisdiction over conjugal rights as determined by Hindu law, and enforce them according to their own [British Indian] modes of procedure'.

The judges dismissed as irrelevant any distinction between restitution and institution on the ground that 'the gist of the action for restitution of conjugal rights is that married persons are bound to live together'. Neither Hindu nor English law contemplated that consummation was necessary to complete the marriage. Whether the withdrawal from cohabitation occurred before or after consummation, a violation of conjugal duty 'necessarily' followed and entitled the injured party to the restitution of conjugal rights. The only discretion the courts could exercise was to refrain from ordering an infant wife to join her husband.[32]

The judges saw it as no reason to exercise discretion on the fact that Rukhmabai, who did not have a voice in the choice of her husband, had never adopted her guardians' choice. Since it was not argued that 'the marriages of Hindu children are not perfectly valid without the exercise of any volition on their part', the judges remarked:

> ... the Court is virtually asked to disregard the precepts of Hindu law, which treats the marriage of daughters as a religious duty imposed on parents and guardians, and to look at the matter from the purely English point of view, which sees in marriage nothing but a contract to which the husband and wife must be consenting parties.

The judges reversed Pinhey's decree. But because he had judged without calling on the defence, they remanded the case to the Division Court for a decision on the merits after hearing the defendant's case. Costs of the appeal were to abide the result.

III

An inherent prejudice about the position of woman as a wife lay behind Dadaji's case against Rukhmabai. Its starkness surfaced only occasionally during the proceedings. When it did, it revealed the erasure of the woman as a person in her own right. On one such occasion, explaining Dadaji's claim over Rukhmabai, Vicaji argued that 'the wife formed a portion of the husband's body and should live with him'. This was just the stuff Bayley's satire, ensconced in European notions of superiority, felt compelled to ridicule: 'How would you apply that rule to the Thakore of Bhownuggur, who according to the Rajput practice, married four wives the same day?' Vicaji replied manfully: 'Well, the Thakore's identity was then divided into four fractions.'

The laughter that greeted this exegesis of the Hindu law was understandable. Not so Bayley's belief that the likes of him were above the attitude towards women that their laughter reviled. Nursing the memories of Gretna Green marriages, he had conveniently forgotten the unromantic detail that not long ago 'subsumption' was pivotal to English family life as well. The learned judge overlooked the fact that an important English legal assumption of his day was a vestige of the same principle of subsumption. The wife, in this view, was so completely a part of her husband that the English law even denied her the right to sue him in a civil court.

The ruling people's belief in their own superiority tended to make them overlook traces of cross-cultural analogues that were subversive of that belief. A Bayley could laugh at the subsumption expounded by a Vicaji, and remain oblivious to the deep-rootedness of the same notion in his own culture. Such people could barely recall the original Christian rationale for prohibiting levirate: 'Hear the decree of the synod: "A surviving brother shall not enter the bed of a dead brother." For the Lord saith: They shall be two *in* one flesh; therefore the wife of thy brother is thy sister.'[33]

Nor were they impressed by the arguments advanced by subtle comparativists of law among Indians. In his Tagore Law lectures, which Bayley must have seen, Gooroo Dass Banerjee had put the matter in perspective:[34]

> The Hindu law, while it yields to no system in maintaining the unity of man and wife, is more equitable than other systems such as the English, as it leaves to women a much larger share of freedom in the exercise of their rights during coverture... the identity of person between man and wife does not extend to civil purposes;... the peculiar and often embarrassing consequences of the legal identity of husband and wife in the English law, such as that the husband cannot make a gift to the wife, and that the wife cannot sue or hold property alone, do not exist in our law.

Though the judges took shelter behind the non-availability of discretion in this case, and Sargent frequently sounded deceptively radical during the proceedings, their judgment squared with their assumptions about women, marriage and social stability. Bayley expressed his concern that Pinhey's verdict would embolden women to treat their marriages as dissolved once they took, 'rightly or wrongly', a dislike to their husbands.[35] In the final analysis, Sargent was little different. The oppressed woman disappeared from his cognitive map as he speculated upon the 'immense' effect of a judgment that would scruple to force a non-consensual marriage upon an unwilling woman:[36]

> ... ladies would look upon their position in a new light. A great many ladies would say, 'Oh, the court won't oblige me to go to my husband; and the marriage treaty is a nullity'.

Bayley was protected by self-complacency. But Sargent, we shall recall, had said: 'No woman who has not entered the married state with her free consent should be ordered to go to her husband if she does not like it.' He, too, subordinated this conviction sufficiently in order to realize the serious repercussions of unquestioned deference to existing social arrangements. Women, he did believe, should *obey* their husbands while men should *love* their wives.

What escaped Sargent hit Rukhmabai as she reflected on the reversal of Pinhey's verdict:[37]

> The hard-hearted mothers-in-law will now be greatly strengthened, and will induce their sons, who have for some reason or other, been slow to enforce the conjugal rights to sue their wives in the British Courts, since they are now fully assured that under no circumstances can the British government act adversely to the Hindu law.

Yet the judges could not risk appearing impervious to the liberal thrust of recent English legislation and the verdicts by Melvill, Markby and Pinhey. They were confronted in the Rukhmabai case with the typical imperial dilemma of having to arbitrate rival forces within the native society. They veered towards the escape route—the subject people's egregious orthodoxy—the colonial relationship had made available to the rulers.

Their reluctance to disturb the existing social order alerted the judges to chinks in the arguments that favoured Rukhmabai. For the same reason, they missed the convoluted nature of their own reasoning. They could, consequently, turn on its head Telang's evidence from the *Vyavahar Mayukha* and justify, in the name of Hindu law, the exercise of powers it specifically restrained.

Notwithstanding the pains they took to argue otherwise, their defense for admitting this suit rested not on Hindu law but on section 260 of the Civil Code, which was an importation. The existing law, they admitted, was out of harmony with morality. Also, that it 'may be advisable that the law should not adopt stringent measures to compel the performance of conjugal duties'. But, as long as the law remained what it was, the civil courts:

> cannot with due regard to consistency and uniformity of practice (except perhaps, under the most special circumstances) recognize any plea of justification other than a marital offence by the complaining party, as was held to be the only grounds upon which the Divorce Courts in England would refuse relief in *Scott v. Scott.*

The judges made no attempt to demonstrate that section 260 was in consonance with Hindu law. They just ignored Latham's powerful demonstration that the section applied where suits for restitution of conjugal rights were maintainable, which they were not among Hindus.[38] Instead, they accepted the legal fiction that justified the civil courts' wresting of jurisdiction in Hindu cases of restitution of conjugal rights. They violated for the purpose, as they did the *Vyavahar Mayukha* fragment, the spirit and objective of the Privy Council decision in *Ardaseer Cursetjee v. Perozebye.* While recognizing the right of Indians to obtain, in a certain class of cases, relief from British Indian courts in accordance with their own laws and customs, the Privy Council had added the chastening warning:[39]

> It may be that such laws and customs do not afford what we should deem, as between Christians, an adequate relief; but it must be recollected that the parties themselves could have contracted for the discharge of no other duties and obligations than such as, for time out of mind, were incident to their own caste; nor could they reasonably have expected more extensive remedies, if aggrieved, than were customarily afforded by their own usages.

It was as if the arrogance of power had overtaken the relative modesty of this ruling. What was with the Privy Council an obligation had become in the Rukhmabai case a right which was the rulers' duty to exercise. This transformation reflected how the post-1857 consolidation of the Indian empire had fostered a more vigorous view of imperial responsibilities than was available to the Privy Council in 1856, when Dalhousie's aggressive policies had spread anxiety among the authorities in England. Moreover, massive codification of indigenous laws and usages had meanwhile induced a sense of knowledge about the subject people, and an attendant sense of power that could dispense with the earlier hesitancy and uncertainty. The British would now be the sole arbiters in India, even settling cases relating to the subjects' private lives. They would assume the powers of the king and the functions of the caste.

Rather than administer indigenous laws and usages in consonance with the ruling they had invoked, the judges would take pride in the 'systematic administration of justice' the British had introduced in India.[40] They would not only exercise jurisdiction over conjugal rights as determined by Hindu laws, they would enforce those rights according to their own modes of procedure.

The singularization of the notion of 'systematic' and the consequent insistence on a uniform procedure bespoke an impatience with and devalorization of plurality. It permitted, or hid from view, the violation of not just the objective and spirit but also the substance of the judicial policy earlier laid down by the Privy Council. In its grossness, the violation implied the administration of indigenous laws and usages according to English legal practices. As the reference in the Appellate Court's judgment to *Scott v. Scott* shows, the courts assumed unrestrained jurisdiction in matters of Hindu law, but the limitation of the authority to administer the Hindus' conjugal obligations was sought in the practice of English divorce courts. Similarly, suits for the restitution of conjugal rights were entertained putatively on the authority of Hindu law, but the guilty were judged and punished according to procedures imported from England. At a subtler level, the violation consisted in the deadening of customary laws and usages as a result of the imperialist fetish for 'consistency and uniformity of practice'.[41]

There was something arbitrary about the judges' interpretation of authority and their refusal to be drawn into 'fine distinctions'. So when Telang argued that 'the Hindu law books do not recognize a compulsory discharge of marital duties, but treat them as duties of imperfect obligation to be enforced by religious sanction', they pleaded incompetence to 'entertain any objection which goes to the root of the jurisdiction'. This was a convenient incompetence. It enabled the judges to resist the review of a questionably acquired jurisdiction, even as they virtually defied the very authority that they were invoking.

The reality of the allegiance professed towards indigenous laws was exposed by J.H. Nelson. Around the time the Appellate Court offered its ambivalent exposition, the eccentric judge-scholar from the Madras Presidency wrote with devastating candour:[42]

> We may bind the people by new laws, if we will; but at present we are *pretending carefully* to maintain the existing laws and customs of the country, good, bad or indifferent. (Italics added).

Telang, who interpreted Hindu law dynamically in response to the changing needs of his society, lost out to the likes of Macpherson, Bayley and Sargent, who held this law in derision even while betraying some of its more noxious assumptions, and supporting many of its reactionary aspects.[43] That Telang and other similar interpreters also lost out to those like Mandlik, who loved their society in a different way, is another facet of the same tangled tale to which we shall return later.

For the present we may follow the swift disposal of the case by Justice Farran.

IV

It was, from a narrow legal point of view, a walk-over for Dadaji when, eleven months later, the case came up before Justice Farran on 3 March 1887. The confidence instilled by the Appellate Court's judgment in those who had made Dadaji's cause their own is reflected in the fact that they could now do without the shrewd advocacy of Macpherson. The old combination of Vicaji and Mankar could be trusted to carry the case to its foregone conclusion.

The confidence in Dadaji's camp was in strong contrast to the resignation among the counsel and supporters of Rukhmabai. This resignation, however, was only about the immediate judgment in the case. Their hope was now focused on the Privy Council where, it was felt, issues of principle and morality would outweigh trivial technicalities and merits. Rukhmabai, as the *Indian Spectator* wrote two days after the Appellate Court's verdict, would have to 'face another trial at the High Court before representing her sad condition, and of too many of her sisters, to the final *court* of appeal, the Privy Council'.[44]

With the gaze fixed on the final arbitration, it was important to maintain a superior moral stance in the High Court. Latham being away in England, Inverarity was recalled to join Telang as Rukhmabai's counsel. Their plan was to steer clear of the mire of merits and technicalities. They refused even to mention the fact, which could constitute a possible technical objection, that Farran had, as a lawyer, drawn Dadaji's original plaint. Beyond reiterating the morality of Rukhmabai's stand, her counsel would not occupy the High Court's time.

The hearing began with Vicaji recapitulating the facts of the case. Farran then asked for the evidence for the defence. Inverarity exposed the futility of the exercise. He could prove that Rukhmabai never consented to the marriage which was now sought to be enforced; that she never regarded Dadaji as her husband; and that, besides being unhealthy, he was too poor to maintain her. Absence of consent having been pronounced by the Appellate Court to form no defence in this case, it was pointless to offer evidence in this regard. The same applied to evidence relating to the grounds which had been 'practically admitted' in the testimony of Dadaji and his witnesses in Pinhey's court. Rather than furnish evidence, therefore, Inverarity would 'content himself with protesting against the decree which the court would no doubt consider it proper to make'.

Rukhmabai backed this protest with a climactic moral gesture that transfigured her defense into a cause. She let it be known to the court, with due deference, that rather than accept a verdict that directed her to live with Dadaji, she would submit herself to the maximum penalty admissible under the law. The gesture revealed, more than her abhorrence for the man, her faith in the rightness of her resolve not to live with him. Her readiness to 'bear the consequences' of her defiance—six months in jail or attachment of property or both—converted the walk-over in Farran's court into a moral victory. Her willingness to suffer was more eloquent than the most impassioned advocacy.[45] And it acted upon sympathizers as also upon those who were hostile.

Extraordinary by any reckoning, Rukhmabai's defiance is even more impressive because it was made before passive resistance had captured either political theory or popular imagination. It further stands out for having been made by a woman when—let alone India where physically as well as mentally 'respectable' women were confined to the zenana—even in the West women's groups were in the early stages of developing a gendered critique of life, and still uncertain about ways of seeking change.

There was no going back for Rukhmabai. She was aware enough in 1884 to want to resist the injustice of which she had been a victim. Each stage of this momentous litigation further steeled her determination. Gone was her initial diffidence when, struggling to justify her resistance to the man who claimed to possess her, she looked uneasily around for support. She had now acquired a moral lucidity and strength to categorically declare 'No' to both entrenched orthodoxy and the colonial dispensation. That lucidity also gave her the imagination to anticipate a mode of resistance towards which groups of oppressed women and men would turn in due course.

The atmosphere, though, had begun to resonate with inchoate notions of passive martyrdom. Malabari often proposed such martyrdom in the face of injustice. The display around this time of public anger against the imprisonment of Surendranath Banerji in the famous *Shaligram* case—and the fact that Bihari Lal Gupta disregarded his position as a covenanted civilian and visited Banerji in jail—indicated the process by which these inchoate notions were tending to affect political practice.[46] Yet, Rukhmabai's defiance was unparalleled; she had asked for martyrdom, whereas it was almost thrust on Banerji who had been jailed in spite of his apology to the Calcutta High Court.

To return to Farran's court, Inverarity pushed the other party still further into a morally defensive position and asked that, 'as a matter of courtesy', notice be given to Rukhmabai before a bailiff was sent to her house. With the same end in view, he suggested that Dadaji should pay Rukhmabai's costs in the case.

Vicaji was not touched by the moral offensive. Or so he pretended. His learned friend, he coolly said, 'had surrendered all along the line', leaving the court with 'no other alternative but to name a particular day' for Rukhmabai's return to Dadaji's house. He also cited cases to oppose Inverarity's request for costs.

Farran, mindful that the suit was for restitution *or* institution of conjugal rights, ordered Rukhmabai to 'go or return' to Dadaji's house within one month and inform the court accordingly. As for the costs, he found it hard to make a husband 'pay the costs for the restitution of his conjugal rights'. Responding legalistically to Rukhmabai's defiance, he said that if she had 'expressed her intention of obeying the decree', he would have given a different order about the costs. But unrepentant as she was, she had to pay the costs of the original hearing, and each party was to bear the costs of appeal.[47]

NOTES

1. The expansionist drive of the British Indian legal system can be seen as part of a larger imperial enterprise, as also of a modernist knowledge system intolerant of plurality in the cognitive domain, the three forming an integral discursive whole. The same expansionism can also be described to have belonged intrinsically to that legal system by virtue of its being a species of 'modern' law. In the latter sense, the phenomenon is expressed succinctly by Galanter when he says that 'official law of the modern type does not promote the enrichment and development of indigenous legal systems; it tolerates no rivals; it dissolves away that which cannot be transformed into modern law and absorbs the remainder'. Marc Galanter, *Law and Society in Modern India*, Delhi, 1989, p. 36.
2. Macpherson was delighted to explicate the judge's comment. 'And a number of very pernicious results would ensue,' he chuckled, 'if Mr Justice Pinhey's view of the question was given effect to. [Laughter.] *Times of India*, 13 Mar. 1886.

3. It was futile, after this, for Sargent to ask: 'Does not the defendant admit that she was married?' 'Yes,' Latham admitted happily, 'but that would not matter in the least.' A harassed Macpherson could only re-echo Sargent: 'She admits it, and he swears to it.' The Chief Justice saw the risk of having to hear the case for two or three days just to 'find out that no marriage has been proved'.
4. *Moore's Indian Appeals*, vol. XI, pp. 570–1, 614.
5. Because ecclesiastical courts possessed no means, except excommunication, to enforce their process, they were compelled to seek help from courts of common law and equity. The latter courts interfered on the ground of contempt of ecclesiastical courts.
6. See *Moore's Indian Appeals*, vol. VI, pp. 348–91.
7. Such perpetuation of error through case law had already attracted the attention of, and elicited contradictory opinions from, lawyers and scholars. The balance of contemporary opinion seems to have favoured deference towards case law even when based in error. Its rationale, as stated by Gooroo Dass Banerjee, was: '... where a decision, though erroneous, has been followed as a precedent in a series of cases, the solution of the question involves some difficulty. For, though it is wrong to perpetuate an error, it would hardly be right to rectify the error by unsettling the law and overruling a precedent which might have long been the basis of men's expectations and conduct. Where there has been a uniform current of decisions, notwithstanding that they may be erroneous, the reasons for following them will, on the whole, be found to preponderate, unless the error appears to be so clear as to lead to a fair presumption that the rule laid down in the decisions could not have been uniformly accepted as settled law by the profession or the public.' *Hindu Law of Marriage and Stridhan*, p. 16. The opposite view, exposing the harm done by erroneous case law and arguing for a drastic reopening of the whole question of 'Hindu' law, was forcefully presented by J.H. Nelson in his *A View of the Hindu Law as Administered by the High Court of Judicature at Madras*, Madras, 1877. For a summary exposition of his views, see his spirited reply of April 1882 to Justice Innes' vicious attack on his legal nihilism. Here is an excerpt from Nelson's reply to Innes: 'I have never yet been able to appreciate the reasonableness and propriety of the principle which you appear to consider to be one of an elementary character, that where an English Judge, who has no Sanskrit, has decided after a few hours' consideration one of the most complex and difficult questions of Hindu law that can present themselves for resolution, and has had his decision duly recorded, every person in the country is to be stopped for evermore from essaying to establish in the courts a contrary view of that question... In other words, in innumerable instances an ordinary judgment in a suit between A and B is... converted practically into a judgment in rem, or rather into an eternal and immutable law.' Pp. 14–15. I have seen Innes' criticism and Nelson's reply in the copy bearing India Office Library No T 8055 of *A View of Hindu Law*.

8. The proposed change was dropped by the Select Committee because of the apprehension that it would work badly in Panjab. Home, Judicial Proceedings, June 1887, nos. 189–92. National Archives of India (NAI).
9. When, in answer, Macpherson referred to a decision by Justices Norris and Ghose, which had been reported in the *Indian Law Reports* of Feb. 1886, Latham countered that the wife was not the defendant in that case. This was an important point that related to the 'recovery of a wife' as distinguished from restitution of conjugal rights, a distinction that was not usually observed. Section 259 of the Civil Procedure Code provided for the recovery of a wife out of the possession of any person harbouring her. Section 260 of the Code applied in cases where a husband or wife had withdrawn from the society of the other without sufficient reason.
10. Seton-Karr observed: '... nor do I think that the provision for imprisonment of the party [according to section 200 of the Civil Procedure Code of 1859, which then was the law] against whom the decree is made and for attaching his property ought, or was intended, to apply to such a case. Surely it would be a harder course to imprison a reluctant wife than to deliver her to her husband who wishes to cohabit.' *Bengal Law Reports*, vol. XIV, p. 302.
11. Markby explained this in terms of the English courts' tendency towards liberalism. He dwelt on the underlying presuppositions of the Canon law to show how the Church attempted to control the conjugal relations of its adherents 'in the minutest particulars'. The civil courts were differently inclined: 'The law of England has in modern days to a very great extent rejected these pretensions and modified these views, but they have not as yet been radically removed; rather, however, in my opinion because they produce but small practical evils than from any approval of the principles on which they rest.' Ibid., pp. 305–6.
12. For the judgment, see ibid., pp. 298–306.The law of England, Markby believed, should be looked upon as a guide only where it was 'in harmony with the general principles of equity and jurisprudence'; not where it was 'exceptional'. Which is what, in its letter, it was in the matter of enforcing conjugal rights.
13. Macpherson may have offered the assurance on an impulse. But the suspicion that his not exactly honourable clients might not honour the assurance must have prompted discretion. Even this should have galled Narayan Dhurmaji, if not also Dadaji. A quick short message, through Vicaji or directly to Macpherson, would have forced the final recoil.
14. Pinhey said: '...neither the law nor the practice of our Courts either justifies my making such an order, or even justifies the plaintiff in maintaining the present suit.' *Indian Law Reporter*, Bombay Series, vol. IX, p. 534.
15. Sargent, too, seemed clear on the point: 'I cannot see how we are to support the judge in the court below, except on the ground that we have that discretion and may exercise it.'

16. See *2 Adam's Ecclesiastical Reports*, pp. 249–53.
17. When Latham mentioned *Molony v. Molony*, Sargent asked him: 'What year is that?' On learning that it was 1824, Sargent commented: 'Oh, I thought you were going to give us something since the new Act [1857] was passed.' Latham promised to 'come to that presently', as indeed he did, and made quite a persuasive job of it. *Times of India*, 19 Mar. 1886.
18. See *Probate Division*, vol. V, pp. 19-24.
19. Though his reply was in keeping with the submision about iniquitous hardship, Latham felt that he had conceded more than was warranted. So he quickly added: 'Nor do I see what real hardship the man would suffer.'
20. Sargent remarked: 'If the first wife does not live with him, he can get another; and if she is barren, he can take a third wife. It seems to me the Hindoos are better off than the Mahomedans in this respect.' [Laughter]
21. The Hardwicke Act (1753) was intended to do away with the problem of run-away clandestine marriages, especially of young and rich heirs and heiresses, which had for almost a hundred years acquired a degree of notoriety . Except for the Quakers and Jews, the Act stipulated that 'no marriage other than one performed by an ordained Anglican clergyman in the premises of the Church of England after thrice-called banns or purchase of license from a bishop or one of his surrogates' would be valid; also that those under twenty-one could marry only with parental consent. See John R. Gillis, *For Better, For Worse: British Marriages, 1600 to the Present*, Oxford, 1985, pp. 140–2; and Lawrence Stone, *Road to Divorce*, pp. 119, 122–4. Latham's assertion about early marriages in England may seem to be contradicted by the findings of historical sociology in recent years. However, insofar as they admit too wide a range of regional and other variations to make one feel comfortable with their generalizing hypotheses, these very researches would induce one to take Latham's point seriously. See Peter Laslett, 'Characteristics of the Western Family Considered Over Time', *Journal of Family History*, vol. 2, no. 3, Summer 1977, pp. 89–115. For examples of the early marriages mentioned by Latham, see Frederick J. Furnivall, *Child-Marriages, Divorces, and Ratifications, &c. in the Diocese of Chester, A.D. 1561–6*, London, 1897.
22. Latham sealed the argument about absence of precedent by showing the inapplicability of the two Indian cases Macpherson had cited in this context. These were *Khooshal v. Bhugwan Motee* and *Kateeram Dokanee v. Mussamut Gendhenee*. The wife was not a party in the first, and in the second she was a minor.
23. Even Markby, while admitting that suits for restitution of conjugal rights would lie in India, refused to concede that the courts had no discretion in the matter: 'That the Courts are not hemmed in by any such absolute necessity is, I think, indisputable.' *Bengal Law Reports*, vol. XIV, p. 303.

24. This process is a variation of, and also different from, the 'interstitial' law-making power of the courts which H.L.A. Hart discusses in his *Essays in Jurisprudence and Philosophy*, Oxford, 1983, pp. 6–7.
25. Justice Melvill provided this summary in his judgment in *Ardesar Jahangir v. Avabai* on 11 Sept. 1872. See *Bombay High Court Reports, 1872*, pp. 293–7.
26. The illustration pertained to the following exceptions contained in section 21 to which the Specific Relief Act could not apply: 'A contract which runs into such minute or numerous details, or which is so dependent on the personal qualifications or volition of the parties, or otherwise from its nature is such, that the Court cannot enforce specific performance of its material terms'; and 'A contract the performance of which involves the performance of a continuous duty extending over a longer period than three years from its date'. See D. Sutherland, *The Indian Contract Act (Act IX of 1872) and the Specific Relief Act (Act I of 1877) with a Full Commentary*, Calcutta, 1879, pp. 259–63.
27. 'Your lordships,' Latham added, would consider it 'most desirable that a case like this should go there.' Predictably, the Chief Justice replied: 'Oh yes, it would be most desirable.' *Times of India*, 13 Mar. 1886.
28. See *Probate Division*, IX, pp. 52–7.
29. As the Hardwicke Act (1753) applied only to England and Wales, marriage 'shops' cropped up just across the English border in a Scottish village named Gretna Green where couples under twenty-one could repair stealthily to get married without parental consent. See Lawrence Stone, *Road to Divorce*, pp. 81, 130–1, 133–5. In a delightful cross-cultural comparison, Gooroo Dass Banjerjee pointed to the resemblance between the runaway Gretna Green marriages and the Gandharva form of marriage. *Hindu Law of Marriage and Stridhan*, p. 86.
30. The point made by Telang a hundred years ago is repeated by Ludo Rocher in his 'The Theory of Matrimonial Causes According to the Dharmasastras' wherein he quotes Sen-Gupta, *Evaluation of Ancient Indian Law*, London, 1953, p. 46, to make the following remark: '... disputes between husband and wife are not vyavahar because "vyavahar means litigation before the King's Court while these disputes were matters for domestic tribunals"...' In J.N.D. Anderson (ed.), *Family Law in Asia and Africa*, London, 1968, p. 113.
31. The inspiration for this brilliant manoeuvre seems to have come from the following formulation in the Privy Council judgment in the Buzloor Ruheem case: 'Of authority negating the jurisdiction there is none.' *Moore's Indian Appeals*, vol. XI, p. 372. Patrick Olivelle of the University of Texas, Austin, suggests that, although Telang did not think of it, the well-known *Purvamimamsa* maxim, *yavadvachanam vachanikam*, demolishes Macpherson's argument. Kane thus explains the maxim: '... in the case of an authoritative text that much only is to be accepted as covered by it which is expressed by the words used and that it should not be made applicable to other cases on the ground of similarity or analogy.' P.V. Kane, *History of Dharmasastra*, Poona, 1962, vol. V, p.

1348. Macpherson went much farther than similarity and analogy in employing absence as decisive evidence.

32. The judges added that following the remarks made by Justices Mitter and Markby in *Kateeram Dokanee v. Mussamut Gendhenee*, even the right of the infant wife to remain at her natal home until her puberty could not be considered 'free from doubt'.

33. Jack Goody, *The Development of the Family and Marriage in Europe*, Cambridge, 1983, p. 62. The belief represented by Bayley in the normative contrast between the two cultural-legal systems was unlikely to be affected by the most glaring similarity between them. For example, when Macpherson alluded to an English legal practice to strengthen Dadaji's case, his enunciation made the English practice appear humane in contrast to its Hindu counterpart. He referred to the formulation by the Queen's Bench of the principle that because the husband 'was the wife's protector and guardian', she was bound to live with him; and claimed that nothing prevented 'a Hindu from obtaining the privileges given to the European'. But, then, he described the attendant English practice in a way that did away with its harshness: "They [the English courts] did not, however, go beyond putting the wife before the husband's door.' (In contrast to the Indian provision for delivering the wife bodily to the husband.) Whether the operation demanded 'putting' her before the husband's door or 'driving' her across the dreaded threshold, it reflected a cross-cultural similarity about the status of women.

34. Gooroo Dass Banerjee, *The Hindu Law of Marriage and Stridhan*, p. 138. For details of the comparison, see pp. 139–45.

35. There was, for once, more than a lawyer's readiness to echo a sympathetic judge as Macpherson added his own alarm: 'And a number of very pernicious results would ensue if Mr Justice Pinhey's judgment was given efffect to.' The laughter that ensued indicated a more general sharing of those assumptions.

36. To this was also added his concern that it 'would be putting a new revelation upon the Hindoo wording if the woman, on arriving at the age of puberty, was to consider whether she should go and live with her husband'. The entire discussion of the proceedings in the Appellate Court is based on their detailed coverage in the *Times of India*, 13 and 19 Mar. 1886, and on *The Indian Law Reports*, Bombay Series, vol. X, pp. 301–8.

37. Rukhmabai's letter of 18 Mar. 1887, in Ramabai Saraswati, *The High Caste Hindu Woman*, pp. 66–7.

38. This was in marked contrast to their keenness to reason away Pinhey's plea about 'delicacy of feeling'. The courts, they contended, could not 'draw fine distinctions between a woman who has never lived with her husband and is averse to joining him and one who has lived with him and perhaps acquired a physical or moral loathing for him, and objects to returning'. For the Appellate Court's judgment, which was delivered on 2 Apr. 1886, see *The Indian Law Reports*, Bombay Series, vol. X, pp. 308–13.

39. *Moore's Indian Appeals*, vol. VI, pp. 391–2.
40. Its matter of fact assertion in the Appellate Court's judgment—occurring as a mere parenthetical clause in a long sentence—shows that the rulers no longer needed to establish the grand claim. They assumed, perhaps rightly, that it would be taken for granted by the rulers and the ruled alike.
41. Without referring to the very large body of literature dealing with this subject, one may quote Gallanter's brilliant summing up of the complex and long-drawn-out process of the displacement of traditional law in colonial India: 'Even where Indian rules were available, their application by the British transformed them. Mere restatement in English legal terminology distorted the Hindu and customary rules. English procedure curtailed some substantive rights and amplified others. The British insisted upon clarity, certainty and definiteness of a kind foreign to Hindu tradition. Neither the written nor the customary law was "of a nature to bear the strict criteria applied by English lawyers". Rules seemed vague and requiring of definition, and this was accomplished by English methods. The mere process of definition had the effect of creating rights of a kind that did not previously exist.' Marc Gallanter, *Law and Society in Modern India*, p. 22.
42. J.H. Nelson, *A Prospectus of the Scientific Study of Hindu Law*, London, 1881, p. 149.
43. In 1877 Nelson had written: 'Translations of texts are interpreted and dealt with in a thoroughly unsympathetic spirit, by men who appear to know nothing of, and care nothing for, the Hindu religion.' *A View of Hindu Law*, pp. 12–13.
44. *Indian Spectator*, 4 Apr. 1886.
45. Cf. Lillian Hellman's remark: '... if you are willing to take the punishment, you are halfway through the battle.' *An Unfinished Woman*, New York, 1968, p.10. Quoted in Martha Ronk Lifson, 'The Myth of the Fall: A Description of Autobiography', *Genre*, XII (Spring 1979), p. 52.
46. See Surendranath Banerji's own account of the incident in his *A Nation in the Making*, Bombay, 1963 (first published in 1925), pp. 69–78.
47. For the proceedings in Farran's court, see *Times of India*, 4 Mar. 1887. For certain minor variations in the reporting of these proceedings, see *Bombay Gazette* of the same date. The latter report was reproduced in *Madras Mail*, 8 Mar. 1887.

4

A Challenge to Civilized Society

The debate that had begun with Pinhey's verdict was revived with greater stridency and a new sense of urgency by Farran's order and Rukhmabai's defiance. Even the stolid colonial bureaucracy was shaken by the embarrassing prospect of the young rebel's imprisonment. Her supporters, for their part, organized a powerful Rukhmabai Defence Committee with a view to averting that prospect. To buy time for the expensive expedient of moving the Privy Council, an appeal against Farran's order was filed in the Bombay High Court. This flurry of activity, and the support influential quarters in England extended to Rukhmabai, upset those who believed that the threat to social stability had disappeared with the dismissal of Pinhey's verdict. They reacted with renewed determination and even warned of popular discontent if the authorities succumbed to pro-Rukhmabai forces. But they also felt timorous about her moral defiance and, unsure of how best to grapple with it, endeavoured to defuse the crisis without risking a loss of face. And most of these divergent responses carried within them varying degrees of ambivalence about women's position vis-a-vis men.

One of the best articulations of Rukhmabai's cause came yet again from Malabari, who stressed the human-ethical dimension of her martyrdom. Hers was an ineluctable tragic predicament. Even if the court did not order cohabitation in her case, she would not—unlike her husband—be free to remarry. There was for her no release from this 'brutal embrace'.[1] Keen to take the fight to the bitter end, Malabari hoped that Farran's order would be a prelude for a final ruling from the Privy Council so that life became easier for future Rukhmabais.[2]

Rukhmabai's great triumph, Malabari argued, was her rejection of 'the preconceived idea of woman's inferiority' and the attendant 'duty to be everything to everybody—to father, brother and husband'. She had shown that the notion of woman as 'a thing to be trampled under foot' was sustained by both native orthodoxy and colonial law.[3] Malabari anticipated, and ridiculed, the attempt the English and Anglo-Indian press and the public opinion would make to exonerate their government. The following excerpt conveys his rage against the combination that perpetuated women's subjection in colonial India:[4]

> But the High Court of Bombay, working under Letters Patent from Her Majesty the Queen-Empress, hold a tournament of chivalry, and these Christian umpires rule that a mere woman can have no right to consult her heart, or, may be, her honour. Caste enforces on this Hindu girl a marriage to which she was as much a party as any of the Judges of the High Court. And the Judges countenance this outrage, in fact offer to serve as constable and jailor. What could they do?—poor men—such is supposed to be the law of the Hindus. And what could the British Government do?—poor Government—their mission is to perpetuate inequalities. So Rukhmabai should either go to jail or live under the protection of her so-called husband's protectors. Perhaps the husband who loves her so, may one day bring another 'wife' to keep her company. What even then? The High Court will go on grinding the dead-bones of law, and the Government will go on whistling in sympathy with the process which is grinding the womanhood out of the women of Hindustan.

This could appear disloyal. But it was also imbued with faith in the British.[5] The belief, which never came to be tested, in the certainty of a favourable verdict from the Privy Council was part of this faith. Reflective of this ambivalence, attacks on the rulers were also appeals to their moral sense. When it came to the predicament of women in India, special appeals were made to their British sisters. Malabari, consequently, called upon 'the women of England to witness this new form of Suttee, set up by British law and Christian morality'.[6]

Directing his sarcasm against caste orthodoxy, Malabari emphasized that the Hindu shastras had never contemplated such an 'unmanly' idea as restitution of conjugal rights. Nonetheless, if 'caste' had become 'educated' enough to import that idea without at the same time importing adult marriage, it might do so. But it must not seek assistance from an alien legal system; and the latter must leave 'caste' to its own resources.[7]

While he hoped to shame some people by his sarcasm, Malabari also sought to allay the fear that Rukhmabai's action would erode Hindu marriage. He called for 'the least liberal position that unprejudiced minds should take' on the issue. A letter in the *Bombay Gazette* by Vaman Abaji Modak, Principal of the Elphinstone High School, seemed to provide such a position. The letter traced 'the very root of the question' to the 'jumbling' of two discrete principles of marriage in the existing British Indian law.[8] Restitution of conjugal rights assumed a marriage that was contracted freely by parties alive to its obligations. Its coupling with the Hindu law of marriage, without regard to the latter's rationalizing principle, gave Rukhmabai's case its 'unfortunate turn'. It was likely to cause 'even greater hardship hereafter'. Women circumstanced worse than Rukhmabai might in future be implicated in such cases, to be either 'compelled to fulfil the marriage engagement' or 'be sent to jail for no crime of theirs'.

Modak felt that Rukhmabai's grievances were not grave enough to entitle her to general sympathy. But he recognized her right to personal freedom, 'the most sacred and inalienable right of every human being under normal conditions'. He wanted Indians to realize the 'utter want of consent' on Rukhmabai's part to the marriage to which she was expected to submit. It was 'only' on this ground that, while sympathizing with Dadaji as well, he sympathized with Rukhmabai more.[9]

From Malabari's reformist viewpoint, Modak may have done 'strict justice to both sides'. But, whatever he may have said about Rukhmabai's grievances, he spoke a language—the language of inalienable individual rights—that was bound to alienate the proponents of sacramental Hindu as against contractual western marriage.

The man who thundered against the orthodoxy in the language of the majority of his co-religionists, lay and pundit alike, was Raghunath Rao. Rukhmabai's imminent incarceration, he declared, was 'the result of the national sin of having violated the pure, liberal and just laws of our star-like Rishis'. Unlike the secular language of western law, with its direct link between crime and punishment, the idiom of sin presumed no simple correlation between the agents of sin and the subjects of retribution. Rukhmabai's martyrdom, while it presaged 'the emancipation of our Hindu sisters', was also the realization of the shastric prophecy 'that in this era persons not cognizant of the Law shall ascend royal seats and shall administer as law that which is no law'.[10]

The wrathful reference to 'the national sin' was a brave attempt to touch people where they were especially vulnerable. It posited guilt in the very heart of collective pride. They, the people, had violated just the law on which had rested national greatness. Against the fear of societal breakdown owing to Rukhmabai's resistance was pitted the national sin that had provoked her martyrdom. National revival demanded that the rishis' law be cleansed of later distortions, including those introduced by the British. Rukhmabai must be supported, not condemned.

Raghunath Rao, his anger notwithstanding, was no modern Durvasa. He could also appeal to individual filial sentiments to neutralize hostility towards Rukhmabai. When T. Madhavarao, the veteran statesman whose pronounced orthodoxy was tinged with sympathy for social reform, demanded punishment for her contumacy, Raghunath Rao appealed to his adversary's heart. He urged Madhavarao to imagine whether, were his own grand-daughter circumstanced like Rukhmabai, he would like her to be sent to jail. Or, would he like the grand-daughter's husband to be in jail if he refused to receive her into his house? The latter question was intended to disarm the suspicion that Rukhmabai's supporters were partial towards women. Raghunath Rao concluded:[11]

> 'Do to others as you would wish to be done to you', is a golden principle... To send a girl to the company of felons or liars, simply because she refused the company of a husband or a would-be-husband, is so barbarous that it is a wonder to me how any sane man can think of it.

As the shift here from ordinary affection to a principle of decent behaviour and the surprise about deviance therefrom suggests, both impassioned anger and gentle persuasion were used to sustain an offensive in order to shake the opposition out of an extreme illiberal position. The offensive exposed the contradictions of the orthodox position vis-a-vis Rukhmabai. Because the general reformist argument relied heavily on shastric exegesis and the controversy over the Rukhmabai case was part of a larger conflict over the meaning of tradition, the reformists felt tempted to meet the orthodox on their own ground. This offered a chance to pin the orthodox down to their liberal professions, or else be exposed. Besides reminding the orthodoxy of its own professions, this offensive also elicited from, or filled into, them a meaning that squared with what was seen as universal principles.

One such offensive came from the *Indu Prakash*. Abstracting the principles at stake in the case, it focused on Rukhmabai's status as a person.[12] Because she was an independent agent capable of thinking for herself, the important thing was her feelings in the matter, and these were 'now well-known'. But Dadaji, as her husband, claimed to be the master of her 'person and property'. This raised the larger human question: Could a man be forced on an unwilling woman? This resembled Modak's invocation of inalienable human rights. But the *Indu Prakash* took care to situate the issue in a specific socio-cultural context. It asked: 'Does the Hindu law sanction the use of any pressure, direct or indirect?' The answer, the weekly proposed, was obvious: No orthodox Hindu could countenance a law that forced 'a man on an unwilling woman or vice versa'. It reminded the orthodox of Markby's view that the idea of a husband's proprietary right over his wife was 'wholly abhorrent to the Hindu law'.[13]

This involved a principle that was dear to all indigenous orthodoxies, Hindu as well as others. It related to the preservation of a minimum cultural-legal space outside the pale of colonial control. Since the Hindus possessed their own laws to deal with the issues involved in this case, there was no reason for inflicting alien laws. Those cherishing this autonomous space, the *Indu Prakash* wrote, were 'bound' to support Rukhmabai whom 'the machinery of a foreign law' was set to punish for refusing to give 'the custody of her person' to a man she disliked.

As for the argument, put forward by the orthodox, that the law acted as a deterrent, the weekly brought out the underlying self-deprecation of the belief that force alone could restrain recalcitrant wives: 'What becomes then of the much vaunted efficacy of our institutions to foster wifely affection, independently of foreign laws?' 'If,' it continued, 'suits for restitution have been few and far between it is not because of the existence of Section 260 of the Civil Procedure Code but because of the moral sense of the community which has from ages past held that it is barbarous to compel two people, by direct or indirect means, to live together when they cannot agree.' That 'artificially created laws' did not generate 'conjugal affection' was 'fully recognized' by 'our ancestors'. The same recognition 'ought to guide us and our Courts in these days'.[14] After all, 'with all its indignation against the lady', even the reactionary *Hindoo Patriot* had shown the provision of imprisonment to be violative of both Hindu law and sentiment. How could the orthodox, then, oppose the Rukhmabai Defence

Committee, set up as it was to prevent her imprisonment?[15]

The question showed those who extolled the humanitarianism of Hindu socio-legal organization the incongruity of their rationalization of its oppressive functioning. They hid their hostility to reform behind 'sophistry and cant', and created the impression of opposing not reforms but certain objectionable modes of effecting them. 'We have not discovered a man yet among educated natives who says he is opposed to reform,' wrote the *Indu Prakash*, and went on:[16]

> But the wonder is people will still criticise harshly the attempts that are being made in the direction of reform; that they will call those who make these attempts 'over-zealous', 'rash', and 'hasty' and in a number of ingenious ways apologise for existing customs, —all the while taking care to say that they want reform too. Zeal, enthusiasm, and outspokenness, which are rightly admired in *political* actions, are derided as rashness and madness when they are displayed in *social* matters. In the former, nothing is before the time; in the latter, the vague doctrine of 'slow and sure' is constantly heard, while no one knows what that 'slow and sure' means...

The reformist position, however, was not without its own constraints and inconsistencies. Seeking equality between women and men in 'ancestral' law, it in effect treated men as more equal than women. It argued, in good faith and unmindful of the similarity with the orthodox argument on the point, that the Hindu law, which denied remarriage to a woman who refused to live with her husband, punished a deserting husband just as adequately by making him pay her maintenance. The acceptance of this differential punishment as non-discriminatory marked the limits of the contemporary reformist notion of gender equality. 'Beyond this,' the *Indu Prakash* wrote, 'there is neither reason nor sound authority for contending that our Courts should go in the supposed interests of morality and order.'[17]

Demarcating reason—universal reason—from authority—the authority of ancient law—and also bringing them together in commanding the same end, this pregnant formulation betrays a more abiding tension that marked the reformist position. Rukhmabai's supporters, it shows, invoked an uncorrupted 'tradition' to which the laws provided by 'our ancestors' were integral. They also invoked a reason from which flowed universal principles, such as those of inalienable human rights, and that made possible the idea of universal justice. Rather than face the difficulties involved in the exercise, they took recourse to exegetics that almost always discovered a convergence between 'tradition' and 'reason'. Very rarely was the dilemma of a clash between the two posited and resolved discursively.

II

Rukhmabai's opponents framed the case within what they saw as the crisis of the Hindu community. In their responses crystallized some of the deeper fears which colonialism had inspired. These fears spanned a wide range from the dark depths of individual sexuality, via socially organized domesticity, to the simultaneously public and private domain of the politico-cultural confrontation between the community/nation and the alien rulers.[18]

The Hindus, the *Native Opinion* claimed, were 'the only people directly concerned in the issue'. Barring an 'inconsiderably small section' with its 'misdirected over-zeal for reform by any means', they were happy that the alarm over Pinhey's verdict had been laid to rest. Unhappy that an ordinary marital dispute should have generated a 'war in discussion',[19] and that an appeal to the Privy Council was being planned, it wanted the controversy to be buried.[20]

Confirmed in its original understanding that Pinhey's judgment was 'unwarranted by Hindu Law as well as by long established practice', the *Native Opinion* highlighted three objectionable propositions of that judgment: (1) A marriage is not consummated according to Hindu law by the ritual performed at its celebration. (2) It is invalid for want of consent when one of the parties happens to be a minor. (3) Law courts have no jurisdiction to compel a wife to go to her husband. Exploiting the socio-psychological obsession with domestic stability and legitimacy of birth to create an 'absurd panic',[21] the *Opinion* warned that these propositions would mean:

> that all marriages among Hindus hitherto performed and not actually consummated are illegal and void, that the progeny of persons married during their minority is illegitimate and that neither husband nor wife can have the aid of law to secure the company of the other.

Heightening the effect, it insinuated that these grave consequences were courted because:

> Rukhmabai is an educated lady, has a large fortune, and was brought up in a fashionable family while her husband is poor, uneducated, sickly and unable to provide his wife the means of life suitable to her position.

It developed the argument it had briefly made in 1885, one that presented the *status quoists* as well-wishers of women. Many educated men had uneducated wives who were unfit to be their life mates. Pinhey's verdict, if upheld, would have given those men 'good reason' to forsake their wives; and it would have been 'barbarous and cruel for a court of justice to give the wives any remedy'. The *Opinion* gave this argument a wanton twist to suggest that what really motivated the reformers was their weakness for women. The 'name of a female' worked upon them 'like a magic charm'. They supported anything that seemed to benefit a woman immediately, no matter how detrimental its long-term repercussions might be for women.[22]

Despite its share of meanness, the *Native Opinion* was restrained compared to the *Kesari*. The Marathi weekly from Poona, though officially edited during most of the Rukhmabai controversy by reform-minded Gopal Ganesh Agarkar, was actually controlled by Bal Gangadhar Tilak who, in spite of claiming support for social reform, ardently backed reactionary Hindu orthodoxy.[23] Affecting an air of objectivity to effect greater credibility, the *Kesari* conceded that Rukhmabai had been a victim of oppression. The conjugal cart, it moralised, could never move along smoothly with an unwilling woman forcibly yoked to it. It expressed the hope that Dadaji would realize the woman's resistance and not press his claim.

Nevertheless, the Poona weekly strongly propounded the orthodox Hindu position. Would it be 'proper to take a position against the law because of one or two cases?' Could occasional hardship be a reason to admit the superiority of consensual over parentally arranged marriages? The two systems produced about equal conjugal strife. Viewed in terms of larger societal welfare, as against narrow individualism, there was little justification for the fuss over Rukhmabai's lack of consent in her marriage.[24]

This could sound reasonable. Soon the *Kesari* warmed up to scorn the 'reformers' rubbish' and savagely attacked those who cited the *shastras* to defend Rukhmabai. It mocked Pinhey as a *maharshi* whose judgment had propounded a new *dharmashastra* that some sturdy souls swore by even though the High Court had set it aside. Feigning allegiance to tradition, they privileged their own consciousness as sovereign, and cared neither for any authority nor for social order.

Countless Hindu men lived happily with their ill-educated wives. Here, in an exceptional case, an educated woman had run to seek legal redress against her uneducated husband. Those who claimed justice for her forgot that even the English law did not permit a woman divorce on the ground of mere dislike for her husband.

Facts, in this account, were subtly modified to achieve the desired effect. Rukhmabai, not Dadaji, was said to have rushed to the court. Further, while she only wished not to be forced to go to her husband, she was accused of demanding divorce for herself and, by extension, for Hindu/Indian women at large, and for a reason even the English considered preposterous.

To this misrepresentation was added a sarcasm particularly suited to tickle reactionary instincts. 'May you be blessed, Rukhmabai!', the *Kesari* exclaimed in mock celebration, 'You have by your action ensured the salvation of your ancestors, and offered a wonderful example to your Indian sisters.' In a society that worshipped its ancestors, and believed that on the virtuous acts of the progeny depended their salvation in the world hereafter, the message was clear. Let alone the living, Rukhmabai had shamed even the dead.

The *Kesari* then turned to the reformers' opposition to Rukhmabai being sent to jail. They had used Pinhey's verdict to argue that her case had no basis in Hindu law. Why should they complain if the same High Court sent her to jail? If the courts were powerless to implement their decisions, what was 'the point in making a demand on them to sit in such cases?' Earlier such cases would go to caste panchayats which could drag a woman by her hand to the husband's house. Once the law courts had assumed that jurisdiction, the right to punish also must belong to them.

The *Kesari* employed to great effect the kind of ambiguity with which the worst resistance to reform was passed off as reformism. The ambiguity thrived by meaning different things to different constituents and was especially geared to convey an intended meaning to those inclined towards oxthodoxy and, if necessary, contend that the very opposite had been stated. For example, after it had castigated the reformers for opposing imprisonment in a suit for restitution of conjugal rights, and lectured them on why 'the courts must have some means of enforcement by way of fine or imprisonment', the *Kesari* added parenthetically: 'We have always maintained that men-women relations are so delicate that coercion should be avoided.'[25]

The orthodoxy demanded punishment for recusancy, including imprisonment, and also self-righteously recoiled from coercion. It even waxed eloquence, as the *Indian Mirror* did, about the Hindu moral economy. The penalty of imprisonment was condemned as a 'barbarous and savage' English interpolation that was 'foreign to us, foreign to the spirit of our religion, foreign altogether to our sociology, and in utter conflict with our notions of the almost Divine respect we pay to women.'[26]

The image of an ideal Hindu/Indian woman lay at the heart of the controversy. Rukhmabai's defiance, for the orthodoxy, was not martyrdom but an 'act of madness'. The ideal she ought to follow was *streedharma*, whereby the wife gladly suffered even a brute and patiently transformed him into a loving spouse. She could still 'accept the court's verdict and, by reforming her husband, live happily with him'. 'In this alone,' the *Kesari* said sagely, 'consists her true courage, her true accomplishment.'[27]

The advice, obviously, was not meant to win back Rukhmabai to the ideals of womanhood she had reneged. It was to reassert the ideal. As for the renegade, following the time-tested technique of gossip and revilement—'the perverse logic of image making that degrades the most courageous female models of liberation'[28] —Rukhmabai was projected as irrepressibly licentious. This was intended to demoralize Rukhmabai personally and also reject the reformers' notion of an ideal woman. The *Kesari*, which had in 1885 insinuated a liaison between Rukhmabai and Pinhey,[29] now published a burlesque, entitled 'The Final Scene in the Rukhmabai Farce'. It portrayed her as a promiscuous woman who would rather exhaust her own and others' money in litigation and even go to jail, than be with her husband.[30]

The burlesque dismissed the reformers' comparison of Rukhmabai with Dr Anandibai Joshi. The first Indian woman to have trained as a doctor in the USA, Anandibai had prematurely died a couple of years earlier, soon after returning home. Hindu orthodoxy, building its pantheon of ideal women for a larger cultural hagiography, was keen to appropriate her as a tragic figure whom patriotism had driven to a distant land. There, legend would have it, rather than make the dietary and vestural adjustments required to fight the Philadelphia cold, she wooed the disease that killed her young. The burlesque called it a *mahapataka*—a great sin—to equate a dissolute woman with one whose 'renowned epic' would inspire 'Hindus so long as they maintain their Hindutva'.[31]

The *Kesari* burlesque shared its vulgarity with much of the orthodox antagonism to Rukhmabai. For example, in a lecture delivered under the respectable auspices of the Bombay Brahmo Samaj,[32] K.R. Kirtikar lashed out at her character. Denying that she stood for women's emancipation, he argued speciously: 'Rukhmabai is dependent on her well-wishers. Where is her independence?' He gave a suggestive twist to this dependence and asked: 'Does it constitute a state of freedom to secure the opportunity of living in association with educated European friends instead of an uneducated husband?' Sinking deeper into his prurient rhetoric, he queried: 'What will happen to her after another ten years?' Warning parents not to make Rukhmabais of their daughters, this self-professed reformer advised: 'Educate your women not to abandon their husbands and lead a roving sensational life, but teach them to construct a happy home and maintain a high tone of life.'[33]

Such vilifiction must have made Rukhmabai despair. How often had she wished it was all over, that it had never begun. It was mortifying to be cast within a widely shared stereotype of the westernized woman, and have her life eroticized as a 'golden lady' and 'Girl of the Period', as it was, for instance, by the *Hindoo Patriot*:[34]

> an accomplished young lady who can sing and dance and play on the piano, and whose proper sphere is the ball room at night, and the Apollo Bunder or the Bandstand at time of the setting sun...

The villain, yet again, was 'western education'. But for the 'fine notions of independence and freedom' it instilled into her, 'the Bombay young lady' would not have 'rebelled against the authority of her husband'. She would have known that, however unworthy, Dadaji was 'nevertheless her husband'.[35]

The self-evident power of the phrase—*nevertheless her husband*—telescopes centuries of internalized acceptance of the husband's authority. It reflects the longevity of an androcentrism nursed by injunctions like Manu's: 'Though destitute of virtue, or seeking pleasure [elsewhere], or devoid of good qualities, [yet] a husband must be constantly worshipped as a god by a faithful wife.'[36]

However, to bring in a necessary digression, this was not very different from the Victorian valorization of matrimony and maternity. Idealizing her service and sacrifice, the seductive phrase, 'angel in the house', encouraged the woman to dedicate her body and soul to her husband. As Charles Kingsley proclaimed in his *Yeast, A Problem* (1850), 'for true woman, the mere fact of a man's being her husband, put it on the lowest ground that you choose, is utterly sacred, divine, all-powerful'. Frederick Denison Maurice, the oracle of Christian Socialism, expressed similar views in his 1863 essay 'On Sisterhoods'.[37]

To come back to Rukhmabai, she was projected as a threat to social well being. Misled (in this reckoning) by the freedom made available by the English Raj, she and women like her, to use the conventional phraseology of the *Hindi Pradip*, were devouring the pure moon of *satitva*—the ideal of female chastity. This sad thought made the Allahabad monthly—edited by the well-known writer Balkrishna Bhatt—carry an elegy on the chaste Hindu/Indian woman. Was it still the land of those goddess-like women whose tales cleansed people of all sins?[38]

Orthodox feelings were further exacerbated by an official circular, which we shall discuss in the next chapter. It proposed the introduction of divorce among possible measures to avert the recurrence of the Rukhmabai kind of embarrassment. This was worse than the worst that Privy Council could do in the event of an appeal in the Rukhmabai case. It confirmed the suspicion that the British policy of non-interference in the religious affairs of the ruled was not entirely trustworthy. The rulers, the *Hindi Pradip* observed, might as well admit that they aimed to Europeanize the Hindus and wipe out their religion.[39]

Fears got exaggerated in this state of agitation. They were fed by a deep-seated anxiety about female sexuality. Supposed to be insatiable, female sexuality was believed to require constant vigilance and control.[40] Like the deification of the Hindu husband, attitudes to female sexuality and its controlling mechanisms also had a long unbroken tradition.[41] For those socialized in this tradition, divorce was not only corrupting and anti-shastric, it also appeared—despite the wide prevalence of customary divorce—to be the negation of marriage. Considering that men, even without divorce, were not particularly constrained, the prospect of freedom it might give women was the only reason for apprehending chaos from the introduction of divorce. Hence the *Pradip's* panic that every woman—men, for obvious reasons, are not mentioned in this context—might as well live with whomsoever caught her fancy and leave him the moment she spied someone better.[42]

The *Hindi Pradip* reflects a mentality that apprehended social chaos as the inevitable consequence of Rukhmabai's stance. At the same time, the monthly supported Malabari on the issue of early marriage, and favoured a system that provided for the spouses' consent without dispensing with the parents' role in arranging marriages. Further, though not sparing Rukhmabai, the *Pradip* was critical of Dadaji who, disobeying the shastras and custom, had invoked the authority of the king—the State—in a conjugal dispute. The king possessed no power over a person's heart. Even if Rukhmabai was forced to live with him, she would bring Dadaji no happiness.[43]

That a Hindu should have moved a colonial law court to get possession of his *dharmapatni*, as the Bengali monthly *Prachar* put it, signalled a larger crisis. A double embarrassment, it exposed the ineffectuality of the community's venerable role models and of its internal disciplinary mechanisms. The Hindus had lost their Hindutva.[44]

The *Indian Mirror* offered another variation of the Hindu response to Rukhmabai. True to its liberal image, the Indian-owned English daily from Calcutta[45] found in the case an illustration of 'how heavily a girl may be punished for what, after all, is only very natural in the case of a young girl, a dislike to live with a person she does not care for.' 'Our instincts,' it wrote, 'must necessarily revolt against a contract under such circumstances as came to light in her case.' Compared to the Hindu view of marriage 'as a sacred tie, above human laws, and beyond juristic interference', the European idea of contract was 'more advanced'. It placed conjugal relations on an intelligible basis and recognized men and women as equals who entered matrimony after comprehending its implications.[46] Yet, rather than press for reform, the daily justified the existing arrangements, and did so fairly aggressively. It sang of the 'sacredness' and stability of *sanskaric* marriage;[47] predicting 'in fact, a degeneration of the institution' in the event of marriage becoming a contract.

Such ambivalence seems to have been pervasive. Whatever the lure of the West and discontent with tradition, there was always the realization of the reality of subjection and the consequent risk of cultural subversion. The sense of a beleagured community/nation could, in such an ambience, prove compelling: the 'disruptive forces' released by the colonial connection provided the 'necessity' to uphold marriage as a sacred institution. To achieve this, law needed to be 'held supreme'; and for its sake natural instincts and human conscience could be 'stifled'. If the law contained 'outrageous' anomalies, as indeed it did, these 'must be for a time tolerated' to safeguard the 'social traditions' which constituted the 'backbone' of the nation.[48]

Yet another mode of short-circuiting the logic of admitting injustice to Rukhmabai was to project it as an individual instance of hardship. One could, then, philosophize without being 'cruel to such an eminent lady as Rukhmabai':[49]

> the order of society requires here and there a sacrifice to propitiate it, and we must perforce look on coldly, as it were, while the innocuous lamb is being led to the altar, though we wish from the bottom of our hearts to save it from the impending knife.

The admission of injustice to an individual, or a minority within the society, could also be used to turn the tables upon the reformers: 'Is the happiness and peace of the whole society to be disturbed in order to do sentimental justice to a single individual?'[50] This was a shrewd rhetorical move. A favourite strategy of the orthodox, it shifted the charge of tyranny from the opponents to the proponents of social reform. A small minority, the reformers were accused of imposing their will on the majority.[51]

Ambivalence could also cause injustice to be perceived as the opposite of itself. This is what happened when the *Indian Mirror*, reverting to the Rukhmabai case after an interval of two months and forgetting all its earlier reservations, wrote ecstatically:[52]

> Our ideas of marriage are at utter variance with European ideas of marriage. With us it is not a mere legal contract. With us marriage is a sacrament, blending of two souls, a holy binding of spirit with spirit, the union of man and woman for working out our common salvation. Man does not forge the matrimonial chains; he cannot break them. That work is Divine. The very name which the Hindu wife assumes immediately after marriage, and the name by which she is popularly called is suggestive of this spiritual fact. That name is *svadharmini*, that is, a spiritual companion of her husband. Can any idea of womanhood and wifehood be more sacred, more elevating, more ennobling than this? It will be centuries before Europeans attain to the Hindu ideal. And because this marriage among Hindus is a spiritual fact and factor of all potentiality, therefore it is that the separation or divorce was neither understood nor dreamt of...

In this ecstasy—or terror—were fused visceral fears about women's liberation and politico-cultural anxiety about the community/nation. The imperilling of *sativa*—the woman's chastity and fidelity to her husband—presaged familial and larger socio-cultural disintegration. But what gave it the dark strength of the irrational was the fear of female licentiousness in the wake of freedom.[53] Hence the imaginary portrayal of Rukhmabai's meretricious life-style, and the credibility of the portrayal. In her was believed to have come true the shastric prophecy that 'in this Iron age [Kaliyuga] wives would grow recalcitrant and defy the authority of their husbands'.[54]

As the portrayal defied all evidence to the contrary, the reformers fretted about the poetry of *sanskaric* marriage that survived their prosaic demonstration of its unreality:[55]

> It is marvellous to see how the point at issue is being ignored and a marriage is called a 'sacred relation', with Providence and several other holy things to bear witness, when the husband can marry as many wives as he likes even in the lifetime of the first victim, while the wife cannot re-marry even after the husband's death.

The deep psychic terror struck many as a function of patriotism. The threat to their community/nation bound them to defer—resist —the reform of what they admitted was indefensible. Insisting on the primacy, in a subject country, of political reform, they argued against creating internal divisions in the pursuit of social reform. The threat also induced a curious perceptual trans-formation whereby what was indefensible became worthy of universal emulation.[56] When the seamy reality of lofty cultural claims threatened to obtrude, the sheen of high ideals needed to be particularly preserved. Minds so agitated could scarce heed the delicate reformist logic that their fears constituted the worst castigation of 'pure' Hindu women and the sacred Hindu marriage.

III

The opposition to Rukhmabai was widespread. Feeding an array of impulses from the existential to the political, it was accented to say different things to different people at one and the same time. Its semantic fluidity—which they saw merely as a ruse—frustrated some of Rukhmabai's supporters. But there were others who, willy-nilly, recognized the representative character of that opposition and felt forced to accommodate it. Of the latter, Telang's is a telling example.

When influential Indians and Europeans in Bombay decided to form the Rukhmabai Defence Committee, Telang was naturally invited to join in. He did so on the understanding that the Committee's exertions would be confined to avert Rukhmabai's imprisonment. He soon felt, however, that the Committee was inclined to question the very validity of child marriage. Taking exception to this, he submitted a memorandum to the Committee which indicates how much he felt obliged to give in to the opposition.

Telang began with what the Committee ought *not* to do. Resiling from his own argument as Rukhmabai's counsel, he wanted the Committee not to question the courts' jurisdiction in a suit for the restitution of conjugal rights where the parties were Hindus. Nor did he want it to argue that what was asked by Dadaji was not 'restitution' in the strict sense of the word. Concerned with adverse popular perception of reformist activities, he worried that the Committee was *supposed* by the public to be working to upset the institution of early marriage.

To 'disarm reasonable opposition', Telang also backed away from the course of action on which were centred all hopes for Rukhmabai. He asked the Committee not to support an appeal to the Privy Council. Hindus, he argued, might want to file a suit in conjugal disputes 'where everything is not innocent'. The doors of justice should not be shut against them.

Telang further warned the Committee of 'irreconcilable opposition' from 'the whole Hindoo community'—and that would include him—if it accepted Raghunath Rao's suggestion to question the validity of Rukhmabai's marriage on the ground of absence of consent. Echoing orthodoxy, he used the rarity of consensual marriages among Hindus to ask the familiar question: 'Are we, then, prepared to take any step that shall render all this immense mass of marriages questionable at law?' He stressed that his emphatic 'No' was '*at least* as much in the interests of the female as the male parties to these marriages'.

Telang's daunting list of don'ts ended with an admonition to the Committee not to approach the legislature for relief to Rukhmabai on the ground that she had not been a party to her marriage. As one opposed to 'legislative interference in our marriage customs', he could not countenance a request that meant inviting 'such interference in a most objectionable form'.

Turning to its 'proper objects', Telang expected the Committee to prevent Rukhmabai 'from being *imprisoned* for disobedience to the decree for "restitution"', and do it in a way that ruled out the recurrence of similar situations in future. For that purpose, Rukhmabai's marriage with Dadaji had to be assumed to be as binding in law as it was 'by the custom and usages of the community' to which they belonged. The Committee, consequently, should recognize that 'such a marriage should be enforced in certain ways', but represent against enforcement 'by the penalty of imprisonment'.

This would be in keeping with enlightened opinion which had come round to opposing imprisonment generally as a mode of enforcing decrees in civil suits. The English legislature had abolished imprisonment entirely for enforcing 'restitution' decrees, and almost entirely for nonpayment of debt. The Indian legislature was about to follow suit in the matter of debt, and the law relating to conjugal obligations, too, should be correspondingly altered.

Realizing, however, that people were gripped by 'a genuine feeling of alarm', Telang was anxious to allay popular misgivings about reformist moves, especially in the matter of legislation. Neither the Rukhmabai case nor the proposed alteration implied that things were amiss with Hindu marriage:[57]

> the change of law required is not in the case of Hindoos only, but also of Mahomedans, Parsees and Christians; it is required not merely in cases of infant or early marriages, but also of adult marriages; it is required not only in cases of marriages without consent, but of marriages where the fullest consent has been given; and it is required not merely in cases of 'restitution' inaccurately so called, but also in cases of what is properly called 'restitution'.

Telang endeavoured to remove the general alarm that the conjugal bond would weaken once the deterrent of imprisonment was gone. Married young and without their consent, Hindu spouses grew up to show the same 'smoothness and mutual love and affection' that characterised 'married couples under other systems'. But the fear of the 'awe-inspiring remedy of imprisonment' was scarcely the reason for the success of this system of marriage.

Having testified to the general health of the Hindu household, Telang met the orthodoxy more than half way. Though he personally favoured abolition of imprisonment, he suggested, 'in this period of transition', the lesser alteration that *ordinarily* imprisonment would not be provided in restitution cases. He argued that, given the rare and often insignificant ownership of property by women in India, the other punishment provided by law—attachment of property—would be either inadequate or nugatory. The mere presence of the penalty of imprisonment could, in such a situation, have some utility. In any case, recourse to imprisonment, if made exceptional, would be 'quite sufficient' for the cicrcumstances laid bare by the Rukhmabai case.

Telang warned the Hindu orthodoxy that he would accept this compromise only if the latter agreed to its immediate implementation. And he assured the Rukhmabai Defence Committee that the orthodox would not oppose limited legislation. The warning as well as the assurance suggest that, having fancied himself in the role of a mediator, Telang expected to create a consensus around this as the minimum acceptable change. He was obviously taken in by the orthodox indictment of imprisonment as a 'barbarous' English importation.

Telang was not the only one in 1887 to believe in the possibility of altering the law. Even the Legislative Department of the Indian government thought likewise. It would take years and a great deal more public acrimony before the organized Hindu orthodoxy agreed to any reform. Telang's premature death saved this well-meaning mediator the stark disillusionment that forms the subject of chapter five.

Telang's response in 1887 shows how powerfully the colonial ambience influenced people's attitudes. He was willing, he said, to make even unreasonable concessions 'in order to reconcile public opinion in India'. The concessions he made, and forced the Rukhmabai Defence Committee to accept, reflected more than an anxiety to remove 'reasonable misconception' about reformist efforts. They verged on a capitulation to just about *any* misconception among the orthodoxy. Telang behaved as if he himself shared the politico-cultural fears of orthodoxy. Keen to reach out to an audience larger than his formal addressees, he had his letter to the Rukhmabai Defence Committee published *verbatim* in the *Times of India,* to the acute embarrassment of Rukhmabai's sympathizers and to the delight of her opponents.

This acquiescence was in marked contrast to Telang's stern attitude towards English public opinion. That opinion, he agreed, could activate the Indian legislature along desired lines. But he felt disinclined to take advantage of it because of the way the press in England had covered the Rukhmabai case. This coverage, he observed:[58]

> impresses me so unfavourably, shows to my mind, so complete a misconception of the true conditions of the problem, that while I am willing to accept aid from that quarter, I am not prepared to deviate a hair's breadth from the path which lies plainly before us in order to secure that aid.

If Telang found the English reaction so exceptionable, it must have galled those who suspected even in well-meant criticism an assault on their culture, religion and nation. What was that reaction like?

IV

The London *Times* set the pattern for the coverage of the Rukhmabai case in the English press. Besides carrying the despatches of its India correspondent and commenting on the case editorially, it published letters from persons like Max Mueller, the Bishop of Carlisle, Pinhey, Latham and Rukhmabai herself. Many other English newspapers and periodicals, too, reported the case. But, setting aside professional rivalry and political differences, they mostly followed the conservative London daily.

The Times had fixed ideas about India. Believing in the Britons' civilizing mission, it saw in India rampant evil and backwardness that justified the belief. If it noticed any stirrings there in the direction of social reform, these were *ipso facto* an upshot of English education and other liberating forces released by the British. Political agitation, by the same token, reflected the Indians' natural resistance to be regenerated.

The archetypically imperial gaze of *The Times* characterized even those among the British who disagreed with it on issues not colonial. It was an omniscient and manichean gaze. Never in doubt, it cast the rulers and the ruled in terms of the opposing forces of good and evil, light and darkness, order and anarchy. What held India together was the British presence. Its diverse population would otherwise be at each other's throats.[59]

In *The Times*' story of the Rukhmabai case, the entire culpability rested with Hindu law which the English judges, knowing that it was an instrument of oppression, perforce administered: 'At every stage in the case there was the utmost sympathy expressed by the Judges for the wife, but the law was clear and was against her.' The impugned law was not section 260 of the Civil Procedure Code, but the Hindu marriage law. In 'the disguise of law'—Hindu law—was enacted 'a tale of monstrous wrong and of injustice' as the judges' personal sympathy 'went for nothing'.[60]

The humanitarianism of the English judges and the perversity of Hindu law symbolized, for *The Times*, a self-evident civilizational dichotomy: 'There can be no doubt to which side opinion in this country will incline.' In contrast, as was illustrated by the Madhavbag meeting,[61] Rukhmabai's own countrymen found 'nothing shocking or revolting in the end' their law had been employed to serve.[62] That law, over 'thirty centuries', had got so 'closely interwoven with the moral and religious sentiments of the people' as to course through their 'daily conduct'.[63]

The Times nonetheless hoped that the British Indian judicial system would not send Rukhmabai to jail. It was one thing for the court 'to give a judgment on a matter of fact, and quite another for it to set the administrative machinery in motion to enforce an order against which the conscience of the Judge revolts'. In its resolution of October 1886, precipitated by the Madhavbag clamour, the government of India had reiterated that it would not interfere with indigenous social customs.[64] This left Rukhmabai's 'countrymen and countrywomen' free to excommu-nicate her; and she would in the event have to 'put up with the inconvenience'. But the government could not be obliged to enforce the community's sanctions. If Dadaji moved the court to send his recusant wife to jail, he could be refused on the ground that his request entailed the kind of interference the government was bound to avoid. The *Times* capped its innocent legalism with the rhetorical query 'whether we govern India in order that we may send to prison a woman who will not live with a husband against whom her whole nature rises up in most justifiable abhorrence'.

Suspecting that the worst could nonetheless happen, *The Times* in a precautionary move philosophized about Rukhmabai's possible imprisonment. Six months in jail, 'a heavy sentence, out of all proportion to the offence', would be 'lighter by far than the life-long misery which would follow her from compliance with the order which Mr Justice Farran has *felt it his duty to pronounce*'.

(Emphasis added.) Also, there was 'a minority of dissentients' in India that made penalties 'not very dreadful to those who can dare to face them'. Moreover, if her example inspired 'even a few' Indian women, Rukhmabai would have 'dealt no light blow at the law which has driven her to revolt'. In any case, 'customs of thirty centuries' could not be 'uprooted at a stroke'.

The Times credited this 'first act of open rebellion' by an Indian woman against 'the superstitions and prejudices of her country' to the liberating influences, like female education, that the British had released in India. It would teach Indian women 'the rights of their sex elsewhere' and lead to 'a general enfranchisement of the sex'. And, as the women's struggles in western Europe showed: 'When the day comes at which the women refuse to be bound by the tyrannical rule imposed upon them, the men may resolve as they will, but they will be forced to yield nevertheless.'[65]

The conviction about the villainy of Hindu law and the liberating power of colonial mediation flourished in the face of contrary evidence. Indeed, it then tended to work itself into the kind of self-righteous rage to which the Bishop of Carlisle gave expression in *The Times.* Oblivious to Pinhey's judgment about the culpability of the colonial law, he wrote:

> Is it necessary that a Government which abolished suttee should respect such a venerable relic of barbarous and cruel tradition and custom as that which compels wise and large-hearted Judges to become the means of inflicting intolerable torture upon defenceless women? Respect for native prejudices and feelings is necessary no doubt, but respect which practically leads to brutal cruelty is very unrespectable and ought to be made to give way to the laws of God and conscience and humanity.

However well-meaning, this offensive ranged very respectable considerations—the laws of God and conscience and humanity—against native customs, traditions and sensibilities. Not even did the evidence coming from pro-Rukhmabai quarters soften the belief in native degeneracy and imperialist rightness. The *Times*, for example, reported Lepel Griffin's forceful defence of Rukhmabai in which the British Resident at Indore had accused the English law of compelling 'her to go to her husband against her will'. 'Such a law', Griffin had said, 'was a disgrace and an outrage upon human society.'[66] Latham, too, told the *Times* that Rukhmabai could have tided over the customary sanctions that would have followed her refusal to live with Dadaji. 'Unfortunately for her, the English law stepped in.'[67]

Max Mueller made the same point in *The Times.* No Indian law book required 'that a young girl who refuses to fulfil a contract to which she was no party, or objects to being made a wife by force, should be sent to prison for six months... Why, then, should the English law offer to aid in the restitution of conjugal rights, supposing that conjugal rights exist?' Whether the rights existed could be debated by 'Hindus and Hindu lawyers'. The English—'more than all, Englishwomen'—could see to it that their law was not 'rendered infamous in aiding and abetting unnatural atrocities'.[68] Pinhey, too, sought to remove the misconceptions about Hindu law in a quasi-pseudonymous letter to *The Times.*[69]

But nothing shook *The Times*' and the general British belief about the brutality of Hindu and the superiority of English law. The belief continued even though the daily felt obliged to somewhat modify its position about the responsibility of Hindu law in Rukhmabai's case. It carried the above mentioned letters and also accused Indians, not just Hindus, of being inured to cruelty:[70]

> we see no reason why the sanctions of the English law should be employed for the enforcement of practices and customs which are utterly repugnant to English feeling, and to which, indeed, only the hardening effect of long usage could reconcile the people of India.

Alive, at the same time, to the risks of meddling with these practices and customs, *The Times* also counselled caution. But it did this without forsaking its aggressive moralism. On the contrary, it converted the rulers' lapse from high precepts into a principle with which to defend them against the charge of despotism:[71]

> The government of India by England is, we are often told, autocratic, despotic and irresponsible. Is there any other dependency of any other country where an outrage—against which the feeling of every member of the ruling and many of the better men among the ruled people revolted—would be nevertheless reluctantly connived in, out of respect for the degrading custom of the subject race?

There was no winning against this logic. Claiming credit for both Pinhey's verdict and its reversal, it proclaimed the rulers' duty to root out native savagery and also justified their passivity. Their choice always sprang from principles; with them even the avoidance of obligation was an obligation. Their democratic ethos obliged them to tolerate the native law in Rukhmabai's case.

This, in general terms, was the British view as they reacted with anger and concern to the Rukhmabai case. Its lines were etched in a question tabled in the House of Commons within days of Farran's order. Coming from a Liberal member of parliament who had been a non-conformist judge, the question stressed the inequity of the Hindu as compared to the western marriage system, and it welcomed the liberation of Indian women through exposure to English influences.[72]

Even self-critiques of the colonial intervention were self-celebrations, irrespective of whether they came from the Liberals or the Tories. The decision in the Rukhmabai case was 'eminently unsatisfactory' because: 'A young woman, by the action of our English Courts of Law, will go to prison for doing what, from an English point of view, we feel she is perfectly justified in doing.' The criticism implied herein was eclipsed by an explication that redounded to the colonizers' credit:[73]

> We do our best to raise the women of India out of the condition of helplessness and social slavery and degradation... and then, when the natural results follow, and they attempt to behave like women of education and refinement, we allow our laws to become an instrument for riveting their chains.

These sentiments, so kindred to *The Times*', were expressed by the *Indian Magazine*, that stout defender of the Indian Empire. Far removed from both, the radical/liberal *Westminster Review* struck a similar stance.[74] Piqued that a Hindu lady should 'under British law' be subjected to a penalty abolished 'at home', it reached the familiar conclusion that the Rukhmabai case was 'the most striking illustration yet to hand of the evils involved in Hindu child-marriage'. So stated, the net impression it created was one of colonial mediation releasing liberating influences and the native society resisting them; of India—'a society that still loves the ways of the ancient world'—being exposed to the 'Zeitgeist of modern Europe'.

The rulers, the *Review* realized, could still be blamed for reinforcing, through their judicial nexus, 'regulations which lacked any precise sanction in the original state of Hindu society'. But given the stubbornness of native conservatism, the best course was to trust the irresistible process of change they had initiated, of which Rukhmabai herself was a personification.[75] Meanwhile, in the immediate context of the Rukhmabai case, the *Review* favoured Markby's idea of making restitution decrees merely declaratory:

> In this way the sanction of the penalty for refusal of cohabitation would

> again be left to the displeasure of caste, and to whatever machinery of supernatural menace might be employed.

This relief, the *Review* exulted, would 'gracefully commemorate the reign of a Queen which numbers amongst the greatest triumphs of civilization it has witnessed the immense improvement that has taken place in the position of women'.[76]

True to the script, the *Saturday Review*—certified as 'generally sober' by the *Indian Spectator*[77]—admitted that Farran's order 'may appear to cloak rank injustice under the forms of law'. It wished that Rukhmabai had embraced Christianity and claimed dissolution of her marriage under 'Sir Henry Maine's excellent Act passed in 1866'.[78] Without this extreme step, too, the *Review* expected Rukhmabai to obtain relief from an appeal to a Divisional or full Bench of the Bombay High Court. It could 'hardly imagine any justices, civilian or barrister, who will not find the means, not indeed of evading the provisions of the law, but of adapting its spirit to equity and reason'. Having among its contributors such old India hands as Joseph Arnould, Alexander Grant, W.S. Seton-Karr and Maine himself, the *Saturday Review* was not innocent in judicial matters. Yet it expressed the hope that, feeling 'something like Sir Robert Hazlewood, who Scott tells us, would have died rather than commit the solecism of sending a captain of dragoons to gaol', the Divisional or full Bench would set aside Farran's order.

The fancy that their judges would prefer death to punishing a victim of social oppression indicates the generous conception the British had of their own incapacity for injustice. It was protected by a variety of rationalizing devices which helped any deviation from justice appear anything but what it was. Thus the *Times*, too, had expressed its faith that, in the event, no injustice would come Rukhmabai's way through the British Indian judiciary; and it had also stressed the beneficial fall-out of Rukhmabai's incarceration. The *Saturday Review*, which apparently would not even hedge, resiled the most as it maintained that Pinhey's verdict had been 'rightly' reversed.[79]

Underlying these protective devices was a fear of political danger. The fear itself was rarely admitted. One such admission came from the *Spectator*. The weekly favoured dissolution 'of a marriage anywhere whenever the husband turned out a boor'. But it advised against meddling with the Indian marriage laws. That would be 'politically too dangerous': 'India would revolt.'[80] Relating native conservatism to political agitation was a disguised expression of the same fear.[81] Once the tenacity with which 'they' held on to tradition was recognized as the defining trait of Indians, it was easy to stress the futility, rather than the danger, of external mediation.[82]

An even finer camouflage came in the form of a Burkean defence of native customs and practices. The *St. James' Gazette* arraigned the 'young native radical reformer' who would 'clamour for parliamentary institutions' but 'not stir a finger to free the Hindoo women from their wretched condition', and called the Hindu marriage law 'the greatest evil afflicting our fellow-subjects in India'. Yet, in the context of British inaction, it described Hindu laws and customs as 'most suited to the necessities of the race', which the rulers 'must elect to maintain'.[83]

The *Pall Mall Gazette* was rather exceptional in commenting on the Rukhmabai case without condemning the Indians outright. It regretted the 'constant injustice' caused by the colonial judiciary enforcing 'that vague body of rules of caste and religion which hitherto have had their only sanction in opinion'. That gave 'an extra turn to the screw of those very customs and superstitions which the well-wishers of India desire to see gradually relaxed without revolutionary confusion or violence'. The *Gazette*, however, couched these comments in a non-incriminatory language. It even expressed, albeit a little cautiously, faith in the ultimate triumph of British justice. Should Rukhmabai appeal, it concluded, the Privy Council was 'very unlikely' to retain the decree of imprisonment.[84]

The solitary rejection, perhaps, of the ideology of *The Times*' master narrative came from the *Echo*. Following its motto—'Be just, and fear not'—the inexpensive London radical paper admitted the injustice done to 'the Native lady who has appealed unsuccessfully to the Courts to release her from a marriage contracted in childhood'. 'It is horrible,' wrote the *Echo*. But, it asked, 'is it so much more horrible than our own law?', and answered unmincingly:[85]

> True, there is no child-marriage with us, but once a girl is married, the law compels her, let her repulsion be great as it may, and great with cause, to live with her husband, unless and until she can prove adultery or cruelty... we should do well to look at home, and remember that with us alone among the civilised nations suits for restitution of conjugal rights are known.

The *Echo*, too, got its story from *The Times*. But its radically different social vision permitted it to see through the master narrative. True, the *Echo's* facts were not impeccable. The English law as it impinged upon women was even harsher. Only men could obtain divorce on simple grounds of adultery or cruelty. A woman was required to prove aggravated adultery by her husband —adultery combined with cruelty or incest.[86] But the paper was right in rejecting the holier-than-thou attitude of its countrymen and women.

For the majority of *Echo's* countrymen, it was natural to respond the way they did. More so as, manifesting yet another comforting ambivalence, they could combine anxiety about women in India with varying degrees of opposition to feminism at home. The Victorian ideal of domesticity providing the norm for man-woman relationship, the 'natives' had to come up to the ideal and the 'feminists' had to learn not to transgress it. Hence, for example, the *Saturday Review's* invocation of the English judges' chivalry and, to quote Deirdre David, its 'notorious opposition to feminism and intellectual women'.[87]

The *Echo's* countrywomen, too, betrayed a similar response. The imperialist discourse cut across internal barriers of class and gender. For instance, the *Queen*, a popular women's magazine which lionized Rukhmabai, saw her as a product of the liberating colonial intervention, who had taken 'the spirit of the age' 'into the privacy of Indian zenanas'. With this spirit acquiring 'ever-accelerating velocity', the sort of 'outrages on human liberty' witnessed in her case would be over in the 'not distant future'.[88]

Although armed by a sense of superiority and mission, sympathy for Rukhmabai among British women also indicated a growing solidarity for the women's cause. They saw Rukhmabai as a fellow victim and as an exemplar for feminist struggle. They were especially stirred by her resolve to court suffering to resist injustice. Theirs was no *Times*-like moralizing about martyrdom. Beneath their imperialist self-assurance remained a sense of shared vulnerability with women in India, as elsewhere. Given the melancholy realization that the fruition of women's emerging struggles lay in the distant future, they could intuit the liberating power of the will to mock the consequences of defying authority.[89] As three Welsh women put it in an epistolary expression of camaraderie with Rukhmabai: 'Each woman who raises herself now is but before the age which is to be... but the raising will be due to them—to her... may it never be submission to a wrong!' Their letter 'hoped and prayed':[90]

> 'that you may go to prison rather than to that man. You will show what a woman can do, and future ages when women are free and justly treated will bless you as their pioneer. It must be so!

A similar letter, with over a hundred signatures, expressed the Scottish women's 'hearty co-operation' with Rukhmabai and those 'Indian sisters, who desire to escape from the bondage under which the custom of ages has placed you'. Commending Rukhmabai's preference for imprisonment to 'the worst form of slavery', these Scottish women enclosed with the letter a poem which began:[91]

> The coded doom has fallen! I, who asked,
> For *Justice* must be satisfied with *Law.*

Invoked by women, the distinction between law and justice was an instrument for exposing rather than rationalizing the injustice of authority. An anonymous correspondent to the *Times of India* —from among the ruling people but distinguishing herself as 'Only a Woman'—emphasized the criminality of law uninformed by justice. Maintaining that Pinhey's 'spirited' judgment was 'a boon to the cause of justice and freedom', she dismissed the attempts to present its reversal as 'a true rendering of the law':[92]

> Laws weakly expounded, or weakly administered, become the tools of tyranny, and it seems to me that even when judgments are delivered in accordance with the law, but in conflict with justice and the main principles of our national laws, the Courts do not fully comprehend the sacredness of their duty when they fail to qualify these judgments with a recommendation to the Government, to deal with the sufferers in the light of equity and justice.

'Only a Woman' wanted her people to offer justice and not excuses. If 'this odious decree be law,' she exhorted, 'now is the moment to vindicate our national principles by an immediate reprieve': 'To grant it [the reprieve] only can be just, while to withhold it can be little else than criminal.' Yet, as the anxiety about 'our national principles' shows, her criticism was not above the kind of superiority to which Telang had objected. Imperialist poetry burst forth as she wrote of the liberatory British mandate:[93]

> She [Rukhmabai], a pure, but brave young woman, has broken the bondage of a custom viler than slavery, and is looking to our boasted laws for protection;... You [Rukhmabai] have friends in plenty, who will stand by you till you have successfully fought the fight, and till every woman, be she Hindoo, Mussulman or Christian is entitled to be judged

> by that British law which proclaims to the stranger and sojourner that the ground upon which he treads is holy, and is consecrated by the genius of universal emancipation.

Such—from the *Queen* to 'Only a Woman'—was the range of British and Anglo-Indian female reactions to the Rukhmabai case. Admired and lionized, the young rebel evoked an uncanny realization of the commonality of women's predicament across the board. But she also became a measure of the emancipatory possibilities the British had created among a benighted people. With all their internal variations, these reactions shared a resistance to any fundamental questioning, such as the one voiced by Pandita Ramabai who had the clarity to see and the courage to say that compared to 'the native society and religion', the English had proved 'a worse tyrant' for women in India.[94]

V

The British in India were no less partisan. The *Times of India*, disclosing that Rukhmabai was the 'Hindu Lady', recalled her 'hard story': 'a lady of considerable culture—even from a European standpoint', she was justified in refusing the consummation of 'a distasteful marriage'. In 1885 the paper had hailed Pinhey's verdict as the 'vindication of the rights of Indian womanhood'. Now it found his verdict was 'not sound law', which the subsequent judges had done 'right' to reverse. It dismissed as 'somewhat too feminine' the indictment of 'Only a Woman'; adding gratuitously that feminine instinct, though quick, was 'not always quite logical'.[95]

Like the London daily that had inspired its christening, the *Times of India* pressed home the advantages of Rukhmabai's incarceration. It would provide 'a capital text for agitation here and in England' to press for legislative changes which 'ought to do much towards rescuing the daughters of India from slavery and degradation'.[96] This, at least, sounded like celebrating her martyrdom. But the daily also added that imprisonment would offer Rukhmabai, who wanted to be a doctor, 'enforced retirement' for preparatory studies. However, it solicitously asked 'the leaders of Bombay society' to ensure that she was not rendered 'out of pocket by the costs of her trial'; and others who 'felt for a helpless woman in a difficult and painful position' to do their bit to make her 'sojourn' in jail 'as pleasant as possible'.[97]

The moral buoyancy that characterized the *Times of India's* coverage of the Rukhmabai case in 1885 had given way to a realism that did everything to rationalize the *status quo.* The paper played up Rukhmabai's 'martyrdom', but with the attendant caution that in matters relating to native social life, it was 'difficult no doubt for an Englishman to arrive at an unprejudiced opinion'.[98] Gradually its interest in Rukhmabai's well-being also tapered off.

The problem, in the British and Anglo-Indian reckoning, was the non-availability of the emancipatory British law to Indians. Once in a while anger was directed against the amoral expediency of retaining unjust laws. But nothing disturbed the faith in western superiority. This anger coexisted with the justification of official inaction.[99]

The *Statesman,* for example, assumed consent to be a universal principle of civilized marriage: 'It is the conflict of Hindoo law with this principle, or the ignoring of it by the practice of infant marriage, that creates the present difficulty.' 'No civilized tribunal' could ignore this principle, 'let the law be what it may.' Otherwise, bereft of any means to differentiate marriage from violence, the tribunal would do what lay beyond the competence of law: it would legalize crime.[100] Yet, the Calcutta daily blamed Inverarity for offering in Farran's court the 'simple' defence that Rukhmabai had never consented to her marriage.[101] Further, in line with the London *Times,* it valorized the imperial refusal to abuse 'the power we possess as foreign rulers in the most despotic and fatal manner'.[102]

The *Pioneer* felt that the 'extremely guarded policy' contained in the October 1886 resolution 'ought to have saved' Rukhmabai. Hindu marriage customs, being 'on the same plane as *suttee*', should have been interfered with. It held that 'the law—if the judgment against her was legal—can scarcely be left in its present state'. The 'public voice' was 'crying aloud' for action by the government, and even high officials 'openly' recognized that 'the cry must have a response'.[103]

Within two weeks, however, the *Pioneer* was worrying lest Rukhmabai's prayer for an officially fixed minimum age of marriage, commended by the *Times,* should receive favourable consideration. 'More harm than good,' it warned, 'is likely to be wrought by asking for reform at lightning speed.'[104] The warning may not have been unfounded. But the anxiety behind it sat ill with the *hauteur* of the daily's condemnation of 'Hindu marriage customs' as *suttee.*

This view of Hindu marriage justified the query that, given a choice, would Rukhmabai not 'prefer suttee':[105]

> Is not the custom which would force a woman like Ruckhmibai [sic] to consent to be tied for life to a man like he whom the Bombay High Court has decided to force upon her as her husband, and to invest with a husband's right over her—is not such a custom equally barbarous, if not worse?

The Anglo-Indian press had in mind a *'suttee'* different from Malabari's 'new form of *suttee* set up by British law and Christian morality'. The *Civil and Military Gazette* considered Malabari's description 'rather unfair' as it wrote with unusual moderation: 'We are under the impression that the lady goes to jail by Hindu law, and that the bulk of the native papers are more pleased than disgusted.'[106]

The uncertainty behind the word 'impression' was, however, accompanied by the assertion that 'if ever a decision was given in accordance with the views, alike of the leaders of Hindu opinion and of the uneducated peasant, it was that ruling which bade Ruckmibai to go to her "husband", or go to jail'.[107] That uncertainty finally gave way to the conviction that the verdict in the Rukhmabai case was a 'grim folly' whereby the 'Government and law are now making themselves ridiculous, alike in the eyes of the native population, and in the judgment of the critical historian of the future.' Hindu law-makers, the *Gazette* admitted, who were 'wiser than our legislators of to-day', recognized that no 'legal contract whatever' was possible in the case of children getting married without knowing what the relationship meant. Rukhmabai's persecution was due to 'English Civil Law, and has nothing to do with Hindu law'. 'Let us not,' the Lahore daily appealed, 'prostitute our civilization to perpetrate a legal injustice which native customs never permitted, nor demanded.'

Armed with this understanding, the *Gazette* saw through the paradoxical reaction typified by the *Times*:

> We strike a magnanimously reluctant attitude, and lament that our tender regard for native susceptibilities compels us to violate our own sense of justice to womanhood; while, as a fact, we are only forging a new legal weapon for applying force to woman, which native susceptibilities regard with the utmost abhorrence.

Because the 'barbarity of the situation' was of their 'own creating', the *Gazette* continued, the 'duty of reparation' lay with the British. They ought to get over the 'blindness' and the 'confusion in terms' whereby they had ignored their own role in the 'grim folly'.[108]

The *Civil and Military Gazette* itself took time to discern the collective 'blindness' that for the ruling people must have been comforting and functional. The one Anglo-Indian paper that possessed this clarity all along was the *Bombay Gazette.* Its defence of indigenous marital arrangements against the attack of 'A Hindu Lady', which we noticed in the first chapter, may have seemed reactionary. But it believed that neither indigenous nor British laws had been exclusively progressive or reactionary in their impact on Indian society. The *Gazette's* editor, Grattan Geary, acted on this understanding as he fought to stave off Rukhmabai's imprisonment. A man of conviction and uncommon empathy for alien cultures, Geary had left the *Times of India* to build the *Bombay Gazette* into a worthy rival. His efforts on behalf of Rukhmabai were sustained by his wife, who joined the Rukhmabai Defence Commmittee, and by a passion that survived his vexatious implication in a libel suit filed by Narayen Dhurmaji to force Rukhmabai into submission to which we shall turn in the next chapter. Indeed, he used the suit as an occasion to expose those among whom Rukhmabai had been judicially condemned to live.

'Fate and the High Court are dealing harshly with Rukhmabai', bemoaned the *Bombay Gazette.* Leaving fate to its inscrutable ways, the *Gazette* targeted the High Court. The crucial blow had come from the Appellate Bench: 'Every point of law upon which the defence could have hoped successfully to resist the action had been decided against her.' After that she could only resolve for 'martyrdom'.

However nice the word might sound, the *Gazette* realized, the immediate consequences of martyrdom would not be pleasant for Rukhmabai. Consequently, it refused, unlike the *Times* and the *Times of India,* to turn Rukhmabai's moral stance to any extraneous advantage. In fact, should the worst materialize, the *Gazette* raised a technical objection in the hope of having her prison term reduced from six to two months. Had Rukhmabai been a Parsi, her contumacy would have invited only two months in jail. Different punishments, the *Gazette* argued, could not be justly meted out for the same offence.

The courts, the *Gazette* argued, had always exercised discretion in deciding Hindu suits relating to conjugal rights. The legislature had never meant them to be 'blind and mechanical executants of local law'. Nor had their practice ever been 'an exact reflex of the custom of the castes'. They had, indeed, 'advisedly and wisely ignored' certain elements of the Hindu conjugal system. But, the *Gazette* scathingly wrote, the Appellate Court had abdicated this discretion in 'heroic indifference to the human aspects of the case', and refused to make 'fine distinctions'.[109] The verdict against Rukhmabai, it argued, involved the assertion by the High Court of 'a coercive jurisdiction' which no Hindu king ever affected.[110] Managed, ironically, with 'a little Hindu law and a good deal of the judgments of the English Divorce Court', that jurisdiction made the British Indian courts 'more Hindu than the Hindus'.[111] Violative of both 'policy and equity', the jurisdiction justified the use of English 'precedents and warrants' to enforce the obligations of a marriage law 'wanting in any one of the attributes of a contract'. Rukhmabai, who could not have been so helpless 'if the Court were guided wholly by the Hindu law as it stands, or by the English law as it stands', could well:[112]

> complain that so much of the English practice as tells against her has been imported into the operations of the Court, but that she is refused the benefit of its leniencies—leniencies, moreover, which are measured out in England to wives who deliberately break contracts into which they have freely entered.

The resultant transformation of Hindu law constituted 'the heart of the whole question'. The 'considerate reticence' and 'usual elasticity' of Hindu law, that made 'a silent provision' for hard cases, were taken away by 'the mischievous application' of English law, giving it 'an oppressive character that has not hitherto belonged to it'. Rukhmabai's refusal to live with her husband, 'based on exceptional circumstances, would not be held to be contrary to the spirit of the engagement entered into in the names of the children who are affianced to one another in infancy'. Such couples were bound by 'religious duties of uncertain obligation'. Realizing that these duties or obligations could not be 'safely' enforced by the civil courts, Hindu law left them 'to the discretion of the caste and the punchayat'. Rukhmabai, not liable under this law to imprisonment, 'would be left to argue the matter with the discreet elders of her caste'.

Implicit in the *Bombay Gazette's* defence of indigenous marriage laws and practices was an important argument that Rukhmabai would soon employ in her 'Reply' to Dadaji's 'Exposure'. Incidents of refusal to cohabit occurred among the Hindus 'from time to time'. What led to 'the scandal of the present case' was Dadaji's recourse to law 'to compel the cohabitation of a reluctant girl whose friends approve of her refusal'.[113] Should Hindu husbands be eager for the enforcement of their 'law by procedure invented by English ecclesiastical lawyers', the *Gazette* observed, 'let it be the better procedure of today', and not the one already repudiated by the English legislature.[114]

This could be done 'without creating alarm amongst the Hindus for the safety of any custom or institution amongst them that is worth saving'. The *Bombay Gazette* cited the *Mahratta*, 'the organ of the Poona Brahmins', to suggest the existence among the Hindus of 'a very evident desire' to be 'freed from the stigma of even appearing to be accomplices' in coercing a reluctant wife by sending her to jail.[115] This was more a move to allay Hindu anxieties than a description of actual Hindu feelings. The *Bombay Gazette* knew the *Mahratta* and its likes too well to ignore their contrary pronouncements. They were wedded to the system Rukhmabai was 'so stubbornly resisting'.[116] Yet it was worth trying to corner them into conforming with their humane pronouncements.[117]

The *Gazette* believed, and hoped thereby to neutralize orthodox fears that Rukhmabai's success would bring harm to Hindu society. A decision in her favour would not encourage Hindu wives to desert their husbands. Caste authority was not dependent on orders like the one issued by Farran to safeguard domestic order. In any case, Rukhmabai was an 'exceptional woman', and the number of Hindu wives following her example would be small. There always was 'a relativity in contentment'. The Hindu wife, having known marriage as an irrevocable sacrament—'so far at least as her own will is concerned'—could hardly long 'for the free status of a consenting wife'.[118] Indeed, the 'school of experience' taught wives in all male dominated societies to endure husbands who were hard to endure. 'Neither the Hindu law nor the Canon law,' the *Gazette* added ironically, 'gives wives the right to marry husbands by twos or threes, or by the dozen, until they are mated to their satisfaction'.[119] Rukhmabai's rebellion notwithstanding, even the 'most aggressive' social reformers could not inspire 'the millions of Hindu wives' to long for the freedom of contractual marriage. They had 'enough in hand without desiring to go far into the large field which is brought into view by Rukhmabai's case'.[120]

Compared to its outburst against the High Court, the *Bombay Gazette* may have seemed charitable in its criticism of Hindu orthodoxy. But it did not absolve the latter. It knew the 'truth':[121]

> that the orthodox party, under the garb of an enlightened conservatism, seeks to perpetuate the depressed condition of females, and would even utilise the hated interference of Government.

This was enough, in the frenzied perception of the 'orthodox party', to make the *Bombay Gazette* indistinguishable from the general run of English and Anglo-Indian papers. Those who two years ago had been avid readers of its criticism of 'A Hindu Lady' were now blinded by its defence of Rukhmabai. They appreciated neither its *exposé* of the British legal mediation nor its defence of healthy conservatism.

With even a voice like the *Bombay Gazette's* sounding adversarial, Telang understandably felt driven to concede to the opponents of Rukhmabai much more than he would normally have done. Equally understandably, he carried the day when, on 8 May 1887, the Rukhmabai Defence Committee met to discuss his memorandum.[122]

NOTES

1. The powerful phrase is Malabari's: 'So they have a law by which they would not mind surrendering girls of ten to the brutal embrace of their husbands.' *Indian Spectator*, 27 Mar. 1887.
2. So keen was Malabari to have the law settled by the Privy Council that, even at the risk of sounding personally cruel to Rukhmabai, he hoped that there would be no pardon for her. *Indian Spectator*, 10 July 1887. At the same time, he taunted the government for its inability to intercede on behalf of Rukhmabai as she waited to be sent to jail. He recalled that more than twenty years ago William Muir, 'one of the wisest and most careful of our administrators', had proposed the non-recognition of unconsummated infant marriages by the law courts. But the government had held back. 'Has the Native community', Malabari asked, 'made no progress during the interval?' Irrespective of how one answered the question, the need for action remained. If the community had progressed in the meanwhile, why was the government not acting? If it had not progressed, how much longer was the government to wait for an initiative to come from the community? Ibid., 6 Mar. 1887. Malabari kept hoping till the end for a Privy Council ruling. Less than two weeks before the compromise that brought the case to an anti-climactic end, he wrote: 'But for our part we would much rather seek a pronouncement from the Privy Council, and be done with it once for all.' Ibid., 24 June 1888.

3. For example, the English law of marriage, which in England was a matter of imperfect obligation and did not admit infant marriages, was used in India to enforce restitution of conjugal rights in cases 'where a real marriage had not taken place nor certainly been consummated!' 'The High Court of Bombay,' Malabari illustrated the argument, 'professes to administer the Hindu law, and yet it imports into this Hindu law a point of the English Church law which has nothing to do with the marriage law of the Hindus.' 'Why should the British Government,' he asked, '*enforce* infant marriages, any more than slavery?' Ibid., 13 Mar. 1887.
4. Ibid., 6 Mar. 1887. Two weeks later, referring to the possibility of pardon for Rukhmabai, Malabari wrote with unconcealed anger: 'His Excellency could give free pardon to a murderer, but not to a girl married in infancy, who has never been to her husband, so called, and never can go. After all, you see, it is only a woman, and nobody is going to bother himself about such a thing.' Ibid., 20 Mar. 1887.
5. 'Faith in colonialism despite an understanding of its exploitativeness - this was the paradox of educated consciousness in colonial India.' I have elaborated this in *The Oppressive Present*, pp. 17–70.
6. *Indian Spectator*, 20 Mar. 1887.
7. Ibid., 27 Mar. 1887.
8. The deleterious consequences of the pitchforking of English principles and procedures into indigenous laws were not confined to marital causes alone. Writing, coincidentally, in the very year of Farran's order, J.H. Nelson developed this theme in his *Indian Usage and Judge-Made Law in Madras*, London, 1887. The following excerpt captures his basic argument: '... Sanskrit law was pursuing a course of spontaneous development; this has been interrupted, and English doctrine has been pitchforked into Sanskrit texts. Is it likely that a satisfactory result will ever follow? The whole subject is now in a chaotic state, and so great is the uncertainty that valuable property is commonly sold for a thousandth part of its value. So far the present policy cannot be viewed with complacency.' pp. 4–5.
9. Because of this extra sympathy, Modak sent his 'little mite of subscription' to the Rukhmabai Defence Fund; a subscription that was more a token than the measure of his sympathy for her.
10. *Indian Spectator*, 13 Mar. 1887. Carried away into comparing Rukhmabai to Jesus, Raghunath Rao wrote: 'If Rukhmabai did not consent to be given in marriage to the man who claims her as his wife, then the judgment of the court, under which she may be sent to jail, is more preposterous and unjust than the judgment of the Jews who convicted Jesus and got him crucified. I look upon Rukhmabai as a redeemer of the girl-wives of India, offering herself as a sacrifice for her sisters.'
11. *Bombay Gazette*, 20 May 1887. For Madhavrao's letter—writing under the psuedonym 'Native Thinker'—see *Madras Times*, 8 May 1887.
12. Clearing the ground for the discussion of the principles involved in the

case, the *Indu Prakash* of 13 June 1887 dismissed Dadaji's projection of Rukhmabai as 'a mere tool' in the hands of her avaricious relatives. It detailed the 'absurdly palpable' inconsistencies that marked his charge to show that Dadaji's was an unreliable testimony proffered by a questionable character. Moreover, irrespective of who she lived with, Rukhmabai was herself competent to dispose of her property.

13. The powerful effect of Markby's judgment on reformist thinking is epitomised in the following remarks: 'If, therefore, such a penalty is repugnant to the letter of the English law and foreign to the spirit of the Hindu law and when its working is found to exceed the requirements of justice why should it not be done away with? Law is certainly as progressive as civilization and society, and if the law could be less harsh with safety to society in a previous stage of progress, it stands to reason that the law should be as little harsh at present.' *Sind Times*, 2 July 1887.
14. *Indu Prakash*, 13 June 1887. An additional argument this write-up advanced was: 'Refusal to live with a person you do not like is not a positive offence; and it is only positive offences which the law ought to punish.'
15. Deviating awhile from its usual sober and conciliatory tone, the *Indu Prakash* added: 'We are all more or less on our trial and it will be a matter of great interest to know how many of us stand up for imprisoning a lady because she refuses to live with a man she does not like or care for, and how many plead for the abolition of the penalty of imprisonment... *Opinions* will not be numbered but weighed, and we entertain no doubt the Government will not deviate from the honest work they have taken in hand.' (Emphasis in the original.) Ibid.
16. Ibid.
17. Ibid.
18. The conflation of the fear for the community as fear for the nation formed part of a larger synonymization of Hindu and Indian which I have discussed in *The Oppressive Present*, pp. 116–44.
19. *Native Opinion*, 11 Apr. 1887.
20. Ibid., 4 Apr. 1887.
21. This expression is inspired by the following in Pierre Saint-Amand, 'Terrorizing Marie Antoinette', *Critical Inquiry*, No. 20, Spring 1994, p. 400: 'Indeed, the phallocentric status quo will yield to an intelligent dissolution only when we have found the means of combatting base resentment, absurd panic at the new, and above all recourse to the female scapegoat: when we are able to avoid the mythic repetition of a fateful history.'
22. *Native Opinion*, 11 Apr. 1887.
23. I am indebted to Ram Bapat who explained to me the *Kesari's* writings on the Rukhmabai case and suggested, on the basis of stylistic evidence, that some of these were penned by Tilak.
24. *Kesari*, 8 Mar. 1887. It made fun of the claim that consent was essential to a valid Hindu marriage. Were that so, it quipped, how many

reformers could claim legitimacy of birth? It also dismissed a similar suggestion about the necessity of consummation of marriage. A marriage exists, the paper proposed, when people think that it does. The *Mahratta*, which belonged to the *Kesari* group, insisted that the Hindu marriage law caused no hardship, 'except probably in isolated cases of the kind now brought before the Court'. Even though Hindu marriage was a sacrament, castes did 'allow separation between husband and wife in cases of cruelty &c'. The Hindu wife was not much worse off than 'her free English sister'.

25. *Kesari*, 5 Apr. 1887.
26. *Indian Mirror*, excerpted in *The Madras Mail*, 19 Apr. 1887. Like Telang before the Appellate Court, the *Mirror* maintained that 'with Hindus, sociology and religion are not two distinct and opposite things as in the West'.
27. *Kesari*, 22 Mar. 1887.
28. My debt to Pierre Saint-Amand continues. See note 21.
29. Employing an ambiguous phrase that carried titillating resonances without being clear enough to invite legal action, the *Kesari* wrote, in its issue of 13 Oct. 1885, that the judge and the lady were 'one and the same'—*ekaroopa*—and wondered why the husband was adamant to secure the company of such a wife: 'After all, the native people do not repose dignity or prestige about that kind of women. There is no dearth of such women!'
30. Rukhmabai had not, the burlesque concluded, 'hesitated to act in each and every possible way with all the powers of her body, speech and mind, to sow the seeds of strife among the numberless households living a life full of happiness and peace; to achieve in the shortest possible time the degradation of the entire womenfolk by detaching them from religion and proper conduct… ' Ibid., 29 Mar. 1887.
31. The burlesque wrote: 'Anandibai did not give up even in the minutest bit her own religion, proper conduct as a woman, or our own customs and conventions. She realised that otherwise people would call her *dharmabhrashta*—fallen from religion—that women from her society will not honour her, and… as a result, she would not be able to secure the good of her sisters and reform them.' Ibid. For a fictionalized account of Anandibai Joshi's life, see S.J. Joshi, *Anandi Gopal*, translated and abridged from the Marathi original (published in 1962) by Asha Damle, Calcutta, 1992.
32. Posing as a reformer, Kirtikar regretted that Dadaji should have been maligned as a coolie, but maintained that no good would accrue from harassing Rukhmabai. Dadaji should 'bid her a distant good-bye'. Kirtikar, maintaining that the litigation originated in Sakharam Arjun's designs on Rukhmabai's property, dismissed any connection between her case and the issue of social reform.
33. Ibid., 19 Apr. 1887; *Madras Mail*, 22 Apr. 1887.
34. *Hindoo Patriot*, 4, 18 Apr. 1887. The Bengali monthly, *Prachar*, in yet another vicious example of character assassination, wrote that

Rukhmabai, a low caste woman, had got the moon in her possession. For, carried away by her beauty and bent on introducing corrupt alien ways of life, both *vilayati* and native sahebs considered her unfortunate. She could now cancel her present marriage and wed one of these sahebs. The monthly bemoaned that *Hindus*—as if upper caste Hindus alone answered to the description—were obliged to take cognisance of the marital goings-on of the lowliest of the socially low. See *Prachar*, vol. III, 1293–94 B.S., pp. 390–9. I am beholden to Indira Sen-Gupta who, showing uncommon generosity in sharing her research material, gave me a copy of this essay; and to Biswaroop Das for helping me with the Bengali text. The most elaborate fictionalised account of Rukhmabai and her case, however, appeared in a Marathi play which was published soon after Farran's order. See *Tarunishikshan Natika*, Poona, 1887. I am grateful to Ram Bapat for bringing this text to my notice and for explaining it to me.

35. *Hindoo Patriot*, 14 Mar. 1887.
36. Manu, 5.154.
37. See Susan P. Casteras, 'Virgin Vows: The Early Victorian Artists' Portrayal of Nuns and Novices', in Gail Malingreen, ed., *Religion and the Lives of English Women, 1760–1930*, London, 1986, pp. 136–7. See also Malingreen's 'Introduction' in which she uses a memorable phrase, the 'triumph of social myth over female reality', and writes: 'A class-bound Victorian domestic ideology of female service and self-abnegation, confused and confusing in its effects, fuelled the multifarious projects of female philanthropy and social improvement which male commentators like Dickens alternately ridiculed and sentimentalized.' Ibid., pp. 3,9. Recent scholarship has shown how, following European expansion in Africa and South America, androcentric Christian ideas rooted out traditional social arrangements that tended to assign to the sexes complementary and equally valued roles. See Ramon A. Gutierrez, *When Jesus Came, the Corn Mothers Went Away: Marriage, Sexuality, and Power in New Mexico*, Stanford, 1991; Margaret Jean Hay and Marcia Wright (eds.), *African Women and the Law: Historical Perspectives*, Boston, 1982; Elsa Malvido, 'The Role of the Female Body in the Mexican Colonial Period as Seen Through Studies of Historical Demography', *Journal of Women's History*, IV(1), Spring 1992, pp. 119–32.
38. For an analysis, both diachronic and synchronic, of the pervasive androcentric ideology of *pativratya*, from which *satitva* is indistinguishable, see Vanaja Dhruvarajan, *Hindu Women and the Power of Ideology*, New Delhi, 1989.
39. *Hindi Pradip*, Aug. 1887.
40. From Manu to Bankimchandra Chattopadhyaya (1838–94), to mention two paradigmatic figures, the genealogy of the fear of female sexuality seems to have been uninterrupted when Rukhmabai rebelled. Here is a random selection from Manu: 'It is the nature of women to seduce men in this world; for that reason the wise are never unguarded in the

company of females.' 'For women are able to lead astray in this world not only a fool, but even a learned man, and to make him a slave of desire and anger.' 'Women do not care for beauty, nor is their attention fixed on age; thinking "it is enough that he is a man", they give themselves to the handsome and to the ugly.' 'Through their passion for men, through their mutable temper, through their natural heartlessness, they become disloyal towrds their husbands, however carefully they may be guarded in this world.' (ii, 213–14; ix, 14–15.) A similar obsessive fear is expressed in Bankim's novel *Krishnakanter Will* (1878) which shows Rohini, who had until then lived loyally in self-exile with her lover, betraying him for a stranger she had barely set eyes on.

41. One of Manu's famous commandments says: 'Her father protects her in childhood, her husband protects her in youth, and her sons protect her in old age; a woman is never fit for independence.' Also: 'Women must particularly be guarded against evil inclinations, however trifling they may appear; for if they are not guarded, they will bring sorrow on two families.' (ix, 3, 5.)
42. *Hindi Pradip*, Aug. 1887.
43. Ibid.
44. See *Prachar*, vol. III, 1293–94 B.S., pp. 390–9. We may note the use of the term *Hindutva* in different Indian languages at this time, and also their concern to arrest its decline.
45. For example, the *Civil and Military Gazette*, 16 Apr. 1887, regretted the position taken on the Rukhmabai case by 'the organ of progress' from Calcutta.
46. *Indian Mirror*, excerpted in *The Madras Mail*, 19 Apr. 1887.
47. See also the *Mahratta* which claimed universal validity for sacramental, as against contractual, marriage. It asserted: 'We say that not only Hindu marriages but marriages among the European communities also partake of this character. Why is there otherwise any necessity of appearing before a priest? Why are such marriages again distinguished from purely civil marriages… ?' 27 Mar. 1887. A somewhat differently accented defense of Hindu marriage was provided in A.T. Banerjee's letter to the *Indian Daily News* of 14 Apr. 1887. He wrote: 'The fact is that Rukhmabai's case, which is no doubt a hard one, is one of those necessary evils that form part of the world's constitution—one of those evils which we cannot attempt to remedy without throwing the whole system out of order.' As he was addressing an Anglo-Indian paper, Banerjee added: 'Such necessary evils are by no means unknown even in the highly refined European system of marriage by courtship. But no one there even thinks of condemning that system because of the occasional evils that arise out of it; and so, indeed, I do not see why such a fuss should be made about Rukhmabai's case, which, though a hard one, does not vitiate the system of which it is the outcome.'
48. The *Indian Mirror* ended on a pragmatic note to justify its virtual retreat into inaction: 'A rush often means a fall. Hindoo society is not

in a state now to go so far as to say that marriage is only a contract voidable at all, although, at times, we see that injustice is the natural consequence of a strict application of law to old customs, and that lifelong misery may be the penalty of a technical crime.' Excerpted in *Madras Mail*, 19 Apr. 1887.

49. A.T. Banerjee's letter to the *Indian Daily News*, 14 Apr. 1887.
50. *Mahratta*, 10 Apr. 1887.
51. It was used with great effect by Bankimchandra Chattopadhyaya. He wrote, for example, movingly about the cheerless lot of Hindu women, especially widows. But he refused to support the minority of social reformers. They should, the ideologue of neo-Hinduism argued, patiently convert the majority to their viewpoint. From here it was but a short step to accuse the reformers of tyranny: 'If it is a cruelty not to relieve the miseries of a handful of widows, then it must be a barbarous inhumanity that causes mischief to thousands of individuals by inaugurating widow-remarriage.' 'It is no piety,' Bankim delivered the punch, 'to gift a pair of shoes after killing a cow.' I have discussed this in *The Oppressive Present*, pp. 100-15.
52. *Indian Mirror*, 25 June 1887, in *The Voice of India*, July-Aug. 1887, p. 340.
53. In his note of 14 Sep. 1887 on the proposed modification of the law relating to the restitution of conjugal rights in the aftermath of Farran's order, W. Kaye, the Commissioner of Agra Division, bluntly stated: 'The real truth is, that Hindus dread any change tending to make the control of the husband over the wife less complete than it is at present.' *Home Department, Judicial Proceedings*, May 1890, nos. 410–715, (National Archives of India).
54. *Mahratta*, 20 Mar. 1887.
55. *Indian Spectator*, 7 Aug. 1887. The immediate provocation for this remark came from the *Liberal*, the organ of the reformist New Dispensation faction of the Brahmo Samaj headed by Keshabchandra Sen, which wrote: 'Marriage is a sacred relation and is brought about by Providence. It is for time and eternity. Both in the Hindu Shastras and in the Christian scriptures, it is so regarded. The New Dispensation has taught us very high doctrines about marriage. Let us all keep faithful to our ideal and oppose any unwise attempt to upset it.' The *Spectator* was prepared to support the ideal of marriage as a sacrament. 'But what on earth,' it asked, 'has it to do with *infant* marriages and their enforcement by a foreign tribunal, or with sending an unwilling wife, the victim of this accursed union, to jail?' 'Our Hindu friends,' the *Spectator* wrote on another occasion, 'have gradually departed from that ideal, till they have entirely lost the spirit of it and are clinging to the dead form.' Ibid., 27 Mar. 1887.
56. Cf. Principal Wordsworth's letter of 1 Nov. 1887 about the proposed alteration of the existing law of restitution of conjugal rights: '... at the present moment there is a strong reaction manifesting itself among a large section of educated natives against western institutions, ideas and

morals. This reaction is closely associated with the "patriotism" which is so much in fashion just now, and which prides itself on the immense superiority of Hindu morality, religion, and social order to anything that the world has to show elsewhere. It seems to be becoming a point of honour among the young Hindus to defend these ideas...' *Home Department, Judicial Proceedings*, May 1890, no. 421 (National Archives of India).

57. Telang did admit, 'in the most public, emphatic and unreserved manner,' that there were defects in the Hindu marriage system. Yet, he felt obliged to affirm, 'our Hindoo households will be found to be, in fact, quite as well constituted—when you have due regard to the other differences of conditions—as households among the Christians or other communities which are free from those particular defects'. *Times of India*, 26 May 1887.
58. Telang's letter, dated 24 April, ibid.
59. Frequently carrying such stories, the *Times* of 17 Sept. 1888, for example, dragged in the Indian National Congress while reporting the ill-usage of two child-wives: 'If the native Congress would address itself to the reform of horrible social abuses, their efforts would enlist European sympathy in every direction; but no personal capital could be made out of a social reform agitation, and consequently these barbarous customs are accepted apathetically, without the faintest attempt at amendment.' Similarly, reporting 'serious disturbances between Hindus and Mahomedans during Mohurrum' in different parts of India, its issue of 1 October 1888 claimed: 'Were it not for the impartial and determined attitude of the Government officials in the maintenance of peace and order, it would be almost impossible to prevent these rival races from settling their religious and political disputes by force of arms.'
60. Even the *National Reformer*, the organ of free thought edited by Charles Bradlaugh and Annie Besant, followed *The Times* in attributing Rukhmabai's suffering to the English judges' sombre duty to administer the Hindu law. Also, betraying the typical inconsistency of British reaction, it praised both Pinhey and the judges who reversed his verdict. It admired the judges for the following reasons: Pinhey for refusing to send 'a refined and highly cultivated girl' to a husband who 'was too poor to support her, was utterly ignorant and uneducated'; Sargent and Bayley for feeling 'compelled' to overrule Pinhey despite 'their entire sympathy with Rukhmabai'; and Farran for realizing that he 'had no option save to' pass the order he did. *National Reformer*, 20 Mar. 1887. The *Globe*, an evening daily from London, did a more convincing job of praising all the four judges. Pinhey, according to it, was inspired by justice while the other judges had reluctantly obeyed the law. *Globe*, 14 Mar. 1887.
61. This refers to a mammoth public meeting organized by the Bombay Hindu orthodoxy in Sept. 1886 to demand official non-interference in religious matters. *The Times*, 13 Sep. 1886.
62. *The Times* of 11 April 1887 developed the contrast between the Indian

and British reactions by imagining that the Privy Council had ruled against Rukhmabai. Despite the 'native community', it asserted, 'the force of English and Anglo-Indian opinion' would then 'certainly compel the Government to alter the law'.

63. It added: 'They inflict the social penalties which are the main sanction of the law, and without which the law would speedily fall into disuse.' It overlooked the fact that neither the thirty-century-old law nor the social sanctions that sustained it were responsible for Rukhmabai's predicament. Also, that the British Indian judicial system was now bolstering up that law. Ibid. Like 'thirty centuries', another term used to suggest the antiquity of this law and its absorption into people's thought structure was 'immemorial usage'. *Methodist Recorder*, 17 Mar. 1887.

64. It is a measure of the close interest *The Times* took in Indian affairs that, like the Madhavbag meeting, it covered the Government of India resolution at length in its issue of 18 October 1886. Its India correspondent thus summarized the resolution approvingly: 'Reforms which affect the social customs of many races must be left to the improving influences of the time and the gradual spread of education.' For a critical reaction to the resolution, see the communication entitled 'The Hindoo Child-Widow', Ibid., 15 Oct. 1886.

65. Ibid., 14 Mar. 1887. At least one notable Anglo-Indian paper commented unfavourably on the *Times*' shifting position. Referring to the question, 'whether we govern India in order that we may send to prison a woman...', the *Civil and Military Gazette* sharply commented: 'This open question, *The Times* does not undertake to answer in the only way in which a question, whether the law should perpetuate a monstrous wrong and injustice ought to be answered. All the consolation which our London contemporary can offer to Rukmibhai (sic) is, that six months' imprisonment is lighter by far than the life-long misery of living with such a husband;...' 8 Apr. 1887.

66. *The Times*, 4 Apr. 1887.

67. F.L. Latham's letter of 15 Mar., ibid., 18 Mar. 1887.

68. F.M.M.'s letter of 17 April, ibid., 21 Apr. 1887. Max Mueller returned to the Rukhmabai case in the *Times* of 22 August 1887—refuting the charge, primarily on the testimony of Pandita Ramabai, that Rukhmabai was a puppet in the hands of her avaricious mother—and of 14 January 1888 wherein he said, *inter alia*: '...such a punishment, under the plea of restitution of conjugal rights, is utterly repugnant to the spirit of ancient Hindu law... What the friends and supporters of Rukhmabai object to is this introduction of a novel English penalty for refusal of conjugal rights; and what they are anxious for is that the Anglo-Indian Code should be amended without further delay, and imprisonment abolished as a means of coercing the wife.' The question of property was discussed earlier in *The Times* of 25 Apr. 1887 by its India correspondent in connection with Dadaji's *Exposition*. The correspondent's own verdict on Dadaji's testimony was: 'Even if his

statements were correct they are not likely to induce the public to change its opinion of the case, seeing that almost every line shows complete indifference on his part to Rukhmabai's wishes and feelings.' The *Kesari* of 20 Sept. 1887 took serious note of Max Mueller's letter of August and warned its readers against what it described as 'the axing of Hindu religion by the trinity of Pandita Ramabai, Max Mueller and Rukhmabai'.

69. Pinhey thus summarized the matter: 'Rukhmabai, a Hindu lady, is declared subject to the provisions of the English law of procedure in a suit for the restitution of conjugal rights, and to imprisonment under the provisions of the Indian Code of Civil Procedure in the certain event of her refusing to go to live with her husband in obedience to the decree of the Court, and... she does not get the benefit of the statutory relief without which the rigour of these decrees in England has been found to be intolerable.' Dated 21 April 1887, Pinhey's letter was signed 'R.H.P.', initials too well known to be missed by informed readers in England or India. Published in *The Times* of 27 Apr. 1887, the letter was reproduced in the *Bombay Gazette* of 17 May 1887, which took no chances and decoded the initials for its readers.

70. *The Times*, 22 Aug. 1887.

71. *Times*, quoted in the *Civil and Military Gazette*, 8 April 1887.

72. The question tabled by Cozens-Hardy ran:

 'Whether this lady, when only a child of 11, was married without her consent:

 'Whether she has received a high English education and developed considerable literary power:

 'Whether, while she is a lady of refinement, her nominal husband is a labourer earning only 10 rupees a month, unable to support her, and suffering from consumption:

 'Whether the Judges of the High Court have ordered her to join her nominal husband within a month, and whether she will be liable to be sent to prison for six months if she refuses to do so:

 'And, whether the Government propose to take any action to prevent the Courts of Law from being used to compel adult Hindoo women, whose child marriages have never been followed by cohabitation, to live with their nominal husbands.'

 See J&P, 1887, No.481, India Office Library. The file contains interesting details relating to the drafting of the government's reply to the question.

73. *Indian Magazine*, May 1887. The *Magazine* would not, however, face the full logic of its criticism of the colonial administration. It brushed aside the charge that there was 'too much law and too little justice' in India. It admitted, though, that 'something must be wrong when', as in the Rukhmabai case, 'the exact administration of the law produces manifest injustice'. The *Magazine* returned to Rukhmabai and her case in June, Aug. and Oct. 1887, and Aug., Sept. and Nov. 1888. Reporting in its Aug. 1888 issue the termination of the case following a

compromise, it hoped that the Indian government would bring in legislation to 'prevent the recurrence of similar suits in the future'.

74. Along with the Whig *Edinburgh Review* and the Tory *Quarterly Review*, the *Westminster Review* constituted the 'great triumvirate' of nineteenth-century English periodicals. Started in 1824 under Benthamite influence, and enjoying its heyday during John Chapman's forty years of editorship (1854–94), the *Westminster Review* is believed to have been, in the 1870s, so advanced in its liberalism in some areas as to represent liberal opinion even a hundred years later. Walter E. Houghton, ed., *The Wellesley Index to Victorian Periodicals 1824–1900*, Toronto, 1979, vol. III, p. 528.
75. Saddling the natives with the entire responsibility of corrective action, it wrote: 'Once the wedge is inserted [by Rukhmabai's kind of individual action] the worst part of the system must ultimately relax and decay. This is all that can be gained at present. Violent legislative interference with the child-marriage customs of the Hindus would be as impolitic as it is impossible... an ignorant agitation in this direction, if successful for the moment, would inflict a most cruel injustice on a vast number of Hindu women sought to be benefited. It would inevitably degrade them to the position of outcasts and *declasses* in their own society.' *Westminster Review*, May 1887.
76. Ibid., pp. 181–7. For an elaboration of the great benefits bestowed upon India by the British system of justice, and of imperial duty and universal laws of nature, see ibid., Mar. 1888, pp. 342–51. The *Review* could be radical in its criticism of the double standards of British law with regard to women, especially in relation to divorce and the custody of children. But it would not support equality between men and women: 'That women should be entitled to the same privileges as men in so far as to have seats in Parliament is a question open to grave doubt, and to accord those privileges would be a step for which the country is certainly not prepared.' Lecky's *History of European Morals* (vol. II, p. 380) was quoted to support the view that morally women were superior to men. But no authority was considered necessary to back the contention that women were 'physically and (generally speaking) intellectually inferior'. Ibid., Sep. 1887, pp. 698–710.
77. This is how the *Indian Spectator* described the *Saturday Review*, 14 Aug. 1887. See also 23 Oct. 1887.
78. This was Act XXI of 1866. Section 19 of this Act provided for the dissolution of the marriage of a Hindu convert to Christianity. See Gooroo Dass Banerjee, *The Hindu Law of Marriage and Stridhan*, pp. 129–31, 134, 194–5.
79. *Saturday Review*, 19 Mar. 1887.
80. *Spectator*, 19 Mar., 9 Apr., 11 Oct. 1887. A staunch supporter of imperialism and keen to avoid anything that might risk the Empire, the weekly subscribed to the theory of imperial expansion in a fit of absent-mindedness: 'The Empire grows, as it were, by its own volition. Nobody that we know of wants Zululand, but we have had to annex

that State.' Ibid., 21 May 1887. For a recent critique of the theory, see Anne McClintock, *Imperial Leather: Race, Gender and Sexuality in the Colonial Contest*, New York.

81. It is tempting to relate to this nineteenth century British view the received wisdom—which is slowly beating a retreat—that divides nationalist politics in colonial India into the binary categories of 'moderate' and 'extremist', and assumes that the moderates supported social reform whereas the extremists were die-hard reactionaries.

82. In a fine specimen of the moral justification of passivity, Justice J. Scott of the Bombay High Court, then vacationing in England, wrote: 'The Indian people cannot be made moral by Act of Parliament, and Western interference in their social polity without their agreement and sanction would only retard real progress.' *The Times*, 27 Aug. 1887. Similarly, the *Globe and Traveller* sadly reflected: 'The Hindoo traditions relative to marriage are far too deeply rooted to be got rid of by legislation', 14 Mar. 1887. To cite another example, the *Saturday Review* maintained that since 'all real progress' had been 'forced' on Indians by 'the civil and military servants of Government', social reform could not be left 'to native opinion, education and time'. At the same time, it maintained that this was a process 'which English statesmen can only urge, and which English laws, if passed, might only retard'. Consequently, it admonished the 'platform agitators', rising 'in every part of India', not to pose as 'advanced Liberals'—'quite ready to abolish the House of Lords, to give self-government to Ireland, and to disestablish the English Church'—but to promote 'Indian reform'. 19 Mar. 1887.

83. *St. James' Gazette*, 14, 18 Mar. 1887. It also put forward the argument that 'change must come from within, not from outside'. The position taken by the *Gazette* was approvingly reported by the *Madras Mail*, an evening daily, on 15 Apr. 1887.

84. *Pall Mall Gazette*, 4 Apr. 1887. Earlier in its issue of 22 Mar., the paper produced long excerpts from the despatch of the *Times*' India correspondent. It had also reported the decision of the Appellate Court on 12 April 1886. The *Gazette's* understanding of the judicial process in India seems to have been influenced by Raghunath Rao, whose article on the subject in the *Asiatic Quarterly Review*—offering a comparative analysis of the British Indian courts with their codified laws vis-a-vis the traditional 'equity courts of the Panchayats'—was reviewed in its issue of 24 Mar. 1887.

85. *The Echo*, 14 Mar. 1887.

86. As against this understatement, in another context the *Echo* overstated the case against English law. It is not true, as we have seen in chapter 3, that England alone, 'among civilized nations', permitted suits for restitution of conjugal rights. The only nation not permitting such suits was the USA.

87. Deirdre David, p. 17. Similarly, the *Globe* was not prevented by its hostility to the women's cause at home from publishing the Rukhmabai

story on its front page as a confirmation of the worse-than-slaves position of Indian women, 14 Mar. 1887.

88. *Queen*, 19 Mar. 1887. In its issue of 16 Apr. the weekly devoted its opening editorial to a discussion of the letters of Bishop Carlisle and Rukhmabai in *The Times*. The *Queen* was a glossy magazine that, besides substantial advertisements, published material on fashion, music, literature and general matters affecting women, such as manners and embroidery. It did not take a radical position on issues related to women. It opposed, for example, legislation that assumed equality between women and men. In taking this view, the weekly distinguished itself from 'the advanced women's party' that looked upon adoption by women of their husband's name 'as a symbol of slavery and degradation' insofar as the prefix 'Mrs' demonstrated 'to the world that they are the possessors of such appendages as husbands'. Ibid., 28 May 1887.
89. For a sensitive discussion of the notion of martyrdom in Victorian femininity, see Trev Lynn Broughton, 'Making the Most of Martyrdom: Harriet Martineau, Autobiography and Death', *Literature & History*, Third Series, Autumn 1993, pp. 24–45.
90. *Bombay Gazette*, 20 June 1887.
91. Ibid.
92. The reversal, 'Only a Woman' contended, was 'neither in consonance with justice, nor with one of the fundamental principles of British law, viz. that every man and woman is the only and absolute proprietor of himself or herself, and that none other possesses the right to dispose of his or her person without his or her own honest consent!' The letter is reproduced in the *Civil and Military Gazette*, 24 Mar. 1887.
93. Ibid., 24 Mar. 1887. 'Only a Woman' strongly urged Rukhmabai 'to appeal to the highest legal tribunal in England' where the decision of the Bombay High Court 'would certainly be upset'.
94. At the end of a letter, dated 22 May 1887 and unsparing in its criticism of the British who could do anything to serve 'their own interests in India', Ramabai felt constrained to tell Miss Dorothea Beale, an eminent educationist and well-wisher of India: 'I hope you will not be offended with me; I have said the truth, and am not sorry for it.' A.B. Shah (ed.), *The Letters and Correspondence of Pandita Ramabai*, Bombay, 1977, p. 178.
95. *Times of India*, 24 Mar. 1887. The paper, however, admitted that there was 'something wrong here'. What was wrong was the application of 'the principles of English law, designed to meet purposes altogether different, to the enforcement of laws in which consent is not necessary'. Were she an Englishwoman, Rukhmabai would not have been compelled to 'return to the roof of a husband of whom she knew nothing'. Treated under Hindu law, 'she would still have had an option in the matter'. Instead, 'the terribly intricate machinery of both countries' had been brought to bear upon her. A law had come into being, 'by a pure accident', which was foreign both to England and to India. This was legal. 'But legality, like everything else, has its limits, and here, we

think, the limits have been over-reached.' The following day, the paper wrote: '...it seems at once cruel and absurd to attempt to regulate the difficulties and complications arising out of infant marriages by employing laws which have been condemned and discarded at home.' Neither of these editorials mentioned Pinhey though the point was lifted straight from his judgment. For a discussion of the Victorian variant of the patriarchal stereotype of women being without reason, see Deirdre David, pp. 14-20.

96. Ibid., 5 Mar. 1887.
97. Ibid., 24 Mar. 1887. Saying that a sum of rupees five thousand was required, the paper reported that 'we are still a long way from the total amount'.
98. Ibid., 25 Mar. 1887.
99. Even Lepel Griffin's, in the final analysis, was a typical Anglo-Indian stance. He described the existing law—'if this be the law'—as 'vile' and 'shameful', and regretted 'the strange spectacle of a civilized tribunal of a great and free nation declaring that the woman, united when a child to a man without her consent by a ceremony falsely called marriage, is still compelled, when she has come to years of maturity and discretion, to surrender herself to this so-called husband whom she loathes, or accept the alternative of imprisonment'. But rather than implicate the government that had introduced this law, he observed: 'The British Government has not so far been fortunate in its dealings with the marriage law, and with the best intentions has thrown back the cause of Indian women 50 years.' In keeping with the same attitude, he called upon 'Hindu reformers' to 'never rest until' the vile law 'be altered or repealed'. See *Civil and Military Gazette*, 6 Apr. 1887.
100. Reproduced in *Times of India*, 22 Mar. 1887.
101. Ignoring that Rukhmabai's defense rested entirely on principles, the paper also blamed Inverarity for not offering evidence before Farran.
102. Reproduced in *Madras Mail*, 19 Apr. 1887. The *Statesman* added with the same ostensible sagacity: 'It would be to disintegrate native society altogether, and would produce incalculable mischief, and a deep and just sense of outrage in the minds of the people.'
103. It wrote: 'If to force a woman to live with a man against her will because she was made to go through a form she did not understand when a little girl, be not opposed to "morality and public policy", we do not know what is.' Reproduced in *Madras Mail*, 4 Apr. 1887.
104. Ibid., 18 Apr. 1887. The age prayed for by Rukhmabai was twenty years for boys and fifteen for girls. Besides maintaining that the proposed change was 'quite unnecessary in order that both parties should understand the meaning of the marriage vow and be held responsible for taking it', the *Pioneer* pointed out that it meant going 'further than we have gone in Europe'.
105. *Indian Daily News*, 18 Mar. 1887. *Civil and Military Gazette*, 22 Mar. 1887, reproduced this excerpt, and in its issue of 19 Apr. used the expression *suttee* on its own.

106. *Civil and Military Gazette*, 12 Mar. 1887.
107. Ibid., 5 Apr. 1887. Even the use of inverted commas to describe Rukhmabai's husband may have been inspired by Malabari's persistent questioning of the relationship between Rukhmabai and Dadaji.
108. Ibid., 19 Apr. 1887. It wrote: 'The native community would be justified quoting our scripture to us: "These things are a matter of your customs and of your law: look ye to it".' Believing that indigenous customs were not so barbarous as the rulers believed, it opposed Rukhmabai's suggestion for regulating the minimum age of marriage. That for it was 'an instance of the dangerous lengths to which this blunder may be carried'. In its issue of 23 Apr., the *Gazette* reproduced from the *Englishman* of Calcutta an 'instructive letter' by Surendra Nath Ghose, an 'educated gentleman of culture', who maintained: 'The unmerited sympathy which Rukhmabai has attracted from the Anglo-Indian press and from some of our native social reformers is remarkable, as showing the extent of human depravity which high civilization is capable of leading to... the alleged evils in the Hindu marriage system are purely imaginary... Whatever may have been the conduct of Rukhmabai, it is certain that she has been dealt with with rigour. But the fault is not due to any provision of the Hindu law... You largely import English law in this country, and when you see that the consequences prove disastrous you find fault with this and that institution, although it may have a strong hold on the minds of the people.'
109. *Bombay Gazette,* 5 Mar. 1887. A fortnight later it wrote: '...the absolutely binding character of that [Hindu] law has never been recognized by the Legislature, and... some portions of it are interpreted by the Law Courts with a good deal of freedom. The Courts certainly exercise a discretion in recognizing customs, despite the general rule that custom shall have the force of law and shall operate in modification of the written law.' Ibid., 19 Mar. 1887.
110. It complained that the Bombay High Court was 'more solicitous for the application of Hindu law of marriage than its native predecessors are known to have been'. Ibid., 19 Mar. 1887.
111. It wrote: 'The sanction which could not be found in the Hindu law books the court found in English reports and in the judgments of English commentators. Manu and the Smritis might be silent; but Blackstone and Sir James Hannen, who must have had the conjugal problems of Indian society as little in their mind as those of Laputa, were called upon to make up for the defects of the Hindu law books.'
112. Ibid., 19, 22 Mar. 1887.
113. Ibid., 22 Mar. 1887.
114. Ibid., 31 Mar., 24 June 1887.
115. 'It is not so much Hindu law which has provoked a protest as English procedure,' it commented, 'and they are under no necessity to approve of the latter no matter how they may cling to the former.' Ibid., 24 June 1887.
116. Thus the *Bombay Gazette* commented on the *Mahratta's* advice to Dadaji

not to press for Rukhmabai's imprisonment: 'This is by far the most sensible thing that has yet been said on that side, and the most astute.' Explaining the whence of the thing, it remarked: 'The champions of Rukhmabai have not spoken in vain.' Ibid., 28 Mar. 1887.

116. The *Bombay Gazette* of 28 Mar. 1887 observed: 'The absurdity of denying any of the qualities of a contract, and at the same time endeavouring to enforce it by measures appropriate only to the enforcement of contracts or other secular obligation, is too obvious to need insisting on.' On 31 March it complained of 'the anomaly which supplies a coercive English provision to enforce a Hindu religious obligation which is not enforced by Hindu law'. See also issues for 4, 5 and 8 Apr. 1887.

118. Ibid., 5 Mar. 1887. The *Gazette's* realistic assessment was that Rukhmabai's action would bear 'fruit of both kinds': 'The reactionists will derive some benefit from an incident which emphasizes the absolute control which the law gives to the husband over a non-consenting wife. What the liberal is to gain cannot precisely be foreseen. Rukhmabai has done more than anyone hitherto to protest against a system which, whatever its general results may be, certainly brings hardship in its train. There are thousands who feel as she has done, but who have not had the courage to resist in the fashion that she has chosen for bringing her grievances and theirs before the world. She is doing them a service in ascertaining her own rights, though it may be that she will have to wait long before her sacrifice bears fruit.'

119. Ibid., 8 Apr. 1887. Highlighting the superfluity of legal compulsion, it wrote: 'Cupid collared and handcuffed by a Court beadle! Venus in the lock-up, and doing six months! Household affections enforced in the Houses of Correction by Captain Walshe! What are we coming to?'

120. Ibid., 5 Mar. 1887.

121. Ibid., 8 Apr. 1887.

122. Even Raghunath Rao, who was present at this meeting and whose position Telang had specifically assailed in his memorandum, quietly gave in. Ibid., 11 May 1887.

5

The Brutal Embrace: Let it Stand

Rukhmabai's resistance in Farran's court raised to a new plane her challenge to both colonial law and indigenous social authority. In her defiant submission to the former and open revolt against the latter she affirmed, as a person, the ultimate authority of her own moral convictions. Neither colonial dispensation nor organized orthodoxy was quite ready to cope with the force of a gesture such as this. Just when her principled stand seemed to count for nought, and the only chance lay in a further round of litigation, the gesture transformed her defeat into an exuberant triumph. It drove her detractors to counsel caution and propelled the bureaucracy into urgent activity.

The Bombay government, afraid that the young lady was 'determined not to obey' the court's verdict, requested the government of India for quick remedial action.[1] The latter was on its own seized by anxiety. The very day the Bombay SOS was despatched, Viceroy Dufferin, who was then on tour, telegraphed his Law Member: 'I hope you are keeping your eye on the Rukhmabai case. It will never do to allow her to be put into prison.'[2]

The SOS was a plea for legislation. Besides emphasizing Rukhmabai's decision to defy the court, it mentioned the 'demand by a section of the community' for 'an alteration in the law'. The demand, it added significantly, was likely to receive support in England.[3] The legislation proposed was to exempt from imprisonment a person against whom a decree for the restitution of conjugal rights had been given.

The central government replied two and a half months later, on 17 June 1887, that 'before considering the matter' it was 'desirable to ascertain the views' of the other local governments and of 'the leaders of Native opinion'. Meanwhile Rukhmabai had appealed against Farran's order and there was no immediate risk of her being imprisoned. The Legislative Department, however, believed that there would be 'no difficulty in carrying out any amendment'. The Law Member, A.R. Scoble, concurred 'entirely' with the proposal of the Bombay government, which he understood to mean bringing section 260 of the Indian Civil Code in line with the English Matrimonial Causes Act of 1884. He did not expect the change to 'offend native susceptibilities'.[4] The reply to the Bombay government and the letter asking for the views of the local governments were sent the same day. The central government, besides being anxious to have a wide range of reactions before moving further, was also keen to avoid the impression of doing nothing in the matter. Consequently, it made its letter to the local governments public.

'The suit for the restitution of conjugal rights,' the letter said, was 'an useful one, provided that no means which are indefensible on moral or social grounds are adopted to enforce compliance with a decree given in such a suit.' The question was 'in what way the State ought to interfere to enforce' the performance of conjugal duties. The earlier practice of the Indian courts, whereby 'the wife was given bodily into the husband's hands', had since been substituted by 'that of subjecting a reluctant wife to imprisonment'.[5] Both the practices being 'alike repugnant to modern ideas', the best remedy, the letter declared grandly, was 'to follow the movement of the English law' and bring Indian legislation 'into greater conformity with the ordinary practice of civilized nations'.[6]

The British had erred in importing into India the English legal practice of enforcing the restitution of conjugal rights by imprisonment. The proposed legislation continued with this error. It recommended that English law, including the provision of separation and divorce, be applied in its entirety in India.[7] Since Hindu orthodoxy had attacked the provision that sent housewives to prison, there may have been reason to infer that its abolition would not offend 'native susceptibilities'. But the clause about divorce could only have exacerbated existing fears and damaged the prospect of legislation.

Two months later, in August 1887, before any local government had responded to the proposed amendment, the issue of legislation was once again forced upon the central government by a memorial from the Rukhmabai Defence Committee. The memorial repeated the now familiar proposal to modify section 260 of the Civil Procedure Code insofar as it related 'to the execution, by process against the person, of decrees for the restitution of conjugal rights'. Since Rukhmabai's case was urgent, the memorial pressed for 'a short Act' to do away with imprisonment 'in the case of married persons who have never cohabited'.[8]

It took the authorities a little over a month to reply that they were considering 'the general question of amending the law in the direction indicated by the memorialists'. The request for a special short act was, however, turned down. No replies from the local governments having been received, the central government did not want to prejudge the question. In any case, there was no urgency now that Rukhmabai had appealed against Farran's order. The authorities, moreover, knew of developments behind the scene which suggested that any attempt to enforce the decree through Rukhmabai's imprisonment was in 'the highest degree improbable'.

Caution was the key to the government's handling of the situation. Thus, when the Law Member wanted the Rukhmabai Defense Committee to be assured that there was 'no urgent need for special legislation to meet the circumstances of this particular case', the Home Secretary, A.P. MacDonnell, objected that this could be taken as 'a pledge to legislate for the particular case, should the necessity arise'. J.B. Peile, the Home Member, concurred: 'Yes; I would say we are not prepared to undertake special legislation to meet the case.' So did Dufferin.[9] No wonder, little sense of urgency marked the official discussion about modifying the existing law. With the exception of Coorg, replies from most governments came in towards the end of 1887 and the beginning of 1888. Punjab responded as late as in January 1889.

II

Meanwhile a compromise brought the historic Rukhmabai case to an anti-climactic end in July 1888. Dadaji accepted two thousand rupees from Rukhmabai 'in satisfaction of all costs' and, in return, agreed not to execute the decree against her. Ostensibly the *cause celebre* ended the way it had begun—as a private marital dispute—leaving unresolved the momentous issues it had raised. The compromise, however, was not exactly a private agreement arrived at between the rival litigants which they asked the Appellate Bench to issue as a consent decree. It was hammered out over a year of intermittent and often hard behind-the-scene negotiations through influential mediators who were keen to save their society from the crisis over the case. Even the top bureaucracy, anxious to avert the young woman's imprisonment, had followed these developments with concern.

Since the day Farran ordered Rukhmabai to go to her husband, and she let her intentions be known, the leaders of organized orthodoxy had been keen not to precipitate matters further. They were willing to risk neither her martyrdom through imprisonment nor an appeal to the Privy Council. The first exposed to avoidable strain their professed regard for women; the second could mar an interpretation of Hindu marriage which, to their great satisfaction, had resulted in Farran's order. It was important for them to prevent Dadaji from seeking to enforce the decree against Rukhmabai. He was persuaded in all sorts of ways, even being asked if he would accept a woman like Rukhmabai whose 'ways' were public knowledge.

We do not know if the two thousand rupees Dadaji obtained from Rukhmabai remained with him or went to Narayan Dhurmaji who had financed the litigation during its anonymous phase. But having contributed not a farthing to the cost of the case, materially he could not have been a loser. Maybe he found himself better off than he was as his uncle's dependent, once leaders like Mandlik began testifying to his good conduct and public money became available for his case after Pinhey's verdict. It is possible that he even received, or extracted, some reward for agreeing to a compromise the orthodox were so keen on. Be that as it may, and whatever the *Kesari's* grumble about the dead loss to him from his marriage with Rukhmabai, Dadaji was able to celebrate the compromise without any loss of time by wedding another woman.

Dadaji was never more than a willing pawn in this litigation. It could not have been difficult, first, for Narayan Dhurmaji to talk him into the suit and, then, for the orthodoxy to make him accept the compromise. But why did Rukhmabai drop a fight that, until a year ago, she was determined to take to the finish? The answer seems to lie in a disenchantment that set in within months of her stirring defiance in Farran's court on 3 March 1887.

While her character was being subjected to a public assassination that revelled in the lascivious, Dadaji came out, on 11 April 1887, with what was titled 'An Exposition of Some of the Facts of the Case Dadajee Vs. Rakhmabai'. Ghost written by K.R. Kirtikar—if Rukhmabai's plausible suspicion can be trusted—the 'Exposition' presented Dadaji as fighting for the cause of Hindu religion, and denied the truth of Rukhmabai's charges. Not sure whether to ignore or expose it, Rukhmabai eventually published her 'Reply' on 29 June. Therein she stated, among other things, that Narayan Dhurmaji had a mistress 'living in his house for some 14 years', and added: 'to avoid whose tyranny the lawful wife of this man had once jumped into a well. I did not wish to live in the same house as the companion of this woman.'

Buoyant after Farran's order and also keen to harass them into submission, Narayan Dhurmaji brought a libel suit against Rukhmabai and her grandfather. He also sent a legal notice to the *Times of India* and the *Bombay Gazette*, both of which had on the same day published the 'Reply', to produce the original text in order that its authorship could be ascertained. The *Times of India* complied, and sent the proof slip of the 'Reply' which it had received from the *Bombay Gazette*. Rukhmabai had sent her text to the *Gazette* and its editor, Grattan Geary, had passed on the proof slip to the *Times of India* in order that the 'Reply' reach a wider readership. Geary, taking a principled position, refused to supply the original, and Narayan Dhurmaji dragged him, too, in the libel suit.

The suit, at one level, served Rukhmabai's cause. She was defended by Pherozeshah Mehta, one of the most eminent nationalists of the day who, as we shall see later, retained his interest in the principles of her defense against Dadaji. The suit was decided against Narayan Dhurmaji and established many unsavoury details about his mistress and his wife's attempted suicide.

Yet, it caused Rukhmabai much anguish and humiliation. Narayan Dhurmaji having employed an English lawyer as uncouth and unfeeling as himself, the going in the case was tough for everyone, not excluding the magistrate. It was, obviously, most so for Rukhmabai because she was the most vulnerable. Snide remarks apart, she was treated by this lawyer with a cavalier disrespect. Once, for example, while arguments were going on which did not require Rukhmabai's presence in the court-room, he abruptly enquired as to where she was and refused to continue until she was brought into the room. Considering the delicacy normally observed with regard to women's presence in court-rooms when they belonged to 'respectable' families, as Rukhmabai did, her presence forced her into becoming a spectacle.

Also crushing was a certain loss of credibility so soon after she had demonstrated her will to suffer the worst. One of the unkindest cuts came from the *Times of India*, for which she could not have been prepared despite the paper's waning enthusiasm for her cause. After all, it had with great alacrity published her 'Reply' merely on the receipt of a proof slip from the *Bombay Gazette*. But when the libel suit was filed, the *Times of India* saw in the 'Reply' no principles but mere 'family squabbles of which we can know nothing'. True, this was largely an attempt to explain away its own pussilanimity in contrast to Grattan Geary's readiness to face litigation and assert an important editorial right.[10] But not all its readers would have seen it that way. Rukhmabai had reason to feel let down. Had it not been in realization of the truth behind the family squabbles that the *Times of India* had promoted her cause when she least expected it?

Disillusionment had, in fact, begun earlier. Rukhmabai could not quite understand what her supporters were prepared to do, and what they expected of her. It was gratifying that so many 'big' men and women had formed a committee to defend her, and reassuring to be invited in their midst with her grandfather. But in practical terms that could determine her future life, what were these people planning to do? Telang's letter of 24 April 1887 to the committee was unnerving enough. Once the committee felt obliged to accept it, giving in so much to Hindu orthodoxy, even an appeal to the Privy Council did not seem a viable option. Unless, of course, she was prepared to alienate powerful sections of her supporters, and go along with a few uncompromising reformers like Malabari.

Even if she braved all odds and moved the Privy Council, where was the certainty of a favourable decision? And an adverse verdict from that tribunal would remove whatever chance there was of a humane alteration of the existing law. In any case, she had fought the battle long enough to show the urgency of legislative interference, which was for others to accomplish. Her faith in legislation, as contradistinguished from a judicial decision, was no rationalization for her compromise. In the letters of 'A Hindu Lady' she had pleaded for certain minimum changes in the existing law. A fortnight before Farran's order, knowing it would be against her, she reiterated her 'simple' solution that 'marriages performed before the respective ages of 20 in boys and 15 in girls shall not be confirmed in the eyes of the law if brought before the Court'.[11]

Twenty-six year old Rukhmabai could, in this frame of mind, apprehend nothing but a life of increasing isolation and uncertainty. Wanting to be a doctor—there was a great need for women doctors in her society—she had received a generous offer of hospitality and money for her medical education in London. Could she afford to decline the offer, or defer a decision indefinitely? She, too, deserved a life of her own. The time had come for her to reject the tyranny of reformist expectations and refuse to be sucked inextricably into the role of a martyr. Having asserted it in rejecting Dadaji's demand for cohabitation, she also had to assert her right to life as a person in the matter of planning a future for herself. Not the least so because, for a woman who had abnigated a married life, there could be no substitute for self-reliance.

Notwithstanding a nagging self-doubt Rukhmabai could feel justified in thinking of a compromise in these circumstances and at this point in the fight. But the terms of the compromise had to be honourable. Giving two thousand rupees in settlement of 'all costs' in such an expensive suit was by no stretch of imagination a surrender. The man who claimed a right over her person had shown his real worth in settling for this amount. Once she realized the wisdom of buying her freedom, this was no great price to pay. In a final confirmation of her resolve not to have a life with Dadaji, immediately after the compromise Rukhmabai left for England to take up her medical studies while the man busied himself with a new wife.

Once the two parties had agreed upon the terms of the compromise and decided to ask the Appellate Bench to issue a consent decree in the case, each tried to create the impression that it had been sought by the other. This exercise in face saving was paralleled outside the court-room as similar attempts were made by both the reformers and the orthodox. The tussle began as Jardine, appearing for Rukhmabai, told the Appellate Bench that 'proposals have been made to us'. 'By mutual friends,' quickly interjected Vicaji, Dadaji's persevering counsel. Unruffled, Jardine continued that 'on behalf of Rukhmabai I have seen my way to accept' the proposals. Vicaji again countered: 'I may say that the proposal, though it was a wise one, did not emanate entirely from us; but the arrangement was brought about through the assistance of mutual friends.' Claiming victory out of a none-too-favourable bargain, he said:[12]

> The point has been decided in the plaintiff's favour; but since the defendant has apparently no affection for the plaintiff, I think he has acted well in determining not to press his claim further.

Improving upon Vicaji and avoiding the term 'compromise' altogether, the *Native Opinion* created the impression that Dadaji had won the case:

> The Rukhmabai case has at last been finally decided, the Court of Appeal confirming the decision of Mr Justice Farran commanding the recalcitrant wife to go to her husband and awarding the husband his costs.

The *Native Opinion* accused Rukhmabai and her supporters of prolonging the suit to denigrate the Hindu social system. 'So long ago as about a year and a half,' it claimed, Dadaji had 'told the public' that he 'never' desired 'to execute the decree against his wife by putting her in prison.' 'What he wanted was the vindication of his rights as against his wife, who denied them.' This achieved, for him the matter was over.[13] The claim overlooked simple facts like Macpherson's retreat from the assurance that Rukhmabai's imprisonment formed no part of his plea. Later, during the year and a half specifically mentioned by the *Native Opinion*, Inverarity's request that prior notice be given before Dadaji sent a bailiff to execute the decree against Rukhmabai was summarily rejected; and organs like the *Mahratta* had to exhort him to hold his hand.

These wrangles were also part of the fight over the proposed legislation. To show that all was well with the existing law, the orthodox argued that 'fortunately for social economy', the final settlement in the case was a triumph of law. In an admonition obliquely directed at the government as well, it hoped that 'meddlesome people will take to heart the lesson read to them by Dadaji, and profit by it in future'.[14]

Those pressing for a modification of the existing law insisted that if reformist forces had not bent the orthodoxy into 'judicious surrender', Rukhmabai would have been in jail. The orthodoxy, as the *Bombay Gazette* pointed out, had 'the law on their side, and there were no technical obstacles at all'. The obstacles they floundered against 'were of a moral rather than a legal character'.[15] It was progressive public opinion in Bombay that had saved

Rukhmabai from the worst manifestation of the existing law. But a woman in similar circumstances in the mofussil was unlikely to be so protected. The full realization of Rukhmabai's 'vindication of personal rights and liberties' required changing the law. More so because the 'lame and impotent conclusion' of the case had left 'the matter, as effecting the general community, much as it was'.[16]

Malabari, too, could think of legislation as the only saving grace of the Rukhmabai case. Unhappy over the compromise, he understood why, after 'all their brag and bluster', the orthodox party made up 'at the eleventh hour'. But the reformists should have gone to the Privy Council which 'would have knocked on the head the present barbarous law'. He now hoped that, in order 'that we may never again hear of another Rukhmabai', the government would change the law in discharge of a 'duty so clearly indicated by public opinion'.[17]

These opposing claims about the government's duty in the aftermath of the Rukhmabai case were intended to influence the fate of the proposed legislation.

III

The compromise further eased the sense of urgency about legislation. Indeed, now that the issue was divested of the tragedy/embarrassment of Rukhmabai's imprisonment that once seemed so real, even the perception of what lay at stake was significantly affected. Representing this changed perception, Law Member Scoble, who in 1887 had responded to the Bombay government's SOS by supporting legislation along the lines of the 1884 changes in England, now felt that 'the less we meddle with the matter the better'.[18]

But one seasoned Anglo-Indian official saw this as an opportune moment to be done with legislation. Auckland Colvin, the civilian with a liberal image who four years ago had advised Malabari to obtain some test decisions, was 'certain' that the law of restitution of conjugal rights, hitherto 'very rarely' used, would soon begin to be more frequently utilized. That would exacerbate the 'conflict between the more advanced and the less advanced' within Indian society, and make the confrontation between progressive English opinion and Hindu orthodoxy dangerous. Rather than follow the English law of 1884, Colvin proposed the abolition altogether of suits for the restitution of conjugal rights. He apprehended very little opposition if the government acted immediately, 'at a time when public opinion, which at some date not very distant may be prominently turned to the matter, is not yet excited'.[19] Colvin's perception was exceptional. Unlike his peers, he suggested a radical legislation that was far ahead of his times, arguing that this could be passed with ease when the public was not agitated. Abolished in England only in the 1970s, suits for the restitution of conjugal rights still survive in India.

Colvin also used the familiar argument that those 'who oppose the abolition of the law as at present constituted, themselves admit that it is not in accord with Hindu law and custom'. They recognized, moreover, that 'actual imprisonment will not give the relief sought for, as no Hindu of respectability would take back a woman who had undergone it, or had even been in immediate danger of it'. More people, Colvin assured, disapproved of imprisonment than was indicated by the responses to the government's inquiry. Because divorce was coupled with the proposed abolition of imprisonment, many among those opposed to imprisonment held back for fear of subverting the institution of marriage.[20]

The Rukhmabai case, as Colvin saw it, prefigured the fury of the emerging social confrontation the British had set in motion in India. As a pioneer female actant in the confrontation, Rukhmabai had directed the authorities' attention to the problem of protecting 'a class of the community which has especial claims on the English Government, namely, the women who in India have educated themselves after Western methods'. Nonetheless, as the executive head of the North West Provinces, where native opinion was generally hostile to change, Colvin needed to convince himself, as he did, that the abolition of restitution suits would not be abused by women. 'Not one in a million,' he observed, 'would be aware of it for many years to come.' Even that one, if she chose to desert her husband, would remain subject to conventional sanctions which could 'weigh upon her through the remainder of her life'. Sensitive to the kind of reasoning that underlay Telang's letter to the Rukhmabai Defence Committee, Colvin opposed the suggestion to do away with restitution suits only in the case of infant, rather than all, marriages. Singling out infant marriages would amount to an attack on Hindu marriage.[21]

Colvin's logic, that passage of time would make legislative intervention increasingly difficult, was met by his counterpart in Bengal, Steuart Bayley, who found public excitement already strong enough to warrant avoidance of legislation. Writing in February 1888, before the compromise in the Rukhmabai case, Bayley doubted if 'either the practical inconvenience or the moral insufficiency of the existing law' justified legislation. He was certain that 'alteration of the law in the manner proposed' would give rise to 'much misunderstanding and some resentment on the part of the Hindu community'. The 'diverse' replies received by his government indicated:[22]

> the impossibility of devising any alteration in the law, which shall be equally applicable to the conditions and requirements of the two main sections of the native community.

Imprisonment, Bayley admitted, was 'distinctly a blot on the civilization of the country that retains it'. But 'in legislation concerning marriage' it was inadvisable to proceed 'too far in advance of the social and moral sentiments of the community concerned'. He reported, unlike Colvin and others, 'considerable persistence and remarkable unanimity' among the Hindus about 'retaining the punishment of imprisonment'. They favoured the punishment, however, not as an inexorable sequel to non-compliance with a restitution decree, but 'as a discretionary remedy' against improperly motivated or insufficiently grounded recusancy. He, therefore, suggested that the courts be armed with discretion in the matter of ordering imprisonment. He knew that every caste possessed a penal arrangement that functioned effectively 'quite outside the operation of the law'. But, unlike Colvin, he did not see that as a reason to divest the courts of the authority to order imprisonment.[23]

The replies from other administrations fell within the range that separated Colvin and Bayley. Inter-administration differences apart, the opinions expressed by different branches of the same administration were often divergent. While the Bombay governor's executive, for instance, pressed for urgent legal change, the Bombay High Court opposed it. All official responses were nonetheless informed by a common impulse, that of caution. It inspired differently circumstanced and inclined officials to propose divergent solutions even when there was analytic agreement among them.

The critical exercise in much of this discussion was to make sense of the paradoxical orthodox Hindu position vis-a-vis imprisonment. The larger politico-cultural context and the resultant intractability of that position were, perhaps, best grasped by the Assam administration. The paradox, as the Assam Chief Commissionerate posed it, was: 'Hindus proper'[24] had reason to oppose the proposed measure for the dissolution of marriage. But why should they also condemn the amendment regarding imprisonment, something to which 'they would as a rule never think of resorting?' Most administrations recognized the paradox, and attributed it to anxiety about Hindu marriage owing to the insertion of divorce in the proposed amendment. The Assam administration went a step further in its analysis. The anxiety about marriage, it realized, related to a whole culture. For 'the mass of conservative Hindus' the attack on their marriage system was 'a piece of aggression on the part of Europeans and the handful of advanced natives who adopt European views'. This made the issue intractable:[25]

> It would probably be impossible to get this idea out of their minds, and it will accordingly remain as an element to be reckoned with in the further discussion of the question.

Dennis Fitzpatrick, who as Chief Commissioner designed the Assam reply, and later as Chief Commissioner of Coorg submitted a 'Note' on the subject, admitted the 'abuses' that the Hindu system of marriage was 'apt to lead to'. But he was struck by the 'ignorance or narrowness of view' that characterized 'most of the attacks' on that system and the 'crude suggestions' made to reform it. These issued from people who, being incapable of thinking 'beyond the range of the canon law and the Mahomedan law', were blind to the rationale behind Hindu marriage.[26] Fitzpatrick wanted the government to keep supporting the besieged system, for it formed 'the very basis of native society'.[27] He subscribed to the common belief that the deterrent of imprisonment operated:[28]

> beneficially both in restraining the erratic tendencies of wives, and in inducing them to return to their husbands when a decree has been passed, and the consequences are explained to them.

Fitzpatrick wanted the law to be left untouched. At the same time, to counter the abuses of Hindu marriage, he felt inclined to vest the courts with discretion in the matter of imprisonment. Further, to protect those married in infancy and unwilling to accept the marriage on coming of age, he proposed that the institution of conjugal rights, as distinguished from restitution, be not covered by section 260.[29]

Fitzpatrick, thus, surpassed Bayley in the matter of suggesting changes after insisting that the existing law be left alone. Such inconsistency was not exceptional. Caught in the intractability of the problem, most officials chafed at inconsistencies in their colleagues' arguments, and did no better themselves. Each official's contradictions were rooted in his particular understanding of the problem. The Rukhmabai case, as Fitzpatrick saw it, had 'directed public attention to a very serious difficulty' in the existing law. A girl married in infancy could decide on maturity not to accept a marriage that, 'owing to peculiar circumstances', had not been consummated. Though it could arise 'at any moment', the difficulty was 'likely to be of extremely rare occurrence'. Conditioned as Hindus/Indians were to consider parentally arranged marriages as natural, the notion of personal choice was 'foreign' to their ideas about marriage. Rukhmabai's, after all, was not the first marriage in which consummation was deferred until the woman had 'reached an age to think for herself'. Still no difficulty of this sort was known to have arisen previously. Nor—'until things change very much in India'—were girls likely to emulate Rukhmabai in the rare event of their cohabitation being uncommonly delayed.[30] However—and hence Fitzpatrick's inconsistency[31]—once the difficulty was known to exist, it was 'desirable to provide against it'.[32] The law needed to be both left untouched and altered.

Fitzpatrick favoured the retention of imprisonment because he wanted the decree for restitution to be enforceable, and not merely declaratory. Attachment of property alone—the point was made by a majority of administrations—would not serve the purpose. Since very few women in India owned property, abolishing imprisonment would mean abolishing 'the decree for restitution as an enforceable decree'. Moreover, a law that annulled imprisonment and retained attachment of property to enforce compliance would operate unequally:

> A woman who happened to have a considerable amount of property would be subject to a severe form of compulsion from which other women would be free.

The issue for Fitzpatrick was pragmatic, not moral. England may have changed its law of restitution of conjugal rights.[33] But that did not make it more just or moral, there being 'nothing in the enforcement of a decree for restitution against either justice or morality'. The issue needed to be decided:

> with reference to all the circumstances of the particular society with which we are dealing, and especially with reference to the conditions under which restitution proceedings are instituted, to the prospect of the process effecting its object and to the sentiments commonly entertained in the society.

Barring exceptions like Coorg, most of India required the retention of restitution suits. In the Assam Valley districts, with which Fitzpatrick's report was primarily concerned, the annual incidence of such suits was 'considerable'. But the province he especially remembered in this context, on the basis of his experience as a judge of the Chief Court there during 1876–77, was Punjab.[34]

Obviously things there had not changed since. The Punjab government reported early in 1889 that 'the Native gentlemen consulted are practically unanimous in deprecating the legislation proposed'. The consensus was particularly striking in that it brought together 'men of the old school' and those 'thoroughly acquainted' with the English system of law. Their attitude, centring around the belief that 'in the interests of family life and of morality women ought to be under strong control', was thus summarized by the Punjab government:

> ...the threat of imprisonment is useful in compelling recalcitrant wives to return to their husbands; and any relaxation of the husband's power of control is deprecated as likely to lead not only to frequent instances of revolt against the marital authority and infidelity, but also to the aggrieved husbands taking the law into their own hands even oftener than they do at present.

Yet the Punjab government found it 'impossible' to support a law under which 'either party to a marriage effected during the infancy' could be ordered 'to cohabit with the other against his or her will'; more so 'when the girl or woman, if recusant, is liable to be imprisoned at the instance of the man'. However, like most administrations, it opposed any alteration in the substantive law of marriage. The change it recommended, as one unlikely to present 'much difficulty', was to arm the courts with discretion.

It also suggested that unconsummated infant marriages be treated at par with betrothals. This had been the rule in the province until 1872. Accordingly, and this was the 'best part' of the old Punjab Civil Code, damages in an action for failure to carry out an infant marriage on the girl's coming of age were paid by her parents or guardians. To prevent husbands evading such a rule by forcing their girl-wives into early cohabitation, the Punjab government proposed that the age of consent be raised from the exisitng low of ten to a relatively decent fifteen. It did not, however, expect early action on this and other proposals.[35] One of these other proposals was that the courts' exercise of discretion must be regulated by rules.[36]

IV

The Home Department secretariat in Calcutta soon submitted, on 8 April 1889, a note for consideration by the superior authorities. It proposed abolition of imprisonment as an alteration that could be safely made even though Indian opinion was 'on the whole against any change'.[37] Its safety assumed, the alteration was invested with a moral purpose: 'This Government is not bound to enforce Hindu marriage laws in a way opposed to modern ideas'. The British were bound by 'principles not actively to interfere except in cases where caste or custom enjoins a practice which involves a breach of the ordinary criminal law'. This policy was designed to facilitate the demise of native customs that no longer possessed 'a sufficient sanction without the aid of the law'. That, indeed, was the 'only' way to bring about 'extensive reforms'. As for the issue under discussion:[38]

> All that it seems necessary or desirable to do is to abolish imprisonment as a means of enforcing conjugal rights, thus avoiding all interference with Hindu laws or customs.

When the papers reached J.P. Hewett, Under-Secretary in the Home Department, he noticed the absence of any opinion from the Calcutta High Court where, inexplicably, the circular of 17 June 1887 had not been sent. It seemed 'essential' to obtain this opinion in view of the strong opposition the proposed alteration had elicited from some of the High Courts and the Chief Court of Punjab. 'Fortunately,' moreover, legislation had 'ceased to be a very urgent matter'. A.P. MacDonnell, the Secretary, agreed, but added: 'we should request a reply within a month if possible.' The judges seemed willing to oblige, and sent in their opinions within three months. Nine of them supported the abolition of imprisonment. The remaining two, Justices Ghosh and Banerji, favoured discretion to the courts.[39]

Legislation may have lost its urgency, but Hewett was fast at work. Within a week he was ready with a note that; in the event, became the basis of official policy on the subject. He disagreeed with the departmental note of 8 April, and found 'great weight' in the arguments that opposed the abolition of imprisonment if the suit for the restitution of conjugal rights was retained. And retained it must be, lest the Hindu community be alarmed. Hewett favoured making 'execution by imprisonment discretional'. Besides having received 'very strong support', this course was 'free from the objections raised by the orthodox people to the abolition of imprisonment'. He saw no need for immediate legislation and recommended amendment when the Civil Procedure Code next came under revision.[40]

The waning of a sense of urgency was reinforced by the appointment of Charles James Lyall as Home Secretary within two days of Hewett's note of 14 August 1889. As Secretary to the Assam Chief Commissioner, Lyall had convinced himself—and his boss Fitzpatrick—that arming the courts with discretion was the only alteration needed in the existing law.[41] The conviction deepened as he studied the relevant papers. Lyall added his own 'decided opinion' to Hewett's advice that Rukhmabai's being 'one of those hard cases which make bad law', 'it would be injudicious to take it as the basis for legislation'. Others, too, had invoked the axiom. But Lyall gave it a subtle twist to warn lest the attempted solution prove counter-productive. The Rukhmabai case, he argued:

> arose in a wholly exceptional state of circumstances, and to provide specially for it would, unless we are extremely cautious, result in those circumstances becoming the reverse of exceptional.

Lyall also gave a sharp edge to the argument that wives constituted a precious article among the lower classes. Imprisonment, he remarked, was 'the poor man's only remedy'. To this solicitude for the male poor was added a concern for conjugal morality. Marriage customs among the lower orders were alreay 'deplorably lax'. Repeal of imprisonment in restitution cases would make marriage even more lax, whereas the object should be to ensure 'fixity for the tie'.[42]

It was mid-January 1890 when the papers were circulated among the Viceroy's Council. The members had other business on hand.

The matter, 'though important', was 'not pressing'. Moreover, time for the annual summer exodus from Calcutta to Simla was nearing and some leisure during the early days could, as usual, be expected there. The matter journeyed, for the second successive year, from the winter to the summer capital.

Lansdowne, the Viceroy, agreed that 'all' they could 'safely do' was 'to give the Courts a discretion in regard to enforcing a decree for restitution of conjugal rights by imprisonment'. This change 'could be best made' when the Code was next revised. Five days later, on 15 May 1890, an order to that effect was passed by the Council and the matter was shelved for the time being.[43]

V

It was revived three years later by A.E. Miller. Having succeeded Scoble as Law Member and possessing, unlike his predecessor, the courage of his convictions, Miller told the Home Department sharply:

> I think it monstrous that any woman—or man either for that matter, but the hardship is more obvious in the case of a woman—should be forced by law to consort with a man she does not like... anything like 'specific performance' of the marital contract is to my mind so shocking that I do not trust myself to characterize it.

Miller would rather abolish imprisonment than trust the courts with discretion to enforce cohabitation by means of imprisonment.[44] Even for women, the best law was one that did not force their husbands into cohabitation. A wife, he observed:

> whose husband refuses to live with her is obviously entitled to maintenance so long as she remains his wife, and, having regard to social feeling and custom, would be worse and not better off if divorced or judicially separated, and certainly worse off than either if he was constrained to take her back into his home against his will, when he would be very unlike a European husband if he did not make her life a burden to her.

Miller expected this to 'be accepted with equanimity by all except the small but noisy body who object to any interference with social custom as an attack on religion'.[45] But, to avoid needless complications, he would have nothing to do with judicial separation or divorce.[46]

Miller's initiative annoyed Hutchins, the Home Member, who tried to stall it by suggesting that, besides upsetting the simplicity of the existing legal procedure, it disregarded the decision of 1890 with regard to both the change proposed and its timing. He decided to 'trouble His Excellency' to settle the issue.[47] His Excellency admitted that the Law Member was free to reopen the issue. But he would need to wait: 'If legislation is to be resorted to at all upon this point, it must be after my term of office has come to an end.' Lansdowne, drained by the Age of Consent Act of all appetite for controversies, would rather have a reposeful final five months.[48]

Miller held his ground, and reiterated two days after Lansdowne's note:

> all that I really care about is the abolition of the power of imprisonment in these cases. I do not think a husband or wife ought *ever*, under any circumstances, to be imprisoned merely for refusing to live with the other.

Realism persuaded the Law Member, however, that what he cared about could not be realized all at once. Holding out an olive branch to his fellow councillors, he assured them that he would be 'glad to get any alteration of the existing law in the right direction, on the "instalment" principle'.[49]

Hutchins responded with a conciliatory note the following day, but took care to put it on record: 'I understand that the Hon'ble Legal Member will accept what I think was agreed to in 1890, though he would prefer going further.' The sudden friendliness, nipping the previous week's budding friction, was apparently preceded by an understanding that, it seems, was left prudently unrecorded. The Council agreed, on 20 July 1893, to accordingly amend section 260 of the Civil Procedure Code. The amendment, introduced by Miller on 12 August 1893, provided:[50]

> that no decree for restitution of conjugal rights shall be enforced by imprisonment of the defendant, unless the Court shall, for sufficient reasons to be stated in writing on the face of the order, think fit so to direct.

The amendment, it may be noticed, required the courts to exercise discretion when imprisonment was required, not when it was not required. Miller, having compromised on his ultimate objective, wanted discretion to be as near a substitute for abolition of imprisonment as deft drafting could ensure. Requiring the courts to exercise discretion only when ordering imprisonment was meant to effect just this.[51]

Miller's amendment quickly ran into trouble.[52] The first shot was fired within the Select Committee by Baba Khem Singh Bedi who presented a note that vied with the worst that Rukhmabai's opponents had written. Fourteenth in the direct line of descent from Guru Nanak, Khem Singh was sure to carry weight by dint of the spiritual and secular eminence of his family in Punjab. This note expresses uninhibitedly, and at the highest level of decision-making, a conception of women that more minds harboured than were willing to admit. A Sikh of the finest vintage, he spoke as a Hindu, reflecting between the two identities a community of feeling despite the emergence of separate communal sentiments and their institutional crystallization.[53] He remarked with chilling equanimity:

> To the Hindu mind the wife is but his property. The 'Dharma Shastras' rule the same way. She is given in a 'Dan' by her parents, who have nothing to do with her after the marriage. Her moral, legal and religious duty is therefore to live with him as long as he lives.

The Baba then generalized about India as a whole: 'Women in this country are amla (never free).' If a woman left her husband, 'the law must force her to return' to him or 'to go to jail'. Mercifully, he wanted that done under certain constraints. No force ought to be used against a woman who could not be guaranteed against ill-treatment in the event of being sent to her husband. She must also have the freedom to stay away from her husband, but not to remarry, if he embraced another religion, suffered from leprosy, was insane, 'and under similar circumstances'. Khem Singh noted with satisfaction the rarity of actual recourse to imprisonment. Barring 'one or two cases out of a hundred', the 'mere threat' of imprisonment achieved the desired result. Following the conventional 'happily-ever-after' ending, he reported that these women 'afterwards lived a peaceful life blessed with several children'. But: 'If they did not return, they would have been subject to many sins, and the law would have been responsible for it.' The provision of imprisonment served the material and moral interests of women.

Khem Singh also expressed the pervasive belief that the law did not discriminate against women. He had little use for the theoretical fig-leaf that men and women were alike liable to imprisonment for recusancy. Instead, he used the familiar conflation of the wife's entitlement to maintenance and the husband's claim on the person of his wife, as he queried:

> If a man does not like to keep his wife, she is entitled to a maintenance allowance against his will. Why then should they [women] not be

compelled by the force of the law to return to their husbands if they do not like to go to them?

When, as we have seen, even well-wishers of women could accept the conflation, those who viewed women as 'property' and *amla* could scarce be alive to the difference between a man doling out a pittance for what he considered good riddance and a woman forced into the arms of a man she found insufferable.[54] Nor for such people—as we saw in the imaginary portrayal of Rukhmabai as a licentious woman—could a woman who left her husband be capable of an honourable life. Hence Khem Singh's final lament that Miller's amendment would 'give encouragement to wicked *women*, and the *people* will suffer'.[55] The pregnant, unconscious distinction between 'women' and 'people' says it all!

Miller thought he could corner the obscurantist Baba and go ahead with the amendment. He was quickly disabused as he encountered the hostility of the Anglo-Indian bureaucracy. Two weeks before Khem Singh hit out, Miller was subjected to a vicious attack by Dennis Fitzpatrick, who had now become the Lt. Governor of Punjab. In what was obviously a mere ploy, he claimed that he would have accepted the amendment 'at once' if the Law Member had not designed it to serve the end he 'personally' thought desirable, 'viz., that no decree for the restitution of conjugal rights would be enforceable at all'.[56] Supporting discretion 'only in the rarest cases', he proposed that the courts should exercise discretion when imprisonment was not required, not the other way around.[57]

The Bengal government, too, wrote that the existing 'irritable condition of Hindu society' was no time for the 'practical abolition' —which is what the proposed discretion meant—'of all legal coercion over married women who may be reluctant to live with their husbands'. It admitted that sending recusant women to jail was repugnant to Hindu feelings, but dismissed the inference that the repeal of imprisonment would not alienate the Hindus. 'Popular opinion' in India expected a court that decreed restitution to be also 'in a position to enforce that decree by actually making over the wife to her husband.' The provision of imprisonment, once it had got into the statute book, was seen as the instrument that, by its mere presence, enabled the courts to exercise authority.[58]

It was, therefore, 'inadvisable to alarm the orthodox and conservative class of Hindus by passing a measure for which it appears that there is little urgent necessity'.[59] The Bengal government also thought of the mute 'lower classes'—men—who, 'very much' used as they were to 'suing for the restitution of a run-away wife', would be 'most affected' by the amendment:[60]

> The classes from whom the officials and non-offcials are drawn, whose views are represented, do not bring suits of this nature, but it is important that the Legislature should take especially tender care of the interests of those who have the most difficulty in making themselves heard.

Miller had believed while planning the amendment that it was 'mainly a Bombay question'.[61] Faced with opposition from within the officialdom, he was helped little by the Bombay government's insistence on disallowing imprisonment entirely for enforcing a restitution decree.[62] Miller's measure was doomed. The Baba's minute was a mere excuse.

The *coup de grace* came on 20 February 1895 when the Select Committee dropped Miller's amendment.[63] None of his colleagues within the supreme government stood by him. Pherozeshah Mehta, the Parsi nationalist leader, sought to salvage the amendment when the Imperial Legislative Council met on 28 February to consider the Select Committee's report. He proposed, in deference to the common criticism against Miller's amendment, a mode of discretion that required the courts to state their reason(s) in case of *not* enforcing a restitution decree by imprisonment. Mehta's modest motion read:

> Provided that no decree for restitution of conjugal rights shall be enforced by imprisonment of the defendant if the Court shall, for any sufficient reason, to be stated in writing on the face of the order, think fit that it shall not be so enforced.

Mehta maintained that his motion was not meant to obtrude his 'personal predilections on the subject'. Rather, it represented the best 'conservative and orthodox view of the matter'.[64] Making a conciliatory speech, he opposed any 'meddling with so peculiar and complex a system of social life and religion as Hinduism'. His motion, he said, was based on the joint minute of Justices Ghosh and Banerji of the Calcutta High Court, both of whom were 'devout and sincere' conservatives. Touching nothing that was 'essential' to the Hindu social order, it was directed against an 'excrescence' which had 'got itself grafted from an extraneous jurisprudence'. His motion could give no just ground for complaint to Hindus or Muslims.[65]

Mehta contended, contrary to official assertions, that the papers placed before the Council indicated 'a weighty consensus of Indian opinion' in favour of altering the law. Still the Select Committee had pronounced the country 'not yet ripe' for the change. True, 'one section of the community' had been hostile. But that section, as R.C. Dutt had observed, would 'stop all reforms' and revive 'the burning of widows'.[66] The government obviously could not wait for unanimity among the ruled before it legislated.[67]

Miller fully supported Mehta's motion. It was an unexceptionable motion which did not attract any of the criticism provoked by his own official amendment. Its principle had been supported, with the sole exception of Mohini Mohun Roy, by every member of the Council who had spoken on the issue. Supporting Mehta's contention that the existing law was an excrescence, Miller recalled how, as late as in 1877, the then Law Member, Whitley Stokes, had 'entirely on his own responsibility introduced a few words into section 260' which took away the courts' discretion.[68] This was done although no difficulty had 'ever risen' since 1855, when restitution decrees first began to be made by the British Indian courts. As against the smooth functioning of the pre-1877 system, the 'very serious scandal' of the Rukhmabai case had demonstrated the enormity of 'the application of this excresence (sic) of English law on the top of the Hindu marriage law and opposed to its general principles'.

Gangadhar Madhav Chitnavis was another member who supported Mehta's motion. 'Even the strongest advocate of the husband,' he argued, 'would admit that there might be cases where it would be cruel to force the wife to go to the husband'. Mehta's 'very mild' measure would cover just such cases. Moreover, the disgrace that was bound to result among the 'higher and respectable classes' from a wife's incarceration meant that:

> if the machinery of the present law is ever set going, it can only be with a view to the gratification of vindictive feelings and not to secure the society of the wife.

The legislature had no reason to 'aid and abet a Hindu in the commission of an act so repugnant to the dictates of his personal law and religion'. The official plea about the 'lower classes' was invalid because this motion:[69]

> while it does not take away what ought to be considered as a sort of protection which the present law afforded to some sections of the people, only allows a discretion to the Court in cases where the motives of the suitor can be clearly perceived to have been actuated by resentment or revenge pure and simple.

With this even the Maharaja of Durbhanga, who had helped

kill Miller's amendment, agreed. Since there was 'absolutely nothing in the Hindu religion to force an unwilling wife to cohabit with her husband', he felt no anxiety about opposition from Hindu orthodoxy, of which he was a leader. What had 'forced' him to oppose the amendment was the 'chance', as he learnt from Khem Singh, of 'the fanaticism of the Sikh community' causing 'grave political consequences'.[70]

Charles Elliott, the Lt. Governor of Bengal who had but a month ago warned against alarming 'the orthodox and conservative class of Hindus', conceded that the proposed change would not be unpopular with 'Hindus of the higher classes, both the orthodox and the more advanced'. But, ignoring the fact that Mehta's motion risked nobody's restitution rights, he reiterated the legislature's duty towards the unrepresented lower classes.

The most commanding articulation of the official position came from A.P. MacDonnell, the Home Member, who enjoyed the image of 'a liberal-minded ruler.'[71] Proud of the Empire and conscious of the role of rhetoric in sustaining it, he knew that, given Miller's sympathies, it was for him to destroy Mehta's motion. 'I entirely sympathize', MacDonnell commenced his grandiose discourse, 'with the spirit of this amendment.' But, unlike Mehta whom—contrary to Mehta's own pronouncements—he understood to represent 'the most advanced Hindu opinion in Bombay',[72] those 'concerned with the government of this great Empire' had to think beyond their own sympathies:

> It would be easy to rule India if we had merely to deal with the most advanced classes. The difficulty of the administration in India is that it has to deal with classes and sections of the community that are not so advanced, and among whom a wave of religious fanaticism would undo in a very brief space of time all that the advanced classes have done in the space of half a century.

This good work, carried out to consolidate the gains of the advanced classes, was not arbitrarily done. MacDonnell had been 'most anxious' not to influence the decision in 'a question intimately connected with the religious feelings of the Hindus and their marriage system'. It had to be made 'by the Native members of the Select Committee alone'. That the decision they finally reached, which was both 'right and patriotic', 'greatly satisfied' him was incidental. For, although the Rukhmabai case had shown 'the Hindu system at its very worst', the evils it exposed were not systemic. This, combined with the wisdom that hard cases made bad laws, rendered it 'inadvisable for the Government of this Empire to legislate against the feelings and wishes of the people'.

MacDonnell wound up as he had begun. In a morally charged pragmatism—the oxymoron indicating the imperial power to reconcile the irreconcilable—he offered an indefinitely deferred hope:

> Although I, with the hon'ble friend Mr. Mehta, look forward to the time when such an amendment will be placed on the Statute-book, yet I think as practical administrators we cannot conclude that that time has yet come.

MacDonnell's was a model of imperialist prose. Its authority lay as much in self-belief as in the awe it inspired. Not the prose of the implicated, it belonged to one chosen to arbitrate. There could be nothing petty or calculating about it. Those involved in the conflict, heeding their own narrow interests and considerations, would seek to fight it out. The one in command would mediate justly and practically. Even his pragmatism was altruistic. What looked like a surrender to reaction was meant to consolidate the progress made possible by imperial mediation. As the agent of that magnificent mediation, he could not be proved wrong by small details. Nor, since he had to negotiate the contradictory pulls and pressures of native society, could his decisions be unmarred by apparent inconsistencies. His infallibility was beyond challenge. MacDonnell could, thus, attribute the Rukhmabai case to the evils of, and also exonerate, the Hindu system without fear of being charged with inconsistency. He could, similarly, ignore the role of English law in causing Rukhmabai's woes, and the fact that solicitude for the 'lower classes' was not vitiated by discretion to the courts.

The finalé was a charming little essay in imperialist cunning by the Viceroy. Pleased that his own views had been 'very well expressed' by MacDonnell, he benignly added: 'I have great sympathy with the feelings which have prompted this attempt to amend the law, and I should hope that the time will come, and perhaps at no very distant date, when that amendment can be carried out.' For the present His Excellency was 'certainly' against it.

Mehta's motion was thrown out by a division of two—Mehta himself and Chitnavis—against fifteen. Miller, to his great credit, and Durbhanga were among the four who did not vote.

At the end of a decade of debate, the authorities were unprepared to convert into law even a fraction of the demand the Rukhmabai case had shown to be just.

VI

Those who had assailed Rukhmabai's cause as subversive of Hindu/ Indian domesticity were relieved that the fears brought to life by Pinhey's judgment were finally laid to rest. However, their reaction to the defeat of Mehta's motion was not one of triumphal declaration of the defeat of reform. It tended, rather, to be couched in terms of a conservatism which would wait for society to be gradually prepared for change. The colonial bureaucracy was not alone in supporting the *status quo* as a preparation for future changes.

The polyphonous *Mahratta* placed itself with those members of the Council who, though in sympathy with Mehta's motion, opposed it because the time for it had not come. It shared MacDonnell's fear that religious fanaticism could undo the gains made by the advanced classes. But whereas MacDonnell apprehended resistance from 'important sections' as well, the Poona weekly twisted his speech to suggest that fanaticism would erupt among the lower classes alone. At the same time, it opposed Mehta's motion in the name of 'the general Hindu community' on the ground that the existing law had 'stood the test of time' and 'not worked any mischief'.[73]

Leavened with sympathy for Mehta's motion, resistance to change seemed to acquire respectability. In any case, it made sense to appear reasonable in the moment of victory. This reasonableness, moreover, was underscored by exaggerating the reformers' demands. As it reported with satisfaction the disappoint-ment of 'the sympathizers of Rukhmabai's cause', the *Native Opinion* overlooked what—as exemplified by Mehta's motion—they had finally accepted. It maintained that they had all along pressed for 'the abolishment of the punishment of imprisonment'.[74]

There were unrestrained outbursts as well, revealing the wide spread of the sentiments voiced by the likes of Khem Singh Bedi and Mohini Mohun Roy. For example, the *Gujarat Mitra*, an Anglo-Gujarati weekly from Surat, justified the existing law thus:[75]

> In the present state of the Indian society much shuffled from its past calm aspect, with many of the old bonds loosening, the place of which is hardly supplied by others and better ones, we looked upon this

only check to a wild and uncontrolled life in some quarters to be a wholesome one.

While organized orthodoxy, including its 'extremist' nationalist elements, disingenuously defended the government of India, the reformists with their 'moderate' nationalist stance accused it of having crushed 'the most elementary rights of womanhood'. It had done so on 'very insufficient grounds', imagining obstacles where none existed. Mehta's motion was based on the views of conservative Hindus who commanded 'a high influence' among their castes, including 'so hopelessly orthodox a Hindu judge as the late Sir Muthuswami Iyer'.[76] Even 'the so-called uneducated classes', it was claimed, held opinions no 'different from those of their educated leaders'.[77] The motion, moreover, had in principle been approved by 'all its opponents in Council, except one'. Yet, Elgin's government[78] had defeated the motion, caring neither for its 'justice and necessity' nor for the 'distinct pledge' his predecessor had given in 1890. As for the regard it flaunted for public opinion:[79]

> On the one hand, Government passes the terrible Police Amendment Bill against the united voice of the people; on the other, it rejects a harmless little measure, timid and tentative, against all the weight of authority that it is possible to be ranged in its favour, and against the most obvious claims of justice, of humanity, of common decency.

In fact, 'the pretence of respecting the prejudices of the orthodox' was meant to neutralize the government's 'unpopularity in other directions'.[80] The message was unmistakable: 'where the smallest amendment of a law is needed to further the end of equity or justice, you may as well whistle for it to the end of your days.'[81]

Sparing neither the orthodox, who never relented in their demand for non-interference, nor the rulers, whose neutrality could not mask 'their position of shame to themselves and wrong to he women of India', the *Indian Spectator* wrote:[82]

> What did the fool of a husband do before our so-called neutral Government interfered in the case in 1877?[83]... Has Caste died since then?... Why can't they manage their own domestic affairs, instead of calling upon a foreign Government to play the part of—what shall we call it? It is an ignoble part for Government... And much more humiliating it is for the Hindu community to avail itself of this crutch of a Christian law, a relic of barbarous times, given up even in Christian countries, in so delicate a family matter as the relations between wife and husband.

The shameful incongruity of their behaviour as champions of non-interference apart, the *Spectator* noted, neither Mohini Mohun Roy nor Khem Singh Bedi represented the Hindu community. Roy spoke for none but himself.[84] Bedi was at best 'supposed' to represent the Sikh community. Assuming that he did, it did not follow 'that the Sikhs represent the whole of the Panjaub, much less that the Panjaub represents the whole of India.'[85] In reality this man, who had raised 'false spectres of possible political complications in the Panjaub', did not represent even his own community.[86] Soon Bedi was accused, apparently with good reason, of having been officially 'goaded' into opposing Miller's amendment.[87]

To those who had taken up Rukhmabai's case as a crusade for 'the rights and liberties of women', the defeat of Mehta's motion spelt the end of a decade of hope. The cause of social reform was seen to have been put back 'by some years' as a 'blood-thirsty orthodoxy', entertaining views 'worthy of medieval barbarism', had obtained a new lease of life.[88] Section 260, that 'deep blot on the statute-book of the country', continued to be 'a standing threat against wronged women', 'practically' empowering 'the most profligate and cruel of husbands to keep his wife in custody like his cattle'. The struggle to empower women needed to be renewed. Otherwise, the 'savage notions' that had caused this setback would 'spread far and wide', and make social progress 'an impossibility'. To achieve such progress, it was important to effect 'a reasonable and equitable equality between man and woman', and prevent any unnecessary or unkind restraining of 'the liberties of the weaker sex'.[89]

In the renewed struggle no hope could be placed on the colonial officials. Enjoying a monopoly of power, they claimed a monopoly of wisdom as well.[90] They rationalized any position that helped to ensure their power and safety. They had developed cold feet on the question of altering the existing law for fear of popular discontent. The only way left open to the reformers was to begin an agitation 'quite contrary to what Government expected' from the repeal of section 260.[91]

No agitation worth the name was in those days conceived in India without an eye on the dynamics of political power and public opinion in England. The experience of the ten years leading to the frustration of 1895 itself indicated that the officialdom in India had at no point been more inclined to alter the law than when sympathy for Rukhmabai was at its peak in England around 1887.

The lesson was confirmed by the critical role of English opinion in the passing of the Age of Consent Act. Neither resolutions of self-reliance nor disillusionment with the authorities in India militated against exertions in England. The *Indian Social Reformer*, thus, warned the government of India that it could not 'long evade passing the amendment', for pressure would be 'brought to bear upon them from England'.[92] Malabari also, knowing from his experience the efficacy of this remote control, kept an eye on the effect his writing would have in England as he lashed out at the authorities in India for letting the women down. As he spelt out the consequences for India of the 'fall' from the days of Bentinck to those of Elgin, he also mentioned the 'very serious' risk to which it exposed England. Hinting at the moral, and eventually political, erosion that the 'fall' of its representatives in India might cause in the 'parent' country—not an uncommon theme those days—he wrote:

> Let leaders of public opinion in England see to this in time. If they realize what it is that the Government has been frightened into backing out of, they will understand what we mean.[93]

In keeping with the ambivalence felt towards the colonial connection, however, the disillusioning aftermath of the Rukhmabai case also prompted some rethinking about the axiomatically progressive role of colonial intervention in Indian society. Reformist leaders like Telang and Ranade—by no means hostile to westernization *per se*—had even earlier made suggestions to this effect. It was not coincidental that the *Indian Spectator* took up those suggestions for serious consideration in the wake of the defeat of Mehta's motion. It invited its readers to ponder whether 'the rigid pressure of British rule' had not adversely affected 'the spontaneous tendency towards growth and improve-ment which was going on in Hindu society as long as it was left to itself.'[94] Telang died young without pressing this line of enquiry. Ranade too, although he lived longer, did not follow it far enough. Despite continuing ambivalence with regard to both 'tradition' and the culture of the colonisers, the frame of cognitive validation in the emerging pattern of dominant consciousness almost inexorably tended to come from the latter. In that sense, going against the grain of contemporary understanding among both the colonisers and the colonised, the alternative line of enquiry could not, perhaps, have had more than an occasional cautionary function.

It is symptomatic that, in the immediate context that had

prompted it, MacDonnell's booming rhetoric carried little conviction. But the larger faith at which the rhetoric was directed survived the disillusionment symbolized by the defeat of Mehta's motion.

NOTES

1. *Home Department, Judicial Proceedings*, June 1887, nos. 189–92 (National Archives of India).
2. Both the Bombay government's confidential despatch and the Viceroy's telegram were dated 30 March 1887. Ibid.
3. The general importance for the Indian administration of opinion in England apart, it is instructive that the issues of the London *Times* that discussed the Rukhmabai case were among the papers requisitioned by John Prescott Hewett before he made up his mind about the Bombay government's communication. A senior member of the government secretariat, Hewett became the Viceroy's Private Secretary a year later. Ibid.
4. Another note, showing agreement within the Legislative Department, was similarly reassuring: '... we shall certainly not be offending against native law and ancient prejudices, for, as I have shown, the law under which imprisonment is possible is British in origin and quite new in its application to India.' Ibid.
5. The issue of restitution of conjugal rights was most of the time discussed as if only the wife was liable to be punished.
6. The provisions of the English law, listed in the letter, were as follows: '(1) a decree for restitution of conjugal rights shall not be enforced by process against the person (section 1);
   '(2) when the application is made by the wife, the Court may order that, in the event of the decree not being complied with, the respondent shall make payments as for alimony (ibid.);
   '(3) when the application is made by the husband, the Court may order the property of the wife to be paid or settled for the benefit of the petitioner and children of the marriage (section3);
   '(4) the Court may vary any order for payment as it may think just (section 4);
   '(5) non-compliance with the decree shall be deemed desertion, and a suit for judicial separation may be forthwith instituted. If a husband has also been guilty of adultery, the wife may petition for dissolution of marriage (section 5);
   '(6) the Court may make order for custody, maintenance, and education of children (section 6).' Ibid.
7. It was proposed that, instead of causing imprisonment, 'non-compliance with the decree shall be deemed desertion, and a suit for judicial separation may be forthwith instituted. If a husband has also been guilty

of adultery, the wife may petition for dissolution of marriage'. The proposal was thus justified by Scoble: 'Among Mahomedans, divorce is facile, among Hindus, though forbidden by the written law, it is common among many castes; in all cases, in which self-respect did not prevent an application to the Court, I think a satisfactory money arrangement would remove scruples that might otherwise be felt.' Since, however, a circular meant for public consumption could not so directly state the power of money to neutralize scruples, it proposed matter of factly: 'As divorce is easily arranged among Muhammadans, and as it is also common among many castes of the Hindu community, although forbidden by the written law... non-compliance with the decree should be made a ground for dissolving the marriage upon the application of either party, provided - '(a) that compensation were given to the party divorced; and '(b) that a suitable and effective arrangement were made for providing for the children of the marriage.' Ibid.

8. Home Department, *Judicial Proceedings,* Sept. 1887, no. 299 (National Archives of India).
9. In a noting reminiscent of Malabari wishing publicly that Rukhmabai be sent to jail, Dufferin wrote with laconic irony in the file: 'It would be a good thing for the cause if Mrs or Miss (?) Rukhmabai were sent to prison; but still we must prevent it somehow.' Ibid.
10. Appreciating the *Bombay Gazette's* refusal to hand over the original text of Rukhmabai's reply - an act the *Times of India* described as 'quixotic chivalry'—the *Indian Daily News* extracted the following from the latter's unconvincing self-defense: 'When we published the letters of "A Hindu Lady", we accepted the fullest responsibility for them, and we were bound to keep her secret. But when Rukhmabai writes to us over her own name, about family squabbles of which we can know nothing, we leave the primary responsibility with her.' 3 Aug. 1887.
11. For Rukhmabai's letter of 17 Feb. 1887, see Appendix A. This faith in legislation she retained even in her old age. See Dr. Rukhmabai, M.D., 'Purdah: The Need for Its Abolition', in Evelyn C. Gedge and Mithan Choksi, (eds.), *Women in Modern India: Fifteen Papers by Indian Women Writers,* Bombay, 1929, pp. 144–8.
12. *Bombay Gazette,* 7 July 1888.
13. *Native Opinion,* 8 July 1888. Drawing a contrast between Dadaji and Rukhmabai, the weekly wrote: 'Although the wife through her counsel called him all manner of names, he never did or uttered a single thing that was compromising to his self-respect. And we are glad to see that he preserved that dignified attitude to the last.'
14. Ibid.
15. *Bombay Gazette,* 7 July 1888.
16. *Indian Daily News,* 9 July 1888.
17. *Indian Spectator,* 8 July 1888.
18. See Home Department, *Judicial Proceedings,* Mar. 1895, nos. 1–80. Similarly, when A.P. MacDonnell pointed out in early 1890 that discretion to the courts had been overruled by the government of India

in June 1887, Hutchins, the Home Member, countered: 'At that time it may have been considered not to go far enough.' Note of 2 Feb. 1890, Ibid.

19. Colvin argued 'that it would be well to take measures necessary to avoid the difficulty before it is urged upon the Government in a more startling form, evokes from the English public a pressure more difficult to resist, and precipitates into more violent collision the conflicting views of the English and the Hindu through the bitterness caused by test cases at a time of public excitement'. Ibid., May 1890, no. 459.
20. Colvin thus wound up the argument: 'So that in abolishing suits for the restitution of conjugal rights we should not be violating any ordinance of the Hindu law, but abolishing a compromise merely, which has been shown to be ineffective; which has not been resorted to by those for whom it is intended; and which, should it ever be more generally resorted to, will probably be used at the moment when it will attract the greatest reprobation and censure, because it will be at a time when the suitableness of the law to the circumstances of the society in which it is applied is prominently brought into view.' Ibid. Colvin was one among many to believe that the orthodox opposition would yield under the weight of its own irreconcilability. But he went farther—he strained the Hindu criticism of imprisonment to justify the abolition of suits for the restitution of conjugal rights. He may not have anticipated, nor did others, that orthodox Hindus would unembarrassedly oppose the abolition of imprisonment even while denouncing it as a barbaric importation. But there was little justification for his inference that, because of their criticism of the penalty of imprisonment, they would acquiesce in the abolition of restitution suits *per se.* They had, after all, rejected the contention that such suits were alien to Hindu law.
21. Colvin, however, appreciated the logic underlying the proposal to confine the measure to infant marriages. He wrote: 'A process which may be defended in the case of the woman who has cohabited with her husband as at least consonant with the freedom of the individual, becomes indefensible in the case of those who have never been consulted as to their marriages, and who, on arriving at the time when they can judge for themselves, repudiate the contract made for them during their infancy.' Ibid. The Punjab government, too, favoured keeping unconsummated infant marriages within the purview of the Civil Procedure Code, though it proposed that in such cases the court's decree should be merely declaratory and not enforceable. Ibid., no. 546.
22. Illustrating the 'impossibility', he wrote: 'On the one hand, the Mahomedans do not require or wish for imprisonment as a means of enforcing conjugal rights. Their own law, with its system of divorce and forefeiture of dower, provides a sufficient sanction; and the substitutes for imprisonment, which are provided by the English statute, are not required by them.' He contrasted this with the Hindu community's insistence on retaining imprisonment. Ibid., no. 447.
23. Though Bayley received some reports suggesting that 'all chances of

harshness or hardship will be eliminated by giving an absolute discretion to the Courts', he favoured a more cautious procedure. He proposed the retention of imprisonment for contempt of court, and explained it to mean: 'the Judge should first be compelled to proceed by attachment, and if the judgment-debtor still continued in contempt, he should have a discretionary power to commit to jail for a limited period.' Keeping in mind the speculation in England and India whether, even after completing a term in jail, Rukhmabai could not be sued again by her husband, Bayley added mercifully: 'The penalty, once suffered, should be regarded as having purged the contempt, and no further penalty should be enforced to compel restitution.' Ibid.

24. Considering the varying levels of Hinduization among the Assam population, the use of the term 'Hindus proper', distinguished from those on the margins and periphery of Hinduism, is understandable.
25. From the Secretary to the Chief Commissioner of Assam to the Secretary to the Government of India, Home Department, 6 Feb. 1888, Ibid., no. 667.
26. Elaborating the point, Fitzpatrick wrote in his 'Note' of 5 Oct. 1887: 'It is almost impossible for us, accustomed as we are to give full play to "sexual selection" in marriage, to realize a state of things under which it never occurs to either party to exercise a choice and under which accordingly it is not felt as a grievance to be debarred from exercising a choice, but this is the state of things which as a matter of fact at present exists among the mass of natives of this country.' Also: 'The present system as I have said has its defects, but so far as the contentment of married people is concerned, I have no hesitation in saying that from all I have seen and heard, in a service of 28 years, I believe it works a very great deal better than the critics suppose, and all things considered very tolerably.' Ibid.
27. Note by D. Fitzpatrick, Officiating Chief Commissioner, 5 Oct., 1887, Ibid.
28. Explaining why he was talking of wives alone, not of spouses in general, Fitzpatrick wrote at the outset: 'I have for the sake of simplicity treated the question throughout as if it referred only to restitution suits instituted by a husband. I have never known one instituted by a native wife.' Ibid.
29. Preliminary enquiries made Fitzpatrick feel that, given the improbability of Rukhmabai's kind of cases, most Indians would not care much as to what was done in such cases. But he could neither ignore the 'danger of a cry of sacrilegious interference with native laws and breach of our promise to observe them being raised'. He also felt that an infant marriage that was disputed by a spouse on coming of age should be allowed to be dissolved 'on the application of either party'. But, uncertain about people's reaction, he reserved his opinion on that issue for the time being. Ibid.
30. Of the examples of socialization given by Fitzpatrick, one relates to 'a highly educated and very intelligent native official of somewhat high

standing in the service' whose infant marriage had been consummated 'after both the parties had reached an age to think for themselves'. Asked if there was not a risk 'that before the marriage was consummated one of the parties might conceive a dislike towards or at least find it impossible to conceive a liking for the other and on that ground object', he said, *inter alia*: 'It is no greater hardship than when one of us is given in adoption to a stranger, perhaps to a man whom he would not choose for his father if he had a voice in the matter.' In another example, which also explains something of the public animus against Rukhmabai, figures 'a girl, a Government ward, who had been left unmarried up to an age when it could be at least pretended that she had views of her own on the subject'. She had, 'at the instigation of interested parties', objected to the husband proposed for her and expressed a liking for another man. When, during discussions 'with some native gentlemen', an English official worried lest the girl should not flinch, their answer was: 'You need not fear that, *no decent girl among us would ever think of such a thing*.' (Emphasis added.) Ibid.

31. Perhaps realizing that he was deviating from his conviction that the law be left untouched, Fitzpatrick felt constrained to add: 'I would say to the people "we have every respect for your marriage system, and our Courts will do all they properly can to uphold it; but in a case of this sort where the system has owing to your default or to other ca[u]ses beyond the control of the girl resulted in a miserable failure we can't undertake to help you to compel her to live with her husband".' Ibid.
32. Noticing, like Sargent, the role of a different kind of socialization in her case, but without the Chief Justice's acerbity, Fitzpatrick described Rukhmabai as 'the innocent victim of a failure of the system brought about by circumstances beyond her control'. Ibid.
33. Fitzpatrick argued that extra-legal influences deterring a wife in England from leaving her husband were 'so numerous and so powerful that she would not think of taking such a step unless things had gone so far that there was no reasonable hope of a reconciliation'. Because the chances, in such a situation, of forcing her to go back to her husband seemed 'extremely small', people developed a 'natural reluctance' to sanction what they thought was a 'brutal remedy'. In India, except among the higher classes and castes—and they did not take recourse to restitution proceedings—women were often 'quarrelsome and petulant', running away 'in a fit of passion' to their own families and friends who were usually willing to receive them because a woman was 'in more ways than one a useful article'. 'In these cases,' he observed, 'a decree for restitution enforceable by imprisonment is the only remedy; and leaving out of account a handful of advanced natives who desire to be more English than the English themselves, and who, however estimable they may be, represent no one, it would never cross the mind of any human being high or low, to conceive that there was anything in the adoption of such a remedy to shock anybody's feelings'. Ibid.
34. In a passage reminiscent of Markby's judgment, but drawing an opposite

result of more clearly perceived principles of justice and morality, and when they are it is our duty to follow them in this country; but as far as I can see there is nothing in the enforcement of a decree for restitution against either justice or morality.' Ibid.

35. One of these proposals was to declare dissoluble, on suit by her, the marriage of a girl under 15 to a man 25 years or more older than her, if no cohabitation with her full consent had followed. Ibid., no. 546.
36. The other two suggestions, laying down when the courts should not order imprisonment for recusancy, were: (1) Where the court was satisfied that the paintiff-husband kept concubines; or frequented prostitutes or catamites; or was a habitual drunkard; or was of a violent temper and addicted to assault; or was suffering from leprosy or venereal disease. (2) When the defendant-wife could satisfy the court that she was leading a chaste life and had reasonable grounds, other than those already specified, for objecting to cohabitation. The second suggestion, by its blanket character, immensely enlarged the court's discretion. Ibid.
37. That besides, understandably, papering over differences and contradictions, the note also tended, not quite understandably, to be less than faithful to some administrations' positions will be clear from the summary it provided: 'The reports submitted by the Local Governments and Administrations show the Madras, Bombay, North-Western Provinces, and Burma Governments approve of the proposal that a decree for restitution of conjugal rights should not be enforced by process against the person. The Chief Commissioner of the Central Provinces would retain it except where the person at the time of his or her marriage was a minor, and has not after attaining majority ratified the marriage by cohabitation. The Bengal and Punjab Governments would give the Courts a discretionary power to commit to jail, while the Assam Government would leave the law unaltered except by enacting that no suit for institution of conjugal rights should be instituted against a wife whose marriage has not been consummated.' Note by R.W.C., 8 Apr. 1889. Ibid.
38. The note would not limit the proposed legislation to infant marriages alone. That would appear as 'an insidious attack on infant marriage' and increase Hindu opposition 'greatly'. For the same reason, and also because a declaratory decree could 'occasionally be useful', it ruled out as 'unnecessary' Auckland Colvin's suggestion to abolish restitution suits altogether. But it used his logic about altering the law forthwith: 'If this is to be done, early action is advisable.' It admitted that the abolition of imprisonment would have 'a considerable effect among the lower classes where wives are expensive articles'. But it opposed, for the present, any pre-emptive safeguards, arguing that 'it would be easy hereafter for Government to re-establish the penalty of imprisonment in certain cases, and it could then be guarded by conditions which it would be impossible now to introduce without giving rise to stronger opposition than is likely to be offered to its total abolition'. Ibid.

39. *Home Department, Judicial Proceedings,* Mar. 1895, nos. 1–80, Appendix K. For the joint minute by Justices Chunder Madhub Ghosh and Gooroo Dass Banerji, dated 12 Jul. 1889, see ibid., May 1890, no. 715.
40. Abolishing the suit for the restitution of conjugal rights only in the case of infant and unconsummated marriages would appear to Hindus as an interference with their marriage system; and they would not accept its total abolition because their internal sanctions had become 'an inefficient substitute in the present day for the ordinary legal sanction'. Ibid.
41. Lyall disclosed in his note of 1 Nov. 1889 that he persuaded Fitzpatrick to accept this departure from his position that the law should be left as it was. Ibid.
42. Lyall took more than two months to write his note. He was new to the charge and many pressing matters must have claimed his attention. But that his note took three weeks to reach the Home Member, Hutchins, illustrates the lack of urgency that had come to surround this question. Hutchinson, for his part, needed six weeks to reach 'precisely the same conclusion' as Lyall's. Ibid.
43. Lansdowne prepared a note on 10 May and that became the basis for the Council's decision on 15 May. Ibid.
44. Miller, however, added that the courts 'would be entitled to treat any active contempt—such as refusing to comply with an order to hand over the children to the other parent—in the usual way'. Note, dated 17 June 1893, *Home Department, Judicial Proceedings,* Mar. 1895, nos. 1–80, K.W.
45. Miller laid down the following formula for the government to act in relation to the small noisy body: 'On the opposition of these men to *every* reform we must make our account: when the matter at issue is one of preference or sentiment merely, I should be inclined to defer to them to a very great extent, but when an intelligible and important principle is involved—e.g., in the age of consent question—we have, I think, no choice but to go on our way regardless of them.' Ibid.
46. About judicial separation or divorce following upon an unenforced decree for the restitution of conjugal rights, Miller wrote: 'I see no reason why the recalcitrant party should be released from any consequence of the judgment except that of physical consortium, and—though it might sometimes be an appropriate remedy in the interest of the other party—I think it would be too great an interference with the social arrangements of the great bulk of the population to be wise or desirable.' Ibid.
47. Miller, Hutchins complained, was proposing to replace the simple Indian procedure with elaborate English legal provisions which would be 'as much out of place as a steam plough in a paddy field'. The complaint referred to the following in Miller's note: 'I should like to alter the law so as to bring it into practical conformity with the first four sections of 47 & 48 Vict., c. 68, saying nothing about section 5 and expanding section 6 so as to enable the Court to make any order about the custody of the infant children it thought just, at any time, so long as the decree

for restitution remains uncancelled and uncomplied with.' Hutchins also objected that introducing discretion would practically amount to abolishing imprisonment: 'I may mention that suits by wives will almost always take the form of a claim for maintenance; and when once the imprisonment has been declared discretionary, that form will probably become universal.' Note of 7 July 1893, Ibid.

48. In an obvious reference to Miller's plan to abolish imprisonment, Lansdowne hoped that, even after he had left, legislation would not go beyond what was agreed upon in May 1890. Lansdowne's note of 12 July 1893, ibid.
49. Miller denied having ever 'dreamt of introducing a system of settlements on the English model into India'; though he thought that 'the Court should have the power of dealing with the property of the spouses so as to do justice as far as possible to the party in the right'. Miller's note of 14 July 1893, Ibid.
50. Ibid., no. 1; Appendix A, p. 23.
51. When an earlier draft of the amendment seemed equivocal to him, Miller gave it the requisite clarity and explained: 'Section 260 required, I think, more specific reference to the fact that the discretion of the Court was to be exercised when imprisonment was required, not when it was not required, than appeared in the original draft.' Ibid., K.W.
52. The 'contentious' drafting of the amendment was immediately noticed by S.H. James, a Legislative Department official who had been involved with the question of legislation since it was mooted in 1887. Ibid.
53. Khem Singh Bedi himself provided leadership to the separate Sikh identity that was then beginning to be more sharply defined and was seeking organizational expression.
54. Around the same time an Anglo-Gujarati weekly from Surat remarked: 'When ill-treated wives have a remedy in suits for alimony against their recalcitrant husbands, the injured husbands, too, should have remedy for them for the restitution of their conjugal rights when their better halves turned worse and obstinately and persistently refused to make them happy.' *Gujarat Mitra,* 17 Mar. 1895, in *Indian Spectator and Voice of India,* 31 Mar. 1895.
55. Italics added. See Appendix E.
56. In what was an undisguised attack on Miller on account of his want of Indian experience, and an assertion of the authority Fitzpatrick claimed by virtue of his varied local knowledge, the amendment was said to raise a 'most serious' question 'on which persons unfamiliar with the very various conditions of domestic life in this country may easily go wrong'. He even refused to be bound by the decision of May 1890 to alter the law. Whatever was agreed to, Fitzpatrick asserted, 'was agreed to by the Members of the Supreme Council as then constituted'; and of this he was not aware. R.E. Younghusband, Offg. Junior Secretary to Government, Punjab and its Dependencies, to the Secretary to the Government of India, Legislative Department, 2 Oct. 1894. *Home Department, Judicial Proceedings,* Mar. 1895, nos. 1–80.

57. He argued: 'All objections which could be urged against the enforcement of a restitution decree by imprisonment would, as a rule, be equally good as objections against the passing of such a decree, and it would as a rule be only in cases where something fresh had supervened after the passing of the decree that there would be any justification for refusing it in the regular way.' Ibid., Appendix U.
58. This argument, strikingly, suggests that abolition of imprisonment would practically result from the amendment, and proceeds as if that is what the amendment was formally meant to achieve. Ibid., Appendix N. The letter was dated 1 Oct. 1894.
59. Charles Elliott, the Lt. Governor of Bengal, it may be noted, identified four broad positions vis-a-vis the amendment: those absolutely for or against it; those favouring or opposing it with hesitation and modifications. Given 'this conflict of opinion', he said, he felt inclined to express his views with 'some reserve'. There was, however, no trace of reserve in the reassertion of his earlier, provisional opinion. H.J.S. Cotton, Chief Secretary to the Government of Bengal, to the Secretary to the Government of India, Legislative Department, 8 Jan. 1895, Ibid.
60. Ibid. Even the administrations that seemed to offer qualified support to Miller's amendment served to confirm the categorical opposition voiced by the Punjab and Bengal governments. The letter sent by the Assam administration referred generously to the views expressed by Fitzpatrick when he was Chief Commissioner of Assam. It commented, *inter alia*: '...unless the process of imprisonment continues to be recognized as the ordinary means of enforcement of a decree, to be departed from only upon due cause shown, there is reason to fear that such decrees will in most cases prove impossible to execute at all.' The Offg. Secretary to the Chief Commissioner of Assam to the Secretary to the Government of India, Legislative Department, 2 Oct. 1894. Ibid., Appendix P. This point was made with particular force by G. Godfrey, judge of the Assam Valley district, who observed: 'I see no justice in giving the judgment-debtor an undue advantage in the matter such as is given in the proposed section [of the amendment]. If a decree is just and proper, as it must be presumed to be, it seems only fair that the person against whom it is given should make out sufficient grounds for stopping its execution in the only way which it is possible that it could be executed.' Ibid. The letter from the N.W.P., it would seem, was designed to be self-subversive. Having replaced Auckland Colvin as the Lt. Governor, the arch reactionary Charles Crosthwaite submitted an opinion that effectively neutralized his predecessor's relatively liberal opinion while ostensibly reiterating it. After supporting the amendment and alluding to the risk posed by 'Hindu agitators', Crosthwaite had the letter mischievously add: 'This has no doubt been considered by the Government of India.' Secretary to Government, N.W. Provinces and Oudh, to the Secretary to the Government of India, Legislative Department, 26 Sept. 1894. Ibid., Appendix M.
61. Note of 29 Aug. 1894, Ibid.

62. W. Lee Warner, Secretary to Bombay government, to the Secretary to the Government of India, Legislative Department, 6 Oct. 1894. Ibid. Among the Bombay officials who strongly pleaded for abolition of imprisonment was Satyendranath Tagore. Son of Debendranath Tagore and the first Indian to break the British monopoly over the covenanted Indian civil service, Satyendranath wrote on 28 Aug. 1894: 'The present amendment investing the Court with a discretion in the matter is undoubtedly a step in the right direction. It is, however, a half-hearted measure, and I am of opinion that the legislature would do well to abolish the penalty of imprisonment altogether in such cases.' Ibid.
63. On 3 Jan. 1895 the committee was enlarged to include the Maharaja of Durbhanga, Prince Sir Jahan Kadr, Mirza Muhammad Wahid Ali Bahadur, M.M. Roy and Griffith Evans.
64. Mehta said that he would 'probably' have kept silent if there had been in the Council someone from Bombay or Madras—the presidencies that had supported Miller's amendment—'who would have voiced the best Hindu view of either of these Presidencies': 'In the absence of any such member, I think it a duty to represent what, I believe, would have been the views put forward if, for instance, there was sitting at this Council a Hindu like my late friend Mr Justice K.T. Telang, a true and sincere Hindu of Hindus, from whom I, as well as many others, have learned to respect and appreciate many valuable lessons of Hindu social and religious philosophy.' C.Y. Chintamani (ed.), *Speeches and Writings of the Honourable Sir Pherozeshah M. Mehta, K.C.I.E.*, Allahabad, 1905, p. 409.
65. Mehta was liberal in citing the views of such Hindus as Telang, R.C. Dutt, Satyendranath Tagore and Justice Muthuswami Iyer. The views of Iyer, he said, were particularly 'entitled to the greatest respect' because: 'his devout and sincere conservatism was as unquestioned as his knowledge of Hindu law and usage was profound.' Mehta also cited the note submitted on behalf of the Central National Mahomedan Association in favour of Miller's amendment. Ibid., pp. 409–13.
66. Ibid., pp. 409–13, 415–17. See also H.P. Mody, *Sir Pherozeshah Mehta: A Political Biography*, Bombay, 1921, vol. I, pp. 335–7. Mehta's speech in the Council can also be seen in Home Department, *Judicial Proceedings*, Mar. 1895, nos. 1–80.
67. That, the *Bengalee* argued in its issue of 16 Mar. 1895, would imply undertaking legislation when it was redundant; the people by then 'will have outgrown the law'. The same point was also made in terms of impossibility: 'If such a change in the law of the country, which does not at all clash with any religious doctrines or social customs, should be thought to produce political consequences of a dangerous character, then legislation itself must be impossible.' *Madras Standard*, 11 Mar. 1895.
68. So arbitrary was this decision of Stokes that when in 1887, the courts wanted to find out the rationale behind it before deciding to annul it, they found themselves clueless after perusing the relevant documents. Home Department, *Judicial Proceedings*, June 1887, nos. 189–92.

69. Besides advancing these powerful arguments, Chitnavis also gave a subtle twist to a technical point that was intended to hoist the *reactionaries* with their own petard. He said: 'The principle underlying the provision of section 260 of the present Code appears to be that marriage is an ordinary civil contract, and a refusal to perform its obligations is like breaking a contract; therefore the same penalties that attach to non-compliance with the order of the Court to specifically perform a contract should also apply to the refusal to abide by the decree for restitution of conjugal rights. But among Hindus marriage is not a contract, but a religious sacrament, being the last of the initiatory rites prescribed for the regenerate classes, and the only one for women and sudras. Non-compliance with the duties and obligations of a religious rite should not, according to Hindu ideas, be visited with worldly punishment.' Ibid., Mar. 1895, nos. 1–80.
70. Another non-official member, Griffith Evans, maintained that he was 'very reluctantly' led to oppose the proposed alteration in law because of Khem Singh, although 'personally' he considered it 'a very good thing for many reasons'. An advocate of the Calcutta High Court and a member of the Viceroy's Legislative Council since 1877, Evans, having referred to 'a very large body of orthodox and conservative Hindus who, whether their reasons are good or bad, very strongly object to this change', said about Mehta's motion: 'However, this change which has been proposed, is such a small one, and its effect would be so very beneficial in preventing such a scandal as that of Rukmabai's case, which very nearly led to strong agitation in England, which would have been exceedingly inconvenient, that I would have been inclined to run a certain amount of risk of disturbing the feelings of certain classes of Hindus, had it not been that in Select Committee, when the Hon'ble Khem Singh Baba, who, as we all know, is a Guru among the Sikhs, and whose opinions carry the very greatest weight amongst them, was absolutely and irreconcilably opposed to it. Enquiries were made from him; we got other Native members of the Committee to discuss it with him; it was discussed, so that there could be no misunderstanding, and we found that his attitude was resolute and uncompromising.' Ibid.
71. The following, written in spite of his crucial role in the success of the infamous Police Bill and the defeat of Mehta's motion, is a fair specimen of educated Indians' feeling: 'Nonetheless we consider Sir Antony MacDonnell to be a liberal-minded ruler.' *Bengalee*, 9 Mar. 1895.
72. This led Mehta to remonstrate: 'I thought I had made it clear that I was only representing the conservative and orthodox view of the matter in the Presidency of Bombay, as well as in that of Madras and Bengal.' C.Y. Chintamani (ed.), pp. 414–17.
73. *Mahratta*, 10 Mar. 1895.
74. *Native Opinion*, 10 Mar. 1895. It did mention that the Law Member, instead of going so far, agreed to make imprisonment discretionary. But while describing how his amendment was dropped by the Select Committee, it wrote as if the reformers, not satisfied with the

amendment, were happy that it was aborted: 'This amendment did not only meet with considerable opposition from those who entertain no sympathy for recalcitrant wives, but it did not satisfy the reformers also. In one way they will welcome the fate that has befallen it.'

75. *Gujarat Mitra*, 17 Mar., in *Indian Spectator and Voice of India*, 31 Mar. 1895.
76. For Justice Iyer's minute of 4 Oct. 1887, see *Home Department, Judicial Proceedings*, May 1890, no. 411.
77. The claim on behalf of the masses of Bengal was made by the *Bengalee*, 16 Mar. 1895; and of the other two Presidencies by the *Hindu* of 14 Mar. 1895. A similar claim was indirectly made for the 'lower classes' of the Bombay Presidency by the *Indu Prakash*, 18 Mar. 1895. Their marital affairs, the weekly remarked, were 'as a rule' determined by caste meetings and not through litigation in the colonial courts.
78. While criticizing MacDonnell, the *Indian Spectator* came down heavily on Elgin: 'But difficult as it is to follow Sir Antony McDonnell, it is simply impossible to understand the head of the Government talking of 'I shall certainly oppose' [this is how Elgin had ended his speech in the Council]... We admire his Excellency's courage, but must beg him to forgive us if we wrong him in thinking that the courage seems to have been inspired more by the solid majority at his back than by his own conviction. What India needs, in a case like this, is the courage of personal responsibility towards God and man.' 10 Mar. 1895.
79. This paragraph is based on *Indian Messenger*, 3 Mar., *Indian Spectator*, 10, 17 Mar., *Indian Social Reformer*, 16 Mar., and *Bengalee*, 16 Mar. 1895. The *Advocate*, a weekly brought out from Lucknow in English, even accused the Select Committee of 'defying public opinion' in dropping Miller's amendment. 12 Mar. 1895. See also *Indian Spectator and Voice of India*, 31 Mar., 7 Apr. 1895, for excerpts from these and other journals. The *Indian Mirror* wrote about Elgin: '...he has by this time placed himself completely at the service of the officials, and the period of positive unpopularity has already begun for him... and willing as we are to find apologies for Lord Elgin's policies, we are unable to invent even a single decent excuse.' 5 Mar. 1895.
80. *Indian Social Reformer*, 16 Mar. 1895. Like the *Indian Messenger* and the *Indian Spectator*, the *Reformer* also wrote: 'The English Government cares not a brass farthing for public opinion so-called when it has to get through the Council a Police Act or a Zemindari Bill, however loud may be the clamour that may be raised against them.'
81. *Indian Spectator*, 10 Mar. 1895.
82. Ibid., 31 Mar. 1895.
83. This was in answer to a 'Hindu friend in the north' who had asked as to what a husband would do 'without the strong arms of the law to help him'. Ibid. Earlier the *Indian Spectator* had employed this argument against Khem Singh Bedi: 'And what did even the Sikhs do before the miserable relic of the Church Law of Europe was imported into India about seventeen years ago?' Ibid., 17 Mar. 1895.

84. The *Indian Spectator* remarked about Mohini Mohun Roy: 'If he spoke for the Bengalis, he has done them a very bad turn indeed. If his speech represented his own views, he shows himself unfit to be the spokesman of any intelligent race that has character or reputation to lose. This comes of 'representation' in Council!' 24 Mar. 1895.
85. Ibid., 10 Mar. 1895. After conceding for the sake of argument that Khem Singh was right about Sikh feelings on the issue, the *Indian Spectator* continued the following week: 'But to ask Hindus and Mahomedans of the rest of India to wait till the Sikhs are ready for the measure, would be to give the latter a degree of importance in social and religious matters, which the former have never conceded to them. We have seen strange results emerge from the habit of Government to adhere to the strict letter of their professed neutrality in social and religious affairs; but we are very much mistaken if this setting up of the Sikh in a position where he can lay down the law to Hindu and Mahomedan alike, while he himself is neither the one nor the other, though perhaps something of both, is not the strangest of them all.' 17 Mar. 1895.
86. *Bengalee*, 16 Mar. 1895. It wrote: '...we cannot bring ourselves to believe that the proposed alteration which sought to leave so much to the discretion of the court, would have affected the domestic tranquillity of the Sikhs...'
87. Ibid., 28 Apr. 1895. Reading the Punjab government's replies between the lines, it seems plausible that Fitzpatrick had something to do with Khem Singh's 'Note'.
88. Describing these people, and locating them primarily in Bengal, a province that, 'neither in politics nor in matters of social advancement', represented 'the best, the most enlightened or the most moderate type of Indian opinion', the *Hindu* of 14 Mar. 1895 observed: 'They would assume that whenever a Hindu wife is sent to jail, she is sent to jail with perfect justice, and that when a Hindu husband and his wife quarrel, the former is invariably innocent and the latter invariably guilty.' The Madras weekly, however, distinguished enlightened orthodox Hindus from this blood-thirsty orthodoxy.
89. *Madras Standard*, 11 Mar. *Subodh Patrika*, 10 Mar. 1895; *Bengalee*, 16 Mar.; *Advocate*, 12 Mar. 1895. The fact that the *Advocate* was owned by a Hindu and edited by two Muslim graduates from Cambridge lends additional significance to its observation that section 260 was 'a disgrace to the entire Hindu and Mahomedan population.'
90. This helplessly anguished statement of Pherozeshah Mehta was quoted by the *Indian Spectator* of 21 Apr. 1895.
91. *Advocate*, 12 Mar. 1895.
92. *Indian Social Reformer*, 16 Mar. 1895.
93. *Indian Spectator*, 24 Mar. 1895.
94. Ibid., 21 Apr. 1895.

Epilogue

Rukhmabai believed that with the reversal of Pinhey's 'humane decision' a wonderful opportunity had been lost. Had it been upheld, the decision 'would have altered the fate of millions and millions of daughters of India, and the longed-for freedom would have been easily secured'. 'But', she wearily added, 'it seemed the will of God that it should not be so.'[1] She was not alone in expecting momentous consequences from Pinhey's verdict. Hence the social drama, and the investments made by antagonistic social forces to direct its denouement. Judicial decisions, along with legislation, appeared—and still do—to be powerful instruments of social engineering.

In retrospect, however, the hopes and fears that animated the developments from Pinhey's decision to the defeat of Mehta's motion seem to have been exaggerated. This is elliptically reflected in the cheerless irony that the moment that forms the theme of this monograph still stays with us. The debate provoked by Pinhey's 'humane decision' was rehearsed a hundred years later in independent India as two different High Courts gave conflicting judgments on the validity of suits for the restitution of conjugal rights. I shall return to this presently.

The Rukhmabai case highlighted the enormity of the law relating to the restitution of conjugal rights. It also illustrated the power of a morally charged individual resistance backed by an alternative, albeit minority, public opinion. Rukhmabai's misfortunes were not exceptional. In fact, as Vaman Abaji Modak pointed out, many more women were subjected, objectively, to even greater hardships. What led her into open defiance, while the others gave in or resorted to less confrontational expedients, was her exceptional strength of character.

Notwithstanding the support her stepfather and, later, grandfather gave her in resisting Dadaji's efforts to obtain her company, Rukhmabai received a less than fair deal—at best, she was left unkindly alone—during her adolescence. Without the steel she developed on her own, the support that gradually came her way could not have taken her very far with the trying litigation and the witch-hunt to which she was subjected.

Rukhmabai's self-education gave her an amazing capacity to question what in her culture was assumed to be ideal. This enabled her to evolve, from the pain of her existential predicament, a fundamental critique of the meaning of marriage, and to assert her right to her person. In another striking rejection of received assumptions, she refused to accept a vow pressed on her by her grandfather as she was leaving for her medical education in London. The old man asked her to abide by three conditions: avoidance of beef, not to marry an Englishman and not to embrace Christianity. She accepted the latter two. But the first made no sense to her in spite of her Hindu upbringing, and she began eating beef soon after she arrived in England.[2]

Then, years later, something happened that, *prima facie*, may not seem to square with the strength of her character. Dadaji died in 1904 and Rukhmabai, who had refused to accept him as her husband, decided to don the Hindu widow's garb.[3] The martyr who had braved the combined tyranny of the colonial state and indigenous society, and been exposed to western feminism during her years in England,[4] suddenly became a picture, as it were, of conformism. This happened at a time when, unlike the socio-legal offensive of the 1880s, she was under no perceptible social pressure.

Rukhmabai's 'conformist' gesture does not make her an apostate to the cause of reform. Yet it reveals the power of organized social authority to command obedience through the sheer pressure of implicit expectations. As a lady doctor in Surat, combating the resistance of its small-town conservative population to sending their pregnant women to her hospital, she had to worry about her image among them. This resistance was strongest among the city's Hindus—more than amongst the Muslims and Parsis—and this would have made Rukhmabai, as a Hindu, particularly sensitive to what the local Hindus thought of her. The good work of eight years, that had transformed the 'golden girl' of orthodox imaginings into a doctor respected by the people, could have been threatened by her refusal to accept her widowed status.

She had, moreover, before her the example of a friend whose

commitment to the cause of women she admired. Pandita Ramabai, even after embracing Christianity, never deviated from the sartorial requirements of a Hindu widow. For her mission to be successful, Ramabai knew, it was important 'to reach Hindu women as Hindus'.[5] She and those others who worked for the upliftment of their Hindu sisters needed to be 'correct in their morals and conduct'.[6] Having chosen to fade out of the limelight, and do quiet medical work in a local arena, so important in the context of her times, Rukhmabai could not have neglected the pressure to be 'correct' in terms that made sense to the beneficiaries of her efforts.[7]

Also, while it made sense to repulse a husband who inspired revulsion but demanded cohabitation, the fight may have seemed to her futile once he was gone. The finality of death may have affected her even more profoundly, making her wonder if, after all, she had not been unjust to this man. Death, we know, can be surprising in its retroactive transformation of human feelings. Dadaji dead could have induced in Rukhmabai a tenderness that she had never felt towards him, a tenderness born of the relief that she could now really be what she had practically been all along, a widow.[8]

The old fire of youth may have mellowed in the two decades between the court case and his death, making her more prone in her forties to the force of that nebulous and virtually untranslatable category called sanskar. Whatever they were, in this moment of death—of sadness and liberation—her feelings could not have been unmixed. Kalidasa creates in the *Raghuvansham* a moment that encapsulates a woman's transition from one emotion to its very opposite. In a visibly advanced state of pregnancy, Sita is brought to a forest by Lakshman and informed that Rama has exiled her under suspicion of infidelity. She swoons with shock, recovers and, still distraught, sends a message to Rama. She asks Lakshman to tell 'that king'—not his brother, or her husband, not even Rama or the king—that he had witnessed her ordeal through fire that had established her purity. Does it become the illustrious house to which he belongs that he should thus renounce her for fear of hearsay? The Sanskrit verb used here for 'telling' the king, we may note, is one that denotes censure. From this angry denunciation, Sita's message dissolves into a rationalization of Rama's behaviour by blaming her own deeds in a previous birth. She resolves, once she has borne him a son (sic), she would undergo a *tapasya* that would make her his consort in the next life, and bind them together forever.[9]

Kalidasa's imaginative encapsulation of diametrically opposite affective responses perhaps reveals a structure of consciousness that has persisted over the centuries. It offers us a possible insight for reconciling Rukhmabai's behaviour in 1884 and 1904.

At play in Rukhmabai's defiance and 'conformance' is the dialectics that binds law, public opinion and social change in an interpenetrating causality. And in the dramatic nature of the two gestures, their unpredictability, appears the play, however vital or limited, of individual volition in the operation of this dialectics. Determined to have Pinhey's verdict reversed, and the law on the restitution of conjugal rights unchanged, organized orthodoxy discovered the futility of reliance on law. It could not invoke the penal measure—imprisonment—which was believed to give the existing law its power of deterrence. Rather, it accepted restraint as the better part of valour

So long as Rukhmabai was determined to rebel, neither the distant prospect of an adverse judgment nor, later, its imminence could hold her back. Her 'capitulation' came long after she had exposed the powerlessness of the legal system. If the contemporary Hindu/Indian society teemed with Rukhmabais whose potential rebelliousness remained repressed, it was because they were all along held back, as Rukhmabai eventually was,. not by law but by the weight of orthodox opinion and their socio-cultural schooling—*sanskar.*[10] In the continuing confrontation between orthodox and reformist forces, it only marginally mattered as to which of them had the law tilted in their favour.

The much touted deterrence of the imperious provision of imprisonment—one that even the courts could not moderate—was more imagined than real. The *de facto* helplessness of the penalty in Rukhmabai's case apart, its *de jure* 'terror' does not seem to have entered people's consciousness. No law that is not seen as terrible can terrify. For example, giving his opinion about the proposed amendment of the existing law, Lindsay Neill, the officiating commissioner of Nagpur division, could not understand 'the fuss and commotion' over the Rukhmabai case, because:[11]

> The provisions of section 260 of the Civil Procedure Code are permissive not imperative. Rukhmabai need not be imprisoned if she continue [sic] to refuse to go to her husband, and I would not, if I had to deal with the case, imprison her. Probably no Judge would think of doing so.

Neill's confident explication of what he believed to be the existing law stands out all the more sharply on account of its repudiation of the highest judicial and executive authorities' understanding of that law. Because the discretion enjoyed by the courts had, in 1877, been withdrawn by Whitley Stokes almost on the sly, the change escaped the notice of even many of those whose business it was to administer the laws. Moreover, the text of section 260 of the Civil Code easily lent itself to Neill's kind of interpretation. It provided:[12]

> When the party, against whom a decree for the specific performance of a contract or for restitution of conjugal rights, or for the performance of, or absetention from, any other particular act, has been made, has had an opportunity of obeying the decree or injunction, and has wilfully failed to obey it, the decree *may* be enforced by his imprisonment, or by the attachment of his property, or by both. (Emphasis added.)

The operative part of the provision 'may' seems to suggest that the courts possessed discretion in the matter of punishing recusancy. It is unlikely that there were no other Anglo-Indian officials who thought like Neill, although they may, unlike him, have discreetly assumed from the proposed amendment that they had been mistaken. In fact, even the Home Department officials took time, after receiving the Bombay government's SOS in 1887, to realize that the revised code of 1877 had divested the courts of their discretion.

The subject people, whom the law was expected to deter, knew no better. Even those among them who were otherwise well-informed shared Neill's view of the existing law. The eminent Parsi, Sir Jamsetji Jeejeebhoy, opposed any alteration on the ground that, enjoying 'ample discretion', no court was 'bound to enforce the penalty of imprisonment if it should not think fit to do so'. Kazi Shahabuddin, who had been an administrator in Kutch and Baroda and a member of the Bombay legislative council, believed that the courts possessed discretionary powers with regard to restraining both the person and the property of the recusant party.[13] Even assuming, hypothetically, the autonomous power of law over human behaviour, section 260 could not have exercised the kind of deterrence attributed to it, when there was such inadequate appreciation of its actual provision.

If deterrence was still exercised, it was a function of the strength possessed by organized social authority. This strength, despite the growing challenge of alternative ideas, not only ensured a fair measure of compliance from the people, but could also oblige the government to leave its own Law Member in the lurch, as it did when Miller's much diluted motion was unceremoniously dropped.

The higher judiciary, for its part, had an uncanny way of reflecting the transient balance of social forces, i.e. public opinion, within the larger society. The highest executive authorities, who also controlled legislation, called for detailed information and weighed the pros and cons before taking any significant policy or administrative decision on sensitive social matters. The judges, more often than not, ended up giving in these matters decisions that were unlikely to embarrass the executive. Acting neither in collusion nor in subordination, and always seemingly adhering to the facts presented before them, they tended to interpret the given laws generally in conformity with the dominant view thereof within the society.

There were, of course, differences within this larger cognitive uniformity. High Courts occasionally took conflicting positions about interpreting a given law, or about the need to alter it. But these differences remained properly constrained. However, when an aberrant decision, like Pinhey's, issued forth from these hallowed precincts of conservatism, the judicial process could be trusted to rectify the damage—and do so without lowering the rulers' moral superiority. Nor was this moral superiority, generally speaking, forsaken by others within the colonial administration and by the Anglo-Indian and English public opinion. Possessing, like the orthodox in India, their own polyphony, they also possessed, unlike the native orthodox, a logic—the masters' logic[14] —that converted their compromises and surrenders into a pursuit of principles by other means.

The higher judiciary in India has inherited, among so many other things, its colonial precursor's uncanny pragmatism. The balance of social forces, during the hundred odd years since Rukhmabai's case, has tilted just enough in favour of reformist ideas to make the exisiting law of restitution of conjugal rights about as liberal as the reformed English law of 1884. Though not impressive, this shift has resulted in decisions which reveal an appreciation of changing times. Illustrative of this is a tendency, albeit not undisputed,[15] towards an interpretation of 'cohabitation' that accommodates circumstances that require spouses to live separately. On balance, however, the attitude towards women and their status in marriage remains similar to the one that had caused the reversal of Pinhey's verdict.

This brings us to the tragic irony of the re-enactment, with cosmetic variations, of the drama of the 1880s in the 1980s. The irony illustrates the persistence of an elusive hard core of social consciousness beneath what feels like exponential change. In 1983 Justice Choudhury of the Andhra Pradesh High Court ruled that the remedy of restitution of conjugal rights, provided in section 9 of the Hindu Marriage Act, was void. Situating his judgment within the framework of the Indian Constitution, he declared that the remedy violated the right of privacy and human dignity. It transferred from the individual to the State the choice to have or not to have marital intercourse, and to allow or not to allow one's body to be a vehicle for the creation of another human being.

Available theoretically to both the spouses, the remedy actually operated as an engine of the wife's oppression by the husband. By treating the husband and the wife as equal, while in reality they were unequal, the remedy violated the rule of equal protection under the law. Since, moreover, it subserved no social good, Justice Choudhury pronounced the provision of restitution of conjugal rights arbitrary and void. He also drew pointed attention to the barbarous and imported nature of the provision. Introduced by the British in India, it had never been contemplated in the Hindu matrimonial law even though that law 'fully upheld the duty of the wife to surrender to her husband'. He regretted the continuance of the provision in India even after its abolition, in 1970, in England.[16]

This was in July 1983. Four months later, in *Harvinder Kaur v. Harmander Singh*, Justice Rohatgi of the Delhi High Court took a different view and upheld the validity of suits for the restitution of conjugal rights. The object of restitution, he ruled, was to enable the spouses to live together and preserve the marriage. The remedy involved no discrimination between the husband and the wife. Not accepting the stress laid by Justice Choudhury on sexual intercourse in marriage, Justice Rohatgi saw it as but one of the constitutive elements of marriage, and by no means its *summum bonum.*

Besides upholding the legality of restitution suits, Justice Rohatgi actually ordered the woman in this case to go to her husband, and did so in circumstances that highlight the deference higher judiciary still offers to conventional modes of thinking about women vis-a-vis men and marriage. The woman had told the court that she was willing to live with her husband if he set up an independent residence. What she objected to was living in the husband's joint family which she found 'irksome'. This Justice Rohatgi dismissed as 'trivial', and ordered her to resume cohabitation with her husband in the joint family.[17] It is important to note that the material circumstances of the husband, in this case, were such that he could, if he so desired, afford a separate residence.

Justice Rohatgi's judgment, which took great pains to refute Justice Choudhury's reasoning, is an index of the dominant mentality within the higher judiciary in relation to the changed circumstances, expectations and demands of women. Confronted with the conflicting claims of a wife and the joint family, this judicial authority supports the latter. It does so ostensibly to save *marriage* and not the *joint family.* In that a marriage is saved to save a family—that being the site for enacting the tragi-comedy of conjugality—Justice Rohatgi's utilization of the law of restitution of conjugal rights to save the joint family shows how, for this judiciary, the joint family continues to be the family. The deference traditionally shown to the *idea* of the joint family, consequently, obliterates the simple fact that nothing threatens conjugal harmony more than the joint family does. Derrett, unyielding in his advocacy of retaining the provision of the restitution of conjugal rights for Hindus, puts it bluntly: 'It is a very common thing for a wife to run away (not so much from her husband, who may be inert or stupid, as from her mother-in-law)...'[18]

The uncertainty caused by the conflicting interpretations of the Andhra Pradesh and Delhi High Courts lasted less than a year. In August 1984 the Supreme Court overruled Justice Choudhury and upheld the validity of the restitution of conjugal rights. Acting as a check against the break-up of marriage, the apex court ruled, the remedy served a social purpose. Also, that the Hindu Marriage Act contained sufficient safeguards to prevent marriage from becoming a tyranny.[19]

The identical fate of Pinhey's and Choudhury's powerful verdicts represents the persistence of certain dominant attitudes and beliefs. One is reminded of an entry in the diary of an eminent contemporary of Rukhmabai, Govardhanram Madhavaram Tripathi (1855–1907). An advocate of the Bombay High Court and a man of letters who, in the privacy of his *Scrap Book*, subjected to ruthless introspection what he experienced within and around him, Govardhanram wrote on 27 February 1906:[20]

> New circumstances will probably bring about some happier compromise. In the meanwhile, orthodoxy, with nature's gift of instinctive self-preservation, must hold its own as an iron wall, and reformers grow wiser and less sorrowful with their frequent knocking of heads against the wall, until the wall begins to crumble and the heads grow stronger by frequent exercise in knocking and breaking; and a new scheme of reciprocal adaptation between Family, Caste and Justice sparks out of the friction.

Described by Govardhanram with a degree of sympathy for the reformers, the process offers them few false hopes. By its very nature it does not admit of decisive resolutions of difficult social questions. We may recall that in the decade-long drama that forms the theme of this book, part of the orthodox role was directed to showing concern for women's interests. In its re-enactment a century later, what most upset Justice Choudhury's critics, including the Supreme Court, was his penetrating observation that restitution of conjugal rights acted as a legal facade for the oppression of women.

It is clear that the restitution of conjugal rights has brought no relief to women. We may recall that Justice Hannen, who precipitated the removal of the teeth of the restitution law in Victorian England, had 'never known' a restitution case not instituted for the ulterior purpose of enforcing a money demand. To that ubiquitous avarice is added in the Indian context—perhaps not there alone—the vindictiveness of husbands and the ready availability *to them* of forced sex within marriage. The additional motivation, however, does not justify the lofty spirit in which a Justice Choudhury is reminded that sex is only one of the elements that constitute marriage—more so a *sanskaric* marriage—and his verdict is set aside. Nor does it reflect much concern for women.

Hegemonic illusions have sustained the belief that the provision of restitution of conjugal rights subserves women's interests. To the extent women, and liberal reformers, share this belief, they continue to support a savage legal provision which, whatever it may or may not do, does little to help women. Once this clarity is widely shared, and reflected in public opinion, it may elicit from the ever pragmatic judiciary a decision accepting as legal, not aberrant, the Rukhmabai kind of refusal to be coerced into cohabitation. Whether it comes through legislation or judicial ruling, the desired resolution will have—following the familiar dialectics of law and public opinion—lessened the need for the reformed law. Meanwhile, the experience of a hundred and fifty years of legislative effort to remove certain social practices, such as child marriage, and promote others, like widow remarriage, warns against undue optimism. There is an inexorability about the process described by Govardhanram.

NOTES

1. Rukhmabai's letter of 17 February 1887 to Miss Goodwin, *Times*, 9 Apr. 1887.
2. Mohini Varde, *Dr. Rukhmabai: Ek Aart*, pp. 103–4.
3. During the long fifty-one years that she lived after Dadaji's death, Rukhmabai dressed only in white and also gave up other marks, such as putting on vermilion, traditionally reserved for a *sadhawa* woman, i.e. one whose husband is alive. Ibid., p. 96.
4. Already known to them when she reached England, Rukhmabai was readily welcomed by feminists. One of them, Millicent Garrett Fawcett, wrote about Rukhmabai in the newly launched but already important monthly, *The New Review*, no. 18, Nov. 1890. Earlier, in its Sept. 1890 issue, the *Review* had carried Rukhmabai's 'Indian Child Marriages: An Appeal to the British Government', pp. 263–9. For a critical evaluation of Millicent Garrett Fawcett, see Barbara Caine, 'Millicent Garrett Fawcett: a Victorian liberal feminist?', in Barbara Caine, E.A. Grosz and Marie de Lepervanche (eds.), *Crossing Boundaries: Feminisms and the Critique of Knowledge*, Sydney, 1988, pp. 166–79.
5. I take this perceptive observation from Rachel L. Bodley, the evangelical doctor who, having earlier helped Anandibai Joshi prosecute her medical studies in Philadelphia, organized an effective campaign to support Ramabai's scheme of shelter for young and high-caste child-widows. See her Introduction to Ramabai's *The High-Caste Hindu Woman*, p. XXIII.
6. This observation was made by Ramabai during her evidence before the Education Commission in 1883 in the context of providing female teachers for girls. Ibid., p. xvii. But, as her own example shows, it would apply to all those who, in a broad cultural sense, were seen as Hindu by the women among whom they worked. Even as a Christian, therefore, Ramabai continued to be an exemplar of Hindu conduct and morals. Such pragmatic considerations do not, however, rule out the possibility of deeper cultural impulses behind preferring certain 'Hindu' modes of conduct and behaviour.
7. Rukhmabai's choice of a modest arena was, in fact, part of a larger movement to make available female doctors to Indian women. Considering the problems of women's seclusion, the National Association for Supplying Female Medical Aid to the Women of India, popularly known as the Countess of Dufferin Movement, was organized around this time. Rukhmabai was the first doctor to be given charge of a

dispensary established at Surat under this scheme. Such was her dedication to her work, and the popularity she won, that the dispensary, named after Sheth Morarbhai Vijbhukhandas, the donor who provided money for it, continues to be popularly known as the Rukhmabai Hospital even today, a hundred years after she joined it. Significantly, the local legend does not remember her as a martyr to the cause of women's emancipation.

8. In the opening pages of *Brothers Karamazov*, Dostoevsky thus describes the reaction of Fyodor Pavlovich Karamazov on hearing of the death of his first wife, with whom he had had little connection: '... the story is that he ran out into the street and began shouting with joy... but others say he wept without restraint like a little child... It is quite possible that both versions were true...'

9. *Raghuvansham*, Chapter 14, verses 61–6. I have benefitted from my father's sensitive reading of these verses.

10. Citing as an example Manu's command that a 'virtuous wife' ought to revere her husband 'as a god' even if he be 'unobservant of approved usages, or enamoured of another woman, or devoid of good qualities', Gooroo Dass Banerjee remarks by way of showing the power of socialization: 'Nor have precepts like these been without their effect. The feelings which they serve to engender, often enable the wife calmly to bear her lot however unhappy, and to try to propitiate a cruel husband; and often prevent those vain bickerings which can only embitter life.' *The Hindu Law of Marriage and Stridhan*, p. 120.

11. *Home Department, Judicial Proceedings*, May 1890, nos. 410–715, National Archives of India.

12. The following is the full text of section 260 which related to a decree 'for specific performance or restitution of conjugal rights':
'When the party, against whom a decree for the specific performance of a contract or for restitution of conjugal rights, or for the performance of, or absetention from, any other particular act, has been made, has had an opportunity of obeying the decree or injunction, and has wilfully failed to obey it, the decree may be enforced by his imprisonment, or by the attachment of his property, or by both.
'When any attachment under this section has remained in force for one year, if the judgment-debtor has not obeyed the decree, and the decree-holder has applied to have the attached property sold, the property may be sold; and out of the proceeds the Court may award to the decree-holder such compensation as it thinks fit, and may pay the balance (if any) to the judgment-debtor on his application.
'If the judgment-debtor has obeyed the decree, and paid all costs of executing the same which he is bound to pay, or if, at the end of one year from the date of the attachment, no application to have the property sold has been made and granted, the attachment shall cease to exist.'
Section 342, relating to the term of imprisonment, provided:
'No person shall be imprisoned in execution of a decree for a longer period than six months;

'or for a longer period than six weeks if the decree be for the payment of a sum of money not exceeding fifty rupees.' J. O'Kinelay, *The Code of Civil Procedure, Act XIV of 1882 With Notes and an Appendix*, Calcutta, 1883, pp. 239-40, 313.

The use of 'may', not 'shall', in section 260 could create the impression of the provision being permissive. Similarly, 'a longer period than six months' in section 342 suggested that the resultant imprisonment could be for less than six months. Yet, the law was taken to imply that, on an application being made by the decree-holder, the courts were bound to send the judgment-debtor to jail for six months.

13. *Home Department, Judicial Proceedings*, May 1890, nos. 410–715.
14. Cf. Jean-Francois Lyotard, *Toward the Postmodern*, New Jersey, 1995, the chapter entitled 'On the Strength of the Weak', pp. 62–72.
15. For example, according to the Punjab and Haryana High Court ruling in *Kailash Vati v. Ayodhya Prakash*, the husband has the right to decide the place of the matrimonial home, and the wife must give up her job in order to live with him. 1977 *HLR*, 175..
16. *Sarita v. Venkata Subbayya* in 1983 AP 356. In what seems a striking omission in view of the way his judgment resonates Pinhey's, Justice Choudhury's impressive citation of case law does not include Pinhey's judgment.
17. 1984 Delhi 66.
18. J.D.M. Derrett, *A Critique of Modern Hindu Law*, Bombay, 1970, p. 326.
19. 1984 SC 1562.
20. Kantilal C. Pandya (ed.), *Govardhanram Madhavaram Tripathi's Scrap Book, 1904–06*, Bombay, 1958, vol. III, p. 67.

Appendix A

Rukhmabai's Letter in *The Times* of 9 April 1887

Bombay, February 17, 1887

My dear Madam,—I would thank you very much for the interest you so kindly take in my unfortunate trial, and in my native sisters in general. I learn from my friend... that you would like to know the particulars of my still pending case more minutely than I had written to you in my first letter.

Before explaining my own troubles, I should like to state a few facts concerning our disastrous child-marriage custom, which has enslaved the daughters (and even sons to a certain degree) of India for centuries. In our vast country, right from the Himalayas to Cape Comorin, it has become a rule that every individual must be married; be it a lame, blind, or diseased one. And by this rule it has become customary to betroth every child, male or female, at the age of five or six; but in higher classes at the minimum of one or two years of age; and sometimes (girls) even before they are born. Among the Hindoos only there are more than a thousand different castes, and inter-marriages even between the sects of slightest differences are strictly prohibited. This being the case, and by the pressure of child marriage, every parent is obliged to marry its child within the limit of the age and within the limit of its own caste, be it a fit or unfit match. In this way a robust promising youth gets a rickety consumptive wife, while an intelligent girl gets an inferior husband. Now for the Sastras and the Hindoo laws. It is clearly stated in our religious books that a boy should be entitled by the moony or thread ceremony to become a regular student from the age of eight years. After that he should study for 12 years, and then after having a good experience in the world for four years more should be allowed to marry at the age of 22 with a girl of suitable age and with his own accord. Well, for girls also it is stated that they should be allowed to marry when they become of age and with their own choice, though nothing has been said for their education. We find in ancient history marriages taking place between the boys and girls of mature ages and with their own liking. But these good laws have ceased to be observed and other pernicious customs have taken their place, the results of which lie before us in many horrible forms. As for castes, no more than four distinct classes—the Brahmins, the Kshatrias, the Vayshias, and the Sudras—are mentioned in our religion. But during the past two or three thousand years there has been a growing tendency to split up these four classes into many divisions, so that in some castes there are scarcely a few hundred people. By this fact it is clearly difficult for parents to find suitable and reasonable marriages for their children. Both the father of the boy and of the girl in looking for a husband or a wife for his child pay greater attention to the respectability and standing of the family than to the personal attributes of the child itself.

Lately, by the descent of India's fortune stars, all the worthy commands and precepts of our sacred religion were disobeyed and uncared for through ignorance and superstition, the consequences of which have proved deadly fatal, and India's material, physical, and spiritual condition has been totally ruined, and now she has piteously and helplessly to look to foreigners to get through the folly of her own people.

Now for my own misfortunes I belong to the second class of castes, in which, fortunately, widow re-marriage is allowed. In 1867 my own father died, leaving me, an orphan of two-and-a half years of age, in the care of my mother (then 17 years of age) and my maternal grandfather. Six years after that my mother was re-married with a celebrated doctor in Bombay, who proved an unusually kind stepfather to me. He protected and loved me as his own child throughout his life, but by the will of the Almighty his useful life was cut short, and for these 22 months, dear lady, he rests very far from us, leaving his widow and five children behind lamenting in vain. Well, according to the above-mentioned facts, I was married at the age of 11 years (an age rather beyond the limit of the fixed marriageable age in girls) with a boy of 19, on conditions that he should thoroughly be provided by us, but that he should study and become a good man. To these conditions he, his mother (who died a few months after the marriage), and relations had quite agreed. However, in a few months after the marriage in 1876... he began to neglect his duties, leaving the school, and, disobeying my father and grandfather, fell into bad companies. I should rather say the consequence of which was that he fell sick, and was attacked with consumption, confined to his bed for three continuous years, in such a state that he was not expected to live another season. But by God's grace he recovered a little day by day... Now, as for myself, being of much reserved disposition from childhood, I had a great liking for study while a great disgust for married life; and though not fortunate enough to attain school after the age of 11 years to complete Marathi studies, I began to learn English at home after leaving the school. I used to ask a number of pronunciations and meanings of English words at a time whenever my European lady friends happened to call. Day by day my love for education and social reform increased, and I continued to pursue my studies as much as I could; but in this country it is very hard for women to study at home. But constant association with the people who had tried to devote their lives to the social reform of India, and by the aid of the little education which I had been able to gain I began seriously to consider the former and present condition of our Hindoo women, and wished to do something, if in my power, to ameliorate our present sufferings. On the other hand, the... habits of the man with whom I had been given in marriage added more to my natural distaste for married life. However, my father, considering his constitution, habits, and unfitness for any work, resolved not to send me to his house to live as his wife. He also seemed indifferent to the matter... but by some former disputes between the leaders of our castes and the constant instigations of wicked people (very common in India), and in the hope of getting my little money, he was induced to file a suit making me to go and live as his wife. On the 19th of March, 1884, he filed it in the Bombay High Court, thinking that by this action my father would be afraid of losing his reputation (because to have a suit of this kind in a Court is considered a greatest disgrace among us Hindoos), and would quietly send me to his house with all that I possessed. Our party, having resolved long before never to send me to his house, did not care for his suit in that point (but, of course, money matters and the result of the suit were the points of deep interest), and so we began to prepare ourselves for the defence as it became necessary. On the 21st of September, 1885, the humane decision was given in my favour by Mr Justice Pinhey without taking our defence. The decision, if it had been supported, would have altered the fate of millions and millions of daughters of India, and the longed-for freedom would have been easily secured. In the same way Mr Justice Pinhey's name would have been made immortal. But it seemed the will of God that it should not be so; for the man appealed the case, on which it was decided on the 2nd of April, 1886 by the Chief Justice, Sir Charles Sargent, and Mr Justice Bayley that the first decision should be reversed, and that the case should be sent back for re-trial. Since then it is still pending in the Court.

In our matrimonial laws, or rather in the prevailing customs, a man can marry any number of wives at a time, or whenever he chooses to do so, keeping all of them with him, or driving away those for whom he does not care much; while a woman is wedded once for all. She cannot remarry even after the death of her first husband, nor can she deny to live with him even on reasonable grounds. He may ill-treat her, beat her, drive her away a thousand times, keep her without food, but she must submit to her lot and stay with him (if he keeps her) till she dies a natural death or is killed by him, her sole lord and master. Is it not inhuman that our Hindoo men should have every liberty while women are tied on every hand for ever? If I were to write you all about this system of slavery it would require months to complete it; but I refrain from doing so as everybody, even in England, is aware of it to some extent. The only thing I can hope is that it should be amended some day. Oh! but who has the power to venture and interfere in the customs and notions of such a vast multitude except the Government which rules over it? And as long as the Government is indifferent to it I feel sure that India's daughters must not expect to be relieved from their present sufferings. From some of the quotations in our old religious books I find it stated that women may marry in case of following five misfortunes:—(1) if she is a child widow; (2) if her husband has become a saint; (3) if he is wanting in manhood; (4) if he has converted; and (5) if he is a leper. None of these suit me in my misfortunes; but I also find that a woman can deny to become his wife before the consummation of marriage. However, these quotations are not unfortunately *reckoned* in the English book on Hindoo laws.

It seems to me to be an inevitable duty of the present Government (in spite of our old laws and customs) to have the most urgently required reform, suitable to the present age and state of the country. Evervwhere a law needs revision in at least a few centuries, to suit the prevailing ages; and how is it possible that our Hindoo matrimonial laws, formed about thousands of years ago, suit the present age (an age half-Europeanized)? The only way to face the difficulties is the law reform. For many years social reformers are trying to eradicate these pernicious customs, struggling hard in vain. Lately Mr Malabari (a Parsee gentleman) and his colleagues have roused the whole of India through their formidable efforts among innumerable opponents and few advocates; they have created a great stir throughout India to abolish child marriages and enforced widowhood. But alas! what can one person do without unity and support? By their continuous perseverance and requests the Indian Government was kind enough to make inquiries into the matter, asking the opinions of many influential Hindoo gentlemen: but to the greatest dissatisfaction of every reformer, the numbers of the opponents to the intended reform surpassed that of advocates, and all the aspirations of anxious reformers were thus at an end.

Everywhere it is considered one of the greatest blessings of God that we are under the protection of our beloved Queen Victoria's Government, which has its worldwide fame for best administration. If such a Government cannot help and unyoke us Hindoo women, what Government on earth has the power to relieve the daughters of India from their present miseries?

This 50th year of our Queen's accession to the most renowned throne is the jubilee year in which every town and every village in her dominions is to show their loyalty in the best way it can and wish the Mother-Queen a long happy life to rule over us for many years with peace and prosperity. At such an unusual occasion will the mother listen to an earnest appeal from her millions of Indian daughters and grant them a few simple words of change into the books on Hindoo law—that 'marriages performed before the respective ages of 20 in boys and 15 in girls shall not be considered legal in the eyes of the law if brought before the Court'. This mere sentence will be sufficient for the present, to have enough check on child marriages, without creating a great vexation among the ignorant masses.

This jubilee year must leave some expression on us Hindoo women, and nothing will be more gratefully received than the introduction of this mere sentence into our law books. It is the work of a day if God wished it, but without His aid every effort seems to be in vain. So far, dear lady, I have dwelt on your patience, for which an apology is necessary. With best compliments,

I remain, yours very sincerely.

RUKHMABAI.

To the Editor of *The Times*

Sir,—The sympathizing tone of the leading article on the case of Rukhmabai which appeared lately in *The Times* makes me feel confident that you will be willing to find space in your columns for the accompanying letter, which has been received by a member of my family from the poor woman herself. No words can plead her cause more eloquently than her own. Here is a woman whose letter testifies to her intelligence, her refinement, her elevation of character, condemned to the disgrace of imprisonment or to a life which to such a woman must be a living death. Is it necessary that a Government which abolished suttee should respect such a venerable relic of barbarous and cruel tradition and custom as that which compels wise and large-hearted Judges to become the means of inflicting intolerable torture upon defenceless women. Respect for native prejudices and feelings is necessary no doubt, but respect which practically leads to brutal cruelty is very unrespectable and ought to be made to give way to the laws of God and conscience and humanity.

How far Rukhmabai's suggestion of reform is capable and worthy of adoption I do not know. I send it to you because it is in her letter, not because I am prepared to support it as the best suggestion possible. But I am quite certain that I shall carry you, Sir, and all your readers with me, when I say that the appeal of the poor afflicted Hindoo woman to the Queen, with the reference to the jubilee, is infinitely pathetic. Your columns have lately teemed with jubilee suggestions and the merits of many schemes have been debated. There would be no difference of opinion, no debate, either in your columns or elsewhere, as to the propriety and superlative glory of a jubilee scheme which should emancipate our Indian sisters from a most degrading bondage.

I will only add that I send you Rukhmabai's letter as received—with the exception of the rectification of a few words in respect of orthography and the omission of one or two sentences which are suitable for a private letter but not for a public utterance. It will, of course, be understood that the responsibility of publication rests with me, and not with the writer of the letter. I feel confident, however, that in such a cause she will forgive me for the liberty which has been taken.

I am, Sir, your obedient servant,

HARVEY CARLISLE

Appendix B

Justice Pinhey's Letter in *The Times*, 27 April 1887

Sir,—The Case of Rukhmabai continues to excite the interest of the British public, and the letter which appears in the columns of *The Times* to-day, under the well-known initials 'F.M.M.', induces me to offer this contribution to the discussion of the subject, because what I have to say supports the view taken by 'F.M.M.' and I have special knowledge of the case. The notices of the case which have hitherto appeared in the public prints are I think misleading because incomplete. For instance, from the notices of the case which appeared lately in the leading articles of *The Times,* your readers have probably arrived at the conclusion that Mr Justice Pinhey, before whom the case was first tried, dismissed the suit simply because he sympathized with Rukhmabai, and considered that it would be a monstrous hardship to compel a young woman of 22 years of age, and of cultivated taste and possessed of many intellectual gifts and acquirements, who had gone through the ceremony of marriage without her consent during her infancy, to go and live with her husband, an ignorant journeyman carpenter, against her will, in order that the marriage might be consummated. The newspaper-reading public probably have no idea that Mr Justice Pinhey delivered a judgment of some length, in which he considered the provisions both of Hindoo law and of English law applicable to the case, and gave his reasons for considering that under neither law was the plaintiff entitled to a decree. The public seem to think that the judgment of the Court of First Instance was based on sentiment only, and that it was only when the case was brought before the Appellate Court, when Mr Justice Pinhey's judgment was reversed, that law was really applied to the case. I should like to dispel this illusion; for not only had Mr. Justice Pinhey a good deal to say on the law of the case, but the grounds on which he proceeded to dispose of the case are in effect the same as those stated in a more colloquial form by 'F.M.M.', and are those on which the case will be argued before the Privy Council, if (as is probable) the case is appealed to England.

Dealing with the case under Hindoo law, Mr Justice Pinhey pointed out that under Hindoo law a case such as this could not have come before the King—that is, before the Civil Court—but before the caste, and if the caste decided that Rukhmabai ought to go and live with her husband, it would only proceed to enforce its decision by ecclesiastical censures and penalties, such as excommunication and the like. As the parties to the case are Hindoos, who are entitled to have their own law administered to them, this would have been conclusive of the case if it had not been for the later action of the English Courts in suits for the restitution of conjugal rights. The English Courts, however, have of late years taken upon themselves to deal with suits for the restitution of conjugal rights between Hindoos, and the practice has prevailed too long for the local Courts in India now to refuse to recognize them. But as these suits are as between Hindoos the creation of English law, Mr Justice Pinhey in considering the case under English law held that he was not bound to carry the practice of the Court further than he could find precedent for doing. He pointed out that the case of Rukhmabai was not really one for the restitution of conjugal rights as ordinarily understood, but for the completion of the contract of marriage to which she had never given her consent by compelling her to go to her husband to have the marriage consummated. He also pointed out that no Court either in England or in India had gone the length of ordering a virgin wife to go and live with her husband, and finding no precedent for the order which he was asked to make, he refused to make such a precedent. Then Mr. Justice Pinhey went on to point out that the remedy sought, if to be enforced by imprisonment, was, even in England, where suits for the restitution of conjugal rights were of older origin, a discredited one; that in a late case in England (that of Mrs Weldon) the Court had refused to imprison a recusant husband who would not obey the mandate of the Court requiring him to go and live with his wife; and that, later still, the English Legislature had by statute done away with imprisonment as a mode for enforcing a decree for the restitution of conjugal rights. The result, of course, is that under the view of the law applicable to this case taken by the Appeal Court Rukhmabai, a Hindoo lady, is declared subject to the provisions of the English law of procedure in a suit for the restitution of conjugal rights, and to imprisonment under the provisions of the Indian Code of Civil Procedure in the certain event of her refusing to go and live with her husband in obedience to the decree of the Court, and that she does not get the benefit of the statutory relief without which the rigour of these decrees in England has been found to be intolerable.

The above statement will, I conceive, throw a new light on the case of the unfortunate Rukhmabai and give the British public further reason for extending to her its sympathy.

To carry on the history of the case. The plaintiff, Dadaji, brought the case before the Court of Appeal in Bombay, and that Court held that by taking cognizance of suits for the restitution of conjugal rights the Court had assumed to itself the jurisdiction formerly exercised by the caste, and was bound to give such relief as was the logical consequence of the exercise of such jurisdiction. The Appeal Court therefore reversed Mr Justice Pinhey's decree and remanded the case to the Court of First Instance for disposal on its merits, as the case had been stopped by the Judge at the first trial so soon as the case for the plaintiff was closed, without the case for the defence being gone into.

Intermediately, Mr Justice Pinhey had left India and so the case was called on before Mr Justice Farran, in order that the case for the defence might be considered. The defence pleaded by Rukhmabai was that her husband, Dadaji, was in bad health and too poor to maintain her. In dismissing the suit at the first hearing, Mr Justice Pinhey had noticed that this defence, even if supported by evidence, was no defence, and that a poor man was as much entitled to the companionship of his wife as a rich one. Consequently, no evidence was led for the defence before Mr Justice Farran, and that learned Judge, as a matter of course, gave effect to the judgment of the Appeal Court by decreeing that Rukhmabai should go to her husband.

Rukhmabai has now filed an appeal against Mr Justice Farran's decree in the Appeal Court in Bombay as a necessary preliminary to bringing the case before the Judicial Committee of the Privy Council. The Appeal Court in Bombay will, of course, reject the appeal, as there are no new facts in the case in addition to those which were before the Court when it reversed Mr Justice Pinhey's decree. As soon as the formal decree of the Appeal Court in Bombay is given, an appeal will be made to the Privy Council.

Rukhmabai has but small means. They are wholly insufficient to meet the costs of an appeal to England. Europeans and natives have joined in raising subscriptions in Bombay to enable Rukhmabai to bring her case before the final Court of Appeal in England. Many in England have professed sympathy for her. What will they do?

April 21.

R.H.P.

Appendix C

An Exposition of Some of the Facts of the Case

Dadaji Vs. Rakhmabai

The recent decision of the Hon. Justice Farran in the case of *Dadaji Vs. Rakhmabai* has caused no little public excitement in the press and elsewhere. While others, with and without knowledge, have been freely commenting on the case, my mouth has been closed and I have suffered in silence. While the case was *sub judice*, I did not think it right or prudent to place my views before the public, though I was reproached and maligned in many quarters times without number; but as the case is now concluded, and the anticipated decision has been pronounced, I now submit a few of the facts of the case to show how grossly I have been misrepresented by a portion of the Anglo-Indian and the English Press as well as by a few self-styled 'Reformers'. In some instances these misrepresentations were made in ignorance, in others in wilful malice, while in all there is an absence of 'fair play'. The facts are these. At the time of my marriage with Rakhmabai, I was 20 years of age and my wife was 13 years. One Junardhun Pandurang was the natural father of my wife. After his death, which occurred in 1867, his widow, Jaentibai, married the late Dr Sakharam Arjun, re-marriage in our caste being permitted. Some time after the re-marriage of Jaentibai, my marriage with Rakhmabai was solemnized, according to the most approved form of our religion, with the full consent and approval of my wife's stepfather, Dr Sakharam Arjun, her mother, Jaentibai, and her grandfather, Mr Harichandra Jadowji. The marriage was sought for by Rakhmabai's family. Seven months after her marriage, my wife, Rakhmabai, reached puberty. The marriage was not at once consummated because Dr Sakharam

Arjun volunteered the opinion that an early consummation would result in the issue of a weak progeny, and he told me this in a friendly way, while I accepted his advice in the same friendly spirit. My wife, Rakhmabai, was therefore, in deference to Dr Sakharam's wish, permitted to remain with her mother and stepfather. In 1884 I asked that my wife might be allowed to come and live with me, as I thought the probation period had lasted long enough. To my surprise this request was the signal for the open hostility, not of my wife, Rakmabai, be it remembered, but of her mother, Jaentibai, and her grandfather, Mr Harichandra Jadowjee, who feared that if Rakhmabai came to live with me, she would assert her right to the property of her deceased father, the late Mr Junardhun Pandurung, and which property is of the estimated value of upwards of Rs.25,000. This property devolved upon my wife, Rakhmabai, upon the remarriage of her mother, Jaentibai, with the late Dr Sakharam Arjun. My mother-in-law, Jaentibai, and her father, Harichandra Jadowji, are now in the enjoyment of the said property. I have never quarrelled with Rakhmabai, nor have I ever given her occasion to dislike me. In this little history of property lies the whole secret of the world-wide case of *Dadaji vs. Rakhmabai.* There is property in the case, and also a mother-in-law, both very good things in their way, but beyond these two great social factors there is nothing special, and absolutely nothing Hindu, in it. The case might have originated in any non-Hindu family, and amongst persons of any caste or class, as very frequently happens amongst those other classes, as all the Indian world knows.

In order to prove that neither the late Dr Sakharam Arjun nor my wife, Rakhmabai, nor her mother, Jaentibai, nor her father, Mr Harichandra Jadowji, regarded my marriage with Rakhmabai as objectionable on account of my education or my physical health, I here transcribe Dr Sakharam's letter to my solicitors, Messrs. Chalk and Walker. It is dated the 22nd of March 1884, and was written in reply to my request to allow my wife, Rakhmabai, to come and live with me:

> 'Gentlemen,—In reply to yours of the 19th instant, I have to inform you that Rakhmabai, mentioned therein, has not been detained at my house against the wishes or demands of your client, Mr Dadaji Bhikaji. Her stay at my house hitherto has been by the consent of the relatives on both sides, because of the unfortunate circumstances of your said client.
>
> 'I have not the slightest wish to detain her even now, and I shall be rather glad if your client provides her with a suitable house and takes

her away, which is however his own look out. He is at liberty, so far as I am concerned, to take her away at any time.

Yours faithfully,

(Sd.) SAKHARAM ARJUN

It will be perceived that the only ground of objection raised in this letter to my removal of Rakhmabai to my own family-house is the objection of my 'unfortunate circumstances' and the want of a 'suitable house'. These are clearly both after-thoughts, as no change had taken place in my 'circumstances', and our family-house was neither better nor worse than it was when I married Rakhmabai. The objections are just those that would occur to a man who had no real objection to offer. The reference which is made to 'the consent of relatives on both sides' refers to my acceptance of Dr Sakharam's advice not to consummate my marriage at an early period, and which I thought had gone far enough in 1884. Had the subsequent charges which were made against me by the persons who were fighting the property-battle behind the scenes, and who put these charges into the mouth of my wife, Rakhmabai, had any, even an atom of foundation, to sustain them, they would certainly have been made by such an intelligent and observant man as the late Dr Sakharam, and would have found a place in his letter to my solicitors. Dr Sakharam was anxious to let Rakhmabai go, but, like King Pharoah with the Israelites, somebody was 'hardening his heart' and pulling at the reins. For how does he conclude his remarkable letter? He says he (Dadaji) is at liberty, so far as I am concerned, to take her (Rakhmabai) away at any time. From this statement it is quite manifest that Dr Sakharam had no objection to the removal of my wife to my family residence: the real obstruction was elsewhere, and was with the holders of the property.

It will be observed that at this period in the history of the case I had made a demand, through my solicitors, that I should be allowed to take home my wife, Rakhmabai, and that I had been met by evasion, innuendo, and equivocation, and many neighbours knew what had happened. Whether it was in consequence of these occurrences, and the spreading of the intelligence that my demand to have my wife was illegally resisted, I am unable to say; but I know that certain anonymous communications were received by Dr Sakharam as to his conduct in harbouring my wife in an unjust way against my wishes. Dr Sakharam sent for me and told me that my wife's grandfather, Mr Harichandra Jadowji, suspected me as the author of these communications; and he added that it would be to my interest and advantage if I would give him a written statement, saying that there was no truth in the said communications; at the same time he produced a draft of a letter in his own handwriting to this effect, and asked me to sign it and present it to him. I became indignant, felt that a trap was prepared for me, and refused to sign the letter, knowing that the statements which were contained in the letters which Dr Sakharam had received were perfectly true, although the letters were not written by me. On my refusing to sign, Dr Sakharam lost his temper and left me.

On the day after my solicitors received the letter from Dr Sakharam previously referred to, I sent my brother, Mr Damodhar Bhikaji, my uncle, Mr Narayen Dhurmaji, and my solicitor's clerk, to Dr Sakharam Arjun's house to invite my wife, Rakhmabai, to accompany them to my house, according to the custom of my caste, with a promise that I would provide for her according to my means. My brother and uncle were informed that my invitation was declined, and they were dismised, having completed a fruitless errand. I was thus publicly disgraced before my caste, and was entrapped into sending an inviting party to Dr Sakharam's house by the terms of his letter to my solicitors to 'take her away at any time'. The relations between the two families had thus become still more strained than they proviously were: the rich considered it their right to insult and disgrace the poor. Then some further correspondence ensued, which exhibited a still greater Pharoaic hardness of heart towards letting Rakhmabai go. I was thus driven to the necessity of appealing to the law, and I filed a suit for the institution or restitution of my conjugal rights. My wife, Rakhmabai, was necessarily made the defendant of this suit, and under the influence and advice of her grandfather, Mr Harichandra Jadowji, and my mother-in-law, Jaentibai, filed a written statement with the view of resisting my claim. The grounds of defence set forth in this statement were now for the first time, on happy second thoughts, enlarged to—

(1) 'the entire inability of the plaintiff to provide for the proper residence and maintenance of himself and his wife;'

(2) 'the state of the plaintiff's health in consequence of his suffering frequently from asthma and other symptoms of consumption;' and

(3) 'the character of the person under whose protection the plaintiff was and is living in the house in which the plaintiff called on the defendant to join him'.

There is nothing about 'consent' or 'loathing' in this deliberately prepared statement: these were subsequent promptings, and may be increased *ad infinitum* if found useful.

As to the first allegation, I say I never refused to provide my wife with a maintenance. The means of my family enabled me to make quite as good a provision as is made in hundreds of other Hindu families in similar circumstances. From a Hindu point of view, and after a marriage had been made, the allegation in the objection is peurile. If placed before any panchayat in India, it would be at once rejected.

The second allegation is quite baseless. It was proved on undoubted medical evidence at the hearing of the case that my health was sound then as it is sound now. Dr Gopal Sewaram, one of the leading native medical gentlemen in Bombay, gave the following evidence:

> 'I examined plaintiff yesterday evening and found the lungs quite clear. The bronchial tubes are not affected. I treated him about two weeks ago. I should call him a robust man.'

Dr Vithul Rao Pandurang gave the following evidence:

> 'Plaintiff has no consumptive tendency; at least none is manifested at present. I have examined his lungs since the attack of pneumonia. They are a little weak, owing to his getting a recent cold.'

The allegation in regard to 'asthma' and 'consumption' is thus completely dispelled by careful medical examination.

As to the third allegation, in regard to the questionable character of a person who was living in our family-house, the attempt to prove it completely broke down at the trial.

Both during the hearing of the case and subsequently, I have repeatedly been described as an ignorant, uneducated person, and my wife, Rakhmabai, as a woman of high education and great intellectual refinement. The statements have been made to my injury, and the comparison has been instituted to injure me still more. Both statements are untrue. My education is equal to the education of my wife, Rakhmabai; but of this let those who sufficiently know us both be the judges. This supposed intellectual disparity between myself and my wife has been made the most of, and the intelligence has been spread alike over India and over Christendom. My wife, Rakhmabai, put in a written statement in the case of *Dadaji vs. Rakhmabai*, which will be found on page 12 of Suit 139 of 1884. It was necessary that she should attest this statement; but how and under what circumstances did she do so? She affixed her signature in two places, not in English, but in Marathi. Being unable to understand her own statements as they appeared on the record in English, they had to be interpreted to her at the time of attestation. The record of the case shows that the statements were 'interpreted (to Rakhmabai) by me, Narayen R. Malpeker, Sworn Interpreter, 5th July 1884'.

It is with the utmost reluctance that I dissipate the gross fiction that my wife, Rakhmabai, was the writer or author of the English letters which appeared in the *Times of India* over the signature 'A Hindu Lady', but, as I have been compelled to publish the facts of the cases of *Dadaji vs. Rakhmabai* the truth must be told, and I say that my wife, Rakhmabai, is not the author of the English letters referred to: this fact is notorious over a large circle of native society. The intellectual degradation with which the fiction-loving journals accredit me, appears to be one of the necessary characters in the case. If the heroine is to be represented as a great scholar, then a hero must be furnished who is a great fool. I claim no high intellectual qualities; all I contend for is that Rakhmabai is by no means my intellectual superior. At the same time it is my duty to confess that although I have myself put together these notes in English, they have been revised by a male friend.

An attempt has been made by some newspapers to show that my wife, Rakhmabai, has been fighting out the case of *Dadaji vs. Rakhmabai* on behalf of the millions of her countrywomen. It is complete ignorance of the realities of the case that has enabled these leaders of public opinion to arrive at this conclusion. I trust that the facts of the case which I have now given will render it quite evident that that scrupulous gentleman, Mr Harichandra Judowji, has alone caused this family rupture, and that a question of property has been represented to the public as a question of Hindu marriage. Can astute jugglery be carried further than this? If the name Harichandra is substituted for the name Rakhmabai in this case, its realities will be better understood but its poetry will be gone. How careful should Anglo-Indian journals be when they allow themselves to get "mixed up" in questions of caste dispute. I say deliberately, and with a full knowledge of the facts, that the rupture between me and my lawful wife, Rakhmabai, has not been caused by any intellectual inequality between us, by any poverty of mine, or by any active or latent disease in my system, but solely by the cupidity and love of gain on the part of persons behind the scenes, who have not the courage to come forward and do openly the mischief which they are doing secretly. Is the case of *Dadaji vs. Rakhmabai* a Hindu matrimonial question, or is it simply a question of human frailty? Let the reader judge. I here transcribe translation of a Marathi will, the will of the late Mr Janardhun Pandurang, my wife's father, for the purpose of proving the chief matter in the suit.

SHREE (PROSPERITY)

WILL.—The 16th day of the month of June in the year 1867. On that day, I, Junardhun Pandurang, not being in a good state of health, and knowing that there is no certainty of this body, do, in my sound mind and understanding, write my will as follows:

There are the property belonging to my deceased father, Tirthroop Pandurang Manikji, and my own property as follows:

1. A dwelling-house and a chawl adjoining it and the ground underneath the same bearing Nos. 27 and 28.
2. Another house which is on the back road, Gamdevi, together with the land bearing Nos. 21 and 22.
3. A house and a garden, No. 237, which is on the Chowpatty road, a share therein being a moiety thereof is mine, and the remaining moiety belongs to Rajeshri Bhasker Wittoba.
4. Besides what is written above, the household furniture and ornaments, & c., and all other articles whatever there may be.

My wife, Jaenti, is heir to all the abovementioned landed estate and furniture, and for the purpose of taking care of that estate, I have appointed my father-in-law, Rajeshri Harichand Judowji, executor. He is to manage this my estate with the consent of my wife, and when she will find it convenient she is to adopt, with the consent of my executor, a good son for the purpose of my ancestors' name. No one else besides my wife has a right of inheritance of this my estate. Out of the above mentioned estate a legacy of Rs.300 to be paid to my sister, Ladubai, the wife of Dhakji Nanaji, and a legacy of Rs.300 to be paid to another sister, Benabai, the wife of Raghoba Bhikaji, and Rs.100 in cash are to be paid to the person who will perform my funeral ceremonies; and the marriage ceremony of my daughter, Rakhmabai, is to be performed according to my respectability; and a legacy of Rs.200 is to be paid for the marriage expenses on the occasion of the marriage ceremony of Chirwanjiwi Gungabai, the daughter of my sister. I have made this will of my free will and pleasure, and in my sound sense and understanding, in the presence of four several respectable gentlemen.

(Sd.) JUNARDHUN PANDURANG

Attestation.

(Sd.) WITTOBA JEEWANJI

(Sd.) GUNESH RAMJI

From this will it be perceived that my mother-in-law, Jaentibai, was left sole heiress to the property of her first husband, Mr Junardhun Pandurang. By her second marriage with the late Dr Sakharam Arjun she became disinherited, and my wife, Rakhmabai, became the sole heiress. If this will and this property had had no existence, there would have been no case of *Dadaji vs. Rakhmabai*, and there would have been no separation between myself and my lawful wife.

The only way in which the case of *Dadaji vs. Rakhmabai* can affect Hindu marriage reform is by attracting irreligious, disobedient, wilful, and unscrupulous persons to follow the course which that case points out. What will this do for Hindu social life, and what will be its effects upon society? If religious pledges are to go for nothing, then where does morality begin? It is both a precept and a divine law to the Hindus that it is a wicked and an undutiful act on the part of girls or women to form matrimonial connections without the consent of their parents or relatives. When such unions are made with care and consideration, as was my marriage with Rakhmabai, I ask if it is not incumbent on every Hindu, man and woman alike, to do all that in them lies to render the union happy? Non-Hindus did not understand this matter; it has formed no part of their religious training; but to a Hindu it is at once conscience, reason, and religion. No censure which non-Hindus may apply to the system, no ridicule which they can throw upon it, can change the faith in this doctrine of the Hindu who values his religion. The true Hindu will suffer martyrdom for it. I appeal with boldness to all my co-religionists, for they alone can understand my feelings and the power of the doctrine which I have endeavoured to explain. My wife, Rakhmabai, is made to say that a pure mutual affection cannot be maintained in a poor and humble abode. This is what is meant by reproaching me with the terrible sin of poverty. My wife's counsel took the greatest delight in tormenting me about questions with a view to elicit my poverty in order to prove—and perhaps he thinks he has proved—that

Rakhmabai is incapable of loving, or living with, a poor man. I know that persons do constantly marry against the advice and remonstrances of their parents, other relatives, or guardians, and that some of these over-wise persons are Hindus. But I know, too, that the end of most of these unions is life-long misery and torment, if not something worse. May I not appeal to my European readers to help me in this question? Hindu marriage is a sacrament and not a civil contract. The ceremony of seven steps makes it complete and binding on both sides. And this has been my marriage with Rakhmabai. That being so, the custody of my said wife's person and her property belong as a right to me as her lawful husband. If I am a poor man in the conventional sense, does my poverty place me outside the pale of justice? It does not. If I am to-day an unmarried man legally wedded to Rakhmabai, and if my wife, Rakhmabai, is to-day a married woman without a husband, we have not been placed in this unfortunate position by Hindu law or by the Hindu marriage system, but solely by persons whose conduct I will not more plainly criticize than is unfolded in the facts set forth in this my first and only public defence.

If there happens to be a woman in the case I am sorry for it; that woman was thrust into that position; it was given to her as an inheritance; and she is now compelled for very shame's sake to play out the part allotted to her. I feel my misfortune in having to write one word against a woman, and have endeavoured, by every means in my power, to soften my remarks to the very uttermost that the case will allow, for I know how imaginationists, and sentimentalists, and the busybodies in the affairs of their neighbours, will prepare to apply their unctuous criticism to me. But I write for those who can judge the case of *Dadaji vs. Rakhmabai* with reason, and with a full knowledge of the Hindu religion and Hindu feeling; and perhaps also for some who, though not Hindus, can discern the central and salient facts of this case, and to these readers I will leave the final decision. When all the world, including the London *Times,* was discussing my case, and I remained silent, I knew I was losing ground; but my friends advised me to await the termination of the case before placing myself at the bar of public opinion. I have waited for this termination of the case. It has now terminated in so far as I am concerned. I was treated cruelly and maliciously, and was maligned, caricatured, and grossly libelled by third parties lurking privily and securely behind the scenes; by fourth parties writing ignorantly, if not maliciously, in the press;

and by fifth parties who took entire charge of their neighbours' affairs for the purpose of settling the matrimonial affairs of the world; and under all this undeserved obloquy I remained silent, and have suffered by my silence. I have now been driven to put in this written defence. Let the readers endeavour to imagine themselves in my circum-stances, fighting known but unseen foes, forced into a case which had the outside features of a case of honour and morality, but which was within a mass of corruption, covetousness, and deceit. The Hindu religion and the Hindu marriage system has had nothing whatever to do with it, and as a Hindu, and one of the first persons concerned, I contend that I am entitled to pronounce unerring judgment upon this material point in the case.

I have been awarded the costs of this suit by the Hon. Justice Farran. I am influenced by no revengeful feelings against my persecutors, and if I could afford to do so I would be indifferent about the costs. But the case has put me and my family to very great expense, which I cannot well afford. My circumstances will therefore compel to [sic] me to demand the payment of these costs. Unless my persecutors are prepared to afford proof to all the world that they have been wholly influenced by money and not by love to Rakhmabai, they will themselves contribute from their own purses the costs which they have brought upon Rakhmabai, and will not allow Rakhmabai or her European friends to pay the costs of their inconsiderate and selfish conduct. I can only say that it is but the barest justice that I should have my costs, including the costs of the appeal, which are too heavy and not yet awarded, and the persons who forced on the action should pay these costs.

BOMBAY, 11th April 1887 DADAJI BHIKAJI

Appendix D

Rukhmabai's 'Reply' to Dadajee's 'Exposition'

There appeared some time since over the signature of Mr Dadajee Bhikajee in the newspapers, as well as in a separate pamphlet form, what is called 'An Exposition of Some of the Facts of the Case of *Dadajee vs. Rukhmabai*'.

As most of the facts mentioned in this 'Exposition' are fictions, pure and simple, I could not do Mr Dadajee Bhikajee the injustice of crediting him with a knowledge of what has been put before the public in his name. Mr Dadajee Bhikajee cannot write or well understand English; he knows nothing about the Jews in Egypt, or who was *Phaorah* [sic], and these references show that a *Christian* hand has helped to write the so-called 'Exposition'. But some of my friends think that several of the statements in the 'Exposition' should receive public contradiction from me; I defer to their wishes, though in doing so I remember that I am in an exceptionally delicate position.

The following are some of the assertions made in the 'Exposition', and which the public is asked to believe.

ASSERTION	CONTRADICTION
1. At the time of my marriage my wife was 13 years.	I was only 11 years.
2. The marriage was sought for by Rukhmabai's family.	It was sought for by Mr Dadajee's mother, who had for years importuned my mother and grandfather to marry me to one of her sons.
3. This was a signal for open	Mr Hurrichand Yadowjee did

hostility of her mother and her grandfather.	not meddle in these matters, as everything with regard to me was then done by Dr Sakharam.
4. My health was sound then as it is sound now.	Quite untrue.
5. The property is of the estimated value of upwards of Rs.25,000.	It was not worth even half that sum.
6. My mother-in-law and her father are now in the enjoyment of the property.	Neither of them is.
7. The statement that any circumstances had changed is an after-thought.	They are not after-thoughts; the change in Mr Dadajee's circumstances was that four months after the marriage his mother died, and his family house was broken, and he went to live with persons of objectionable surroundings and gave up studies and good habits.
8. I asked for the removal of my wife to my family house.	This is a misnomer. Mr Dadajee had no family house. As he correctly puts it, in his plaint, what he should say is the 'house he resided in'.
9. I have never quarrelled with Rukhmabai, nor have I given her occasion to dislike me.	There is some truth in the first assertion, the other is untrue.

Some of these points I give in detail below.

Both my late lamented step-father, Dr Sakharam Arjun, as well as Mr Dadajee's mother, the chief contracting parties to my marriage, are dead.

As I was married by Dr Sakharam, and as he looked to my education, &c. everything relating to me was referred to him. Mr Hurrichund Yadowjee was only formally consulted as he was my natural father's executor.

My mother and my grandfather are said to be in the enjoyment of my property: I cannot understand in what sense the word 'enjoyment' is used. My mother is not connected with my property in any manner whatever. My grandfather, as my executor, collected rents, &c. for a long time, but he submitted the accounts to me, and I checked them myself. Since 1882, long before Mr Dadajee filed his present suit, I had opened an account with the Bank of Bombay in my own name.

The death of Mr Dadajee's mother wrought a great change in his 'circumstances'. Mr Dadajee began to lead a wild reckless life, and went and lived with an uncle whose surroundings are most objectionable. I should have stopped here, but the person who writes for Mr Dadajee has the audacity to say that 'in regard to the questionable character of a person who was living in our family house, the attempt to prove it completely broke down'. In paper book containing the evidence in the present suit, printed under the superintendence of Mr Dadajee's attorneys, it will be found on pages 21, 28, and 31, that Mr Dadajee, his brother, and his uncle admitted the fact that what is conveniently called a person lived in the house of his uncle. The relationship of that person to Mr Dadajee's uncle would have been proved if witnesses on my side had been examined. But the presiding Judge did not think it worth while to take any defence. It is abusing language to say after this, that the attempt completely broke down. I have to reluctantly observe that *this person* is no other than a mistress of Mr Dadajee's uncle, who has been living in his house for some 14 years, as admitted by him; and to avoid whose tyranny the lawful wife of this man had once jumped into a well. I did not wish to live in the same house as the companion of this woman. If Mr Dadajee never quarrelled with me, it is because I have been never with him since the day of my marriage; when he says that he gave me no occasion for disliking him, he is mistaken. He abused my relatives, including my mother, in language which was shameful. He set at defiance the efforts made by my father and grandfather to educate him, and took to ways which a woman's lips cannot utter. Mr Dadajee went through every course of dissipation till my aversion for him was firmly settled. Having watched his movements for the last five or six years, I gave him as irreclaimably lost, *and made up my mind to wash my hands of him for ever.*

The person who has written the 'Exposition' for Mr Dadajee asserts that I am merely a tool in the hands of others, and that I am compelled to fight out the suit by those who are behind the scenes, and who are in possession of my property. There is not a particle of truth in this. My mother inherited the property absolutely by the will of my father, and that I received it is purely due to her affection for me. Before marrying the late Dr Sakharam Arjun, she could have, if she had wished, claimed and disposed of it herself.

Mr Dadajee's writer conveniently omits a few words in the copy of my father's will, that he gives to the public so as to change the meaning. In the will the reference to me is 'the marriage ceremony of my daughter, Rukhmabai, is to be performed according to my respectability, and a *legacy of Rs. 200 is to be paid to her.*' The word [sic] in italics are purposely omitted by Mr Dadajee.

Another person has insinuated that it is my grandfather, Rai Bahadoor Hurrichand Yadowjeė, who has interfered. Even when my step-father, Dr Sakharam, lived, and I had the benefit of his guidance and advice, Mr Hurichand Yadowjee managed my estate and rendered to me accounts of rents, &c. This he did because he was my executor. The present suit was filed while Dr Sakharam lived. Mr Dadajee is aware of this, and also knows that my mother inherits in her person from my father, Dr Sakharam, money over and above what I inherited from my natural father. He knows that each of her other children is better provided for than myself. He also knows that Mr Hurichand Yadowjee is a well-to-do man, whose long and faithful service has been rewarded by Government with a special title and a special personal allowance in addition to his pension. Knowing all this, Mr Dadajee wants the public to believe that both of them have combined for the nefarious purpose of depriving me of my property, of what belongs to me of right, and brought about this separation, as a means of attaining that end.

Another base suggestion made by an irresponsible party is that Dr Sakharam Arjun wanted to secure my (Rukhmabai's) money to his own family. Need I say that all these insinuations with regard to property are entirely false and made to divert the public mind from the real issues in the matter? I am so far satisfied with their treatment of my property that I have no hesitation in regarding these statements with the contempt they deserve. Mr Dadajee wants the public to believe that he was and is in a position to provide a suitable house for me; I have therefore out of sheer necessity to tell the public what Mr Dadajee said about his earnings in his evidence in the Court. 'Besides my uncle, during the last year I earned no money from any one except Rs. 2 or 4 for preparing plans. I did work for Narayen Wittoba, and he paid me Rs. 5. This was the largest sum I got from an outsider.' Mr. Dadajee made an attempt to show that he got annually Rs. 500 or 600 for work done for his *uncle.* But when asked to support this statement, he admitted that he had not a scrap of paper to prove his statement.

The uncle, though contradicting Mr Dadajee in several material points, said that he paid him Rs. 450 or 500 annually for superintending the work *of brick-layers, carpenters and labourers.* But when asked to show by documents what sums he had paid to Mr Dadajee, the convenient answer was, that he kept no accounts, made no entries and took no receipts. About the evidence on this point, the learned Judge observed: 'The plaintiff (Dadajee) gave much false evidence as to his pecuniary position, and his uncle, who was examined on plaintiff's behalf on the same point, gave, if possible, evidence less credible still.' But even assuming for a moment that Mr Dadajee got the money he professes to get annually, it will be seen that he was entirely dependent for his income on the sweet will of his uncle, as he could scrape together nothing more that Rs. 5 or 10, if so many, during a year, from any other source. Naturally Mr Dadajee is therefore under the control of an uncle, the less said about whose surrounding the better. This uncle has it in his power to turn Mr Dadajee out of his house, and then where would be Mr Dadajee's family residence, and his means to provide a suitable lodging for his wife? Lately an attempt has been made to show that Mr Dadajee is able to earn Rs. 35 a month, 'not a cooley's, but a graduate's salary in these days', as one of his friends say [sic]. If the detailed circumstances of this employment, its nature, and its duration be stated, it will be found that obliging friends cannot provide convenient berths always, and I hear that Mr Dadajee has again reverted to his dependence on his uncle.

Mr Dadajee, relying upon the evidence of the two native medical gentlemen, who were called on his behalf, and who said that at the moment they examined him, they found his lungs not affected, exclaims that the allegation in regard to 'asthma and consumption' is thus completely *dispelled by careful* medical *examination.* My late father, Dr Sakharam, had been treating Mr Dadajee off and on for years, and he was in a better position to judge of his general health than a couple of doctors, called at a particular moment, and whose opinion was given off-hand. He shunned the medical examination to which he was invited by my solicitors in their letter of 25th July 1884. First, Mr Dadajee's solicitors wished exactly to know, what I believed Mr Dadajee to be suffering from; when a specific statement was made, Mr Dadajee quietly declined to submit to the examination. A particular Hindu Doctor, moreover, whose sympathy for Dadajee yields in intensity only to his desire to abuse and vilify me, says: 'Dr Sakharam had entertained sanguine hopes of Dadajee turning out an ordinary school boy, but *disease weakened* him, or call it, if you so please, perversity, indolence, or dullness prevented him from reaping the fruit of early education.' Again, Mr Dadajee's brother said in his evidence: 'Plaintiff's health has *deteriorated for some years past.*' This is the testimony of men who cannot be accused of saying anything in my favour, and who had better and more constant opportunities of seeing Mr Dadajee, than the two doctors whose evidence he quotes.

Mr Dadajee's writer gets hold of the fact, that my written statement in the case, was signed in Marathi, and declares that I could not understand my own statement, it had to be interpreted to me, and therefore I signed in Marathi. The statement was interpreted to me as a mere *formality*, and I was asked to sign it in my usual way. I naturally signed it in Marathi. If I had attached any importance to the fact, I should have signed in English. If the statement had to be interpreted to me because *I did not understand English*, why was it interpreted to Mr Dadajee, who is capable of writing the 'Exposition,' and it is asserted, had studied up to the VI Standard! If the reader cares to see, let him refer to suit No. 139 of 1884, page five, and he will find the record of the case was interpreted to Mr Dadajee in the same way as it was done to me, and signed by Mr Narayen R. Malpeker, sworn Interpreter, 24th April 1884. How far Mr Dadajee under-stands English, much less Marathi, will be seen from the following portion of his evidence. It will also show his habit of making reckless assertions, and then backing out of them. In the plaint which was interpreted to him, Mr Dadajee asserted that I was prevented from going to live with him by my mother and grandfather, because in that case 'She should assert her right to the property of her deceased father', which the plaintiff *contends devolved upon the remarriage of the said Jayentibai with Dr Sakharam Arjun.* When questioned on this point in the Court, Mr Dadajee replied (see pages 23 and 25 of the said suit):

'I have not read the will carefully and cannot say whether under it, defendant takes only a legacy of Rs. 200, and her marriage expenses.' 'I have read the will, but have forgotten its contents! The instructions for my plaint were given by me so far as I know. I stated the facts of the case to the managing clerk, and he got the plaint drawn. I gave some of the instructions for this para, so far as I knew them to the managing clerk, and the case was framed by the managing clerk. I did not tell the managing clerk that her father's property devolved upon my wife on the marriage of her mother. I cannot say whether the property has devolved upon my wife. I make no such contention. The managing clerk put it into the plaint.'

Let the reader contrast the foregoing assertions made on *oath* with what appears in the 'Exposition,' and test the veracity of Mr Dadajee. On page 2 of the 'Exposition' appears: 'This property devolved upon my wife Rukhmabai upon the remarriage of her mother Jayentibai with the late Dr Sukharam Arjun. My mother-in-law Jayentibai and her father Hurichand Yadowjee are now in the enjoyment of the said property.' Which of the two statements is true, that made on *oath*, or that made to deceive the public? I have shown previously how conveniently Mr Dadajee omits the words from the copy of my father's *will* which gave me a legacy of Rs. 200 and left the property absolutely to my mother. It has been asserted against me that I instructed my counsel to call Mr Dadajee a cooly; I need hardly say I never did. If this word was uttered by my counsel, it must have been by his own choice, and of course I could have had no previous knowledge about it.

Again Mr Dadajee seeks to 'dissipate the gross fiction', that I wrote the letters which appeared two years back in the *Times of India* over the signature of a Hindu Lady. I wonder if Mr Dadajee understands the words he uses. Has Mr Dadajee read my letters? I subscribe the first para. of my first letter for his benefit.

'Not being much accustomed to write in English, particularly to newspapers, I submitted this letter to the inspection of a friend, who has kindly *looked over and corrected it where he thought correction was necessary*. But for this friend's kindness I should have not, I am afraid, *dared to address you*, I have to thank this gentleman not only for the *literary help* given by him, but for the genuine sympathy he feels for our condition.' (I have underlined some of the expressions now.)

The public will thus see that I have acknowledged in the amplest terms, the help I got from a friend. As regards the sentiments of the letters, I had been writing to vernacular newspapers *on this very subject*, long before Mr Malabari brought them into prominence.

By omitting the material words in my father's letter to Mr Dadajee's solicitors, and quoting only such words which detached from the context, may mean anything but what is intended, Mr Dadajee asserts, that he was 'entrapped into sending an inviting party'. Mr Dadajee's uncle admitted in his evidence, that when he came to invite me, on Mr Dadajee's behalf, he was told that 'I would go if Mr Dadajee can provide a separate lodging'. Mr Dadajee conveniently omits to mention this little thing, and says, 'I was thus publicly disgraced before my caste'. I suppose Mr Dadajee had advertised publicly, that he was sending an inviting party to me! Had there not been scores of cases in our caste, where wives had to refuse to live with their husbands? But those husbands had not, like Mr Dadajee, prosecuted their wives, served them with solicitors' notices, and dragged them to Court.

On pages 10 and 11 of the 'Exposition' Mr Dadajee lectures me and my sympathizers on morality and Hindu marital law. But I hope to have shown that money and property considerations are at the bottom of the persecution with which he and his advisers follow me.

It was I who had persuaded my mother and grandfather to my side when I finally made up my mind to wash my hands of Mr Dadajee once for all, and though my late father Dr Sakharam always sympathized with me in this matter, the influence of my mother and grandfather was sufficiently strong to force him to make several attempts to settle my unfortunate case out of Court. But Mr Dadajee, instigated by evil counsellors, repulsed these advances, forgetting that it was this same father of mine who had heartily fed and clothed him and his brothers for years.

RUKHMABAI.

P.S. About the same time as Mr Dadajee published his 'Exposition' and couched in somewhat similar style, there was uttered against me and against men who have sympathized with me, a lot of nonsensical declamation by a certain young Hindu doctor. Naturally this and Mr Dadajee's Exposition are by some persons assumed to be components of a joint effort, their style of thought and writing is so similar, and I may be expected to reply to it; but in my humble opinion, while Dadajee's Expositions call for an answer as coming from a party directly interested in our dispute, the other effort lacks this, the only element which invests these utterances with any importance. Besides, when I recollect that the writer of the declamation, which bristles with abuse of my dead father, is the same individual who, whilst studying at College only a few years back, was dependent on the good-will of my father who was then alive. Witness these quotations from the writer's own letters addressed to Dr Sakharam Arjun: 'You have laid me under further obligation for which recompense at my hands is next to impossible, but you will find me attached to you henceforth as a grateful friend... I feel it deeply that my connection with you has been a continuous source of gain to me, and those near and dear to me.' When I recall to mind these and other similar assurances of my and my dead father's present calumniator, who has assumed this role for more than two years past, I consider him and his essay to be beneath even the expression of contempt.

R.

Appendix E

Note by Baba Khem Singh Bedi, C.I.E.

As to the amendment to section 260 of the Civil Procedure, I most respectfully beg to submit that I am strongly opposed to the above amendment. The enforcing of the decrees for the restitution of the conjugal rights cannot be affected without at least the threat of imprisonment.

To the Hindu mind the wife is but his property. The 'Dharam Shastras' rule the same way. She is given in a *'Dan'* (gift) by her parents, who have nothing to do with her after the marriage. Her moral, legal and religious duty is therefore to live with him as long as he lives.

If she being married and having lived with him for some time leaves him and does not like to go back to him even if she is guaranteed against ill-treatment, the law must force her to return to her husband or to go to jail.

I am quite prepared to admit that in cases of the husband's conversion from one religion into another, or being subject to the disease of leprosy or crackedness of the head and under similar circumstances, she may be allowed to remain away from her husband, and the practice prevails to the effect to some extent, but even then she cannot re-marry according to the Hindu Law. Divorce is not allowed nor re-marriage except after the death of the husband, and even that among the Hindus of an inferior status. The high caste Hindus look upon it with contempt and disgust, and any one practising it meets with excommunication. It is never celebrated like a marriage and is termed 'Chadir Audazi'.

Women in this country are 'Amla' (never free). Before marriage they are under guardianship of their parents, after marriage under their husbands and after their death under their children. So long as their husbands live, they have no right to leave them. Imprisonment is a mere threat to force them to return to their husbands, as in one or two cases out of a hundred have they actually been imprisoned. They have always preferred returning to their husbands, and I have seen several instances in which they have been forced to return to their husbands and have afterwards lived a peaceful life blessed with several children. If they did not return, they would have been subject to many sins, and the law would have been responsible for it.

If a man does not like to keep his wife, she is entitled to a maintenance allowance against his will. Why then should they not be compelled by the force of the law to return to their husbands if they do not like to go to them.

I think the public, the Dharam Shastras and the practice prevailing are against it, but, however, a wider expression of opinion from towns and villages may be obtained before passing the amendment, as it is apt to give encouragement to wicked women, and the people will suffer.

(*Home Department, Judicial Proceedings,* Mar. 1895, nos. 1–80, K.W.)

Index

Hindu Women and Marriage Law

Hindu Women and Marriage Law

From Sacrament to Contract

MONMAYEE BASU

To my father

My Source of Inspiration

Acknowledgments

In the preparation of the present work, I received invaluable assistance from many quarters. I would like to express my deep regard for my parents who have not only been a constant source of inspiration, but have been of immense help in giving valuable suggestions, collection of materials and in the preparation of the first draft. I am deeply indebted to my respected supervisor, Dr B.K. Sinha, Professor at Patna University (Retd), whose kind and indispensable help and guidance steered the project to its fruitful end. I also express my profound gratitude to Dr B.N. Mukherjee, Carmichael Professor of the University of Calcutta, but for whose unfailing cooperation and encouragement this work would not have seen the light of day. No words, however, would be adequate to record my deep sense of gratitude for Dr Parthasarathi Gupta, Professor of Delhi University, who very patiently went through the manuscript and helped in making important rectifications in the process of giving final touches to the work. I am sure that this is a better book as a result of his keeping my nose to the grindstone.

I have had suggestions on how to improve the book from a large number of people who have seen the preliminary versions. I should acknowledge my debt in particular to my cousin, Shri Moy Roy, my friend Geeta Kudaisya and my respected brother-in-law Shri Pradeep Kumar Basu, who rendered very useful suggestions in the course of my work.

Shri C.P. Sood and Shri Satish Kumar have placed me under

deep obligation by getting many versions of the manuscript typed and retyped in their spare time. I am very grateful to them. At the same time, my thanks are due to the authorities of all the libraries and institutions for their ungrudging help and cooperation in the collection of facts, figures and other information.

I am grateful to my husband Prabeer Basu who very patiently bore all kinds of inconvenience on account of my preoccupation with this project. And in the end, I must extend my affectionate acknowledgment to my thirteen-year-old son Amitabha who most ungrudgingly and sincerely typed and compared many important things in connection with my work.

Contents

Preface

This work, which was submitted for the doctorate degree of the Patna University in 1990, attempts an in-depth study of some of the matrimonial problems of Hindu women extending over the period 1856 to 1956. Remedial legislative measures to ameliorate their problems have also been discussed in considerable detail. This is followed by an assessment of the impact of those legislations on the position and status of Hindu women.

There was a strong temptation to deal with the problems of married women in general, but it was necessary to limit the scope of this work. So, women belonging to tribes and communities other than the Hindu community have been kept outside the ambit of the proposed study because that would have made the narrative rather sketchy. Further, this work is with special reference to Bengal, which has played a leading role in the feminist movement of our country. The study, therefore, is set mainly against the background of Bengali society which, to an extent, was representative of Hindu society then existing in other parts of India.

The two terminal points of the monograph—the Hindu Widow-Remarriage Act (1856) and the Hindu Succession Act (1956)—are very significant as they stand for two very important landmarks in the history of social legislation. Both these legislations were designed to bring about a transformation in the status of married Hindu women. The former aimed at giving widows the right to remarry and rehabilitate themselves, while the latter boosted their social status by granting them the right to full ownership of property like any male successor. These two pieces of legislation have left an indelible impression upon the history of reforms for women.

However, these reforms are to be seen against the historical background of the period. The remedial measures as well as the events leading to them throw light on the redeeming features of the time. The reforms were made in consonance with the prevailing spirit of the age. A few words regarding the historical backdrop of the period are, therefore, essential.

In fact, the story is not of the period of Indian nationalism alone but also of the age of Hindu revivalism and the reawakening of the past. The promotion and idealization of Western ideas and attitudes had led to an inevitable counter-movement towards Indianization. For whatever temporary rotting and destruction this crude impact of European life and culture has caused, it gave three needed impulses. It revived the dormant intellectual and critical impulse; it rehabilitated life and awakened the desire of new creation; it put the reviving Indian spirit face to face with novel conditions and ideals, and the urgent necessity of understanding, assimilating and conquering them. The national mind turned a new eye on its past culture, reawoke to its sense and import, but also, at the same time, saw it in relation to modern knowledge and ideas.[1] The trend reflected itself, *inter alia,* in the field of social reforms as well. It had its beginnings in the days of Rammohan Roy, who had to face fierce orthodox opposition to his actions, and that went on gathering momentum till it developed into a dominant and positive feature of the Indian Renaissance at the turn of the century. The urge of Dayananda Saraswati to 'go back to the *Vedas*' and his foundation of the Arya Samaj, the Theosophic movement led by Mrs Annie Besant, Sri Aurobindo's vision of Mother India as *Bhawani* or *Bharat Shakti,* 'the infinite energy composed of the *shaktis* of all the millions of units that make up the nation, just as Mahisha Mardini sprang into being from the shaktis of all the millions of gods assembled in one mass of force and welded into unity',[2] Bankimchandra's interpretation of Sri Krishna as a nation-builder and a statesman endowed with the far-sightedness, dexterity and zeal of a shrewd politician whose aim was to unify India,[3] the rejuvenation of Hinduism by Vivekananda at the Parliament of World Religions in Chicago, and Tilak's stress on Shivaji and Ganapati festivals were nothing but mighty expressions of the revivalistic spirit of that age. In fact, all the great movements in India of the time—the Brahmo movement, the Arya Samaj, the movement associated with the great names of Ramakrishna and Vivekananda—symbolized this characteristic spirit of the age and attempted a wide synthesis of tradition and modernity. Reform through revivalism and the consequent fusion of the old and the new, therefore, created the central pivot around which the renaissance of India revolved. To quote Sri Aurobindo,

> India can best develop herself and serve humanity by being herself and following the law of her own nature. This does not mean, as some narrowly and blindly suppose, the rejection of everything new that comes to us in the stream of Time or happens to have been first developed or powerfully expressed by the West.[4]

The story of women's reforms was inevitably woven into this predominant ideal of the time. Even Vidyasagar, while he was advocating widow remarriage, was not free from this trend, which assumed a dominant character much later. Although a student of the Sanskrit College during the thirties, the 'decade of the Derozinians', the challenge of the Young Bengal only made his traditional values and nationalist feelings stronger. In his endeavour to get the widow-remarriage legislation passed, he quoted extensively from the *Dharmashastras*, particularly the *Parasar Samhita*, to meet and satisfy the old mentality and the new, the traditional and the critical mind, and to convince the contemporary Hindu society of the assent of our scriptures to the great reform. In the preface of his tract on the marriage of Hindu widows, Vidyasagar wrote,

> It is true that I do feel compassion for our miserable widows, but at the same time I may be permitted to state, that I did not take up my pen before I was fully convinced that the *Shastras* explicitly sanction their remarriage. This conviction I have come to, after a diligent, dispassionate and careful examination of the subject and I can now safely affirm, that in the whole range of our original *Smritis* there is no one single text which can establish anything to the contrary.[5]

The Arya Samaj too, while stressing the importance of the *Vedas* as the foundation of Hindu life, encouraged inter-caste marriage, decried child marriage and fixed the minimum marriageable age for boys and girls at twenty-five and sixteen, respectively. In support of divorce, the old customary practices, and the ideas of Kautilya (See *post*, p. 32) have been referred to.

It is against this historical backdrop of oscillation between the past and the present, the old and the new, that the question of the women's reform movement is to be traced.

It is true that a great deal has already been written on movements for rights of women, and any fresh attempt to write on such a topic, even for a select period, must involve some risk of repetition. Yet, much has been left out by previous writers, and fresh research on the subject invariably brings to light new facts hitherto unknown. Most studies so far have been of a general character. I propose to deal exclusively with a particular section of women, namely, women belonging to the Hindu community. Moreover, among the unending problems of Hindu women, only those relating to their marriage are selected for study. The monograph will, therefore, be a micro-study in nature. I also propose to deal with the legal aspects of their marital problems. The remedial legislative measures, how these ultimately came up through long-drawn and tardy legislative procedures as well as the extent of their success will also be discussed at length. This, I hope, would contribute a new perspective to the subject. Problems such as dowry, and the condition of women in general, have been dealt with by many other researchers. However, none of these earlier works have dealt with the remedial measures in any detail. I have, therefore, analysed the extent of the success of these legislations to improve the lot of women in our Hindu society. In short, my work attempts to examine the following questions:

i. Some marital problems of Hindu women.
ii. How these were looked upon by Hindu society in various stages of its evolution, and what endeavours were made by Indian reformers to improve the status of married Hindu women.
iii. Whether the attempts made by Hindu society and its reformers succeeded in solving the marital problems of Hindu women, and, if at all, to what extent?

iv. Attempts made by the legislature to solve these problems and how far they succeeded in achieving their purpose.

The first chapter is devoted to the study of the condition of Hindu women during the mid-nineteenth century which will serve as a background. Bengal has been taken here as a case study and, on the basis of contemporary literature and other writings, the true condition of the married and widowed women of the time has been depicted. Girls were married off at a very early age and were sent to their husbands' homes as soon as they attained the age of puberty. With no prospect of education or freedom, confined within the four walls of their homes, they were plunged into a hackneyed and tedious life of ceaseless domestic duties and of producing and rearing children. The plight of the widows was far worse. The condition prevailing in Bengal was, to a large extent, representative of the situation then existing in other parts of the country. The second chapter analyzes the concept of Hindu marriage, tracing its evolution through different stages over the years. The problems of child marriage and efforts made for its eradication are dealt with in the third chapter. The fourth chapter examines the problem of widow remarriage, the enactments for its eradication and its repercussions on Hindu society. Acts and laws which aimed at the improvement of the status of Hindu widows have also been analyzed. The fifth chapter discusses the dowry system which has made the lot of Hindu women so pitiable, and looks at the Dowry Prohibition Act of 1961. The legislative proceedings for ameliorating the situation emerging from the widely prevalent dowry system began in 1958, and culminated in the passing of the Act of 1961, both dates being outside the purview of my study. Even so, I have discussed them in detail in my work because the problem of dowry is inextricably woven into the marriages of numerous Hindu women. In the sixth chapter I analyse the matrimonial relief provided by the Hindu code. The Hindu Marriage Act 1955—the first part of the Hindu code—has amended and codified the law relating to marriage; while it has simplified the conditions for a valid marriage, it has also repudiated the age-old concept of Hindu marriage as an essentially sacramental institution. Chapter seven discusses women's right to property and the Hindu Succession Act of 1956. In the last chapter, I have tried to draw conclusions from the study.

Apart from a number of social scientists writing on various specific and general aspects of women's development through the ages (their books are listed in the bibliography), a number of monographs in this field have come out within a short span in the past few years. A discussion, for example, on the reform of the religious personal laws of the different communities and the place that women find in them;[6] a legal discourse on the availability of different legal provisions designed to protect married women from the Vedic times to the present day;[7] a survey of the legal measures enacted with the object of protecting women against the manifold difficulties and handicaps in different spheres of life, like unequal remuneration, the *devadasi* system, maternity benefits, termination of pregnancy, violence against women, as well as marital issues like *sati*, dowry, problems in matrimonial homes arising out of independent employment of husband and wife in different places and separate homes set up by both, etc.,[8] a study of the social legislations (including within its horizon some matrimonial as well as social laws relating to issues like prostitution, education, labour, employment, etc.) enacted for the benefit of Hindu women and the impact of these legislations on the outlook and social position of Hindu women living in Varanasi;[9] a general study portraying the lifestyle of the women of India in general and of Bengal in particular;[10] a detailed analysis of the progress of Indian women in diverse spheres from the nineteenth century till the modern times—a movement started by Indian men and then taken over by women themselves;[11] have confined my discussion to a narrower field to avoid the risk of repetition. A close scrutiny, nevertheless, reveals that particular aspects have still been left out like issues exclusively dealing with marital issues and their remedies, leaving room for further research on the topic. Intricate questions such as the traditional concept of Indian society about the role of women in their matrimonial homes, the consequent problems faced by women as a result of the prevalent social ideas, how social reformers and legislators attempted to solve these problems through several legislative measures and the changes brought about in the position of women in society by these measures have not yet found adequate place in the consideration of social scientists. I have, therefore, chosen these issues as the subject of my research. The need for specific periodization, along with the selection of themes, dictated the choice of the chronological limits of 1856 and 1956. Not only do these two years only stand for two epoch-making events, but the intervening period, too, represents massive transformations in the social history of India.

There is no dearth of materials for the proposed work. The primary data upon which the above chapters are based are the proceedings of the Council of the Governor-General of India, Assembly Debates, Parliamentary Debates, Government Reports and Pamphlets, Census Reports, the Gazette of India, India Council Acts, autobiographies and private papers and various other journals besides secondary books. Assembly Libraries and State Archives, the National Archives of India, New Delhi, the National Library of Calcutta, the Nehru Memorial Library of Delhi, libraries of Patna University and the A.N. Sinha Institute for Social Studies, as well as the Sinha Library of Patna have rendered valuable information.

Notes and References

1. Sri Aurobindo, *The Renaissance in India*, Pondicherry, Sri Aurobindo Ashram, 1966, pp. 18–19.
2. Nirodbaran, *Sri Aurobindo For All Ages: A Biography*, Pondicherry, Sri Aurobindo Ashram, 1990, p. 51.
3. Chattopadhyaya, Bankimchandra, *Krishna Charitra*, published in Bibidha, ed. Brajen Bandopadhyaya and Sajanikanta Das, Calcutta, Bangiya Sahitya Parishad, Pous, 1346 B.S.
4. See Note 2 above.
5. Vidyasagar, Ishwar Chandra, *Marriage of Hindu Widows*, Calcutta, K. P. Bagchi and Company, 1976, Preface.
6. Parashar, Archana, *Women and Family Law Reform in India*, Delhi, Sage Publications, 1992.
7. Sharma, Vijay, *Protection of Women in Matrimonial Home*, New Delhi, Deep and Deep Publications, 1994.
8. Diwan, Paras and Piyushi, Diwan, *Women and Legal Protection*, New Delhi, Deep and Deep Publications, 1994.
9. Sahai, Sheila, *Social Legislation and Status of Hindu Women*, Jaipur and New Delhi, Rawat Publications, 1996.
10. Chakravorty, Sambuddha, *Andare Antare: Uneesh Shatake Bangalee Bhadramahila*, Stree Prakashan, Calcutta, 1995.
11. Forbes, Geraldine, *Women in Modern India*, The New Cambridge History of India series, vol. IV. 2, New Delhi, Cambridge University Press, 1996.

1

Condition of Hindu Women during the Second Half of the Nineteenth Century

It is not easy to evaluate the condition of Hindu women during the second half of the nineteenth century. The life of an average Hindu woman was difficult and pitiable owing to the existing social customs and practices of the time. The present study is made against the background of Bengali society which is not very different from Hindu societies existing in other parts of India. Bengali society has been chosen particularly because Bengal took a leading part in the feminist movement in the nineteenth century under great social reformers such as Raja Rammohan Roy and Pandit Ishwar Chandra Vidyasagar.

In the early periods of Indian history, some Hindu women were highly educated and played an important part in society. In the pursuit of knowledge and virtue, performance of rituals, composition of hymns and in other activities, temporal or spiritual, women were considered the equals of men. Famous women like Gargi and Maitrayee, both teachers, were renowned for their intellectual and spiritual attainments, as well illustrated in the famous dialogues between Maitrayee and her husband, Yajnavalkya, in the Brihadaranyaka Upanishad iv. 5, and Gargi Vachaknavi in Brihadaranyaka Upanishad III, 6.8. Hindu women displayed outstanding capabilities as administrators and warriors, and did not lag behind in statecraft either. Meerabai, for example, distinguished herself as the poet-queen of the fifteenth century. Ahalya Bai of the Holkar state in Central India and Rani Lakshmi Bai of Jhansi, were rulers who displayed exemplary courage and rare determination. Lakshmi Bai intensely resented the annexation of her husband's state in 1853 by the British who applied the Doctine of Lapse after her husband's death. She joined the sepoy mutineers and, dressed in male attire, gallantly defended Jhansi till she was killed while fighting on 17 June 1858. Ahalya Bai became the ruler of the Holkar State, succeeding Malhar Rao Holkar, her father-in-law. She administered the state with great wisdom till her death in 1795 and is still revered for her benevolence and saintliness. She is immortalized by the numerous temples she built in various parts of India, such as the temple of Annapurna at Varanasi and the Vishnu temple at Gaya. In Bengal, too, women distinguished themselves in different spheres of activity. Some like Rani Bhawani of Natore exhibited rare ability in managing their estates; others excelled in qualities of learning and imagination. Hati Vidyalankar, a Bengali resident of Varanasi, and Shyammohini Devi of Bengal were two eminent Sanskrit scholars.

These are however, examples of extraordinary women. The condition of Indian women in general, and of Hindu women in particular, began to deteriorate after the Muslim conquerors settled in India. By and large, women lost their opportunities and freedom, and became increasingly dependent on men. This was largely due to a natural social response to the challenge posed by the disturbed conditions following foreign invasions as well as internecine conflicts. The consequent political and economic unrest arrested the development of Indian society as a whole and women in particular. Worse still, undesirable social customs crept in, which gradually reduced the Indian woman to a state of perpetual bondage. When raids and warfare became a common occurrence, the fear of insecurity which affected unmarried young women was, perhaps, largely responsible for the emergence of the system of early marriage. This most probably led to the beginning of the cruel and reprehensible dowry system which has prevailed for centuries and persists even today. The fear of insecurity was, to a great extent, responsible for the growth and continuance of the system of sati.

The emergence of the purdah system and seclusion of women was another byproduct of such fear. With no organized system of education to sustain her, a female child was often married even before she had learnt the alphabet, remained unlettered and absolutely dependent upon men, economically and otherwise. The effect of these disabilities was awesome. Gradually, the belief grew in Indian society that women were destined to a status inferior to men.

By the beginning of the nineteenth century, the position of Indian women had reached the 'lowest depth of degradation'[1]. Although India's contact with the modern West at this time had a tremendous impact upon Hinduism as well as the social reformers of India, feminism did not make much headway. Notwithstanding the abolition of sati, social evils pervaded Indian society throughout the nineteenth century. Social legislations, such as the Widow-Remarriage Act 1856, the Age of Consent Act 1860 and similar measures, were more in the nature of reforms on paper than actual accomplishments. Therefore, any discussion of the condition of women during the second half of the nineteenth century must analyse in detail the social customs with the accompanying evils which prevailed in society. The position of women in the family has to be examined first in order to determine their social status because, in early Indian society, women exercised influence mostly in their families.

The family was of prime importance in the life of an Indian. The joint family, which included father, mother, grandfather, grandmother, brothers, sisters and other relatives, was the traditional pattern of the family. The western concept of the nuclear family consisting of only a husband, wife and children had not emerged then. There was so much bias against women that it was considered an act of immodesty if a husband happened to show any outward expression of attachment for his wife. She was, however, expected to show concern and care for all the members of the family without any discrimination. Marriage was a social institution and the union of a couple was regarded as a social alliance between the families of the bride and the bridegroom.[2] It was believed that the woman's sole aim in life ought to be to ensure the happiness and well-being of her husband's family—her own happiness was of the least importance. The chief objects of Hindu marriage were three: *dharma* or religious duties to be performed by the couple, *proja* or procreation, and *rati* or conjugal love.

This lofty concept of Hindu marriage, however, was vitiated in the nineteenth century. The concept of an ideal mother, was also eroded by the common misuse of power by the mother-in-law in the day-to-day management of the family, as a result of which the only role left for a young wife was one of appeasement. Vivekananda says,

> It is perfectly true we have made almost a caricature of some of these great ideas. It is lamentably true that the fathers and mothers are not what they were in the olden times, neither is society so educated as it used to be, neither has society that love for individuals that it used to have.[3]
>
> The fact is that, by and large, women fell prey to abhorrent social customs and came to occupy a very abject position in Hindu society.

Child marriage, known as *gouridan*, was a bane of Hindu society. Girls were often given in marriage at the age of ten or even below. The Age of Consent Act 1860 determined the minimum age of ten for the marriage of a girl. This was raised to twelve after the amendment of the Act on 19 March 1891 (Act X). The young girl, after her marriage, went to her husband's house and found her life a crown of thorns. She had no freedom and was under the complete control of her husband's family. The mother-in-law was the supreme authority of her new home and the young wife had to obey her, please her and submit to her will till she herself grew old and became a mother-in-law herself. A young couple would never speak to each other before elders. The wife never ate in her husband's presence. If by any chance the husband happened to appear while she was eating, she had to stop eating immediately, and he had no option but to move out of sight into another room.[4]

The common practice in a typical Hindu family was that as soon as the daughter-in-law stepped into the house, the mother-in-law and sister-in-law retired, as it were, and the newcomer was burdened with all kinds of responsibilities.[5] The girl was often scolded for any minor fault by her husband, mother-in-law and any other elder member of the family.[6] Most mothers-in-law had little sympathy with the young daughter-in-law and often ill-treated her, so that she felt miserable in her new home and was forced to live in a state of tension and fear. To quote M. Fuller,

> The girl from the very moment of her birth to her death undergoes one continuous life long suffering as a child wife, as a child mother and very often as a child widow.[7]

Giribala Devi, a distinguished Bengali writer and the winner of the 'Lila Prize' (a prize awarded by the Calcutta University to the best Bengali writer of the year) has narrated the story of her life, giving a vivid picture of the daily duties of a young housewife. Born towards the close of the nineteenth century (1892), she depicted the conservative traditions of Bengali society at the beginning of the twentieth century. The story is not much different from that of the nineteenth century. No young housewife, rich or poor, was allowed to sit idle. She had to perform a variety of domestic chores ceaselessly from morning till midnight. Besides cooking food, she had to perform religious duties with all care and punctiliousness. The young housewives made various types of sweets and milk-based preparations because the widows of the family were not permitted to eat sweets bought from the market.

Women were expected to wear veils and were not permitted to speak to the elders, a practice considered a mark of respect. They had to talk to the younger family members in a low voice. They had to obey the mother-in-law and other elders of the family alike. Allowed to have meals only after the elders had been fed, they had to wait for them to retire before they could go to sleep. The elder members of the family were always free to take them to task for the most trivial matters. The young housewives, as a rule, could never meet their husbands during the daytime, the couple were allowed to meet only at midnight. They were thus expected to go to bed late at night and get up early in the morning. These mistreated girls had become so used to restrictions that they never even expressed any resentment.[8] When the young daughters-in-law themselves grew old and occupied the superior position of a mother, they enjoyed more power, authority and freedom, but always within the framework of the household, never beyond it. They were really dependent housewives, but were trained from their very childhood to adapt themselves to this subordinate position without any grudge or resentment. It was with a sigh of relief that they went back to their parents for a short visit, weeping profusely while leaving for their husbands' houses. Their heart-rending sobs could be heard by the neighbours as they proceeded on their way in the palanquin.[9]

Ishwar Chandra Vidyasagar said that the Hindu religion prescribed laws that applied equally to men and women. According to the Hindu scriptures, it was necessary to examine the family roots, tradition, etc., of both the boy and girl before fixing a marriage. Just as a man could marry again if his wife was dead or barren, a woman had the same right in a similar situation. If it were shameful for a widowed woman to marry again, it should be just the same for a man. After marriage both husband and wife were expected to make each other happy. Unfortunately, men disregarded these laws and saddened the lives of women, laments Vidyasagar:

> A man's heart breaks, at the deplorable condition of the present day India. The practice of keeping women in happiness and care almost disappears. By and by, some so-called wisemen even go to the length of thinking that it is quite foolish to give them peace and comfort. On close examination it becomes quite evident that at present women's status is lower than that of maid servants in the family.[10]

Volumes of Bengali literature refer to the injustices and indignities inflicted on women during the second half of the nineteenth century. *Subarnalata*, for instance, written by Ashapurna Devi, particularly refers to the evils of child marriage, and *Kari Diye Kinlam* by Bimal Mitra is also the story of an unhappy woman belonging to a rich family of Bengal.

Even more tragic was the lot of upper caste Hindu widows in society. Often looked upon as a drudge in the family, a widow invariably led a miserable life. The condition of a child widow was still worse, neglected and ill-treated from her very childhood, she grew up as a helpless being, destined to suffer. The number of such child widows was very high during the period under review. The renowned social worker, Kamala Devi Chattopadhyaya, in her book *Indian Women's Battle for Freedom*, referred to a survey in Calcutta in 1891 which found 10,000 widows below the age of four in and around the city which then had a total population of only four lakhs. In upper caste Hindu society, even child widows were not permitted to remarry, contrary to the norms of Hinduism which give equal marital rights to men and women.

A widow had no freedom—whether economic or personal. Women in Hindu society had no right of succession to property, the absence of which made them dependent on men.[11] A Hindu widow, therefore, inherited nothing on either side and was only entitled to bare sustenance in her husband's family till her death. Even a millionaire's wife became virtually a pauper in widowhood and, since widows had no economic security, they came to be looked upon as parasites.[12]

A widow could not enjoy any luxury, and could dress only in white. She could not wear ornaments and her diet was strictly vegetarian. A widow was allowed only one major meal a day, and that, too, in one sitting. If she left her seat before finishing her meal, she was no longer allowed to eat it, because then she would be guilty of taking two separate meals in a day. She was frequently required to keep a fast while performing various religious rites in the family. Since her very presence was regarded ominous on auspicious occasions, she was prevented from taking any active part in marriages being held in the family and was not even permitted to touch anything used for ceremonial rites. Her duty on such occasions was to perform all routine domestic work, however hard that might have been. With a view to improving the lot of widows, the Hindu Widow-Remarriage Act (Act XV) was passed on 26 July 1856, through the untiring efforts of Vidyasagar. The Act, however, failed to serve its purpose and the attempt to encourage the remarriage of Hindu widows did not make any substantial progress.[13]

It was found that ninety per cent of the prostitutes at the time were widows,[14] a fact revealed in Rabindranath Tagore's novel *Chokher Bali* and Bankimchandra's novel, *Krishnakanter Will.*

Dowry system was yet another evil that prevailed in Hindu society during the period under investigation. Dowry had to be paid, as a rule, at the time of the girl's marriage. A daughter was a perennial source of worry in the Hindu family since she had to be married at the right age and within the accepted caste framework.

Neither intercaste marriage nor marriage below one's social status was socially acceptable. The father of a girl sometimes found it very difficult to meet these requirements and, taking advantage of his difficult situation, an exorbitant dowry was often demanded by the bridegroom's father. The girl's father had no option but to agree to this high demand, resulting in great hardships for the bride's own family after her wedding. Thus the term *duhita* (daughter) acquired a perverted meaning. Originally the term meant a girl who milked cows for the family's consumption, but it gradually came to mean a daughter who squeezed her parent's family dry. The parents were often humiliated for their failure to give adequate gifts and often insulted and ridiculed for not fulfilling all the promises of dowry. When her parents failed to meet the demands of the husband's family, the girl was tortured by her mother-in-law and frequently by her husband too. Sometimes she was sent back to her parent's house, never to be brought back.[15] Rabindranath Tagore has vividly described the evil effects of dowry in his short story, *Dena Paona*.

Purdah was another great hindrance for women who, shut in the innermost part of the house and living in strict seclusion, had little scope for widening their ideas and broadening their outlook. Young housewives were not permitted to even step out of the house.[16] The upper caste Hindu family had a separate inner apartment, where the women lay condemned to a life-long prison, helpless, prostrate and pathetic figures—with enfeebled health, then naturally keen senses dulled through inaction, without the light of knowledge illuminating their vision, steeped in ignorance and prejudice, groping in the dark—martyrs to the conventions of the society in which they had been born.[17] They had to cover their heads and faces with their sarees worn as long veils throughout the day, even when they remained inside a room. A young wife with a shorter veil was sure to be abused and vilified as a shrewd and bad woman.[18]

The common transport for women either in a village or in town was the palanquin.[19] It was considered a great offence for a young husband to go out openly with his wife in the street. Keshab Chandra Sen, who belonged to an old Brahmo family, defied this convention as a mark of protest against injustice to women. On 13 April 1862, Keshab along with his wife in a *palki*, went down from 'Kolutola to

Jorasanko',[20] an act that can be regarded as a significant step towards the women's liberation movement.

In a Hindu family, women were often neglected, no care was taken of their health and they had to do a great deal of household work even during an illness. They were denied nutritious food and, for want of a proper diet and health care, often suffered from serious diseases, which worsened with the passing years. A pregnant woman at the time of childbirth was segregated in a small thatched room, newly built or temporarily improvised in an open space in the inner part of the house,[21] and often damp, unhealthy and uncomfortable. Early marriage and childbirth increased the death rate of both mothers and infants.[22] Many women, in these circumstances, did not live long and the death rate of young women was much higher than that of men.

There were several laws of marriage in the Hindu shastras, some of which stated that a man had the right to remarry only if his first wife died or was barren. In the latter case, the husband had the right to remarry, even while the first wife was alive. Of course, in the *Ramayana*, we have the example of Dasaratha who had three wives all of whom lived at the same time under the same roof of the royal palace. Dasaratha however, was compelled to marry them under very special circumstances. Dasaratha had to marry again because he had no son by his first wife and he was getting on in years. He married a third time only when his second wife also failed to bear him a son. At last, four sons were born to his three wives when he was very old. Further, it must be remembered that the rules which the Hindu shastras prescribed for the common people, did not apply to kings.[23]

During the second half of the nineteenth century, upper caste Hindus practised polygamy without any restraint.[24] The system was widely prevalent among the *Kulin* Brahmins of Bengal, who often married more than a hundred wives. In 1871, it was found that thirty-three Kulin Brahmins of Hooghly District were married to two thousand and fifty-one women. Ishwar Chandra Vidyasagar records in anguish,

> With the Kulin brahmin, the sacred rite of matrimony had been notoriously degraded to a system of shameful traffic. These men

> for the sordid gain of some paltry sum, visited village after village, accepting the hands of crores of maidens, the great majority of whom were destined never to enjoy the blessings of a wedded life.[25]

The Kulin Brahmins were mostly uneducated and since they were incapable of earning a decent living, they took to the practice of marrying many wives as a means of livelihood, visiting their wives by turn mostly to collect gifts and money.[26] The unfortunate girls, married to a man they shared with others, got neither the love of the husband, nor any status in society as they lived in their parent's house throughout their lives, awaiting the visits of their husbands patiently. Such visits were sometimes so few and far between that it did at times prove difficult for a young girl or the members of her family to recognize the husband when he visited his wife after very long intervals.

One of the reasons for the persistence of the evil custom was that the Kulin girls could not be given in marriage to anyone of a lower caste rank. On the other hand, in accordance with social custom, they had to be married at an early age. The Kulin Brahmin men exploited this situation and demanded very high dowry. These circumstances compelled the poor girls to marry old, diseased or otherwise undesirable men, if indeed they were able to marry at all. In order to avoid scandals which might bring their families into disrepute, many were murdered secretly. Dwaraka Nath Gangopadhyaya, a pioneer of women's liberation made personal enquiries and found that in his own village within ten years about thirty-two Kulin Brahmin girls, who purportedly died of cholera, were in fact poisoned to death. Dwaraka Nath was so moved at their miserable lot that he brought out a journal entitled *Abala Bandhav,* for the purpose of highlighting the wretched condition of these unfortunate women, born in high Kulin society. He related his personal experiences in *Abala Bandhav,* an extract of which runs thus:

> The tremendous sufferings of the Kulin girls of this country are not beyond knowledge of those who have eyes. Those who have eyes are still blind and remain ignorant of the fact. I myself would have remained blind unless one heart-rending event opened my eyes. One exceedingly beautiful Kulin girl was killed with poison

> by her relatives. I was then seventeen. The news came to us through gossip of the people. We were overwhelmed with grief by this unnatural tragic death of that girl, because the girl was personally known to us. We further came to know from a contemporary that this event was not a rare one; this happened every year. By inquiry I came to know that what he said was true. Within 17 years 32/33 women died by the same process in one village. A man's heart unless turned into a stone cannot but melt under this circumstance. In our early days, by studying the *slokas* of Chanakya, we became anti-women. We felt amused in mocking and jeering at them. Now we realise that there was nothing to laugh at them. They were really poor creatures. From that time a tender affection for women grew in our hearts. We thought that our lives would be really meaningful, if we could do a bit to assuage the sufferings of these unfortunate women. With this purpose in view Abala Bandhav was born.[27]

The 'Bidhumukhi Abduction Case' was a sensational event of the time, revealing the plight of women. Bidhumukhi Mukhopadhyaya was a close relative of Baroda Nath Halder, a resident of Bikrampur. The guardians of Bidhumukhi decided to give her in marriage to a very old man with thirteen wives. To sabotage the marriage, Baroda Nath and his brother Sarada Nath fled with the girl, with her consent. Bidhumukhi's guardians tried to find her with the help of the police, but in vain. Instead of bringing Bidhumukhi directly to Calcutta, the Halder brothers, took her to the house of an acquaintance—Durgamohan—at Barisal. The guardians filed a suit in the High Court against the Halder brothers on the charge of abduction of Bidhumukhi, after which Dacca's magistrate issued a warrant of arrest for Baroda Halder. On behalf of Baroda, it was argued before the High Court that Bidhumukhi had been confined secretly for her own good, i.e. to save her from an immoral marriage and that her guardians had thus forfeited their right of guardianship. On 20 September 1870, Justice Couch and Justice Locke heard the case in court, held the warrant of arrest in abeyance and ordered the production of all papers connected with the case. In January 1871, the case was heard in the court of Justice Jackson and Anukul Chandra Mukhopadhyaya. Baroda's lawyer, Manmohan Ghosh pleaded the case very efficiently and the judges decided that the action of the accused was one of protection against the evil of a prevailing social custom and for the benefit of their relative, Bidhumukhi. They set the young men free and praised them for their courage.[28] Later Bidhumukhi was married to Rajaninath Roy, a brilliant scholar of the Calcutta University and ex-Deputy Controller of Paper Currency, Government of India.

Such was the condition of women in Hindu society during the late nineteenth century. There were, no doubt, some exceptional instances of enlightened and progressive families, particularly in the Brahmo Samaj, where women were duly respected, given an education and treated more or less on an equal footing with boys.

There were also some upper caste Hindu families, though very few, where women, though required to abide by the strict conservative social rules, were not harassed. They were treated by the mother-in-law and others with much care and affection and widows were sympathised with and respected. For example, Kadambini Basu and Surjamukhi Basu were the first lady graduates of Calcutta University (1883).[29] Kadambini Basu completed her medical studies in the Medical College of Calcutta, and then went abroad for higher studies. She was the second wife of Dwaraka Nath Gangopadhyaya, of whom mention has already been made, and was the first woman doctor of Bengal. As a doctor, she moved about freely from place to place to treat her patients. She spoke English fluently as if it were her mother tongue, wore attractive modern clothes and decorated her drawing room in a style that displayed her superb taste and imagination.[30] Other girls of her family also had similar opportunities for a better life. For instance, Punyalata Chakravorty, the granddaughter of Dwaraka Nath by his first wife, her sister and their relatives also went to Bethune School for their education. They experienced the pleasures of life not accessible to most women at that time, such as the circus, puppet shows and travel with their parents to different parts of India, thereby broadening their mental horizons.[31]

Girls of other enlightened families also had opportunities for education. Rani Chanda, (a student of Visva Bharti, a Bengali writer and a close associate of Rabindranath Tagore) and her sister went to Eden School of Dacca. Sarala Ray, the founder of Gokhale Memorial Girls' School of Calcutta, Abala Das (later Lady Abala

Basu) who passed the entrance examination in 1881, Kumudini Khastigir, (later Kumudini Das), the first Principal of Bethune College, were all educated women of their times. Other girls were inspired by them to acquire learning.

Giribala Devi[32] frankly admitted that it was mainly due to the help and guidance of her husband that she could develop her literary potential. A typical young housewife of a conservative family, busy with domestic duties all day long, she was not allowed to meet her husband before mid-night. Still, at that late hour, her husband taught her, taking her through her first lessons. Giribala also had the support of her father-in-law, who was a patron of learning with great regard for women's education. Giribala went on to become a poet of renown and received the 'Lila Prize' of Calcutta University at a very old age in 1983.[33]

Kusum Kumari Das, mother of the great poet Jibanananda Das, was another distinguished woman of the time (1875) who studied in Bethune School. She belonged to a middle class family and lived the life of an ordinary housewife. Jibanananda writes:

> . . . our house was full of people at Barisal. I saw my mother and aunt always engaged in domestic work. They were not spared of hard physical labour, nor did they want to be spared; indeed they were not afraid of hard work. They were conscious of their duties and never thought of avoiding responsibilities.[34]

Kusum Kumari was an upright, conscientious person who did whatever she thought was correct. She was known to help neighbours in trouble—day or night. She ignored criticism and went to Western India for a change of climate and better medical treatment for her sick son, Jibanananda.[35] Domestic duties never stood in the way of her pursuit of studies and the habit of writing. In about 1896, Kusum Kumari wrote a collection of poems for children entitled *Kabita Mukul.* She was closely connected with the Brahmo Samaj, attended its meetings and gave short discourses during its gatherings. Jibanananda writes '... she sat on the altar erect, quiet and self composed, did not repeat—she reminded me of Cardinal Newman ....' Kusum Kumari was awarded the Sarojnalini Gold Medal in an essay competition. Titled *Ideal Womenhood,* the essay revealed her thoughts on women's liberation.

She wrote that female power in this country was still dormant, so the nation remained half dead.[36] She was involved in social work and with women's associations, and was the secretary of *Barisal Mahila Samiti*, an active women's centre. She also wrote an article entitled, *Women's activities and their sphere of activities*.[37]

Rani Chanda's is one of the positive accounts which record that in those days there were a few families in Bengal where women, even when they were widowed, were treated with love and respect. Her eldest aunt had lost her husband on the fourth day of her marriage, yet she held the highest position in the family next only to her mother-in-law. She did not return to her parents' house in spite of their entreaties, and spent her life freely and happily in her husband's family. Her brothers-in-law and sisters-in-law loved and respected her. They teased her, amused her, and always looked upon her as one of them, holding her in high esteem. She was very cheerful in their company. A young girl when she was married, she hardly remembered her husband; still she had an abiding love for her husband's family.[38]

Sarat Kumari Chaudhurani's short story *Didima* portrays a child-wife who was treated with love and sympathy. The grandmother of the house and other women elders of the family showered love and affection upon the young housewife, who was hardly ten years old. They were anxious to give her sufficient food and other comforts, and as she was a young girl, she was freed from domestic duties. If she made a mess of the work she did, she was not rebuked. Rather the grandmother explained to her how to do it and trained her patiently. She was allowed to meet her young husband during the day. Aware that the little girl might be homesick, the grandmother voluntarily made arrangements for her visit to her father's house. She also attended to little details of the little girl's comforts—she made sure the young bride was given sufficient amount of milk to which she was used in her own home.[39]

The women of *Thakur Bari* (the family of Rabindranath Tagore) were symbols of happiness in nineteenth century Bengal. To others they showed the way to progress and culture. It is true that many of them led the traditional life of a conservative family, mostly confined to the *andarmahal* (inner part) of a big house, and they did not move out without a palki. They occupied themselves with different types of domestic duties, managing the household, cooking food, rearing their children and looking after the needs of their elders. They were, however, quite happy and comfortable[40] received care and affection at par with the male members of the family, and joined the other family members for meals. Most of them were given good education and training,[41] and developed refined qualities of mind and heart. Well-versed in literature, music and art, some of them were writers and poets who wrote stories, novels, poems, autobiographies, selected translations, etc.

Swarna Kumari Devi and Jnanadanandini Devi of the Tagore family were well known for the active interest they took in women's emancipation. Jnanada brought about a radical change in ideas about the social condition of the women of Bengal. Swarna Kumari Devi had no interest in domestic chores and she never lived the life of an ordinary housewife. Always immersed in studies, she was a talented writer who contributed much to Bengali literature.[42] The other girls of the Tagore family were also brought up in an enlightened atmosphere, and much care and attention was given to their education, including music and art. Sarala (the daughter of Swarna Kumari and later famous as Sarala Devi Choudhurani) was the first to receive the Padmavati Gold Medal, donated by Rashbehari Ghosh, for passing the B.A. examination from the Bethune College in 1890. Indira (the daughter of Jnanadanandini, and later known as Indira Devi Choudhurani) was also awarded the Padmavati Gold Medal for standing first in the B.A. Examination in 1892. The men of the Tagore family contributed immensely to the progress and enlightenment of the women of their family. Satyendranath, (Rabindranath Tagore's elder brother) stood behind his wife, Jnanada, in all her progressive work; Hemendranath took the utmost care to ensure the education of the women of the family; Jyotiridranath rode openly with his wife Kadambari on horseback;[43] Rabindranath was the inspiration of all the women of the house.

Another name worth mentioning in the realm of Bengali literature is Jyotirmoyee Devi. The granddaughter of Sansar Chandra Sen, the Dewan of the Maharaja of Jaipur, she was born in 1894, and took up her pen to bring to light the misery of the depressed section of the population, especially women—the helpless widows of Varanasi, the prostitutes, the oppressed womenfolk of Rajasthan and the downtrodden Harijan women.

However, not all educated families of Bengal welcomed the waves of modernity, preferring to cling to the traditional and orthodox ways of life. In the course of my discussion so far, I have referred to some enlightened families who favoured modernization and progress amidst the general milieu of conservatism and stagnation. But the discussion remains incomplete without a word about the highly educated, cultured yet conservative families of Bengal who were well known for their knowledge, education and scholastic achievements, but were still in favour of conforming to old social values and ideals. The family of Bhudev Mukhopadhyay is one of them. He was a student of Hindu College, well-versed in English literature, including the works of Bacon, Shakespeare, Milton as well as the historical writings of Hume, Mitford, Fergusson, Gibbon, Elphinstone and Russell. He had at a point of time read the Bible with immense interest, and was later influenced irrevocably by his study of Hume, Tom Paine, Gibbon and Voltaire. In his hours of leisure, he read European poetry and the intimate portions of his letters to his sons as well as of his diary were written in English. Yet he never saw anything above the 'practical skills' of Europe to be worth learning and stuck very strictly to all traditional and Brahmanical codes of conduct. He considered it essential that Indians should draw inspiration from their own past and traditions because he felt that there was nothing else of worth left for the Indians but to preserve their own orthodox ways of life. His *Samajik Prabandha* (Essays on Society) and *Pariwarik Prabandha* (Essays on Family) clearly depict his ideas and beliefs with regard to social issues in India. In *Satir Dharma*, he made his disapproval of the dissolution of marriage very evident. Child marriage was totally acceptable to him because, as Dr. Tapan Raychaudhuri points out, 'he had seen it blossom into abiding love ... his own child bride grew into an ideal and much loved companion.'[44] To him, widow remarriage was anathema. He believed that women need not gain knowledge by reading books and scriptures but should concentrate on learning how to handle domestic chores because running the household efficiently was their primary concern. Education for women, in his mind, meant training in domestic work. In his article

Stri Shiksha (Female Education), he showed no preference for school or college education for women, while his observations on dowry were quite interesting. He felt that the elite were trying to get educated and university-qualified bridegrooms for their daughters despite the fact that such bridegrooms were very few, while brides of good families were available in large numbers. Moreover, as educated boys did not believe in polygamy, getting a university-educated bridegroom was a stupendous task and the girl's father would have to spend money lavishly to achieve such a mission. Bhudev sympathized with neither the girls nor their fathers. He sympathized with the educated bridegrooms as their fathers behaved inconsiderately and cruelly for the greed of money, burdening their sons with any girl whose father agreed to pay the highest dowry. Money, it seems, became the prime consideration with the boys' fathers rather than the qualities of the girls.

Bhudev's reverence for tradition and conservative outlook strongly influenced his talented grand-daughters—Anurupa Devi and Nirupama Devi—well-known women writers of the late eighteenth and early nineteenth centuries. Alarmed by the attack on Hindu culture and civilization, the sisters devoted their works to the task of defending and protecting the traditions, customs and rituals of Hindu religion and society. The basic qualities or spiritual and social aspirations such as self-sacrifice, altruism, social well-being, love for God and religion, which mark Hindu thought, are expressly evident in all their writings. The underlying strength of the sacramental Hindu marriage has been stressed in Nirupama Devi's *Didi* And Anurupa Devi's *Mantrashakti*, both written in 1915. *Didi* narrates how a series of complicated events finally succeed in uniting Amar and Surama, husband and wife, after a long separation which was the consequence of misunderstanding and a clash of egos. She stresses the supremacy of the everlasting bond of Hindu marriage and the depth of the husband-wife relationship.

The very same concept is emphasized in Mantrashakti by Anurupa Devi. Insurmountable Hindu customs had forced Bani, the daughter of an aristocratic *zamindar* family to marry Ambarnath, who belonged to an ordinary priestly family, but her inherent pride prevented her from accepting him as her husband. In the end, however, the age-old sacred Vedic hymns chanted at the time of marriage cast their magic spell. Slowly, the hymns transformed Bani's mind and sowed the seeds of love and respect for her husband in her heart, and finally succeeding in uniting the couple after a prolonged separation. So it was the Mantrashakti, that is, the power of the hymns (here used in the sense of marriage hymns), which won at last.

In her famous novel *Ma,* Anurupa Devi works on the same idea when she depicts the eternal love of a wife devoted to her husband. Arabindo, the husband, obeyed the orders of his father to desert his wife Monorama, who then spent the rest of her life with her son in her father's house. Instead of protesting against the heartless behaviour of her husband, Monorama looked upon it as an extreme sacrifice by her husband, who, she was certain, suffered terribly because of his separation from his beloved wife, but bore it silently and patiently as a duty towards his father. Monorama never allowed even her son, Ajit, to protest against his father's injustice. Monorama's unflinching devotion to her husband was the ideal of ancient Hindu society.

At any rate, the examples of enlightened women from educated and progressive families do not obliterate the fact that most Hindu women were steeped in extreme ignorance and misery. The number of the emancipated was very slender, almost negligible, in contrast with the vast majority of unfortunate women who were compelled by circumstances to a very sorry existence. They remained mere child-producing machines or glorified domestic workers.

Notes and References

1. Madhavananda Swami and R.C. Majumdar, *Great Women of India: Ideal and Position of Indian Women in Social Life,* Almora, Advaita Ashrama,1953, pp. 43–4.
2. Urquhart, M.M., *Women of Bengal,* Association Press, Calcutta, 1925, pp. 32–3, 39–40.
3. *Complete Works of Swami Vivekananda,* vol. III, Almora, Advaita Ashram, 6th edition, 1948, pp. 408–9.
4. Swami Vivekananda, *Bharatiya Nari,* Calcutta, Ubdodhan Karyalaya, pp. 16–7.
5. Chanda, Rani, *Amar Ma'r Baper Bari,* Visva Bharati, Granthan Bibhaga, Calcutta, 1977, p. 27.

6. Shastri, Sivnath, *History of the Brahmo Samaj*, vol. I, Calcutta, R. Chalteye Publishers, 1974, 1977, p. 33.
7. Fuller, M.B., *The Wrongs of Indian Womanhood*, Edinburgh, Oliphant, Anderson and Ferrier, 1900, p. 13.
8. *Desh*, 26 March 1983, pp. 43–4.
9. Chanda, Rani, op.cit. p. 49. See note 5 above.
10. Halder, Gopal (Ed.), *Vidyasagar Rachana Sangraha*, vol. II, Calcutta, Vidyasagar Smarak Jatiya Samiti, Saksharata Prakashan, 1972, p. 157.
11. Mayne, J.D., *A Treatise on Hindu Law and Usage*, Madras, Higgin Botham & Company, 1906, pp. 601–5.
12. Nehru, Uma, 'Whither Women', published in Nehru, Shyam Kumari (Ed.), *Our Cause: A Symposium by Indian Women*, Allahabad, Kitabistan, 1936, p. 416.
13. Majumdar, R.C., Majumdar A.K. and Ghose D.K., (Ed.) *The History & Culture of Indian People*, vol. X, part II, Bombay Bharatiya Vidya Bhavan, 1965 p. 278.
14. *Amrita Bazar Patrika*, 11 March 1896.
15. Chatterjee, Suniti, Brojen Banerjee, and Sajani Kanto Das, (Ed.), *Samaj*, published in *Vidyasagar Granthabali*, Ranjan Publishing House, Calcutta, 1939, p. 255.
16. Chanda, Rani op.cit. p. 60. See note 5 above.
17. Ray, P.C., *Life and Times of C.R. Das*, London, OUP, 1927, p. 4.
18. Folklore, '*Nak Ghomta Buk Tan Oito Bou Saitan*'.
19. Chaudhurani, Sarala Devi, *Jibaner Jharapata*, Calcutta, Shishu Sahitya Samsad, 1958, p. 23.
20. *Desh*, 2 April 1983, p. 15 (article by Smt. Jhara Basu).
21. Chanda, Rani, op.cit. p. 71. See note 5 above.
22. Rajwade, Lakshmibai, 'The Indian Mother and Her Problems', Published in Shayam Kumari Nehru, (Ed.) *Our Cause: A Symposium by Indian Women*, Kitabistan, Allahabad, p. 81.
23. Halder, Gopal (Ed.), *Vidyasagar Rachana Sangraha*, vol. II, See note 10 above, p. 173.
24. Census Report, 1891, vol. I, p. 254.
25. *The Friend of India*, 30 March 1865.
26. Majumdar, R.C., A.K. Majumdar, and Ghose, D.K. (Ed.), p. 261. See note 13 above.
27. *Sanjibani Patrika*, 2 July 1898. Vide, Gangopadhyaya Prabhat, Banglar Nari Jagoran, p. 59. (Prabhat Gangopadhyaya was the son of Dwaraka Nath Gangopadhyaya).
28. Collet, M. (Ed.), *Brahmo Year Book*, London, Williams & Norgate, 1879.

29. Nag, Kalidas (Ed.) *Bethune School and College Centenary Volume* (1849–1949), p. 218.
30. Chakravorty, Punyalata, *Chhele Belar Dinguli*, Calcutta, New Script, B.S. 1388, pp. 8, 109.
31. Ibid., pp. 20–21, 25.
32. *See ante*, p. 5.
33. *Desh*, 26 March 1983, p. 13.
34. Das, Jibanananda, *Amar Ma, Baba*, Uttar Suri, (December–February) 1954.
35. *Desh*, 26 June 1982, p. 12 (article by Sumita Chakravorty).
36. Ibid., pp. 12–13.
37. Ibid., p. 12.
38. Chanda, Rani, op.cit. pp. 8, 38–9. See note 5 above.
39. *Bharati Patrika*, June–September, B.S. 1316.
40. Dev, Chitra, *Thakur Barir Andar Mahal*, Calcutta, Ananda Publishers Private Limited, B.S. 1387, pp. 8, 221.
41. Tagore, Jyotirindranath, *Jiban Smriti*, Sharadiya Sankhya, *Desh*, 1956, p. 138.
42. Chaudhurani, Sarala Devi, *Jibaner Jharapata*, See note 19 above, pp. 3, 12, 29.
43. Ibid.
44. Roychaudhuri, Tapan, *Europe Reconsidered: Perception of the West in Nineteenth Century Bengal*, Delhi, OUP, 1988, p. 28.

2

The Changing Concept of Hindu Marriage

Marriage has been, since ancient times, one of the most important social institutions. Sociologists have offered several different explanations, among them being Westermarck's definition of marriage 'as a more or less durable connection between male and female, lasting beyond the mere act of propagation till after the birth of the offspring'.[1] In the words of George A. Lundberg, 'marriage consists of the rules and regulations which define the rights, duties and privileges of the husband and wife.' Otto Larsen, one of the greatest scholars of American sociology, defined marriage as a 'contractual agreement which formalizes and stabilizes the social relationships which comprise the family'. The concept of Hindu marriage has undergone continuous modifications through the ages, and traditions of thousands of years are dissolving. An analysis of the concept, therefore, has been rendered extremely difficult. In fact, the most significant change the concept of Hindu marriage has undergone is its transformation from sacrament to contract. Here, I endeavour to analyze in brief how the transformation took place.

Marriage in the Vedic period was regarded as a *sanskara*. Sanskaras are very deeply rooted in the Hindu social system. The *Vedas* do not mention the word, but a reference to it is found later in the *Grhyasutras* which are based on the Vedas. Sanskaras are certain performances and undertakings which are aimed at making the life and the personality of a person complete, and marriage is one of them. According to Manu, several impurities enter the body through the womb of the mother owing to the parental relationship, but Man can get rid of these impurities through sanskaras.[2]

Generally, a Hindu marriage is solemnized with the customary rites and ceremonies practised by both the families involved. One of the most important Hindu marriage rituals is *saptapadi*, i.e. seven steps taken together by the bride and the bridegroom around the sacred fire. It is only after the seventh step of saptapadi is taken, that the marriage ceremony is considered complete. Through these rites and customs, especially of marriage—regulated by law—a Hindu, whether male or female, attains full personhood. As *Satapatha Brahmana*, an exposition of Vedic religious rites and practices, says, 'He alone is a perfect man who consists of his wife, himself and his offspring. A man who does not win a wife is really half and he is not a full man as long as he does not beget an offspring'[3]. Similarly, Manu expresses the idea that men are created to be fathers and women to be mothers. So marriage is obligatory for both man and woman, though even in olden times there were a few exceptions like Gargi in the *Brihadaranyaka Upanishad*, Sulabha in the *Mahabharata* and Sabari in *Ramayana*. In the Mahabharata there is a story of the daughter of Sage Kunigarga who did not want to marry and was practising severe penance by remaining celibate. When she was about to die, she was told by the great Sage Narada that she would not attain heaven as her body was not consecrated by the sacrament of marriage. It is said that she then requested another Sage Sringavat, to marry her and stayed with him one night so that she could go to heaven.

Marriage in the *shastras* was viewed as a sacrament. The relationship of husband and wife, once established through proper customs and rituals, was believed to be irrevocable. In Hindu marriage, custom is sacrosanct, which is why a marriage ceremony is considered to be complete only when the customary rites and rituals are fully performed. Of course, customs vary from place to place and from society to society. Hindu marriage in the early Vedic and later Vedic age was categorized by Kautilya into two broad classes—*dharmiya* (sanctioned by religion) and *adharmiya* (disapproved by religion). The Grhyasutras have mentioned about eight forms of marriages—*brahma, daiva, arsha, prajapatya, asura, gandharva, rakshasa* and *paisacha*. These forms are uniformly referred to in all the *Dharmashastras*, ancient treatises relating to *dharma* (religious ordinances or rites), its contents, chronology and other kindred matters. The different forms of marriage have been translated by Kane in the following words:[4]

> The gift of a daughter, after decking her (with valuable garments) and honouring her (with jewels) to a man learned in Vedas and of good conduct whom the father himself invites is called Brahma form of marriage ....
>
> When the father gives away his daughter after decking her (with ornaments) to a priest who duly officiates at a sacrifice during the course of its performance, it is the Daiva form of marriage.
>
> When there is a gift of one's daughter after taking one pair of cattle (a cow and a bull) or two pairs only as a matter of fulfilling the law (and not as a sale of the girl) that is named Arsa.
>
> The gift of a daughter after the father has addressed the couple with the words 'may both of you perform your religious duties together' and after he has honoured the bridegroom (with madhuparka) is declared to constitute the Prajapatya form.
>
> When the girl is given away at the father's will after the bridegroom gives as much wealth as he can afford to pay to the relatives of the girls and to the girl herself, that is called the Asura form.
>
> The union of a girl and the bridegroom by their mutual consent is known as Gandharva which springs from the passion of love and has intercourse as its purpose.
>
> The forcible abduction of a maiden from her house while she weeps and cries aloud after her kinsmen have been slain, wounded and their homes are broken open is called Rakshasa form.
>
> When a man has intercourse with a girl stealthily while she is asleep or intoxicated or disordered in mind (or unconscious) that is the Paisacha form which is the most sinful of all forms.

Kautilya stated that the first four forms belonged to the *dharmiya* category and the latter four to the *adharmiya* category. In fact, the latter four forms are presumed to be the earliest forms of marriage, since they prevailed at a time when there was no established institution of marriage. So the different forms of marriage, in a way, represent the evolution of the institution from the earliest times. It is worth noting that in all these forms of marriage, except gandharva, the consent of the girl was not a matter considered at all. This indicates that in matrimonial affairs, the lines and destinies of women were definitely controlled by men. Out of the eight forms, *paisacha* and rakshasa ceased long ago, as evidenced by the fact that *Apastamba* and *Vasistha* do not feel the need to even mention them.[5] The first four forms which were brahma, daiva, arsa and *prajapatya*, were regarded as the best forms of marriage in the *Sutra* period and also in the *Smriti* period.[6] At objective levels, Hindu tradition stipulates that the important aims of marriage are religious duty (*dharma*), progeny (*praja*) and conjugal love (*rati*). According to Hindu traditions, marriage is an instrument for the pursuance of higher goals of life, rather than a means for personal gratification which was given the least priority. For this reason, dharma or religious duty is regarded as the most important purpose of Hindu marriage. A man has to perform various religious rites and ceremonies throughout his life, and these ceremonies would remain incomplete without the presence of a wife since the husband and wife are supposed to perform these religious obligations together before the sacred fire by offering oblations. This was perhaps the reason why king Ramachandra had to place a golden image of Sita beside himself at the time the *Asvamedha Yajna* was performed. Therefore, on the death of his wife, a householder is supposed to remarry so that his religious duties remain unhampered.

The other important aim of marriage is praja, i.e. progeny or procreation. Procreation is essential for the continuance of the family line. A son, it is said, saves his father from going to hell.[7] Moreover, debts to ancestors (*pitririna*) are discharged through procreation. The *Avesta* states that bachelors were inferior to married men who, if childless, were definitely inferior to those who had children. Furthermore, the marriage of a daughter or *kanyadan* involves a drain of wealth from the girls father's to her husband's house. A son, on the other hand, carries out the religious duties of the family and performs the last rites of his parents, thereby paving their path to heaven and preserving his father's property through inheritance and succession. The perpetuation of one's *kula* (lineage), which according to the *Dharmashastras* is the cardinal function of marriage, can be done only by the the son and not by daughter as the latter, after marriage, automatically assumes the *gotra* of her husband. The continuity of a person's *kula* through his progeny is not intended to involve only simple biological replacement but, more importantly, the preservation and continuance of the culture and customs of the family. Marriage thus involves union not only for the purpose of biological reproduction, but also to maintain an orderly replacement of the family culture.[8]

The role of *rati* or sex in marriage is regarded as very insignificant in Hindu tradition. Though sex is accepted as one of the functions of marriage, it is less important in Hindu marriage than dharma and *praja*. The three higher *varnas*, namely the Brahmanas, Kshatriyas and Vaishyas, are believed to have been born for the purpose of achieving the higher goals in life. Personal pleasures like rati, therefore, are not supposed to play a vital role in their lives and sex is to be treated only as an essential means for perpetuation of procreation. The marriage of a Sudra, however, was believed to be for pleasure alone because a Sudra was looked down upon as a lowly being having no high purpose in life.

Since Hindu marriage is regarded as a means to establish relations between two families, utmost care is taken to ensure maximum cultural compatibility between the two. Therefore, regarding the selection of mates, a number of prohibitions and restrictions were followed, the most important of these being exogamous restrictions. According to the *Oxford Wordfinder*, 'exogamy' means the marriage of a man outside his own tribe, and 'endogamy' means marrying within the same tribe. In Hindu exogamy, a person had to marry firstly outside his or her own *gotra* and secondly, to avoid marrying a person who is a *sapinda*. The former is called gotra exogamy and the latter, sapinda exogamy. Two persons who have a common ancestor are sapindas. Thus a son is a sapinda of the father and grandfather. Similarly, he is the sapinda of the mother and the maternal grandfather, being connected with them by a close blood relationship (in a literal Sanskrit translation 'sapinda' means 'of the same body' or a connection of particles of the body). Further, in the *Rig Veda*, the word gotra was not quite used to mean 'descendants', but rather referred to different things at different times like 'cow stable' or 'herds of cows'[9] or 'clouds'[10]. Sometimes, of course, it was used to mean *samuha* or assemblage which can be taken to refer to a group of persons.[11] However, the Rig Veda hymns clearly indicated that marriage should take place between strangers[12]. The ancient treatises, *Aitareya Brahmana* and Satapatha Brahmana, mentioned the condemnation of Prajapati for his incestuous behaviour with his daughter.[13] It was in the Sutras that the gotra and *pravara*, which meant one or more illustrious ancestors, have been discussed at length. In the Brahmana period and specially in the *Upanishads*, it indicated blood relationship or genealogy. As Krishna Nath Chatterjee has pointed out, in most of the *Sutras*, gotra and pravara had the same significance and marriages were prohibited within the same gotra or pravara.[14]

Exogamy was accepted as a general rule during the Smriti period also. Manu distinctly prohibited marriage between identical gotras as did *Yajnavalkya* (third century AD), Vishnu in the *Vishnu Smriti*, Narada (sixth century AD), Parasara in the *Parasara Smriti* as well. Regarding sapinda exogamy also, the *Sutrakars* and the *Smritikars* were all of the same opinion that marriage between sapindas should be prohibited, although they differed regarding the degrees of blood-relationship to be avoided. Most of them, including Manu, maintained that a sapinda relationship extended up to the seventh degree from the father's side and five degrees from the mother's side. Parasara, however, was an exception as he prohibited marriage, as a general rule, till the fifth degree from a common male descent, but was ready to condescend to marriage in the fourth degree where there were local or family traditions in its favour. In general, the prohibited relations are: father and daughter, son and mother, father-in-law and daughter-in-law, mother-in-law and son-in-law, brother and sister, father's brother's wife, brother's wife, mother's brother's wife, father's brother and sister, uncle and niece, aunt and nephew, or of the children of a brother and sister or of children of two brothers or of two sisters.[15] There is no doubt that in Hindu tradition, the observance of custom is supreme. And if custom prevails, marriages between sapindas or within the prohibited degrees of relationship are also permissible. For instance, in

Southern India, a marriage between a maternal uncle and niece is valid whereas in Northern India it is unthinkable due to the absence of such a custom. In the south there has been a preference for the marriage of a girl with her father's sister's son and, less generally, with her mother's brother's son or with her mother's younger brother. Some castes practice direct exchange, which takes place when the marriage of a boy is fixed on the condition that his sister would simultaneously get married to a boy of his bride's family.[16]

Coming to the question of endogamy, the Hindu ethos upholds marriage within one's own caste or varna. Initially there existed only two classes of people—the Aryans who had sharp features and were fair, and the native people, that is, the non-Aryans or the *Dasas (Dasyus)*, who were dark and snub-nosed. The *Rig Veda* is full of references to the constant strife between these two rival groups. Gradually, in course of time, the Dasas came to be absorbed as the lowest classes of the community and were called the Sudras. The Aryans themselves became divided into three groups or classes according to their profession or occupation—Brahmanas, Kshatriyas and Vaishyas. There is no reference to Vaishyas in the Rig Vedic hymns though mention has occasionally been made of Brahmanas and Kshatriyas. It was only as late as the *Purusa Sukta* that the four varnas were spoken of. The three upper castes formed one endogamous unit as distinct from the Sudras who were the lowest class, so although inter-marriage could take place among the first three castes, there was an insurmountable barrier between the Sudras and three other castes as far as marriage was concerned. Slowly, however, the distinctions among the three upper varnas, too, became quite rigid and the four-fold division took a concrete shape. The *Satapatha Brahmana* clearly mentions the four castes and lays stress on the superior qualities of the Brahmanas.. From this emerged the concept of *Anuloma* and *Pratiloma* marriages. The marriage between a man of a higher caste with a women of a lower caste is called an anuloma marriage and when a man of a lower caste marries a woman of a higher caste, it is called pratiloma. The *Sutras* have recognized such marriages, although they seem to have been more prevalent during the time of the Upanishads. The Sutras, the Smritis, the epics and the *Dharmashastras* regarded Pratiloma marriages with disfavour. While the Grhyasutras never mention pratiloma marriages, the *Apastamba Dharmasutra* goes a step further and looks upon Anuloma marriages with scorn. In the Mahabharata, we find numerous examples of anuloma marriages like Agastya's marriage with Lopamudra, Jamadagni's marriage with Renuka and Risyasringa's marriage with Santa. That Manu, too, was averse even to anuloma marriages, besides his disdain for Pratiloma marriages, is evident when he says:

> Children of a Brahmana by women of the three lower castes, of a Kshatriya by wives of two lower castes and of a Vaisya by a wife of the Sudra caste, all these six are called base born.[17]

Vedic literature generally endorsed monogamy and was considered the best practice of the highest virtue. However, polygamy was also in practice, especially among the nobles. A number of such instances of polygamy are available not only in later Vedic literature, but also in the *Rig Veda.* In fact, polygamy was sanctioned by the ancient law givers under certain specific circumstances. For example, Manu and Yajnavalkya approved of second marriages under special circumstances such as the wife's barrenness or lack of religious-mindedness, that is, if she was unfit to participate in the performance of the religious rites of her husband. The husband had the right to remarry if the wife failed to deliver a male child, so that he could beget a son. For example, Dasaratha in the *Ramayana* married three times for the want of a son.

There is no reference to polyandry in Vedic literature except in a few sporadic instances like the marriage of Surya, Savitri's daughter, with the twin Asvin brothers. In the *Mahabharata,* Draupadi married the five Pandava brothers. However, Draupadi's marriage took place under unusual circumstances—the Pandavas were compelled to marry her in order to abide by the wish of their mother whom they held in highest esteem. Even so, the marriage was bitterly opposed by Draupadi's father and brother and Yudhisthira, the eldest Pandava, had to use all his persuasive powers to convince them, and eventually won their consent by citing a precedent in support of his arguments. This incident, if anything, shows that polyandry was not the customary practice in the Vedic age .

Widow remarriage was permitted under special circumstances in the Vedic age as evident in a hymn in the *Rig Veda* which is addressed to a widow weeping beside the body of her dead husband. Her husband's brother tells her: 'Rise, come into the world of the living, O woman, come, he is lifeless by whose side thou liest. Wifehood with thy husband was thy portion, who took thy hand and wooed thee as a lover'[18].

This system of remarriage with the husband's brother was called *niyoga*. The *Atharva Veda* also refers to remarriage when it says 'whenever woman having married one husband, marries another, if they (two) offer a goat with five rich dishes, they would not be separated (from each other)[19].

There is a reference to a widow's son in *Taittiriya Samhita* which suggests that widow remarriage was an accepted practice at that time. Some Sutras also speak of widow remarriage, the example being *Vasistha, Dharmasutra,* according to which a woman who leaves the husband of her youth and after living with another person, re-enters the house of the husband; or one who takes another husband after leaving an impotent, outcaste or lunatic husband or after the death of the first husband, is a punarbhu. Narada mentions another category of punarbhu, that is, a maiden whose hand was taken in marriage, but whose marriage was not consummated. The word punarbhu, therefore, is generally applied to a widow who has remarried.[20] The Grhyasutras, however, are silent about widow remarriage, which implies that there was a general prohibition of the custom by that time. Manu was strictly opposed to widow remarriage. He clearly said, 'In the *mantras* on marriage such a commission (widow remarriage) is never mentioned and the second marriage of a widow is not spoken of in the rule of marriage.'[21]

As far as the appropriate age of marriage is concerned, it appears that in the Rig Vedic and also the later Vedic age, girls were supposed to be married at a mature age because consummation was prescribed immediately after three nights following the marriage ceremony, indicating that the girls were sufficiently grown up. The *Brahmanas* and the *Samhitas* do not shed much light on this aspect though the Grhyasutras speak of *nagnikas* as the best brides. There is a difference of opinion among scholars as to what the word *nagnika* actually meant, though it is generally taken to mean a girl who had not yet reached puberty. The *Grhyasamgraha* also has the same explanation of 'nagnika'.[22] According to Manu, it was desirable to give a girl in marriage after she reaches the age of puberty. He says, 'A girl having reached the age of puberty should wait three years (for a husband); but at the end of that time she should choose a husband of like (caste)'.[23] However, Manu thinks that a girl could be given in marriage even before puberty only if an exceptional suitor was available. 'One should give a girl in marriage according to rule to that suitor who is of high (family), handsome and of like (caste), even though she has not reached (the age of puberty)'.[24] Yajnavalkya, however, was of the opinion that a girl who was not given in marriage before puberty 'would be visited by the sin of the destruction of the foetus at every time of her menses'.[25] The marriage of a girl after puberty is regarded as sinful by other lawgivers like Yama, Marichi and Parasara as well.

The system of dowry or marriage gifts in the modern sense was not in practice in ancient or medieval India. There is no specific mention of marriage gifts or dowry in the Vedic literature, though there are some sporadic references to them. For example, in the brahma and daiva forms of marriage, the father gives away the daughter, richly adorned with ornaments. In the *Ramayana*, Sita, and in the *Mahabharata*, Draupadi, Subhadra and Uttara were given valuable presents of horses, elephants and jewels by their parents at the time of marriage. However, in that era, the parents or the guardian of the bride were free to give only what they could easily afford and it was never a compulsion or a condition of marriage. The main considerations for marriage were caste, status, family position, and so on. Gifts or money from the bride's family were never used as a pretext to harass the bride by her in-laws. In other words, the dowry system had not taken its roots in the ugly and naked form it is today. Rather, Manu says, 'a man who takes a consideration through greed is a seller of (his) child'.[26]

The concept of marriage underwent significant modifications under the influence of Buddhism and Jainism, which emerged as challenges to the prevalent Brahmanical order. The most important change was that, unlike the Vedic and post-Vedic literature which looked upon marriage as a sanskara without which a man's life is incomplete, Buddhism regarded marriage as rather an impediment to a spiritual life or attainment of *nirvana*. This is why Lord Buddha severed all his matrimonial ties before he started on his quest for enlightenment. Marriage was not considered a sacrament either, but was a contract between the husband and the wife. As a result, widows were free to remarry, though the custom was rare and, as B.C. Law points out, there is reference to only a single instance of widow remarriage in the Sri Lankan chronicle *Mahavamsa*. Buddha repudiated the notion of caste, which meant that caste barriers in marriage were done away with. Even marrying one's own cousin was not unusual. The marriage of Ajatasatru with the daughter of his mother's brother can be cited as an example.[27] Ananda, the favourite disciple of the Buddha, was enamoured by the beauty of his father's sister's daughter, Uppalavanna, and wanted to marry her.[28] In Buddhism, the *Theris* or elder ladies, composed religious songs known as *Theri Gatha* (songs of the Theris) which, formed a part of the Buddhist canon. These were brief accounts of the lives of the Theris which threw light on the prevailing social customs of the time. For example, the story of Ishidasi indicates that if a woman severed her marital bond with her husband and married another man, it was accepted. The story of Utpalavarna suggests the existence of polygamy. Utpalavarna, the daughter of a rich merchant, was deserted by her husband after her daughter's birth. Her daughter stayed on with the father and Utpalavarna married a man who was enchanted by her beauty, but she later discovered that he was already married. To her great shock, she learnt that his first wife was none other than her own daughter. In deep anguish and frustration, she renounced the world and became a nun in a Buddhist convent.[29] From this episode, it appears that polygamy was in practice in those days. However, polyandry was not common and Buddhist literature contains but one reference to polyandry in the *Kunala Jataka*.[30] Dowry is hardly mentioned in Buddhist literature, except for one or two stray instances mentioned in the *Dhammapada Commentary*, vol. I, which refers to the case of Visakha who received a fabulous dowry from her father, Migara, a Savatthian treasurer, on the occasion of her marriage.[31] As in the Vedic age, in the Buddhist period also, early marriage was not the custom but there are many instances of girls being married at the age of sixteen, Yasodhara, Buddha's wife, being one of them.

Although Jainism, like Buddhism, rejected the sacramental notion of marriage and considered marriage inferior to celibacy, it accepted many of the marriage customs of the Hindus and intermarriage between the Hindus and the Jains slowly came into practice. From Jain literature, it appears that child marriage started by this time and there is reference to the custom of sati as well, though it was not prevalent in society.

However, this temporary progressive phase was followed by a strong *Brahmanical* revival. The Brahmanas revised the orthodox tradition and codes of conduct with a vengeance as is evident from the Smritis and the *Puranas* to which reference has already been made. An example of this trend is that although there is no reference to child marriage in the Vedic literature, the later law-givers like Yajnavalkya, Yama, Marichi and others (with the exception of Manu), insisted on pre-puberty marriage.[32] The customs of *niyoga* and widow remarriage were prohibited in the three higher degrees,[33] and the Brahmanas strictly adhered to endogamous restrictions. The custom of sati also began to be practised in this period. *Vishnu Dharma Samhita* seems to have mentioned it first,[34] later Vatsayana in the *Kamasutra* and *Brahaspati Smriti*, *Parasara Smriti* and *Agni Purana* referred to the practice.[35] Thus the later Brahmanic period witnessed a marked degradation in the position of women in India.

The analysis remains incomplete without any reference to Kautilya, the celebrated Chancellor of Chandragupta Maurya, who assumed power in or about 323 BC. Kautilya's *Arthasastra* remains an ideal exposition of social principles and the political theory of ancient India, and the laws of Kautilya reflect the fact that reactionary movements had not influenced society yet as there was no trace of the later maxims which denied property rights to women. His laws, therefore, justly recognized the daughter's claims[35] to her mother's property and permitted divorce as well as remarriage of young widows.[36] Kautilya wanted matrimonial relations to be established between families of equal status, saying, 'a wise man may marry an ugly girl from noble family, but he should not accept a beautiful and good natured girl from low family.'[37] However, Kautilya contradicted his own words when he said 'nectar from poison, gold even from dirty place, knowledge from the auspicious, wife even from a low family—all these should be accepted'.[38] He regarded serving the husband and obedience to him to be the highest duty of a married woman as he said, 'woman who without the permission of her husband performs *vrata* and fasts, lessens the age of her husband and herself goes to hell.[39] And again, 'A woman does not get as much piety by giving offerings, or by keeping fasts, or by visiting holy places as she gets by washing the feet of her husband'.[40] Such statements show that like Manu, Kautilya too played a part in degrading the position of women.

The position of women deteriorated further with the advent of the Muslim invaders and, consequently, customs and practices like purdah, polygamy, and infant marriages slowly took deep roots in Hindu society. Since the invaders held the womenfolk of their fallen foes captive, the practice of sati became prevalent as the women preferred to burn themselves on the pyres of their dead husbands in order to save themselves. In places like Rajputana, women committed mass self-immolation called *jauhar brata*. Tod described jauhar as 'that horriable rite, where females are immolated to preserve them from pollution or captivity when a kingdom fell into the hands of the Muslims'. It is said that thirteen thousand ladies of Chitor performed jauhar along with Rani Padmini when the fort of Chitor was captured by Ala-ud-din Khilji, the Sultan of Delhi on 26 August 1303. Further, even in times of peace, women were confined within the four walls of the house to protect them from lustful abduction. Consequently, they were denied all freedom and became totally dependent on their menfolk for even their basic needs.

The security of young girls was a problem for parents and they saw giving them away in marriage very early as a solution; so early marriage became a custom. The Hindus felt that the arrival of the Muslims endangered their own religion and social practices, and the protection of each person's caste became a fight for survival resulting in the four castes turning into strict endogamous units. Even within the broad outline of these four castes, there were sharp distinctions of hierarchy and these began to be scrupulously adhered to in matters of marriage. Finding a suitable bridegroom for a daughter within a narrow caste grouping became more and more difficult. Desperate parents, therefore, began giving their young daughters away even to old infirm men who already had a number of wives. This established polygamy and child-marriage firmly in Hindu society and, as a natural consequence, society was faced with numerous problems emanating from the practice of child-marriage—

child-mothers, a high mortality rate among child-wives and the children born to them, and the most distressed, the child-widows.

By the time the British came to India, Hindu women were already beset with numerous problems. Hindu marriage was still considered to be a sacramental institution groaning under the burden of restrictions related to gotra and sub-castes—an alliance in which the woman was compelled to occupy a position much inferior to her husband and was dependent on her male relations in every way.

Through their efforts at social reform, the British succeeded in passing Regulation XVII in 1829 which declared sati illegal and punishable by courts. The position of women in the nineteenth century was changing, thanks to the endeavours of social reformers like Rammohan Ray, Ishwar Chandra Vidyasagar and others—gradually, they attempted a solution to each of the multitude of problems suffered by Indian women. Indian legislators actively sought to work out solutions through legislation, the result of which was the chain of legislative measures passed by the Assembly. These legislations will be discussed at length in the following chapters. It is worth noting, however, that women themselves were slowly equipping themselves mentally, educationally and socially to fight for their own rights. The cumulative effect was a radical transformation in the position of Indian women. This trend can be attributed to the following factors:

1. Increasing industrialization.
2. The efforts of Indian reformers to improve the status of Indian women.
3. The spread of education among Indian women, which helped them see beyond tradition and customs.
4. The freedom movement which brought women out into the struggle for national liberation leading to independence and to the Constitution which guaranteed equal rights to all citizens, including women.
5. The weakening or disintegration of the joint family system. In 1951, the Census Commissioner of India said that joint family was breaking up.[41] The techno-socio-economic system affected the structure of families as, under economic exigencies, people were forced to migrate to urban and industrial areas in search of

> jobs, leaving the extended family. The spread of education and the new administrative machinery of the British period opened up prospects of bright careers for young men who then moved away from the joint family and their native place. Education for women brought about a tremendous change in Hindu marriage and in family ideals and practices.[42] Women gradually came out of the four walls of the house, looking for opportunities for independence and self-realization. In fact, 'capitalism' in the economic field, liberalism in the ideological domain and the principle of equality in the social and political systems became the order of the day. All these proved fatal for the joint family system.

Since the position and outlook of women are so remarkably transformed over the years, it is quite natural that the concept of marriage as well as its traditions would undergo a radical change. This was recognized by Nyayamurti Mahadev Govind Ranade, a judge of the Bombay High Court, well-known not only as an erudite scholar and thinker but as a prophet of the cultural renaissance of India. As he declared, legislation is one of the important methods of changing the social structure and elevating it to a higher level. In fact, one of the distinguishing characteristics of modern society is the heavy reliance on law to bring about social change. The struggle for legal equality, therefore, has been one of the major concerns of women's movements all over the world.

In India, the first movement for women's marital rights centred round the three major problems of infant marriage, enforced widowhood and property rights for women. The concern of social reformers at this stage was primarily a concern for women as a part of the patriarchal Hindu joint family. Their endeavour was to ensure that women were better equipped socially to undertake the roles of mothers and wives in the new social conditions that were emerging. On the other hand, the concerns of women activists such as Pandita Ramabai were to focus attention on the gender-based oppression of women.

The second major debate was triggered off during the freedom struggle and the discussions on the Indian Constitution. These mainly centred round the Hindu Code Bill and the debate was largely within a framework which recognized that women were not accepted as the social, economic or political equals of men and that these discriminations could be effectively reduced, if not eliminated, by passing appropriate laws and evolving an effective machinery to implement these laws. And so, after independence, there was a phase of legal reforms, progressive and bold legislative initiatives, which translated constitutional commitments and guarantees into laws to improve the legal status of women. The Hindu Code Bill is a great landmark in the field of marital problems of Hindu women in general and those belonging to the upper castes in particular, because the educated upper castes, especially those of the urban areas, were those who made the best use of the advantages procured by the Hindu Code Bill.

The traditional concept of marriage is now greatly changed and Hindu marriage today has assumed more or less the nature of a contract for the mutual benefit of the parties concerned, duly aided by different legal provisions and reforms. It is, however, necessary to realize that there are limits to the extent to which changes can be effected by law. Attempts to bring about changes in the status of woman either through legislation or judicial activism can achieve little success without a simultaneous movement to transform the social and economic structures and the culture (values, ideologies and attitudes) of society.

Notes and References

1. Edward, Westermarck, *The Origins and Development of Moral Ideals*, London, New York, MacMillan Company Limited, 1906–8, p. 364.
2. वैदिक: कर्मभि: पुण्यैर्निषिकादिर्द्विजन्मनाम् ।
   कार्य: शरीरसंस्कार: पावन: प्रेत्य चेह च ।।१।।२६
   ग्राभेहोमैजतिकर्म चौड़मौञ्जी निबन्धनै: ।
   वैजिकं गार्भिकं चैनो द्विजानामपमुज्यते।।
   मनु: २।२६-२७
3. अर्धो ह वा एष आत्मनो
   यज्जाया तस्माद्यावज्जायां न
   विन्दते नैव तावतप्रजायतेऽसर्वो
   हि तावद भवतित्यथ यदैव
   जायां विन्दतेऽथ प्रजायते
   तर्हि हि सर्वो भवति।

   शतपथ ब्राहमण: ५/२/१/१०

4. Kane, P.V., *History of Dharmasastra*, vol. II, part I, Poona, Bhandarkar Oriental Research Institute, 1974, p. 517.
5. Chatterjee, Krishna Nath, *Hindu Marriage—Past and Present*, Varanasi, Tara Publications, p. 44.
6. Ibid.
7. पुन्नाम्नो नकरात्त्रायते इति पुत्रः ।
   Quoted by Avasthi, Abha in *Hindu Marriage in Continuity and Change*, Lucknow, Pradeep Prakashan Kendra, 1979, p. 21
8. Ramu, G.N., *Family and Caste in Urban India*, Delhi, Vikas Publishing House, 1977, p. 33.
9. विश्चा यद् गोत्रा सहसा पवीवृता मदे सोमोऽस्य हम्हितान्यैरयन्।
   त्वं गोत्रमङ्गिरोभ्योऽवृगोरपोता त्रये शतहुइेषु यातुवित् ।
   I, 51.3
   Vide also Chatterjee, p. 65
10. वृहस्पते भीममिमत्र-दम्भनं रक्षोहणं गोत्रमिदं स्वर्विदम्।
    Rig Veda II. 23.13
11. नव श्रिये व्याजहीत पर्वतो गवां गोत्रमुदसृजो यदङ्गिरः।
12. Rg Veda II. 23.18 ride also Chatterjee, p. 65. See not 5 above.
13. Chatterjee, op.cit. p. 62.
14. Chatterjee, op.cit. p. 117.
15. Social Welfare, vol. XXX, No. 12, March, 1984 (*Marriage under Hindu Law* by Leelavathi Chari, p. 5)
16. *Towards Equality*, Report of the Committee on the Status of Women in India, Ministry of Education and Social Welfare, Government of India, 1974, p. 62.
17. Das, R.M., *Women in Manu's Philosophy*, Jalandhar, ABS Publications, 1993, p. 65.
18. *Rig Veda*, XVIII, 8.
19. Chatterjee, op.cit. p. 260.
20. Kane, P.V., *History of Dharmasastra*, vol. II, part I, p. 608. See note 4 above.
21. Manu, Lect. IX.
22. नग्निकान्तु वदेत कन्या यावन्नुर्मती भवेत्।
    ऋतुमंती त्वनग्निका तां प्रयच्छेत्वनग्निकाम्।।
    Grhya Samgraha II, 17.
23. Manu, Lect. IX, 90.
24. Manu, Lect. IX, 80.
25. Thomas, P., *Indian Women Through the Ages*, Delhi, Asia Publishing House, 1964, p. 225.
26. Manu, Lect. III, 51.

27. Law, B.C. *Women in Buddhist Literature*, Varanasi, Indological Book House, 1927, p.2.
28. Ibid., p. 3.
29. *Jataka*, No. 536.
30. Law, see not 26 above, p. 12.
31. See ante, p. 30
32. Kane, P.V., *History of Dharmasastra*, vol. II, part I, op.cit. see not 4 above, p. 693.
33. Avasthi, Abha, *Hindu Marriage in Continuity and Change*, op.cit. See note 7 above, p. 80.
34. Ibid.
35. Bandopadhyay, N.C., *Kautilya*, Varanasi, Indological Book House, 1982, p. 273.
36. Ibid.
37. वइयेत्कुलजां प्राज्ञो विरूपामपि कन्यकाम।
    रूपशीला न नीचस्य विवाह: सहशे कुले ।।१४।।
    चाण्क्य-नीति-दर्पणं:, प्रथमोऽध्याय:।
    Taken from *Chanakya Neeti Darpan*, Chapter I, translated by Mann, Gian Singh, in *Chanakya*, Delhi, Amar Prakashan, 1986, p.5.
38. विषादप्यमृतं ग्राहयममेध्यादपि काञ्चन।
    नीचादप्युत्रमां विद्यां स्त्रीइत्नं दुष्कुलादपि।।१६।।
    Ibid., Chapter 1, p. 6.
39. पत्युराज्ञां विना नारी उपोष्य व्रतचइिणी।
    आयुराहरते भर्तु: स नारी नरकं व्रजेत।।१।।
    Ibid., Chapter 17, p. 100.
40. न दानैं: शुद्धयते नारी उपवासशतैरपि।
    न तीर्थसेवया तद्वदभर्तु: पादोदकैर्यथा ।।१०।।
    Ibid Chapter 17.
41. Kaur, Inderjeet, *Status of Hindu Women in India*, Allahabad, Chugh Publications, 1983, p. 41
42. Kapadia, K.M., *Marriage and Family in India*, Bombay, OUP, 1958, p. 253.

3

Age of Marriage

The movement against child marriage started in Bengal about mid-nineteenth century. A few Bengali women from Chinsura had, however, already ventilated their grievances through newspapers even earlier. Their complaints were focused in the form of questions in the *Samachar Darpan* in 1835 as follows:[1]

1. Oh, father and brother: Why should you deprive us of the scope of education which the women of other countries do avail? Do you think that education would make us unfit for domestic duties?
2. Why don't you allow us to live and move freely as women of other countries do?
3. Why are we transferred like cattle at the tender age of 4, 5, 10 and 12 to unknown men who have no education, wealth or beauty? Why do you treat us so cruelly?

These grievances of the women of Bengal did not go unheeded, and contributed much to the agitation against the traditional system of marriage. In July 1847, the *Samvad Pravakar* pointed out that early marriage was detrimental to the education of young boys.[2] Early marriage was likely to distract their attention, hamper their studies and spoil their future.

In August 1850, the *Sarvasubhakari Patrika* published an article written by Pandit Ishwar Chandra Vidyasagar pointing out the evils of child marriage. Early marriages led to premature childbearing, often damaging the health of young parents who, as a consequence rarely had strong and healthy children. Moreover, young boys and girls developed little understanding of each other because, before marriage, as a custom, they were never allowed to see or know each other. Therefore, real conjugal love seldom grew between them. 'Oh God,' Vidyasagar exclaimed, 'when will you save us from this precarious condition? Will any bright light shine at all? After how many years?'[3]

The movement against child marriage gathered momentum throughout the sixties and seventies of the nineteenth century. *The Bamabodhini Patrika* published an article denouncing the evils of child marriage, pointing out many abuses caused by it, such as early death, ill health, lack of education, poverty, etc. It burdened growing young men, hampered their studies and led them to the horrors of poverty.[4] The weekly paper, *Somprakash*, was very critical of child marriage and polygamy, and wrote strongly against it. Early marriage, it observed, was the root of numerous evils and the main cause of the gradual decay of the human race. Just as strong trees could not grow from weak seeds, so a prosperous mankind could never grow from physically weak and mentally undeveloped boys and girls.[5]

During the 1860s, the younger members of the Brahmo Samaj under the leadership of Keshab Chandra Sen, after a split in the Samaj, propagated marriage reforms. The years 1871 and 1872 witnessed an important Reform Act, the earliest piece of legislation which sought to deal with early marriage. In fact, it was in 1861 that Devendranath Tagore, the leader of the older group, had first introduced a simplified and reformed Brahmo marriage ceremony from which the idolatory aspects of orthodox Hindu rites were excluded.[6] The younger *Brahmos* under the leadership of Keshab Chandra Sen went a step further and introduced inter-caste marriage in December 1867. A number of old rituals were dropped. In the place of *sampradan*, (the Bengali term for *kanyadan*, i.e. gift of the bride), mutual vows were exchanged, the ceremony thus taking on a Western tinge.[7]

In 1868, the question of legal validity of these changes was raised and the Advocate General declared the marriages performed according to the Brahmo Samaj rites legally invalid.[8] Keshab Sen, discussed the matter with the authorities in charge of legislation, particularly Sir Henry Maine who was then the Law Member of the Viceroy's Council.[9] Henry Maine believed that the Brahmo sect was new and, like all newly formed religious bodies, its doctrines and principles were not in a definite shape. He, therefore, proposed a comprehensive measure making the Brahmo ceremony a kind of civil marriage. It was called the Native Marriage Bill, and was applicable to all non-Christians. He introduced the Bill on 18 November 1868 and circulated it among the local government officials for their views. The opinion poll went against the proposed Bill on the ground that it was likely to introduce far-reaching changes in 'native' law and would interfere with native social relations.[10] The orthodox Hindus, the landholders of Bengal, and the Pandits of Varanasi all opposed the Bill, as they were afraid of heterodox unions amongst their communities. The Bill was, therefore, kept in abeyance for two years.

One of the contested points in the controversy was the acceptable marriageable age of Indian girls. In April 1871, Keshab Sen, as the President of the Indian Reform Association, addressed a circular letter to eminent medical practitioners of the country and sought their opinion.[11] The medical authorities of Calcutta determined the age of fourteen as the minimum marriageable age for girls. Fitzjames Stephen (Sir James Stephen), who succeeded Maine as the Law Member, considered the opposition from the orthodox Hindus, and modified the Bill after receiving the Select Committee's report in March 1871. The Bill became one intended exclusively for the Brahmos under the name of the Brahmo Marriage Bill, according to which fourteen years was fixed as the minimum marriageable age for girls.[12]

By the year 1865, the Brahmo Samaj had been divided into two camps—the Conservatives and the Progressives. The former, called the Adi Brahmo Samaj and led by Devendranath Tagore, at once sent a deputation which met the Law Member in the morning of the day on which the Bill was to be passed and pressed its objections against the measure. Stephen found good reason to postpone the passing of the Bill till July. In that month, the same deputation of the Adi Brahmo Samaj proceeded to Simla from Calcutta and presented a memorial to Stephen against the Bill.[13]

The first objection of the deputationists was that its application would extend to the whole body of Brahmos, although the majority of the Brahmo Samaj members did not feel the necessity for such an enactment, nor had they applied for any legislation on the subject of Brahmo marriage. Secondly, they objected that such a law would tend to cut off the Brahmos from the general community of Hindus of which they formed an integral part. Such a state of affairs, they said, would only injure their cause. Their third argument was that the form prescribed by the Bill for registration of marriages would reduce it to a mere civil contract. The fact that the parties to the marriage would not be required to go through any religious ceremony was extremely revolting to the feelings of the members of the Bramho Samaj and it would be hard for them to reconcile themselves to the forms and practices enjoined in the proposed law. Fourthly, the provision with respect to the age of the parties contracting the Brahmo marriage was inconsistent with the usages of the country, because the marriageable age of girls in India was considered to be below fourteen years. Fifthly, the passing of the proposed law would lead to serious complications with regard to the question of succession and inheritance of the descendants of those who would avail of the provisions of the proposed enactment and marry out of the pale of Hindu society. There was nothing in the existing law to regulate the succession of the children of such a marriage to the property left either by the father or the mother.

Considering the objections of the Adi Brahmo Samaj, the Bill was again postponed for a few months and came up next before the Council of the Governor-General of India on 16 January 1872, when Stephen moved the Bill in the Council and narrated the background of the measure. He urged the immediate passing of the Bill.[14] Inglis, a member of the Council opposed the Bill on the ground that calculating people with base designs in mind might take advantage of certain provisions of the Bill to entrap lads of good families, infatuated with dancing girls, into marriage which would end in disgrace and ruin. So he suggested that the Bill be circulated once again throughout the country and referred to the local governments in order to obtain public opinion on its provisions.[15] Cockerell, another member of the Council, also supported the further delay. Only Temple agreed with Stephen against any postponement of the Bill. Inglis' motion was put to vote and was carried by nine votes to two.

On 19 March 1872, the Bill came up again before the Council.[16] Inglis moved the amendment that the Bill be referred back to the Select Committee for necessary alterations because native opinion did not favour the measure. He read out letters from eminent persons holding high positions in the Government of the Madras Presidency. For example, V. Ramiengar, Additional Member of the Council of the Government of Fort St. George wrote on 28 February 1872, that 'It (Bill) appears to me to differ little from Sir Henry Maine's Bill, so universally condemned and withdrawn'. Sachish Sastri, the head *seristadar* (head ministerial officer of a court) of the Madras Revenue Board, wrote on 12 February 1872, that 'It is highly injudicious on the part of the government to undertake to legislate on matters connected with the social and religious movement of the people.' The Acting Collector of Madura, Mc. Quhae said that a few Hindus objected to the Bill on the ground that it was founded on the same principle as the Act which legalized the remarriage of Hindu widows and Act XXI of 1850.[17]

Stephen pointed out, on the other hand, that he had also collected the opinions of a number of Indians which were sufficiently favourable to justify the government in pressing on with the Bill. Hannyngton, the Acting Collector of the Kistna District, gathered the views of the 'native gentlemen' of his district and wrote that 'the deduction which may be drawn' from their opinion is 'that they consider the Bill not entirely necessitious, but on the whole a measure to be desired'. Mac Gregor, the Collector of Malabar wrote that he had consulted several Hindus of his district and they had no objection to the proposed measure.[18]

Stephen moved that the Bill as amended be passed. The motion was carried by eight votes (including those of the President and Commander-in-Chief) to five.[19] In view of the opposition of the Adi Brahmo Samaj, the new Bill was, however, renamed as the Special Marriage Bill, and three days later it was passed into law as Act III of 1872. The Act abolished early marriage and made polygamy penal, sanctioned widow remarriage and inter-caste marriage.

The Act of 1872 was passed, but the storm it roused within the Brahmo Samaj did not subside. Raj Narayan Basu, an eminent leader of the Adi Brahmo Samaj circulated a pamphlet voicing agitated protests, entitled *An Appeal to the Brahmos*, in which he expressed deep sorrow that such a 'Godless' marriage could be introduced in the Samaj. He also expressed regret that the Brahmos had on their own sacrificed their rights and liberty at the feet of a foreign government and entitled it to intervene in the social affairs of the country.[20]

Tattvakaumudi, on behalf of the younger Brahmos, defended the Marriage Act of 1872 on the ground that religious mediation was a vital feature of this new form of marriage. The registration of marriage was only an extra act added to the existing rites, so it was wrong to suppose that this marriage system was devoid of the blessings of God. Tattvakaumudi also argued that there were different forms of marriages prevailing in India. For example, the Sudra form of marriage was quite different from that of the Brahmins, and in Bengal among the Vaishnavas, the exchange of garlands was the only rite observed in the marriage ceremony. All forms of marriages were equally accepted as valid in Hindu society, so what was wrong with the Special Marriage Act 1872 if it introduced a somewhat new pattern, different from the traditional one? Besides, the registration of a marriage was needed from another point of view. Since the presence of men was regarded as essential during a Hindu marriage, registration would only serve as testimony that the marriage ceremony had taken place. *Tattvabodhini Patrika*, however, refuted Tattvakaumudi's arguments and severely criticized the new Act. In its view, the marriage ceremony as envisaged in the Act of 1872 was definitely 'Godless'. Since registration was included as an essential part of marriage, God had been denied His supremacy.[21]

Since the inception of the Bill, some of its provisions were subject to criticism also by *Somprakash*, a weekly newspaper. Since the Bill provided that both the spouses must be Bramhos, the *Somprakash* pointed out that this provision must be explicit and must clearly state that any person other than a Brahmo would necessarily be converted into a Bramho a year before marriage, or else serious consequences might follow. As, for instance, a shrewd prostitute with an evil motive might become a Brahmo a day before her marriage, and marry a young rich Brahmo. If the young-man died prematurely, the prostitute would inherit a large fortune, and re-start her business, her purpose of marriage having been fulfilled.[22] Secondly, according to the *Somprakash*, the age of marriage as prescribed in the Act was also opposed. It was argued that, in India's tropical climate, girls attained puberty much earlier, so the girls' marriageable age should be lowered to twelve. As for doctors' opinions referred to by Keshab Chandra Sen, it was argued that eminent doctors like T. Charles, J. Fayhar and Mahendra Sarkar looked at the problem from only one point of view and ignored the others.[23] The argument continued that, after puberty, girls felt an urge for cohabitation, and that raising the age of marriage to sixteen would result in harm to the young girls due to suppression of their natural desires.

The Special Marriage Act (1872), however, gave more rights to women than those permitted in the traditional form of marriage. Under this Act, a husband could not marry a second time during the lifetime of the first wife. On the demise of the husband, who was married under the Special Marriage Act, his widow succeeded to his estates, and was not helpless. Further, the raising of the marriageable age came as a relief to young girls who were relieved to some extent from the hazards of early marriage.

However, the Act of 1872 could not stop the evil practice of early marriage. The orthodox Bengalis still supported child marriage and raised serious objections against Garrett's (the officer of the British government in charge of education) proposal to the Director of Public Instruction that married boys should not be allowed to sit for final examinations. The progressive section, however, endorsed Garrett's proposal, because they believed that early marriage was a pernicious practice. In August 1878, nearly four hundred students held a meeting in Albert Hall, a public hall in Calcutta, and resolved that no student would marry until he turned twenty-one.[24]

The agitation became stronger in the eighteen eighties. Behramji Merwanji Malabari, the well-known Parsi social reformer, had been agitating to secure legislation against child marriage and published his notes on *Infant Marriage and Enforced Widowhood* in 1884.[25] In his notes, Malabari exposed the abuses of early marriage and suggested remedies for the social evil. These were that: (1) married boys ought not to be allowed by universities to sit for examinations, (2) the government should prefer unmarried men to married ones in the matter of appointments for jobs, and (3) a National

Association for Social Reform be created with the existing societies as branches and its members were to be most prominent government officials, from the Viceroy to the Governors.[26]

Lord Dufferin, the Viceroy of India, did not approve of Malabari's proposal because the provincial governments and the chief government officials refused to interfere with Hindu marriage customs. Dufferin believed that the Government of India was guided by certain principles and could intervene in national and social matters only when those came in conflict with the Criminal Procedure Code. The question of infant marriage did not come under any civil or criminal law of the country, and so, any legislation in this respect would directly antagonize public opinion.[27]

Max Muller, the renowned German philosopher, well-versed in Indian philosophy and culture, did not support the government's attitude. In reply to Malabari's notes, he wrote in 1886:

> My attention has been drawn to the war you have started against infant marriage. So far I have not written anything about it, because I do not like to express my opinion on all matters. In my opinion the Government should stop whatever is unnatural. It is beyond expectation that men will do everything themselves, law should help them, because legislation is nothing but a focus of public opinion.[28]

Malabari's movement roused great excitment all over India. The leading Indian supporters of Malabari were Justice M.G. Ranade, the erudite scholar and thinker, also known as a prophet of the cultural renaissance in Western India; K.T. Telang, a Judge of Bombay High Court and a thoughtful social reformer; Dayaram Gidumal, an Assistant Judge of Ahmedabad; Bepin Chandra Pal, the famous orator, freedom fighter and social reformer; Mahendra Lal Sircar, eminent in the field of medicine, and others. In early January 1885, Tilak, the great nationalist leader, organized a number of meetings in which he vehmently urged that it was humiliating to appeal to the alien government to remedy an Indian social evil. He did not deny the harmful effects of early marriage but was of the opinion that education and not legislation was required to eradicate the evil.[29] There was opposition in Bengal too, where Malabari was severely criticized by many vernacular newspapers.

The liberal Hindus, however, supported his social campaign. The controversy over the question reached its height towards the end of 1890 when the government sponsored a Bill known as the Age of Consent Bill which aimed at raising the age of consent from ten to twelve.

The Indian Penal Code, enacted in 1860, had made rape an offence and had prescribed punishment which might extend to transportation for life. The offence extended to a husband who had sex with his wife if she was below ten years of age.[30] Gidumal proposed that the IPC be amended so as to raise the age of consent for girls from ten to twelve and, as before, the offence was to be applicable to married wives below twelve as well. But there was fierce opposition from the orthodox section, particularly from Bengal.

The problem was also raised in the Indian National Social Conference. Ranade strongly supported Gidumal's proposal of the amendment. The third annual session of the Conference held in Bombay in 1889 resolved that in order to prevent early consummation of marriage, which leads to the impairment of the physical health of both husband and wife, cohabitation with wife below twelve years of age should be punishable as a criminal offence.[31] In the fourth session of the Indian National Social Conference held at Calcutta in 1890, the following resolution was passed:

> This Conference is of opinion that the practice of child marriage be discouraged by public sentiment and that within the sphere of the various caste and communities strenuous efforts be made to postpone the celebration of the marriage rites till 12 in the case of girls and 18 in the case of boys.[32]

The agitation spread throughout the country. Fifty-five women doctors from different parts of India appealed to the Viceroy to pass a law prohibiting consummation of marriage with girls below fourteen.[33] Sixteen hundred Indian women sent a similar petition to Queen Victoria.[34] Many reformers, including Sir R.G. Bhandarkar, an enlightened scholar, cited the Indian *shastras* in support of the Age of Consent Bill. He explained that Manu sanctioned late marriage.

In Bengal, though orthodox sentiment was against the measure, the proposal for raising the age of consent received support from many sections. The Brahmo Samaj supported the Bill wholeheartedly. A public meeting held at 12, Wellington Square in Calcutta on 15 February 1891 formed a committee which sent a memorial in favour of the Bill signed by 8000 persons to the Government of India.[35] The prominent supporters of the Bill were the Nawab of Dacca, Narendra Nath Sen, Editor, Indian Mirror; Sarat Chandra Roy, Editor, Saturday Herald; Babu Krishna Kamal Bhattacharjee, Principal, Ripon College; Peary Mohan Roy, grandson of Rammohan Roy, among others. A group of 155 women of different faiths—Hindu, Brahmo, Muslim, Christian—worked for it.

The Bill, however, was vehemently opposed by Tilak and his orthodox friends. Although he felt deeply for girls who suffered the unfortunate consequences of child marriage, Tilak strongly resented the idea of interference by a foreign race in Hindu social and religious customs.

On 9 January 1891, the issue of the age of consent was placed before the Viceroy's Council.[36] Andrew Scoble, a member of the Council, while introducing a Bill in the Council to amend Indian Penal Code and Code of Criminal Procedure 1882, cited the Hari Maity case, in which Hari Maity, aged thirty-five, caused the death of his wife Phulmoni, aged only nine, by forcing her to have sexual intercourse. He said that under section 375 of the Indian Penal Code, the offence of rape was committed when a man had sexual intercourse with a woman under certain circumstances, one of those being intercourse with or without the consent of a girl under ten years of age. No exception was made in favour of married persons. On the other hand, it was stipulated that sexual intercourse by a man with his own wife, provided that the wife was above ten years of age, could not be classified as rape. Scoble proposed that the age of consent be raised both for married and unmarried women, from ten to twelve years.

According to him, the objects of the Bill were two-fold. It was intended to protect female children: (1) from premature prostitution, and (2) from premature cohabitation. While justifying the Bill, he referred to the eloquent speech of Pandit Sasadhur Tarkachuramoni, an eminent Sanskrit scholar, an extract of which runs as follows: 'It is true we advocate early marriage … but we believe it to be a great sin to cohabit with a girl before her puberty and we believe it to be the terrible cause of our degeneration.'[37]

Ramesh Chandra Mitter, an Indian member of the Council, opposed the Bill. He stated that it was an anomaly in the Indian Penal Code that a husband could be guilty of rape when the woman was his own wife. Section 375 of the Penal Code was, already, a dead letter. If the amended section was also likely to prove irrelevant, there was no need to enact it.[38] In his opinion, the proposed amendment regarding the husband's criminality would cause widespread discontent in the country and would be a departure from the government's policy of non-interference, because that would amount to interference with the religious rites of the Hindus. He said that he would be glad to support a policy that protects child wives from personal violence, if it were not a departure from the wise, just policy of the government not to interfere where such intervention was not needed for the repression of crimes, even if it had the effect of remedying, to an appreciable degree, the evils of early marriage. So far as the protection of child wives from personal violence was concerned, he said, they were sufficiently protected by the provisions of the existing criminal law, under which a husband was criminally liable for acts which constituted offences like causing death by a rash or negligible act, of hurt, simple or grievous, or of an assault on his wife, even if they were done with her consent, if she was under ten years of age. The existing law, therefore, afforded sufficient protection to a wife under ten years of age from violence by her husband. Thereupon he gave his note of dissent saying, 'After careful consideration of all that has been said for and against it, I am still of the opinion that the proposed amendment of the exception to section 375 of the Indian Penal Code, is likely to cause more harm than good.'[39]

Though Ramesh Chandra Mitter opposed the Bill, all Indian and other members of the Council spoke in favour of the measure. Rao Bahadur Krishnaji Lakshman Nulkar, an Indian member of the Council, supported the Bill and said that any discontent that arose in certain sections of the society would only be temporary.[40] He also referred to Dr. Chever's *Manual of Medical Jurisprudence for Bengal* (published in 1856) describing the artificial means employed to prepare child-wives for the earliest possible intercourse with their husbands. On the basis of Dr Chever's Manual, Nulkar pointed out that the legislation undertaken by the government was a great necessity.[41]

Hutchins, a member of the Governor-General's Council, remarked:

> ... the evil at which the Bill is directed was brought prominently to our notice by the case of Hari Maity .... The post mortem examination of the girl Phulmoni showed that either the private parts had undergone artificial enlargement with a view to early consummation or that, she had been subjected to repeated acts of intercourse. The abominable state of things cried out loudly for a remedy and the Bill was absolutely necessary.'[42]

Andrew Scoble, while describing the situation in Bengal, quoted an extract from Stewart Bayley which ran thus, 'the custom appears to be universal ... but it prevails generally over Bengal proper, especially over Eastern and Central Bengal'.[43] Scoble also cited the official documents.[44] In one such document, Leyall, the Commissioner of Chittagong, had reported that the practice of consummating marriage with immature girls was universal in his division as it was in the whole of Bengal. The records of the criminal courts pointed to the same situation. In the Sessions Court in Rungpur, a man called Dhulamasga was tried in March 1890 for committing rape on his wife and was sentenced to three months' rigorous imprisonment. Similarly, at Hooghly, Jamiruddin was charged with having caused the death of his wife Parijan in December 1889.

On the basis of these cases, which were but an indicator of the real scale of the practice, Andrew Scoble asserted that Hari Maity's was not an isolated case and that the existing law needed further protective clauses. The Marquis of Lansdowne, the Viceroy and Governor-General of India and the President of the Council, declared:

> We justify our proposal on the ground that British Law would fail to provide adequately for the safety of the children of this country, if it failed to protect them from a particular form of ill usage infinitely more revolting and more disastrous in its direct as well as in its remote result than any form of ill treatment to which they are liable.

The Bill was passed on 19 March 1891 as Act X of 1891. By virtue of this Act, the age of consent prescribed in the Indian Penal Code 1860 was amended and raised from ten to twelve.[45] Although the immediate effect of this Act was not very encouraging, a silent change in social attitude gradually became visible. This was perhaps due to the spread of education and the consequent change in the thinking of the people. This change was noted by many eminent persons. Manmohan Ghose, the elder brother of Sri Aurobindo, said in his address at the meeting of the National Indian Association held in 1895: 'As regards child marriages, though I regret I cannot say that the practice has been discontinued, there has undoubtedly been a remarkable progress of late.' Two Indian princely states, which adopted measures to abolish child marriage, deserve special mention. First, the Mysore Government passed the Infant Marriages Prevention Regulation in 1894 to stop marriage of girls under eight and to prevent marriage between man and woman of very unequal age, particularly of girls below fourteen. Second, the Gaekwad of Baroda, in the face of a good deal of opposition, passed the Infant Marriage Prevention Act for his state in 1904, which absolutely forbade the marriage of girls below the age of nine and allowing girls below the age of twelve and boys below the age of sixteen to marry, only if the parents first obtained the consent of a tribunal consisting of the local Sub-Judge and three assessors of the petitioner's caste.[46]

The Census Report of 1911 also states:

> The practice has been denounced by many social reformers since Malabari opened the campaign a quarter of a century ago; and the Social Conference which holds its meeting, annually, in connection with the National Congress has made the abolition of child marriage, one of the leading planks in its platform. It is strongly discouraged by the Brahmos in Bengal and the Aryas in North India.[47]

Efforts to fight this evil continued. In 1924, Sir Hari Singh Gour introduced in vain a Bill to amend section 375 of the Indian Penal Code so as to raise the age of consent of girls from twelve to fourteen.[48] On 1 September 1925, Sir Alexander Muddiman, the Home Member, introduced a Bill prescribing thirteen as the age of consent in marital cases and fourteen in extra-marital cases. The

Home Member explained that he was only the stepfather of the Bill; the credit for the measure must go to Sir Hari Singh Gour.[49] M.K. Acharya, the leader of the opposition, objected to penal legislation for social reform and criticized the authors of the Bill. Shanmukham Chetty, a member of the Legislative Assembly, also opposed it. However, after a long debate, Hari Singh Gour moved that the age be raised to fifteen. His amendment was rejected by sixty-three votes to forty-two.[50] On 3 September 1925, Dr S.K. Datta, another member of the Legislative Assembly moved in the Assembly that the age of consent for the marriage of girls be raised to fourteen, instead of thirteen as provided by the Bill. He said his amendment was for educating the community. He referred to the unhealthy growth of children in Calcutta, holding the low age of marriage responsible for it and stating that the remedy was to raise the age of consent.[51]

However, the Bill of 1925 was not treated as finally settled, either by the Government or by the Assembly; and early marriage persisted in the early part of the twentieth century. The Census Report recorded the following figures of infant marriages in 1921:

Number of wives up to the age of 5	1,04,850
Number of wives up to the age of 10	2,016,687
Number of wives up to the age of 15	6,330,207
	8,451,744

A Hindu woman from Bengal wrote a letter to the editor of the newspaper, *Young India*, describing a girl's tragic death in Calcutta. The girl was ten years old. After living two nights with her husband, she refused to live with him any further. A few days later, she was sent by her mother to give *paan* (betel leaf) to her husband. After handing over the paan, she wanted to return but the man shut the door and refused to let her go. After a while, a pitiable groaning was heard, and when the door was opened, the girl was found dead with injuries on her head.[52] One can only speculate about how many cases of that nature went unreported.

A large section of people, however, continued to support child marriage even in the twentieth century on the ground that early marriage was a universal custom of Hindu society and it was improper to say that the Hindu *sastrakars* were entirely wrong in prescribing child marriage. In their view, early marriage was not the cause of weak health. On the contrary, they believed that as the marriageable age continued to rise, the race was becoming weaker. The argument was that fifty or a hundred years ago men and women were stronger by far, so early marriage could not be condemned.[53]

In December 1925, the All India Social Conference, presided by Sarala Devi Choudhurani, emphasized the need for further raising the age of marriage both for boys and girls in view of physical degeneration and other evils resulting from early marriage.[54] The first All India Conference of women held at Poona, in January 1927, under the presidentship of the Maharani of Baroda adopted the following resolution:

> This Conference deplores the effect of early marriage on education and urges the Government to pass legislation to make marriage below the age of sixteen a penal offence... .[55] It demands that the age of consent be raised to sixteen.

On 1 February 1927, Rai Saheb Harbilas Gour Sarda introduced a Bill on child marriage among Hindus. The Bill was called the Marriage Restraint Bill, popularly called the Sarda Bill. It prohibited marriages of girls below the age of 12 and of boys below the age of 15. The Bill was referred to the select committee on 15 September 1927 but was kept in abeyance for two years. In the meanwhile an Age of Consent Committee was appointed by the government of India on 25 June 1928. The Comittee as finally constituted, consisted of Sir Moropant Vishvanath Joshi (Chairman), Rai Bahadur Pandit Kanhaiya Lal, A. Ramaswamy Mudaliyar, Khan Bahadur Mahbub, Mian Imam Bakshi Kadri, Mrs M. O'Brien, Beadon, Rameshwari Nehru, Satyendra Chandra Mitra, Pandit Thakurdas Bhargava, Maulvi Muhammad Yakub and Mian Muhammad Shah Nawaz. On 8 September Harbilas Sarda moved before the Assembly that the Bill be recommitted to a select committee as the bill had been before the country for about two years and wanted that the select committee should report within three days. The move was ardently supported by Lala Lajpat Rai.[56] On the same day, ladies of all shades of opinion and representing every women's society of Bengal accorded unanimous support to the Child Marriage Restraint and Age of Consent Bills in a crowded meeting in Calcutta under the presidency of Lady Mukherjea.[57]

After amendment by the select committee, the Bill came up before the Assembly on 29 January 1929. The first amendment that the select committee made to the original Bill was that the Bill was to be applicable to all classes and communities in British India. Secondly, clause 6 of the original Bill, i.e. the conscience clause, was completely eliminated. Thirdly, originally the intention was to declare all objectionable marriages of boys or girls below a certain age to be invalid; instead the select committee introduced a provision to make it penal. Finally, not only the substance of the Bill, but also the very title and preamble were altered. Harbilas Sarda moved the Bill in the House and delivered a forceful speech. He stated that, despite its reference to the select committee, the principle of the Bill had not been changed. The government had agreed that the principle was that there should be legislation with regard to child marriage. He further stated that the Bill was circulated to the public for eliciting their opinion. Hundreds of conferences were held in the country; women's associations and *sabhas* met and passed resolutions supporting this Bill and there was not a single instance of a public meeting of women protesting against the Bill.

Sasha Ayyangar, a Member of the Legislative Assembly, however, opposed the Bill on the ground that the original Bill had been so vitally changed, both in form and substance, by the select committee that it almost appeared to be a new Bill. In the first report of the select committee, it was said that the Bill had been 'so materially altered by us that in our opinion it requires republication.'[58] It was hence necessary to obtain sanction for the new Bill again from the Governor-General.

M.K. Acharya, Member, Legislative Assembly, said that the consideration of the Bill should be postponed until the Age of Consent Committee's report was published and the report became available to the members of the Council. His motion was put to vote and was carried by fifty-three against thirty-four.[59]

On 26 August 1929, the Report of the Age of Consent Committee, popularly called the Joshi Committee, was published.[60] The

Committee recommended that the age be raised to fifteen in marital cases, consummation before fifteen be treated as 'marital misbehaviour' and the offender be punished with imprisonment of either description for ten years and a fine when the wife was under twelve, and imprisonment for one year or a fine, or both, when she was between twelve and fifteen. In extra-marital cases, the age was to be raised to eighteen. In the case of any sex relation with a girl under sixteen, the offender was to be punished with transportation for life or with imprisonment of either description for ten years. If, however, the girl was above sixteen and below eighteen, and had given consent, imprisonment up to two years with or without fine could be awarded. With a view to protecting younger girls, the Committee further recommended that the marriage of a girl under fourteen should be prohibited and made penal. It further recommended that the definition of the offence of rape should be amended so as to exclude a husband and that, instead of the present provision, a new offence to be termed 'marital misbehaviour' should be provided. In order to give better protection to a girl against rape by a person who was not her husband, the age of consent was to be raised to eighteen years.[61]

After publication of the Report of the Age of Consent Committee, the Bill once again came up to the Legislative Assembly on 4 September 1929, but was severely criticized by M.K. Acharya, who raised a number of points.[62] In the first place, the voluminous report of 363 pages was published only a week before the session and, within such a short period, it was neither possible to read the whole of it, nor to scrutinize it in detail. Secondly, the Committee was not fully representative, and none of the original six members could properly represent the orthodox Hindu opinion. Moreover, the report contained contradictory statements.[63] The most serious charge was that the report was based on inadequate evidence. Questionnaires had been sent to 7930 persons, of whom only 1200 responded, which is only fifteen per cent. The Committee also claimed the support of women, but Acharya pointed out that the telegrams from women—one from Krishna and one from Kumbakonam—both opposed the Bill. So the Report of the Committee ignored everything that was unfavourable and magnified the points in favour.

Sasha Ayyangar also cited many instances where women had

opposed the Bill.[64] He claimed that women's meetings held in Kumbakonam, Triplicane, Madras, and also in Cocananda just a week before, were all thoroughly representative, and they called it the most pernicious Bill that was aimed at undermining the Hindu religion in the country. In Madras, Collectors of almost every district, such as Salem, Anantapur, Krishna, Chittoor, Coimbatore, Madras, Tiruchinapalli, reported that the *Dwija* (Brahmin) communities of those districts invariably opposed the Bill. In addition to this, there were many conferences throughout India, for example, at Varanasi, Calcutta, etc., where all the leading communities protested against the Bill on the ground that it was likely to sap the foundations of the Hindu society, because marriage was a part of religion. Most Bengali members of the Assembly spoke against the Bill. Amar Nath Datta of Burdwan opposed the Bill because, in his opinion, no legislation had any right to impose any rule of conduct upon the people.[65]

K.C. Neogy of Bengal pointed out that, in the provinces of Madras, Bengal, the Punjab, Bihar and Orissa, there were mixed reactions.[66] The Government of Punjab, for example, suggested that it should not be immediately promulgated; the Government of Madras rejected the Bill; the Bihar and Orissa Governments contended that they had nothing to do with it; and the Government of Bengal recommended that the Bill be dropped.

K.C. Neogy pointed out that, towards the end of August 1929, the meeting of the Bengal Provincial Hindu Sabha Conference was held at Dacca under the Presidentship of N.E. Kelkar, member of Legislative Assembly, and a resolution in support of the Sarda Bill was defeated by an overwhelming majority—a sufficient indication of Bengal's public opinion on the Bill. He also attempted to ascertain the opinion of the people by sending a few thousands of letters inviting public opinion on the measure. In response, he received a large number of telegrams and letters, of which not more than half a dozen were found to be in favour of the Bill.

A.H. Ghuznavi of Bengal (from the Muslim constituency) supported K.C. Neogy in his protest on behalf of the Hindus of Bengal. He cited an extract from the Bengal Government's report which ran as:

> In reply, I am to say that selected Bar Libraries and recognised associations and certain selected officers are consulted and copies of the replies received are enclosed for the information of the Government of India. It will be seen that most of the associations are opposed to the proposed legislation as affecting religious rights and usages.[67]

D.K. Lahiri Chaudhuri, a member from Bengal also held that such a legislation should not be allowed to go through. He, disagreed that infant mortality was in any way related to child marriage.[68] The Census Reports of 1911 and 1921 also showed that where the percentage of child marriage was the highest, infant mortality was the lowest. K.C. Roy was one of the few Bengalis who wholeheartedly supported the Bill. He vehemently protested against K.C. Neogy's arguments attacking the measure and his contention that the Bengal Government really opposed the legislation. Regarding the view of the Bengal Government he said: 'In conclusion I am to say that in the opinion of the Governor in Council, the question is one for the Hindus and if Hindu opinion is on the whole in favour of the legislation, he would not oppose it'.[69]

The torrent of arguments raged unabated against the Bill. Notable among the supporters of the Bill were Pandit Motilal Nehru, Pandit Madan Mohan Malaviya, N.C. Kelkar, M.A. Jinnah, M.R. Jayakar and others. The upshot of their arguments was that early marriage was a great evil which resulted in many women becoming widows and even hindered women's education.[70]

Sir James Crerar, the Home Member, explained the standpoint of the government in the House.[71] In his opinion, the Joshi Committee had rendered a great social service. The measure was then put to vote, and the motion was carried by sixty-seven votes against fourteen.[72] On 23 September 1929, the President declared the Bill as amended and passed.

Though the Bill was passed, the discussion centred on it continued for several days in the Assembly House. On 26 September, at the Simla Session, Mohammed Yakul, the Deputy President of the Assembly, severely criticized the government's attitude towards the Bill. He said:

> The Government of India seems to have lost its statesmanship, farsightedness, imagination and strength, and appears to be demoralised like a vanquished army. The passing of the Child Marriage Bill by the Legislative Assembly in the teeth of Moslem opposition must be an eye-opener to the Moslems. What is the guarantee that the Moslem religion and religious rites will not be made invalid and trampled upon in future when full responsible government is established?[73]

An attempt to fix the age of marriage for girls at twelve was lost without a division as the members of the Council of State favoured a deferment. P.C.D. Chari moved the postponement of the consideration of the Bill to the Delhi Session; Surpat Singh also favoured postponement. Ramaprasad Mukherjee agreed with the Bill, but pointed out that some modification was needed. The proposal for postponement of consideration of the Bill was put to the House and was defeated.[74] The public encouraged the Marriage Bill and sent letters to the editors of newspapers in favour of it. It became an Act on 1 October 1929 (Act No. XIX of 1929) and came into force on 30 April 1930. It fixed the marriageable age for boys at eighteen and for girls at fourteen.[75]

The Act was endorsed by women's associations in general. Dr Muthulakshmi Reddy, Deputy President of the Madras Legislative Council in her presidential address to the Andhra Mahila Mahasabha held at Bezwada on 3 November 1929, observed:

> Rai Bahadur Harbilas Sarda, the author of the Child Marriage Restraint Act, will go down to posterity as a great humanitarian and saviour of Indian womanhood because the Child Marriage Restraint Act is nothing but a measure to protect the rights of children.[76]

The Oudh Women's Conference held at Lucknow on 23 November 1929 under the presidency of Iravati Mehta also supported the Bill and resolved that the conference cordially welcomed the action of the Legislative Assembly in passing the Sarda Bill and thereby preventing the evil of early marriage.[77]

The British Press claimed that in the passing of the Bill, Indian opinion at last had yielded to the reformist pressure exerted by the government.[78] Quite contrary to this claim, however, the proceedings of the legislature will show that the efforts to raise the age of marriage in India were entirely due to Indian initiative and persistence. In fact, the Indian movement against early marriage had begun at least sixty years before this Act.

Despite these efforts, the Act did not affect the validity of child marriage, because once the marriage was performed, it was validated after the payment of a nominal fine. Sadly, the Act lacked teeth and failed to serve its purpose.

The most glaring defect of the Act was that it did not make child-marriage a cognizable offence, so no action could be taken by the government for its breach, unless a complaint was made within one year of the performance of the marriage. Secondly, such a complaint had to be lodged in a court of the Presidency Magistrate or a District Magistrate or a Magistrate of the First Class. Further, nearly six months lapsed between the date on which the Act was passed and the date on which it came into force. As a result, the passing of the Sarda Act was followed by a frantic rush of parents to marry off their minor children before the Act came into effect. Gujarat and Bengal in particular witnessed thousands of child marriages, and other parts of India were not far behind. An interesting account of such marriages appeared in the paper *Liberty* which wrote, 'A matrimonial wave is just passing over the country. Bride in embryo is being mated to groom in the cradle. The Sarda Act is coming into force and ... the poor girl just learning to suck the feeding bottle is being carried to the wedding bower.'[79]

Such a spate of infant marriages even attracted the attention of the law courts and criminal cases followed. In Nasik, the court had to stop the marriage of a Brahmin girl of ten to a deformed cripple, nearly four times her age. Her father's plea was that the Act would shortly be in force and it was against the *shastras* to keep the daughter unmarried till she was fourteen.

Early marriages, in fact, did not stop even when the Act came into force. This will be evident if the Census Report of 1931 is compared with that of 1921. No practical improvement took place in this respect, even two years after the passing of the Sarda Act.[80]

Number of Wives

Age	Year	Year
Years	*1921*	*1931*
1	9,066	44,082
1–2	11,595	63,954
2–3	32,197	1,14,099
3–4	60,755	2,32,813
4–5	1,04,850	3,46,904
5–10	2,016,687	4,200,534
10–15	6,330,207	7,269,208

Number of Widows

Age	Year	Year
Year	1921	1931
1	759	1,515
1–2	612	1,785
2–3	1,600	3,485
3–4	3,475	9,076
4–5	8,693	15,019
5–10	1,02,293	1,05,482
10–15	2,79,124	1,85,339

The above figures show that notwithstanding the Act, child marriages went on increasing. For example, in 1921 there were 9,066 wives under the age 1, in 1931 there were 44,082—an increase of nearly five times while the population increased only by one-tenth. Under the age group 10–15, there were 6,330,207 wives in 1921, and 7,269,208 wives in 1931. Again in 1921, there were 759 widows under 1, and in 1931, the number was 1,515. Under the 10–15 age group, there were 2,79,124 widows in 1921 and, in 1931, the corresponding number was 1,85,339. The successive census figures showed only a microscopic improvement.

During the period when the Sarda Act was in the offing, the law in England permitted a girl to marry at twelve and a boy at fourteen. This shows that child marriage was prevalent in England as well at that time. In 1929, a Bill was introduced in the House of Lords making sixteen the lowest age for a valid marriage, effectively abolishing the custom of child marriage.

The movement to raise the age of marriage did not stop with the passing of the Sarda Act. The fervour of agitation did not die and, even after 1929, the movement carried on. However, in view of the turmoil in the country triggered off by the pressing political developments emerging from the freedom struggle, and the outbreak of World War II during the late thirties and uptil the mid-forties, the issue of the age of marriage was kept in abeyance. The issue was taken up again by Pandit Thakurdas Bhargava after India's independence in 1947. This was but a continuation of the efforts that had been undertaken by the Government of India in 1928, when it had appointed the Age of Consent Committee even before the passing of the Sarda Act. On the basis of the recommendations, Pandit Thakurdas Bhargava moved three Bills on 4 April 1949 to amend the Indian Child Marriage Restraint Act 1929 or the Sarda Act. The Bills were designed to give effect to certain recommendations of the Age of Consent Committee of 1928. The first sought to raise the marriageable age of boys from eighteen to twenty and that of girls from fourteen to fifteen. A clause was also sought to be introduced to prevent girls below the age of eighteen from being married to men over the age of forty-five. The other Bills sought to make offences under the Child Marriage Restraint Act cognizable. The Bills had the general support of the members, though there were some difficulties as to the details, and they were ultimately referred to a select committee on 25 August 1948.[81] The select committee considered the three Bills together and submitted a revised Bill which sought to raise the marriageable age of girls from fourteen to fifteen, and of boys from eighteen to twenty, stating that the punishment of a fine prescribed for offences against this had not been sufficiently deterrent. The select committee recommended that the courts should be vested with the power to award simple imprisonment in suitable cases. For serious offences, compulsory imprisonment was the punishment considered suitable.

The select committee also recommended that offences under the Act should be cognizable, bailable and non-compoundable and that

Circles Inspectors of Police be authorized to investigate offences under the Act.[82] Members of the Constituent Assembly differed in their views. Pattavi Sitaramayya was opposed to offences being made cognizable because that would be tantamount to putting another weapon in the hands of the police to encroach on privacy and possibly turn any investigation to their own pecuniary gain.[83] Ananthasayanam Ayyangar, Deputy Speaker of the Constituent Assembly, welcomed the provisions of the Bill, but was opposed to the clause making violation of the provisions a cognizable offence. He maintained that simple imprisonment was deterrent enough. Professor Shibban Lal Saksena and Ram Narayan Singh supported the Bill. Both favoured offences under the Act being made cognizable although they realized that the police might misuse the power. N.V. Gadgil, Minister for Works, Mines and Power, said that so far as the Government of India was concerned, he was not sure whether the proposed difference of one year in the marriageable age of girls from fourteen to fifteen would in any way promise a remedy. As time went by, child marriage before the age of fourteen practically did not exist in the upper classes of society. Poorer people, too, for various reasons did not marry at an early age any more. Therefore, Gadgil said, there was no particular need for a legislation in this matter.[84]

A compromise was, however, effected and the Bill was passed with certain important amendments. It raised the marriageable age of girls to fifteen; the marriageable age for boys was, however, retained at eighteen, as provided in the Act. Clause 6 of the Bill making offences under the Act cognizable and vesting the power to investigate an offence in police officers was deleted.

The Bill when put to vote was adopted without amendment.[85] It came to be known as the Marriage Restraint Act and came into force along with other matrimonial Acts of the first part of the Hindu Code in 1955. When the first part was passed in 1955, the age of marriage for girls was retained at fifteen. *The Amrita Bazar Patrika* had already commented, however, 'Whatever might have been the case in the days gone by, child-marriage was gradually going out of vogue in all parts of India.'[86] In fact, it began to disappear quickly during the forties and fifties, and the age of marriage of girls rose far beyond the expectations of legislators and reformers. The credit for the reforms, however, was not due to social or educational progress, but mainly due to the fact that society at that time was adversely affected by political and socio-economic changes. World War II and the inflation that followed it disrupted the economic situation of the country. Further, many educated middle class families in certain parts of India—especially the provinces of Bengal and the Punjab—were badly affected by the Partition of India. Economically hard hit middle classes were forced to defer the marriages of their daughters because of their inability to meet the heavy expenses of weddings.

Notes and References

1. *Samachar Darpan*, 21 March 1835.
2. *Samvad Pravakar*, July 1847.
3. Halder, Gopal (Ed.), *Vidyasagar Rachana Sangraha*, vol. II, p. 2. See note 10 in chapter 1.
4. *Bamabodhini Patrika*, November 1864.
5. *Somprakash*, June, 1868.
6. Shastri, Sivnath, op.cit. p. 256. See note 6 in chapter 1.
7. Ibid.
8. Ibid.
9. Proceedings of the Council of the Governor-General of India, 1872, p. 1820.
10. Ibid.
11. Shastri, Sivnath, op.cit. p. 158.
12. Proceedings of the Council of the Governor-General of India, 1872, p. 28.
13. *Tattvabodhini Patrika*, June, 1872, an article—Civil Marriage Act.
14. Proceedings of the Council of the Governor-General of India, 1872, pp. 15, 51–3.
15. Ibid., pp. 53–6.
16. Ibid., pp. 149–50.
17. Act No. XXI of 1850 was passed by the Governor-General of India in Council, 11 April 1850. 'So much of any law or usage now in force within the territories subject to the Government of the East India Company as inflicts on any person forfeiture of right or property or may be held in any way to impair or affect any right of inheritance by reason of his or her renouncing or having been excluded from the commission of any religion, or being deprived of caste, shall cease to be enforced as law in the courts of the East India Company and in

the courts established by Royal Charter within the said territories' (India Council Act, 1850).

18. Proceedings of the Council of the Governor-General of India, 1872, p. 187.
19. Ibid., p. 205.
20. Chakravarti, Ajit Kumar, *Maharshi Debendra Nath Tagore*, Calcutta, Jijnasa, 1971, pp. 504–30.
21. *Tattvabodhini Patrika*, October 1879.
22. *Somprakash*, April 1871.
23. Ibid., July, 1871.
24. *Somprakash*, August 1878.
25. Gidumal, Dayaram, *The Life and Lifework of Behramji M. Malabari*, London, T. Fisher Unwin, 1888.
26. Heimsath, Charles, *Indian Nationalism and Hindu Social Reform*, Bombay, OUP, 1964, pp. 89–90.
27. *Somprakash*, August 1884.
28. Ibid., June 1886.
29. Tahmankar, D.V., *Lokmanya Tilak*, London, John Murray (Publishers) Ltd., 1956, p. 46.
30. Indian Penal Code, Section 375 dealing with rape and Section 376 dealing with punishment for rape.
31. Report of the Third National Social Conference, 1889, Appendix G.
32. Report of the Fourth National Social Conference, 1890, Appendix A.
33. Heimsath, Charles H., op.cit. p. 168. See note 26 above.
34. Report of the Fourth National Social Conference 1890, p.6.
35. *Journal of Indian History*, vol. 49 (April, August and December), The University of Kerala, Trivandrum, 1971, p. 295.
36. Proceedings of the Council of the Governor-General of India, 1891, p. 8.
37. Ibid., p. 10.
38. Ibid., p. 16–7.
39. The *Statesman*, 7 March 1891.
40. Proceedings of the Council of the Governor-General of India, 1891, p. 119.
41. Ibid., 1891, p. 119.
42. Ibid., 1891, p. 131.
43. Ibid., 1891, p. 11.
44. Ibid., 1891, pp. 77–80.
45. Ibid., 1891, p. 154.

46. Census Report, 1911, vol. I, part I, chapter vii, p. 272.
47. Census Report, 1911, vol. I, part I, chapter vii, p. 271.
48. India in 1924–5, p. 111.
49. Mitra N.N. (Ed.), *The Indian Quarterly Register*, Calcutta, the Annual Register Office, 1925, vol. II, p. 170.
50. Ibid.
51. Ibid., p. 173.
52. *Young India*, 7 October 1926.
53. Ibid., 9 September 1926.
54. Mitra, N.N. (Ed.), *The Indian Quarterly Register*, 1925, vol. II, p. 400.
55. Mitra, N.N. (Ed.), *The Indian Quarterly Register*, 1927, vol. I, p. 427.
56. Mitra, N.N. (Ed.), The Indian uarterly Register, 1928, vol. II, p. 168.
57. Ibid., p. 3.
58. Legislative Assembly Debates, 29 January 1929, (Official Report), vol. I, pp. 197–9.
59. Ibid., p. 204.
    Modern Review, Chatterjee, Ramananda (ed.), February 1929, vol. 45, p. 284
60. India in 1929–30, p.7.
61. Joshi Committee Report, 10ff. 123ff. p. 196.
62. Legislative Assembly Debates, 4 September 1929, p. 240.
63. Some statements of the Report were contradictory. Paragraph 232 of the Report (p. 102) stated that 'maternity contributes very largely to maternal and infantile mortality.' Paragraph 262 stated, on the other hand, that in some provinces as 'Burma where hardly a girl is married below 15, 200 infants die per 1000 births'. These two statements could not be reconciled—one in para 232 and the other in para 262.
64. Legislative Assembly Debates, 4 September 1929, (Official Report), vols iv & v, pp. 262–4.
65. Ibid., pp. 259–62.
66. Ibid., pp. 275–8.
67. Ibid., 11 September 1929, pp. 657–8.
68. Ibid., p. 650–1.
69. Ibid., 5 September 1929, p. 349–50.
70. Ibid., pp. 343–9, 369.
71. Ibid., p. 273.
72. Ibid., 23 September 1929, p. 1315.
73. *The Statesman*, 26 September 1929.
74. *The Statesman*, 28 September 1929.
75. Gupte, S.V., *Hindu Law of Marriage*, Bombay, Tripathi, 1961, p. 15.

76. Mitra, N.N. (Ed.), *Indian Quarterly Register,* 1929. vol. II, p. 397.
77. Ibid., p. 498.
78. Chatterjee, Ramananda (Ed.), *Modern Review,* November 1929, vol. 46, p. 601–2.
79. *Liberty,* 13 March 1930 (Quoted in Census Report, 1931, part I, vol. I, 230–3).
80. Census of India, 1931, part I, vol. I, chapter vi, p. 224.
81. *Amrita Bazar Patrika,* 26 August 1948.
82. Ibid., 5 April 1949.
83. Ibid.
84. Ibid.
85. Ibid., 27 August 1948.

4

Shackles for the Widow

As we come to the nineteenth century, we find the widow bowed in misery. Many widows were compelled to burn themselves on the funeral pyres of their husbands. Thanks to the endless efforts of Raja Rammohan Ray, the practice of *satidaha* was prohibited and made a penal offence in 1829, but there were other problems faced by Hindu widows. Law could not stop the pangs of widowhood which lingered in other ways. All the sages prescribed a life of severe discipline for widows. 'Until her death,' said Manu, 'Let her be patient of hardships, self-controlled, and chaste…'[1] Manu further said, 'at her pleasure let her emaciate her body by living on pure flours, roots and fruits; but she must never mention the name of another man after her husband died'.[2] The abject misery Indian widows lived in has been described in the previous chapters.[3]

From the 1930s, Bengali reformers began feeling the need to ameliorate the condition of young widows. The widows themselves expressed their miseries through newspapers. A letter from a woman from Shantipur described their predicament and narrated how widows were denied even good food and clothes. In her letter, she complained that while widowers were free to enjoy the company of concubines and prostitutes and could still hold high positions in society, the widows were deprived of even their basic needs. She appealed to the government to give justice to the women of Bengal.[4]

It was during the middle of the nineteenth century that the *Tattvabodhini Patrika* first took up the cause of widows, and focused the attention of the public upon their plight. It succeeded in creating an urge for reform in different spheres of Indian society, with articles lamenting that the Indian woman was never independent, and had to rely on her husband to be her guide, philosopher and friend. She had a respectable status in society as long as her husband was alive, but as soon as he died, she became a miserable creature, doomed to a life of forced servility in the family, and looked upon by her relatives as a drudge. Her relatives were unkind to her, ill treated her and hurled abuses at her. Even the servants of the family would begin to insult her.[5] The women, therefore, preferred to die with their husbands. This is the reason why the Tattvabodhini Patrika started a reform movement for ameliorating the lot of widows in Bengal. Soon people in other parts of the country also realized the necessity of bringing about social change or national regeneration, and devoted their energies to bettering the condition of widows. Many remedies were considered and it was concluded that widow remarriage was the real solution to the problem.

Ishwar Chandra Vidyasagar was the most ardent advocate of widow remarriage. He published an article in *Tattvabodhini Patrika*, highlighting the scriptural sanction of widow remarriage.[6] He pointed out that the *Parasar Samhita* was the scriptural authority of the *Kaliyuga*, so during the nineteenth century, we must follow its dictates sanctioning widow remarriage. Parasara Samhita openly declared that on receiving no tidings of a husband, on his demise, on his turning an ascetic, on his being found impotent, or on his degradation, a woman could have another husband.[7]

A number of widows jointly wrote to the editor of *Somprakash*, expressing their views on widow-remarriage. The following is an extract of that letter:[8]

> We, a few *Kulin* brahmin widows of district Midnapur, make this appeal to you that we lost our husbands in early childhood and have since been living in the extreme misery of widowhood. Since no effective solution has been found till now to relieve us of our sufferings, we have been enduring many harmful experiences. Of late, we have come to know that Sri Iswar Chandra Vidyasagar has been proclaiming that widow remarriage is perfectly justifiable, being dictated by *Sastras* themselves, and has cited the *Parasara Samhita* in particular. It is indeed lamentable that the scholars of

> our country, instead of supporting the statements of Vidyasagar, are raising many obstacles to oppose him. But do they not realise that the widows in their own families, unable to endure the unbearable rules of Brahmacharya are going morally astray?
>
> Therefore, we exhort all of you to put this Act into practice and follow the dictates of Parasara, so that we may put an end to playing hide and seek with ourselves. If you fail to propagate the Act, you will become morally involved in and liable for the sin of countless abortions.

A student wrote in the *Somprakash* that the pamphlet in support of widow-remarriage written by Vidyasagar had created a sensation throughout the country. It stirred Bengali society to its very depth, and elicited replies from a host of opponents, most of which were worthless arguments. Though Vidyasagar was being criticized at the initial stage of his endeavour, as Rammohan was, once the Act was passed, he would be thanked as the champion of liberal social reforms of our country.[9]

Protests against widow remarriage soon filled the pages of many newspapers. The *Samachar Sudhavarshan* complained that the Widow-Remarriage Bill, if passed, would undoubtedly affect a vital part of the Hindu *shastras*.[10] It further stated that if the Act of Widow-Remarriage was introduced, and if widows should remarry, they would no doubt be regarded as social outcastes according to the customs of the country.[11] Ishwar Chandra published a series of articles and pamphlets propagating widow-remarriage and it was mainly through his untiring efforts that the Hindu Widows' Remarriage Act (Act XV of 1856) was passed on 26 July 1856. The important provisions of the Act read as follows:

> Section I—No marriage contracted between Hindoos shall be invalid, and the issue of no such marriage shall be illegitimate, by reason of the woman having been previously married or betrothed to another person who was dead at the time of such marriage.
>
> Section II—All rights and interests which any widow may have in her deceased husband's property by way of maintenance or by inheritance to her husband, shall upon her remarriage cease and determine as if she had then died, and the next heirs of her deceased husband, or other persons entitled to the property on her death, shall thereupon succeed to the same.

Section III—On the remarriage of a Hindu widow, if neither the widow, nor any other person has been expressly constituted by the will, the guardian of his children, the father or paternal grandfather, or the mother or parental grandmother of the deceased husband, or any male relative of the deceased husband may petition to the highest court for the appointment of some proper person to be the guardian of the said children and thereupon it will be lawful for the said court, if it shall think fit, to appoint such guardian in the place of their mother.

Section IV—Nothing in this Act shall be construed to render any widow who at the time of death of any person, leaving any property, is a childless widow, incapable of inheriting the whole or any share of such property if, before the passing of this Act, she would have been incapable of inheriting the same by reason of her being a childless widow.[12]

The Widow-Remarriage Act elicited mixed reactions in Bengali society. Some supported it while others denounced it. Some newspapers wrote in its favour, others wrote against it. But widows themselves were happy and conveyed their gratitude to Pandit Ishwar Chandra Vidyasagar. A widow named Vidya Devi wrote a letter to the editor of *Samvad Bhaskar*, an extract of which is as follows.[13]

Oh! this is indeed an auspicious day! It was beyond our dreams that God would show us such compassion! We will not any longer yearn for release of death. Great is Vidyasagar, great indeed his achievements; glory to him; women of India will ever remain indebted to him. Respected editor, when I was seven, I was given in marriage to a husband 44 years old, old enough to be my grandfather. He died a year after our marriage. Since then I have been passing my days in great difficulty, in utter penury. Vidyasagar's efforts have proved successful, that is to say, Widow Remarriage Act has been promulgated. I cannot express how happy I am over this.

Through your support, this terrible social institution has been abolished and widow remarriage will take place. But it will take a long time to be effective. For me there is no possibility of enjoying the bliss of married life. For I fear I will not live that long. But I feel happy that I will die with the great joy of remembering that I myself am deprived of it, but hundreds of widowed women

> will enjoy it. Rammohan had the practice of *sati* abolished, thus bringing an end to our physical sufferings, but Vidyasagar has freed us, not only from physical suffering, but mental sufferings as well.

A correspondent wrote in the *Bengal Spectator* that widow-remarriage was not new in the history of India.[14] It was prevalent among the people of Western India under the name of gandharva or *netra* marriage. The Malbunees of Gujarat and Brahmins of Jodhpur also accepted it. Raja Jay Singh of Jaipur and Rana Galim Khan of Kota made immense efforts to make the practice more widespread and effective, and Sri Chaitanya Mahaprabhu himself preached the necessity for remarriage of widows. The correspondent concluded that it was undoubtedly true that placing our women on an equal footing with men will remove the cause of much disgrace and misery, and contribute to the happines of about half the Hindu population.

A reader wrote to the Editor of the Samvad Bhaskar:

> The Widow-Remarriage Act XV of 1856 has been published in the Calcutta Gazette. The day is an everlasting memorable day in the history of Bengal. Raja Rammohan abolished the *Satidaha*, I thought that I shall not live long enough to see the widow marriage, but with the grace of God I am still living to rejoice this day. Oh God! you are kind and merciful; you fulfil the heartiest wish of every body; and you have fulfilled mine too.[15]

Another person wrote:

> Ah! what an auspicious day has dawned on our country. Ah! it has brought a message of hope to the unfortunate widows. They would be now saved from the cruel social rites of fasting; the parents of the widows would breathe a sigh of relief. They would be free from the intense pain of seeing the untold sufferings of their daughters. The sacred land of India would no longer resound with the crippling cries of the poor, helpless, unlucky widows; no longer it would be polluted with foeticide.[16]

Notwithstanding the fact that some widow marriages were celebrated, the Act was not a big success. *The Englishman* regretted that no widow remarriage had taken place in Calcutta till the end of 1856.[17] The Special Marriage Act (Act III of 1872) which tried to popularize widow marriage was a progressive law, but failed to improve the lot of Hindu widows because its provisions were not utilized to any great extent for the remarriage of widows. The total number of marriages celebrated under it in Bengal during the decade 1901–10 was only 335, of which two-thirds took place in Calcutta and, in thrity-four cases, the only widows who did marry were brides whose marriage ceremonies had not been consummated.[18]

In the whole of India, no fewer than eleven per cent of the females aged fifteen to forty were widowed. Among the Hindus the proportion was twelve per cent; while in Bengal it exceeded sixteen per cent.

The Census Report gives the following Table:

Number of widows per thousand females	Year
187	1881
176	1891
180	1901
173	1911

The number of widows per thousand females which was 187 in 1881, fell to 176 in 1891; it rose to 180 in 1901 and fell to 173 in 1911, the lowest on record. It would seem that the prejudices against widow-remarriage were gradually dissolving. The proportion of Hindu females who were widowed in 1911, though larger by two per mile than in 1891, was less by nine per mile than it was in 1881.[19]

The prohibition of widow-remarriage was seen as a badge of respectability. Castes which did not allow it ranked higher in social estimation. This was carried to the extent that castes were sometimes divided into two sections, one following and the other forbidding the practice.[20] Many social reformers raised their voices against the condemnation of virgin widows to perpetual widowhood, and pointed out that the custom was a modern innovation which was unknown in Vedic times. In many provinces, there were cases where such widows were given in marriage a second time, not only among Brahmos and Aryas who naturally led the way, but also among the orthodox Hindus. From the 1870s onwards, the issue of widow remarriage created a considerable stir in South India. Kandukuri Viresalingam delivered the first of his series of lectures on widow-remarriage on 7 July 1879 at the Maharaja of Vizianagram's Girls School. Citing ancient examples of the custom, he stressed that Hindu sacred texts sanctioned the performance of widow-remarriages. Under his auspices, the first widow-remarriage was celebrated in Rajahmundry amidst lot of protest on 11 December 1881.[21] A very well-known instance occurred in Calcutta where a high class Brahmin who held a distinguished official position[22] gave his widowed daughter in marriage a second time.[23] Gandhiji strongly advocated widow-remarriage many years after the Act XV of 1856 was passed. [24]

In Bengal there were numerous organizations working towards a change of social attitude and an acceptance of widow- remarriage. Due to their efforts, widow-remarriages were reported from Pabna, Mymensing, Bakargunge, Jalpaiguri and Rajshahi. Figures culled from the Bengal Census Report of 1931 show that a greater number of widow-remarriages took place during the third decade of the present century. The figures are as follows.[25]

1931

Hindu Female

Age	Married	Widowed
4–6	47,106	3,711
7–13	6,13,402	19,905
14–16	5,36,094	30,261
17–23	13,55,654	1,49,949
24–26	6,28,750	1,31,555
27–33	8,57,504	3,06,953
34–36	3,01,864	1,87,791

It is to be noted from the above figures that the maximum number of girls got married when they were between seven and twenty-three years of age, but surprisingly enough, the percentage of widowed girls was the minimum in this age-group, i.e. a little above one cent. The percentage of widowed girls was highest in the age-group of thrity-four to thirty-six, i.e. a little above fifty per cent.

Statement No. VI–3[26]
Ratio per 1000–1921 & 1931 in Bengal

Ratio	1921		1931	
Place	Married	Widow	Married	Widow
	460	197	514	176
Burdwan	462	267	500	235
Presidency	477	230	518	207
*Rajshahi	458	181	520	167
Dacca	457	168	523	150
**Chittagang	442	149	497	133

* With Cooch Behar
** With Tripura State

Subsidiary Table[27]
According to age, the ratio per 1,000 in Bengal—1931, 1921, 1911.

Hindu Female Age	1931		1921		1911	
	Married	Widow	Married	Widow	Married	Widow
0–5	26	2	7	1	5	1
5–10	260	9	85	6	120	6
10–15	505	22	584	38	671	34
15–20	866	83	867	94	874	93
20–40	739	248	713	276	724	266

It is, therefore, evident that the general ratio of widowed females had decreased in 1931 as compared with 1921. On an average, for example, out of 460 married women in 1921, the number of widows was 197, while in 1931, it was found that, out of 514 married girls, only 176 were widows. This could be ascribed to the fact that widows were getting married in increasing numbers so the total number of widows was decreasing. Even so, nearly all correspondents were in favour of limiting the number of widow-remarriages, restricting it to those who were of a young age. Moreover, they also insisted that the consent of widows for remarriage should always be taken. They resented the way orthodox

Hindus treated women as chattels or wards of some male relative.[28]

It is evident from the records of the census that widow- remarriage was, to some extent, popular and the number of widows was also decreasing; even so, the improvement was not remarkable. A vast majority of widows never availed of the provisions of the Act and Hindu society was too conservative to accept it. By and by, the social reformers came to realize that, without the strength of education, the problems of the Hindu widows could never be solved.

Since the days of Raja Rammohan Ray, enlightened men had recognized that education was essential for widows. It is strange that a great social reformer like Keshab Chandra Sen did not include the education of widows in his scheme of reforms, though he had fought for the remarriage of widows. The first major effort to educate widows in Bengal was made by Sasipada Banerji who, in 1884, opened a small school in his house at Baranagar to teach adult women and widows. This school did not last long, but the idea remained embedded in the mind of the founder of the school till it found a fruition in the establishment of a Home for Hindu widows in 1887. The idea was undoubtedly revolutionary and no less important than the idea of widow-remarriage, because it also intended to provide the unfortunate widows with support and some means of enabling them to lead their lives honourably. The Christian missionaries also took up the idea and worked towards uplifting the lives of Hindu widows. Ramabai's *Sarada Sadan*, primarily a home for widows, was established in 1889 at Bombay and then moved to Pune in 1890. It was well known that Pandita Ramabai, though herself a Christian, conducted the Sarada Sadan primarily on Hindu lines.[29] Annie Besant also felt that action must be taken to educate Indian widows, and the Theosophical Society took shape in this direction.

Dhonodo Keshab Karve of Poona, an ardent advocate of widow remarriage, also felt that it would take a long time to prepare public opinion in favour of this reform and that it was very hard to push forward the cause, however admirable work a few individuals might do for it. Years of service to the cause of widow-remarriage and a long period of contact with the public led Karve to feel that the best way to advance the cause was to educate the widows.[30] With this object in view, an independent institution named the Hindu Widows'

Home was established by Karve in Poona on 1 January 1889.[31] He also started the Widows' Home Association on 14 June 1896[32] with R.G. Bhandarkar as its President and himself as its Secretary. Thus the first steps were taken to remove the basic root of widows' problems rather than those of their remarriage, though progress of the reform was very slow during the earlier part of the present century.

Soon after India became independent, the Hindu law was codified and women were granted substantial rights, which promised to change the very face of the Hindu society. Unfortunately, the problem of widows remained unsolved and widow-remarriage seldom took place. The reasons are not far to seek. In the first place, incidents of child-marriage declined rapidly and, as a result, the problem of child-widows also disappeared. Consequently, the sympathy which child-widows used to evoke in society ceased gradually. Moreover, the sufferings of the widows also lessened because, with time, the social customs were changing and the widows no longer had to bear extreme social stigma if they did not follow the strict laws of living prescribed for widowhood. Naturally, the keenness to encourage remarrying of widows with the intention of solving their problems began to die because the problems themselves were no longer as acute as before.

Further, the socio-economic conditions of the country changed to a great extent towards the mid-twentieth century. World War II and the partition of India disrupted the natural course of social life and also affected Hindu society and its women. Innumerable families were uprooted from their homes and were hit hard economically. The struggle for existence was their primary concern. They had no time to think of their daughters' marriages. Parents in such Hindu families were so incapacitated financially that they were unable to afford the heavy expenses of a daughter's wedding; so the marriage of Hindu girls began to get delayed and late marriage, instead of early marriage, became the problem of the day. Under circumstances such as these, many Hindu women, remained unmarried all their lives. When the situation was such that girls could not get married even once, how could the widows hope to get remarried? Gradually, the issue of widow-remarriage withered away.

The mid-twentieth century saw a radical change in the outlook and attitudes of people. Women had access to education and many went in for higher studies and earning money by taking on jobs.

The same was true of Hindu widows, many of whom made immense efforts to get an education, earn a living and stand on their own feet. During this transitional period, old ideas about institutions such as widowhood, marriage and the family also underwent radical changes. New and modern ideas were brought to bear on traditional problems such as that of Hindu widowhood.

Another aspect to be considered is the economic import of the Widow-Remarriage Act of 1856. Did it improve the status of the Hindu widow economically? Did it in any way give her a greater right to property? It can, however, be said that the Widow-Remarriage Act of 1856, in particular, had two serious limitations. First, the widow was heir to the deceased husband's estate only if there was no son. Second, her right to property was also subject to many restrictions. The Court records contained many cases where reversioners (heirs of the last full owner) had no plea of abuse or waste, but still questioned the alienation of the property by the widow. The net result was that her position, whether she inherited any property from her husband or not, was not very much better in practice.

Section 2 of the Act of 1856 dealt with the effect of remarriage on the right of inheritance and maintenance which a widow possessed in the property of her husband or his lineal successors at the time of remarriage. This section deprived the widow of any right or interest which she had at the time of her remarriage in the property of her late husband. A Calcutta case raised the question whether this section applied to all Hindu widows who remarried (irrespective of the religion of the person they married) or whether this was limited only to Hindu widows remarrying Hindus under Hindu law as provided by the Act. The Full Bench of the Calcutta High Court held that the section was of universal application and was not limited to widows marrying Hindus. Where a Hindu widow inherited the property of her deceased husband and afterwards married a second husband, who was not a Hindu, there was a procedure provided by the Act III of 1872. After she had first made a declaration, as required by section 10 of the Act, that she was not a Hindu, it was held that by her subsequent marriage she forfeited her estate in her late husband's property in favour of the next heir.[33]

Thus the Act of 1856 did not provide the Hindu widow with an absolute right to her husband's property and she could be deprived of it as soon as she remarried. This limitation of section 2 of the Act of 1856 was removed by the Act of 1956 of the Hindu Code hundred years later. The Hindu Code explicitly stated that, even after remarriage, the widow could not be deprived of her husband's property.[34]

Section 4 of the Act of 1856 was intended to render the right of inheritance to a widow in default of a son. The section stated that the widow of any childless person who died leaving property was capable of inheriting the whole or any share of such property. The author of the well-known Mitakshara school of Hindu law maintained that when a man died separated from his co-heirs and had not reunited with them, leaving no male issue, his widow, if chaste, inherited the estate in the first instance. In other words, the widow was entitled to inherit her husband's property if he died separated from his family or if he did not have a son to inherit his property.[35]

The laws of the Mitakshara school, mainly based on the text of Yajnavalkya, were largely acceptable in all of British India. The laws of the Dayabhaga school prevailed only in Bengal. Mitakshara also gave the widow the right to succeed to the self-acquired property of her husband even where he died undivided from his family. If he left both joint and self-acquired property, the joint property would pass to the other members of the undivided family, whereas the self-acquired property would be inherited by the widow alone.[36]

Jimutvahana, the founder of Dayabhaga, maintained, on the other hand, that a widow was entitled to inherit her husband's property in all cases, whether he was joint or separate from the family in the event of his dying without male offspring.[37] In Bengal it was also held that a widow could not be deprived of her right to maintenance by any provision in her husband's will. Although a father in Bengal could make a testamentary deposition of his property so as to deprive his son even of maintenance, he could not by his will deprive his widow of her right to maintenance. The right to maintenance of the widow arose by marriage, and was a legal obligation which was attached with the property of her husband. Also, a husband could not gift his entire estate without reserving maintenance for his wife. In such cases, it was laid down that the donee would take the property subject to the widow's right to maintenance.[38]

Mitakshara did not impose any restraint on the widow's power of disposition of her deceased husband's estate. The author was in favour of the unqualified right of the widow. According to this school, the widow of a divided family took the whole estate of her deceased husband which devolved upon her by inheritance.[39] The Mitakshara rule of the unqualified right of a widow was, however, restricted by the Widow-Remarriage Act 1856, which was based on Dayabhaga texts. Jimutvahana, the author of Dayabhaga, prescribed definite restrictions on the widow's right to alienate property inherited from her late husband. The widow was allowed only to enjoy her husband's estate during her lifetime; after her death the estate passed to the heirs of her deceased husband. She had no right to make a gift, mortgage or sale of it at her pleasure.[40] Dayabhaga thus made it clear that property inherited by a widow from her husband was not her property whereas Mitakshara treated such property as *stridhan*.

The Dayabhaga doctrine was wholly upheld by the highest judicial tribune in British India. The subsequent India Council Acts imposed further restrictions on widows' rights. Let us take, for example, Act No. 1 of 1877, the Specific Relief Act. Section 42 of the Act stipulated in para (e):

> The widow of a sonless Hindu alienates part of the property of which she is in possession as such. The person presumptively entitled to possess the property, if he survives her, may in a suit against the alienee, obtain a declaration that the alienation was made without legal necessity and was therefore void beyond the widow's life-time.

Para (f) said:

> In case a Hindu widow in possession of property of her deceased husband, adopts a son the person presumptively entitled to possession of the property on her death without a son may, in a suit against the adopted son, obtain a declaration that the adoption was invalid.[41]

Para (m) stated:

> In case a Hindu widow in possession of her deceased husband's property, commits destruction of the property without any case sufficient to justify her so doing, the heir expectant may sue for an injunction to restrain her.[42]

A widow's right to inheritance was modified by the Act No. XXXIX of 1925. By Section 33 A of this Act, when the intestate had left a widow and also lineal descendants, one-third of his property was to belong to his widow and the remaining two-thirds to his lineal descendants. Where he had left no lineal descendants, but had left persons who were his kindred, one-half of his property was to belong to his widow, and the other half to those who were related to him. If he had left behind no person, either lineal descendent or kindred, the whole property should belong to his widow. Further, where the intestate had left a widow but no lineal descendants and the net value of his property did not exceed five thousand rupees, the whole of his property should belong to his widow. In cases where the net value of the property exceeded the sum of five thousand rupees, the widow should be entitled to rupees five thousand in addition to her share in the remaining estate.[43] The subsequent legislation, therefore, gave greater, though limited, rights to Hindu widows.

Hindu widows' rights were further widened by the Hindu Womens' Right to Property Act of 1937 and its amendment in 1938. The rule was modified to say that when a Hindu governed by any school of Hindu Law or customary law died intestate, leaving his own property as well as interest in the joint family property, the same principle would apply to both cases. The man's separate property and his interest in the joint property devolved upon his widow along with his lineal descendants, if any, in the same way that it devolved upon a son.[44] However, the Act further stated that any interest devolving on a Hindu widow was to be a limited interest known as Hindu woman's estate, subject to the rights of the reversioners.[45] That is, the widow's property would devolve on her death to the reversioners. So under the Act of 1937, the Hindu widow had no power to dispose of her property. She was a limited owner, only for as long as she lived.

The Hindu widow's right to property was greatly enlarged by the Hindu Succession Act 1956. Section 14 of the Act stated that any property possessed by a female Hindu, whether acquired before or after its commencement, was to be held by her as a full owner and not as a limited one.[46] This had a significant implication—section 2 of the Widow-Remarriage Act[47] (Act XV of 1856) was immediately repealed by this Act, because the Act stated that any other law in force immediately before the commencement of this Act was to become void so far as it was inconsistent with any provisions in the Act.[48] By section 2 of the Act 1856, the right of a Hindu widow in her husband's property, whether inherited from him or his lineal successor, ceased on remarriage. Section 2 of the Widow-Remarriage Act of 1856, being inconsistent with the provision of section 14 of the Hindu Succession Act of 1956, was consequently repealed. However, the widows who had remarried before the passing of the Act of 1956 could not in any way claim the benefits provided by this Act because these benefits were not given retrospectively. Act 30 of 1956 also provided that widows were not heirs if they had already remarried on the date the Succession Act came into force.[49] The reversioners in such case would be entitled to claim possession.

Notwithstanding the fact that the widows' proprietorial rights were fully recognized by the Hindu Code of 1956, problems continued to exist because the two primary needs of women—education and economic stability—which alone could remove the problems of widowhood were not fully realized. It is true that under the pressure of circumstances, women had begun to get educated, even so, a very large number of women, including widows, continued to be denied education. It is again true that economic rights of women were sought to be recognized on an equal footing with men by the Hindu Code and other laws of the post-independence era, but there were not enough safeguards for a widow's economic security. Very few people in India could leave an estate sufficient to sustain the widow, and her problems were expected to remain as complex as ever unless she was properly educated and could earn enough to become self-sufficient. Even after the attainment of independence, most Indian women continued to remain confined to their homes, helplessly depending on others. It must be said, though, that many women from all parts of India came forward, acquired education and took an active part in different spheres of life.

Therefore, till the middle of the present century the Hindu widows were classified into two categories—(1) those who were uneducated and financially dependent, and (2) those who were educated and self-reliant. The condition of the former was as wretched as that of the nineteenth century widows while those who had access to education and financial independence were better off.

It is true that Ishwar Chandra Vidyasagar was the first man who initiated some concrete action for widows; but his movement was suitable and relevant only in the conditions of the mid-nineteenth century, especially in so far as child- widows were concerned, and it only solved the problem of how to get widows remarried where marriage was possible and desirable. Where widows—for whatever reason—did not or could not remarry, there was no option for a better life available. For this section of women, legal and social reforms were needed to increase their access to education and self-reliance.

Notes and References

1. Manu, V. 158.
2. Ibid., V. 157.
3. See *ante*, pp. 6–7.
4. Extract from *Samachar Darpan*, 14 March 1835, cited in Banerjee, B.N., *Samvad Patre Sekaler Katha*, Acharya Bangiya Sahitya Parishad, Calcutta, 1339.
5. Extract from *Tattvabodhini Patrika*, March 1854, (cited from Ghosh, B. (Ed.), *Samayik Patre Banglar Samaj Chitra*).
6. Extract from *Tattvabodhini Patrika*, February 1856 (cited by Ghosh, B., op. cit. vol. II, p. 145).
7. *Parasar Samhita*, p. 2.
8. *Somprakash*, 24 May 1856, (Quoted by Ghosh, B., op.cit. vol. IV, pp. 769–70).
9. Extract from *Somprakash*, 24 May 1855 (cited in op. cit.) by B. Ghosh, p. 771).
10. Extract from *Samachar Sudhavarshan*, 29 December 1855 (cited by B. Ghosh, op. cit. pp. 138–9).
11. Ibid.
12. India Council Act 1856.
13. Extract from *Samvad Bhaskar*, 21 August 1856 (cited by Ghosh. B., op.cit. vol. III, p. 483).

14. Ghosh, B., op.cit. vol. III, p. 79.
15. Extract from *Samvad Bhaskar,* 2 August 1856, (cited by Ghosh, B., op.cit. p. 313).
16. Extract from *Samvad Bhaskar,* 18 December 1856, (cited by Ghosh, B., op. cit. pp. 357–8).
17. *The Englishman,* 25 , 26 , 29 , November 1856.
18. Census of India (Report on the Census of Bengal, Bihar and Orissa), 1911, vol. V, chapter VII, p. 322.
19. Ibid.
20. Ibid., p. 274.
21. Leonard, John Greenfield, *Kandukuri Viresalingam, 1849–1919; A Biography of an Indian Social Reformer,* Hydrabad, Telegu University Publication, 1991, pp. 112–3.
22. That great man was Sir Ashutosh Mukherjee.
23. Census of India, Bihar and Sikkim, 1911, vol. I, part I, p. 274.
24. See Appendices I and II.
25. Census Report of Bengal and Sikkim, 1931, Census of India, vol. V, part I, chapter IV, p. 201.
26. Census Report of Bengal and Sikkim, part I, Census of India, 1931, vol. V, chapter IV, p. 205.
27. Ibid., p. 221.
28. Ibid., p. 402.
29. Karve, D., *Looking Back,* Poona, B.D. Karve, Hindu Widow's Home Association, 1936, p. 60.
30. Ibid.
31. Ibid., p. 61.
32. Ibid., p. 58.
33. Justice Mitter, D.N., *The Position of Women in Hindu Law,* New Delhi, Inter-India Publications, 1984, pp. 427–8.
34. See *Post,* p. 141.
35. Mitakshara, chapter II, section 1 and 2 (Colebrook's translation).
36. Mitakshara, section II, pp. 1 and 5.
37. Mitter, D.N., op cit., p. 468. See note 33 above.
38. Ibid., p. 418.
39. Mitakshara, chapter II, section 1.
40. Dayabhaga, chapter IX, section I, pp. 56–7, 61–3.
41. India Council Act, 1877, Act I, chapter VI, section 42.
42. Ibid., chapter X, section 54.
43. India Council Act, 1925, Act XXXIX, part V, chapter II, Section 33.
44. India Council Act 1937, Act No. XVIII, section 3.
45. Ibid., 1937, Act No. XVIII, section 3, sub-section 3.

46. Act of 1956, Act No. XXX, section 14.
47. See ante, p. 65.
48. Act of 1956, Act XXX, section 4.
49. Ibid., section 24.

5

Dowry

The dowry system in India has a long history. The Hindus believed that kanyadaan was a pious duty. Kanyadaan means, literally, the gift of a virgin, and the ideology to which high-caste groups tried to conform and which was respected by low-caste groups as well, was the kanyadaan marriage. The Act of *dana*, according to religious requirements, made it incumbent on the parents to give something more besides the bride, so that the ritual of *kanyadaan* could be complete. Marriage thus implied the gift of a daughter bedecked and bejewelled with expensive ornaments and laden with presents. The gifts, including jewellery, were voluntarily given to the bride for her comfort as well as a better status in her in-laws' house. Hindu religious scriptures are replete with instances where even Lord Shiva and Rama received valuable items like jewels, gold, horses, elephants, cows, etc., in the shape of dowry.[1]

This being the ideal, any element of explicit bargaining was supposed to be discreet and covert, so that the dominant ideology was not violated. According to this ideology, the groom's family could not explicitly demand gifts; but the reality was quite the reverse. Insofar as household goods and other gifts were concerned, the bride's mother-in-law was supposed to have the highest authority to decide how these items should be distributed. It was largely women, especially elderly women, who controlled the flow and pace of gift-giving both within the household and outside it. If any sum of cash was involved, it was likely to be under the immediate control of the father-in-law. It was up to him to decide whether some portion of these funds should be earmarked for the future use of the young couple or they should be merged with the general funds of the household. The bride herself was supposed to have little say in what happened to her dowry once she left her parents' home. As a new bride, she was expected to behave in a modest and self-effacing manner, and the way to ensure her own future happiness and earning the new family's favours, was by not asserting her own wishes. There was always the possibility of a conflict between the couple and the husband's parents on this issue, for it was not only that the bride had limited control over her dowry, but even her husband could find it difficult to assert her rights in it, owing to the close relationship between seniority and authority in the family.[2]

Another implied ideology governing dowry was that it was a means of pre-mortem inheritance for the girl from her parents' wealth, which if probed, would be found to be equally violated. Under the Mitakshara system, a woman was not entitled to a share in the parental wealth, and the system of favouring the daughter with a handsome dowry during marriage seemed to have been introduced to overcome this restriction. However, dowry does not represent a fixed share of a particular divisible estate; the amount is fixed in accordance with the prevailing trends of the marriage market and the financial capability of the bride's family, that is, how much they can afford at the time the marriage takes place. Moreover, dowry is not paid to the bride but to her in-laws. Contrary to the dominant ideology and the terminology of traditional Hindu Law, the property acquired through dowry is not women's wealth, rather it is wealth that goes with women. So the two principles governing dowry—one as the form of a gift associated with *kanyadaan* and the other as a form of inheritance—are both defunct.

Dowry is often confused with *stridhan*. The two are very different from each other. *Stridhan* is traditionally accepted as women's absolute property. Dowry, on the other hand, goes to her in-laws. According to Hindu Personal Law, the *stridhan* passes on to the woman's heirs after her death; dowry does not. *Stridhan* is a woman's asset, while dowry could make the woman a liability to her parents because it is not always her fair share of property willingly given.

Stridhan enhances the economic status of the Hindu woman as it stands in good stead when she needs financial support. Unlike dowry to which a woman has no access, stridhan sustains the woman, particularly in situations such as desertion by her husband.

The question that then needs to be addressed is how the classical notion of a woman's marriage wealth or stridhan has been violated. How does dowry become a property of the bridegroom and his kin and not hers? This is a complex question which cannot be answered satisfactorily without delving into the underlying structure of tradition and society. Therefore, whatever may have been the notion of classical *stridhan*, it has been distorted to a dowry which is to be transmitted to the bridegroom and his kin in the contemporary transitional Indian society. As the economy was changing with the progress of industrialization, and a variety of industrial products began to flood the market, many people chose a straight and shorter route to fulfilling their desire to possess them. Marriage was the easiest way to procure them, giving rise to an increased demand for dowry. Dowry as a social practice took deeper and deeper roots, and social norms transformed with the changing economy. In fact, the emergence of novel socio-economic forces in the country gradually changed the 'harmonic' social structure into a 'disharmonic' or discordant one. The unequal socio-economic developments during and after the colonial period became heterogeneous in terms of occupation, income and education. The values and means of status measurement in terms of acquisition of wealth have distorted the spirit of the stridhan. Since modern laws and legislations are not very effective, women can easily be dispossessed of their stridhan.

The universal form of marriage in the nineteenth and the early twentieth centuries was marriage by purchase, that is, payment from the bride's family to that of the bridegroom in the shape of *tilak* or *dahej*.[3] The amount varied with the wealth and position of the families involved. While a poor man was not expected to pay as much as a rich man, he had to pay more than his position would allow if he sought a matrimonial relationship with a family which had a higher social position. Educational qualifications enhanced the price of a bridegoom and, in spite of the increasing numbers of highly educated bridegrooms, their prices did not diminish. In the nineteen-fifties, a Kayastha father, for instance, in Champaran district of Bihar was presented Rs. 700 for a son who had passed the entrance examination (the school-leaving final examination which was the examination for entrance to college), whereas he would otherwise have received only Rs. 300. The price of a graduate bridegroom from Bihar shot up to Rs. 3,500, and at the same time in the richer provinces of Bengal, the price of a Kayastha matriculate or graduate usually varied from Rs. 500 to Rs. 3,000; there were even instances of Rs. 40,000 being demanded and paid. It should be added that besides paying such an excessive amount of dowry, the bride's parents were mostly expected to meet the expenses of educating their sons-in-law. The payments were thus sometimes spread over several years, and there was the prospect of a good investment if the boy had calibre.[4]

Dowry, therefore, like everything else in India, took different forms in different regions and communities. The custom was, however, near universal. During the mid-twentieth century and even later, the dowry system became an evil of tremendous magnitude, particularly after the influx of business and black money into the country. Dowry no longer remained a voluntary gift to the daughter, nor was it an expression of concern for her future happiness. It was more like a yoke clamped on a woman or like a sale coupon tagged on the bridegroom to fetch more money in the matrimonial market.

So, dowry came to be associated with the groom's price, which assumed an ugly form in the nineteenth century. This cruel social custom has been well illustrated by the classic story *Dena Paona* by Rabindranath Tagore. The author describes the social condition of the time and portrays dowry problems through the story of an innocent girl who met with a tragic end only because her poor father could not fulfill the promise of an exhorbitant dowry demanded by her in-laws. Nirupama, the only daughter of Ramsundar was given in marriage to the son of a rich family. A sum of Rs. 10,000 was settled as dowry during the negotiations for marriage, but Ramsundar failed to pay the sum in time. He was not well-off but, even though the amount of money was too much for him to pay, he agreed to the fabulous sum in the fond hope of ensuring the happiness of his beloved daughter in a rich family.

However, after marriage, Nirupama suffered because of her father's failure to fulfill his promise of dowry. She was harrassed and tortured by her mother-in-law who frequently hurled sharp abuses at her. She was never allowed to visit her father's house. Whenever Ramsundar came to meet Nirupama, even though he was seldom allowed to do so, he was cold-shouldered and ill-treated. Nirupama was very saddened by the humiliation of her poor father. Unable to bear the situation for long, Nirupama fell ill, and breathed her last—her dying wish to see her parents remaining unfulfilled.[5]

During the early years of the present century also, the custom was no less a torture. Dowry problems and resultant evils prevailing in the nineteenth century became more virulent at the turn of the century. My grandmother told me about a tragic incident which she personally witnessed at Vikrampur in Dacca, East Bengal, about 1914–15. A girl named Snehalata burnt herself to death to save her father from the heavy burden of dowry demanded on the occasion of her marriage. Her marriage was settled on the condition of an excessive amount of money to be paid as dowry. Snehalata knew that the exaction of so much money would ruin her father completely; so a few days before her marriage, she committed suicide. The incident created a great sensation and was published in the local newspapers of the time. People were greatly agitated over her sad death and poems were written in her memory.

Such incidents were far from uncommon in the nineteenth as well as the early twentieth century and were flashed in the newspapers from time to time. In East Bengal, for example, an organization known as Jnanvikashini of Korhari sent a letter in January 1885 to the editor of *Education Gazette*, a local newspaper, denouncing the evil of the bride price. This custom, the letter stated, resulted in one family becoming rich all of a sudden, while another being reduced to utter penury, and some girls remaining unmarried all their lives because of their fathers' inability to pay dowry. The organization resolved that the pernicious system should be up- rooted.[6]

Other anti-dowry news was also published in the *Education Gazette*. For example, at the annual session of Dharma Rakshini Sabha in January 1885, at Navadweep in Bengal, some traditional pundits refused to sign the Dowry Prohibition Resolution. There was great excitement and agitation in the meeting and sharp abuses were hurled on the pundits.[7] This is a clear indication that even in those days dowry was looked upon as a serious menace.

As a general trend among the educated urban Bengalis, however, in the mid-twentieth century, dowry was never openly demanded. The amount of gifts depended wholly on the discretion of the brides' parents and were generally held to be the sole property of the bride and the bridegroom.

During the first decade of the present century, the British administrators cast a disapproving eye on the practice of dowry. The Indian social reformers also began to realise the enormity of the problem. The problem of dowry became the focus of attention of social thinkers only since the middle of this century. More women's organizations took up cudgels and voices were raised in indignation; but even so, the social evil of dowry continued to thrive.

The Government of India, as well as the state governments, took steps to eradicate the evil. The Bihar Government passed the Bihar Dowry Restraint Act in 1950 (Bihar Act 25 of 1950). In the south, Andhra Pradesh also enacted the Dowry Prohibition Act in 1958 (Andhra Pradesh Act I of 1958).[8] The concrete result of the efforts of the social reformers were first perceived in clause 93 of the Hindu Code, Part II where it was clearly stated that dowry would be deemed to be the property of the bride. Its recipient should hold it in trust for the benefit and independent use of the bride, and transfer it to her on her completing the age of eighteen. Though its provisions did not prohibit, they prescribed certain checks or restrictions on the use of dowry.

Hence, the anti-dowry movement continued. The need seriously felt for an all-India enactment prohibiting dowry was fulfilled in the year 1961. It so happened that on 5 December 1958, Jugal Kishore of Uttar Pradesh introduced a Bill in the Rajya Sabha[9], entitled the Dowry Restraint Bill (1958). The object of this Bill was to prohibit the evil practice of giving and taking dowry, a problem which had been agitating the minds of high government officials for quite some time. Efforts were made to enlarge the property rights of women provided by the Hindu Succession Act 1956. The Bill, however, excluded presents in the form of clothes, ornaments and household items, which are customary at marriages, provided their value did not exceed Rs. 2000. Such a provision appeared to be necessary to make the law workable.[10] Consequently, on 3 December 1959, the Lok Sabha held an inconclusive debate on the Dowry Restraint Bill.[11] Meanwhile, the Bill had been referred to a joint committee of both the Houses on 6 August 1959. Two changes in the original Bill were suggested. R.M. Hajarnovis, Deputy Minister of Law, explained the significance of the changes made by the joint committee in the original Bill, the first change being that the offenders under the Act could now be punished with both imprisonment and a fine, amending the original Bill's proposal of either imprisonment or fine. Another important change proposed by the committee was that it abolished the exemption limit of Rs. 2,000 for presents like ornaments, clothes, etc., made at the time of marriage, to either party. Its effect would be that if a present worth even one rupee was made at the time of marriage, it would constitute an offence and would be liable to punishment.

In the course of the debates in the Lok Sabha, some members supported the Bill, while others opposed it. Narayan Kutty Menon, a Member of Parliament, welcomed the Bill, though he had doubts about whether the pernicious system could be ended by mere legislation. He cited the instance of the utter failure of the attempt to banish prostitution from this country and pointed out that though the Immoral Traffic Act was very much in force, not a single sex-worker had been removed from the streets of Calcutta. Pandit Thakurdas Bhargava said that it was true that dowry was a social evil which needed to be remedied, but it was not an evil of such magnitude that the bride or bridegroom and their parents should be sent to jail. Dowry, he said, was confined to the higher classes or those literate people who wanted money for sending their sons abroad for higher studies, etc. So why should age-old customs be stopped?[12]

Subiman Ghosh, Hem Barua, Ila Pal Chowdhurani, Parvati Krishnan, Manjula Das, Renu Chakravorty and others supported the Bill. Manjula Das said that although according to Hindu custom, *shalankara kanya* (daughter bedecked with jewellery) was supposed to be given in marriage, it did not mean that marriage should be settled on monetary considerations. Renu Chakravorty argued that in view of his strong ties of affection for the daughter, the father would naturally like to make ample provisions for her life, but what happened in many cases was that when a bride went to her husband's house, most of her property in the form of furniture, cash, jewellery, etc., was grabbed by her greedy in-laws. In most cases, the bride could not recover them even if she so desired.[13]

The next controversy arose over the question of the meaning of the term 'dowry'. The amendment moved on 7 December 1959, made it clear that any present made at the time of marriage in the form of cash, ornaments, clothes or other articles (which by custom were made at the time of marriage) would not be deemed as dowry.[14] Pandit Thakurdas Bhargava said that stridhan and other gifts voluntarily given at the time of marriage should not be stigmatized and the amendment should be accepted.

Some members opposed the amendment. T.C.N. Menon, for example, said that the amendment would legalize dowry and completely nullify the effect of the Bill. On 9 December1959, Narendrabhai Nathwani, a Member of Parliament since the formation of the first Lok Sabha in 1952, put up another amendment to the original Bill which provided that the law court could take cognizance of the offence only on a complaint made within a year.[15] Nathwani's amendment sought to enlarge the powers of the law courts to take cognizance of the offence as that would make the implementation of the Act more effective. The amendment sought to vest the magistrates with discretionary powers to award punishment according to the nature of the offence. As to the punishment, his amendment proposed that the offender be punished with imprisonment for up to six months or with a fine of up to Rs. 5000, or with both. The Bill, after passing through the select committee, provided that the offender would be punishable with imprisonment which may extend to six months and concurrently with a fine of up to Rs. 5,000.

Nathwani pressed an amendment which sought to penalize the person who gave dowry because if the giver of dowry was completely excluded from punishment, the Bill, in his opinion, would be weakened. This amendment was lost by one hundred and forty-one votes to forty-one.[16] The Bill, however, could not be passed in the Lok Sabha. On 30 November 1960, the Rajya Sabha also made it clear that it would refuse to accept the clause making it punishable to offer a dowry. H.N. Kunzru felt that the Bill was not constructive. He emphasized that the most important clause of the Bill was clause

6, which laid down that even if one was forced to give dowry in the form of cash or of property, that should belong to the bride, a clause more constructive than the penal clause.

Winding up the debates, the Law Minister, A.K. Sen, proceeding along the lines of Kunzru's argument, pointed out that a social evil like dowry could not be fought or remedied only by legislation. Giving a vivid picture of the appalling condition of women in India, the Law Minister said that many fathers tried to deprive their daughters of a share of their property, despite the Hindu Succession Act of 1956. Drawing attention to clause 6 of the Bill which made dowry a trust property of the wife for her heirs and the civil rights which vested in her the right to obtain possession of the trust, Sen said that, in his view, this provision would be more effective than the penal provisions in fighting the dowry evil.

The Rajya Sabha's vote was taken on the Law Minister's motion that the House members 'do not insist' on its amendment. There was an overwhelming voice against the Law Minister's motion and only a stray voice in its favour.[17] Due to such controversies, the passing of the Bill was withheld and this led to a joint session of both the Houses. Under Article 108 of the Constitution, the President might notify both the Houses of his intention to summon a joint meeting to settle the differences between them, if either House rejected a Bill passed by the other, or if the two Houses disagreed finally on the amendments to a Bill, or if after a Bill had been passed by the one House, the other House took over six months to pass it. Ultimately, the joint session cleared the Dowry Prohibition Bill, and it received the President's assent on 20 May 1961 and came to be known as the Dowry Prohibition Act (Act XXXVIII of 1961). It was enforced with effect from July 1961. It was a penal statute, and a small enactment consisting of only ten sections. Section 3 prescribed punishment for both giving and taking of dowry and Section 6 laid down that dowry, if and when given, was to be treated as a trust in favour of the bride for whose benefit it was given. The section also prescribed punishment for such persons who failed to transfer the dowry in favour of the bride within the stipulated period. Section 8 provided that offences under this Act were non-cognizable, bailable and non-compoundable. Section 9 authorized the Central Government to make rules under the Act for carrying out its purpose and publish them in the Official Gazette. Finally, Section 10 repealed the Andhra Pradesh Dowry Prohibition Act 1958 and the Bihar Dowry Restraint Act of 1950 and thus made the law relating to prohibition of dowry applicable uniformly throughout the country.[18]

Unfortunately, however, the Dowry Prohibition Act has proved to be a complete failure. The Committee on the status of women in India[19] remarked:

> We are compelled to record our findings that the Dowry Prohibition Act 1961, passed with the ostensible purpose of curbing this evil, if not eradicating it, has signally failed to achieve its purpose. In spite of the growth of this practice, there are practically no cases reported under the Act ....[20]

On analyzing the causes of its failure, it was felt that there were some legal loopholes in the Act of 1961 which had rendered the enactment infirm.[21] First, Section 3 penalized both the giver and the taker of dowry. This provision was not equitable and was likely to frustrate the very object of the legislation, for to put both in the same category would be extremely unjust. Secondly, since Section 7 of the Act made the offence non-cognizable, and a magistrate could not act *suo moto*, it meant that there must be a complaint to set the machinery of law in motion. But who would file the complaint? The taker was undoubtedly the offender. If the giver was an offender along with the taker, he would be the last person to come forward with a complaint for no amount exacted as dowry would compel even the most bitter father to shatter the domestic happiness of his daughter in a new family by his complaint. Unless a third party came in, there would be no case and no punishment. But why should a third party bother to load a burden on his own purse and time, and, in case of failure, in prosecution to bear the consequences of filing an unsuccessful complaint? On this ground, Sri Sinhasan Singh submitted a note of dissent in the Joint Committee. Section 6 had its own weaknesses. The section provided that if the person receiving dowry failed to return it to the woman concerned within the requisite period, he would be liable to imprisonment. But the section did not touch upon the criminal liability of the persons giving and taking dowry, or demanding dowry in any way. The section further provided that if a woman entitled to dowry dies before receiving it, her right to receive the items devolved on her heirs. The section was silent as to what would happen if the person receiving the dowry on behalf of the woman died before making it over to the actual claimant.

One of the crucial reasons for the failure of the Act was the lack of social support for the anti-dowry laws, showing that the main obstacle for the satisfactory enforcement of any legislation is the lukewarm attitude of people. In spite of the legislative enactments to banish dowry, the evil is present in its ugliest form even today, and the incidents of dowry deaths are multiplying rapidly. Dowry deaths are reported to be higher in the western zone comprising the Union Territory of Delhi, Punjab, Haryana, Rajasthan and Uttar Pradesh. These areas account for more than three hundred and ten dowry deaths out of a national total of three hundred and forty-five. West Bengal, which was more or less free from this social evil, is also affected.[22] The Chief Minister Jyoti Basu had given a written statement in the State Assembly that between January 1981 and December 1983, there were one hundred and sixty-five bride killings.[23] The Calcutta High Court awarded its first death sentence on 2 April 1985 to the husband and father-in-law of the dowry victim, Devjani Banik, who was murdered. Davjani had brought a handsome dowry when she was married to Chandan Banik. Her in-laws, however, tortured her to fetch an even greater amount of money.[24]

In 1984, a proposal for amending the Dowry Prohibition Act of 1961 was placed before the Lok Sabha on 9 May, the closing day of the Parliament session.[25] It was proposed to make the offence cognizable so that the police and recognized welfare institutions, in addition to parents and relatives of aggrieved persons, could report such offences to the court. The amending Bill also sought to make the punishment more stringent. Section 3 of the Act of 1961 had provided for imprisonment for up to six months or a fine of upto Rs. 5000, or both, for giving or taking dowry, the amending Bill proposed to award punishment extending from six months to two years and to double the amount of the fine to Rs. 10,000. Section 6 sought to reduce the time- limit from one year to three months within which dowry was to be restored to the bride.[26] The amendment Bill was passed and came to be known as the Dowry

Prohibition (Amendment) Act 1984 (Act 63 of 1984). It was enforced from 2 October 1985.

Even this amendment to the Dowry Prohibition Act was found inadequate in view of the existing situation. The amendment did not reflect grave concern about the ever increasing dowry deaths because it failed to bring forth a strong and effective legal provision to end this abominable social evil. The next Bill was presented in the Parliament on 6 March 1985.[27] On 22 August 1986, the Dowry Prohibition Amendment Act 1986 was passed which, besides enhancing punishment for taking dowry, defined for the first time the term 'dowry death' by making it an offence under the Indian Penal Code[28].

However, this enactment also failed to serve its purpose, making it evident that mere legislation is not enough to banish the hydra-headed monster, dowry, from Indian society. One must rely on social rather than legal reforms, spearheaded by the actions of committed individuals and groups to eradicate this practice.[29] Dowry may disappear some day, but such a hope seems distant at the moment when many more bride-burning cases appear in the newspapers with depressing regularity. A few cases of a single year, i.e. 1983, are given below. The year 1983 has been taken at random only to illustrate how the menace of dowry, despite the legislation and movement organized to curb it, is still prevalent in our society in a frightening way. In that year alone, the newspapers reported the following events from Bengal:

(1) Twenty-two year old Champa Rani Mandal of Sridharpur village in the Gargi Thana area of Burdwan district was burnt after kerosene oil was poured on her by her in-laws because her father had not been able to give a dowry that matched their expectations. The victim's father, Mr. Konar, had alleged in a written complaint to the police that though he fulfilled the demand for dowry made when his daughter was married to Dilip Mandal, she was frequently tortured by her in-laws. They wanted her to bring more money and she was burnt to death when she failed to satiate their increasing greed.[30]

(2) In Calcutta, near the Kasba area, a housewife aged twenty-six, named Mala Das, was burnt to death on 10 April 1983. Mala was married to Swapan Das for five years and had a son. Mala's parents were not even informed of her death. Mala's father alleged

that after her marriage, her in-laws had been demanding thirty thousand rupees from her parents. As her father could not afford it, she was tortured and humiliated. The neighbours suspected that kerosene was poured over her and she was burnt to death.[31]

(3) The hearing of the case of fifteen-year-old Rina was resumed by B.P. Bose, Judge, City Sessions Court, Calcutta, on 5 May 1983, in proceedings against her husband, Vijay Gupta and his mother Shyama Devi, who were being tried under Section 306 I.P. Code. Usha Gupta, the victim's mother, stated that her daughter was married to the accused on 31 January 1981and they gave 25 *tolas* of gold, Rs. 7,500 in cash and furniture at the time of marriage, but greedy for more, the accused persons demanded a washing machine also after two or three months of the marriage. A machine was purchased for Rs. 2,500 and delivered to the accused, but then Rs. 20,000 was demanded for Vijay's ghee and oil business as well as a tape-recorder. When she pleaded that she had no more money to satiate their greed, they said that unless the tape-recorder was given, Rina would die. Rina complained that she was asked by the accused to commit suicide by taking poison or hanging herself; and when she refused, they burnt her to death on 16 July 1981.[32]

(4) Mrs. Manjula Sett, a twenty-year old housewife and her nine-month-old son Dipak died of burn injuries at the Calcutta Medical College Hospital on 24 September 1983. According to the Deputy Commissioner of Police, 'physical and psychological torture over dowry' was the reason for death. In her statement made in the hospital, Manjula Sett said that she was being 'tortured for dowry' and her husband and parents-in-law were arrested.[33]

Notes and References

1. Krishnabala, 'Marriage and Violence: An analysis of cruelty related to the practice of dowry', in *Women and Violence*, edited by Dr Niroj Sinha, New Delhi, Vikas Publishing House, 1989, p. 82.
2. Hooja, S.L., *Dowry System in India*, Delhi, Asia Press, 1969, pp. 9–11.
3. Census of India, 1911, vol. V, part VII, p. 316.
4. Ibid.
5. Tagore, Rabindranath, *Dena Paona*, taken from *Galpaguchcha* (a collection of Tagore's short stories), Visva Bharati Granthan Bibhag, Calcutta, (1926).

6. Extract from *Education Gazette*, 9 January 1885, (cited in *Samayik Patre Banglar Samaj Chitra* by Ghosh, B., op.cit., vol. III, p. 196).
7. Ibid., 27 January 1885, (cited by Ghosh, B., op.cit. p. 203).
8. Anand, R.L. and Sethi, Gargi, *The Prohibition of Dowry Act*, Act 28 of 1961, section 10, Allahabad, Law Publishers, 1962
9. Rajya Sabha Debates, Official Report, 5 December 1958, vol. XXII, p. 1234.
10. Gazette of India, 1959, Ext. Pt. II, section 2, p. 397.
11. The *Indian Express*, 4 December 1959, New Delhi, p. 9
12. Lok Sabha Debates, second series, vol. xxxvi, 4 December 1959, pp. 3454–7.
13. Lok Sabha Debates, second series, vol. xxxvi, 7 December 1959, p. 3710.
14. Ibid.
15. Lok Sabha Debates, second series, vol. xxxvi, 9 December 1959, pp. 4229–4231.
16. The *Indian Express*, 10 December 1959, p. 9
17. The *Statesman*, 1 December 1960.
18. Anand, R.L. and Sethi, Gargi, op.cit. Introduction and Sections 3–10. See note 9 above.
19. See Appendix IV.
20. Towards Equality, Report of the Committee on the Status of Women in India, Ministries of Education and Social Welfare, Government of India, 1974, p. 115.
21. Anand R.L. and Sethi, Gargi, op.cit. p. 58. See note 9 above.
22. *Amrita Bazar Patrika*, 23 May 1983.
23. Ibid., 3 March 1986.
24. Ibid., 3 April 1985.
25. Lok Sabha Debates, 9 May 1984, c. 479–80.
26. The *Statesman*, 16 May 1984.
27. *Amrita Bazar Patrika*, 9 March 1985.
28. Ibid., 24 August 1986.
29. *Manushi*, No. 1, Delhi 1979, the article entitled 'Price of a Life', p. 16.
30. *Amrita Bazar Patrika*, 24 February 1983.
31. *Jugantar*, 11 April 1983.
32. *Amrita Bazar Patrika*, 6 May 1983.
33. Ibid., 25 September 1983.

6

Severing the Sacred Tie

In Hindu society, women suffered from various disabilities. They were victims of many evil practices, some of which have been discussed in the foregoing chapters. One such evil was unilateral divorce by the husband. The right to separation, annulment of marriage and divorce was not available to women. That was because in Hindu society, marriage was regarded essentially as a '*dharmik* institution' which was indissoluble. The social reformers were, therefore, actively engaged in devising ways and means to remedy the situation and arm women with certain rights, which would empower them with the freedom to choose a better life.

The Widow-Remarriage Act of 1856, the Age of Consent Act of 1891, the Child Marriage Restraint Act 1929 were some of the reforms intended to help Hindu women to break centuries-old fetters. But these were not considered adequate solution to their marital problems, so the movement for greater relief started. The result was the Hindu Marriage Act of 1955, which amended and codified the existing laws relating to marriage. Besides simplifying the conditions for a valid marriage, it also repudiated the concept of a Hindu marriage as being an essentially sacramental institution. A Hindu marriage was no longer regarded as indissoluble. The provisions of the Act dealing with matrimonial reliefs firmly stressed the concept of matrimonial equality and equal right of spouses to obtain suitable remedies.

It will not be correct to say that Hindu law prior to the passing of the Hindu Marriage Act of 1955 did not provide for any matrimonial relief to the wife. The remedy of restitution of conjugal rights was made available to women at the end of the nineteenth century by the courts.[1] The right to a separate residence and maintenance of married Hindu women was recognized by legislation in 1946.[2] Relief of nullity and annulment of marriage was also judicially recognized by the courts prior to the passing of the Hindu Marriage Act.[3] As regards divorce, Hindu law always acknowledged the right of divorce by virtue of custom, though it was generally practised more often by the so-called lower castes. Specific laws for matrimonial remedies had not yet been prescribed.

This situation was drastically changed by the passing of the Hindu Marriage Act in 1955 which, for the first time, gave all Hindu women specific matrimonial remedies and introduced a new basis for the matrimonial law of the Hindus. The Act of 1955 provided for four types of matrimonial reliefs:

i. Restitution of conjugal rights,
ii. Judicial separation,
iii. Declaration of nullity and annulment, and
iv. Divorce.

Divorce was the most radical social reform. The *dharmasastras* did not recognise divorce. However, the Hindu adherence to the doctrine of the indissolubility of marriage did not mean that the need of divorce was not realized. Customary modes of divorce were easy, very few formalities were needed to dissolve a marriage. Many times it was purely a private act of the parties but, in some communities, a forum was necessary—such as a *panchayat* or a family council. Customary divorce was the privilege of the lower castes and higher castes seldom followed customs which permitted divorce.[4] Nevertheless, by 1955 marriage came to be accepted as essentially a contract. The issue of divorce then came as a natural consequence. Though people started to think seriously in terms of divorce, it was still reserved as the last resort. This led to development of the concept that marriage could be dissolved only in those cases where a party to the marriage violated its sanctity by his acts or behaviour.

Adultery, according to the Indian Divorce Act of 1869 (meant for Christians only), was supposed to be an act which destroyed the sanctity of marriage. Similarly, desertion and cruelty came to be regarded as sufficient grounds for divorce and judicial separation.[5] Adultery, desertion and cruelty were looked upon as 'matrimonial offences' which needed to be punished, and divorce was used as an instrument for punishing people guilty of such offences. This was initially called the 'offence theory of divorce'.[6] Later, insanity was added as a ground for divorce and came to be regarded as a 'matrimonial offence', though insanity or unsoundness of mind is a misfortune, not a cause for guilt. With insanity being recognized as a ground, some other diseases like leprosy also came to be considered as grounds for divorce. Since diseases like insanity could not be categorized as an offence, the 'offence theory' was renamed as the 'fault' theory. That is, if the respondent had some 'fault' which made continuance of cohabitation almost impossible, the petitioner was entitled to divorce. It was against this background of the Indian Divorce Act of 1869 that the Hindu Marriage and Divorce Bill came before the Parliament.

On 20 September 1938, G.V. Deshmukh, a Member of Parliament, introduced the Hindu Women's Right to Divorce Bill to give the right to divorce to Hindu women under certain circumstances.[7] On 12 December, he moved that the Bill be circulated to elicit public opinion on the issue by 15 February 1939.[8] On 18 February 1939, Deshmukh moved that the Bill be referred to a select committee.[9] Nripendra Nath Sircar, the Law Member, pointed out that very few opinions had been received by 15 February. The opinions of the provincial governments were not in favour of the Bill either, so a discussion on the motion to refer the Bill to a select committee had to be postponed for the time being.

The discussions on the Bill actually started on 11 April 1939.[10] Deshmukh made it clear at the outset that since the Bill was an enabling measure, those women who did not want to take advantage of it and were willing to bear with the agony and the wrongs of a married life were free to do so. The Bill would not interfere with them. He argued that the Bill was entirely in accord with the spirit of Hinduism, which was always in favour of change. That is why, he said, it had secured the approval of persons like C. Rajagopalachari and V.D. Savarkar who would have refused to support any anti-Hindu measure.[11]

Sir N.N. Sircar pointed out that Deshmukh had wrongly assumed that the majority of Hindus were in favour of the Bill and wanted the introduction of certain conditions, not the rejection of the Bill. Sir N.N. Sircar said that the preponderance of Hindu opinion, on the other hand, was severely against the measure.[12] He also clarified the government's attitude towards such measures. The only exception which the government had made in the rule of not interfering in the religion and social customs and practices of the people of India was when the ordinary sense of morality was impinged on even though the majority opinion was against interference. But in the present case, even this condition justifying interference did not exist. He next analyzed the provisions of the Bill and pointed out the difficulties which lay in the way of a woman seeking shelter under such provisions. The ground of impotency or incurability, for example, he said, could not be easily decided in a court of law.

Another ground urged for divorce was that of a husband marrying another woman while the first marriage existed. But, as Sir N.N. Sircar pointed out, a scoundrel could get round this by maintaining concubines. The last ground put forward by the Bill was desertion for a period of three years. But what would Deshmukh say to a husband who returned to his wife after a lapse of two years, eleven months and twnety-nine days? Further, Deshmukh had not provided for a case of cruelty by a husband or a case of a husband leading an immoral life which would remain beyond the reach of law. Another important matter which this 'one clause Bill' overlooked, according to Sir N.N. Sircar, was the question of custody of children. Nine out of ten women, he asserted, could not take recourse to this law for the sake of their children.

Bhulabhai Desai sympathized with Sir N.N. Sircar's criticism[13] of those parts of the resolution which were considered to be far too wide to serve any useful purpose. He further criticized the connotation which was attempted to be given to the term 'divorce'. To think, he asserted, that there was a 'right' to divorce was entirely to misunderstand the relation between man and woman, and the meaning of the term 'marriage'. He believed that one might come across a difficulty or a danger in marital life but that it could not be construed that a 'right' to divorce followed.

The debate on the Hindu Women's Divorce Bill proceeded. On 31 August 1939, when the Assembly again discussed Deshmukh's Bill to confer the right of divorce on Hindu women, Bhai Parmanand, Lalchand Naval Rai and Baijnath Bajoria, the members of the Congress Party, opposed the Bill.[14] Bhai Parmanand's objection was that the Bill sought to introduce in India a system which had brought unhappiness and misery and had wrecked homes in the West. Apart from that, it was argued that the Bill was one-sided because, although the original intention of the Bill was to protect woman against marital sufferings, it was unreasonable to deny the right of divorce to the husband. For, just as there were cases in which women suffered from the cruelty of husbands, there were also cases in which husbands suffered from ill-treatment by wives. Lalchand Navalrai asserted that Deshmukh knew nothing of the conditions that existed outside Bombay. If he had, he would not have brought forward a Bill of this kind. Bajoria took a stand on the Hindu *shastras* and quoted a number of Sanskrit verses in support of his thesis that, as marriage was a sacrament, there could be no severing of that sacred tie even by death. Ninety-nine per cent of Hindu women themselves were opposed to the Bill because they were convinced that it would disrupt Hindu society and culture. In India 'divorce was looked upon as an epidemic like small pox and a pest like the rinderpest'.[15] M.S. Aney, leader of the Congress Party said that the institution of marriage could be considered either as a sacrament or as a contract. If it was a contract, then it should be fair to both the parties. On that basis, the privilege of divorce should not be given to women alone, and denied to men as the Bill sought to do. The conviction, however, was that Hindu marriage was a sacrament and the shastras did not recognise divorce. He looked at the position from a different point of view. Was Hindu society ready for this new reform? The House should remember that the legislature had nearly eighty years ago passed the Widow-Remarriage Act. How many Hindu widows had taken advantage of it? Aney proceeded to refer to many defects in the Divorce Bill, such as absence of any provision with regard to inheritance or the maintenance of the children of the divorced wife.[16]

Sir Yamin Khan, speaking on behalf of the Muslim League, said that he would be untrue to his heritage as a Muslim if he opposed a measure embodying a principle which Islam had handed on as a torch to other nations in the world. Islam, he said, was the first to recognize the right of men as well as women to separate if they could not live together, and Protestant Christians had adopted the system too and incorporated it in their law. Umar Ali Shah quoted verses from the *Mahabharata* and the *Ramayana*, which supported the theory that the right of divorce was exercised by Hindu women in the olden days. Maulana Zafar Ali endorsed the view of Umar Ali and supported the principle of divorce.

On 15 September 1939, the Legislative Assembly rejected Deshmukh's motion to refer his Bill on the Hindu women's right to divorce to a select committee by 22 votes to 15. J.A. Thorne, the Home Member, made it clear that the attitude of the government to the Bill, as announced by Sir N.N. Sircar in April, remained unchanged. What struck him was that not a single Hindu, with the exception of the mover (Deshmukh), supported the Bill and the only support had been from Muslims. Thorne, however, held that the government could not in any way be opposed to the principle of such a measure and would examine it as they had examined this Bill strictly on its merit.[17]

The failure of the Bill, however, could not demoralize Dr Deshmukh who again, on 22 December 1940 ,introduced a Bill to give married Hindu women a right to separate residence and maintenance under certain circumstances and to provide for judicial separation and divorce among Hindus. It was forwarded by Akhil Chandra Datta, the Deputy President of the Assembly, and the Bill was adopted in the legislature.[18] On 28 October 1941, he introduced another Bill to amend the Special Marriage of Act, 1872.[19] In the meantime, a resolution of the Government of India had appointed a law committee on 25 January 1941 under the chairmanship of Sir B.N. Rau, a Judge of the Calcutta High Court and India's permanent member in the UN, with a view to overhaul and codify Hindu law dealing with Hindu intestate succession and Hindu marriage. Deshmukh's Hindu Women's Right to Separate Residence and Maintenance Bill was referred to the committee for its perusal and advice along with many other acts and bills. The committee submitted its report in June 1941 in which it recommended the preparation of a complete code of Hindu law beginning with the law of succession, to be followed by the law of marriage and, in due course, by other topics of Hindu law.[20]

The Hindu Married Women's Right to Separate Residence and Maintenance Bill was later referred to the Select committee on 6 March 1946, and the report of the Select committee was presented by Deshmukh in the Assembly House on 21 March 1946.[21] A debate followed and the Bill received the assent of the Governor-General on 23 April 1946 and was passed into law.[22]

Meanwhile, the Hindu Law Committee Report of June 1941, accompanied by two draft bills, one dealing with Hindu intestate succession and another with Hindu marriage, was laid before the Joint Committee of both Houses of the Parliament on 2 April 1943. As a result of the Joint Committee's report, the Hindu Law Committee was revived on 21 January 1944 and under its Chairman, Sir B.N. Rau, a draft code was prepared dealing with succession, maintenance, marriage and divorce, minority and guardianship and adoption. It was this code which was given the name of the Hindu Code Bill and was published in April 1947.[23]

The Hindu Code Bill, which was recommended by the Rau Committee was referred to a select committee under the chairmanship of B.R. Ambedkar, the Law Minister, on 9 April 1948.[24] On the basis of the changes suggested by the select committee, the Hindu Code Bill came up for consideration on 24 February 1949.[25]

Ambedkar elaborated the changes suggested by the select committee on the original Bill. To the first part of the Bill, which dealt with marriage and divorce, the select committee added two clauses relating to the restitution of conjugal rights and to judicial separation. These were specifically absent in the original Bill. Those who drafted the original Bill were content with a simple reference to the Indian Divorce Act 1869, which contained provisions relating to the restitution of conjugal rights and judicial separation. The select committee felt that, since this legislation was going to be a complete code of Hindu Law, it would be desirable to embody the two provisions in the code itself, instead of leaving them to be invoked by reference to the Indian Divorce Act.[26]

Ambedkar further pointed out that the section relating to marriage and divorce was a perfect synthesis of the old and the new. He discussed the three points of controversy which were:[27] first, the abolition of castes as a necessary requirement for a valid marriage; second, the prescription of monogamy and third, the permission for divorce. So far as the abolition of castes was concerned, Ambedkar said, the Bill attempted a compromise between the old and the new by allowing any Hindu who wanted to follow the orthodox system requiring the bride and the bridegroom to belong to the same varna, to do so freely as there was nothing in the Code which prevented him from fulfilling his wishes or what he regarded as his dharma. At the same time, the law regarded as equally valid the marriage of a Hindu who was a reformist and chose to marry a girl outside his *varna*. Regarding monogamy, although it was a new introduction, Ambedkar argued that it was not true to say that a Hindu husband had at all times an unfettered, unqualified right to polygamy. With regard to the controversy about the right to divorce, Ambedkar said that this was in no way an innovation. Everybody in the House knew that the Sudras practised customary divorce. The Sudras, in his view, formed practically ninety per cent of the total population, while the regenerate class formed only ten per cent. What he was contending was whether they were going to adopt the law of the ninety per cent of people as the general law of the country, or were they going to impose the law of ten per cent of the population on the majority. Ambedkar's submission, therefore, was that so far as the law of marriage and divorce was concerned, the provisions laid down were both just and reasonable, supported not only by our shastras but the experience of the world as a whole.

Kamath criticized the reactionary views and said that, as regards marriage and divorce, the policy should be that marriage becomes easy and divorce difficult. Kamath referred to the fact that he had received a letter from outside the House urging him to oppose the Bill in the name of God, in the name of Gandhi and in the name of Subhash Chandra Bose. He said that this was all the more the reason why he should support the Bill—in the name of God in whose eyes men and women were equal; in the name of Gandhi who all along upheld the equality of status and justice for women, and in the name of Subhash Chandra Bose who sought and accomplished the complete emancipation of men and women to the extent of calling women to battle on par with men. He congratulated Dr Ambedkar for supporting the Hindu Code Bill which aimed at granting equality of status to women.[28]

H. Siddaveerappa, who also supported the Bill, said that as regards the provisions relating to divorce, a time limit should be fixed within which nobody should be allowed to get the benefit of the provisions for divorce.[29] He said that as soon as a man or a woman wanted proceedings to begin for a divorce, he or she should be asked to first live together for a certain period of time and only then to file for divorce if their differences were not mended within the time allotted.

N.V. Gadgil, Minister for Works, Mines and Power, said there was nothing revolutionary about the provisions for divorce,[30] nor was there anything inconsistent with the principles of the shastras and smritis. In his own province, Gadgil said, ninety-five per cent of the people supported some form of divorce as a matter of custom, and the small fraction of the educated class who opposed it were now in favour of it, 'I agree that divorce must be not very cheap' added Gadgil, 'but at the same time marriage should not be considered as a life sentence if it comes to that.'

Some correspondents wrote to the Editor of The *Hindu* supporting the Bill.[31] One said that it was a familiar idea that Hindu society had been leading a peaceful life without the ideas of divorce newly introduced by the Bill. True, so long as the practice of sati and child-marriage existed, nobody thought along the lines of widow remarriage or divorce. Marital incompatibilities were hardly taken into consideration, but there has been a great change. Marriages no longer take place between children but between adults. However, pre-marital friendship is discouraged and the couple barely know each other at the time of the marriage.

There is no guarantee whatsoever that such marriages would be successful, and no wonder there are so many unhappy marriages today. Is it not the duty (dharma) of our society to give a practicable solution to such unhappy couples by making divorce possible? Will we not be more Hindu in character if we contribute something towards the betterment of our society instead of talking about the glory of our ancient culture and doing nothing about it? How could we possibly turn a deaf ear to those unhappy countrymen?

The *Hindu*, however, in its editorial, denounced it as an unwanted legislation.[32] The editiorial observed:

> ... Imagine what a remarkable fact of consolidation would be achieved by allowing within the same society two different and diametrically opposed sets of marriages and divorce laws. It was a familiar charge against the Code that it aimed to disrupt the traditional joint family. But it was out to do something far worse, that of laying the axe at the root of the family itself as an institution.

The Hindu also criticized Dr Ambedkar's statement that 'Sudras' who formed ninety per cent of the Hindus as against ten per cent of what were called the 'regenerate class' had customary divorce, a statement which, according to it, was palpably false. Besides, it asked, would it be proper, as Ambedkar assumed, to impose the law of the majority on the ten per cent minority? The Hindu argued that the Constitution had framed an elaborate charter of fundamental rights. Thoughtful minds in the West were bitterly regretting that the destruction of the family and the reduction of society to an automatic conglomerate was fast bringing to an end the culture and civilization which the world had known and cherished. Should we allow ourselves, the editorial asked, to be dragooned by a rootless minority jumping into the whirlpool in the wake of the West?

By the time the first Parliament of the Government of India met, experience had taught that the entire Code was too bulky to admit of satisfactory treatment at one time. Therefore, although the first part of the Code, dealing with marriage and divorce, was taken up, only that part which proposed to deal with civil marriages was brought before Parliament first in order to test the temper of the house. Accordingly, on 28 July 1952, C.C. Biswas, the Law Minister, introduced a Special Marriage Bill which aimed at legalizing inter-communal marriages which were not sanctioned or countenanced by any of the religions practised in our country.[33] It was intended to be a permissive measure which enabled two persons, both citizens of India, to marry according to its provisions. The Bill was referred to a Joint Committee of both Houses consisting of forty-five members on 16 September 1953.[34]

The report of the Joint Committee on the Special Marriage Bill,

1952, was presented at the Council of States on 18 March 1954 and it came up for discussion on 29 April.[35] The Joint Committee had added three new chapters to the original Bill. The first chapter dealt in detail with all the provisions under which divorce and dissolution of marriage would be permitted. In another chapter, provisions regarding procedure, the steps to be taken, how divorce was to be obtained and so forth, were discussed. The third chapter dealt with provisions for restitution of conjugal rights and judicial separation. Debates followed, and finally the Bill was passed by the Council of States on 8 May 1954 with many other Acts and Bills.[36]. The Bill received the President's assent in October 1954. Under the Act, Hindu males who married under it were automatically severed from their joint family, and both the spouses and their children were to be governed by the Indian Succession Act in respect of the devolution of their property. Divorce by mutual consent was provided for, and this had a curious relevance for Hindus because if they married in sacramental form and chose to have their marriage registered as a civil marriage (both parties being twenty-one years of age), all the results which flowed from a marriage under this Act were to be available to them just as if they had originally been married under the Act.

In the meantime, a motion was adopted on 20 December 1952 in the Council of States that the Hindu Marriage and Divorce Bill of 1952 be circulated for eliciting public opinion.[37] The Law Minister, C.C. Biswas, while introducing the Bill, clarified that it was only the first instalment of the Hindu Code Bill. The Hindu Code had been taken up for consideration by the Provisional Parliament several times but nothing concrete had evolved, and the Bill had lapsed. As the question of reviving the Bill arose, he strove, keeping in view the discussions which had taken place in the Constituent Assembly and also at the Congress Party meetings, to introduce a Bill in a much simpler form without affecting the important features of the original Bill in any way. The result was the Hindu Marriage and Divorce Bill of 1952. Since the Special Marriage Bill had been introduced, all reference to marriage in that form was deleted from the Hindu Marriage and Divorce Bill which was meant to deal exclusively with Hindu marriages—that is, marriages between Hindus. This was a significant change because, in the original draft of the Hindu Code

Bill, provision had been made not only for orthodox Hindu marriages, but also for civil marriages.

The Bill referred also to marriages contracted by Hindus outside India. Moreover, full recognition had been given to customs and usages where they departed from the orthodox law—like marriages between uncle and niece, marriages with maternal aunts, a sister's daughter, and so on. As divorce was to be allowed, it was decided to make procedures for divorce applications easier by allowing the parties concerned to seek relief from the nearest civil court instead of the High Court. Unlike the draft Hindu Code Bill, which left out any reference to *sapinda* and other prohibited relationships, and had given a list specifying the persons between whom marriages will not be allowed on these grounds, the new Bill specifically defined these relationships. In this Bill, the narrower limit of *sapinda* relationships, i.e. five degrees on the paternal side and three degree on the maternal side, was accepted. Finally, one of the most important objects of the Bill was to ban polygamy.[38] The Bill came up for discussion in March 1954. On 16 March, a motion was adopted to refer the Bill to a joint committee of forty-five members of both Houses of the Parliament.[39] The committee submitted its report in the Rajya Sabha on 26 November 1954.[40] It included certain relations like the brother's widow, the widow of the paternal or maternal uncle, the widow of the grand paternal or maternal uncle, and children of brothers and sisters within the prohibited degrees. Further, the minimum age for a valid marriage under clause 5 was raised by the Joint Committee from fifteen to sixteen years in the case of a female and from eighteen to twenty-one in the case of a male. The Joint Committee looked upon clause 9 dealing with restitution of conjugal rights with scorn and sought to delete it because in its view, it was inhuman and immoral to compel two persons to live as husband and wife if one or both found it impossible to do so. However, it was retained on the ground that the court could not force the party to abide by its decree if any failure to comply with a decree of restitution of conjugal rights had been made a ground for divorce. This offered a more dignified way of obtaining a dissolution of marriage.[41]

However, D.P. Karmakar, the Minister for Commerce, pointed out that in many cases extraneous influences operated to disturb the harmony of the married life of a couple. In such cases, the remedy provided by this clause would afford an excellent opportunity to bring the parties together, and minor differences between the parties could be settled in this manner.[42]

Although it is difficult, for lack of space, to summarize the long and stimulating debates that followed, one cannot refrain from pointing out an interesting argument by S. Mahanty that the Bill made a discrimination against those Hindus who had faith in an indissoluble tie and were also in favour of bigamy on the ground 'only of religion'. He felt that the Bill, as it had emerged from the joint committee, was *ultra vires* Article 15(1) of the Constitution. So he felt that it should not be called the Hindu Marriage and Divorce Bill, but the Indian Marriage and Divorce Bill, applicable equally to all sections of the population. He was supported by H.P. Saksena who also argued that the Bill was being imposed only on the Hindus while the government did not have the courage to touch the personal law of the Muslims, the Parsis, or the Christians.[43]

On 14 December 1954, the Rajya Sabha passed an amendment which was more concerned with polygamy. 'The Rajya Sabha decided in favour of extending to wives of polygamous Hindu marriages solemnised before the commencement of Hindu Marriage and Divorce Bill, the right to divorce.'[44]

Finally, the right to divorce was granted to women by the Hindu Marriage Act of 18 May 1955. The principal grounds of divorce were:[45] (1) living in adultery, (2) conversion to another religion, (3) suffering from any incurable disease for three years, (4) suffering from leprosy for three years, (5) suffering from a venereal disease for three years, (6) renunciation of the world, (7) respondent not heard of, (8) no cohabitation after judicial separation, (9) failure to comply with the decree of restitution. The three additional grounds on which the wife alone could seek divorce were rape, sodomy or bestiality.[46] Divorce by mutual consent was provided for in Section 28. No hasty divorce could be obtained on this ground, and the couple had to live separately for a period of at least two years before filing a petition. No decree could be passed for dissolving the marriage unless a period of one year had elapsed after the presentation of the petition.

The Hindu Marriage Act 1955 also granted two other matrimonial remedies. These were the restitution of conjugal rights and judicial separation, two provisions which were absent in the original Bill.

As has already been said, the authors of the original Bill felt that mere reference to the Indian Divorce Act of 1869 was sufficient. The law of restitution of conjugal rights provided that:

(i) When either the husband or the wife has, without reasonable excuse, withdrawn from the 'society' of the other, the aggrieved party may apply, by petition to the district court, for restitution of conjugal rights and the court, being satisfied of the truth of the statements made in such petition and that there is no legal ground why the application should not be granted, may decree restitution of conjugal rights accordingly.

(ii) Nothing should be pleaded in answer to a petition for restitution of conjugal rights which shall not be a ground for judicial separation or for nullity of marriage, or for divorce.[47]

Undoubtedly, the remedy of restitution of conjugal rights is a unique matrimonial relief provided in the Act of 1955. Nullity of marriage, judicial separation and divorce are contrary to the laws of our sages, but restitution of conjugal rights falls in line with their ideals of marriage. The restitution of conjugal rights is the only matrimonial relief which empowers the court to direct the party at fault to take some positive action.

It must, however, be admitted that, though the provision for restitution of conjugal rights aims at upholding marriage, it does not seem to have much practical utility. Except in a few cases of minor differences where the provisions might be useful, the court's order for restitution of conjugal rights is more often violated, because a mere order of the court is not expected to change the mind of a spouse who has severed all connection with the other. As a matter of fact, such a decree would be ineffective without an adequate enforcing mechanism. It had been admitted while moving the Bill that a decree would not be enforced against unwilling spouses, so there was no effective measure to force the parties to come together, even after the decree. It is difficult to believe that a person who has severed conjugal tie, with or without reasonable excuse, would return willingly, after being a defeated in the legal battle.

Another difficulty is the 'delay' suffered by the parties in matrimonial proceedings under the scheme of existing laws. Sometimes the courts take more than ten years to finalize matrimonial disputes, and often without any relief in its true sense. The relief would certainly not be worth much if the petition for restitution of conjugal rights was finally dismissed after nearly a decade, wasting ten years of the spouses' youthful lives. In matrimonial cases, delay in justice would naturally amount to denying a happy married life to people who have to wait till the slow and tardy legal proceedings are over. In fact, English law, realizing the practical difficulties of enforcing the decrees for restitution of conjugal rights, has abolished this relief from the country's matrimonial laws.[48] Indian matrimonial laws have retained it although it is outdated, unsuitable and practically unenforceable in the present day pattern of society, and in spite of the fact that arguments in favour of this relief based upon the theory of the 'indissolubility of marriage' do not find much support today.

Judicial separation is a relief quite contrary to the restitution of conjugal rights. The main provision reads as follows: [49]

> Either party to a marriage, whether solemnized before or after the commencement of this Act, may present a petition to the district court praying for a decree for judicial separation on the following six grounds: (1) desertion, (2) cruelty, (3) virulent form of leprosy for one year, (4) venereal disease in communicable form for three years, (5) unsoundness of mind for two years, or (6) on the ground that the other party has after the solemnisation of the marriage had sexual intercourse with any person other than the spouse.

These are the grounds for obtaining a judicial separation. In the Special Marriage Act 1954,[50] the grounds for judicial separation and grounds for divorce are identical, but in the Hindu Marriage Act 1955, the conditions required for divorce are more stringent than those necessary for judicial separation and some distinctions are maintained between the two reliefs. Keeping in view the moral ideals which the Hindu community has always aspired for, the aim was not to make divorce easy and to frame the law accordingly to provide the maximum opportunities for mutual adjustment. The scheme of this Act is, therefore, slightly different. The joint committee introduced some major changes in Clause 10. These are: (a) cruelty has now a self-contained definition; (b) one act of infidelity to the marriage partner now furnishes a ground for judicial separation instead of continued adultery as proposed in the original Bill; and (c) the definition of 'desertion' has been so widened to expressly include wilful neglect of the respondent.[51]

Living in adultery is a ground for divorce, not one single act of infidelity. Divorce terminates a marriage, but judicial separation does not. The real purpose of judicial separation is to provide the estranged spouses, while keeping the marriage intact, a chance of coming together again. The grounds include the three matrimonial offences—desertion, cruelty and adultery. In the interest of women, some more grounds, such as habitual drunkenness or gambling, show of temper and impotency, have been added in the statute.

The only effect of the decree of judicial separation is that, after the decree, it shall not be obligatory on the part of the petitioner to cohabit with the respondent. As the decree of judicial separation does not dissolve the marriage, the relationship between the husband and wife continues. Therefore, if the respondent dies intestate after the decree, the petitioner, as the heir of the respondent, is entitled to inherit the property of the respondent or vice-versa.[52]

The law of judicial separation is no innovation in the Hindu Code, but is rather a repetition of the earlier Act, i.e. Act No. 19 of 1946, which gave a married woman the right to separate residence and maintenance under certain circumstances. The grounds of separate residence and maintenance are:

1. If he (the husband) is suffering from any contagious disease,
2. If he is guilty of such cruelty towards her that it is unsafe or undesirable for her to live with him,
3. If he is guilty of desertion,
4. If he marries again,
5. If he ceases to be a Hindu by conversion to another religion,
6. If he keeps a concubine in the house, and
7. For any other justifiable cause.

The amount of maintenance given to the wife by the husband would be decided by the court, according to the social standing of the parties and to the extent of the husband's means.[53]

The grounds for a right to separate residence and maintenance are, to a large extent, similar to those for judicial separation in the Hindu Marriage Act 1955. As a matter of fact, the principle of the Separate Residence and Maintenance Act 1946 has been adopted in the Hindu Code under the term 'judicial separation.'[54]

In the Hindu Code, an attempt has been made to blend the law of nullity and divorce. The Hindu Marriage Act distinguishes between void and voidable marriage, Section 11 dealing with the former and Section 12 dealing with the latter. Void marriages are those, when firstly, a party has a living spouse at the time of the marriage and secondly, when a marriage is contracted between parties within the prohibited degrees of relationship between *sapindas*[55]

The grounds of voidable marriage under Section 12 are impotency, idiocy and lunacy, or obtaining the consent of the petitioner or the guardian of the petitioner by force or fraud. A void marriage is void *ab initio*. In a voidable marriage, the parties are husband and wife, and children begotten of such marriage are always legitimate, till it is annulled by a decree.

The scheme of the Act shows that it makes a distinction between decrees for divorce and decrees for nullity of a marriage. The decrees for divorce stipulate that the parties cannot remarry until a specified period expires, while in the decrees for nullity, there is no such restriction. Any Hindu marriage which has taken place after the passing of this Act of 1955 can alone be declared as null and void by the decree of nullity, which is not applicable to marriages solemnized before the Act came into force.

It must be admitted that divorce laws under the Hindu Marriage Act have some shortcomings. The greatest lacuna that virtually makes all divorce laws ineffective is the difficulty in procuring evidence sufficient for an action for divorce. Except in cases where the grounds can be proved by medical evidence, for instance, in the case of leprosy, or any communicable venereal disease, it is not always possible for a party to produce reliable and convincing evidence to prove grounds like adultery.

Secondly, adultery has been recognized as a ground for divorce in all the divorce laws in force in the country. However, the law, as contained in the Hindu Marriage Act, makes a difference between continued living in adultery and a single act of adultery. In the former case, it is a valid ground for divorce under Section 13(i) of the Act, but in the latter case, it enables the injured party to seek a right of judicial separation only. It would be insensitive not to realise that adultery causes mental agony to the injured, whether it is a single act or many.

Another flaw of the Hindu Marriage Act is that cruelty has not been recognized as a ground of divorce, thought it finds place in the Indian Divorce Act of 1869, and the Mohammedan Law. It is astonishing indeed that the framers of law felt that Hindus, as a class, would treat their wives better than Muslims or Christians. There appears to be no logical reason for awarding special consideration to a Hindu husband to the detriment of the Hindu wife by not providing cruelty as a ground for divorce. Likewise, desertion has not been provided as a ground for divorce for Hindus. Considering the fact that the majority of Indian women are not only illiterate but are unable to earn a livelihood for themselves and their children, desertion appears to be a more serious ground than adultery and cruelty. In the case of desertion, the wife suffers more than the husband, as for her it is not only the loss of marital company but is coupled with monetary insecurity also. It is therefore necessary that desertion for a number of years should be a ground of divorce, instead of only being a ground for judicial separation as it is now.

So far as the other grounds of divorce, such as insanity for three years, incurable leprosy for three years and a contagious venereal disease for three years, are concerned, it is necessary that the time limit for obtaining the decree for divorce in all these cases should be either abolished or reduced. Retaining the three-year period is not justifiable on a humanitarian basis and the law should recognize that the existence of these diseases is sufficient ground for seeking a divorce. If the law forces them to live in misery till the expiry of a certain period, the provision only serves to prolong the agony of the couple for another three years. Therefore, specifying the time limit to institute a suit for divorce on the basis of the above three grounds as given in Section 13(i) of the Hindu Marriage Act should be seriously reconsidered.

The Hindu Code, especially the Act dealing with the dissolution of marriage, created a storm of controversy. A fraction of public opinion went in favour of the law, and some newspapers and journals hailed it as a great landmark in the social history of India.[56] The *Modern Review* supported it strongly and remarked that it was passed by the Lok Sabha with a degree of unanimity which contrasted sharply with the controversy it had raised.

As expected from his unremitting support to the Hindu Code, Nehru, the Prime Minister, made it a point to take part in the reading. He saw the Bill as the first attempt to shake the rigid structure of society and said that it was essential for social freedom to be integrated with political and economic freedom. The Prime Minister paid high tributes to the women of India. He was very proud and had faith, he said, in their sense of duty, grace, charm, intelligence and spirit of sacrifice. He was not afraid to allow them to go forward.[57]

In his biography of Nehru, professor S. Gopal has pointed out that, towards the end of his life, Nehru regarded the enactment of the Hindu Code as the greatest real advance achieved under his leadership. But, irrespective of all arguments and debates in favour of a common code that preceded the enactment, Nehru could not secure it because of his consideration for the sensitivities of Muslims. To quote his eminent biographer, 'Nothing could be done for Muslim women because that might alarm the Muslim community.'[58]

Some economic problems resulting from the Hindu Marriage Act 1955 dealing with marriage dissolution were pointed out in The *Statesman*.[59] What should happen to the property of the spouses once a divorce is granted? Property might be the joint property of husband and wife, for example, joint bank accounts or their individual property. How far does the court which grants a divorce have the power to pass orders for the readjustment of proprietary relations of the spouses? This power was conferred on the court by Section 27 of the Act of 1955. The section reads:

> ... the court may make such provisions in the decree as it deems just and proper with respect to any property presented at or about the time of marriage, which may belong jointly to both the husband and the wife.

By its wording, this section was confined to property jointly belonging to the spouses. Could the court, by some other power, deal with a case where property belonging to the wife (such as jewellery) was in the husband's possession? Could such property be restored to the wife? Such problems would naturally arise which the limited power of Section 27 could not solve. The Delhi High Court, however, held that return of individual property in possession of the other person could not be ordered under Section 27 of the Hindu Marriage Act. It held that the wife should file a separate suit before an ordinary civil court to claim return of the jewellery and other valuables. But to expect a woman, who has already spent time, money and energy in filing and pursuing a petition for divorce or judicial separation, to take separate proceedings for recovery of property is insensitive.

As a matter of fact, the Hindu Marriage Act displayed a peculiar conservatism, a strange faltering attempt at reform, a half-hearted endeavour to move with the times. The assumption that Hinduism is conservative and orthodox, and that Hindu society will not tolerate any rapid or radical reforms of its law made the law-framers proceed very cautiously. One point forgotten was that the *dharmashastras* had touched the common people only at the fringe. The lower classes of the Hindu community—who had always formed a large section of the society—always had very liberal law for divorce. Conservatism and orthodoxy in this matter have prevailed mostly among the elite.

Suffering from the delusion that Hinduism symbolized conservatism or orthodoxy, the reforms made in the Hindu law of marriage and divorce were far from being satisfactory. The Hindu Marriage Act 1955 did not represent a picture of progressive law when it was enacted. The guilt theory, which loomed large in the minds of the framers of the Act, was made more rigid by the framers of the Hindu Marriage and Divorce Bill, so much so that, in the Act of 1955, it became virtually a reactionary theory. The three traditional fault or guilt grounds—adultery (i.e. a single case of adultery), desertion and cruelty were no longer grounds of divorce.[60] Strangely, one act of adultery was not considered to undermine the foundation of marriage and therefore 'living in adultery' was made a ground of divorce.[61] In fact, the dichotomy of the fault theory based on the premise that one party was at fault and the other was innocent was enacted in Hindu marriage alone.

Notes and References

1. Kane, P.V., *History of Hindu Dharmasastra,* vol. II, part I, p. 570.
2. The Hindu Married Women's Right to Separate Residence and Maintenance Act, 1946.
3. Raghavachariar, N.R., *Hindu Law: Principles and Precedents*, Madras, MLJ office, 1970, pp. 29–36.
4. Mayne, John Dawson, A *Treatise on Hindu Law and Usage,* Madras, Higging Botham and Company, 1906, pp. 175–6.
5. The Indian Divorce Act, 1869, section 10.
6. Diwan Paras, *Modern Hindu Law, codified and uncodified,* Allahabad, Allahabad Law Agency, 1979, pp. 71–3.
7. Legislative Assembly Debates (Official Report), vol. VI, 8th Session, 20 September1938, p. 2830.
8. Ibid., vol. VIII, 8th Sesstion, 12 December 1938, p. 4414.
9. Ibid., vol. II, 9th Session, 18 February 1939, p. 1116.
10. Ibid., vol. IV, 9th Session, 11 April 1939, p. 3540.
11. Mitra, N.N. (Ed.), *The Indian Annual Register,* 1939, vol. I pp. 140–1. Legislative Assembly Debates, 11 April 1939, p. 3540–1.
12. Ibid.
13. Ibid., 12 April 1939, vol. I. p. 142.
14. Ibid., 31 August 1939, vol. II, pp. 89–90.
15. Ibid.
16. Ibid.
17. Ibid., 15 September 1939, p. 592–6.
18. Legislative Assembly Debates, 22 December, vol. V, 12th Session, 1940, p. 996.
19. Ibid., 28 October 1941, vol. IV. p.177.
20. Report of the Hindu Law Committee, 1941, Government of India Press, Simla, 1941, p. 23.
21. Legislative Assembly Debates, vol. IV, 21 March 1946, p. 2719.
22. Act No. XIX of 1946.
23. Derrett, J.D.M., *Hindu Law Past and Present.* Calcutta, A. Mukherjee and Company, 1957, pp. 74–5.
24. Constituent Assembly of India (Legislative) Debates, vol. V, part II, 9 April 1948, p. 3628.
25. *Hindustan Standard,* 25 February 1949.
26. Constituent Assembly of India (Legislative) Debates, vol. II, part II, 24 February 1949, pp. 826–8.
27. Constituent Asembly of India (Legislative) Debats, vol. II, part II, 24 February 1949, pp. 831–34.

28. Ibid., 1 March 1949.
29. Ibid.
30. Ibid., 2 March 1949.
31. The *Hindu,* 2 April 1949.
32. The *Hindu,* 26 February 1949.
33. Council of States Debates, vol. I, 28 July 1952, c. 2102.
34. Council of States Debates, vol. IV, 16 September 1953, c. 2575–6
35. Ibid., vol. VI, 29 April 1954, c. 4553
36. Ibid., vol. VI, 8 May 1954, c. 5761.
37. Ibid., vol. II, 20 December 1952, c. 2649–50.
38. Council of States Debates, vol. II, 20 December 1952, c. 2650–54.
39. Ibid., vol. VI, 16 March 1954, c. 2887–88.
40. Rajya Sabha Debates, vol. VIII, 26 November 1954, c.7.
41. The Hindu Marriage and Divorce Bill, 1952, Joint Committee Report, p.x.vi
42. Rajya Sabha Debates, vol. VIII, 6 December 1954, c. 939
43. Rajya Sabha Debates, vol. VIII, 7 December 1954, c. 1058–78.
44. *Daily Press,* 15 December 1954.
45. Act No. 25 of 1955, Section 13.
46. Act of 1955, sub-Section 2 of section 13.
47. The Hindu Marriage Act, 1955, section IX.
48. The Matrimonial Proceedings and Property Act, 1970, section 20, para 4, p. 12.
49. The Act No. 25 of 1955, section 10.
50. Special Marriage Act 1954 contains the first secular law of India relating to marriage and divorce which any Indian can make use of.
51. Report of the Joint Committee, 25 November, 1954 p. IV. Gazette of India, Extra, part II, dated 4 December 1954.
52. Chaudhuri D.H., The Hindu Marriage Act, 1955, Calcutta, Eastern Law House, 1966, p. 180.
53. The Act No. XIX, 1946. Sections 2 and 3.
54. *Desh,* 12 March 1983, p. 60.
55. Chaudhuri, D.H., op.cit. p. 50.
56. *Hindustan Standard,* 22 March 1949.
57. *Modern Review,* 1955, vol. 97, p. 431.
58. Gopal, S., *Jawaharlal Nehru: A Biography,* vol. II, Delhi, Oxford University Press, 1979, p. 313.
59. The *Statesman,* 20 February 1984.
60. The Hindu Marriage Act, 1955, Section 10.
61. Ibid., section 13(i)

7

Right to Property

In early Hindu society, women had no legal status. The Hindu law of inheritance had deprived women of the right to property (except the right to their stridhan) and, as a result, their economic security was completely dependent on the pleasure of the man—husband, father, brother. The movement to strengthen the position of women in society began from the second half of the nineteenth century. The earliest attempts may be traced back to 1865, with Act X of that year as the first step towards conferring economic security upon Indian women. The Indian Succession Act 1865, (Act X of 1965) laid down that 'no person shall, by marriage, acquire any interest in the property of the person whom he or she marries nor become incapable of doing any act in respect of his or her own property which he or she could have done if not married to that person'.[1]

The Married Women's Property Bill 1874 was a natural consequence of this Act. On 24 February 1874, the Council of the Governor-General of India met at Government House to consider the Bill.[2] The Bill was passed into Act III of 1874, which was the first law in modern times extending the scope of stridhan. It declared that the wages and earnings of any married woman, any property acquired by her through the employment of her art and skill, and all her savings and investments shall be her separate property, and that a married woman can file a suit in her own name in respect of her own property. This Act, though a radical one, did not create stir in Hindu society because, until 1923, the Act applied only to

Indian Christian women. Married women belonging to Hindu, Mohammedan, Sikh and Jain communities remained outside the purview of the Act.[3]

In 1923, the Married Women's Property Act of 1874 was amended by Act XIII of 1923 so as to bring Hindu women and others within its jurisdiction. On 15 February 1923, on the motion of Kamath, the select committee's report on the Bill to amend further the Married Women's Property Act of 1874 was taken into consideration. Kamath's Bill intended to provide a policy of insurance which would be for the benefit of the wife, or the wife and children of the insurer. The Bill was finally passed into law in March, 1923.[4]

The year 1923 constitutes a landmark—this was the year that the Hindu woman's independent right to property was recognized for the first time, although to a limited extent. No doubt, Section 4 of the Widow Remarriage Act 1856 entitled the childless widow to a share of her husband's property, this right was limited in scope.[5] So the attempt made in 1923 may be regarded as the first move to ensure that women's economic rights were honoured.

The Married Women's Property Act of 1874, was further amended in 1927 by Act No. XVIII of that year. Its aim was to safeguard the interests of husbands. James Crerar, the Home Member, moved the Bill, a part of which was meant to limit the liability of a husband when his wife had obtained a probate or letter of administration and was a trustee, executrix or administratix either before or after marriage. The motion was adopted.[6]

Apart from safeguarding the interest of wives and husbands by the Acts of 1923 and 1927, respectively, another Act was passed in 1929, which aimed at giving preference to some nearer degrees of female heirs over certain remoter degrees of male heirs. The seeds of this Act were sown in 1923 when, on 15 February of that year, besides Kamath, T.V. Seshagiri Ayyar, also moved a Bill in the Legislative Assembly to change the order of inheritance in the Hindu family so as to give priority to certain female members.[7] What was sought to be done in this Bill was that in matters of inherritance, after the father's father and before the father's brother, the son's daughter, daughter's daughter, sister and sister's son be given preference over the father's brother. This Bill sought to ensure that the inheritance rights of female heirs were between those of the father's father and the uncle. The House agreed to refer Seshagiri's Bill to a select committee.

After the select committee reported, the Bill again came up in the Legislative Assembly on 27 March 1923. J.N. Mukherjee of Calcutta suggested that before considering the report of the select committee, the Bill be recirculated so that more opinions could be voiced. In his view, opinions of competent men should be considered on the issue, because it was improper for individual members to suggest amendments without consulting the country. His objection to the Bill was that it stopped with the son's daughter and excluded the grandson's daughter. The father's sister had been also completely ignored, although these two heirs were very important in a Hindu family.

Seshagiri argued that the principle of Hindu law on property was based on three elements of *bandhus—atmabandhus*, that is, one's own descendants, *pitribandhus*, that is, the father's descendants and *matribandhus*, that is, the mother's descendants. The second principle of Hindu Law was that the classes of bandhus should not go beyond three degrees, which meant that the grandson's daughter, who was more than three degrees removed, did not come under the category of atmabandhu. the son's daughter and the daughter's daughter came within the three degrees and were within one's atmabandhus, and so they must be given preference over the sister, who was a pitribandhu. That was the principle upon which the order of succession of the Bill was based.[8] When put to vote, Seshagiri's motion for recirculation of the Bill was lost by a margin of eleven votes, and on 19 July 1923, when the Bill came up before the Council of States, it was postponed. Thus Seshagiri's Bill on the Hindu Law of Inheritance remained pending.[9]

Though Seshagiri's Bill was kept in abeyance, the legislators continued their endeavour. It was again moved in the legistative Assembly by Sir Shanmukham Chetty on 12 February 1929.[10] The Bill now laid down that if a person died leaving property not held in coparcenary and not disposed of by will, and if the last persons surviving were the father's brother and a son's daughter, the son's daughter, being the nearer relative, should have preference over the father's brother. That is, a son's daughter, a daughter's daughter, sister, and sister's son, should in the order specified, be entitled to rank in order of succession, next after a father's father and before a father's brother.

An interesting discussion followed the motion by Chetty. Siddheswar Prasad moved the amendment that the Bill be circulated for public opinion, while M.S. Aney supported the amendment on the ground that it was a question which affected everyone who called himself a Hindu, so the opinions of Hindus must be ascertained. He asserted that the reformers had no right to force their views on them. This tendency of the reformers, he felt, amounted to showing disrespect to the dead, contrary to one of the radical beliefs of Hindu society which was its duty to the dead. Because, according to Aney, many people did not make a will as they wanted the natural inheritance laws of the land to prevail in his own case. Laying down new rules of succession meant hurting that sentiment and faith of those dying intestate, while our age-old tradition was based upon the duties of the living to the dead. This tradition would be in jeopardy, Aney believed, if Chetty's motion was carried through. So, if the amendment was not accepted, it would tantamount to striking at the very root of the Hindu people's faith in their *achaars*.[11]

Sir B.L. Mitter, the Law Member, said that the intention of the Bill was to be gathered from the Bill itself and not from the proceedings of the Council of States. He wanted to know whether the reversioners after the death of the limited owners were to be protected or not. He elaborated his point by giving an example. If a man died leaving a widow but no children, the widow became a limited owner of his estate. After the widow's death, a nephew of the man might become the full owner, but one question was whether it would be in the interest of the nephew during the lifetime of the widow since it was only an expectation, a mere chance of succession if he survived the widow. B.L. Mitter questioned whether the expectant heirs were to be protected by accepting the amendment or were they to be placed in the same position as other expectant heirs. According to him, the government would not take any part in such a controversy because, at any rate, the fundamentals of Hindu law were not questioned. The question was only how some nearer degrees of female heirs could be given preference over certain remoter degrees of male heirs.

Pandit Madan Mohan Malaviya was avowedly opposed to the Bill.[12] He said that the Hindu Law of Succession was a personal law and the government had promised not to interfere with such laws. Hence, it was not right on the part of the legislators to alter the law. Pandit Malaviya then asked the Hindu members to record their protests in the official report and to publish it in the newspapers so that the Governor-General-in-Council might take notice of them.

Pandit Motilal Nehru said that as a social reformer he sympathized with the Bill, but as a lawyer he could not support it.[13] The amendment was necessary to protect reversionary heirs, but no man of property died without making a will. If the man died without making any will, it would be inferred that the deceased person's wishes were that the law of succession which had been followed for ages should be applied to his case also, for every Hindu knew the ordinary law of succession.

M.R. Jayakar vehemently opposed the amendment.[14] He said that the Bill, placed a long time ago by Seshagiri Ayyar, had been examined by the select committee and its principles had been accepted by the House. The Bill was then postponed by the Council of States. He said that the Bill was already old and the demand for amendment would only delay its enactment further. He said that no more obstacles should come in its way since the Bill introduced only four female heirs between the father's father and the uncle and stopped there. The intention was that the interests of certain degrees of remoter male heirs should be postponed in favour of those of the nearer degrees of female heirs. Eventually, the amendment, when put to vote, was rejected by forty-eight as against fourteen votes in its favour. Seshagiri's Bill received the assent of the Governor-General on the 21 February 1929, and became a law under the name of the Hindu Law of Inheritance (Amendment) Act 1929 (Act II of 1929).[15]

The provision of the Act introducing the female heirs reads as follows:

> A son's daughter, daughter's daughter, sister and sister's son shall, in the order so specified be entitled to rank in the order of succession next after a father's father and before a father's brother, provided that a sister's son shall not be included, if adopted after the sister's death.[16]

This Act was very limited in its scope and did not make any radical change in Hindu law in favour of women. By this Act neither daughters nor widows were provided with the right of inheritance. The Act only emphasized that certain degrees of remoter male heirs should be postponed in favour of the nearer degrees of female heirs and nothing more. So the provisions of the Act were not particularly radical in support of women's right to property.

Further, Act II of 1929 was limited in the sense that it regulated succession only in the case of the separate property of a Hindu male dying intestate. Its aim was not to alter the law in respect of the property of a female, but only to ensure that when a husband succeeded to his wife's stridhan property, it descended in the same way as if it had belonged to the husband himself, after her death. If at such time, Act II of 1929 was in force, it was that Act which governed succession, and the property could not be deemed to be the property of a female.[17] Thus, the legal position of women, according to Act II of 1929, was far from satisfactory. Realizing this, the legislators continued to fight for greater inheritance rights for women. On 26 September 1929, V. V. Jogia introduced another Hindu Law (Amendment) Bill for the purpose of making 'better provision for certain heirs, under Hindu law, especially with respect to women regarding their rights of inheritance'.[18] On the same day, Munshi Narayan Prasad Asthana introduced in the Council of States the Hindu Law of Inheritance (Second Amendment) Bill, the aim of which was to give some recognition to the rights of women related by marriage to the family of the deceased, for instance, a predeceased son's widow or a brother's widow. This Bill, however, remained pending for consideration in the next session.[19]

Again on the same day, 26 September 1929, Raisaheb Harbilas Sarda introduced the Hindu Widow's Rights of Inheritance Bill to secure a share for Hindu widows in their husband's property, but to no effect. The same Bill was again introduced by Sarda on 21 January 1930. This time it was widely discussed.[20] The principal clause of the Bill was: where the husband of a widow was at the time of his death a member of a joint Hindu family, the widow shall be entitled to such share of the joint family property as her husband would have been. This share would become her absolute property. Under the Hindu law, a widow did not get any share in her husband's property as a son did. A widow's right of inheritance was very limited and this right was often interpreted in courts of law in a narrow sense and entitled her only to maintenance and residence in her deceased husband's house.

The Bill was supported by women all over India who demanded the right of inheritance in women's conferences held in different parts of the country. At the successive annual meetings of the All India Women's Conference—at Poona in 1927 under the Presidentship of Her Highness, the Maharani of Baroda, at Delhi in 1928 under the Presidentship of Her Highness, the Begum of Bhopal, in 1929 at Patna with the Dowager Rani of Mandi as the President and at Bombay in 1930 under the Presidentship of Sarojini Naidu—and at various other provincial constituent conferences of women, the right of inheritance was being demanded repeatedly.

Sir Brojen Mitter, the Law Member, appreciated the object of the Bill and said that it really was a positive step towards improvement of the widow's position in the family. Since the government would be guided by majority opinion, he moved it for circulation and this motion was carried.[21]

On 17 February 1931, Harbilas Sarda tried again to introduce the Bill in the Assembly, after it had been circulated. But due to some opposition, it could make no headway. On 26 January 1932, the discussion on the Bill was held.[22] It was further considered on 4 February 1932.[23] After giving a moving description of the deplorable condition of Hindu widows, Sarda made particular reference to the old Hindu *shastras* by which a woman became the co-owner of her husband's property as soon as she got married. While analysing the provisions of the Bill, he said that when the Bill was being introduced in 1929, most of the criticism was directed against the provision in Clause 3(1) that the share the widow was entitled to get on partition should become her absolute property. In order to disarm opposition, he had in 1931 deleted the words, 'this share shall become her absolute property.'[24]

The Bill was vehemently criticized by a number of members, particularly those from Bengal namely, Amar Nath Dutta, S.N. Sen, S.C. Sen, D.K. Lahiri and others. Amar Nath Dutta emphasized that in Bengal, the lot of Hindu widows was never deplorable. On the other hand, they were in a far better position than in any other province. In Bengal, where the Dayabhaga system prevailed, the childless Hindu widow got the whole corpus of her husband's property. Satyendra Nath Sen also refused to believe that a widow was not given due respect and consideration. He was afraid that if the widows were given the right of inheritance, they would lead a life of luxury and squander their wealth. He quoted from the ancient seriptures to show that the Hindu shastras never approved of the concept of either their independence or of absolute right to property.[25] D.K. Lahiri Chaudhury said that in Bengal, widows always received their legitimate share of maintenance.

Raja Bahadur Krishnamachariar also denied the contention that the lot of the Hindu widow was deplorable. He challenged Sarda to name a single widow who had asked him to introduce the Bill. He said that the judicial authorities cited by Sarda in favour of this measure were unreliable; because these authorities were not Hindus and, therefore, were not likely to be familiar with Hindu social customs or the position of Hindu widows. Besides, he felt that the rate of widow remarriage would increase if the Bill was enacted, for the property of the widows would be enough temptation to men, lured by the prospect of property, to marry them. This showed that he did not approve of widow remarriage either. [26]

The Bill was, however, supported by many. Rai Bahadur Lala Brij Kishore, a member, admitted that the condition of Hindu widows was truly deplorable. They had no legal position and were at the mercy of the male members of the family. Thousands of them were humiliated, disgraced and even driven away from their homes; hence, it was necessary to improve their lot.[27] A. Das, another member supporting the Bill, said that most of the objections raised during the debates were vague and pointless, and that the legislation was overdue.[28]

Sir Hari Singh Gour vehemently criticized the attitude of the government, which only paid lip service to the Bill. He said that a question of such vital importance should not be decided by counting heads but by its righteousness and truth. Addressing the claims of his orthodox opponents, he said that the Bill was only trying to reform laws made by men and that ancient Hindu laws were not sacred or divine. He argued that society then urgently needed such a piece of legislation and that if there were any defect in the Bill, a select committee would make suitable amendments in view of the changing times.[29]

Sir Lancelot Graham, Secretery, Legislative Department, explaining the attitude of the government, said they would not support it unless they were convinced that there was a very strong public demand for passing the Bill.[30] Sir Brojen Mitter, the Law Member, was not sure whether the Bill dealt with a sonless widow, who always inherited the property of her husband, or widows with a son. He criticized the various clauses of the Bill and said that they violated testamentary rights. If the object of the Bill was to give a secure place to a widow in the Hindu social structure, the Bill certainly would not serve the purpose, he believed.[31]

While replying to the arguments in the debate, Sarda said that the government could only retard the progress of the Bill, but could not kill the progress of the society. He said that the government did not consult any women's organization on a social Bill while on political matters it had nominated women to the Round Table Conference.[32] The question whether the Bill should be referred to a select committee was put to vote. The House was divided and the Bill was rejected by fifty-five votes against twenty-six.[33]

The *Modern Review*, a mouthpiece of public opinion, supported the object of Sarda's Bill.[34] It said that all Hindu widows were not necessarily helpless or oppressed, nor were they all happily placed. Discussions as to whether they were miserable or not ought not to be allowed to obscure the principle that a state of dependence was not conducive to the growth of a human personality. Therefore, whether Hindu widows were oppressed or not, they were entitled to be self-reliant.[35]

Undaunted by earlier failures, Harbilas Sarda moved another Bill entitled 'The Hindu Widows' Right of Maintenance Bill' in the Assembly on 29 August 1933. He said that Hindu law gave widows the right of maintenance, but since there was no definite standard to guide judges in fixing the amount of maintenance, this Bill aimed at providing that measuring rod to the judges.

A discussion on the Bill was held on 5 September 1933. The Bengalees vehemently opposed it. Sir Bepin Behari Ghose, the Law Member, wanted a clarification. The Bill proposed that if a widow was sonless, she was entitled to get as maintenance the entire income which her husband's share in the joint family estate would, as on partition, yield. This provision amounted to a compulsory partition; therefore, he proposed that the Bill be circulated.[36] Amar Nath Dutta pointed out that under Dayabhaga, the son was bound to maintain the mother if he inherited his father's property and if there was a partition between the sons, the mother invariably got a share. He agreed with the Law Member on the point of circulation.[37] S.C. Sen criticized the last clause of the Bill which proposed that if a sonless man died, the widow would be entitled to the entire sum her husband left as his share in the joint family estate. That was preposterous according to Sen, and so the Bill needed to be circulated.[38] Rai Bahadur Lala Brij Kishore spoke in favour of the Bill. He said that since nobody could deny that the plight of Hindu widows required amelioration, she was entitled to get maintenance as long as she did not remarry.[39] The Chairman, Sir Shanmukham Chetty, then ordered that the Bill be circulated for the purpose of eliciting opinion on or by December 1933, and the motion was adopted.[40]

The Bill never came up again and, therefore, Sarda's Bill for the Hindu widow's right for maintenance met the fate of its predecessor. But his efforts did not go unrewarded, for his idea caught the imagination of the reformers and a few years later an Act was passed in 1937, which eventually recognized the rights of Hindu widows. The Bill to amend the Hindu law, governing Hindu women's right to property was circulated for the purpose of eliciting public opinion on 17 April 1936.[41] The Bill proposed no innovation, but was merely a measure of restoration. It was referred to a select committee on 15 October 1936 and on 4 February 1937 the Bill, as amended by the select committee was taken up for consideration.[42]

Replying to the arguments advanced by the orthodox Hindus that women could not have the right to property, because they were dependent all their lives, Dr. Deshmukh said that extending the argument to India as a whole, it might as well be contended that because Indians for a thousand years had been dependent, no Indian had the right to hold property. The Bill, as it emerged from the select committee, might not perhaps, mean material gain to a Hindu widow, but it certainly represented moral gain inasmuch as it recognized her right of partition.[43]

Baij Nath Bajoria, holding the orthodox viewpoint, said that Dr. Deshmukh, who was a surgeon and had performed many successful operations on individuals, was now attempting a mass operation on Hindu society. He declared that it was not desirable to give a widow an unfettered right to have partition because she was likely to come under the influence of her relatives, who might deprive her of whatever she obtained by partition. Sir N.N. Sircar, the Law Member, opined that, from the progressive point of view, the Bill was disappointing and he personally thought that it did not go far enough. The Law member, however, concluded by declaring that as an initial step in redressing the wrong, this was a very substantial measure.[44]

Dewan Lalchand Navalrai, while agreeing to the need for reform, pleaded for caution. He reminded the House that educated women were few in India, and it was not right, therefore, to give them unrestricted right of partition.

N.M. Joshi expressed disappointment at the whittling down of the original Bill. How could the government, he asked, be sure that the *Sanatanist* views were acceptable to the country. He felt sure that the government would have received support from the country for a more progressive measure. Dewan Lalchand Navalrai and Baij Nath Bajoria attempted a few amendments to the Bill but they were rejected and the House passed the Bill amidst cheers.[45] The Act was called The Hindu Women's Right to Property Act (Act XVIII) of 1937,[46] the main provisions of which were:

1. When a Hindu governed by the Dayabhaga school or by any other school of Hindu Law died intestate leaving separate property, it would devolve upon his widow along with his lineal descendants, if any, in the same manner as it devolved upon a son.

   Provided that the widow of a predeceased son would inherit in like manner as a son. Provided further that the same provision should apply *mutatis mutandis* to the widow of a predeceased son of a predeceased son.
2. When a Hindu governed by any school of Hindu Law, other than the Dayabhaga school died intestate having at the time of his death an interest in a Hindu joint family property, his

widow would have in the property the same interest as he himself had.

3. Any interest devolving on a Hindu widow would be limited interest known as 'Hindu Women's Estate,' provided, however, that she would have the same right of claiming partition as a male owner.[47]

Act II of 1929 was the first to amend the Hindu law of inheritance and Act XVIII of 1937 was the second. The Act of 1929 made no provision for helpless widows, for whom the legislature had to make better provisions by the Act of 1937.

But this Act of 1937 was criticized on several grounds. Rishindra Nath Sarkar, an advocate of Calcutta High Court, wrote an open letter to the Law Member, N.N. Sircar, pointing out some of its defects. First, according to this law, when a Hindu died intestate, his property would devolve upon his widow along with his lineal descendants, if any, in like manner, as it devolved upon a son. Now the term 'lineal descendants' was a comprehensive term which meant direct descendants like sons, daughters, grandsons and granddaughters by sons and daughters, and so forth. Consequently, the property of a Hindu dying intestate would be liable to be divided into an infinite number of shares. As such, the interest a widow would get could never be deemed to be better than what perhaps the Act intended it to be, as she would merely get a share equal to that of each of the numerous lineal descendents, instead of a share equal to that of a son.[48]

Therefore, a Bill was subsequently introduced in 1938 for the amendment of the Act of 1937. The Law Member, Sir N.N. Sircar, in his speech referred to the Calcutta Weekly Notes in which the defects of the Act of 1937 were pointed out.[49] He said that by 'lineal descendants', the legislators did not mean to give rights to innumerable inheritors of the man dying intestate but only to three types of widows: (i) his own widow, (ii) the widow of his deceased son and (iii) the widow of his deceased son's deceased son. The language, however, he admitted, was ambiguous and needed to be corrected. He also clarified another controversial point in the Act, that is, whether a daughter-in-law's right depended upon whether her mother-in-law was alive. He said that it was not the intention of the Act that a woman's right should be influenced by the existence or otherwise of a widowed mother-in-law. He also corrected another ambiguous point of the Act and made it perfectly clear that if there were more than one widow, say, two widows, both would jointly get the share equal to that of a son. The Amendment Bill of 1938 was therefore passed on 18 March 1938.[50] The Act was called The Hindu Women's Right to Property (Amendment) Act, 1938, (Act No. XI of 1938).[51]

An important defect of this Act was that it gave undue rights to a predeceased son's widow, who got more concrete rights than those of the widow of the deceased owner. Whereas the interest conferred upon the deceased person's own widow was expressly subject to the provision of sub-section (3) which meant that the interest would be known as 'Hindu Woman's Estate', there was no such limitation in respect of the interest conferred on the predeceased son's widow.[52] Besides, under Section 2 of the Widow Remarriage Act 1856, the widow of a deceased Hindu would forfeit the property on remarriage, but it could not be concluded that widows other than the widow of the predeceased owner would also be divested of the property vested in her on remarriage. The Act of 1937 was not specific as to what would happen if a man died leaving a son and a predeceased son's widow and her son. Would she inherit one-third and the son and the grandson get one-third each? Or would the son get half and the widowed daughter-in-law and her son inherit one-fourth each?

Another serious defect of the Act was that it affected the daughters. The Hindu law-givers expressly laid down that the maiden daughter's maintenance till her marriage, and her marriage expenses were to be paid out of her father's estate. By the Act of 1937 and its amendment, a predeceased son's widow was placed before the daughter in the order of succession; but she was not liable to pay any amount to anybody out of the estate which devolved on her. Consequently, the maiden daughter could not enforce her claim to maintenance or her marriage expenses from the predeceased son's widow.[53] In fact, there was no justification in placing predeceased son's widow and the widow of a predeceased son of the predeceased son before the maiden daughter. Any of these widows might turn the daughter out into the street, since her rights were not protected in the Act or its amendments.[54]

In view of the above shortcomings of the Act, a series of private Bills came up. The first Amendment Bill was moved by Akhil Chandra Dutta, Member, Legislative Assembly on 18 February 1939.[55] On 15 September 1939, the motion for the circulation of Dutta's Bill was adopted to elicit public opinion,[56] and on 22 November 1940 a discussion on the Bill took place. [57] Akhil Dutta moved for reference of the Bill to a select committee. His Bill did not seek to amend the Hindu Womens' Rights to Property Act of 1937 but the amending Act of 1938, and related to the right of inheritance of Hindu daughters. Their place in the order of succession, according to the Bill, should be thus: when a Hindu died intestate, the son should come first followed by the grandson, great grandson, then the widow, and after the widow, the daughters. So Hindu daughters occupied fifth place in the order of succession and were sacrificed in the Act of1938 in preference of the daughters-in-law, who had no right of inheritance at all under Hindu Law. The Bill was supported by P.N. Banerjee of Calcutta, M.S. Aney and Syed Ghulam Bhik Nairang, who explained that the Bill was intended to restore the Hindu daughter to the position she enjoyed before the amending Act of 1938 was passed.[58]

The Home Member, Sir Reginald Maxwell, explained that such a legislation must have the support of a large section of the community it affected, and claimed that the mass of opinions received on the Bill was opposed to the principle on which it was based. The government, therefore, would be justified in opposing the Bill.

Akhil Dutta's Bill, therefore, failed. But it was followed by a number of other Bills, such as:

1. The Hindu Women's Right to Property (Amendment) Bill presented by A.N. Chattopadhyay.
2. The Hindu Women's Right to Property Bill introduced by N.V. Gadgil.
3. The Hindu Women's Estate Bill put up by Dr G.V. Deshmukh.

Faced with such a barrage of private Bills, the government appointed a small Hindu Law Committee known as the Rau Committee with B.N. Rau, a Judge of the Calcutta High Court as its chairman and three other lawyers as its members.[59] They were D.N. Mitter, ex-Judge of Calcutta High Court; Gharpure, Principal, Law College of Poona; and Rajratna Vasudev Vinayak Joshi, a lawyer of Baroda. The Committee advocated a Hindu Code—a blend of the finest elements of various schools of Hindu law. On the basis of the various private Bills on property, the Committee evolved a common law of intestate succession for all Hindus in British India. The Code recognized the equality of the status of men and women before law with appropriate obligations as well as rights.[60]

The Rau Committee reported in June 1941 that the Hindu Code Bill should be taken up by compartments:[61] (1) Hindu Marriage, (2) Hindu Succession, (3) Hindu Minority and Guardianship, (4) Hindu Adoption and Maintenance. It was essential to reduce the law relating to each part to a statutory form, and then consolidate the various acts into a single code.[62]

On 24 March 1943, the Hindu Code Bill relating to intestate succession came up before the assembly for discussion.[63] The salient features of the Bill were: that it embodied a common law of inestate succession for all Hindus in British India; that it removed the sex disqualification by which Hindu women in general had been precluded from inheriting property; and that it abolished the Hindu woman's limited estate and converted it into an absolute one. Sir Sultan Ahmed, the Law Member, discussed the background of the Bill and said that, due to the defects of the Act of 1937 and of the amending Act of 1938, a full revision of the Acts had become an urgent necessity.[64]

Bhai Parmananda, opposing the Bill, criticized the government for taking upon itself the task of framing a code for Hindu society, particularly when there was no demand for change among the people. Under the circumstances,[65] the Bill was likely to interfere with Hindu religion, destroy the family structure and lead to fragmentation of property. Babu Baij Nath Bajoria, leader of the opposition to the Bill, moved an amendment for postponement of the Bill.[66] He strongly objected to the Bill being brought up right at the end of the session without giving it sufficient publicity. He argued that if simultaneous heirship of the daughter was recognized as in the Bill, the moral obligation felt by the brother to maintain and marry off his sisters would vanish.

K.C. Neogy of Bengal pointed out that the measure had evoked a great deal of controversy in the province of Bengal at least.[67] Insofar as it had made a departure in essential particulars from the laws of inheritance prevailing in other parts of India, Dayabhaga was itself the result of a reformative movement. He argued that people who were governed by the Dayabhaga school should be the last persons to take exception to the process of reform going on according to modern ideas to suit modern conditions. Unfortunately, however, the opinion in Bengal was mostly opposed to the Bill.

Lalchand Navalrai warned women and the associations of women that 'more or less we are plunged into the ocean of Western ways and we should not allow ourselves to be drowned'. He raised an objection regarding the right of a married daughter who would get a share from her husband's side and also a share in her parental house. Therefore, she would get two shares whereas the son would get only one. He, however, overlooked the fact that the sons enjoyed shares brought by their wives from their parental homes.[68] Amarendra Nath Chattopadhyaya of Bengal welcomed the Bill and said that men and women should have equal rights.[69] He fully appreciated the idea of codification of Hindu Law by which Hindu society would be brought into harmony all over the country. Govind V. Deshmukh supported the Bill and refuted the argument that it would lead to the breaking up of Hindu society, contending that the society was a living organism which could exist and did exist by adopting to the circumstances that cropped up from time to time.[70] P.N. Banerjee pointed out a number of defects in the Bill and supported its reference to a select committee because he felt that it would provoke thought among Hindus throughout India. He demanded that adequate steps be taken to secure the fullest possible publicity and discussion.[71]

Renuka Ray did not think that the Bill could come as a surprise to anyone. She referred to the countrywide agitation that was carried on ten years before the Bill was framed in favour of women's rights, and she maintained that it was not necessary to wait for new elections to determine how far the country was in favour of the Bill. She felt that the denial of property rights to women was based on an old, obscure text which had, in any case, been misrepresented. Refuting the contention that the Bill would lead to disintegration of property, Ray remarked that the suggestion seemed to be that when a man had eight or ten sons and each of them inherited a share of the property, no disintegration took place; but when a man had a son and a daughter, and the daughter got a share, only then disintegration followed. She hoped that the Bill, if passed, would mark the beginning of a new era of social reform in India. However, the Bill, she felt, was quite a conservative measure as the Rau Committee only reframed what was already laid down in Hindu law. She argued that in the Vedic and post-Vedic periods women had a great measure of equality, even in law, as supported by the texts of *Jamini* and *Upasthamba*. Later, due to a multitude of causes, woman lost her position in society and this was reflected in the law. By the time the British came, women's rights had been further curtailed because the pandits and priests who expounded the laws gave the laws a most reactionary interpretation. Moreover, at that time, British common law did not allow women the right to hold property, so the British jurists did not think it strange that Hindu women possessed no such rights either. In that process, not only were Hindu women deprived of their rights, but Hinduism was deprived of some of its finest and most progressive elements. The Rau Committee sought to restore some of these features of Hindu law, not by any revolutionary reform but by attempting to revive the old glory of Hindu law.[72]

Sir Sultan Ahmed, the Law Member, replying to arguments in the debate said that if there was any need, he was prepared to choose two or three experts, particularly from Bengal, who might be of help to the joint committee. The joint committee consisted of Members of both Houses of Parliament while the select committee comprised a number of members of one House of Parliament whose task was to examine special issues and then submit a report before the House. The Law Member gave the assurance that the Joint Select Committee would not be packed with supporters of the Bill but would also include men who held very strong views against it.[73] The House rejected motions for circulation and the Bill was recommended for reference to a joint committee of the Legislative Assembly and Council of States consisting of the following members of the Assembly: Amarendra Nath Chattopadhyaya, Pandit Nilkantha Das, Renuka Ray, Akhil Chandra Dutta, Babu Baij Nath Bajoria, Govind V. Deshmukh, Lalchand Navalrai, Syed Ghulam Bhik Nairang, and Sultan Ahmed.[74]

The *Modern Review* expressed the opinion:

> The great benefit of the Bill is that it provides a uniform code for all India ... Orthdox opposition is intelligible but there is not much in it. The opposition of people who profess advanced views in politics and even in social matters can only be treated as proceeding from interested motives or from mere factiousness.[75]

In a public meeting held in Calcutta on 10 July 1943 to support the Bill, the following resolution was unanimously adopted:[76]

> This public meeting of the women in Calcutta strongly supports the principles of the Rau Committee's Bill relating to Hindu Intestate Succession, which is now before the Select Committee of the Central Legislature with regard to the establishment of one Hindu law all over India, the removal of sex disqualification and the abolition of the Hindu Women's 'Limited Estate'; and recommends that at least two more women should be taken as members of the Assembly to represent the Hindu women's viewpoint and demands that the Bill be referred back to the Assembly for immediate passing into law and not shelved pending the codification of the entire Hindu law.

Atul Chandra Gupta, a lawyer of repute, after explaining the different aspects of the Bill pointed out that the Bill contemplated bringing into force one unified law of inheritance for Hindus throughout India. He felt that the consequences of the Bill had a far-reaching effect on the whole Hindu community in that every one who professed to be a Hindu in India would be guided by it. He emphasized that, to all intents and purposes, the law of succession had nothing to do with religion as such and he failed to understand why one's religion would receive a setback if a daughter was to inherit as in the case of the mother and the brother.[77] The industrialization of India demanded the mobility of capital stagnating in the system of common ownership of the family property. The breaking up of this system was a historical necessity and the Act had done it admirably. According to another lawyer, Risindra Nath Sarkar, the unification of laws was unjustified. In *Amrita Bazar Patrika* and *Hindustan Standard*, he put forward his arguments under the caption, 'No codification of Hindu Law'.[78] The code, in his view, failed to unify the Hindu law as the Central legislature under the Government of

India Act, 1935, possessed no power to legislate on agricultural land. That power was to be exercised by provincial legislatives, and therefore, no unification could be expected. Moreover, the proposed change was to undermine seriously the Mitakshara joint family system; and repealing joint family meant denouncing cooperation. By attacking joint family, the code condemned cooperation while cooperation and united allied action in the form of League of Nations and United Nations had been long recognized as a durable basis for everlasting global unity. Even women's position was not adequately safeguarded by the code as the mother was placed after son, grandson, great grandson, widow, daughter, and even daughter's son. Similarly, predeceased son's widow was also deprived of the right given under the Hindu Women's Right to Property Act of 1937. On the submission of the report of the Joint Committee, the Government of India issued on 21 January 1944, a notification reviving the Hindu Law Committee with B.N. Rau as Chairman to complete the codification of other parts of the Hindu Code Bill.[79] On the occasion of the debates on the Bill, Dr. Ambedkar said that the Bill was 'no revolutionary measure, not even a radical measure'. He did not appreciate the criticism that shares to daughters meant disruption of the family property. 'If we want to stop fragmentation we would have to do something else, not by the law of inheritance but by some other law,' he said.

The Bill as recommended by the Rau Committee was referred to a select committee on 9 April 1948.[80] It came up for discussion in the Legislative Assembly on 24 February 1949. The Hindu Code relating to succession had its repercussions in different parts of India. A letter published in the *Statesman* stated that the Hindu Code was a measure which interfered with the religious and socio-religious life of Hindus and protested that when there was no code for Muslims, Christians and other communities, there was no reason why Hindu society should be made an exception, especially in opposition to the vast majority of Hindus. This violated, it said, all principles of secularism and democracy—the two guiding principles of our national government. The letter went on to say that women who opposed the Code were accused of a slavish mentality and a fondness for their chains. However, if obedience to religious, social and family rules was slavery, obedience to political and legal rules should also be considered as such. According to this view, then, savages and vagabonds were the only free people in this world.[81]

The *Hindu* vehemently attacked the Bill on the basis that the national leaders of this country and their advice were behind it. Dr. Ambedkar seemed, the *Hindu* commented, to regard the Hindu Code Bill as a practical joke. He described himself as a 'progressive conservative' and his job was that of 'repairing those parts of the Hindu system which had almost become dilapidated'. Far from its having become dilapidated and unsafe, the *Hindu* commented, Hindu society rested so strongly on its foundation that Dr. Ambedkar had confessed to a news agency that the orthodox section of the population did not want the proposed Hindu Code and such people were in a vast majority. By what right then, did a microscopic minority seek to impose its own view on the vast body of Hindus in a matter of such fundamental importance to the future of Hindu society and culture? The government could claim no popular mandate for such a measure.

Letters denouncing the Bill were also published in the *Hindu*.[82] Expressing the view that the provisions relating to marriage, adoption, etc., could, with slight modifications, be made acceptable to Hindu society, they protested that when it came to the right of property, both the framers of the Bill and the members of the select committee seemed to have run amuck with their proposals. Rich families could afford to give shares of family properties to all the members alike, but ninety per cent of the people of India lived by agriculture. The fragmentation of agricultural holdings in India would render the agricultural system neither fruitful nor useful. What would become of a family of eight daughters and six sons, with a landed property of fifteen acres? Another letter published on 23 March 1949, stated that Hindu society needed no reform. It said, 'There is absolutely no clamour for the proposed changes except among a few English educated men and women'.[83]

One letter, however, was in favour of the Bill and refuted the argument of the letter quoted above.[84] It said that the notion that these reforms were not needed by Hindu society merely because some of the proposed reforms were Western in character, and some of those responsible for such reforms happened to be 'saturated with Western education', should be given up. Western or Eastern, any idea that would be useful to India should be fully exploited and applied to our conditions. After all, an English educated great man had brought forth the reform of *sati* and people were happy about that.

In Bengal, however, the Hindu Code was more or less supported by the people. It is true that in the Parliament, the Bengali members, except Amar Nath Chattopadhyaya of Burdwan, had opposed the Bill, but a large section of the general public welcomed the Bill. The Hindu Code relating to succession received the assent of the President and became the law of the land on 17 June 1956. The law was named The Hindu Succession Act 1956 (Act No. XXX of 1956).[85] It provided a share to a female even in property owned by a joint Hindu family of the Mitakshara type, and gave a solution to strong divergent views regarding a Hindu woman's position in the order of succession without disrupting the Mitakshara coparcenary.[86]

The Hindu Succession Act of 1956 enacted a new principle. The Hindus were governed by two systems of law—the Mitakshara and the Dayabhaga. According to Mitakshara, the property of a Hindu was not his individual property but belonged to what was called a coparcenary which consisted of father, son, grandson and great-grandson. On the death of any member of this coparcenary, the property passed on by survivorship to members who remained behind and did not pass to the wife and children of the deceased. The Act adopted the Dayabhaga system, under which the property was to be held by the wife and children as personal property with an absolute right to dispose it of.

That was the fundamental change which this Act made, in addition to which the Act sought to introduce four changes.[87] One was that the widow, the daughter, and the widow of the predeceased son all got the same rank as the son in the matter of inheritance, and the daughter was also given a share full and equal to that of the son in her father's property. The second change which the Act made so far as the female heirs were concerned was that the number of female heirs recognized was greater than that prescribed by either Mitakshara or Dayabhaga. The third change made by the Act was that under the old law, a discrimination was made among female heirs as to whether a particular female was rich or poor, whether she was with issue or without issue. All these discriminating points were now abolished by this Act. The last change related to the rule of inheritance in the Dayabhaga. Under the Dayabhaga system, the father succeeded the son in preference to the mother; under the present Act, the position was altered so that the mother came before the father.

Regarding stridhan, the Act made two changes. One was that the stridhan of different categories would be considered as one under the rule of succession. Secondly, the son was also given a right to inherit the stridhan, equal with the daughter. The select committee made another alteration of the existing rule where the husband of a woman in the case of succession came much later under the Hindu law—a provision included in the original Rau Committee. The select committee brought the husband in the line of other stridhan heirs.[88]

Regarding the question of 'women's estate' under Hindu law, a woman earlier inherited what was called a 'life estate' when the property passed after the death of the woman to the reversioners of her husband. The Act now introduced two changes. It converted the woman's limited estate into an absolute estate; and secondly, it abolished the right of the reversioners to claim the property after the widow's death or remarriage. An important provision in this Act also related to dowry. The property given to a girl as dowry on the occasion of her marriage should be treated as a trust property, which the woman would be entitled to claim when she reached the age of 18, so that neither her husband nor any relative of her husband would have any interest in that property.

Nevertheless, certain provisions under the Hindu Succession Act, like Sections 6 and 30, were still unequal and discriminatory. For instance, Section 6, which dealt with the devolution of coparcenary interest left by the deceased Hindu male, discriminated between a son, who was a coparcener with a right by birth over the father's coparcenary interest, and a daughter, who was not a coparcener. Further, a Hindu wife or daughter could be completely deprived of every iota of a share under Section 30 of the Hindu Succession Act which conferred upon a Hindu coparcener the unrestricted testamentary power to will away his property and possessions to whomever he liked. This called for a drastic revision of the relevant provisions of the Hindu Succession Act by placing certain limitations upon the testamentary power of a Hindu male.

Notwithstanding what has been said above, the Hindu Succession Act did bring about certain significant changes in the legal status of women. The growth of the Hindu Law of Succession can be traced from the Vedic period. A female was recognized from the earliest times as the holder of separate property—*stridhan*. It was in 1923 that the married women's rights were somewhat improved by Act XIII of 1923 which amended Act III of 1874 so as to extend its utility to Hindu women too. The rights of Hindu women were also improved by the passing of the Hindu Law of Inheritance (Amendment) Act 1929, and the Hindu Women's Right to Property Act 1937, amended by Act 11 of 1938. But the estate estate which a woman inherited under these Acts was a limited one. The Hindu Succession Act 1956 abolished limited ownership and made a Hindu woman the absolute owner of all property acquired from a male Hindu dying intestate.

Notes and References

1. Act X of 1865, Section 4.
2. Proceedings of the Council of the Governor-General of India, 1874, pp. 47–8.
3. Act III of 1874, Section I.
4. Mitra, N.N. (Ed.), *The Indian Annual Register*, 1923, vol. II, pp. 265 and 296.
5. See *ante.*, pp. 69, 77.
6. Act XVIII, 1927, Section 10. Legislative Assembly Debates, 14 September 1927, p. 4352.
7. Mitra, N.N. (Ed.), *The Indian Annual Register*, 1923, vol. p. 265.
8. Legislative Assembly Debates, 27 September 1923, p. 4041.
9. Mitra, N.N. (Ed.), *The Indian Annual Register*, 1923, vol. II. p. 316.
10. Legislative Assembly Debates, 12 February 1929, p. 7080.
11. *Amrita Bazar Patrika*, 13 February 1929, p. 5.
12. Mitra, N.N. (Ed.), *The Indian Quarterly Register*, vol. I, p. 182. Legislative Assembly Debates, 12 February 1929, p. 734.
13. The *Statesman*, 13 February 1929, p. 15.
14. Legislative Assembly Debates, 12 February 1929, pp. 719–21
15. The India Council Act, 1929.
16. Ibid., Section 2.
17. Bakshi, A.K., *Women's Right to Property*, Dacca, 1939, p. 30.
18. Legislative Assembly Debates, 26 September 1929, p. 1633.

19. The *Statesman*, 28 September 1929.
20. Legislative Assembly Debates, 21 January 1930, pp. 162–8.
21. The *Statesman*, 22 January 1930.
22. Legislative Assembly Debates, vol. I, 26 January 1932, pp. 73–104.
23. Ibid., 4 February 1932, vol. I, pp. 442–80.
24. Ibid., 26 January 1932, pp. 74–9.
25. Ibid., 4 February 1932, p. 450.
26. Ibid., 26 January 1932, p. 84.
27. Ibid., 4 February 1932, p. 449.
28. Mitra, N.N. (Ed.), *The Indian Annual Register*, vol. II, 1932, p. 122.
29. Ibid.
30. Ibid.
31. Ibid.
32. The *Statesman*, 5 February 1932, p. 10. The Indian Government had nominated Begum Shah Nawaz and Smt. Radhabai Subbarayan to the Round Table Conference.
33. Ibid.
34. The *Modern Review*, February 1932, vol. 51. p. 226.
35. The *Modern Review*, April 1932, vol. 51, p. 463.
36. Legislative Assembly Debates, 5 September, vol. VI, 1933, p. 957.
37. Ibid., p. 958.
38. Ibid., p. 964.
39. Ibid., pp. 963–9.
40. Ibid., p. 969.
41. Ibid., 17 April 1936, vol. V, pp. 4153–4154.
42. Ibid., 4 February 1937, vol. I, p. 485.
43. Ibid., pp. 486–92.
44. Ibid.
45. Ibid.
46. The India Council Act No. XVIII of 1937.
47. Ibid.
48. The *Modern Review*, August 1937, vol. 62, p. 220.
49. Legislative Assembly Debates, 18 March 1938, vol. II, p. 1845.
50. Ibid., pp. 1845–9.
51. The India Council Act No. XI of 1938.
52. Ibid.
53. Ibid.
54. Calcutta Weekly Notes, *Xc IX*.
55. Legislative Assembly Debates, 18 February 1939, vol. II, p. 1122.
56. Ibid., 15 September 1939, p. 105.
57. Ibid., 22 November 1940 vol. V., p. 983.

58. Ibid., pp. 988–90.
59. Sarkar, Rishindra Nath, *Hindu Women's Right to Property Act*, Calcutta, S.C. Sarkar and Sons, 1938, p. 3. Gazette of India, 30 May 1942.
60. Rau Committee Report, 1941, p. 24, para 38.
61. Ibid., 1941, p. 23.
62. Ibid.
63. Legisative Assembly Debates, 24 March 1943, vol. II, p. 1406.
64. Ibid., pp. 1408–11.
65. Ibid., pp. 1414–18. *Amrita Bazar Patrika*, 25 March 1943.
66. *Amrita Bazar Patrika*, 25 March 1943.
67. Legislative Assembly Debates, 30 March 1943, vol. II, pp. 1599–1602.
68. Ibid., pp. 1605–11.
69. Ibid., 29 March 1943, p. 1555.
70. Ibid., 30 March 1943, p. 1621. *Amrita Bazar Patrika*, 31 March 1943.
71. *Amrita Bazar Patrika*, 31 March 1943.
72. Ibid., 26 March 1943.
73. Ibid., 31 March 1943.
74. Legislative Assembly Debates, 2 April 1943, vol. II, p. 1742.
75. The *Modern Review*, 5 August 1943, vol. 74. pp. 84–5.
76. Ibid.
77. Ibid.
78. *Amrita Bazar Patrika*, 29 November 1943; The *Hindustan Standard* 25, 26 February 1945.
79. *Amrita Bazar Patrika*, 22 January 1944.
80. The *Statesman*, 10 April 1948.
81. The *Statesman*, 25 February 1949.
82. The *Hindu*, 2 March 1949.
83. Ibid., 23 March 1949.
84. Ibid., 2 April 1949.
85. *Ananda Bazar Patrika*, 19 June 1956.
86. Chaudhuri, D.H., *The Hindu Succession Act 1956, (Act 30 of 1956)* Preface Calcuttta, Eastern Law House, 1963.
87. The *Statesman*, 10 April 1948.
88. Ibid.

Epilogue

Jawaharlal Nehru once said: 'There should not be any lag between the development of law and the needs of a changing society. There should be the closest possible cooperation between jurists and economists or politicians whose object is to study the changing social fabric.'[1] This monograph has attempted to analyze how far the various pieces of legislation passed during the period 1856–1956, with a view to solving the marital problems of Hindu women, have succeeded in meeting their needs in a changing society. In the light of the legal implications of these social reforms and the present-day feminist movement, we may conclude that, though from time to time the status of women in Hindu society has been raised to some extent by Indian laws, many of their problems still remain acute and unresolved. This shows that the social structure and the laws have changed simultaneously with the passage of time, but the social outlook has not been able to keep pace with the changes. A review of these problems of Hindu women would elucidate the point.

The Widow-Remarriage Act 1856 did not achieve any great success, and only a few widows remarried. Even the economic impact of the Act was almost insignificant. The Act suffered two primary limitations. Section 2 of the Act did not provide the Hindu widow with any substantial right over her deceased husband's property, and she could be deprived of whatever right she had as soon as she remarried. Secondly, Section 4 of the Act gave the right of inheritance to the widow only in default of a son. Her right over her husband's property was also subject to certain restrictions.

The Mitakshara rule of the unqualified right of a widow was curbed by the Widow-Remarriage Act of 1856, which was based on Dayabhaga texts. Dayabhaga imposed definite restrictions on a woman's right to alienate property inherited from her deceased husband, allowing a widow to enjoy her husband's estate only during her lifetime. After her death, it was passed on to her heirs, which meant that the widow got only life interest in her husband's property.

The Act of 1872 was the first piece of legislation which prescribed restrictions on early marriage. In 1891, the age of consent was raised from ten to twelve. The Sarda Act 1929 fixed fourteen as the marriageable age for girls, and in the Hindu Code, fifteen was fixed as the minimum age for a girl's marriage. But these laws had little impact on the actual practice of the time.

The Law of Inheritance (Amendment) Act 1929 for the first time tried to amend the Hindu Law of Inheritance, but made no radical change in the law of inheritance in favour of Hindu women. By this Act, neither daughters nor widows were provided with the right of inheritance. The Act only gave certain degrees of preference to nearer degrees of female heirs over remoter degrees of male heirs.

The Hindu widow's right to property was enlarged by the second amendment, called the Hindu Widow's Right to Property Act 1937 and also by the Amendment Act of 1938. According to the Act of 1937, a man's property, after his death, was to devolve upon his widow, along with his lineal descendants, as it devolved upon a son. The Act further provided that any interest devolving on a Hindu widow was to be a limited interest known as the 'Hindu Women's Estate', subject to the rights of reversioners. So, the widow's power remained limited in 1937 too, and she still had no right to dispose of her property. The Amendment Act of 1938 also failed to serve its purpose, since it denied daughters the right to inherit their father's property, while widowed daughters-in-law were benefited by a provision asserting their right to inherit their father-in-law's property.

As a protest, a series of private Bills followed. The government felt the need to bring about a full revision of these Acts and the necessity for the codification of laws on an all-India basis became urgent. The result was the Hindu Code. The part of the Hindu Code relating to property (Act XXX of 1956) provided that the widow, the widow of the predeceased son and daughters, all were to be given the same rank as the son in the matter of inheritance. The Act converted the widow's limited estate into a 'life estate' and abolished the right of reversioners to claim the property after the widow's death. In short, the widow became the absolute owner of the inherited property, which she was entitled to dispose of in any manner she liked.

The Hindu Code, relating to marriage laws of 1955, provided matrimonial reliefs like restitution of conjugal rights, judicial separation, nullity of marriage and divorce. All these intended to set Hindu women free from the bondage of unhappy marriages. The concept of the sacramental Hindu marriage was viewed as a fetter binding the feet of those hapless Hindu women who faced tremendous odds when their marriage was not workable. Judged from this viewpoint, divorce granted by the Hindu Code truly came as a great relief to Hindu women. The Hindu Code, therefore, was a milestone in the history of Hindu life and society, and shook the Hindu psyche to a more realistic understanding of the plight of the Hindu women.

But the law did not work well in actual practice since few women could avail of the legislation granting divorce. Keeping a variety of factors in view, Hindu women of India continue to suffer the consequences of unhappy marriages. One major factor which stands in the way while breaking the chains of marriage is the consideration for the future of their children. Undoubtedly, children are often the worst sufferers of the consequences of divorce; so to provide the children with secure homes, the women continue to suffer the torment of an incompatible marriage. Another important factor preventing women from availing the benefit of divorce is the social attitude, for even today, society looks askance at a woman who has left her husband's home. Moreover, few parents welcome their distressed daughter back, so women are often at a loss about where to go after leaving their husbands. Practical solutions like decent and secure homes for deserted women and steps to provide them with adequate means of livelihood are, therefore, urgent necessities of the day. Apart from these, valuable years of young individuals are wasted in slow, tardy and long-drawn legal processes. The Dowry Prohibition Act of 1961 also proved to be a dismal failure.

It may be admitted, therefore, that social evils could not be eradicated by law alone. While a limited minority of urban women could avail of the opportunities provided by laws like divorce, property rights, etc., the vast majority of rural Hindu women continued to stagger in misery. Their ignorance, illiteracy, social attitude, lack of awareness as well as pecuniary difficulties deprived them of any benefit from the marriage reforms. So, although our Constitution granted equal rights and opportunities to Hindu women, much had yet to be done to enable them to secure these rights and privileges.

The worldwide women's movement and universal concern at the disadvantaged status of women opened the floodgates of feminist movement all over the world. Feminism in Europe as well as in America had been following a trend towards liberalization, while politically, reactionary movements in the West tended to be anti-feminist. Stalinism, for instance, had done away with many innovations of the 1917 Revolution which had improved the lot of the Russian women. When Stalinism was at its height in Russia, the average American woman enjoyed a better social position than her Soviet sister. In spite of this, a decided trend towards women's emancipation in the twentieth century was apparent. Even in the new African states, Turkey, Denmark, Switzerland, Pakistan and others, women started demanding greater equality with their male counterparts. Indian women also began to voice their demands not as mothers, wives or daughters, but as individuals claiming recognition as independent human beings. This was a battle to free women from the shackles of social and legal disabilities.

In the context of the Indian women's movement of the present day, two interesting facts are worth noting. There is a sharp distinction between the character of the women's movement of earlier times and that of today. During the nineteenth and the early part of the twentieth century, the initiative and leadership of women's reforms came from men. Women remained mute spectators, and it seemed inconceivable that women could come out of their cloistered homes to demand reforms. They were fully dependent on men even for their own welfare. In the modern world, the scene has changed significantly. Women's voice is no longer stifled and many more women are actively expressing their problems and asking for solutions. Their fervour for reform has now become sharp, focussed and dynamic, and they are no longer dependent upon men for the redressal of their grievances. The beginning of the change was marked by the emergence of the National Social Reform Conference in 1887. The first modern organization for women—the Women's Indian Association (WIA)— was started in 1917 by the great pioneering woman Margaret Cousins in Madras under the inspiration of Annie Besant. Though functioning mainly in the south, it became, from the very start, a rallying point for women for action on an all-India plane. It even led a woman's deputation in 1917 to Montague, the then Secretary of State for India. The Indian women's movement gathered fresh momentum with the emergence of two additional women's organizations—the National Council of India for Women (NCWI) and the All India Women' Conference (AIWC). The NCWI was founded in 1925 by Lady Dorab Tata, a longstanding member of WIA. It strove to be associated with all women's movements and to form a link with similar national councils of women in other countries through the International Council of Women (founded in 1888 with its first headquarters in Zurich). Another premier women's organization in the country was the AIWC which was founded by Sarojini Naidu, Kamala Devi Chattopadhaya, Margaret Cousins, Muthulakshmi Reddy and others in 1926. AIWC was the first organization to propagate the concept of family planning. The Women's Coordinating Council (WCC), and the All Bengal Women's Union (ABWU) affiliated to WCC are other organizations devoted to the cause of women. The Indian Chamber of Commerce formed the Ladies Study Group. Through these organizations, increasing numbers of women worked ceaselessly to obtain fundamental rights like franchise, property rights and marriage reforms.

On the other hand, the social movements launched by Rammohan Roy and Pandit Vidyasagar were of a different nature. The reformers of early days fought against the legal and social evils to which Indian women were being subjected, but did not fight to elevate women to the same level as that of men. The question then was not of fighting for equality, but against injustice; the problem was not of equality, but of survival, and they wanted to save Hindu women from social evils and oppression. It can be concluded then that, firstly, women fighting for themselves and, secondly, their demand for equality are the most significant and characteristic features of the present-day feminist movement in India.

Since the middle of the twentieth century, the basic demands of women have been economic independence and employment facilities at par with men. The government has taken adequate steps in this direction and has passed many laws aimed at improving the status of women. It has also taken up special projects of non-formal education and income-generating activities for women. Valuable work has also been done by the Committee on the Status of Women in India formed by the Central Government in the International Women's Year. The Committee visited all the states and talked to the people from various walks of life, such as statisticians, politicians, academicians and different women's organizations. The Committee declared unequivocally that discrimination between male and female was remarkable in every sphere. Its commendable report *Towards Equality*, running into almost four hundred pages and published in 1975, is still considered to be one of the major data sources on the position of women. The terminal year of the women's decade, 1985, marked the first official claim that there had been 'substantial progress and achievement' in the status of women in India. The Government of India claimed in its report for the year 1984–5 that remarkable progress had been made by women in the field of education, health-care, employment and economic development, leading to an improvement of their status in society.

Despite all these advances, the fact remains that women are yet to achieve equality of status in society with men. The hindrances blocking the march of women towards such equality are many, some social and educational, and others natural and constitutional. Social hindrances are the social attitudes and outlook of the people of our country which are detrimental to the cause of women's progress. As has already been said, in many cases, parents themselves are responsible for the sad plight of their daughters. In fact, few parents willingly come forward to the rescue of their daughters who are tortured by the husband or by greedy in-laws. Their hesitation is obviously born out of fear of the male-dominated society, which has yet to develop a positive attitude accepting the principle of freedom for women. Illustrating this attitude is the Booker Prize-winning book *God of Small Things* by Arundhati Roy,[3] which portrays a classic example of sharp distinctions made between a son and a daughter in our society in the sixties—quite a few years after the Hindu Code was adopted. It recounts the woeful tale of a young woman with two small children separated from her husband. It is a vivid exposition of the limitation of her rights compared to those of her brother, and the fragility of her position even in her own parental home.

Lack of sufficient education, especially among the rural women, is largely responsible for their lack of progress and confidence, and stands in the way of achieving economic independence, without which any hope of gaining equality inevitably withers away. So, as a reinforcement of governmental efforts, more private voluntary organizations should take up the task of educating the rural poor-men and women—and make them aware of the practical realities and the need for a radical change.

The fact that child-bearing and, to a large extent, child-care are the responsibilities of women, works against them in the sphere of employment. In Japan, for example, more than half the women are working, but their pay is, on an average, sixty per cent less than that of their male counterparts. Managers contend that this discrimination is due to the fact that most women quit work either to get married or to have children. In China as well, the story is similar. According to an article in the March 1986 issue of the *Beijing Review,* after three decades of striving, the nation had 43.24 million working women in 1985, which constituted 36.4 per cent of its work force, compared with 7.5 per cent in 1949, and says that, 'although socialism has opened up new vistas for Chinese women, the problem of allowing women to share equal rights and status with their male counterparts in all fields is far from being resolved'. It further notes that 'although feudalism was subject to criticism after the democratic revolution, ... news about infringements of women's rights and interests is still frequent,' and that it is easier for men to secure jobs in factories or to be enrolled in academic institutions. Among 800 million people living in the countryside, more than two hundred million are illiterate or semi-literate, seventy per cent of whom are women.[2]

If women are to compete on an equal footing with men in every sphere of life, particularly employment, family planning is essential. It is necessary not only for the economic security of the family and the nation, but is also interlinked with the idea of women's emancipation. In earlier times, women had a number of children, whom they could not bring up properly, but now it is becoming increasingly common for women to have a life outside the home.

The position of today's woman can best be summarized in the following words: 'Because women's work is never done and is underpaid or unpaid, or boring or repetitious, and we are the first to get the sack, and what we look like is more important than what we do, and if we get raped, it is our fault, and if we get bashed, we must have provoked it, and if we raise our voices, we are nagging bitches ... and if we love women, it's because we can't get a 'real' man, and if we ask our doctor too many questions, we are neurotic and/or pushy, and if we expect community care for children, we're selfish, and if we stand up for our rights, we're aggressive and 'unfeminine', and if we don't, we're typical weak females, and if we want to get married, we're out to trap a man, and if we don't, we're unnatural ... and if we can't cope or don't want a pregnancy, we're made to feet guilty about abortion and ... for lots and lots of other reasons, we are part of the women's liberation movement.'*

Notes and References

1. Quoted from Nehru's speech at the annual conference of the Indian Branch of the International Law Association, New Delhi, 31 March 1951. From The *Hindustan Times* and *National Herald*, 1 April 1951.
2. *Amrita Bazar Patrika*, 4 March 1986.
3. Roy, Arundhati, *God of Small Things*, New Delhi, India Ink, 1997.

* See Appendix III.

Glossary

Achaar	–	Custom.
Andarmahal	–	Inner apartment.
Anuloma	–	Marriage of a high caste with one of low caste.
Asavarna	–	Of a different caste.
Asura	–	A demon.
Asvamedha	–	Horse sacrifice.
Atmabandhu	–	One's own friend
Bandhus	–	Friends.
Begum	–	A lady of rank, usually Muslim ladies.
Bhagini Sena	–	Sisters' Army.
Brahmins	–	Members of the priestly class.
Brahmo	–	An offshoot of the Hindu religion.
Brahmo Samaj	–	Assembly of Brahmo.
Dahej	–	Dowry.
Dana	–	Presentation.
Dena Paona	–	Giving and taking.
Dharma	–	Religion.
Dharma Rakshini Sabha	–	An assembly of orthodox people formed to protect religion.
Dharmashastras	–	'holy writ'.
Dharmasutras	–	Name of a Jain treatise on religion.
Dharmik	–	Religious.
Dharmiya	–	Of religion.
Duhita	–	One who milks cows, word to describe a daughter.
Gandharva marriage	–	Love marriage.

Gotra	– Race or lineage.
Gouridan	– Giving in marriage a girl who has not attained puberty.
Grhyasutras	– Vedic treatise dealing with the performance of religious rites.
Homa	– A burnt offering.
Jati	– Race.
Jnanvikasini Sabha	– An assembly meant to enhance knowledge.
Kaliyuga	– The fourth age of Hindu mythology.
Kama	– Desire.
Kanyadaan	– Giving away a girl in marriage.
Kayastha	– A caste among Hindus.
Kshatriya	– The second in hierarchy of the four castes.
Kula	– Lineage.
Kulin Brahmin	– A well-born Hindu of the first in hierarchy of the four castes.
Kulinism	– High breeding.
Maharani	– An empress or a queen.
Mahila Samiti	– An assembly of ladies.
Matribandhus	– Friends of the mother.
Nawab	– The title of a Mohammedan ruler.
Niyoga	– A custom by which the widow was remarried to the younger brother of her deceased husband.
Palki	– A box litter for travelling which is borne on the shoulders of four or six men.
Panchayat	– An assembly of men who decide dispute among villagers.
Paan	– A betel leaf.
Pandit	– A man of letters.
Panigrahana	– Wedding.
Patibrata	– A chaste wife.
Pitririna	– Debt to one's father.
Praja	– Progeny.
Pratiloma	– Marriage of a bride belonging to a family of high status and a bridegroom of low descent.
Purdah	– A curtain screening women from the sight of men.
Rakshasha	– A demon.
Rani	– A queen.
Rati	– Sex.

Rishis	– Sages.
Sabhas	– Assemblies.
Sampradan	– *see* Kanyadaan.
Sanatanist	– Orthodox.
Sanskara	– Rite.
Sapindas	– Collateral marriage.
Saptapadi	– Taking of seven steps together by the bride and the bridegroom.
Shastrakars	– One who teaches any branch of Hindu learning, such as law.
Sati	– A chaste women who willingly burns herself on her husband's funeral pyre.
Satidaha	– The rite of widow-burning.
Savarna	– Of the same caste.
Shalankara Kanya	– Bride bedecked with jewellery.
Shastras	– Law books or sacred writings of the Hindus.
Sloka	– Sanskrit couplet or stanza.
Smritis	– Code of ancient Hindu law.
Stridhan	– A term of Hindu law applied to certain property belonging to a woman.
Sudra	– A man of the fourth caste in hierarchy among Hindus.
Swayamvara	– The choice of a husband made by a princess in public.
Talaq	– Divorce.
Tilak	– The vermilion mark applied on the forehead of the bridegroom by the girl's family members after the settlement of marriage.
Vaishya	– Men of the third caste in hierarchy among Hindus.

Appendices

Appendix–I

Gandhiji's reply to a correspondent's letter on the issue of widow remarriage.

A correspondent writes:

'In the course of an article you have said at one time: 'Where marriage is a sacrament, the union is not the union of bodies but the union of souls indissoluble even by the death of either party. Where there is a true union of souls, the remarriage of a widow or widows is unthinkable, improper and wrong'.

'At another place in the course of the same article you say: 'I consider remarriage of virgin widows not only desirable but the bounded duty of all parents who happen to have such widowed daughters'.

'How do you reconcile the two views?'

Gandhiji's reply:

'I find no difficulty in reconciling the two views. In giving away of a little girl by ignorant or heartless parents without considering the welfare of the child and without her knowledge and consent, there is no marriage at all. Certainly it is not a sacrament and therefore remarriage of such a girl becomes a duty. As a matter of fact the word 'remarriage' is a misnomer in such cases. The virgin was never married at all in true sense and, therefore, on the death of her supposed husband, it would be the most natural thing, it would be a duty, for the parents to seek for her a suitable companion in life.'[1]

Appendix–II

Another correspondent writes:

'A bereaved friend sends a pathetic letter describing the plight of a 17 year old girl who has lost in Quetta her husband, two month old child, father-in-law and her husband's younger brother, that is to say, everybody in her father-in-laws house. She escaped unhurt and returned with only her clothes on. She is his uncle's daughter and he does not know how to console her or what to do with her. She herself is not undamaged. Her leg has been injured, though fortunately the bones remained intact'. The correspondent concludes by saying:

I have left her with her mother in Lahore. I gently mentioned to her and other relatives whether the girl might be married. Some listened to me sympathetically, and some resented the proposal. I have no doubt that many a girl must have suffered the same fate as this cousin of mine. Will you say a word of encouragement to these unfortunate widows?

Gandhiji's reply:

I do not know what my pen or voice can do in matters in which age-long prejudices are concerned. I have repeatedly said that every widow has as much right to remarry as every widower. Voluntary widowhood is a priceless boon in Hinduism; enforced widowhood is a curse. And I very much feel that many young widows, if they were absolutely free, not so much from fear of physical restraint as from the opprobrium of Hindu public opinion, would remarry without the slightest hesitation. All the young widows, therefore, who are in the unfortunate position of this bereaved sister from Quetta, should have every inducement given to them to remarry, and should be sure that no blame would be attached to them if they chose to remarry and every effort should be made to select suitable matches. This is not a work which can be done by any institution. This work has got to be done by individual reformers whose relatives have become widows and they have to carry on a vigorous and restrained propaganda in our circles and whenever they succeed they should give the widest publicity to the event. Thus and only thus, there is likely to be tangible relief provided for the girls who might have become widows during the earthquake. It is possible that public sympathy can be easily mobilised whilst the memory of the tragedy is fresh in mind and if once the reform takes place on a large scale, the girls who may have become widows in the natural course, will also find it easy to get married, if they are willing to do so'.[2]

Appendix–III

The (autonomous) Women's Campaign exists in London to further the demands of women within the NUS (National Union of Students). A leaflet/poster produced by the NUS Women's Campaign reads thus:

'Because women's work is never done and is underpaid or unpaid or boring or repetitious and we're the first to get the sack and what we look like is more important than what we do and if we get raped it's our fault and if we get bashed we must have provoked it and if we raise our voices we're nagging bitches and if we enjoy sex we're nymphos and if we don't we're frigid and if we love women it's because we can't get a 'real' man and if we ask our doctor too many questions we're neurotic and/or pushy, if we expect community care for children we're selfish and if we stand up for our rights we're aggressive and 'unfeminine' and if we don't we're typical weak females and if we want to get married we're out to trap a man and if we don't we're unnatural and because we still can't get an adequate safe contraceptive but men can walk on the moon and if we can't cope or don't want a pregnancy we're made to feel guilty about abortion and ... for lots and lots of other reasons we are part of the Women's Liberation Movement.

Appendix–IV

The Government of India felt that a comprehensive examination of all questions relating to the rights and status of women in this country would provide useful guidance for the formation of social policies. For this purpose, it constituted the Committee On the Status of Women by a resolution of the Ministry of Education and Social Welfare on 22 September 1971. The report of this Committee namely *Towards Equality* was published by the Government in

December 1974 and again in May 1975, another report of this Committee was brought out in an abridged form by the Indian Council of Social Science Research, New Delhi, called 'Status of Women in India'.

The Committee was composed of the following:

1. Dr (Smt.) Phulrenu Guha, Chairperson
2. Kumari Mani Ben Kara, Member
3. Smt. Neera Dogra, Member
4. Smt. Savitri Shyam, Member
5. Smt. Sakina Hasan, Member
6. Smt. K. Lakshmi Raghuramaiah, Member
7. Smt. Urmila Haksar, Member
8. Dr (Smt.) Leela Dube, Member
9. Dr (Smt.) Lotika Sarkar, Member
10. Shri Vikram Mahajan, Member
11. Dr (Smt.) Vina Majumdar, Member Secretary.

Notes and References

1. Young India, 26 September 1929.
2. Harijan, 22 June 1935

Bibliography

Official and Government Records

All India Women's Conference—*Artisan in the Indian Society*, Bombay, published by the Committee for Cottage and Village Industries Exhibition of the A.I.W.C., 1949.

All India Women's Conference—*Women in Mines*, published by Aundh Publishing Trust, 1945.

India—Annual Report to the Parliament and Government of India; 1924–30, published by Director, Publication Division, Ministry of Information and Broadcasting, Government of India, New Delhi, compiled by the Research Division.

Indian Quarterly Register, edited by Nripendra Nath Mitra, Calcutta.

Indian Annual Register, edited by Nripendra Nath Mitra.

Legislative Proceedings of the Council of the Governor-General of India, 1872, 1891

Legislative Assembly Debates, 1927,1929,1937, 1938, 1939, 1940, 1943.

Parliamentary Debates, 1949, 1954, 1955, 1956, 1960–61

Report of the All India Women's Conference, Silver Jubilee Session, 1953, Poona.

Report of the All India Women's Conference, Souvenir, 1927–70, New Delhi.

Report of the Administration of Bengal, 1881–2, 1892–3, Calcutta, 1882–94.

Report of the Committee appointed by the Government to consider the question of legislative interference for preventing 'the excessive abuse' of polygamy, Calcutta, 1867.

Report of the Joshi Committee, 26 August 1929.

Report of the Third Annual Session of the Indian National Social Conference, 1889, Bombay.

Report of the Fourth Annual Session of the Indian National Social Conference, 1890, Calcutta.

Towards Equality: Report of the Committee on the status of women in India, Government of India, Ministry of Education and Social Welfare, Department of Social Welfare, New Delhi, December 1974. (Published by the Indian Council of Social Science Research).

Widow Remarriage Papers, National Archives of India, New Delhi.

Conference on work on the Lives of Married Women, Columbia University, 1957. Proceedings of a Conference on Women Power held in October, 20–5, 1957.

Newspapers (Bengali and English)

Biographies & Autobiographies

Athalye, D.V., *The Life of Lokmanya Tilak*, Poona, Anandasahib Chiploonkar Sadashiv Peth,1921.

Banerjee, Chandi Gharan, *Vidyasagar,* Calcutta, Anandadhara Prakashan, 1969.

Chakravarit, Ajit Kumar, *Maharshi Debendra Nath Tagore,* Calcutta, Jijnasa, 1971.

Chaudhuri, N.C., *Autobiography of an Unknown Indian*, London, MacMillan and Co. Ltd., 1951.

Chakravorty, Punyalata, *Chhele Belar Dinguli,* Calcutta, Newscript, 1975.

Tagore, Debendra Nath, *Amar Jiban,* Calcutta, Visva Bharati Granthalay, 1962.

Giribala Devi, *Desh,* March 1983.

Gidumal, Dayaram, *The Life and Life Works of Behramji Malabari,* London, Fisher Unwin, 1892.

Gandhi, M.K., *An Autobiography,* Bombay, third Kitabs Ltd., 1950.

Chaudhurani, Indira Devi, *Jnanadanandini Devi,* Provasi, February–March 1942.

Jnanadanandini Devi, *Smritikatha* in *Puratani,* edited by Indira Devi, 1967.

Tagore, Jyotirindranath, *Jiban Smriti, Desh* (Sharadiya Sankhya), 1363 B.S.

Mitra, Indra Nath, *Karuna Sagar Vidyasagar,* Calcutta, Ananda Publishers Pvt. Ltd., 1969.

Mukherji, N., *A Bengal Zamindar—Joy Kristo Mukherjee of Uttarpara and his time 1808–1888,* Calcutta, 1974.

Rash, Sundari Devi, *Amar Jiban,* Calcutta, Collage Street Publication Pvt. Ltd., 1987.

Tagore, Rabindranath, *Jiban Smriti*, Calcutta, 1959.
Chanda, Rani, *Amar Ma'r Baper Bari*, Vishva Bharati, 1977.
Chaudhurani, Sarala Devi, *Jibaner Jharapata*, New Delhi, 1975.
Shastri, Sibnath, *Atma Charit*, Calcutta, Sadharan Brahmo Samaj, 1953.

Secondary Books

1. Abbot, Edith., *Women in Industry; a Study in American Economic History*, New York, D. Appleton, 1910.
2. Achar M, and Venkanna, T. (Ed.), *Dowry Prohibition Act*, Allahabad, University Book Agency, 1962.
3. Agarwalla, Deokinandan, *The Hindu Marriage Act 1955 (No. 25 of 1955)*, Allahabad, University Book Agency, 1955.
4. Almenas Lipowsky and Angeles, J., *The Position of Indian Women in the Light of Legal Reform*, Wiesbaden, Franz Steiner, 1975.
5. Altekar, A.S., *The Position of Women in Hindu Civilization; from Pre-historic Times to the Present Day*, Banaras, Motilal Banarsidass, 1938.
6. Anand, Ram Lal and Gargi Sethi, *The Prohibition of Dowry Act*, Allahabad, Law Publishers, 1962.
7. Andiappan, P., *Women and Work: A Comparative Study of Sex Discrimination in Employment in India and the USA*, Somaiya Publication, Bombay, 1980.
8. Asthana, Protima, *Women's Movement in India*, Delhi, Vikas Publishing House, 1974.
9. Avasthi Abha, *Hindu Marriage in Continuity and Change*, Lucknow, Pradeep Prakashan Kendra, 1979.
10. A A AS Seminar on Women in Development, Mexico, 1975. Women and World Development, with an annotated bibliography.
11. Bader, Clarisse, *Women in Ancient India: Moral and Literary Studies*, Delhi, Anmol Publication, 1987 (Reprint).
12. Bagal, Jogesh Chandra, *Beginnings of Modern Education in Bengal: Women's Education (mainly based on contemporary records)*, Calcutta, Ranyan Publishing House, 1944.
13. Bagal, Jogesh Chandra, *Women's Education in Eastern India: the First Phase (mainly based on contemporary records)*, Calcutta, World Press, 1956.
14. Bagga, V. (Ed.), Studies in the Hindu Marriage and Special Marriage Acts, Allahabad, The Law Book Co. (Pvt.) Ltd., 1978.
15. Baig, Tara Ali, *Women of India*, Delhi, Ministry of Information and Broadcasting, Government of India, 1958.

16. Bandopadhyay, N.C. *Kautilya*, Varanasi, Indological Book House, 1982.
17. Banks, Joseph Ambrose, and Banks, Olive, *Feminism and Family Planning in Victorian England*, Liverpool, Liverpool University Press, 1964.
18. Bardwick, Judith Mareia, *Women in transition; how feminism, sexual liberation and the search for self-fulfilment have altered our lives*, Brighton, Sussex, Harvester Press, 1980.
19. Barker, Diana Leonard & Allen, Sheila, (Ed.), *Sexual Division and Society: Process and Change*, London, Tavistock Publications, 1976.
20. Barlingay, W., *The Hindu Law of Succession for the Laymen*, New Delhi, All India Congress Comitte, 1957.
21. Barr, Pat, *The Memsahibs; The Women of Victorian India*, London, 1976.
22. Barreto, Duarte, *India's Search for Development and Social Justice: Analysis of Indian Society*, Bangalore, Centre for Social Action, 1976.
23. Basu, Nrisinhadas, *The Law of Succession, containing the Indian Succession Act 1925 and Hindu Succession Act 1956*, Calcutta, Ashok Law House, 1957.
24. Bhave, Binoba, *Women's Power*, Varanasi, Sarva Seva Sangh Prakashan, 1975.
25. Blumberg, Bhoda Lois, *India's Educated Women: Options and Constraints*, Delhi, Hindustan Publishing Corporation, 1980.
26. Boserup, Ester, *Women's Role in Economic Development*, London, George Allen and Unwin Ltd., 1970.
27. Caplan, Patricia and Bujra Janet. M., (Ed.) *Women United; Women Divided; Cross Cultural Perspectives on Female Solidarity*, London, Tavistock Publications, 1978.
28. Chafe, William Henry, *The American Woman; Her Changing Social, Economic & Political Roles (1920–70)*, London, OUP, 1974.
29. Chafe, William Henry, *Women & Equality; Changing Patterns in American Culture*, New York, OUP, 1977.
30. Chakravorti Usha., *Condition of Bengali Women Around the Second Half of the 19th Century*, Calcutta, Firma K.L.M. Pvt. Ltd., 1963.
31. Chakrovorti, Krishna, *The Conflicting Worlds of Working Mothers; a Sociological Enquiry*, Calcutta, Progressive Publishers, 1978.
32. Chapman, George, *The Widow's Tears*, Manchester, Manchester University Press, 1975.
33. Chapman, Jane Roberts and Gates, Margaret (Ed.), *The Victimisation of Women*, Beverly Hills, Sage Year Books in Women's Policy Studies, 1978.

34. Chatterji, Krishna Nath, *Hindu Marriage—Past and Present*, Varanasi, Tara Publications, 1972.
35. Chattopadhyay, Kamaladevi, *The Awakening of Indian Women*, Madras, Everyman's Press, 1939.
36. Chaudhuri, D.H., *The Hindu Marriage Act 1955*, Calcutta, Eastern Law House Ltd., 1966.
    Chaudhuri, Maitrayee, *Indian Women's Movement: Reform and Revival*, New Delhi, 1993.
37. Chaudhuri, Roma, Ray, Renuka and others, *Role & Status of Women in Indian Society*, Calcutta, Firma K.L.M. Pvt. Ltd., 1978.
38. Chaudhury, Rooplal, *Hindu Woman's Right to Property*, Calcutta, Firma K.L.M. Pvt. Ltd., 1961.
39. Maharani of Baroda, Mitra, S.M., *The Position of Women in Indian Life*, London, Longman's, Green and Company, 1912.
40. Chintamoni C.Y., (Ed.), *Indian Social Reform*, part I, Madras, Thompson and Company, 1901.
41. Cormack, Margaret, *The Hindu Woman*, Bombay, Asia Publishing House, 1961.
42. Consins, Margaret E., *The Awakening of Asian Womanhood*, Madras, Ganesh and Company, 1922. *Indian Womenhood Today*, Allahabad, Kitabistan, 1947.
43. Currell, Melville E., *Political Women*, London, Rowman and Little Field, 1974.
44. Darling, Martha, *The Role of Women in the Economy; a summary based on ten national reports*, Paris, O.E.C.D., 1975.
45. Das, Ram Mohan, *Women in Manu's Philosophy*, Jalandhar, A.B.S. Publications, 1993.
46. Das, S., *Purdah: The Status of Indian Women*, Delhi, Ess Ess Publicatoins, 1979.
47. Dasgupta, Jyotiprova, *Girls' Education in India in the Secondary and Collegiate States*, Calcutta, Calcutta University, 1938.
48. Dasgupta, Tamonash Chandra, *Aspects of Bengali Society from Old Bengali Literature* with a foreword by Benimadhav Barua, Calcutta, University of Calcutta, 1935.
49. Datta, Kalikinkar, *A Social History of Modern India*, New Delhi, Mac Millan, 1975.
50. Davin, Delia, *Women-work; women and the party in revolutionary China*, Oxford, Clarendon, 1976.
51. Deb, Chitra, *Thakurbarir Andar Mahal*, Calcutta, Ananda Publishers Pvt. Ltd., O.B.S., 1387.

52. Delamont, Sara (Ed.), *Nineteenth Century Woman: Her Cult and Physical World*, London, Barnes and Noble Books, 1978.
53. Derrett, J.D.M., *Hindu Law, Past and Present*, Calcutta, A. Mukherjee and Company, 1957.
54. Desai, Neera, *Women in Modern India*, Bombay, Vora and Company Publishers Pvt. Ltd., 1977.
55. Desouza, Alfred, *Women in Contemporary India and South Asia*, Delhi, Manohar Publications, 1980.
56. Devadass, T.S., *Hindu Family and Marriage; a Study of Social Institutions in India*, Madras, Dr S. Radhakrishnan Institute for Advanced Study in Philosophy, 1979.
57. Devanandan, P. Thomas, M. (Ed.), *The Changing Pattern of Family in India*, Banglore, Christian Institute for the Study of Religion and Society, 1966.
58. Diwar, Paras, *Modern Hindu Law: Codified and Uncodified*, Allahabad, Allahabad Law Agency, 1979.
59. Diwan, Paras and Diwan, Piyushi, *Women and Legal Protection*, New Delhi, Deep and Deep Publications, 1994.
60. Encel, Sol, *Women and Society*; An Analytical Study, London, Malaby Press, 1975.
61. Etzioni, Amitai, *The Semiprofessions and their Organisations, Teachers, Nurses, Social Workers*, New York, Collier-Mac Millan, Heritage Publishers, 1969.
62. Everett, Jana Matson, *Women and Social Change in India*, New Delhi, Heritage Publishers, 1979.
63. Forbes, Geraldine, *Women in Modern India*, Delhi, Cambrdige University Press, 1996.
64. Fuller, M.B. *The Wrongs of Indian Womanhood*, New Delhi, Inter-India Publications, 1984.
65. Gadgil, Dhananjay Ramchandra, *Women in the Working Force in India*, Delhi, Asia Publishing House, 1965.
66. Gandhi Mohandas Karamchand, *Women and Social Injustice*, Navjivan Publishing House, Ahmedabad, 1947.
67. Gandhi, Mohandas Karamchand, *To the Women*, Karachi, Published by Anand T. Hingorani, 1946.
68. Gavron, Hannah, *The Captive Wife, Conflicts of Housebound Mothers*, London, Routledge and Kegan Paul, 1966.
69. Gharpure, J.R., *Rights of Women under the Hindu law*, Bombay, N.M. Tripathi Ltd., University of Bombay, 1943.
70. Ghatak, Kamal Kumar, *Hindu Revivalism in Bengal: Rammohan to Ramakrishna*, Calcutta, Minerva Associates, 1991.

71. Gopal, S., *Jawaharlal Nehru: A Biography*, Delhi, OUP, 1979.
72. Gray, H., *Indian Women of the West*, London, Zenith Press, 1944.
73. Gujrati, B.S. (Ed.), *Women of East and West*, (the views of Dr. Hardayal, Sir Jadunath Sarkar, Indra Nehru, Madame Kuo, Loo-Tuh Y.M. Rege), Lahore, Hero Publications, 1944.
74. Holder, Gopal (Ed.), *Vidyasagar Rachana Sangraha*, Calcutta, Vidyasagar Smarak Jatiya Samiti, 1972.
75. Hate, Chandrakala, A., *Changing Status of Women in Post Independence India*, Bombay, Allied Publishers Pvt. Ltd., 1969.
76. Hayne, J.D., *A Treatise on Hindu Law and Usage*, Madras, Higgin Botham & Company, 1906.
77. Heinsath, Charles, Indian Nationalism and Hindu Social Reform, Bombay, OUP, 1964.
78. Hooja, S.L., *Dowry System in India*, Delhi, Asia Press, 1969.
79. Howe, Florence, (Ed), *Women and the Power to Change*, New York, McGraw Hill, 1975.
80. Huber, Joan, *Changing Women in a Changing Society*, Chicago, Chicago University Press, 1975.
81. Jain, Devaki, (Ed.), *Indian Women*, New Delhi, Publications Division, Government of India, 1975.
82. Jain, Devaki, *Women's Quest for Power; Five Indian Case Studies*, New Delhi, Vikas Publishing House, 1980.
83. Jeffery, Patricia, *Frogs in a Well; Indian Women in Purdah*, Delhi, Vikas Publishing House, 1979.
84. Kala Rani, *Role Conflict in Working Women*, New Delhi, Chetna Publications, 1976.
85. Kane, P.V., *History of Dharmasastra*, Poona, Bhandarkar Oriental Research Institute, 1974.
86. Kapadia, K.M., *Marriage and Family in India*, Bombay, OUP, 1958.
87. Kapoor, Promilla, *The Changing Status of Working Women in India*, Delhi, Vikas Publishing House, 1974.
88. Kapoor, Promilla, *Love, Marriage and Sex*, Delhi, Vikas Publishing House, 1973.
89. Kapoor, Promilla, *Marriage and the Working Women in India*, Delhi, Vikas Publication, 1970.
90. Karve, Irawati, *Kingship of Organisation in India*, Deccan College, Monograph Series, Bombay, Post Graduate Research Institute, 1963.
91. Katayama, Tetsu, *Women's Movement in Japan*, Tokyo, Foreign Affairs Association of Japan, 1938.
92. Kaur, Inderjeet, *Status of Hindu Women in India*, Allahabad, Chug Publications, 1983.

93. Kaur, Amrit, *Challenge to Women*, Allahabad, New Literature, 1946.
94. Khanna, Girija, Verghese Mariamma A., *Indian Women Today*, New Delhi, Vikas Publishing House, 1978.
95. Kidwai, Mushir Hosain, *Women Under Different Social and Religious Laws*, Delhi, Seema Publications, 1976.
96. Krishnamurti, S., *The Dowry Problem: A Legal and Social Perspective*, Bangalore, IBh Prakashan, 1981.
97. Lalitha Devi, *Status and Employment of Women* in India, Delhi, B.R. Publishing Corporation, 1982.
98. Leonard, John Greenfield, *Kandulkuri Viresatingam 1849–1919: A Biography of an Indian Social Reformer*, Hydrabad, Telegu University Publication, 1991.
99. Lewenhak, Sheila, *Women and Work*, London, Mac Millan, 1980.
100. Madhavananda Swami and Majumdar, R.C., *Great Women of India*, Almora, Advaita Ashram, 1953.
101. Mandelbaum, David., *Society in India*, vol. I, Berkeley, University of California Press, 1970.
102. Manohar, K. Murali, (Ed.), *Socio-Economic Status of Indian Women*, Delhi, Seema Publications, 1983.
103. Majumdar R.C. (Ed.) *The History and Culture of the Indian People, vol X, XI*, New Delhi, Bharatiya Vidya Bhawan, 1969.
104. Mehta, Vimal, *Attitude of Educated Women towards Social Issues*, New Delhi, National Publishing House, 1979.
105. Menon, Lakshmi N., *The Position of Women*, Bombay, OUP, 1944.
106. Mies, Maria, *Indian Women and Patriarchy; Conflicts, and Dilemmas of Students and Working Women*, New Delhi, Concept Publishing Company, 1980.
107. Mitchell, Juliet, (Ed.), *Rights and Wrongs of Women*, London, ALlen Lane, 1974.
108. Mitra, Ashok, *The Status of Women: Literacy and Employment*, Bombay, Allied Publishers, 1979.
109. Mitter, D.N., *The Position of Women in Hindu Law*, New Delhi, Inter-India Publications, 1984.
110. Morgan, Elaine,*The Descent of Woman*, London, Souvenir Press, 1972.
111. Morton, Eleanor, *Women Behind Mahatma Gandhi*, London, Max Reinhardt, 1954.
112. Mukharji, Ila, *Social Status of North Indian Women*, Agra, Shiva Lal Agarwala, 1972.

113. Myrdal, Alva, and Klien, Viola, *Women's Two Roles—Home and Work*, London, Routledge and Kegan Paul Ltd., 1956.
114. Nanda, B.R., *Indian Women, from Purdah to Modernity*, New Delhi, Vikas Publishing House, 1976.
115. Natarajan, S., *A Century of Social Reform in India*, Bombay, Asia Publishing House, 1962.
116. Nehru, Shyam Kumari, *Our Cause: Symposium by Indian Women*, Allahabad, Kitabistan, 1936.
117. Pal, Radya Ballav, *A Glimpse of Zenana Life in Bengal*, Calcutta, S.C. Auddyand Company, 1904.
118. Pandita, Ramabai, *The High Caste Hindu Women*, New York, Chicago, Toronto, Fleming H. Revell and Company, 1901.
119. Parashar, Archana, *Women and Family Law Reform in India*, Delhi, Sage Publications, 1992.
120. Raghavachariar, N.R., *Hindu Law: Principles and Precedents*, Madras, MLJ Office, 1970.
121. Ramanamma A., *Graduate Employed Women in an Urban Setting*, Poona, Dastane Ramchandra & Company, 1979.
122. Ramu, G.N., *Family and Caste in Urban India*, Delhi, Vikas Publishing House, 1977.
123. Raychaudhuri, Tapan, *Europe Reconsidered: Perception of the West in the Nineteenth Century Bengal*, Delhi, OUP, 1988.
124. Robert, Helan, (Ed.), *Doing Feminist Research*, London, Routledge & Kegan Paul, 1981.
125. Rogers, Barbara, *Domestication of Women, Discrimination in Developing Societies* London, Tavistock Publications, 1980.
126. Roy Arundhati, *God of Small Things*, India Ink, New Delhi, 1997
127. Roy, Manisha, *Bengali Women*, Chicago, University of Chicago Press, 1975.
128. Sachchidananda and Sinha, Ramesh P., *Women Rights, Myth and Reality*, Jaipur, Printwell Publishers, 1984.
129. Sahai, Shiela, *Social Legislation and Status of Hindu Women*, Jaipur and New Delhi, Rawat Publications, 1996.
130. Sarkar, Rishindranath, *Hindu Women's Right to Property Act*, Calcutta, S.C. Sarkar and Sons, 1938.
131. Sarkar, Sumit, *Modern India, 1885–1947*, Delhi, Mac Millan India Ltd., 1983.
132. Sarkar Sumit, *Bibliographical Survey of Social Reform Movements in 18th and 19th Centuries*, New Delhi, ICHR, 1975
133. Seetharamu, A.J., *Women in Organised Movements*, New Delhi, Ambika Publications, 1981.

134. Sen, Amiya Prasad, *Hindu Revivalism in Bengal, 1872–1905: Some Essays in Interpretation*, Delhi, OUP, 1993.
135. Sen, N.B., *Development of Women's Education in New Delhi*, New Delhi, New Book Society of India, 1969.
136. Sengupta, Padmini, *Women Workers of India*, Bombay, Thacker and Company Ltd., 1944.
137. Sengupta, Padmini, *Women Workers of India*, Bombay, Asia Publishing House, 1960.
138. Sethi, Raj Mohini, *Modernisation of Working Women in Developing Societies*, Delhi, National Publishing House, 1976.
139. Sharma, Vijay, *Protection of Women in Matrimonial Home*, New Delhi, Deep and Deep Publications, 1994.
140. Sharma, Radha Krishna, *Nationalism, Social Reform and Indian Women*, Patna, Janaki Prakashan, 1981.
141. Shastri, Shivnath, *History of the Brahmo Samaj*, Calcutta, R. Chatterjee Publishers, 1974.
142. Siddiqi, Muhammad Zubayr, *The Social Position of Woman through the Ages*, Calcutta, The University of Calcutta, 1971.
143. Smuts, Robert W., *Women and Work in America*, New York, Columbia University Press, 1960.
144. Srivastava, Vinita, *Employment of Educated Married Women in India: Its Causes and Consequences*, New Delhi, National Publishing House, 1978.
145. Stacey, Margaret and Price Marion, *Women, Power and Politics*, London, Tavistock Publications, 1981.
146. Swami Vivekananda, Complete Works, vol. III, Almora, Advaita Ashram, 1948.
147. Tilly, Louise A. and Scott Joan Wallach, *Women, Work and Family*, New York, Holt, Reinhardt and Winston, 1978.
148. Tripathi, Amalesh, *The Extremist Challenge*, Orient Longmans, Calcutta, 1967.
149. Urquhart Margaret M., *Women of Bengal; a Study of the Hindu Pardanasins of Calcutta*, Calcutta, Assocation Press, 1925.
150. Verghese, Jamila, *Her Gold and Her Body*, New Delhi, Vikas Publishing House, 1980.
151. Westermark Edward Alexander, *The Origin and Development of Moral Ideals*, London, New York, Mac Millan Company Ltd., 1906–8.
152. Wilson, Elizabeth, *Women and the Welfare State*, London, Tavistock Publications, 1977.

Newspapers and Journals

English
Amrita Bazar Patrika, Calcutta.
The Bangal Spectator, Calcutta.
Friend of India, Calcutta.
Gazette of India.
Harijan, Ahmedabad.
The Hindustan Times, Delhi.
Hindustan Standard, Calcutta.
The Hindu, Madras.
India.
The Indian Nation, Patna.
Indian Mirror, Calcutta.
Indian Express, Delhi.
Journal of Indian History
Manushi
Modern Review
New India, Calcutta.
The Searchlight, Patna.
The Statesman, Calcutta.
The Times of India, Bombay.
Young India, Ahmedabad.

Bangali
Ananda Bazar Patrika.
Alochona
Bamabodhini Patrika
Bharati Patrika Desh
Jugantar
Samachar Darpan
Somprakash
Samvad Prabhakar
Samachar Sudhvarshan.
Samvad Patre Sekaler Katha, 2 vols; edited by B.N. Bandopadhyaya.
Samayik Patre Banglar Samaj Chitra, 5 vols; edited by Benoy Ghosh.
Sanjivani Patrika
Tattvabodhini Patrika

Index